VOLUNTARY RELIGION

VOLUNTARY RELIGION

PAPERS READ AT
THE 1985 SUMMER MEETING AND
THE 1986 WINTER MEETING OF
THE ECCLESIASTICAL HISTORY SOCIETY

EDITED BY

W. J. SHEILS
AND
DIANA WOOD

PUBLISHED FOR
THE ECCLESIASTICAL HISTORY SOCIETY

BY

BASIL BLACKWELL

1986

© Ecclesiastical History Society 1986

British Library Cataloguing in Publication Data

Voluntary religion.—(Studies in church history; v. 23)
  1. Church charities—Great Britain—History
  I. Sheils, W.J.   II. Wood, Diana   III. Series
  267′.0941   BV4404.G7

ISBN 0-631-15054-4

Printed in Great Britain by Billing & Sons Limited, Worcester

CONTENTS

CONTENTS

CONTENTS

PREFACE

The theme for the 1985 summer conference and subsequent winter meeting of the society focused on those societies and associations which brought together groups of like-minded individuals for a religious purpose either within or without the life of the broader church. In his presidential address, Professor Patrick Collinson provided a wide ranging assessment of that quintessential voluntary grouping, the English Conventicle, and provided a point of reference for many of the subsequent papers read at the meetings. As a voluntary society itself, certainly with an academic and perhaps even with a religious purpose, the membership had opportunity to explore the workings of such a body during the meetings at Lady Margaret Hall, Oxford and King's College, London. The hospitality provided by both institutions contributed greatly to that 'serious minded sociability' which some contributors identified as a central feature of voluntary organizations, and for that the members are grateful. The society also wishes to express its thanks to the British Academy once again for a grant towards the cost of publication.

W.J. Sheils
Diana Wood

LIST OF CONTRIBUTORS

PATRICK COLLINSON (*President*)
Professor of History, Sheffield University

R.W. AMBLER
Lecturer in Adult and Continuing Education, Hull University

BERNARD ASPINWALL
Senior Lecturer in History, Glasgow University

D.W. BEBBINGTON
Lecturer in History, University of Stirling

JOHN BOSSY
Professor of History, University of York

EUAN CAMERON
Lecturer in History, Newcastle University

CLAIRE CROSS
Reader in History, University of York

MARGARET DONALDSON
Lecturer in Ecclesiastical History, Grahamstown University, South Africa

PETER DOYLE
Prinicpal Lecturer in History, Bedford Institute of Higher Education

GRAHAM GOULD
Research Student, King's College, Cambridge

STUART G. HALL
Professor of Ecclesiastical History, King's College, London

JOHN HENDERSON
Research Fellow, Welcome Unit for the History of Medicine, Universiy of Cambridge

PETER HINCHLIFF
Fellow of Balliol College and University Lecturer in Theology, Oxford

LIST OF CONTRIBUTORS

PEREGRINE HORDEN
Fellow, All Souls' College, Oxford

S. PETER KERR
Tutor in Church History, Lincoln Theological College

JAMES KIRK
Lecturer in Scottish History, Glasgow University

PETER J. LINEHAM
Lecturer in History, Massey University, New Zealand

DERYCK LOVEGROVE
Lecturer in Ecclesiastical History, St Andrews University

RICHARD MACKENNEY
Lecturer in History, University of Edinburgh

HUGH McLEOD
Lecturer in Church History, University of Birmingham

CHRISTOPHER MARSH
Student, Corpus Christi College, Cambridge

R.I. MOORE
Senior Lecturer in History, Sheffield University

DEREK PLUMB
Research student, Corpus Christi College, Cambridge

MIRI RUBIN
Research Fellow in Medieval History, Girton College, Cambridge

W.J. SHEILS
Research Archivist, Borthwick Institute, University of York

JOHN WALSH
Fellow of Jesus College and University Lecturer in Modern History, Oxford

C. PETER WILLIAMS
Vice-Principal, Trinity College, Bristol

JOHN WOLFFE
Lecturer in History, University of York

INTRODUCTION

Marriage is a social transaction and institution which (in the law and traditional practice of the Christian West) requires as its most indispensable constitutent the willingness of the parties whom it principally concerns. Without their voluntary concurrence there can be no marriage. But once entered into, marriage is also subject to involuntary constraint and must conform to legally and socially enforceable norms. These norms are not infrequently disregarded by couples whose cohabitation is entirely voluntary and informal. Such informality is commoner in some societies and epochs and at some social levels than at others. Between informal cohabitation and formal marriage there are more halfway houses than there are supposed to be, while the actively voluntary element sustaining formal marriage is infinitely variable and immeasurable.

Not for nothing did St Paul use the estate of marriage as a metaphor for the bonds connecting Christ with his Church, also reversing the figure to make the Church a model for matrimony. Just as marriages were arranged and enforced, so Christian initiation was, in traditional Christendom, effectively imposed, making the Church as fully compulsory a society as most modern states. Even in more recent conditions of legalised religious pluralism, church membership is subject to involuntary constraints, social, familial, cultural. Nevertheless, baptism is not baptism without out a personal affirmation of repentance and commitment which is formally voluntary, requiring understanding and consent. Thereafter the conduct of a christian life and the ongoing life of the Church, even in situations where theological propositions of extreme predestinarian determinacy prevail, depends upon individual and group responses which in some measure and sense are deemed to be voluntary responses to a variety of invitations and exhortations, ranging from the suppliance of the evangelist to the intimidation of the inquisitor. Although Martin Luther, for one, disapproved, baptismal vows have often been supplemented by a variety of other vows, bonds and convenants, all of them in principle voluntary. This is to conceive of the Church itself in voluntaristic and associative terms, an approach reflected in this volume by the historians of medieval fraternities and by John Bossy in his treatment of sixteenth-century French leagues and associations.

Just as formal marriage and the formalised family have never monopolised the voluntary aspiration to share bed and board, so the impulse of religious cohabitation (as it were) has often sought its ends outside formal ecclesiastical structures, in informal and voluntary associations, fraternities and societies. These can be taken, to constitute voluntary religion, set over against the involuntary religion institutionalised in churches which constrain and discipline their members. To critical and polemical observers, such liaisons may appear promiscuous ('that impious train of *et caeteras*' (Ambler)) and they sometimes are, although more commonly they assume the form of *de facto* or 'common law' arrangements of a settled and quasi-ecclesiastical kind.

So far we speak in mostly ideal-typical terms. In the near chaos of actual religious and social experience, the relation of voluntary to involuntary religion has always been complex. The Church itself, before Constantine, was, in the perception of the state, a voluntary association (Hall) and so it may be regarded by other and more recent governments, like that of the Third French Republic. Many schismatic movements breaking away from established churches to form sects have presently claimed to be themselves true churches, even the one and only true Church. Ernst Troeltsch saw Church and Sect as perfectly antithetical, mirroring each other in the totalitarian grandeur and rigorous exclusiveness of their claims. Excluding both churches and sects, and indeed Richard Niebuhr's denominations, we might resolve to confine the study of voluntary associations and societies, the common subject of the essays contained in this volume, to bodies which at no time *claimed* to be churches, but professed to perform a role which their leaders and adherents understood to be complementary to that of the Church or churches, providing additional emotional satisfaction, social support and fellowship (Walsh, McLeod, Doyle). Peter Lineham points out that voluntary movements which see themselves as complementary to the Church and not substitutes for it by definition cannot exist apart from the Church.

Thus, the English conventiclers whose informal house meetings ran in a more or less continuous tradition from early fifteenth-century Lollardy to late seventeenth-century Dissent often claimed that such private practices were perfectly consistent with the public duties of the parish church. In the age *par excellence* of religious voluntarism, the nineteenth century, a mass of societies arose to absorb energies which the business of the churches, strictly defined, left free to be deployed elsewhere, in evangelistic, pastoral and philanthropic endeavour. Although sometimes designedly inter-denominational or pan-evangelical (see Wolffe on the Evangelical Alliance), or even undenominational and antidenominational (Lovegrove), such movements often existed within churches as specialised agencies (Kerr), just as the religious orders of Catholicism, whilst corresponding typologically to some of the features of the Troeltschian sect, have remained ostensibly obedient to the Church at large. The churches of the reformation had their 'inner rings' of the committed, instructed and patently godly (Cameron, Collinson). Conversely, in Reformation Scotland (Kirk), inner rings without an outer circle became 'privy kirks' with an established future before them. So, in the different circumstances of early nineteenth-century Lincolnshire (Ambler), the apparent disorder of strolling Methodists and vociferating Ranters began to coalesce in a settled chapel life.

The relation of relatively involuntary to relatively voluntary bodies is inherently unstable. The exclusivity of groups with a limited and self-defining membership, when exercised in an area of human experience as open-endedly demanding as religion, may appear prejudicial to those excluded. Prayer meetings are more threatening than fishing clubs. Ecclesiastical authority is particularly liable to feel itself under threat from religious acivity outside its control, and the reactions of authority have often turned into counter-churches movements and associations which initially at least did not see themselves as such. In the collective folk-memory of English Christianity, the people called Methodists represent the classic case of this process, voluntary and involuntary factors acting and reacting in roughly equal measure to create what John Walsh calls 'built-in anomalies of theory and practice', 'taxonomically hard to place'. R.I. Moore presents what may be a less familiar example, from the eleventh and twelfth centuries. As another dimension of the dynamic relation between churches and voluntary bodies, the latter may be thought to have proliferated at times when contracting activity on the part of the Church, or the withdrawal of state support for the Church (Walsh), has created a space which societies and associations have occupied. But only the intolerance of churchmen like Dean Stanley of Canterbury (Walsh) or Bishop Horsley of Rochester (Lovegrove) or most of the six-teenth-century French episcopate (Bossy), would want to argue that voluntary societies are to be wholly explained in terms of nature abhorring a vacuum, as if in ideal circumstances they would not be necessary, since their effect was to weaken rather than strength the Church. Dr Lineham argues conversely, that weak churches will mean weak voluntary movements.

As Peter Hinchliff's essay on the 'voluntary absolutism' of British missionary societies in the nineteenth century suggests, the history of voluntary religion is paradoxical, since bodies which in respect of their external relations, funding and legal status are voluntary and liberal (see Margaret Donaldson) may in their internal struc-tures and modes of discipline function in intensely involuntary and illiberal ways. The young missionary who could not marry without the home committee's consent and had to wait months, even years, for answers to his letters, had doubtless volunteered to serve the Wesleyan Missionary Society, a voluntary association. But no less than the child undergoing baptism or the bride entering into marriage, he found himself in bonds.

It follows that while most Christians, in reciting the Creed, have declared their faith and trust in the Church and have not committed themselves with such mystical abandon to belief in the Church Missionary Society or the Fraternity of the Shaft of the Cross, or even in the Order of St Benedict, let alone a multitude of nameless and unrecorded conventicles, we cannot assume that such voluntary and private associations have necessarily taken second place in the affections and obligations of their adherents. The architectural arrangements of late medieval churches may well suggest that the side-altars of the guilds and fraternities were collectively more valuable than the high altar, and served by many more priests. It may be that the 'public duties' so scrupulously observed by seventeenth-century English Puritans were considered, in our terms, to be political obligations and that as a source of spiritual sustenance they were less esteemed than the private meetings of the godly. Within the relative latitude of the open church fellow-ship, choir or Sunday School or bell-ringers or Christian C.N.D. may matter more, in individual perception, than the parish, let alone the Church in a more ecumenical sense. If what we are sometimes told about the deep roots of 'individualism' is true, we should expect this to be the case in Western Christendom in particular.

The salience of informal religion and its relation to the formal is not, however, a feature of religious history adequately reflected in the literature of the subject. For centuries, ecclesiastical history reigned supreme, subsuming the history of belief and practice within an essentially political framework, and narrative. The history of the Church, or of particular churches, has been called an 'edifying continuum', celebrating, more or less defensively and apologetically, the perdurance of institutionalised truth in the teeth of subversive error. The history of religious orders, or of missionary societies, has indeed flourished as a number of different genres, but has often shared a certain inward-looking self-regard which has limited broader understandings. And beyond the continuum, edifying or not, no history. Late medieval fraternities, long extinct, have had few annalists; more ephemeral conventicles none, unless of course they have been taken for underground or alternative churches, whereupon ecclesiastical historians of every persuasion, both Foxe and Bossuet, have paid them plenty of attention.

It was to make some amends for this neglect and distortion, that the theme of the twenty-third year in the life of that voluntary body the Ecclesiastical History Society was proposed. Fraternities (or confraternities – uncertainty on this score seems to persist!) have found their historians in John Henderson, Richard MacKenney, Miri Rubin and Peregrine Horden; conventicles of the Reformation era in Derek Plumb, Euan Cameron, James Kirk, Patrick Collinson, Richard Marsh, Claire Cross and Bill Sheils; protestant religious societies in more recent centuries, from Societies for the Reformation of Manners to the Scripture Union, in John Walsh, Deryck Lovegrove, John Wolffe, Peter Kerr and Peter Lineham; missionary agencies in Peter Hinchliff, Margaret Donaldson and Peter Williams; the associative principle in Catholicism in John Bossy, Hugh McLeod, Bernard Aspinwall and Peter Doyle.

Although the summer conference followed normal practice in dividing into chronologically defined sections, the discussions proceeded, as it were, in a single room, a cat's cradle of threads connecting in one whole a variety of ostensibly disparate subjects.

INTRODUCTION

Some papers (Horden, Collinson, Walsh, Lineham) assist our conceptual approach to this dimension of religious history, Horden by questioning the quasi-biological concept of a 'drive' to association which is fundamental to much discussion of the topic and which has been an assumption of this introductory essay. Others make their contribution by telling us more than we knew before about particular practitioners of voluntary religion such as the South Buckinghamshire Lollards (Plumb) or the Balsham Familists (Marsh) or Oliver Heywood's north country dissenters (Sheils); revealing, as a matter of particular interest and emphasis, the limited extent of the segregation of all these English 'sects' from the larger, mainstream society. Plumb, Marsh and Sheils all discover, as such microscopic investigations are liable to do, the socially cross-sectional character of such groups, and Plumb and Marsh find that many of their adherents stood higher on the social scale than had been supposed. These are far from the only essays in the collection to contextualise their subjects, making a deliberate strategy of what several contributors distinguish as a horizontal rather than vertical approach. In that respect, the authors mostly exemplify what, without undue hubris, may be called the great strength of current religious historiography: the avoidance of both Scylla and Charybdis in the maintenance of an open-minded curiosity about religious motivation which, while not settling for an excessively narrow 'religious' account of these matters, equally eschews a sterile collapse into socio-economic reductionism. Implicitly, since nobody names him, Max Webers 'elective affinities' have the best of the argument. There are omissions, inevitably. Graham Gould is the only contributor to touch on monastic history. But the religious have had their day, in earlier volumes. With the notable exceptions of John Bossy's and Hugh McLeod's contributions, the political potentialities of voluntary religion have not been much discussed. And D.W. Bebbington's essay on that precursor of both modern cults and 'house churches', the Oxford Group, opens a crack in a door which is not otherwise entered. But such examples of 'voluntary absolutism' as the Scientologists or 'Moonies' would doubtless cross parish boundaries limiting the terrain proper to a society devoted to the study of Church History.

Patrick Collinson.

THE SECTS UNDER CONSTANTINE

by STUART G. HALL

L OOKING back a hundred years after the death of Constantine the historian Sozomen wrote:

Under earlier emperors those who worshipped Christ, though they differed in their opinions, were considered the same by the Hellenizers and were similarly badly treated. They could not interfere with each other because of their common sufferings, and for this reason each group used to assemble without difficulty and form a church, and by keeping up continual mutual contact, even if they were few in number, they were not dispersed.[1]

He contrasted this with Constantine's success in repressing the sects. Sozomen is clearly right as far as he goes. Anti-heresy laws gave powers to bishops they did not have before. He goes on:

But after this law they could neither assemble publicly, because they were prevented, nor in secret, because the bishops and clergy in every city kept them under observation.[2]

We shall look more closely at this change.

From the point of view of the State the Church before Constantine was a voluntary association. It perhaps most resembled those social or craft groups which worshipped some minor divinity. Worshippers of Jesus and the God of the Jews would have posed no threat and suffered no persecution, had they not committed their members to utter rejection of the imperial gods, with consequent ill repute and threat to public order. As they in fact did so, they suffered State persecution from time to time.

In many parts of the Empire the churches sprang up with different collections of scripture, different practices and teachings.

[1] *HE* II. 32,3.
[2] *Ibid.* 32,4.

STUART G. HALL

Walter Bauer has taught us that variety preceded uniformity in most parts of the eastern church. Great centres of Christianity were originally or in the second century predominantly taught and led in doctrines which the third and fourth centuries regarded as heretical.[3] It needs little imagination to document the same variety in Rome itself, which Bauer considered the driving force behind the moves towards uniformity of belief and practice. In the early years of the third century we have evidence, besides the 'catholic' church claimed by Zephyrinus and Callistus, of congregations of Quartodecimans, Montanists led by Proclus, at least one psilanthropist group with a bishop of its own and several named leaders, Elkesaite missionaries, and supporters of Sabellius. Marcionites and various gnostics were also in evidence; and two presbyters, Gaius and Hippolytus, pursued independent doctrinal lines, the latter regarding bishop Callistus as an apostate heresiarch, who had set up a school against the Church. At Alexandria the young Origen could enjoy the patronage and table of a lady who sheltered also a Valentinian teacher. And Origen's own career, like those of Pantaenus, Clement and some Alexandrian gnostics before him, was largely that of a private coach, giving and receiving as a good teacher in Christ should, an activity extra-curricular to the episcopal and presbyteral congregations and sometimes at variance with them, though sometimes he also acted as a theological arbitrator at assemblies of clergy.

The third century saw the development of the Catholic system. Ireneus' ecclesiology had already identified the bishops as the trustees of the true apostolic doctrine. When we get to Cyprian the whole charisma of prophet and teacher has been engrossed by the episcopal hierarchy, now an exclusive priestly caste, which forms the structure of the Church by its mutual acknowledgement and fraternal love. This love expressed itself in letters of mutual recognition, moral support and consultation in crisis, and sometimes in acts of inter-church aid. Unless a Church member could get a certificate of membership from such a bishop he might not be recognized by any other; he did not belong. And not belonging

<hr>

[3] Walter Bauer, *Rechtgläubigkeit und Ketzerei im ältesten Christentum* (Tübingen 1934, 2nd ed 1964); trans. as *Orthodoxy and heresy in earliest Christianity* (London 1972).

could have dire consequences, since many depended on ecclesiastical charity for the necessities of life, others (like slaves, who could expect little kindness after their working life was done) expected to be so dependent in old age, and yet others who had sacrificed their fortune to the Church, literally could not afford to become excommunicate. That means that great power lay with bishops. An offender could of course go elsewhere after lapse and exclusion. But if a bishop admitted one excluded from other denominations, he could come into criticism by the severer minded, as Callistus did from Hippolytus. And although there was some growth in flexibility from the time of the Decian persecution, that was counteracted by the increasing strength of the Catholic Church and its organization. Its very flexibility enabled it to gather members, including the lapsed, from other groups, as Callistus and Stephen did at Rome by recognizing all baptisms. Its preponderance in some localities and universal status everywhere constituted significant parts of its claim to be the trustee of revelation from the one God to the Empire as a whole. The other groups were by contrast often of predominantly local character, like the Montanists in Phrygia and the Paulianists in Syria, or else were constitutionally more congregational, like the Valentinian and other gnostic schools, which had an ethos more monastic, individualist and intellectual than that of their Catholic rivals.

So when Constantine began to take the God of the martyrs seriously, there was only one organization which seemed to have the universal quality he needed. Not only did it seem to be in a position to make unique claims, it also had a constitution which was parallel to that of the Empire itself, with a pattern of urban, provincial and diocesan hierarchy which made it easy for the imperial chancelry to deal with. There was thus an easy transition from the monolithic catholicism of the third-century Church of Cyprian and the Dionysii to the imperial Church of Caecilian, Eusebius and Athanasius. What had begun as a voluntary association of individuals committed to God in Christ, bound by a common faith and the pooling of goods and led by mixtures of teachers, prophets and senior members, had evolved into a system which could pursue individuals with its sanctions across the length and breadth of the Empire, and was ready to become an instrument of that Empire as well as its new soul.

In one sense that was the end of voluntarism. The process, by which bishops had embodied in themselves and their clergy the whole power of the Church, was consummated in imperial support and imperial councils. One may rightly see the surge of monasticism at this time as a new form of protestant voluntarism, a species of nonconformity and revivalism: nonconformity inasmuch as it rejected in its early stages the whole prevailing church order and sacraments, substituting individual or gathered cult for what Church and Empire decreed; revivalism inasmuch as immediate gifts, revelations and miracles from the Spirit were recognized in leading ascetics and cultivated in lesser ones. The bishops formally came to digest monasticism, but the monks went on to acquire an establishment and political influence of their own, and to this day religious orders remain as an alternative power in the churches where they subsist.

We shall follow briefly another process, that by which Constantine and his bishops sought to reduce the substantial but diverse vestiges of Christian groups not in communion with the imperial Church. Some important distinctions must first be made. The older sects should not be confused with those major disputes which occupied more of the Emperor's attention and that of his clergy. The African dispute about the bishopric of Carthage and rebaptism, the doctrinal division of the East over the excommunication of Arius, the Egyptian dispute about the ordinations of Melitius, and the division over the fixing of Easter. These were matters *within* the imperial Church, to be settled by imperially sponsored councils of bishops. Rhetoric might demand that Donatists be insulted as heretics or schismatics, but even after repeated condemnations the Emperor never excludes them from the status of erring members of the Church for which he is God's appointed trustee. That is true even of his minatory letter of 315,[4] and of his disingenuous denigration of the appeal to him by Donatist leaders in the previous year.[5] He certainly thinks the majority of the Donatists are merely deceived by a small minority, and capable of restoration whenever

---

[4] In the Optatus dossier, CSEL 26, 211–212, English text in P.R. Coleman-Norton, *Roman state and Christian church* (London 1966) I pp. 68–69.
[5] CSEL 26, 208–210; Coleman-Norton I pp. 59–61.

God pleases. His aim is 'that the peace of the most holy brother-hood ... should be maintained'.[6] When he writes to Alexander and Arius in 324, he expresses his now disappointed hope that he would find in the East reconcilers for Africa, where some 'had dared to split by ill-advised folly the people's religion into diverse factions', and where the easterns might have been sent as 'helpers for the concord of the persons differing in opinion from one another'. He certainly takes the same view of the Arian dispute itself: it was an unnecessary dispute between brothers, which should never have reached public issue.[7] In Constantine's mind it was to remain so. He might damn Arians as atheistic Porphyrians, but he still offers to meet them and tries to persuade. A submissive Arius can go back to his Church. The speech at the Council of Nicea, which Eusebius attributes to him, makes it plain that it is internal dissent which is in mind. The three issues which the main Council settled, Arianism, Melitianism and the date of Easter, all fell into this class. Private disagreement was permissible, not public or scandalous disunion between believers.

The older sects however, the genuine nonconformists, were a different matter. Here is the characteristic imperial assault on voluntary Christianity:[8]

> Victor Constantinus Maximus Augustus to heretics. Know by this present decree, you Novatians, Valentinians, Marcionites, Paulians and those known as Cataphrygians, and all those in short who constitute the heresies by your own gatherings, how many are the lies with which your vain practice is entangled, and how venomous the drugs of which your teaching consists, so that the healthy are brought by you to sickness and the living to perpetual death. You adversaries of truth, enemies of life and counsellors of destruction. Everything you hold is contrary to truth, according with base acts of wickedness and producing absurdities and fables. By these means you consolidate falsehoods, afflict the unoffending, and deny light to believers. By continual vice under a pretext of godliness you

[6] Eusebius, *Vita Constantini* (= *VC*) II 66.
[7] *VC* II 71.
[8] *VC* III 64–65 (*GCS Eusebius I* hrsg. F. Winkelmann, pp. 117–119; ET NPNF 2 series I pp. 539–540 and Coleman-Norton I pp. 90–92).

stain everything, you wound innocent clear consciences with deadly strokes, one could almost say you rob men's eyes of daylight itself. What need is there to state the details, when to describe your evils as they deserve would need no little time and more than We can spare? So large and immeasurable are your enormities, so disgusting and full of every crudity, that a whole day would not suffice to tell them; and in any case it is right to turn one's ears away from such things and avert the gaze, lest the unstained and pure devotion of our own faith be polluted by the detailed catalogue. Why then should we tolerate such evils any longer? Protracted disregard is allowing the healthy to be polluted with a kind of infectious disease. Why do we not by official action swiftly dig out the roots (so to speak) of so great an evil?

Accordingly, since it is not possible to suffer further this deadly effect of your destructiveness, by this law we proclaim that none of you shall hereafter presume to congregate. We have therefore also commanded that all your houses, in which you hold these assemblies, be confiscated, this purpose extending so far as to prohibit the gatherings of your superstitious folly from meeting, not only in public, but also in an individual's house or any private places. Instead the best course would be that as many of you as care for true and pure religion should come to the Catholic Church and participate in its sanctity, by which you will also be able to attain the truth. But let the guile of your perverted mentality — I mean the accursed and destructive divisiveness of the heretics and schismatics — be utterly removed from the happiness of our times. For it befits that blessedness, which under God we enjoy, that those who live in good hopes should be led from all disorderly error into the straight path, from darkness to light, from vanity to truth, from death to salvation. But in order that the power of this remedy may also be enforced, we have given command, as is aforesaid, that all the congregations of your superstition, all the prayerhouses, I say, of the heretics — if indeed it is right to call them prayerhouses — be confiscated and unequivocally transferred without any delay to the Catholic Church, and the remaining places be designated public property; and that no

facility remain hereafter for you to meet, so that from this present day your unlawful assemblies shall not presume to gather in any place public or private.
To be published.

The first thing is to note the groups addressed, who are presumably the most important heretical sects. The Valentinians and Marcionites belong to the earlier second century, before the Catholic system has fully emerged. The Cataphrygians or Montanists are from the later second century, and constituted among other things a revolt against the institutional aspects of that system. The Novatians derive from a schism in the already existing worldwide episcopate of the 250s, and the Paulianists from the wide local support enjoyed by Paul of Samosata, who as bishop of Antioch was condemned for heresy in 268.

The last two groups received special treatment in the Canons attributed to the Council of Nicea.[9] These Canons did not belong to the primary business of the Council and are not referred to in the primary documents. The Council was concerned to reconcile disputes over Arianism, Melitianism and Easter. But they touch on recognizably contemporary issues, and perhaps derive from some continuing or later conciliar committee. Canon 8 directs that Novatians be reconciled to the Church on very favourable terms. They must renounce specific features of their rigorism, promising to communicate with reconciled penitents and with the twice-married. But their baptisms are accepted as valid, and their ordinations too, subject only to administrative adjustments. Canon 19 does the same for the Paulians, except that all sacramental acts must now be repeated, and the clergy are to be ordained only after scrutiny. It is probable that rebaptism (to which the East was prone) had already become regular in the case of Paulian converts to the main Church. We should note here that there is other evidence that the Novatians were favourably viewed at that time. In 326 Constantine responded to a request from the Novatians and confirmed them, as not being greatly at fault, in possession of buildings and burial-sites, save only properties which before the schism of 251 had belonged to the 'churches of perpetual sanctity'.[10]

[9] Gelasius HE II 32, esp. 32,8 and 32,19.
[10] *Codex Theodosianus* 16,5,2; Coleman-Norton I p. 158.

7

This response confirms the report of Socrates that Constantine had summoned the Novatian bishop Acesius to the Council at Nicea in 325 and reached accord with him on the main business of the Council.[11]

The older sects were not considered at Nicea, and no wonder. They had originated in the period when the word of knowledge and gift of prophecy were not restricted to the universal hierarchy. What organization they had was developed independently, and could not form the basis of reconciliation of officers in post. We know that Cataphrygian baptisms were repudiated by the easterns, and in the 250s Firmilian of Cappadocia had been as intransigent as Cyprian (and one should add, as Novatian) about treating all sectaries as unbaptized. So such heretics now came to the Church as uninitiated heathens.[12]

Already the address in the decree indicates the drift of imperial thinking: 'All those in short who constitute the heresies by your own gatherings'. It is not a divine call that holds them together, nor a universal and therefore valid *ecclesia* they constitute. As a voluntary body, a sectarian assembly is under imperial scrutiny. As such, they are to be informed by decree – not of course by evidence – that their whole religion is a vanity implicated in lies and their doctrine is a deadly poison. Thus both the historical complaints of schismatics and the characteristic teachings of heretics are equally assaulted. The effect of their falsehood is to make the healthy sick and to kill the living. This apparently means that they divert the faithful from their loyalty to the true Church. The point is developed: they are enemies of truth, hostile to life, counsellors, or even plotters, of destruction; they are against truth, use alarming teachings to establish lies, to afflict the innocent and to deny light to believers.[13] To understand this and similar expressions one should consider the likelihood that, as Constantine's reign progressed, the sects flourished. First they had new-found liberty to meet. Then, as rich men crowded into the clericate to gain tax advantages and a stream of indifferent converts came to be baptized, demanding and independent sects would have their attractions, as the desert also did, to the stronger-minded. Later history shows

[11] Socrates *HE* I 10.
[12] 64,1.
[13] 64,2.

8

that puritan Novatianism continued to flourish long after, till weakened by internal dissent. Marcionism was a simple cult of high moral demand, which prized sexual abstinence and dietary restraint. The Valentinians had the added attraction of an intense and complicated literary tradition of spirituality. We hear of their congregations from time to time during the next century. The owners and users of the *Nag Hammadi* codices must have been monks whose ideas would have been dubbed Valentinian by most ancient authorities, not entirely accurately. The Cataphrygians had always been a group with a strong tribal base in Asia Minor, heroic against the persecuting Empire and righteously independent of the compromises of Catholicism: the new alliance of their two enemies would strengthen militancy. And the Paulianists, though they might find the defeat of Arianism (if they thought about it) doctrinally congenial, had a similar record of suffering at the hands of the great Church and the Empire, since it had taken Aurelian's victory over Zenobia to dislodge Paul from his cathedral in Antioch in 272.[14] It is likely that the furious disputes in the imperial Church, especially those at Alexandria and Antioch, led many individual Christians to try their hand at nonconformity.

Constantine's rhetoric points to fear of such conversions. By putting forward falsehoods about the Catholic Church, its truth and its purity, they disturbed the faithful. For all of them would see that church as offering no refuge from divine wrath, as diabolically corrupted. Such a message would afflict the innocent and deny the light they knew. Associated with high standards of morality and asceticism, of conservative piety or spiritual gifts, their message perverts the faithful by wounding their consciences and robs them of daylight. They come to doubt the validity of the baptism (enlightenment) they have received in the imperial Church, and even to join its sectarian enemies.

Further examination of Constantine's text will, I believe, confirm this interpretation. But there is one difficulty to clear away. Many interpreters, including lately Barnes, give the decree against heresies a date before Nicea, about 323 or 324.[15] It is then assumed that Constantine's mind changed as a result of his contact with the

[14] Eusebius, *HE* VII 30,18–19.
[15] Timothy D. Barnes, *Constantine and Eusebius* (Cambridge Mass./London 1981) p. 224.

9

Novatians at Nicea, the conciliatory Canon 8 followed and then the decree of 326 which relieved that sect of the confiscations. I believe a later date is correct for the following reasons:

1. Eusebius clearly states that, after he had resolved the disputes in the Church, Constantine turned to removing the heretics.[16] He puts his account of this decree immediately after Constantine's success with the last of his major inter-church disputes, the riotous affair of the deposition of Eustathius of Antioch and the election of his successor. Eusebius was deeply involved in that affair, and there is no reason to doubt his chronology. But the likeliest date for the deposition of Eustathius is 330, and the earliest possible would be 328.[17]

2. There is nothing in the decree in favour of the Novatians of 326 which requires the decree against heresies to precede it. It is entirely intelligible if the Novatians had requested the restoration to them of property confiscated during the persecutions. Some uncertainty would have followed Constantine's restoration of church properties, and administrators may have varied in their practice where Novatians were concerned.

3. The decree against the heretics implies that some time has elapsed since Constantine came to power: 'Why should we tolerate such evils any longer? Protracted disregard is allowing the healthy to be polluted... it is not possible to suffer further... '. On the other hand all the named sects were stronger in the East than in the West, and certainly the Paulians and probably the Cataphrygians were unrepresented in the West. So the protracted disregard began after the conquest of the East in 324. A date after 330 is therefore more likely than one before 325.

We therefore conclude that the decree against the heretics was designed to counteract their successes in the decade after Constantine's victory in the East. The method adopted is to ban heretical assemblies, to transfer their basilicas (prayerhouses) to the Catholics, and to confiscate any private houses or other places where they might meet.[18] This must have been aimed principally at larger urban churches. Just as Diocletian began his campaign

---

[16] VC III 63,1.
[17] Cf Barnes, *Constantine and Eusebius* pp. 227–228 and see below n.30.
[18] 65,1.3.

against the Church by seizing and demolishing basilicas, so Constantine sees this as the chief way to inhibit the heresies (and incidentally to save money on his programme of church extension). Building and extending basilicas was a feature of his campaign to christianize the Empire. He wanted the healing medicines to be 'on public offer for all to see'.[19] Conversely the poisons of heresy had to be put out of sight. It is the cities which suffered this evil, according to Eusebius' reading of the decree: the heretics were 'corrupters who behind a reverend facade damaged the cities'.[20]

To confiscation Constantine adds persuasion, for which Eusebius in his introduction praises him. Those who really care for true and pure religion should come to the Catholic Church and share its sanctity. But they must leave deceitful guile of heresy and schism, which is divisive and unbefitting the happy state of Constantine's united empire. Error is disorderly, and those who err must with God's aid to be brought back from darkness to light.[21] Eusebius describes with some circumstantial detail how this worked. Some heretics, fearing the Emperor's decree, feigned conversion, and were caught with forbidden books; others appeared as genuine converts. The bishops made careful discrimination between the two classes, banishing some from their congregations and reconciling others after due examination and probation. Those not involved in false doctrine but separated by schismatic quarrels were received back without delay, flocking to regain their native land 'as if returning from long exile', and they recognized Mother Church.[22] This passage swells into a final exordium on the ecclesiastical triumphs of Book III of the *Vita Constantini*. Constantine's decree makes no such clear distinction between heresy and schism. He seems to identify unity with doctrinal truth: one Church, one Empire, one Truth. Nor is Eusebius' account correct in other respects. Apart from smaller unnamed groups the only schismatics were the Novatians. Even the Paulians and Montanists were treated as heretics in the East, since it was false doctrine that invalidated their baptisms. It is exactly the Novatians who figure frequently in the history of Socrates, and whom Sozomen found still openly

[19] Eusebius *VC* II 59.
[20] *VC* III 63,2.
[21] 65,2.
[22] *VC* III 66.

flourishing, 'not much affected by this law' of Constantine. Sozomen attributes this to the mildness of Constantine personally towards them, and his respect for the Novatianist Acesius, by this time bishop in Constantinople.[23] The decree of 326, which got into the Theodosian Code, was doubtless useful to the Novatianists in protecting their position, and was not apparently superseded by the decree we have been considering. Sozomen also notes that, while the other heresies disappeared, Montanism survived in its Phrygian heartland, where it continued numerous.[24] Presumably there was little prospect of transferring churches to Catholic clergy and congregations which did not exist. There were comparable difficulties with the African Donatists.

One last topic deserves attention. Eusebius states that the decree was an exhortation supplementary to a law (*nomos*), and that the law commanded that heretical books be sought out.[25] But there is no need to suppose he had any other document than the decree we are considering. In it Constantine writes that to enforce his cure for heresy he had commanded (*prosetaxamen*) the appropriate confiscations.[26] But there would be no need to do more than circulate the text we have, addressed to heretics, for public display. It would have been sent to magistrates in the first instance, though copies would have reached bishops and others. Eusebius may indeed be describing his own practice in implementing the decree at Caesarea. But the searching out of books is not substantiated in the preserved text of the decree. We may well believe that Constantine favoured the destruction of heretical books, since he decreed book-burning in the case of Arius.[27] Episcopal practice would include a requirement to surrender heretical books in the case of converts.[28] Eusebius, ever seeking Christian acts for which he could praise Constantine, perhaps here gives him credit for something for which he had no actual documentary evidence. We may take Eusebius' statement that there was a separate law as mere deduction from the document he quotes.

---

[23] Sozomen *HE* II 32,5.
[24] *Ibid.* 32,6.
[25] VC III 63,3; 66,1.
[26] 65,3.
[27] Socrates *HE* I 9.
[28] Cf *Acts* 19,17–19; Eusebius *HE* VII 7,1–4.

The Sects under Constantine

The decree was not entirely effective, as we have already observed. Many imperial orders vanished into disuse, perhaps lasting no longer than the papyrus on which they were publicly placarded. The continuing existence of voluntary and particularist groups can be proved from a variety of evidence. One might note the decree dated 376, commanding confiscation of all places of heretical worship in towns or villages.[29] One might think this called in question an earlier act by Constantine, but for the fact that the Emperors note that they are repeating what they have decreed some time ago, but their decree has failed to operate, 'whether through dissimulation by magistrates or through the depravity of profane persons'. The tone and principles set by Constantine clearly prevailed.[30]

University of London
King's College

[29] *Codex Theodosianus* 16,5,4; Coleman-Norton I p. 342.
[30] To the discussion on p. 10 should be added: 1. The title 'Victor' used in the opening was not adopted till 324. 2. An earlier date (326) was proposed by Henry Chadwick, *History and thought in the early Church* (London 1982) cap 13; cf R.P.C. Hanson, *ZKG* 95 (1984) pp. 174–178.

PACHOMIOS OF TABENNESI AND THE FOUNDATION OF AN INDEPENDENT MONASTIC COMMUNITY

by GRAHAM GOULD

T
HE earliest Christian monasticism falls within the definition of voluntary religious societies since it was not the product of institutional reform in the Church directed by bishops or councils. The founders of fourth-century Egyptian monasticism undertook their task voluntarily and without episcopal constraint. As the founders of voluntary and at first unofficial associations, they deserve our attention. I shall examine some aspects of the sources for the life of one, Pachomios of Tabennesi (c.292–346).

There are many lives of Pachomios. It is not the purpose of this paper to re-evaluate the long scholarly debate on their literary relationship and relative historical priority.[1] I shall draw mainly on two lives, the *First Greek Life* (G1)[2] and the *Bohairic Life* (Bo).[3] I believe that both these works have a claim to represent early and precious tradition about Pachomios's life.[4] In most of the passages I shall quote they are closely parallel to one another.

---

[1] A. Veilleux, *La Liturgie dans le cénobitisme pachômien au quatrième siècle*, SA 57 (Rome 1968), pp. 11–114 for a full discussion. But the review by D.J. Chitty, *JTS* ns 21 (1970) pp. 195–9, is critical, as is H. Chadwick, 'Pachomios and the Idea of Sanctity' in *The Byzantine Saint*, ed Sergei Hackel, Studies Supplementary to Sobornost 5 (London 1981), p. 14 n 4, pp. 15–17.

[2] *Vita Prima Graeca* (G1) in *Sancti Pachomii Vitae Graecae*, ed F. Halkin, *sub hag* 19 (Brussels 1932), pp. 1–96. The introduction to this edition also contains a critical discussion of the Greek Lives. ET of G1 in *Pachomian Koinonia*, trans A. Veilleux, 3 vols, Cistercian Studies 45–7 (Kalamazoo, Michigan 1980–82), vol 1, pp. 297–423. References to G1 by chapter number, as in the edition and translation.

[3] Bo in *Sancti Pachomii Vita Bohairice Scripta*, ed L. Th. Lefort, CSCO 89 (Louvain 1925). ET in *Pachomian Koinonia* 1 pp. 23–295. Bo has some *lacunae* which the translation fills from Sahidic manuscripts of the same textual family. See *Pachomian Koinonia* 1 pp. 3–4. This does not affect the chapter numbering of passages I shall quote.

[4] Chadwick, 'Pachomios and the Idea of Sanctity' pp. 15–16.

This paper will be divided into two sections. In the first I shall concentrate on some events in Pachomios's life before he set up a monastic community of which he himself was head. The question to be asked here is, 'What experiences and beliefs led Pachomios to found a new community?' Our sources are of course a later reflection on Pachomios's early life, but as such they shed light on how the Community perceived its own origins and the task of its founder. Besides, I am not absolutely convinced that our sources do not represent Pachomios's own outlook accurately.[5] In the second section of the paper I shall discuss Pachomios's understanding of his Community's position within the Church. Did he see it as *ecclesiola in ecclesia*? Did the Community maintain an attitude of superiority towards those Christians who were outside its monastic life?

I

Three times in G1 (5, 12, 23) and four times in Bo (8, 12, 17, 22), during the period before he sets up his own monastic community, Pachomios has a dream or vision[6] which foretells his role as the founder of a community and guides him towards the fulfilment of this task. These experiences develop the theme which has been established by Pachomios's promise to God at the moment of his conversion to Christianity. In c.312 Pachomios was conscripted into the army of Maximinus Daia to fight against Licinius.[7] While in prison in Thebes awaiting his enforced military service, Pachomios was deeply impressed by the charity of the local Christians towards the conscripts, and he made a prayer, offering himself as

---

[5] G1 3 (Parallel to Bo 6) 10 and 46 all indicate that Pachomios did sometimes make use of his own personal experiences in teaching his monks, so these experiences could have been known accurately to later members of the Community, and the author of G1 seems to want us to think that he has done his research carefully (see also G1 98–9).

[6] G1 5 (parallel to Bo 8): he has a dream and hears a voice; G1 12 (parallel to Bo 17): he hears a voice while praying; G1 23 (parallel to Bo 22): he sees an angel. Bo 12 is a repetition of the G1 5 event, described as a vision.

[7] G1 4 and Bo 7 inaccurately name Constantine as the emperor. See *Pachomian Koinonia*, vol 1 p. 267 n 1 to Bo 7.

a servant of men and God for the rest of his life, if he was delivered from the crisis.[8]

After his release from the army, Pachomios became a catechumen and was baptised in a village called Seneset (in Coptic) or Chenoboskion (in Greek). It was on the night of his baptism that his first visionary experience occurred. According to G1 5:

> On the night on which he was made worthy of the mystery, he had a dream. He saw himself sprinkled with dew from heaven. The dew gathered in his right hand and turned into solid honey, and the honey fell onto the ground. He heard someone saying to him, 'Understand what has happened, for it will be so with you later.'

What Pachomios is to understand is perhaps that he is to become a mediator of God's grace to others.

Pachomios's next visionary experience is a rather more concrete expression of this belief. It occurs after he has become a monk (G1 6, Bo 10), a disciple of the old hermit Palamon. While travelling in the desert on one occasion, he comes to the deserted village of Tabennesi, and here he stops to pray (G1 12, Bo 17). While he is praying, a voice comes to him, saying, in the words of Bo:

> Pachomios, Pachomios, struggle, dwell in this place and build a monastery, for many will come to you to become monks with you, and they will profit their souls.

This is the first reference to Pachomios's foundation of a monastic community. The life of Pachomios and his teacher Palamon was not isolated from other monks.[9] It was however a semi-anchoritic form of monasticism, in which small groups of monks lived near one another in scattered, independent cells. It was not the life of a coenobium, of monks living a fully common life, under a rule,

---

[8] G1 5 and Bo 8 may possibly show signs of anachronism here, as they make Pachomios allude to Scripture or address Jesus directly. See H. van Cranenburgh, 'Étude comparative des récits anciens de la vocation de saint Pachôme', *RB* 82 (1972) p. 282. Our concern remains however with the picture of Pachomios drawn by the Community which he founded.

[9] G1 20 refers to a group of monks around Palamon and Pachomios. Bo 14 (parallel to G1 8) illustrates the sort of destructive rivalry that might exist within groups of anchorites.

in a single enclosure.[10] Not until after Pachomios's experience at Tabennesi do we begin to hear of his wish to set up such a community under his own direction.[11] When he takes this decision, Pachomios's motivation is expressed simply enough: 'Remembering the promise of God, with his brother he began to make the monastery larger, in order to receive those who came to this life.'[12]

We now come to the last and most important visionary experience (G1 23, Bo 22), which I shall set in its context in the *First Greek Life*. In chapter 21 there is an interesting passage about Pachomios's progress in the Christian life:

> Before he had perfect knowledge from the Lord, he seemed to have such perfect faith as to tread underfoot snakes and scorpions... Since he then did these things through uprightness of heart and not yet in perfect knowledge, he was preserved by the Lord, who intended to teach him later how to act... Knowing this, Pachomios used to weep over his ignorance, and used to say in prayer, 'Lord, guide of the blind, I thank you that in this also you have not allowed me to go astray, condescending to my ignorance until you teach me your perfect will.'

Then in chapter 23 we find Pachomios on an island,

> keeping vigil alone and praying to be taught the perfect will of God. An angel appeared to him from the Lord, just as one appeared to Manoah and his wife before the birth of Samson. He said, 'The will of God is to serve the race of men, to reconcile them to him.'

So for Pachomios, to have perfect knowledge is to know what is God's will for him, and God's will is that he should serve men. The service of men which he undertakes is the foundation of a monastic community.

---

[10] Chadwick, 'Pachomios and the Idea of Sanctity' p. 14.

[11] G1 15. A different group of Pachomian lives places this incident after Pachomios's final vision, rather than before it. See the *Third Sahidic Life*, in *Sancti Pachomii Vitae Sahidice Scriptae*, ed L. Th. Lefort, CSCO 99–100 (Louvain 1933–4) pp. 100–30. This incident is found on pp. 106–9, of which an ET (filling a *lacuna* in the *First Sahidic Life*) in *Pachomian Koinonia* 1 pp. 427–9.

[12] G1 15. Pachomios's brother John initially opposed the scheme to build a coenobium.

The Pachomian Community

I want to note two important points about the experiences which lead Pachomios, after this last vision, to found his Community. First, Pachomios's actions were voluntary and not directed by any church authority. The independence of the Community is seen in its foundation by an individual fulfilling his own vocation. Pachomios is portrayed as driven by the power of the Spirit. He is converted by the charity of Christians, 'moved by love for God'[13] when he decides to become a monk, led by the Spirit, inspired[14] and commanded to stay at Tabennesi. His series of visions progressively reveals to him the nature of his ministry. They derive from his initial experience of Christian charity and his promise of service, but it is God who guides Pachomios to the fulfilment of this promise as a monk. In these stories about Pachomios interesting light is shed on the sort of beliefs which may build up in an individual and lead him to found a community. Or at least, we see how the Pachomian Community perceived the forces, the action of God, which moved its founder.

Second, for Pachomios the vocation to have perfect knowledge or be a 'perfect monk'[15] is identical with the vocation to found a community. This is much more clearly true in the case of Pachomios than in that of his older contemporary, Antony (c.251–356). It is true that, as G1 21 comments, as the Lord protected Pachomios, so Athanasios in the *Life of Antony* claims that God guarded Antony so that he could be a teacher of others in the monastic life.[16] Antony's original vocation however is to evangelical poverty[17] and to combat with the devil.[18] A definite sense of vocation to found a community is absent. Despite his great influence over other monks and his ministry to many outside the monastic life, Antony remained at heart a lover of solitude.[19]

Pachomios then, is one whose vocation and promise to God lead him to find his own Christian ministry in the foundation of a monastic community.

[13] G1 6.
[14] Bo 17. This account is fuller than the parallel in G1 12 which does not preserve the references to being led by the Spirit or inspired.
[15] G1 2.
[16] Athanasios, *Vita Antonii*, PG 26, cols 835–976, chapter 46, col 912A–B.
[17] *Vita Antonii* 2–3, cols 841–5.
[18] *Vita Antonii* 5–10, cols 845–60, and *passim*.
[19] *Vita Antonii* 49, col 913B; 84, col 961A–B.

II

We pass now from the founder and his motivation to the Community which he founded. What was its nature? It may seem strange to describe it as voluntary, especially when it is compared with the groups that formed around hermits like Antony or Palamon. Such groups were formed of men who lived independently; the amount of contact they had with one-another and the extent of their asceticism were the voluntary decisions of each, though no doubt respect for tradition and the spiritual father around whom the group formed helped to give it coherence.[20] The Pachomian Community on the other hand lived a genuine common life enforced by the first developed monastic rule. Common life, life governed by a rule and uniformity of life have been singled out as the defining characteristics of the Pachomian Community.[21] The role of the head of the Community was much more defined than in a group of hermits. That he should make good rules, and that they should be obeyed, was much more important for the existence of the Pachomian Community than it was for the survival of a group of the Antonian type.[22]

The *Rules* of Pachomios, which survive in the Latin translation of Jerome,[23] show the stage of development which the Community had reached by the end of the fourth century.[24] But the lives show that the concept of rules and a fixed organisation of the Community emerged early on.[25] In the light of this, what can it mean to say that the Pachomian Community was voluntary? It may be pointed

[20] Some aspects of anchoritic groups and coenobia are contrasted in I. Herwegen, *Väterspruch und Mönchsregel*, Beiträge zur Geschichte des alten Mönchtums und des Benediktinerordens, 33 (Münster i.W. 1977). See also the work cited in next note.

[21] H. Bacht, 'Antonius und Pachomius: von der Anachorese zum Cönobitentum' in *Antonius Magnus Eremita*, 356–1956, ed B. Steidle, SA 38 (Rome 1956) pp. 66–107, especially pp. 70–97.

[22] H. Bacht, 'L'Importance de l'idéal monastique de S. Pacôme pour l'histoire du monachisme chrétien', *Revue d'Ascétique et de Mystique* 26 (1950) pp. 308–26. On obedience: pp. 321–23.

[23] *Pachomiana Latina*, ed A. Boon, Bibliothèque de la Revue d'Histoire Ecclésiastique 7 (Louvain 1932).

[24] For a critical discussion of the *Rules*, A. Veilleux, *La Liturgie dans le cénobitisme pachômien* pp. 116–32.

[25] G1 28, Bo 26.

out that the rules and lives themselves illustrate the Community's voluntary nature, in the sense of its independence of the hierarchical structures of the Church. There is nothing in the Pachomian *Rules* to correspond with Basil of Caesarea's insistence that a bishop should be present when a monk makes his vows or that a bishop should be responsible for the charitable disposal of a new monk's property.[26] Unlike Basil, Pachomios did not combine episcopal office and monasticism in his own person. These differences are reminders of the independence of the Pachomian Community.[27]

Pachomios's attitude to the clergy and non-monastic Christians is defined in an important chapter of the lives which may be considered as a sort of policy-statement. In G1 27 and Bo 25 we read that there were no clergy among Pachomios's early followers, and indeed that he considered this to be a desirable state of affairs, for, as he said,

> It is good not to seek office and glory, especially in a coenob-
> ium, lest because of it strife, envy, jealousy and finally schisms
> arise among many monks... The clerical office is the beginning
> of the thought[28] of the love of power.

Yet this does not mean that the Pachomian Community had a low regard for the clerical office as such or that it separated itself from the sacraments. It is the preservation of the Community from destructive forces acting within it which necessitates that the Community should not have its own resident priest. 'It is better to submit modestly to the Church of God, and whoever at any time we find established by our fathers the bishops, to have him as minister of the priestly office.' G1 27 enforces this point by recording that Pachomios always asked a priest from a nearby church to celebrate the eucharist in the monastery; Bo 25 has a fuller account: Pachomios takes his monks to the village for the Saturday celebration, the priest comes with them to the monastery for that on Sunday.

---

[26] Basil of Caesarea, *Longer Rules* 15, *PG* 31 cols 952A–957A, and *Shorter Rules* 187, *PG* 31 col 1208B–C.
[27] For a comparison of Basilian and Pachomian monasticism see E.A. Amand de Mendieta, 'La Système cénobitique basilien comparé au système cénobitique pachomien', *RHR* 152 (1957) pp. 31–80.
[28] *logismos*: an important technical term in monastic thought for a wicked or demonic impulse.

The lives thus portray friendly relations between the Pachomian Community and the local church. This relationship is strengthened when Pachomios's monks build a church in the local village for the inhabitants who were previously without one (G1 29, Bo 25). Bo suggests that this action was done as a free charitable offering to the people. G1 reports that the building was undertaken with the advice of a local bishop. This difference between the two lives does not seem to me to represent any general tendency on behalf of Bo to understate, or G1 to exaggerate the connexions between the Pachomian Community and the hierarchy (both have the reference to 'our fathers the bishops' which I quoted from G1 27 above), and I do not think it can alter the general picture of the Pachomian Community set up voluntarily, independent in its organisation and devoted to the harmonious development of its common life, but holding such contacts with the local church and the hierarchy as were required.

In all this there is nothing to suggest that the Pachomian Community saw itself as a fully independent *ecclesiola in ecclesia*, let alone as the only true Church. The visit of Athanasios to the Pachomian Community in *c.*328 is further evidence for the good relationships between hierarchy and Community. Indeed, this event perhaps marks the time of transition from a fully voluntary and unofficial to a semi-official or at least approved Community with a recognised place in the life of the Church.[29]

However, two aspects of the Pachomian Community's perception of itself may suggest a different conclusion, and deserve examination. For Pachomios, as we have seen, his initial conversion to Christianity and acceptance of baptism led, under God's guidance, directly to his becoming a monk and founding a community. Did the Community believe that the monastic life in general, or the life of the Pachomian Community in particular, was the only true way in which a Christian could fulfil his baptismal promises? Veilleux argues against this,[30] but there is one passage which suggests that it may have been the case, in G1 140, where Theodore, Pachomios's disciple, says, 'When a man is baptised, if he makes profession of the monastic life, he receives the seal of

---

[29] G1 30, Bo 28. On relations with the hierarchy, see Veilleux, *La Liturgie* pp. 189–94.

[30] *ibid.* pp. 213–25.

the Spirit... '. However, I do not think this passage can be taken as claiming that the monastic life is the only baptised life which claims the 'seal of the Spirit'. Theodore is speaking as a monk to monks, and claims that the monastic life is a complete baptised life, but without making any comment on any other kind of life. 'If he makes profession, then he receives the Spirit' does not imply 'if he does not make profession, he does not receive the Spirit'. Such a passage should not be allowed to overshadow the impression which we have gained of favourable relations between Community, villagers, priests and hierarchy.

Veilleux[31] notes another point about the Community's perception of itself. It sometimes appropriates for itself designations such as 'people of God' which in their biblical context refer to the whole people of God: in the traditional Christian understanding, to the whole Church. Is this not an example of the Community's arrogance or elitism, the point at which a voluntary association becomes a separatist movement? There are two answers to this question which suggest not. First, the Pachomian Community is in effect a local church, a manifestation of the universal Church which, like other local churches can use of itself the epithets of the universal Church.[32] This is, like Athanasios's visit, an indication of the Community's gradual incorporation into the formal, official Church. This does not detract from its original voluntary and independent nature, but shows how a place could in time be found for it within the wider Church and its hierarchy. Second, it is possible that the Pachomian Community saw itself as having a mission towards the wider Church, as a witness of the Christian life.[33] No community could set out to fulfil this role unless willing to apply to itself the biblical descriptions of the universal Church, and the most rigorous standards of Christian living.[34]

---

[31] *ibid.* p. 167, pp. 181–2.

[32] *ibid.* pp. 182–6.

[33] Bo 8 and (more directly connected with Pachomios's attitude to clergy and villagers) G1 29 record the powerful impression which Pachomios's life had on local people: ' ...they were eager to become Christians and faithful. For he was merciful and a lover of souls.' (G1 29).

[34] This view of the value and function of the religious life has found support among both Catholic and Anglican writers. See Francis J. Moloney, *A Life of Promise: Poverty, Chastity, Obedience* (London 1985) and A.M. Allchin, *The Theology of the Religious Life: An Anglican Approach* (Oxford 1971).

I do not think that this motive of witness was the most important motive at work in the formation and life of the Pachomian Community. No doubt desire for a common life in itself was more important.[35] However, the combination of these two motives may help to explain how the Community could have relatively good relations with the hierarchy, and act as a benefactor towards the local church, while at the same time excluding clergy from its own common life[36] because of fears of the tensions which might result.

The Pachomian Community provides an example of how a voluntary community might be formed, by the personal convictions of its founder and the determination of his followers to live a fully common life, and how it might come to find a place within the wider Church.

King's College,
Cambridge.

---

[35] See the articles by Bacht cited above, and Veilleux, *La Liturgie* pp. 176–80.
[36] Or at least, demanding that any cleric who wished to join the Community should submit to exactly the same rule of life as lay monks (G1 27, Bo 25).

THE CONFRATERNITIES OF BYZANTIUM

by PEREGRINE HORDEN

'THE medieval drive to association'. That phrase comes from a monograph by Susan Reynolds. It is to be found in a chapter on guilds and confraternities. And it is representative of the quasi-biological vocabulary to which historians of those institutions seem especially prone.[1] How appropriate is this talk of drives? What, in this context, is the force of 'medieval'? My ultimate purpose is to address those questions from a Byzantine perspective; to ask in effect whether evidence of confraternities from the eastern Roman empire between approximately 400 and the Ottoman conquest will sustain talk of a Byzantine 'drive to association'. The enquiry is, however, worth a preliminary approach on a broader front. This is partly because the historiography of European confraternities shapes the questions that must be put to the Byzantine sources. It is also because, unusually, a Byzantine perspective may illuminate problems arising from the western material. Finally it is because the comparative history of confraternities may, by implication, have a modest contribution to make to the larger question of the differences between eastern and western Christianity. Much energy has been expended on accounting for the 'parting of the ways' – less, perhaps, on measuring the distance between them.[2]

I begin, then, with Europe, particularly with later medieval Europe. For it was, of course, during the later Middle Ages that large, highly formal confraternities proliferated in the West – to the point where there would have been around a hundred in any

---

[1] Reynolds, *Kingdoms and Communities in Western Europe 900–1300* (Oxford 1984) cap 3 (to which I am generally indebted) at p. 77. Cf John Bossy, *Christianity in the West 1400–1700* (Oxford 1985) p. 58; Denys Hay, *The Church in Italy in the Fifteenth Century.* (Cambridge 1977) p. 66.

[2] Cf Peter Brown, 'Eastern and Western Christendom in Late Antiquity: A Parting of the Ways', *SCH* 13 (1976) pp. 1–24.

major city, and where aggregate membership could have represented as much as a fifth of the total population.[3] It may be
tempting to imagine that only the expression of some obscure but
powerful instinct – a drive to association – could lie behind such
an apparently unique phenomenon. The strength of the temptation
is, moreover, likely to reflect the difficulty of arriving at an alternative general analysis. Most attempts to explain the efflorescence
of confraternities are of the functionalist variety. Some of them
come close to circularity of argument. They assert that confraternities satisfied many important lay needs – ascetic, convivial,
political and so on.[4] But often the only substantial evidence of those
needs is that of the confraternities themselves. Other functional
explanations at least avoid merely inferring cause from effect. Yet
they lack chronological specificity. They do not tell us why these
particular needs were met at this particular time.

Confraternities were, for instance, 'of course an artificial kin
group': they embodied the tradition of kinship and compensated
for its supposed decline.[5] The difficulty with explanation in these
terms is that we can say remarkably little about the strength of
kinship in any given period of the Middle Ages.[6] Bonds of kinship
are always dissolving whenever historians catch sight of them, be
it in the ninth century or the fifteenth.[7] Confraternities have also
been thought to reflect a variety of other social changes: a rising
age at first marriage, the weakening of parish loyalties, scarcity of
resources. Yet, again, none of these phenomena can be assigned

[3] Cf in this volume John Henderson, 'Confraternities and the Church in Late-
Medieval Florence', of which he kindly sent me a typescript; Susan Brigden,
'Religion and Social Obligation in Early Sixteenth-Century London', PP 103
(1984) p. 94; Linda Martz, Poverty and Welfare in Hapsburg Spain: The Example
of Toledo (Cambridge 1983) p. 159; Bossy, Christianity, p. 58.
[4] Gabriel Le Bras, 'Les confréries chrétiennes: problèmes et propositions', RHDFE
(1940–41) pp. 310–63 remains the best brief survey.
[5] Quotation from Bossy, 'The Counter-Reformation and the People of Catholic
Europe', PP 47 (1970) p. 58, who is rightly cautious of its implications. Cf Le
Bras p. 310.
[6] Cf Bossy, 'Counter-Reformation', p. 55; Jack Goody, The Development of
Marriage and the Family in Europe (Cambridge 1983).
[7] Cf Jean Devisse, Hincmar Archevêque de Reims 845–882 (Geneva 1976) 2 p. 878
n 361.

with any precision to the right period.[8] Another type of explanation, and a final example, is provided by the historical anthropologist. We are told that confraternities created a 'ritual space' wherein escape from the pressures of living in an 'agonistic' society could be symbolically enacted. This account, ultimately perhaps reducible to a truism about peace and order in the midst of chaos, is specifically intended to apply to the confraternities of fifteenth-century Florence. But with minimal adjustment it could surely be applied to other institutions of different types, and from different places and periods.[9] Until we can show that later medieval society was peculiarly agonistic, and its confraternities peculiarly restful, we shall not have advanced very far. The solution may not, in any case, lie with an improved chronology. As Natalie Zemon Davis has written, 'it seems implausible to explain the confraternity... by the special events of the fourteenth and fifteenth centuries'; its history 'might better be related... to the more slowly changing features of life that influence people's sense of community'.[10] It is easier to applaud such an agenda than to comply with it. To do so would involve abandoning the functionalist stance and developing something more elusive: a sense of context. There are, I suggest, two ways forward.

The first I can no more than hint at. It involves viewing later medieval confraternities in their contemporary setting, not as substitutes for, but rather as complements to, numerous other forms of association – trade guilds in particular, sects, youth groups, networks of kinship and the like. A satisfactory integration of so many areas of enquiry will not easily be achieved. The evidence is seldom sufficient. Worse, our abiding image of the Middle Ages may hinder the proper interpretation of what evidence there is. We knew that the significant bonds of society in that 'world we have

---

[8] Bossy, 'Holiness and Society', *PP* 75 (1977) pp. 120–6, discussing *The Pursuit of Holiness in Late Mediaeval and Renaissance Religion*, ed Charles Trinkhaus and Heiko A. Oberman (Leiden 1974). Cf R.M. Smith, 'The Peoples of Tuscany and their Families in the Fifteenth Century: Medieval or Mediterranean?', *Journal of Family History* (1981) pp. 107–16 on marriage age. On parishes compare Henderson, 'Confraternities'; Brigden pp. 94–6.

[9] Ronald F.E. Weissman, *Ritual Brotherhood in Renaissance Florence* (New York and London 1982). Cf Barbara H. Rosenwein, *Rhinoceros Bound: Cluny in the Tenth Century* (Philadelphia 1982), using a similar model.

[10] *The Pursuit of Holiness* pp. 315, 318.

27

lost' were not only the 'vertical' ones created by king, lord and *paterfamilias*.[11] Yet such a conspectus of medieval 'horizontals' as *Kingdoms and Communities* was none the less a major *desideratum*. It reminded us of how much we knew but had never put together. Still more tellingly, it showed us that horizontal ties were probably as significant in the period before 1300 as during the later Middle Ages.

The second way forward that I propose derives from that assertion of essential continuity across the supposedly transformative twelfth century. It involves asking whether the 'medieval drive to association' was genuinely medieval. Historians acknowledge that confraternities were 'un fenomeno commune a tutta la cristianità'.[12] They then, however, tend to proceed as if evidence from much before 1200 belonged merely to the prehistory of the subject. It is time that the imbalance was redressed.[13] Broadening the scope of confraternity history in this way does not simply replace a functional explanation with a genetic one. Rather, a necessary chronological dimension is added to the context within which the later medieval proliferation of confraternities may eventually become intelligible. Giving due weight to the early Middle Ages does not commit us to the belief that confraternities remained unchanged throughout. (The rise of the mendicants, for example, and perhaps also the consolidation of the doctrine of purgatory, may have decisively altered the character of confraternal devotion.)[14] But the perspective of the *longue durée* does alert us to the possibility that the similarities between early and later associations are at least as noteworthy as the differences – and that the later developed out of the early ones in a less dramatic way than some have thought.

There may for instance have been a sustained period of growth in the early period just as in the later one: growth in the number, distribution and sophistication of confraternities. The crucial phase would, on this account, have been the century or so preceding the

---

[11] *Pace* Peter Laslett, *The World We Have Lost – Further Explored* (London 1983) pp. 7, 10.

[12] Gilles Gerard Meersseman, *Ordo Fraternitatis*, 3 vols (Rome 1977) 1 p. ix.

[13] I have not seen Meersseman, 'Per la storiografia delle confraternite laicali nell'alto medioevo', *Storiografia e Storia, Studi... Theseider* (Rome 1974) 1 pp. 39–62.

[14] Weissman cap 2; Jacques Le Goff, *The Birth of Purgatory*, ET (London 1984) pp. 326–8.

Gregorian Reform.[15] It could, however, be wrong to place too much emphasis on periods of expansion. The small cluster of tenth or eleventh-century Italian confraternity statutes that have come down to us may hint at a development both earlier than we think and more precocious than we can know.[16] Nothing about these texts implies the rarity or novelty of the institutions they describe. The hardly larger collection of statutes from tenth and eleventh-century England is a still more eloquent testimony to a vigorous and highly diversified Anglo-Saxon 'drive to association'.[17] It is surely safer to conclude that Anglo-Saxon society was 'rich in gilds'[18] than to suppose the few we know about to have been merely an isolated anticipation of an essentially later medieval state of affairs.

Evidence of trading or artisan associations might be interpreted in the same light. The guild of (possibly) Frisian traders recorded in runic inscriptions from early eleventh-century Sigtuna is not 'quite evidently witness... to a new age'.[19] We now have a greater sense of certain similarities in commercial organization between the late antique Mediterranean and the Dark Age North. It may therefore be possible to reopen the old question of how much early medieval associations inherited from the classical world.[20] Of course between the merchants of Sigtuna and the last known late antique 'professional' corporations in the West – for example the Neapolitan *saponarii* with whom Gregory the Great concerned himself – there stretch centuries for which little evidence survives.[21] Were merchants and artisans therefore unassociative during that period? The problematic *magistri commacini*, a builders' federation

[15] R.I. Moore, 'Family, Community and Cult on the Eve of the Gregorian Reform', *TRHS* 30 (1980) pp. 56–7; Robert Fossier, *Enfance de l'Europe Xe-XIIe siècles*, 2 vols (Paris 1982) 1 pp. 361–2.

[16] Meersseman, *Ordo Fraternitatis*, 1 pp. 55–65, 95–9.

[17] Benjamin Thorpe, *Diplomatarium Anglicum Aevi Saxonici* (London 1865) pp. 605–17.

[18] Frank Barlow, *The English Church 1000–1066*, 2 ed (London 1979) p. 249. See also pp. 196–8.

[19] Richard Hodges, *Dark Age Economics* (London 1982) pp. 89, 193. Cf Edward James, *The Origins of France* (London 1982) p. 71.

[20] C.R. Whittaker, 'Late Roman Trade and Traders', *Trade in the Ancient Economy*, ed Peter Garnsey *et al.* (London 1983) pp. 163–80.

[21] *MGH Epistolarum* vol 2 pp. 118–19. L. Cracco Ruggini, 'Le associazioni professionali nel mondo romano-bizantino', *SSSpoleto* 18 (1970) pp. 192, 222–4. Cf Fossier 1 p. 538.

of Lombard Italy, suggest otherwise, if only for the highly Roman-
ized Mediterranean.[22]

The search for such continuities has a greater bearing on the
history of the early medieval confraternity than might be imagined.
For the emphatic lesson of the early sources, 'if one removes the
economic spectacles of modern preoccupations, is that economic
motives and interests were much less important to fraternities and
guilds than historians have generally supposed'.[23] Guilds of artisans
or tradesmen might be predominantly devotional and charitable in
character; members of the most pious confraternity might have
many secular interests in common. The early medieval evidence
seldom tells us what the occupations of confraternity members
were.[24] Nor does it describe the full range of any given association's
purposes. No clear distinction can be drawn between 'professional'
and devotional groups – and neither should be neglected by the
religious historian. It is best to envisage a spectrum of possibilities:
the soberly devotional association at one extreme, the wholly secular trade or craft guild at the other, and a large, undivided central
portion where religious, economic and convivial functions are variously but inextricably mixed.

We can then make some sense of the few texts available from
the ninth century and before. Some associations are relatively
articulate. The *collectae* castigated for excessive drinking by Archbishop Hincmar in the ninth century sound like the very model of
a later medieval association. Apart from gathering for a glass of
wine, they were to come together 'in omni obsequio religionis...
videlicet in oblatione, in luminaribus, in oblationibus mutuis, in
exsequiis defunctorum, in eleemosynis, et caeteris pietatis
officiis'.[25] Of the corporate piety of other Carolingian groups
(some perhaps consisting of merchants) we hear nothing.[26] We
should not, however, assume that they had none. More particularly, we should not assume that immoderate conviviality was
always a legacy of some pre-Christian cult. Assuredly certain pagan

---

[22] M. Salmi, 'Magistri Comacini o Commàcini', *SSSpoleto* 18 (1970) pp. 409–24.

[23] Reynolds pp. 72–3.

[24] The Paris MS BN Latin 9430 is exceptional. Cf Meersseman 1 pp. 99–108.

[25] *Capitula Presbyteris Data* cap 16, *PL* 125 cols 777–8. Devisse, *Hincmar* 2
pp. 877–8.

[26] References in Reynolds pp. 67–8. I here omit discussion of monastic confraternities of prayer.

ritual feasts of the newly-converted peoples of north-western Europe had to be transformed beyond recognition or suppressed.[27] But it would be odd if there were no antecedent tradition of conviviality and corporate worship within the Christian congregations into which the least objectionable of those feasts could be incorporated. We know far too little about the internal workings of pre-Constantinian communities to trace the origins of such confraternal worship. The long history of common meals, feasts at martyrs' tombs and collective devotions might none the less be thought to have had some influence on the subsequent development of confraternities. There could still be a sense in which the early Church 'apparut... comme une fédération de confréries'.[28] If that were so it would, moreover, naturally be worth asking whether a comparable federation can be discerned in the immediately succeeding period.

And so to Byzantium. The approach there should be that enforced by the western sources. An ample sense of context is needed; enough to give weight to the early Middle Ages, and to the number of confraternities it may have witnessed. The model of a spectrum of possibilities can be carried over and refined. It is a way of reminding ourselves that the purely 'professional' and the purely devotional association are hardly more than Weberian ideal types; that some mixture of secular and religious purposes is characteristic of the majority of guilds and confraternities. It can also be a way of conceptualizing the shifting relation between highly formal associations (such as those of later medieval Europe) and much looser, more nearly spontaneous groupings (of the type that may now seem to have been virtually inevitable throughout the Middle Ages).

That is the required approach. The evidence to satisfy it is not so easily found. Byzantium presents the historian of western confraternities with two paradoxes. First, the earlier evidence is the more plentiful. There is no obvious later medieval proliferation

---

[27] E.g. Bede *HE* i 30; Gregory of Tours, *Liber in gloria confessorum*, cap 2, *MGH SRM* 1 pp. 749–50. Cf Alcuin, *Ep* 290, *MGH Epp Karolini Aevi* 2 p. 448.
[28] Le Bras p. 312. W.H.C. Frend, *Martyrdom and Persecution in the Early Church* (Oxford 1965) pp. 325–6; Ramsay MacMullen, *Christianizing the Roman Empire* (New Haven and London 1984) pp. 90, 104–5; Wayne A. Meeks, *The First Urban Christians* (New Haven and London 1983) caps 5–6; Peter Brown, *The Cult of the Saints* (London 1981) pp. 26–30.

to be accounted for. Second, the social history which ought to provide the necessary context for the continuities and developments that we may uncover is almost wholly lacking. As with the West, part of the problem is an insidious governing image. In a recent survey, for example, Alexander Kazhdan presents *homo byzantinus*, an isolated individual whose attention is monopolized by imperial autocracy.[29] *Homo byzantinus* is, of course, only another ideal type. Yet the notion that Byzantine society was articulated primarily in a 'vertical' direction is one of which we rid ourselves with difficulty. Evidence has after all adhered best to those who exercised authority. One traverses Byzantine society downwards from the top.[30] No more than a few pioneers have managed to make the refractory texts yield worthwhile conclusions about the strength and character of 'horizontal' ties like those of natural and ritual kinship. The everyday religion of the laity remains comparably obscure; it can only be glimpsed indirectly through the media of sermon, icon and saint's life.[31]

With the obvious exception of monasticism, voluntary religious associations in Byzantium have thus been neglected. In 1975 two editors could still find the important question about confraternities novel enough to be worth stating quite simply: 'did Byzantium stand wholly outside the orbit of events which were transforming the religious life of the laity in the cities of its Catholic neighbour Italy?'[32] The relatively well-documented history of Byzantine craft guilds might have formed part of the answer to that question. Yet guilds, like circus factions and other such 'horizontal' associations, have usually been examined only for their 'vertical' significance:

---

[29] (With Giles Constable) *People and Power in Byzantium* (Washington 1982).

[30] Evelyne Patlagean, *Pauvreté économique et pauvreté sociale à Byzance, 4e–7e siècles* (Paris 1977) shows what can be achieved. Contrast the evidential – and analytical – impoverishment of P.A. Yannopoulos, *La société profane dans l'empire byzantin des VIIe, VIIIe, et IXe siècles* (Louvain 1975) and A.P. Kazhdan and Ann Wharton Epstein, *Change in Byzantine Culture in the Eleventh and Twelfth Centuries* (Berkeley and Los Angeles 1985).

[31] Cf Patlagean's collected papers, *Structures sociales, famille, chrétienté à Byzance, IVe–XIe siècle* (London 1981); *The Byzantine Saint*, Studies supplementary to *Sobornost* 5, ed Sergei Hackel (1981); Peter Brown, 'A Dark Age Crisis: Aspects of the Iconoclastic Controversy', *EHR* 88 (1973) pp. 1–34, a rare perspective on local religion.

[32] J. Nesbitt and J. Wiita, 'A Confraternity of the Comnenian Era', *BZ* 68 (1975) pp. 360–84 at p. 361.

their relations with the state, their disruptive potential.[33] The insistence of a few western historians is even more timely in the field of Byzantine economic history: 'La corporation est aussi une association religieuse. On a trop longtemps considéré la chapelle, les messes et les processions comme des à-côtés secondaires de la vie des *arts*'.[34] To establish the chronological extent and possible scale of guild activity in Byzantium would be to bring to light a principal aspect of confraternal religion. I shall therefore consider craft associations first.

'God be praised that I have overcome the task of describing the guilds and confraternities of Constantinople'. So wrote the seventeenth-century traveller Evliya Çelebi, having recounted in lavish detail the thousand and one guilds of Ottoman Istanbul, their numbers, their patrons, the symbols they carried in procession. Among these associations our sympathies surely extend most readily to the fraternity of 'dung-searchers', whose melancholy but rewarding privilege it was to carry dung from the city's streets to the seashore, there to sift it for coins and jewels.[35] We do not know whether there were any Christians in this fraternity. But we do hear of both Christian guilds and at least one guild of mixed Muslim and Christian membership in early Ottoman times.[36] We also know enough about general continuities between Byzantine and Ottoman economies to warrant extrapolating back from Çelebi's depiction and linking it with possible evidence of guild activity in the thirteenth and fourteenth centuries.[37] That evidence implies some degree of continuity with the period before the Latin conquest. It indirectly puts us in touch with the major sources for the earlier history of Byzantine guilds;[38] and these in

---

[33] Cf Alan Cameron, *Circus Factions* (Oxford 1976); Speros Vryonis Jr, 'Byzantine *Demokratia* and the Guilds in the Eleventh Century', *DOP* 17 (1963) pp. 289–314 with bibliography p. 293 n 13. See however Patlagean, *Pauvreté* pp. 228–9.

[34] Jacques Heers, *L'Occident aux XIVe et XVe siècles* (Paris 1963) p. 308.

[35] *Seyâḥatnâme* pt 2 cap 80. Standard ed by Neib Asim (Istanbul 1896–1900). I have used the translation by J. von Hammer, *Narrative of Travels in Europe, Asia and Africa* (London 1834–48) vol 1 pt 2 pp. 104 *seq*, at pp. 250, 106.

[36] Vryonis, 'The *Panegyris* of the Byzantine Saint', *The Byzantine Saint*, pp. 196–226 at p. 220; Vryonis, 'Byzantium and Islam', *East European Quarterly*, 2 (1968) pp. 236–7.

[37] N. Oikonomidès, *Hommes d'affaires grecs et latins à Constantinople* (Paris 1979) pp. 108–14.

[38] For all which see Vryonis, '*Demokratia*'.

their turn find a starting point in antiquity. Çelebi's testimony thus takes its place as perhaps the richest – if also the most fanciful – in a sequence of texts distributed over the whole of Byzantine history, showing at the very least that the guilds never died out for long.

From Çelebi, too, we gain our most extensive portrait of Byzantine guilds as primarily sociable and ceremonial associations. The details of the portrait conform to what the much older evidence of the pagan guilds or *collegia* reveals. The *collegia*, indeed, answer exactly to the model of a spectrum already proposed. Cult associations at one extreme shade imperceptibly into groups who habitually celebrate together in a temple; the function of providing burial for members can be found at any point on the spectrum between the sacred and the secular; family cults develop gradually into cult associations; conversely, at the 'economic' end of the spectrum, craft associations may include members not of the same craft out of neighbourliness. At no point on the spectrum is there a clear division between different types: virtually every *collegium* is devotional and convivial in tone.[39] Ancient historians have been at pains to stress this general feature as if it demonstrated a radical difference between ancient and medieval European guilds – wrongly, unless the latter are seen through the 'economic spectacles of modern preoccupations'.[40] Some historians have even envisaged a discontinuity between classical and early Byzantine associations. For this they have blamed the 'dirigiste' government of the fourth to sixth centuries that regulated guilds too closely and engendered among them an emphasis on the pursuit of economic and political advantage that had not previously been apparent.[41] The extent of the discontinuity can, however, be exaggerated. It is not clear that all guilds were transformed into single-minded pressure groups.

[39] The most useful modern works are Ramsay MacMullen, *Roman Social Relations* (New Haven and London 1974) pp. 68–83, and *Paganism in the Roman Empire* (New Haven and London 1981) pp. 12, 36–9; Meeks, *First Urban Christians*, pp. 31–2. On burial clubs see Keith Hopkins, *Death and Renewal* (Cambridge 1983) cap 4 pt 3.

[40] Cf M.I. Finley, *The Ancient Economy* (London 1973) p. 138.

[41] Cf J.H.W.G. Liebeschuetz, *Antioch: City and Imperial Administration in the Later Roman Empire* (Oxford 1972) pp. 219–24, with bibliography on monopolistic and restrictive practices p. 222; Ruggini pp. 146–93; Patlagean, *Pauvreté* p. 175.

There is no warrant for assuming that they shed their convivial and neighbourly aspects or their functions as burial clubs.[42] And despite the view of most historians that recruitment to the guilds was compulsory for urban craftsmen in the early Byzantine period,[43] the major pieces of evidence are susceptible of alternative interpretation.[44] The guilds probably remained essentially voluntary associations; and they were still such, it seems, in the tenth century when we again catch sight of them.[45] They had by then acquired patron saints; they took part in religious processions; at the *panegyreis* of the saints (religious festivals that, despite ecclesiastical umbrage, inevitably doubled as fairs) they had a festive and devotional role to play.[46]

Of the guilds' charitable activity less can be said. Some glimpses of it do, however, emerge in the evidence of the various groups that ought to be considered alongside them. Take for instance the *argyropratai* – financiers rather than mere silversmiths. Predictably, financiers could amass considerable wealth and power. Many citizens of Constantinople, and presumably elsewhere, became substantially indebted to them.[47] So it is perhaps appropriate that we should find in Antioch a financier turning to the ascetic life and to good works, and joining a manifestly pious confraternity whose other members were of the same lucrative calling.[48] Here we see something like a guild within a guild – for which a western analogy

---

[42] For the urban geography of crafts compare MacMullen, *Roman Social Relations* pp. 71–2 on antiquity with Vryonis, 'Demokratia' pp. 298–9 on Constantinople c.1000. For Byzantine burial clubs see Patlagean, *Pauvreté* pp. 70, 158.

[43] Cf A.H.M. Jones, *The Later Roman Empire* 3 vols (Oxford 1964) 2 p. 858; Liebeschuetz pp. 219, 221.

[44] Patlagean, *Pauvreté* pp. 169, 173–4 (compare Liebeschuetz p. 223); W.H. Buckler, 'Labour Disputes in the Province of Asia', *Anatolian Studies presented to Sir W.M. Ramsay* (Manchester 1923) pp. 36 *seq*.

[45] Kazhdan and Epstein pp. 39 *seq*; Michael Angold, *The Byzantine Empire 1025–1204*, cap 4; Yannopoulos pp. 161–73 for the seventh to ninth centuries. I gloss over here the question of 'the disappearance and revival of cities' in the latter period: see Cyril Mango, *Byzantium* (London 1980) cap 3. For a different perspective, which makes the proposed continuity of guild life more intelligible, see Hugh Kennedy, 'From *Polis* to *Madina*: Urban Change in Late Antique and Early Islamic Syria', *PP* 106 (1985) pp. 3–27.

[46] Vryonis, 'Demokratia' p. 302, 'Panegyris' pp. 213, 220–3.

[47] Jones 2 pp. 863–4; Vryonis, 'Demokratia' pp. 294–5.

[48] 'L'orfèvre Andronicus et Athanasie son épouse', *Vie et récits de l'abbé Daniel le Scétiote*, ed L. Clugnet, *Revue de l'Orient Chrétien* 5 (1900) pp. 371 *seq*.

is provided by the specifically devotional craft confraternities formed by members of the major guilds in, for example, Renaissance Florence.[49] The trade association was not just a model for voluntary religious groups. The sociability promoted among members of the same profession could directly spawn new, more emphatically devotional, forms of concerted lay activity.

Early Byzantine sources indicate further ways in which professional associations could give rise to charitable groups. Guilds were subject to *munera*, compulsory obligations of various kinds.[50] Some of these were of a distinctly charitable nature, reflecting a wider imperial interest in the needs of the deserving. Shopkeepers in the capital, for example, sustained the scheme that provided free funerals for the entire population; they provided the corps of functionaries known as *dekanoi*.[51] Those in Antioch had to provide monthly assistance to beggars.[52] Against this background we may begin to interpret the activities of that perplexing band, the *parabalani* of early fifth-century Alexandria, who have sometimes been interpreted as forming a confraternity. All we know about them is derived from two passages in the Theodosian Code.[53] 'Parabalanin [sic], qui ad curanda debilium aegra corpora deputantur', had perhaps been behaving too much like the janissaries of the patriarch.[54] Their numbers were thereafter limited and they were to be drawn from the humbler guildsmen who 'pro consuetudine curandi gerunt experientiam' – which had, presumably, been lacking in the past. Much philological and historical energy has been expended on these people.[55] They have been taken as representatives of an inferior grade of the medical profession (otherwise unattested) or a minor order in the Church (which makes no allowance for the connection with guilds); as ambulance-men who brought lepers to hospital or as a group who bathed the poor. An agnostic stance may be wisest. Certainly it is important to resist

---

[49] Cf Weissman pp. 63–5.
[50] Jones 2 pp. 858–9.
[51] Patlagean, *Pauvreté* p. 173.
[52] Libanius, *Oratio* xlvi 21.
[53] XVI ii 42, 43.
[54] *DACL sv* 'Parabalani' (H. Leclercq) col 1575.
[55] W. Schubart, 'Parabalani', *Journal of Egyptian Archaeology* 38 (1952) pp. 97–101 with bibliography; Owsei Temkin, 'Byzantine Medicine: Tradition and Empiricism' *DOP* 16 (1962) p. 112.

the tendency of historians always to relate charitable activity to doctors and hospitals. Byzantine philanthropy was not nearly so centralized, even when managed by a patriarch.[56] And the *parabalani* may have performed a variety of functions to which neither the laconic imperial legislation nor the etymology of their name is necessarily any guide.[57] What deserves emphasis is that for any student of guild *demokratia* the Alexandrians' behaviour has a familiar ring; also that the emperor's solution to the problem they posed was to regulate their activity by turning it into a kind of *munus*, as if the model of a charitable guild were the obvious one in the circumstances.

The context of these professional associations and their offshoots is a suitable one in which to introduce a Byzantine instance of that perhaps surprising phenomenon, the confraternity consisting entirely of priests. It is not obvious that such associations were ever widespread in Europe; and it would be tempting to assume that they must have been at their most numerous in the early Middle Ages, when diocesan organization was relative weak.[58] From late Anglo-Saxon England there is certainly evidence of five priests' guilds. Legislation apparently presupposes, moreover, that priests were generally organized into fraternities of this kind.[59] There were, though, still at least four confraternities of priests in early modern London, suggesting that the institution had not lost its uses.[60] One of these confraternities, that 'of the Holy and Undivided Trinity of Sixty Priests', is reminiscent of two groups that could be found on later medieval Byzantine Corfu. The first of them functioned in the city. From the reign of Manuel I (if not earlier) until well into the fifteenth century, there was a *universitas* (as it is described in the Latin charter surviving from the Venetian

---

[56] *Pace* the latest general account, Timothy S. Miller, *The Birth of the Hospital in the Byzantine Empire* (Baltimore 1985).

[57] *Papyri Iandanae*, ed J. Hummel (Leipzig 1938) pp. 383–7 no 154 lists those to whom wine should be distributed, probably by a church at Oxyrhynchus, *c*.600. It seems to include *parabalani* among the minor clerics. We cannot, however, assume a similarity of function between these and the Alexandrian *parabalani*. Cf Miller p. 129 for the analogous case of the *dekanoi*.

[58] Cf Meersseman, *Ordo Fraternitatis*, 1 pp. 25, 113–35, 154–87.

[59] Barlow, pp. 22–30, 249.

[60] Brigden p. 96 with n 157. Cf Norman P. Tanner, *The Church in Late Medieval Norwich 1370–1532* (Toronto 1984) pp. 75–6 for a further example.

archives) of thirty-two priests, called *oratores*, who enjoyed a number of privileges and exemptions. In the countryside of Corfu there was a similar fraternity known as the *Leutheriotai* (Freemen).[61] They formed a type of caste closely restricted to members of their own families – and for that too there is an English parallel in the 'clerks of St Cuthbert' at Durham.[62]

The charters of these priests' confraternities form a point of transition from the 'professional' to the mainly pious in Byzantine religious associations, and to the one set of confraternity statutes that has survived. Among the *typika* or foundation charters that have come down to us is an informative twelfth-century text.[63] It represents a fresh copy (with a new subscription list) of a lost original dating back to 1048 that is said to have become illegible. It describes a confraternity of twenty clerics and twenty-nine laymen associated with the cult of the Theotokos Naupaktetissa in a monastery of Thebes. The members prayed for one another, their predecessors, the patriarch and others. They functioned as a burial club. And once a month they assembled at the icon of the Theotokos. They carried it in procession, singing hymns the while, to the station elected by the member whose turn it was to look after the image for the month following. There is very little here that a member of a twelfth or thirteenth-century Italian confraternity might have found strange. The *typikon* includes no reference to a common fund for feasting – but then not every Italian confraternity maintained one either.[64] In the West, miraculous altarpieces or wax images of patron saints rather than icons would have been processed around the countryside, but that is the only major difference.[65] The Theban *typikon* is the only one of its kind to survive. But nothing in the text suggests the rarity or novelty of any of its provisions; its uniqueness may simply reflect the accidents of

[61] C.N. Sathas, *Documents inédits relatifs à l'histoire de la Grèce au moyen âge*, vol 1 (Paris 1880) pp. 46–51 no 41; I.A. Romanos, *Deltion tes Istorikes kai Ethnologikes Etairias tes Ellados*, vol 2 (1889) pp. 591–608. See also P. Lemerle, 'Trois actes du Despote d'Epire Michel II concernant Corfu', *Hellenika* 4 (1953) pp. 418–23, 425–6. I owe these references to the kindness of Professor D.M. Nicol.
[62] Barlow pp. 229–30.
[63] ed J. Nesbit and J. Wiita in *BZ* 68 (1975) pp. 360–84.
[64] Cf Meersseman, *Ordo Fraternitatis*, 1 pp. 60–5.
[65] Henderson, 'Confraternities and the Church'; Weissman pp. 54–6. Cf R. Janin, 'Les processions religieuses à Byzance', *REB* 24 (1966) pp. 69–88.

archival preservation. There are no internal grounds for interpreting it as the product of some western influence or of some change in the character of Byzantine society.[66] Other pieces of evidence can, furthermore, be adduced as partial analogues. I here present them in reverse chronological order so that we may work our way back to the early Byzantine period.

Processions of fraternities bearing icons of the Virgin, for instance, seem to have been noted during the later Middle Ages – alas without the vividness of a Çelebi – by foreign witnesses as diverse as Pero Tafur, Clavijo (envoy to the Mongols) and Stephen of Novgorod.[67] Earlier on, Nikephoros Choumnos (c. 1260–1327) noted a group of monks and pious laymen, the *Abramaioi andres*, who met to read the Scriptures and practise charity.[68] An eleventh-century manuscript dealing with events in the 840s tells how an icon of the Virgin had miraculously returned to Constantinople from Rome with the ending of iconoclasm and how a *diakonia adelphon* was formed to help parade it.[69] (It is unfortunately not clear whether these 'brothers' were laymen.) Lastly, the seventh-century *Miracles of Saint Artemius* describe a brotherhood which paid funds into a common treasury for a supply of candles, and met to keep vigil every Saturday night and on feast days in the Constantinopolitan Church of St John Prodromos that contained Artemius's relics.[70]

Serendipity produces no more than these few obscure references dealing mostly with the capital city. But they are sufficient to make the point that voluntary religious groups are evident from a number of centuries between the Arab and the Ottoman conquests. Whether such groups could have been found at every significant shrine, how their numbers and degree of coherence altered over time, and into what sociological context they should be inserted

[66] Yet Kazhdan and Wharton Epstein suppose that 'confraternities began to appear in the eleventh century' (*Change in Byzantine Culture* p. 52) and that the location of the Theban confraternity reflects a new 'decentralization' of Byzantine life.

[67] References in Nesbitt-Wiita p. 382 with n 40.

[68] J. Fr. Boissonade, *Anecdota Graeca*, 2 (Paris 1830) pp. 146–7.

[69] E.v. Dobschütz, 'Maria Romaia', *BZ* 12 (1903) p. 202 no 23. Cf Janin p. 71.

[70] P. Maas, 'Artemioskult in Konstantinopel', *Byzantinisch-Neugriechische Jahrbücher* 1 (1920) pp. 377–80. The *Miracles* were edited by A. Papadopoulos-Kerameus in *Varia Graeca Sacra* (St Petersburg 1909) pp. 1–79. See especially *Miracle* 18.

must all remain matters for surmise. So far, at least, no obvious reason has emerged why they should not have been widespread; Byzantine *mentalités* were not against them.

Reference to the *Miracles of Artemius* has transferred the discussion back to what is usually taken as the earliest distinct period in Byzantine history, the one ending in the seventh century. Here the evidence becomes unexpectedly plentiful – in comparison, that is, with the sources of both late Byzantium and early medieval Europe. It is also in many respects better evidence: narrative and circumstantial rather than cursory and legal. In Jerusalem, Antioch, Constantinople, Berytus, Alexandria and smaller towns the size of Oxyrhynchus (in Egypt if no other province) we find, from the mid-fourth century onwards, groups of those 'devoted to the full Christian life with little, perhaps, to mark outwardly any sharp line between them and the rest of the Christian community'.[71] These associations of *philoponoi* (labour-lovers) or *spoudaioi* (zealots) – as they were often known – are what historians of early Byzantium have come to think of as lay confraternities.[72] They were to be found in Monophysite and Chalcedonian areas alike. Taken as a whole, their membership ranged widely in wealth and age. In some places there were separate associations for men and women.[73]

Their recorded attributes and activities are various. In his *Life of Severus* of Antioch, Zacharias Scholasticus enumerates the qualities of an Alexandrian *philoponos* – orthodoxy, humility, chastity, love of his fellows, compassion for the poor.[74] Orthodoxy was demonstrated in prayer, liturgical chanting and the keeping of

---

[71] Derwas J. Chitty, *The Desert a City* (Oxford 1966) p. 3. S. Pétridès, 'Spoudaei et Philopones', *Echos d'Orient*, 7 (1904) pp. 341–8, to which *DACL sv* 'Confréries' (H. Leclercq) adds little; Ewa Wipszycka, 'Les confréries dans la vie religieuse de l'Egypte chrétienne', *Proceedings of the Twelfth International Congress of Papyrology*, ed Deborah H. Samuel (Toronto 1970) pp. 511–25. See also Miller pp. 124–31, perhaps viewing confraternities too exclusively from the perspective of urban monasticism. Generalizations that follow are largely based on the evidence assembled by Pétridès and Wipszycka, though I cannot always follow their interpretations of it. Full discussion and documentation must be reserved to a forthcoming work.

[72] Zacharias Scholasticus, *Life of Severus* ed M-A. Kugener, *PO* 2 p. 24 shows that *philoponos* was the local Egyptian variant of *spoudaios*, and refers to still other groups of 'companions' who are for obvious reasons virtually untraceable.

[73] The story of 'L'orfèvre Andronicus' (n 48 above) is the clearest evidence.

[74] *PO* 2 p. 12; cf p. 214 (*Life* by John of Beith-Aphthonia).

vigils, participation in ecclesiastical festivals, ceremonies and processions.[75] We do not find icons being venerated, but that is to be expected at this early date.[76] Otherwise the piety of these confraternities clearly has a good deal in common with that of the later ones already mentioned. In this respect there seems to have been no break in confraternity history during the seventh century: throughout the Byzantine period, as throughout the Middle Ages in the West, some form of lay religious association seems to have been more or less inevitable. Zacharias Scholasticus's mention of humility and chastity points, however, towards the more obviously ascetic character of the early associations – sexual abstinence, avoidance of baths, fasting and so forth. Charity towards others, as distinct from the exclusive, fraternal charity characteristic of the Theban group and of so many western confraternities, is also abundantly documented. We hear much of washing the dead, tending the sick, and distributing money or clothing.[77] Members' conviviality is, in contrast, not mentioned in the sources. We know of the *philoponion* or meeting place that some associations maintained or were given, doubtless next to a shrine, but we do not know that there was feasting inside. That omission may simply reflect the nature of the texts. Members of these confraternities had after all intensified their links with the Church much more than they had severed their ties with the world; there remained a good deal in common between them and the ordinary lay worshipper – especially during the day, since their corporate activities were often nocturnal.[78] They did not, with rare exceptions, attain to the feats of miraculous power that their world had come to expect from

---

[75] Wipszycka pp. 513–15; *Vita Auxentii* (Metaphrastic) *PG* 114 col 1380 *seq*; Cyril of Scythopolis, *Vita Theodosii coenobiarchae*, ed H. Usener (Leipzig 1890) pp. 105–6. The strangest function of the Alexandrian *philoponoi* was to remind the Patriarch John 'the Almoner' that his tomb was unfinished: E. Dawes and N.H. Baynes, *Three Byzantine Saints* (Oxford 1948) pp. 228–9.
[76] Ernst Kitzinger, 'The Cult of Images in the Age before Iconoclasm', *DOP* 8 (1954) pp. 83–149.
[77] Wipszycka p. 513. *Philoponoi* or *spoudaioi* might marry, though perhaps live chastely: 'L'orfèvre Andronicus'; L. Clugnet, 'Vies... d'anachorètes', *Revue de l'Orient Chrétien* 10 (1905) pp. 47–8; Sophronius, *Miracles of SS Cyrus and John*, ed Natalio Fernández Marcos, *Los 'Thaumata' de Sofronio* (Madrid 1975) cap 5 pp. 249–51. Charity: 'L'orfèvre Andronicus'; *Cyrus and John* cap 35 pp. 318–22. See also n 93 below.
[78] *PO* 2 pp. 54–5; 'L'orfèvre Andronicus'.

holy men.[79] They were not monks. Some of them could none the less be said to have 'yielded nothing to monks' in their dedication; membership of a confraternity might be seen as a preparation for becoming a monk; and some confraternities might themselves with the passage of time be converted into monasteries.[80]

It is thus easy to conceive of the *spoudaioi* or *philoponoi* as constituting a 'third order' akin to that of the Mendicants in Italy. They certainly appear with some frequency in the texts as a distinct *tagma* or corps intermediate between clergy (or monks) and laity.[81] And they could on occasion be treated as part of the ecclesiastical hierarchy, at least so far as distributions of wine were concerned.[82] Encountering confraternities thus seemingly integrated into the structure of the Church, we may indeed begin to question whether they should be thought of as voluntary lay associations at all. But it would be wrong to envisage all confraternities of the period as having so formal and dependent a character that they were on the verge of turning into monasteries or minor clerical 'orders'.

Again the model of a spectrum suggests itself. A contrast with the extreme of formality and dependence among known lay groups will help to bring the character of the *philoponoi* and *spoudaioi* into clearer focus. At that extreme can be located the groups that are sometimes, perhaps too hastily, taken as the simple equivalent of the *philoponoi* and *spoudaioi* among the congregations of the Syrian Orient, the *benai* and *benat qeiama*, 'sons and daughters of the covenant'.[83] The term had originally embraced the whole Church. With the end of persecution, growth in the number of converts, and a concomitant decline in standards, the *qeiama* came to designate the group of Christians upon whom 'the task fell to carry on the traditions of ascetic Christianity in the heart of the

---

[79] Though cf John Moschus, *Pratum Spirituale*, cap 176, PG 87 col 3044.
[80] Clugnet, 'Vies... d'anachoretès'; *PO* 2 p. 54; Wipszycka pp. 518–19; Pétridès pp. 342–3. Length of service in a confraternity: *Pratum Spirituale* cap 61, PG 87 col 2913; *Miracles of Artemius* p. 19.
[81] Cf 'Fragmente einer Schrift des Märtyrerbischofs Petrus von Alexandrien', ed C. Schmidt, *TU* 5.4 (1901) p. 7.
[82] *Papyri Iandanae* (n 57 above); Berlin papyrus published Wipszycka pp. 522–5.
[83] Arthur Vööbus, *History of Asceticism in the Syrian Orient*, vol 1 CSCO *sub* 14 (Louvain 1958) pp. 97 *seq*, vol 2 *sub* 17 (1960) pp. 332 *seq* gives the 'standard' interpretation. For different etymologies see Sebastian Brock, 'Early Syrian Asceticism', *Numen* 20 (1973) pp. 7–8.

congregations'.[84] In many Syrian churches could thus be found these *tagmata* of men and, less frequently, women who 'shall be continually in the worship service of the church and shall not cease the times of prayer and psalmody night and day'.[85] They assisted in ecclesiastical administration. They acted as nurses in the Church's hospitals and ministered to the poor.[86] In all this they may have resembled the *philoponoi* and *spoudaioi*. But one peculiar feature already emerges in the type of source from which we can learn a good deal about them. The sons and daughters of the covenant emerge most clearly in legislative texts. Their career was nothing if not regulated. Some would have been recruited as children by an itinerant chorepiscopus, who was not above trickery in getting his way with their parents.[87] Adult *benai* could live only with blood relatives or in specially designated dwellings adjacent to the church. They took a vow of virginity, wore distinctive clothes, and were not allowed to wash.[88] Wine and meat were alike prohibited – so much for fraternal conviviality. There is indeed no sign of 'horizontal' ties between members of the *qeiama*. But there are many signs of their strict supervision and maintenance by the Church. It is no surprise to find that ordinands were for preference to be sought among their number.[89]

The sons of the covenant thus represent one clear extreme of 'clericalization' and uniformity in the confraternities of the early Byzantine era; there is more to their coming together than a spontaneous intensification or co-ordination of ordinary lay religiosity. Comparison with them alerts us to the probable heterogeneity and informality which the evidence for *philoponoi* and *spoudaioi* would tend to conceal. Only a few texts hint at the ways in which a confraternity might begin, or might gain in members.

---

[84] Vööbus, *Asceticism*, 2 p. 332.
[85] *Syriac and Arabic Documents regarding Legislation relative to Syrian Asceticism*, ed Vööbus (Stockholm 1960), pt 1 cap 3 no 20.
[86] Vööbus, *Asceticism*, 2 pp. 339–41. Charity: *Vita* of Rabbula of Edessa in *S Ephraemi Syri, Rabulae Episcopi... Opera Selecta*, ed J.J. Overbeck (Oxford 1965) p. 203.
[87] John of Ephesus, *Lives of the Eastern Saints*, cap 16, PO 17 pp. 242–3; *The Canons Ascribed to Maruta of Maipherqat*, ed Vööbus, CSCO 439 (Louvain 1982) no 26.
[88] Vööbus, *Asceticism*, 2 pp. 336–7.
[89] *Canons Ascribed to Maruta* canon 25.

The more 'zealous' and 'industrious' in a congregation naturally distinguished themselves from the rest and consorted with one another;[90] parents no longer had children to care for and so could devote themselves more fully to extra-familial piety; a Chalcedonian shrine isolated in a Monophysite province needed maintaining and defending; students found the energy and the leisure to respond to the challenge of undiminished paganism; while for the philanthropic in a large poverty-ridden city the pooling of resources had obvious advantages.[91] Much, too, would depend on compelling leadership.[92] (The prime example is the Monophysite Paul of Antioch travelling from city to city, establishing in each a *diakonia* or charitable centre and cajoling rich men into running it.)[93] To all this the encouragement and involvement of clerics or monks was perhaps secondary.

A proper account of such *ad hoc* associations would place them in the context not only of guilds (which have already been examined) but of numerous monastic regimes, changing boundaries between cleric and layman, and the obscure growth of heretical sects.[94] There are no clear limits to what may serve as immediate background. That is one lesson to be derived from a comparative investigation. The other is that we should acknowledge the distant beginnings and essential continuity throughout the Middle Ages of the history of confraternities. 'The medieval drive to association' was indeed pan-medieval. Developments in late antiquity and the early Middle Ages merit longer attention than they have so far received. The confraternities and guilds of the medieval eastern empire were closer to European ones in purpose and structure than

[90] Cf *PO* 2 p. 24: 'we found ourselves in the churches with those that one calls *philoponoi*'. References to *spoudaioi laikoi* and such like need not on the other hand always indicate the formation of confraternities. *Spoudaios* and *philoponos* retained their 'non-technical' meanings: cf Athanasius, *Life of Antony*, cap 4, *PG* 28 col 436A for individual *spoudaioi*; Socrates *HE* viii 23. The sixth-century Monophysite philosopher John Philoponos need not ever have belonged to a *philoponion*: that was simply his name (I am grateful to Mr P.M. Fraser for advice here).

[91] 'L'orfèvre Andronicus'; *Cyrus and John* caps 5, 35; *PO* 2 pp. 54–5 – cf W.H.C. Frend, *The Rise of the Monophysite Movement*, 2nd ed (Cambridge 1979) p. 203; Pétridès pp. 346–7; Chitty p. 93. See also n 93 below.

[92] *Cyrus and John* cap 5; *PO* 2 pp. 32–3; *Vita Theodosii* pp. 105–6.

[93] Evidence collected by Patlagean, *Pauvreté*, p. 192.

[94] Heresy: Gilbert Dagron, 'Les moines et la ville', *Travaux et Mémoires*, 4 (1970) pp. 229–76; Patlagean, *Pauvreté*, pp. 134–5.

The Confraternities of Byzantium

might have been thought. And they deserve ample space in any future conspectus – not least because they tell us much about the 'horizontal' aspect of Byzantine society. Whether we adopt the perspective of *la longue durée* or of *histoire totale*, periods of proliferation such as that of the later Middle Ages in the West perhaps come to seem less extraordinary – and certainly less in need of biological summation.[95]

All Souls College
Oxford

Postscript. Dr Judith Herrin has kindly allowed me to read her unpublished paper presented to the Davis Center in March 1985, 'From Bread and Circuses to Soup and Salvation: the Origins of Byzantine Charity'. She there draws attention to evidence of a group of persecuted Chalcedonians attached to the Anastasis church in Constantinople in the 660s whose members sustained one another through correspondence and appear to have continued the traditions of the *spoudaioi*. See Robert Devréesse, 'La lettre d'Anastase l'apocrisaire . . .', *An Bol* 73 (1955) pp. 5–16.

[95] I discussed the topic of confraternities with the late Professor J.M. Wallace-Hadrill only a few days before his sudden death. I take this, the first opportunity of recording a largely scholarly indebtedness to him. I am grateful to Mr. P.M. Fraser, Dr John Henderson and Dr Richard Smith for comments on an earlier version of this paper.

NEW SECTS AND SECRET MEETINGS: ASSOCIATION AND AUTHORITY IN THE ELEVENTH AND TWELFTH CENTURIES

by R.I. MOORE

IT IS always dangerous to proclaim novelty in religious matters, and seldom more so than in relation to the changes of the eleventh and twelfth centuries. In particular the assertions of contemporary observers, bishops, chroniclers and others, that new doctrines were being disseminated or new forms of behaviour detected among the people (a word which, like them, I use in a strict sense to mean the unlettered and the unprivileged, and not simply as a synonym for laity) were usually false, and almost always profoundly misleading. But the assertions themselves *are* new. They are not without precedent, of course: no epoch of the Christian era has been so bereft of the blessings of civilisation as to be entirely unable to produce episcopal denunciations of novelty. But granted the dangers inherent in all such pronouncements it does seem to me that we encounter in these centuries, for the first time since late antiquity, a rising and, as it turned out, continuous chorus of anxiety that the people were acting collectively for religious purposes if not necessarily outside the church, at any rate without its initiation or approval. In that sense it is appropriate to maintain that the modern history of voluntary religious associations, at least as a source of alarm and despondency to those in positions of authority, begins here. Obviously, therefore, it must be a central preoccupation of this paper, though I hope not the only one, to consider to what extent the source of the anxiety lay in the eye of the clerical beholder rather than in the external popular reality, as well as to wonder in either case what needs gave rise to it, and what purpose it served.

The clearest evidence appears when some combination of popular aberration and clerical vigilance gave rise to an accusation of heresy. The group which was arrested, interrogated, exhorted and discharged by Bishop Gerard of Cambrai just after the Christmas of

1024/5 may be taken as quintessential, not least because we have what purports to be a verbatim record of part of their cross-examination. I say purports because what we already knew to be a complex document[1] has now been shown by Duby to have been drawn up by Bishop Gerard as one of a series of manifestos designed to bolster the remnant of the Carolingian political structure at this moment of crisis against what he identified as the subversive forces of heresy, the peace movement and Cluniac monasticism.[2] Nevertheless, what are reported as the words of the accused themselves probably are so, though certainly carefully selected: in this case veracity in reporting what must have been, at least locally, a fairly well-known event would have assisted Gerard's political purpose just as the circumstantial quality of direct speech enhanced his rhetorical effectiveness.

The examination took place at Arras, in St. Mary's church, before a large crowd of clerks and people. The accused, who had been held in custody for three days, and probably tortured,[3] were asked by the bishop 'What is your doctrine, your discipline and your way of life, and how have you learnt it?'

'They replied that they were followers of an Italian named Gundolfo. They had learned from him the precepts of the Gospel and the Apostles, and would accept no other scriptures but this, to which they would adhere in word and deed.'

The bishop now confronted his prisoners with the rumours which had reached him about their teachings. 'To this they replied, "Nobody who is prepared to examine with care the teaching and rule which we have learnt from our master will think that they contravene either the precepts of the Gospel or those of the Apostles. This is its tenor: to abandon the world, to restrain the appetites of the flesh, to earn our food by the labour of our own hands, to do no injury to anyone, to extend charity to everyone of our own faith."'

---

[1] *Acta Synodi Atrebatensis*, PL 142, cols 1271–1312; R.I. Moore, *The Origins of European Dissent* (London 1977) pp. 9–18. Here and throughout, except where it is stated otherwise, quotations in the text are from the translations of R.I. Moore, *The Birth of Popular Heresy* (London 1975).

[2] G. Duby, *The Three Orders: Feudal Society Imagined* (London 1980) pp. 21–40.

[3] See below, n. 45.

In these two answers the men of Arras set out quite explicitly the basis of their own and similar groups in the Bible, and the New Testament in particular. But in the Bible as expounded to them by a teacher, in this case the Italian Gundolfo, of whom we know nothing beyond these words, and who has been the subject of much speculation, as possibly a Bogomil, a merchant, or a figment of Gerard's rhetorical imagination. More to the point, perhaps, is what we can be quite sure Gundolfo was not – namely, a priest licensed by Gerard to minister to the faithful of Arras.

It is no very novel point that the heretics of the eleventh and twelfth centuries founded their faith on the scriptures, but it is one which has received less than due attention in most accounts of them. For one thing it draws an immediate and fundamental distinction between the *literati*, who had direct access to the Latin text, and the *rustici*, who did not. The former may be excluded from this discussion at once. The clerks and regulars who were burned at Orléans in 1022 and the followers of Gerard of Monforte burned at Milan in 1028 were not in any sense drawn from the *populus* and were not concerned to evangelise it, though the latter are said to have 'spread false teachings based on the scriptures' to the peasants who flocked to look at them after their arrest.[4] The inspiration of both groups was wholly intellectual, so far as it can now be discerned, being based on the neoplatonist approach to the interpretation of the scriptures then in vogue in the schools of the north.[5] And in any case the motive of their persecution was directly political. Bautier has shown that the trial at Orléans was an earlier stage of the crisis to which I have already referred, staged to weaken the influence of Queen Constance and her friends at court in the interest of the faction of Eudo of Blois,[6] and Violante implies that

---

[4] Landulf Senior, *Historia Mediolanensis* II, *MGH SS* VIII, 66.

[5] Moore, *Origins* pp. 25–35, corrected on the heresy at Orléans by B. Smalley in *EHR* xciii (1978) p. 855; H. Taviani, 'Naissance d'une hérésie en Italie du nord au xiᵉ siècle', *Annales* 29 (1974) pp. 1241–2; 'Le mariage dans l'hérésie de l'an mil', *ibid.* 32 (1977)) pp. 1074–89; G. Cracco, 'Riforma ed eresia in momenti della cultura Europa tra x e xi secoli', *Riv. di storia e letteratura religiosa* 7 (1971) pp. 411–77.

[6] R.H. Bautier, 'L'hérésie et le mouvement intellectuel au début du xiᵉ siècle. Documents et hypothèses', 95ᵉ *Congrès des sociétés savantes, Reims, 1970, Section philologique et historique* (1975) 1 pp. 63–88.

the affair at Monforte was designed to assist in extending the power of Archbishop Aribert's Milan over the region around Asti.[7]

The illiterate, of course, received the good news directly or indirectly from the learned, but in many cases they also found in the direct study of vernacular scriptures a principal *raison d'être* of their associations. As early as 1043 Bishop Roger II of Châlons-sur-Marne complained to Wazo of Liége that 'if uncouth and ignorant men (*idiotae et infacundi*) become members of their sect they immediately become more eloquent than the most learned Catholics, so that even the pure argument of the truly wise seems to be conquered by their fluency.'[8] It is another century before the attempt which that suggests at direct study of the scriptures is explicitly echoed in the claim of the monk Heribert that 'nobody is so stupid that if he joins [the followers of Pontius who were active around Périgueux *c.*1163] he will not become literate within eight days.'[9] A few years later, if there is any residue of truth in Ralph of Coggeshall's famous but highly conventional and stylised story,[10] the old lady summoned to defend the maiden of Reims who had betrayed herself a heretic by rebuffing the advances of Gervase of Tilbury 'replied so easily' to the arguments of the archbishop and his clerks 'and had such a clear memory of the incidents and texts advanced against her, both from the Old and New Testaments, that she must have had great knowledge of the whole Bible.' The followers of Pontius were probably Cathars (and if so the first whose presence in the Languedoc is attested), whose later use of vernacular scriptures is well known; the group at Reims belonged to the *Publicani*, most probably converted by Balkan Paulicians, as the old lady's knowledge of the Old Testament tends to confirm.[11] But it is by no means to be supposed that interest in the scriptures was the prerogative of aliens, or even of heretics. It

---

[7] C. Violante, 'Hérésies urbaines et hérésies rurales en Italie du 11ᶜ au 13ᶜ siècle' in J. le Goff, *Hérésies et Sociétés dans l'Europe pre-industrielle* (Paris 1968) pp. 172–77; cf. H.E.J. Cowdrey, 'Archbishop Aribert II of Milan', *History* 51 (1966) p. 5.

[8] Anselm of Liége, *Gesta episcoporum ... Leodiensis*, MGH SS VII pp. 226–8.

[9] *PL* 181, col. 1721, and for the date Moore, *Birth of Popular Heresy* p. 79.

[10] Ralph of Coggeshall, *Chronicon Anglicanum* ed J. Stevenson (RS 1875) pp. 121–5; E. Peters, *The Magician, the Witch and the Law* (Philadelphia 1978) pp. 34–9.

[11] Moore, *Origins* pp. 182–5.

was also in the early 1160s, for example, that Lambert le Bègue, priest in the diocese of Liége, made a rhythmical translation of the Acts for the use of members of his congregation who 'when they returned to their houses' after mass on Sunday 'liked to spend the rest of the day until vespers singing hymns, psalms and canticles, thinking over what they had heard in church, and encouraging each other to observe it.' And Lambert claimed that those who accused him on this account of opening the scriptures to the unworthy themselves possessed 'a copy of the psalms translated into the vernacular by a certain Flemish master.'[12] Indeed, though it is not a subject on which I can claim to speak with knowledge, I am inclined to share the view that the use of vernacular scriptures at this time was not a novelty, but one of the manifestations of piety which the reformed church checked in the interest of maintaining its own more comprehensive authority.[13]

However that may have been the largest number of devotees of these sects plainly depended on their leaders for scriptural knowledge and refreshment. Who they were and what their formation is for the most part as obscure as for the Gundolfo who passed by Arras. Some were priests disgusted by the corruption of the church or, like Lambert le Bègue and his contemporary Albero of Mercke, near Cologne, disenchanted by the failure of the reform to live up to its promise; the same may be true of Cyprian and Peter, who followed Henry of Lausanne from Le Mans in 1116 but soon repented, or of Frederick and Dominic William, caught preaching heresy near Trier a few years later, who did not. At least one of Tanchelm's leading followers was a priest named Everwacher, who took over the church of St. Peter (at Ghent?) by force, driving out its venal incumbents much as the Patarenes had done at Milan in the 1050s. St. Bernard's assertion that Henry of Lausanne was a renegade monk is consistent with his capacity to conduct a serious theological discussion, and Peter the Venerable hints that Henry had contrived by some means to circulate a written version of his

---

[12] Frédéricq II pp. 26–32; the passage discussed here trans Moore, *Birth of Popular Heresy* pp. 108–9.
[13] cf. P. Wolff, *Western Languages AD 500–1500* (London 1971) pp. 116–21; R. and C. Brooke, *Popular Religion in the Middle Ages* (London 1984) pp. 130–1.

teachings.[14] Indeed, as the case of Italy, where the Patarene movement was substantially under the leadership of clerks throughout
its history reminds us, the point would hardly be worth making if
we were not still in the habit of assuming far too clear-cut a
distinction between the critics of the clergy and its behaviour who
ended up outside the church and those who made their way to its
pantheon.

In all this we are, in effect, retracing and to some degree extending Stock's recent analysis of the heretics of the eleventh century.[15]
For him they represent a quite new kind of social grouping, based
not on kinship or lordship, or even on habitation or way of life,
but on common allegiance to a particular body of writing – in this
case the scriptures, or parts of them – mediated by a particular
teacher or leader. From this perspective such groups could hardly
have come into existence without the capacity to articulate an
abstract conception of a better society to which they could aspire;
and that capacity must be supposed to be directly dependent on
patterns of thought moulded by the written word rather than
simply by oral discourse. Stock's thesis, to whose power and
originality I am conscious of having done less than justice in a
somewhat ungracious review,[16] offers a much better understanding
of the sectaries of the eleventh century and a new and useful
answer – though not on that account an exclusive one – to the old
question why they appeared then and no sooner. It also has the
advantage of placing both literate and illiterate heretical and enthusiastic groups in a framework which relates them to each other and
to a variety of other social and cultural developments. However,
I would like to make a further distinction within it by observing
that for most of those who have been mentioned the mediator –
the leader – was in some ways more important than the text. The
point is made obviously enough by contrasting the unassuming
men of Arras who were happy to tell Bishop Gerard that they

---

[14] *Tractatus contra Petrobrusianos* ed. J.V. Fearns (CC, *Continuatio Mediaevalis*
X, 1968) p. 5; Moore, *Origins*, p. 93.
[15] Brian Stock, *The Implications of Literacy: Written Language and Models of
Interpretation in the Eleventh and Twelfth Centuries* (Princeton 1983) pp. 88–
151.
[16] *History* 69 (1984) pp. 455–6.

could conceive of nothing more Christian than what he had said to them, and go their way, with the followers of Tanchelm who were inspired by his outrageous blasphemies to terrorise the Flemish countryside for a number of years.[17] We must look at these groups a little more closely, in the hope of identifying some of the bonds which held them together.[18]

We all venerate holy men now. I need not labour to describe how the wild eyes, tattered garments and bare legs of a Robert of Arbrissel or a Henry of Lausanne proclaimed them men free of the corruption of worldly ties and ambitions, and penitents ready to take the sins and misfortunes of their hearers upon their own shoulders, like the hermit Roger of Huntingdon whose 'compassion for the afflicted was such that he could not have born their miseries more hardly if they had been inflicted on himself.'[19] Nor need we do more than remind ourselves in passing that the crucial reward of humility was the power of arbitration, sometimes in great matters as when Vitalis of Savigny threw himself between the armies at Tinchebrai, but oftener, and we must hope with more success, in everyday affairs: Stephen of Obazine's biographer implies the norm in observing that his services to peace were 'non tantum domestica set et totius provinciae.'[20] A well known example is St. Bernard's success, in 1145, in arranging a compromise between the reforming archbishop of Bordeaux and the canons whose benefices he wanted to confer on regulars, which brought an end to a conflict that had caused the city to be under interdict for some seven years.[21] More immediately pertinent, perhaps, as showing how holiness could sometimes circumvent the corruption of established power, was the success of the hermit Edwin of Higney in appealing to the archbishop of Canterbury to uphold the vow of chastity taken by

[17] *Vita Norberti* ed. R. Wilmans, *MGH SS* XII p. 690.
[18] The following paragraphs are largely derived from 'The Cult of the Heresiarch', read to the fourth conference of the Commission internationale pour l'histoire écclésiastique comparée (Oxford 1974).
[19] *The Life of Christina of Markyate* ed and trans C.H. Talbot (Oxford 1959) p. 82.
[20] Orderic Vitalis, *HE* XI 10, ed M. Chibnall; *La vie de saint Etienne d'Obazine* ed M. Aubrun (*Publ. de l'Institut d'Etudes du Massif Central*, 6, Clermont-Ferrand 1970) p. 158.
[21] *PL* 185, col. 411; Ch. Higounet, *Histoire de Bordeaux* II (Bordeaux 1963) pp. 98–9.

the six-year-old Christina of Markyate against the bishop of Lincoln's judgement, obtained by bribery, that it should be overridden in the interests of the betrothal arranged by her socially ambitious parents.[22]

We come closest to observing the problems which might beset relatively humble communities in the very full account which we have of Henry of Lausanne's stay at Le Mans in 1116.[23] His arrival, as Bishop Hildebert was on the point of setting out for Rome, stimulated much excitement. 'When the man's reputation began to grow in our area the people with characteristic frivolity and predictable consequences were delighted', and when he entered the city 'the mob in its usual way applauded the novelty preferring the unknown to the familiar ... they believed that his righteousness was even greater than his fame, which was instantly inflated by gossip.' The tension which that restlessness suggests in the city was confirmed when Henry's disciples declared an economic boycott, refusing to trade with the clerks. Some clerks were driven out of the city, others set upon and beaten up by the citizens. When one of them plucked up courage to deliver a letter in which the clergy denounced Henry's teachings and habits the heresiarch received him in quasi-judicial state, and listened to the accusations with majestic calm, 'nodding his head at each accusation ... and replying in a clear voice "You are lying."' Shortly afterwards he summoned the people to a meeting where he 'proclaimed the new dogma that women who had not lived chastely must, naked before everyone, burn their clothes and their hair. Nobody should accept any gold or silver or goods or wedding gifts with his wife, or receive any dowry with her: the naked should marry the naked, the sick marry the sick and the poor marry the poor, without bothering about whether they married chastely or incestuously.' When his sermon was complete he collected money for new clothes for the purified women, and, anticipating Fulk of Neuilly at the end of the century, invited young men to volunteer to marry them.

Henry's programme, which 'moved the people to subject their every wish and deed to his command' addressed a clearly defined

---

[22] *Life of Christina*, pp. 64–84.
[23] *Gesta Pontificum Cenomannensium*, Bouquet XII pp. 547–51; Moore, *Origins* pp. 83–90.

complex of social grievances. Under the episcopate of the enthusi-astically reforming Hildebert of Lavardin we must suppose that Le Mans had seen the Gregorian drive against marriage within the newly-extended prohibited degrees, and for the treatment of mar-riage as a sacrament, together diminishing the opportunities of marriage available to the poor, increasing its cost and enhancing clerical control over it, and through it over family life.[24] Moreover, Le Mans was, as it would remain, a clerical town. Its population had already demanded a commune in 1070, and failed to get one, as it would continue to do because, as Latouche observed,[25] it was wholly dependent on the church for its living, containing no men of independent substance from manufacture or commerce. The Manceaux were condemned to resentful dependence on the clergy, relieved by occasional eruptions of impotent fury. Henry's attempt to minister to their needs inspired the cry with which they greeted Hildebert on his return from Rome, 'We have a father, a bishop and defender greater than you in authority, fame and learning' and ensured that 'the people had become so devoted to Henry that even now his memory can scarcely be expunged or their love for him drawn from their hearts.'

I have repeated this well-known story in detail because it depicts so clearly not only the basis of religious leadership among the *pauperes* at the beginning of the twelfth century, but also the contexts in which these voluntary associations were formed. By the force of his preaching and the vigour and directness of his attack on the sources of festering grievance Henry enabled the Manceaux to establish among themselves a sense of community and of collective capacity for action. Notice in particular his proud and public defiance of the emissary of the canons, and the facts that his meeting took place in the churchyard of St. Germain and St. Vincent – that is, in the sanctuary by now traditionally immune from seigneurial intrusion, and the centre of communal activity,[26] –

[24] See now G. Duby, *The Knight, the Lady and the Priest* (London 1984) esp pp. 107–20; R.I. Moore 'Duby's Eleventh Century', *History* 69 (1984) pp. 46–7.

[25] R. Latouche, *Etudes Médiévales* (Paris 1968) pp. 21–6, 'La commune du Mans, 1070'.

[26] L. Musset, '*Cimiterium ad refugium tantum vivorum non ad sepulturam mor-tuorum*', *Rev. du Moyen Age Latin* 4 (1948) pp. 55–60.

that the burning of the prostitutes' clothes and hair could symbolise the shedding not only of their old way of life, a venal and humiliating subjugation to those more powerful than themselves, but with it that of their fellow-citizens, and that the collection of money for their replacements again constituted a symbolic but also a practical representation of collective renewal and a fresh start. I cannot offer you any contemporary account of what all this meant to the participants, but there is perhaps food for thought in this experience of the sit-ins in English universities in 1968 and 1969:

> Collective direct action does in fact have a value in itself ... It is not only the experience of comradeship and solidarity, of the disappearance of barriers between people, which those who have known it will never forget. It is that in such a situation, when the conventional hierarchical structure has been for the moment swept aside, a quite exceptional sense of future openness and vast opportunities is born ... [27]

The sentiment described there is precisely that which plays so large a part in Turner's analysis of pilgrimage – of the sense of exaltation and brotherhood produced by the annihilation of worldly differences of rank and wealth in the context of ritual removal from the world.[28] But whereas (a point, I think, which Turner does not make) the pilgrimage may actually reinforce these distinctions in everyday life, bolstering their acceptability both by providing temporary relief from them and by defining their absence as a quality of the ideal world dependent on their presence in the real one, Henry's followers at Le Mans found themselves having achieved the exhilaration of fraternity in the here and now, and consequently – if my analogy with the students of 1969 is legitimate – able to conceive of that annihilation of social barriers as a permanent condition. Very much the same effect would follow, at a symbolic level, from Tanchelm's pronunciation of the marriage vows between himself and his wooden figure of the virgin: the power of the blasphemy was that it united the beholders in awe,

---

[27] A. Arblaster, *Academic Freedom* (Harmondsworth 1974) p. 163.
[28] V. and E. Turner, *Image and Pilgrimage in Christian Culture* (Oxford 1978) pp. 102–3, 133–4.

terror and finally exhilaration as it became apparent that this spectacular assault upon conventional piety was not about to be punished by instant devastation. Tanchelm's virgin stood for many things, but one of them was the worldly authority directly embodied in the canons of Le Mans whom Henry defied as boldly. Marbod of Rennes' famous complaint that Robert of Arbrissel's denunciation of the sins of the clergy was 'not to preach but to undermine'[29] expresses a very potent fear: for the poor – or the *populus* – the holy man was the scourge of the privileged, and the more outrageously he defied the proprieties of the existing order the more profound became the bonds which held them to him, as a being of supernatural power and courage, and to each other as brothers joined in common resistance to an alienating social order. Hence the devotion which led Frederick Barbarossa to have the body of Arnold of Brescia burned and his ashes scattered in the Tiber, and hence also the sense of community which was consecrated in the communion celebrated by those who drank Tanchelm's bathwater, and venerated for more than half a century after his death the ashes of Ramihrdus of Cambrai, salvaged from the hut in which he was burned by the servants of the bishop whom he had denounced.[30]

The cult of the heresiarch characterised the generations of upheaval between the early eleventh and mid twelfth centuries, when there was a strong tendency for all authority, secular as well as spiritual, to be exercised in a very personal way. It is no doubt a freak of the survival of sources that the indications of the use of vernacular scriptures mentioned earlier include none between the 1040s and the 1160s, but it is consistent with the evolution of the framework of dissent. As in the church the heroic age of Hildebrand and Bernard gave way to that of the lawyers, among heretics the wolf at the fold was succeeded by the little foxes among the vines, and Henry of Lausanne, Peter of Bruys and Arnold of Brescia were followed by more anonymous but scarcely less effective missionaries and organisers (the first Cathar bishops appear

[29] *PL* 171, col. 1483.
[30] Otto of Freising, *Gesta Frederici* ed G. Waitz, *MGH SRG* 46 p. 134; *Vita Norberti* ed R. Wilmans, *MGH SS* XII p. 690; *Chron. S. Andreae Cameracesii* ed L.G. Bethmann, *MGH SS* VII p. 540.

in the west in the 1150s), who established sects of considerable endurance.

On the face of it at least the solidarity of the heretical associations was no less tenacious for becoming less obviously charismatic in origin. From the burnings at Cologne in 1143 and again in 1163 through those at Reims in the 1170s and beyond the steadfastness of the heretics in the face of torture and death was a source of admiration and anxiety to Catholic observers. 'I wish I were with you, Holy Father', Eberwin of Steinfeld wrote to Bernard, 'to hear you explain how such great fortitude comes to those tools of the devil in their heresy as is seldom found among the truly religious in the faith of Christ.'[31] The source of that fortitude lay in the bonds which the sectaries had formed among themselves, whether they united in veneration of Ramihrdus' ashes or the *consolamentum* of the Cathars. It goes almost without saying that those acts constituted another vital element in the formation of the sects, and that in uniting the faithful they also excluded outsiders. When a group defines itself by common belief the ceremony of initiation becomes a matter of high importance. That the rejection of infant baptism was the most universal doctrine of the heretics of this period, reflecting the urgency in eleventh-century Europe of forming new communities, as distinct from simply being born into old ones,[32] also points to the rapid evolution of equivalent rites within the sects themselves, from the *baptismum Henrici* of which Peter the Venerable speaks[33] to the *consolamentum*. To stress adult baptism is also, in another of the classic symptoms of sect formation, to proclaim the priority of ties of faith over those of family.[34] When the Patarenes referred to each other as *fideles* they did more than proclaim their allegiance to impersonal and abstract ideals, for they repudiated all former ties and associations in favour of their new way so that, as Andrew of Sturmi put it,

---

[31] *PL* 182, col. 677.
[32] R.I. Moore, 'Some heretical attitudes to the renewal of the church', *SCH* 14 (1977) p. 92.
[33] *Contra Petrobrusianos* p. 14.
[34] cf. J. Goody, *The development of the family and marriage in Europe* (Cambridge 1983) pp. 82–92, applying this point to the early Christians.

'in many households the mother believed with one son while the father disbelieved with another.'[35]

We now find ourselves on the brink of a paradox. Our effort for the greater part of this paper has been to see the sectaries or potential sectaries of these centuries as they saw themselves, taking them at their own valuation and accepting their assessment of the wickedness of the world, and especially of the Church in the world. Yet we seem to have arrived at a conclusion very similar to that of which their enemies, by and large, have convinced posterity, namely that their exclusion from the Church and the christian community at large was their own doing, that they cut themselves off by the very intensity of the narrow flame of their faith. Before attempting to consider whether it was really as simple as that we had better look at the matter from the point of view of those with whom the sectaries found themselves in conflict.

A further merit of Stock's analysis of the texts of the eleventh century is to show how clearly the accounts themselves were shaped from their conception by contrasting interpretations of the origin of heresy closely akin to those with which we still struggle. For Ralph Glaber, the Cluniac monk, or for Adhémar of Chabannes, propagandist of the peace movement in the south-west, heresy represented a recrudescence of paganism and idolatry, an infection carried into the world of the clerks by alien figures from that of the *rustici*, like the old woman mentioned in no other source and quite at variance with the entire character of the episode, to whom Ralph attributes the inspiration of the sect at Orléans. For others, like Paul of St. Père of Chartres, Gerard of Cambrai and Landulf Senior, the fault lay in failures of discipline among the literate.[36] Their attitude was, of course, directly related to the highly conservative position which they adopted towards the broader question of the reasons for the evident corruption of the eleventh-century Church, and the legitimacy of customs which reformers attacked.

---

[35] G. Cracco, 'Pataria: *opus* e *nomen*', in W. Lordaux and D. Verhelst, *The Concept of Heresy in the Middle Ages, Mediaevalia Lovanensia* I, IV (Louvain 1976) pp. 167–71, expanded in *RSCI* xxviii (1979) pp. 357–85; Stock, *Implications of Literacy* pp. 238–9; H.E.J. Cowdrey, 'The Papacy, the Patarenes and the Church of Milan', *TRHS* 5th Series 18 (1968) pp. 31–2; Andrew of Sturmi, *Vita Sancti Arialdi* ed F. Baethgen, *MGH SS* 30 p. 1057.
[36] Stock, *op. cit.* pp. 115, 150–1.

The general identity of the criticisms made of the Church by reformers and heretics and the close association between the architects of the papal reform and many popular attacks on local hierarchies are too familiar to need explication here.[37] The variety of response which enthusiasm encountered in consequence may be illustrated, among the episodes which I have already mentioned, by the contrast between the inclination of Roger II of Châlons to turn the *rustici* whose *furtiva conventicula* he had uncovered over to the secular power and the insistence of Wazo, himself a vigorous advocate of the need for higher educational standards among the priesthood, that they should be countered only by excommunication and patient rebuttal of their arguments;[38] by the fact that in refusing the sacrament from the corrupt hands of those who examined him Ramihrdus of Cambrai did no more than obey the instruction of Gregory VII, who had licensed Wederic of Ghent to preach that very message in Flanders at about this time;[39] that Hildebert's readiness to admit Henry of Lausanne to Le Mans was doubtless prompted by his own adherence to the reforming tradition, or even by his friendship with Robert of Arbrissel, who had died in the previous year, and whom Henry much resembled in his demeanour, appearance and message; and by the recollection that Lambert le Bègue was launched on his turbulent career as a parish priest by a reforming bishop whose standards (at least in Lambert's view) were not maintained by his worldlier successor. In short, behind the general hardening of official attitudes towards critics of the Church and the groupings formed by their admirers and disciples, which continued throughout the twelfth century, there was always an alternative view, embodied in Innocent III's treatment of the Humiliati and the Poor Catholics, that a modicum

[37] See, for example, Grundmann *passim*; K.J. Leyser, 'The Polemics of the Papal Revolution' in B. Smalley ed *Trends in Medieval Political Thought* (Oxford 1965) pp. 42–64; I.S. Robinson, 'Gregory VII and the Soldiers of Christ', *History* 58 (1973) pp. 169–92, and 'The Friendship Network of Gregory VII' *ibid.* 63 (1978) pp. 1–22.

[38] above, n. 8; Stock, *op. cit.* pp. 148–9.

[39] Registrum ed E. Caspar, *MGH Epp Sel* II, 1 pp. 328–9; G. Meersseman in *L'Eremitismo in Occidente nei secoli xi e xii*, Miscellanea del Centro di Studi Mediovali IV (Milan 1965) pp. 171–2.

of obedience should suffice to buy a large measure of independence.[40]

Nevertheless, from the beginning the ordinary response of authority to voluntary association, especially when it involved laymen, or worse still lay women, was one of intense suspicion. Prophecy, appealing to the transcendental authority of sacred text or inner illumination, presents at least an implicit threat to the existing order, which was compounded by social fear when the prophets addressed themselves to the unprivileged. But the most specific reason for distrust of new groups within or alongside the formal structures of the Church was the fear of spiritual élitism, that those who claimed a special insight or skill threatened to cut off the mass of Christians from the faith. From the time of their first appearance this was one of the bitterest reproaches against the Cathars,[41] and it is particularly clearly expressed in relation to the intellectual heresies of the early eleventh century. The stress of late Carolingian exegesis on the spiritual interpretation of the scriptures, the neoplatonist notion that it was through the *interiores oculi* that they were to be rightly read, might easily make true understanding the prerogative of a spiritually competent section of the literate. To that extent there may have been some substance in the charge that the clerks of Orléans had formed a secret circle, and the words that they are reported to have used in initiating Aréfast, that 'Foolish teachings will be shut from your heart and you will be able with a pure mind to receive our teaching, which is handed down from the Holy Spirit'[42] may be thought to imply that there were two versions of Christian teaching, one of which was reserved from most Christians. The same tendency is suggested by the statement of Gerard of Monforte (whose replies to Aribert of Milan were riddled with neoplatonist imagery) that 'I mean by the Holy Spirit the understanding of divine wisdom by which all things are separately ruled'.[43] Certainly it was against the tendency to spiritual

---

[40] Brenda M. Bolton, 'Innocent III's treatment of the *Humiliati*', SCH 7 (1971) pp. 73–82; 'Tradition and Temerity: Papal Attitudes to Deviants 1159–1216', *ibid.* 9 (1972) pp. 79–91; C. Thouzellier, *Catharisme et Valdéisme en Languedoc* (2 ed Louvain 1969) pp. 215–26.

[41] Eckbert of Schönau, *Sermones XIII contra Catharos*, PL 195 cols 13–14, 18–21.

[42] Bouquet X p. 537.

[43] *MGH SS* VIII pp. 65–6.

élitism, as Cracco has shown clearly, that the discourse of Gerard of Cambrai was directed in 1025, its argument that what was required for salvation was not an inside track to divine illumination but a steady and humble attention to the universal public requirements of the Church, and the regular reception of its sacraments. Gerard's purpose, as Cracco puts it, was 'to show the faithful an accessible faith.'[44]

Here is a point of convergence between our two perspectives. I am not aware of any suggestion among the heretics of this period that salvation was not accessible to all who sought it or that any special equipment was needed for the search beyond faith and good will: in this sense Gerard's argument was better directed against the clerks to whom it was in fact addressed (as we shall see in a moment) than to the men who stood before him as he delivered the sermon on which it was based. Nevertheless, it is true that if the heretics were not exclusive or élitist in the sense of denying access to their faiths to any who genuinely sought it, it is also the case that their insistence on the absolute commitment of the informed adult together with the austere habit of daily life which the Cathars and Waldensians at least regarded as concomitant with it, had the effect of setting them apart from the general stream of humanity. The question that remains, to put it rather crudely, is whether in seeing it that way the bishops accepted the inevitable corollary of the sectaries' own self-perception, or made prophecies about them which turned out to be self-fulfilling.

As I have said Gerard of Cambrai's message was not addressed to the men who confronted him at Arras. There is nothing in the text to suggest that they were clerks, which would be a remarkable omission not only in itself but in view of the general nature and purpose of Gerard's exposition; indeed it is explicitly stated that they were illiterate, being unable to understand the Latin confession of faith produced for their endorsement, and having to signify their assent with crosses when it had been translated for them. Moreover, Gerard's references to the *supplicia* employed in their interrogation before the council imply that they were tortured, and that in turn

---

[44] 'Riforma ed eresia' (above, n. 5) pp. 453–6.

that they were unfree.[45] So what happened here was that Bishop Gerard came across a case of popular religious enthusiasm which it suited him to treat as though it had occurred at a more elevated level of society. The leniency of his final decision – the accused were allowed to go free after making their crosses – confirms that he did not take the matter particularly seriously in itself. There is a certain irony here, in that it was precisely the fear of unrest among the *pauperes* which showed itself in the generation of Marbod of Rennes and Guibert of Nogent and beyond as a principal source of suspicion and hostility towards popular religious movements. On the other hand, it shows Gerard doing exactly what Guibert did when he found a revival of Manicheeism behind the evangelism of Clement of Bucy, and what Cohn and Kieckhefer have revealed as the mechanism which transformed the magic of the countryside into the cult of Satan in the later middle ages.[46] In each case evidence of conflict or unrest among the poor was reinterpreted by learned officials to demonstrate the existence of seditious corruption among the more powerful. For Gerard of Cambrai, as Duby has demonstrated, the threat to world order came not from resentful serfs – the process of enserfment, indeed, was still at an early stage in these parts[47] – and still less from resurgent Manichees or Satanic cults, but from the undermining of traditional authority by insubordination in the ranks of the nobility, whose usurpation of royal and episcopal authority was compounded by the peace movement's arrogation to itself of the crown's most fundamental

---

[45] Here, following Stock *op. cit.* p. 123 n., I now accept the view of J.B. Russell, *Dissent and Reform in the Early Middle Ages* (Los Angeles 1965) p. 22; cf. E. Peters, *Torture* (Oxford 1985) pp. 38, 47–8.

[46] Moore, *Origins of European Dissent* pp. 67–9, and 'Guibert of Nogent and his World' in H. Mayr-Harting and R.I. Moore eds *Studies in Medieval History Presented to R.H.C. Davis* (London 1985) pp. 108–10; N. Cohn, *Europe's Inner Demons* (London 1975) esp pp. 225–55; R. Kieckhefer, *European Witch Trials: Their Foundations in Popular and Learned Culture* (London 1976) esp pp. 73–92; for a lucid summary of modern views on the European witchcraze see C. Larner, *Enemies of God* (London 1981) pp. 15–28. All of these, however, need to take account of the specifically political and courtly context of the group of trials around 1300 revealed by E. Peters, *The Magician, the Witch and the Law* (Philadelphia 1978) pp. 112–35.

[47] J.P. Poly and E. Bournazel, *La mutation féodale x–xii siècles* (Paris 1980) pp. 312–19.

responsibilities, and by the Cluniac pursuit of exemption from episcopal jurisdiction.[48]

In choosing to treat the followers of Gundolfo as evidence of these dangers to the social fabric Gerard reminds us of the arbitrariness which, perhaps inevitably, has attended my decision as to what constitutes a voluntary religious association for the purposes of this discussion. For what else were the peace associations? Appearing in south-western Francia towards the end of the tenth century they were usually led though not always launched by bishops; their character was that of free associations entered upon by oath, between those who behaved, at least for this purpose, as equals; and their objectives can hardly be dismissed as secular or material when they adumbrated the entire programme of Gregorian reform, including the purification of the clergy and the regular availability and correct administration of the services and sacraments of the Church.[49] A very small shift of focus might bring before our eyes the guild, of whose ubiquity and substantially religious functions Reynolds has recently reminded us.[50] The word sprang too readily to the lips of this period, as she insists, to bear any narrow or exclusive interpretation – a point which is reinforced by the recollection that one of Tanchelm's disciples, the blacksmith Manasses, formed a guild for his followers.[51] Guilds served a variety of purposes, including in ninth-century Francia (as well as in Wessex) the law enforcement which the peace associations later tried to take over.[52] But the institution, created and renewed by voluntary association, sworn oath, religious ceremonial and (perhaps most universally) communal eating and drinking, must command a prominent place in any comprehensive account of this subject. So must another, destined to become even more universal in its distribution and functions – the parish. For, of course, the European parish as we have known it since the twelfth century

---

[48] Duby, *The Three Orders* passim.
[49] R.I. Moore, 'Family, Community and Cult on the Eve of the Gregorian Reforms', *TRHS* 5 Ser. 30 (1980) pp. 51–3.
[50] Susan Reynolds, *Kingdoms and Communities in Western Europe 900–1300* (Oxford 1984) pp. 67–78. M. Dorothy Ross 'The Role of the Gild in the Religious Life of Anglo-Saxon England' (Manchester University M.A. thesis 1985) is a valuable account of the gild as voluntary religious association.
[51] *ASB* June I, 833.
[52] *MGH Capit.* ii, 375, c. 14.

was created not by any concerted policy, but by a gradual dispersal of parochial rights from the baptismal to the lesser churches, often through the mediation of a noble family, which might alienate them from the former in the ninth century and restore them to the latter in the twelfth.[53] The peace movement itself gave a powerful impetus to the formation of new parishes. One of its earliest and most general objects was to secure the right of sanctuary (*salvamentum*) for the unarmed and their goods in the *cimiterium*. The prohibition of fees for the sacraments of the Church, conspicuously including burial, also fostered parish development, since by depriving the lords of the profits of their *altaria* it tended to encourage their restitution, or at least to reduce its cost.

In broadening my field of discussion I am raising far more questions than I can pretend to answer. However, I have done so with one particularly in mind. In his characteristically persuasive enumeration of the problems which he expects the contributors to resolve our president admonishes them to 'consider what it is to fulfill a religious purpose' and, furthermore, to explore 'the meaning and function of the sociability which we shall encounter within this theme ... without the constraints imposed' by piety on the one hand and Marxism on the other. Fortunate though I am in enjoying equal freedom from both of those disabilities the instruction is one which I am poorly equipped to obey. In the forms of association which we have considered I find myself baffled by the question how to distinguish their religious purposes from their worldly ones. Let me illustrate the difficulty with a final example. It is derived from the recent discovery of Delarun that the familiar description of the last illness and death of Robert of Arbrissel, the *extrema conversatio* by the monk Andreas, is incomplete.[54] It was censored by Petronilla, abbess of Fontevrault, to suppress the undignified circumstances of Robert's translation to his last resting place at her abbey. Delarun's recovery of a complete version has enabled him to undo her work. Robert fell ill at the priory of Orsan in the Berry. The lord of Orsan, Alardus, whose wife was prioress, was anxious to keep the body there, and threatened that

---

[53] Reynolds, *op. cit.* pp. 79–100; R. Fossier, *L'enfance de l'Europe x–xii siècles* (Paris 1982) pp. 345–58.
[54] J. Delarun, 'La véritable fin de Robert d'Arbrissel', *Cahiers de Civilisation Médiévale* 27 (1984) pp. 303–60.

any attempt to remove it would be prevented by the people. Petronilla had made the journey to the deathbed – no doubt with just such an eventuality in mind, for she was a determined and ruthless defender of the rights of her house[55] – and found herself driven to steal Robert's body at the moment of his death, and hide it in the cloister until Archbishop Leger of Bourges, whom she had threatened with all manner of holy terrors including an appeal to Rome, came to her rescue and secured Robert's safe passage to Fontevrault. Twenty years earlier, as Murray has recounted, the men of three townships contended for the remains of another Breton hermit, William Firmatus.[56] His biographer attributes the victory of Mortain to 'its entire clergy and an innumerable crowd of its people' acting on the orders of the count. What brought these people into conflict for the bones of their holy men with as much vigour as if they had been fifth-century Syrians?[57] Orsan was probably, like most Fontevriste priories, a frontier community, founded to clear new land. The people with whose wrath Alardus threatened Petronilla were incomers, probably did not share an ancestral heritage, and were engaged in the process of forming their community; Mortain was not new, but it was again in an area where clearance was in rapid progress at the end of the eleventh century. No doubt its populace found a sense of identity gratifyingly expressed and reinforced in the battle for William Firmatus, as the settlers around Orsan took a step in establishing theirs in defiance of the proud abbess of Fontevrault, even though they failed. Beyond that, if those two stories are placed beside what has already been said about the proliferation of parishes at this time – a great many of them, of course, on newly cleared land – it is worth recalling Gluckman's description of what he called land-shrines.[58] These he defines as shrines which, with their accompanying ritual, are maintained by those whose common bond lies in

---

[55] R.I. Moore, 'The Reconstruction of the Cartulary of Fontevrault', *BIHR* xli (1968) pp. 94–5.

[56] A. Murray, *Reason and Society in the Middle Ages* (Oxford 1978) p. 400.

[57] Peter Brown, 'The Rise and Function of the Holy Man in Late Antiquity', *JRS* 61 (1971), now in his *Society and the Holy in Late Antiquity* (London 1982) p. 113. The influence of this famous paper will be apparent at many points in the present discussion.

[58] Max Gluckman, *Politics, Law and Ritual in Tribal Society* (Oxford 1965) pp. 104–7.

involvement in the cultivation of a particular piece of land. The rituals have the effect of drawing out and reinforcing the principles of cooperation which that task demands. What is particularly interesting from our point of view is that such shrines are often associated with ritual declarations that peace is to be observed at particular times and places, and often with the name of the first settler on the land in question[59] or with a prophet from outside the community.

We have already observed an analogy between the way in which Gerard of Cambrai used the discovery of enthusiasts in his diocese to confirm his thesis of a general conspiracy of evil forces against the social order and the creation of the witch craze in the fifteenth and sixteenth centuries. Twelfth-century writers from Guibert of Nogent and Eckbert of Schönau onwards used the stereotype of the medieval Manichee in the same way.[60] One reason for it is now plain to see. Witchcraft accusations are notoriously associated both with the fission of communities, which tends to produce charges either against or in justification of those who lead the division, and with the attempts of holders of authority to maintain and extend it over assertive local communities. As Mair put it, 'accusations of witchcraft and sorcery are not always connected with rivalry for authority ... but conflicts for authority commonly employ such accusations.'[61] Fission, in brief, may generate conflict, which external authority can exploit.

It does not follow that because the bishops identified the target wrongly there was no target at all. On the contrary, when we are dealing with the formation of communities it is easy to see how the community itself, rallied around the bones of its founding saint or the sanctuary which might often have been its first collective possession,[62] was the object of religious activity and, if you like, the seat of the holy. But it was not only to new communities

---

[59] As is so commonly signified in north-western and western France in our period by place names ending in *erie* or *ière*: R. Latouche, *The Birth of Western Economy* (London 1961) p. 280.

[60] Moore, *Origins of European Dissent* pp. 245–6.

[61] Lucy Mair, *Witchcraft* (London 1969) pp. 116–38; the quotation, from p. 137, refers particularly to the findings of V.W. Turner, *Schism and Continuity in an African Society* (Manchester 1957); Larner, *Enemies of God* pp. 40–59, 192–202.

[62] R. Fossier, *Chartes de coutume en Picardie (xie–xiiie siècle)*. Collection des documents inédits sur l'histoire de France (Paris 1974) p. 35.

that that might apply, and not only to communities which were embodied in or could be identified with a particular settlement or place. The idea of the holy which animated the reform movements of the eleventh century was rooted in collective values and resistance to arbitrary power, opposing *conventio* to *districtio*, *humilitas* to *superbia*, *paupertas* to *potestas*. Such values were expressed in the voluntary association of the community at large, created and confirmed by oath to oppose the arbitrary force of lawless individuals.[63] In resisting the Gregorian transference of the locus of sanctity from the shrine to the priest through increased emphasis on the sacraments[64] and with it the extension of ecclesiastical control over everyday life, through the sacralisation of marriage, the institution of confession, and so on, the heretical sects were doing much the same thing, rooting their allegiance in the collective identity of the sect itself, through their emphasis on rites of initiation *to* rather than those of ordination *within* the sect, through the egalitarian forms of worship which they preferred, – listening to preaching, reading the scriptures, singing the psalms – and through the establishment of distinctive norms of behaviour and demeanour of which the sect itself was the arbiter. When the men of Arras expressed the desire to earn their food by the labour of their own hands, to do no injury to anybody, and to extend charity to everyone of their own faith, and when the girl who had been taken at Cologne in 1163, refusing the sympathy of the onlookers, 'tore herself from the grasp of those who were holding her, and threw herself into the fire with her four companions'[65] the power that moved them was that vested in the association itself, the power of the community held sacred. Whether its sacralisation constituted a religious purpose must be for others to determine.

The University of Sheffield

[63] Moore, 'Family, Community and Cult' pp. 63–5.
[64] R.I. Moore, 'Some heretical attitudes to the renewal of the Church' *SCH* 14 (1977) pp. 89–92.
[65] *Chronica Regiae Coloniensis MGH SRG* 18 p. 114.

CONFRATERNITIES AND THE CHURCH
IN LATE MEDIEVAL FLORENCE

by JOHN HENDERSON

THE confraternities of late-medieval Europe have been seen as associations which were in some ways almost independent of the Church,[1] and drew their special dynamism from the fact that the parish was supposedly in decline and had ceased to provide an adequate religious service to the lay community.[2] However true this may have been north of the Alps, the problem when this proposition is applied to southern Europe, and particularly Italy, is that very little is known about the late-medieval parish to ascertain whether confraternities were really syphoning off the adherence of the local inhabitants.[3] So often our impressions about the state of the Italian church derive from the sporadic visitations of local bishops or the ribald stories of a Boccaccio or Franco Sacchetti, later repeated and taken almost at face value by such influential writers as Burkhardt.[4] But we may also be in danger of seeing late-medieval religion filtered through

---

*Unless otherwise stated, all manuscripts cited are from the Archivo di Stato di Firenze.

[1] J. Bossy, 'The Counter-Reformation and the People of Catholic Europe', *Past and Present*, 47 (1970) p. 59; N.Z. Davis, *Society and Culture in Early Modern France* (London 1977) p. 75.

[2] See, for example, the studies of Northern Europe by P. Adam, *La vie paroissiale en France au XIV^c siècle* (Paris 1964) and J. Toussaert, *Le sentiment religieux en Flandre à la fin du Moyen Age* (Paris 1963). But see the sensitive remarks by John Bossy in *Christianity in the West 1400–1700* (Oxford 1985) pp. 62–63.

[3] Cf D. Hay, *The Church in Italy in the Fifteenth Century* (Cambridge 1977) pp. 23–25, 52–57. Research has begun in this field as can be seen from the conferences on the subject: for example, *Le istituzioni ecclesiastiche della 'Societas Christiana' dei secoli XI–XII. Diocesi, pievi e parrocchie* (Milan 1975) and P. Prodi, P. Johanek eds *Strutture ecclesiastiche in Italia e in Germania prima della riforma* (Bologna 1984).

[4] On episcopal visitations see Hay, *The Church in Italy* pp. 52–57; for S.Antonino's visitations S.Orlandi, *S.Antonino. Arcivescovo di Firenze* (Florence 1959) I pp. 75–89, esp 82–88. J. Burckhardt, *The Civilization of the Renaissance in Italy* (London 1950) pt. VI, where his main target is the regular rather than the secular clergy.

sixteenth-century eyes and taking for granted the correctness of the criticisms of the Council of Trent or for that matter following Luther's gripes that confraternities had become no more than beer-drinking clubs.[5]

The relationship between confraternities and the Church is complex, and varied according to both time and place. Certainly a valid distinction can be made throughout Europe between city and countryside, for in the villages, unlike the towns, many of the local population could easily be enrolled in a company,[6] so that a parish and a confraternity could become almost synonymous. This paper will be restricted, however, to the urban context by examining Florence, one of the largest cities in late-medieval Europe, and the relationship between the confraternities and two parts of the Florentine Church about which we know at least something: the friars and the bishop; only in relation to the latter will the parish begin to slide into view.

Florence, in common with other major cities with populations approaching 45,000, had at least one hundred confraternities by the late fifteenth century.[7] One of the characteristics of many Italian lay religious companies – shared by the Florentine examples – was the diversity of their activities, ranging from the laud-singers and the flagellants to the larger charities, such as Orsanmichele and the Misericordia, to the more specialised groups for children and

---

[5] See, for example, Pierre Janelle's description of the 'disease' within the pre-Tridentine Church, in what has now become a standard work on the Counter-Reformation: *The Catholic Reformation* (London 1971 ed), cap. 1. For Luther's views on confraternities: *Luther's Works*, ed E.T. Backmann (Philadelphia 1960) 35 pp. 67–69.

[6] Bossy, *Christianity* p. 59; D.M. Owen, *Church and Society in Medieval Lincolnshire* (Lincoln 1971) p. 127; N. Galpern, *The Religions of the People in Sixteenth-Century Champagne* (Cambridge, Mass./London 1976) p. 59; W.A. Christian, *Local Religion in Sixteenth-Century Spain* (Princeton 1981) p. 52; J. Chiffoleau, 'Les confréries, la mort et la religion en Comtat Venaissin à la fin du Moyen Age', *MEFRM* 91 (1979) p. 800; C.M. de La Roncière, 'La place des confréries dans l'encadrement religieux du contado florentin: l'exemple de la Val d'Elsa' *MEFRM* 85 (1973) p. 55.

[7] For the population of Florence see D. Herlihy and C. Klapisch, *Les toscans et leurs familles: une étude du catasto florentin de 1427* (Paris 1978) p. 183, and calculation of numbers of confraternities in the city: J.S. Henderson, 'Piety and Charity in Late Medieval Florence. Lay Religious Confraternities from the middle of the thirteenth century to the late fifteenth century' (University of London Ph.D. thesis 1983) p. 32: Table I.2, and Chapters 2–3 for the devotional role of these companies.

artisans. Even though membership was normally restricted to adult males who belonged to trade guilds,[8] it is probable that the majority of this type of Florentine belonged to one or more confraternity. This implies a widespread adherence and also suggests that these organisations were satisfying a very real religious and social need.

By the mid-fifteenth century the most popular type of company was the flagellant, representing almost half of the total number of confraternities in the city. The emphasis on penitence suggests the influence of the friars and indeed when studying where confraternities met we discover that 41 per cent were in churches belonging to the Mendicant Orders.[9] This is not all that surprising given that the Mendicants, and in particular the Dominicans and the Franciscans, had from the mid-thirteenth century been one of the main influences in encouraging the laity to deepen their piety. One of the aims of the famous preaching tours of the friars was to promote a more lasting change in the laity's beliefs and practices, not just by saying Mass and delivering sermons, but also by providing the potential for establishing religious corporations which the laity could run for themselves. The Third Orders were followed by a proliferation of lay companies.[10] The laity on their side were attracted not just by the obvious advantage of having educated men to preach and administer the sacraments, but also by the very size of these huge barn-like structures. Confraternities were provided with space in and around the church, where they could build chapels and construct oratories, neither of which was as easy in the more cramped parish churches. In addition to space for the living the Mendicant friars provided room for the dead and in this way confraternity members could be buried in the company graves inside highly prestigious churches, such as S. Maria Novella and

[8] R.F.E. Weissman, *Ritual Brotherhood in Renaissance Florence* (New York and London 1982) pp. 67–68, 118–120.

[9] Henderson 'Piety and Charity' p. 39 n. 4.

[10] The best introduction to the whole subject is G.G. Meersseman, *Ordo Fraternitatis: confraternite e pietà dei laici nel medioevo* (Rome 1977) 3 vols., and on the Florentine Third Order see the articles by A. Benvenuti Papi, among which 'I frati della Penitenza nella società fiorentina del Due-Trecento', *I frati penitenti di San Francesco nella società del due e trecento*, ed M. D'Alatri (Rome 1977) pp. 191–220.

S.Croce.[11] Furthermore, there was a mutually advantageous arrangement to be had in terms of commemorative masses: the friars provided the personnel to conduct these anniversaries and the confraternity the cash. As we shall see in the case of the *compagnia di S.Pier Martire* in S.Maria Novella, large sums could in this way exchange hands every year.

It is easier to point out the mutual advantages to both confraternities and their hosts of their close association, or indeed the general influence of Mendicant theology in the promotion of flagellation, than to pin down the actual influence of individual religious on specific foundations in Florence. Thirteenth- and fourteenth-century statutes of Florentine companies mention much less frequently the direct involvement of the secular or regular clergy in setting up a company than is true of confraternities in other central Italian towns.[12] However, clerical involvement is implicit in the provisions of many statutes. Although the most important models for statutes were the Commune and the trade guild, most of their religious ceremonies were based closely on the conventual model.

On the one hand, the system of election by lot was taken over wholesale from communal administrative procedures and companies even introduced modifications to their systems in order to

---

[11] Burial sites in these two churches can be traced in their Sepoltuarii: for S.Croce in 1439: 'Sepoltuario di S.Croce', MS 619, and the 1617 'Sepoltuario della chiesa di S.Maria Novella', MS 621. See also M.B. Hall, *Renovation and Counter-Reformation. Vasari and Duke Cosimo in Sta Maria Novella and Sta Croce, 1565–1577* (Oxford 1979) catalogue of chapels and docs. I–II.

[12] One exception among the friaries is the *Laudesi* company founded by St. Peter Martyr in S.Maria Novella in 1244: Conv.Relig.Sopp.102.324, fol 3r; and in a parish church the *Laudesi di S.Frediano*, whose 1323 statutes mention the participation of the local priest in their compilation: Biblioteca Nazionale Centrale di Firenze (cited as BNF), Palatino, 154, fol 6v, as do the 1447 statutes of the *compagnia di S.Maria della Neve* in S.Ambrogio: Capitoli Comp.Relig.Sopp. 606, fol 38r. Examples of clerical involvement in company foundations is more common in other cities, as for example in Siena. The prologue to the statutes of the *Compagnia di S.Domenico in Campo Regio* states that they were 'scritti e composti da savissimi padri nostri frate Giovanni da Sangimignano, frate Ricovaro da Guardavalle e frate Francesco di Missere Gratia': G. Prunai, 'I capitoli della compagnia di San Domenico in Campo Regio', *Bollettino senese di storia patria*, 47 (1940) p. 139; Meersseman pp. 464–465 (Perugia), 596 (Pisa), 603 (Prato). See also the foundation in 1291 of the *compagnia della Vergine Maria* in the Servite church in Siena: F.A. dal Pino, *I Frati Servi di S. Maria dalle origini all'approvazione (1233ca–1304)* (Louvain 1972) 2 pp. 167–168.

comply with new techniques of voting.[13] On the other hand, ceremonies such as the introduction of novices were heavily dependent on the way in which friars were received into a convent. This was particularly true of members of flagellant companies, who wore habits in direct imitation of their hosts. The *vesta* came to have the same symbolic importance for the brother as it did for the friar: as a visual symbol of his intention to lead a reformed, Christian life.[14]

The close relationship between confraternal and Church ceremonies is even more obvious when studying these companies' para-liturgy, which was based very closely on the official liturgy. The main appeal of all these services was the involvement of laymen in virtually all stages of their enactment. The normal psalms were replaced or supplemented by lauds in the vernacular, thus allowing members to participate in a way which would have been impossible in a normal parochial or conventual church. Moreover the services would have been more personalised when compared with masses at the high altar.[15] Instead of taking place among the public, members stood in their own oratory, which was decorated with their own devotional objects, most prominent of which would have been their altarpiece which was commissioned and paid for by the membership.[16]

Although the close dependence of confraternal ceremonies on the liturgy of the Church indicates that these lay groups must have had the expert advice of the clergy when drawing up their statutes, the question which now arises is: how dependent or independent were confraternities once they had been established? The answer is not that straightforward and varied between companies, churches, and different periods. However, it is probably true to say that companies in conventual churches were more rigorously

---

[13] Henderson 'Piety and Charity' Chapter 8 traces this evolution.

[14] See Weissman pp. 82–83; 97.

[15] See the excellent description in C. Barr, 'Lauda singing and the tradition of the *disciplinati* Mandato: a reconstruction of two texts of the Office of Tenebrae', *L'ars nova italiana del trecento* (Certaldo 1978) pp. 2–44; this subject is also treated in detail in Henderson 'Piety and Charity', Chapters 2 and 3.

[16] J. White, *Duccio. Tuscan Art and the Medieval Workshop* (London 1979) pp. 32–45 and esp. 33, on one of the most famous of Florentine confraternity altarpieces, the *Rucellai Madonna*, commissioned by the *compagnia di S.Pier Martire* in S.Maria Novella.

controlled than those in churches which were run by canons or the parochial clergy or those which met in independent oratories. According to the late-thirteenth-century statutes of the *laudesi di S.Gilio*, for example, the captains were required to make sure that the company always had a friar, whose principal duty it was to 'admonish and correct everyone, not just the lesser, but also the more important'.[17] The religious corrector in any company was seen as a neutral figure above other members and officials, who represented the authority of the Church, or as the statutes of the *laudesi* company which met in the Cathedral put it: 'The chaplain [is] in the place of Jesus Christ, and the captains and counsellors in the place of the holy apostles'.[18]

The spiritual advisor's authoritarian function was most in evidence during the regular general confession. Members of the *Compagnia di Gesù Pellegrino* knelt individually on the third Sunday of each month in front of the friar and accused themselves of all those misdemeanours which they had committed against the statutes.[19] The *correttore* then imposed on them a series of punishments, which varied from a gentle tap on their shoulders with a scourge by each of their righteous brothers as they filed past, to a two-mile walk up hill to S.Miniato al Monte, whipping themselves all the way there and back.[20] Some indication of how important was the friar's admonitory role in a flagellant company can be seen from the records of this company during the first five years of its existence. Between 1334 and 1339 ten members were actually expelled each year. This represented about 16 per cent of the membership and was probably only a small proportion of the total numbers punished since only really serious misdeeds warranted the drastic step of expulsion.[21] Offences were predominantly of a moral

---

[17] 'Capitoli della Compagnia di S.Gilio', *Testi fiorentini del duecento e dei primi del trecento* ed A. Schiaffini (Florence 1926) p. 35: 'che ammonischa et corregha tutti, così piccioli di questa compagnia come i grandi'.

[18] Comp. Relig. Sopp. 2176.I, ch II, fol 32r: 'Il sacerdote è in luogho di Gesù Christo et i capitani e consiglieri in luogho de' sancti apostoli'.

[19] *I capitoli della compagnia di Gesù Pellegrino* ed P. Ferrato (Padua 1871) (Nozze Carlotti-Cittadella Vigodezere) pp. 28–29.

[20] Recorded in Comp. Relig. Sopp. 910.6.

[21] Calculated from *Ibid*.

character – best judged by a religious – and ranged from non-attendance at meetings to playing dice or frequenting taverns: all fairly standard failings condemned by the Church.[22]

The corrector seems to have had a powerful position, but his authority was not absolute. While he can be seen as the heir to the religious who helped to draw up the foundation statutes, especially as he had to be present when any changes were made,[23] he himself was bound by them and unable to contravene their provisions. In imposing punishments he was therefore to proceed with discretion 'according to the form of our chapters.'[24] Indeed if the lay officials felt that he had exceeded or even abrogated his authority they reserved the right to dismiss the corrector and replace him with another religious.[25] It should be remembered that the friar or chaplain was, like other employees, paid a salary to fulfil certain functions, which in his case were to say mass, direct ceremonies, and act as a confessor and corrector.[26]

As I have suggested, the relationship between confraternities and the Church did not remain unchanged between the thirteenth and fifteenth centuries. In some convents friars came to exert more authority over lay societies in this period. Thus by the mid-fifteenth century both the *laudesi* companies which met in S.Annunziata and S.Maria Novella included friars among their board of captains

---

[22] R.C. Trexler, *Synodal Law in Florence and Fiesole, 1306–1518* (Città di Vaticano 1971) p. 63.

[23] For example, 'Libro degli ordinamenti della compagnia di Santa Maria del Carmine', in Schiaffini p. 57.

[24] 'secondo la forma de' nostri capitoli' Ferrato p. 24.

[25] A captain of the *compagnia di Gesù Pellegrino* was punished for dismissing the friar without consulting his colleagues: Comp. Relig. Sopp. 910.7, fol 11r (30 Nov. 1366).

[26] See the 1422 statutes of the *Compagnia di Gesù Pellegrino*: BNF, Magl.VIII.1282, ch. XIII, fol 82r and the 1427 statutes of the *compagnia di S. Zanobi*: CRS 2170.I, cap. 8, fol 41r. The *frate correttore* of the first company was elected annually (*Ferrato*, p. 5) and could hold office for a number of years, as can be seen from the company's account book for the period 1411–1431: Comp.Relig. Sopp.919.36. The three correctors during this twenty-year period were: Frate Domenico Ristori, a Master of Theology; Frate Andrea Ducci Betti, a sacristan and later syndic of S.Maria Novella; and Frate Agostino Dominici, Prior of S.Maria Novella. For the lives of these friars see S.Orlandi, *'Necrologio' di S. Maria Novella* (Florence 1955) 2 pp. 126–128, 166–167, and 205–206.

and had their statutes recast by members of their convents.[27] The case of the latter, the *compagnia di S.Pier Martire*, was perhaps somewhat exceptional, but is interesting as an example of how a confraternity might develop. Founded by St. Peter Martyr in 1244 as an organisation to combat heresy and encourage the worship of Mary against the Cathars' denial of her divine motherhood, it emerged as a conventional *laudesi* group with daily meetings and especially splendid festivals at which the members processed around the neighbourhood with painted wax images of their patron saints.[28] It was not long before the company began to be left bequests. Between 1290 and 1389 it received sixty legacies, most of which were pieces of property.[29] By the early fifteenth century the administration of commemorative services had become one of the most important of the company's responsibilities, accounting in 1429 for 67 per cent of all its expenditure.[30] However, due to communal taxation and administrative confusion the company began to lose money. The Dominicans, concerned that one of their sources of income would be jeopardised (they received 93 per cent of all the money paid out by the company on commemorative services), obtained from Eugenius IV a series of papal bulls between 1441 and 1447 which transferred ownership of the company's property to their hands, changing effectively the status of the company from an independent lay corporation to one dominated by the convent. In future half the board of captains would be friars and the two lay members chosen by the Chapter of S.Maria Novella.[31]

The development of the *compagnia di S.Pier Martire* was obviously an extreme case of clericalisation, but reflects a general tendency of the Church, and particularly the friars, to increase their

[27] The 1447 statutes of the *compagnia di S.Pier Martire* in Conventi Relig. Sopp. 102. 324, fols 3r–v; and the 1451 statutes of the *Laudesi di SS. Annunziata* (Capitoli CRS 6, fols 4r–7r) were 'nuovamente coposti et ordinati per me Frate Mariano, lectore in theologia, e per certi altri de' fratelli, per tutto il corpo della compagnia sopracio electi et deputati'.

[28] S. Orlandi, 'Il VII centenario della predicazione di S.Pietro Martire a Firenze (1245–1945)', *Memorie Domenicane*, ns 22 (1947) pp. 47–48, 171–208.

[29] Calculated from BL, Add MS 17, 310: entitled 'Registro, cioè Memoriale di tutti i lasciti e possessioni della compagnia'.

[30] Catasto 293, fol 34r–v.

[31] Conventi Rel. Sopp. 102.324, cap 1, fol 1r. For a more detailed discussion of this process see Henderson 'Piety and Charity' pp. 119–126.

control over confraternities in the fifteenth century. A similar process can be discerned in relation to the large charities, which met in independent oratories. The *compagnia della Madonna di Orsanmichele*, for example, had by the early fifteenth century ceased to provide a significant amount of relief to the poor of the city and instead concentrated on building and decorating its oratory. The changed function was symbolised by the elevation of Orsanmichele into a collegiate church, which came to be staffed by ten priests and two clerics.[32] The Misericordia – the other large charity in Florence – also underwent a transformation in the fifteenth century. When in 1490 it returned after a period of inactivity 'more splendid and ardent in its works of mercy',[33] the composition of the membership had changed drastically. Whereas before it had been almost exclusively lay, in future thirty of the seventy-two members were to be priests.[34]

The relationship between confraternities and the Church before 1400[35] was characterised more by episcopal and papal encouragement than by the ecclesiastical control of the subsequent century. In 1296, for example, the Florentine bishop conceded special indulgences to the members of the *laudesi di S.Croce*, who took part in company processions and attended the daily singing of lauds.[36] But privileges did not simply derive from local ecclesiastical dignitaries. They also came from the Orders which governed the

---

[32] Catasto 291, fol 72r.

[33] *Documenti inediti o poco noti per la storia della Misericordia di Firenze (1240–1525)* ed U. Morini (Florence 1940) p. 59: statutes of 1490: 'Ma ritorni più splendida et più chalda nell'opere della misericordia et charità'.

[34] *Ibid.* cap. 1 p. 60.

[35] Cf. the general remarks by Meersseman, 'Disciplinati e penitenti nel Duecento', *Il movimento dei disciplinati nel settimo centenario dal suo inizio (Perugia 1260). Deputazione di storia patria per l'Umbria*, appendice al bolletino 9 (Perugia 1962) pp. 56–61.

[36] G.M. Monti, *Le confraternite medievale dell'alta e media Italia* (Florence 1927) I p. 165. See also for indulgences to: the *Laudesi di S. Lorenzo* between 1338–1347 (G. Richa, *Notizie istoriche delle chiese di Firenze* (Florence 1757) 5 p. 91) and *S. Giovanni Battista detto lo Scalzo* (Monti I p. 262). Companies hung up lists of their spiritual privileges in their oratories, as in the 1331 (?) inventory of the *compagnia di S. Zanobi* in S. Reparata in Florence: 'Uno suggello nel quale è la figura di nostra donna e l'angelo quando l'anunzia et sedici lettere concedute ala compagnia per cardinali et vescovi et altri prelati dove sono le perdonanze et l'endulgenze': Comp.Relig.Sopp. 2170.4, fol 21r.

churches in which they met, such as the General of the Silvestrines who conceded the right to all the brothers of the *laudesi di S.Marco* to participate in his Order's spiritual goods,[37] or even from the bishops of other cities who gave them indulgences.[38] The favours of the papal court could also be solicited[39] although, as can be seen in the case of the highly prestigious *compagnia de' Magi* in 1467, the brothers might be asked for fairly substantial sums.[40]

While spiritual privileges continued to be granted to Florentine confraternities in the fifteenth century, there is evidence that the archbishop attempted to establish more control over nearly all independent lay groups. This may simply reflect the lack of surviving evidence for the fourteenth century.[41] But it is equally probable that during that period there was no consistent policy for the investigation of company statutes, and that the interest of the Church was less stimulated by the canonists' debates[42] than by energetic bishops, of which there were few in Florence before the fifteenth century. However, from the 1420s the archbishop, as he had now become, seems to have been inspired by the example of

---

[37] Richa 5 pp. 329–330; the *compagnia di S.Pier Martire* in S.Maria Novella from the Dominican Order: Orlandi, 'Il VII centenario', (1947) pp. 118, 178.

[38] The *compagnia di S.Pier Martire* received indulgences from the bishop of Ostia (V. Fineschi, *Memorie istoriche degli uomini illustri del convento di S.Maria Novella di Firenze* (Florence 1790) pp. 118–119), and the *compagnia di S. Zanobi* from the bishop of Fiesole (BNF, Magl. XXXI. 133, p. 17). Meersseman notes indulgences by archbishops to confraternities in Bologna, Imola and Arezzo: pp. 467–469, 931, 933, and indulgences and letters of confraternity to companies of the Virgin in Spoleto, Bologna, Mantua, Vercelli, Arezzo, Perugia, Padua, Piacenza, Lodi and Faenza: pp. 1005–1015.

[39] Monti 1, p. 59 mentions Urban V's privileges to the *compagnia di S.Maria della Croce al Tempio*.

[40] The *compagnia de' Magi* had to pay about 150 ducats for their spiritual privileges in 1467: R. Hatfield, 'The Compagnia de' Magi', *The Journal of the Warburg and Courtauld Institutes* 33 (1970) pp. 151–152.

[41] The episcopal confirmation of the *compagnia della Madonna di Orsanmichele* in 1294 is the only one of its kind to have so far been traced for the late thirteenth century: S. La Sorsa, *La compagnia d'Or S. Michele ovvero una pagina della beneficenza in Toscana nel secolo XIV* (Trani 1902) p. 190. Few episcopal approvals of statutes survive for the Trecento, although see the reference for the *compagnia di Gesù Pellegrino* in 1354 (Capitoli Comp.Relig.Sopp. 502, fol 1v) and the *laudesi di S. Frediano detta la Brucciata* for 1368 (BNF, Palatino 154).

[42] Discussed briefly by G. Le Bras, *Études de sociologie religieuse* (Paris 1955) 2 pp. 448–451.

the Commune[43] and begun to inspect and ratify company statutes. Two periods in particular stand out: the episcopate of Andrea Corsini (1411–1435) and that of Antoninus (1446–1459).[44] The reasons why Corsini should have displayed an interest in confraternities are not clear, but may have stemmed from his general desire to exercise more control over any ecclesiastical corporation, given that the secular clergy was attempting to establish greater independence.[45] It may also, but this is pure speculation, have been related to papal encouragement, for Martin V lived in Florence between February 1419 and September 1420,[46] and there is ample evidence to suggest that when in the following decade Eugenius IV stayed in the city he intervened directly in the affairs of the confraternities.[47] It cannot be entirely coincidental that three out of the twelve statutes which survive with episcopal approbations by Corsini belonged to companies in S.Maria Novella, the site of the papal residence.[48]

But rubber-stamping statutes did not necessarily mean approval of all their provisions, and it gave the archbishop or his vicar the opportunity to amend chapters. Sometimes this simply involved

---

[43] J. Henderson, 'Le confraternite religiose nella Firenze del tardo medioevo: patroni spirituali e anche politici?', *Ricerche storiche* 15 (1985) pp. 77–94 summarises the relations between the commune and confraternities in Florence in the fifteenth century.

[44] On Corsini and Antoninus see D.S. Peterson, 'Archbishop Antoninus: Florence and the Church in the earlier fifteenth century' (Ph.D. thesis Cornell University 1985).

[45] *Ibid.* p. 486.

[46] P. Partner, *The Papal State Under Martin V* (London 1958) pp. 53, 67.

[47] See above n 31 for the Pope's intervention in the affairs of the boys' companies: R.C. Trexler, 'Ritual in Florence: Adolescence and Salvation in the Renaissance', *The Pursuit of Holiness in Late Medieval and Renaissance Religion* eds C. Trinkaus, H. Oberman (Leiden 1974) pp. 207–208.

[48] Approbations have been traced for the following companies: *Gesù Pellegrino*, 20 Nov 1420: BNF, Magl.VIII.1282, fol 8r; *S. Lorenzo*: 12 Jan 1425: N.A. F507 (1423–27) fols 29r–30r; *S Matteo* in S.Spirito, 23 Nov 1420: N.A. S 672 (1417–21) at date; *S. Michele Arcangelo* in SS. Annunziata, 1420: N.A. S659–69 (1378–1456), fols 339v–340v; *S. Zanobi*, Cathedral, 1427 (? no date given): Comp. Relig. Sopp. 2170.I fol 32r and N.A.J 7 (1417–27), at 1427 (no day or month); *S. Giovanni Evangelista*, S Trinita dei Gesuati, 1427 (no day or month): N.A. F507 (1423–27) fols 29r–30r and BNF Magl. XXI.II fols 8v–9r; *S: Benedetto*, S.Trinita, 24 Dec 1431: Capitoli Comp. Relig. Sopp. 635 fol 13r; *S Niccolò*, S. Maria del Carmine, 24 Dec 1431: Capitoli, Comp. Relig.Sopp.439, fols 7r–v. See also approbations of statutes of companies in the *contado* in: N.A. F506 (1412–23), fols 227r–v, 229r, 252v–253r.

the interpolation of phrases such as 'according to the licence of the archbishop of Florence',[49] at others it meant more fundamental changes. In his confirmation of the statutes of, for example, the *Compagnia di S. Lorenzo* in 1425, Corsini introduced a caveat which was to become a constant theme, namely that the parish priest rather than the confraternity chaplain should retain ultimate jurisdiction over the cure of the souls of his parishioners.[50] Emendations to later fifteenth-century statutes make it clear that the archbishop was particularly concerned that members of fraternities should confess and take communion in their parishes at Easter,[51] suggesting that in this sense at least there was something to the sixteenth-century view of a conflict of loyalty between confraternity and Church.

Antoninus, who was one of the most active and scrupulous of Florentine archbishops in the later middle ages, was particularly keen on the proper administration of the sacraments to the laity and ordered parish priests to report to the archiepiscopal courts anybody not fulfilling their basic paschal duties.[52] His interest in the spiritual and moral health of the laity led him to examine company statutes as well as possibly to become involved in the foundation and reorganisation of other confraternities.[53] Although he encouraged the laity to participate in services, he was concerned

---

[49] N.A. F507 (1423–27), fol 29v: 'In prima nel capitolo terzo delle dette constitutioni dopo le parole 'facesse capo' agiunse queste parole cioè "Intervenendoci la licentia di messer l'arcivescovo di Firenze o di suo vicario".

[50] *Ibid.* 'Item in nel decto capitolo agiunse dopo le parole che dicono "l'anime di tutti li huomini della compagnia" queste parole, cioè "Riservate tutte le ragioni e iurisdictioni delle chiese parrochiali"'.

[51] See the approbation of the 1466 statutes of the *compagnia di S.Antonio da Padova* in S.Maria Soprarno: Comp.Relig.Sopp. 137.6 fols 18r–v; the 1476 statutes of the *compagnia di S.Domenico* in S.Maria Novella: Biblioteca Riccardiana MS 3041, fols 25v–27r in Meersseman 2 pp. 740–741. In 1467 the Pope granted the *compagnia de' Magi* the right to take communion in their oratory, with the exception of Easter Day: Hatfield doc II p. 152.

[52] R.C. Trexler, 'The Episcopal Constitutions of Antoninus of Florence', *Quellen und Forschungen aus Italienischen Archiven und Bibliotheken*, 54 (1979) p. 258.

[53] S. Orlandi 2 pp. 211–214, 313–316; R. Moray, *Saint Antonin* (Paris 1914) pp. 89–90. Statutes approved by Antoninus include those of the following companies:

to retain a strict control over their activities. Thus he began his 1455 'Episcopal Constitutions' with a firm statement that:

> no layman in no company or meeting of people [may] presume to dispute the articles of the faith or sacraments of the Church.[54]

The attack stemmed from rumours that people had spoken against the 'reverence and integrity of the holy faith'.[55] He evidently did not want the laity to discuss matters which belonged properly to the clergy. His desire to make sure that the laity did not dabble in matters which did not concern them was echoed by the contemporary policy of the State; while Antoninus was keen to avoid the possibility of heresy, the Medicean government prohibited members from using their companies as places in which to discuss politics.[56] Antoninus's concern to establish a more rigid separation between the worlds of the laity and the clergy was manifested publicly in his new ruling about the general procession on the vigil

---

S.Maria della Neve, Capitoli Comp.Relig.Sopp. 606, fols 50v–51r; *S.Giovanni Battista tra le arcore*: N.A. S 690 at date, published by Orlandi I pp. 187–188; *Purificazione della Madonna ovvero di S.Marco*: BNF, Magl.VIII.1500,II fol 22v; *S.Maria della Croce al Tempio*, 1448 (?), mentioned by G.B. Uccelli, *Della compagnia de S.Maria della Croce al Tempio* (Florence 1864) p. 20, but with no source; *S.Giovanni Scalzo*, Capitoli Comp.Relig.Sopp. 152 fols 1–14, published by Richa 7 pp. 199–200; *S.Andrea dei purgatori e cardatori*: Capitoli Comp.Relig.Sopp. 870 fol 16v (1455). According to Moray, *S.Antonin* pp. 91 n 2, 473–4, Antonino confirmed the statutes of the *S.Giovanni Evangelista; S.Niccolò del Ceppo* in 1450; to F. Moisè, *S.Croce* (Florence 1845) p. 422, the statutes of the *compagnia di S.Francesco* in *S.Croce*; and to Ferdinando del Migliore, 'Registro delle compagnie di Firenze', BNF, Magl xxv, 418 fol 89, those of *S.Lorenzo in Piano* in 1447. According to tradition S.Antonino is supposed to have founded the *Buonomini di S.Martino*, but according to the most recent historian of the company there is no evidence for his direct intervention: A.Spicciani, 'The "poveri vergognosi" in fifteenth-century Florence. The first thirty years' activity of the Buonomini di S.Martino', *Aspects of Poverty in Early Modern Europe*, ed T. Riis (Stuttgart 1981) p. 162 n 10.
[54] Trexler, 'Episcopal Constitutions', p. 256.
[55] *ibid*.
[56] Henderson, 'Le confraternite' p. 85.

of the great Florentine feast of St. John the Baptist.[57] Traditionally the procession had included both the clergy carrying their relics and the lay companies with their *tableaux vivants*. However, Antoninus felt that these 'vain things and worldly spectacles'[58] detracted from the solemnity of the occasion by introducing an element of carnival. From then on the confraternities were to be banned from the clerical procession and required to take part in a separate event on the previous day.

Confraternities, then, for an active archbishop like Antoninus, who was keen to promote the spiritual life of the laity, were to be encouraged but controlled. This remained the policy of his successors, although they did continue to be worried about how lay companies might attract parishioners away from their local church, as can be seen in the acts of the synod of the Florentine church in 1517:

> A great abuse had developed among these fraternities of laymen, so that, gathering together on those festive days, they abandoned the main churches at that hour when mass was sung in them, to open their synagogues and sing their Offices to the people, so that the majority of people was withdrawn from the church.[59]

The problem in interpreting this blanket denunciation is that, as with other diocesan laws, it is difficult to determine whether this ruling represents only the reaction to a specific instance or a more general phenomenon. It is not clear, moreover, whether it involved the town or countryside. Reference was probably being made to the *contado* for complaints had long been heard against rural companies and *opere*, which had come to dominate local parishes.[60] It is possible that some urban confraternities may have been implicated in the Church's condemnation, because in the fourteenth century some of the large charities such as Orsanmichele, the Misericordia, and Bigallo did build oratories.[61] Indeed as early as the 1290s the Dominicans and Franciscans were complaining that

---

[57] On which see R.C. Trexler, *Public Life in Renaissance Florence* (New York, London 1980) cap 8.

[58] Trexler, 'Episcopal Constitutions' p. 265.

[59] *Statuta concilii Florentini* (anno 1517) (Florence 1564), cap 7, p. 26.

[60] Trexler, *Synodal Law*, pp. 118, 120.

[61] La Sorsa pp. 101–114; H. Saalman, *The Bigallo. The Oratory and Residence of the Compagnia del Bigallo e della Misericordia in Florence* (New York 1969).

the Madonna of Orsanmichele was attracting the laity away from their churches,[62] an ironical inversion of the attacks directed against the friars themselves by the secular clergy. But although a few companies were beginning to build independent oratories in the fifteenth century, they were exclusive groups of flagellants,[63] who would have actively discouraged anybody from outside the membership from attending their ceremonies.

If the attacks of the Synod of 1517 were directed primarily against rural companies, the danger remained that any religious corporation offering the eucharist and private burial to the laity could act as a potential danger to the parish. This threat was lessened during the sixteenth century by the establishment in Italy of the new sacramental companies, although the extent to which they were promoted actively by the Church before the Counter-Reformation needs further investigation. These new confraternities bound themselves closely to the parish, and traditional devotional groups – which had drawn members from all over the city – followed suit and were transformed in the sixteenth century into locally based confraternities with a new dedication to the fashionable cult of the Holy Sacrament.[64] The Mendicants' emphasis on the Body of Christ and their encouragement of voluntary flagellation was thus transformed into a devotion based around the eucharist on the altar of the neighbourhood church under the control of the parish priest and therefore more readily supervised by the archbishop.

Wellcome Unit for the History of Medicine
University of Cambridge

---

[62] *Cronica di Giovanni Villani a miglior lezione ridotta* (Florence 1825) 1, VII, clv, pp. 362–363.

[63] The *Compagnia di S.Giovanni Scalzo* bought land in 1407 from the church of S.Pietro del Murrone and subsequently built an oratory: Comp.Rel.Sopp. 1190. A, fols 6r–8v; the *compagnia di S.Paolo* bought in 1438 the existing complex of the Trinita Vecchia: Comp.Rel.Sopp. 1579, fol 58r; the *compagnia di Gesù Pellegrino* built an oratory in 1455 (Comp.Rel.Sopp.906.A, fol 11r) on land belonging to S.Maria Novella, as did the *compagnia di S.Domenico* in 1465: Meersseman p. 698; the *compagnia di S.Antonio Abbate* began theirs in 1490: Comp.Relig.Sopp. 112.13, fol 1r, and the *compagnia di S.Zanobi* of the Cathedral theirs in 1478: Catasto 989, fol 469r.

[64] On Florentine sacramental companies see Weissman pp. 220–235.

DEVOTIONAL CONFRATERNITIES IN RENAISSANCE VENICE

by RICHARD MACKENNEY

PERHAPS the most striking features of the history of Renaissance Venice are its highly commercialised economy and its precocious sense of secular state sovereignty. These characteristics owed much to the city's independence of and isolation from rural and seigneurial influences in the thirteenth and fourteenth centuries.[1] However, the high level of business activity and the confident awareness of statehood could also be related to the weakness of ecclesiastical influence in economic and political affairs. This was the case long before the spectacular conflict of 1606 when Venice was placed under the Interdict. The location of the Cathedral had always been a telling symbol of the place of the Church in Venetian life. It stood at San Pietro di Castello in an isolated area of the city. It is easy to overlook the fact that the centre of religious life, Saint Mark's, was the Doge's private chapel: a constant reminder of the intimate relationship between religious and political power, a material manifestation of the divine favour attached to Venice's wealth and authority, both of which were unmistakably worldly.[2]

Nevertheless, a vigorous religious life flourished among the Venetian laity, especially in the *scuole* or devotional confraternities which made such an impact on the fabric of Venice's 130 or so

---

[1] P.J. Jones, 'Economia e società nell'Italia medievale: la leggenda della borghesia' in *Storia d'Italia, Annali 1: dal feudalesimo al capitalismo* (Turin 1978) p. 340. On the distinctive features of Venetian history see Brian Pullan, 'The Significance of Venice', *Bulletin of the John Rylands University Library of Manchester*, 56 (1974) pp. 443–62.

[2] F.C. Lane, *Venice: a Maritime Republic* (Baltimore 1975) p. 88. On the impact of the Counter-Reformation in Venice see Gino Benzoni, *Venezia nell'età della controriforma* (Milan 1973) pp. 50–78; W.J. Bouwsma, *Venice and the Defense of Republican Liberty: Renaissance Values in the Age of the Counter-Reformation* (Berkeley and Los Angeles 1968).

parish and conventual churches.[3] These institutions have played a prominent part in the recent study of Venice. This interest was awakened by Professor Pullan who showed how the charitable activities of the *Scuole Grandi* contributed to the social stability for which Venice was renowned.[4] This paper seeks to suggest – in a highly speculative manner – that the importance of at least two types of *scuola* should be seen less in terms of their capacity to relieve material hardship through charity than in terms of their role in the political structures of the city and in the metropolitan economy.

The *scuola* was a pious brotherhood which existed for conviviality at an annual feast, the celebration of saints – and especially the Virgin Mary – as intercessors, and the commemoration of dead brethren at mass where candles of remembrance were burned.[5] One observer claimed to have seen 119 of these confraternities at a procession in 1521, and that figure may exclude the religious brotherhoods attached to trade guilds,[6] for the *scuola* took many forms. The largest, richest and most impressive were the *Scuole Grandi* mentioned above. Four of them had been formed in the later thirteenth century. Two more were added in 1489 and 1554.[7] The membership of these institutions was divided into permanent orders of rich and poor – givers of alms and recipients – and wealthy members often helped to fund other charitable projects such as the city's hospitals. There were *scuole* too for various foreign communities resident in the city – Greeks, Slavs, Albanians, even Jews, and for Florentines, Lucchese, Bergamese and Milanese.

---

[3] On the scuole and patronage see Silvia Gramigna and Annalisa Perissa, *Scuole di arti mestieri e devozione a Venezia* (Venice 1981); P. Hills, 'Piety and Patronage in Cinquecento Venice: Tintoretto and the Scuole del Sacramento', *Art History* 6 (1983) pp. 30–43; Peter Humfrey and Richard Mackenney 'The Venetian Trade Guilds as Patrons of Art in the Renaissance' forthcoming in *The Burlington Magazine*.

[4] Brian Pullan, *Rich and Poor in Renaissance Venice: the Social Institutions of a Catholic State* (Oxford 1971).

[5] F.C. Lane, *Venetian Ships and Shipbuilders of the Renaissance* (Baltimore 1934) pp. 72–3.

[6] Marin Sanudo, *I Diarii* ed R. Fulin and others, 58 vols (Venice 1879–1903) vol 30 cols 399–401.

[7] Pullan, *Rich and Poor* p. 38; on the Scuola Grande di San Teodoro, which was closely linked with the mercers' guild, see R. Gallo, 'La Scuola Grande di San Teodoro di Venezia', *Atti dell'Istituto Veneto di Scienze, Lettere ed Arti* 120 (*Classe di Scienze Morali e Lettere*) (1961–2) pp. 461–95.

Other confraternities looked to outsiders of another sort, the 'marginalised', and, adhering to the works of corporal mercy listed in Matthew 25; 42–3, offered help to the condemned, the captive or the crippled.[8]

However, the two species of confraternity which were open to the broadest section of Venetian society were the *scuole piccole* and the *scuole delle arti*. The *scuole piccole* existed purely for devotional purposes and stood above occupation and status as well as parish. The *scuole delle arti* united in Christian brotherhood the practitioners of a particular occupation. Members of these types of confraternity were not divided into 'orders' of rich and poor. Indeed, many of them may have given alms and later fallen into want. These *scuole* recruited amongst merchants and artisans. It may be worth interjecting here that these terms refer not to employers and employees but to a single social group in which status, interests and indeed relationship to the means of production were so diverse that to construct an interpretation of Venetian confraternities along the lines of class would be misleadingly simple.[9]

Looking first of all at the *scuole piccole*, we find that they shared the original principles of the *Scuole Grandi*, but there is little to suggest that they developed their charitable activities in the way that the larger *scuole* did. On the whole, their potential for the relief of material want was restricted by their devotional activities and they did rather more to commemorate the dead than to relieve the living.

The purpose of a *scuola* was made plain in the preamble of its statute. The *scuola di Santa Maria della Celestia*, one of a number established in the fourteenth century, reminded members that 'we do not have a lasting city here, but as the Apostle says, we must

---

[8] For a comprehensive survey of the various types of scuola and an analysis of their functions, see Brian Pullan, 'Natura e carattere delle Scuole', historical introduction to *Le Scuole di Venezia* a cura di T. Pignatti, saggio storico di Brian Pullan (Milan 1981) pp. 9–26. I am very grateful to Dr. Robert Bartlett of the University of Edinburgh for drawing my attention to the connection between the works of corporal mercy and the activities of the scuole.

[9] For a stimulating interpretation of the class basis of charity, see Richard C. Trexler, 'Charity and the Defense of Urban Elites in the Italian Communes' in F.C. Jaher ed *The Rich, the Well-Born and the Powerful: Elites and Upper Classes in History* (Chicago 1973) pp. 64–105.

seek the eternal city and strive to go there'.[10] The merchants of the *scuola di San Cristofalo* advised each other 'you must always have before the eyes of your mind the end of this transitory life and think upon it'. It continues:

> Let there be increase of the church and monastery where we are gathered and exaltation of this blessed *scuola* and comfort and utility for the poor, bearing mind that the more we turn in praise, reverence and devotion to Saint Christopher, the more fervent will he be [on our behalf] before Our Creator.[11]

The confraternity at Santi Apostoli had statutes which lugubriously warned 'you know not the day nor the hour of your death'. Salvation was to be sought through prayer and alms and the reference to Saint James shows how closely linked were devotional activity and philanthropy:

> inspired with divine grace we have begun to ponder on how through brotherhood, prayer and alms, we may acquire the salvation of our souls, recalling what Saint James says; 'pray for one another that you may be saved, for the prayer of a just man is worth much'.[12]

On religious festivals and state occasions, the brethren took part in processions, often with the participation of clergymen who in some cases were formally enrolled in the *scuola*. Members were encouraged to attend mass once a month and, in accordance with canon law, to confess once a year. There were also stern words about the need for mutual correction. Sometimes, as in the *Scuole Grandi*, this took the form of flagellation, but usually fellow members seen to be in a state of sin were reported, examined and told to reform or else leave the brotherhood. This was partly, of

[10] Archivio di Stato di Venezia (henceforward ASV) Index Scuole Piccole, busta 726, Santa Maria della Celestia, Mariegola 1337–1764, preamble.
[11] ASV Scuole Piccole, busta 406, Santa Maria e San Cristofalo, Mariegola 1377–1545, fol 2r.
[12] ASV Scuole Piccole, busta 57 bis, Santi Apostoli, Mariegola 1350–1708, fol 2r.

course, the Church's work in the world, but, since the state controlled the statutes, it was also the state's work among Venetians.[13] For the statutes were vigilantly supervised by the Council of Ten. The Venetian government was somewhat unusual in fairly freely granting permission to form a confraternity.[14] But the state had no time for spontaneous demonstrations of religious fervour. When the Bianchi held an assembly on the Campo San Zanipolo in 1399, they were swiftly dispersed by order of the authorities.[15] Given the suspicion of confraternities shown by other governments, it is a little surprising to find that the internal organisation of the *scuole piccole* in Venice was remarkably loose. This almost certainly reduced their effectiveness as agencies for the relief of material hardship and made them less easily subject to effective political control. The same looseness tells us a good deal about the less obvious functions of confraternities amongst Venetians.

There was, for instance, no standard number of members. One recent estimate puts average membership of the *scuole piccole* at 60 or 70.[16] That figure hides some wide variations. The statute of the original *scuola di Santi Apostoli* of 1288 contains a list of 21 names. In 1325, the *scuola di Sant'Agnese* set a maximum of 550, probably in imitation of the *Scuole Grandi*.[17] Around 1350, however, the

---

[13] The legal status of confraternities was confused. Bartolus observed that their formation was supposed to be authorised by the pope, while in practice their statutes were subject to the approval of the civil authorities. See Anna Toulman Sheedy, *Bartolus on Social Conditions of the Fourteenth Century* (New York 1942) p. 176.

[14] Lia Sbriziolo, 'Per la storia delle confraternite veneziane: dalle deliberazioni miste (1310–1476) del Consiglio dei Dieci, scolae comunes, artifiane e nazionali', *Atti dell'Istituto Veneto di Scienze, Lettere ed Arti* 126 (*Classe di Scienze Morali Lettere ed Arti*) (1967–8) pp. 405–42 charts the pattern of approval. In Florence and London, the authorities were far more suspicious; see John Henderson, 'Piety and Charity in Late Medieval Florence: Religious Confraternities from the Middle of the Thirteenth Century to the Late Fifteenth Century' (University of London Ph.D. thesis 1983) p.36; Ronald F.E. Weissman, *Ritual Brotherhood in Renaissance Florence, 1200–1600* (New York 1982) p. 167; Sylvia L. Thrupp, *The Merchant Class of Medieval London* (Chicago 1948) p. 19.

[15] Benjamin Z. Kedar, *Merchants in Crisis: Genoese and Venetian Men of Affairs and the Fourteenth-Century Depression* (New Haven 1976) p. 113.

[16] Lia Sbriziolo, 'Per la storia delle confraternite veneziane dalle deliberazioni miste (1310–1476) del Consiglio dei Dieci. Le Scuole dei battuti', *Miscellanea G.-G. Meersseman*, 2 (Padua 1970) p. 727.

[17] ASV, Scuole Piccole, busta 1 bis, Santa Maria della Carità, Mariegola 1288, fly leaf, busta 1, Sant'Agnese, Catastico da 1325 in avanti, fol 20r.

records of Santa Maria della Celestia speak of an astonishing 700 members.[18]

Amongst members themselves there was a surprising variety of occupations.[19] As well as those engaged in commercial activity, the *scuole* attracted significant minorities of Arsenal workers, builders and even some engaged in the textile trades. They often rubbed shoulders with nobles. Doge Cristoforo Moro was a member of San Cristofalo dei Mercanti in the mid-fifteenth century. There was room for women too, for the *scuole* sometimes included an organisation of *donne* within the confraternity.

Perhaps the most significant aspect of the composition of membership was that the *scuole* crossed geographical as well as economic and social divisions. In the fourteenth, fifteenth and early sixteenth centuries, the confraternities were 'floating' institutions which operated above the parish and attracted members from all over the city. In each of the four membership lists discovered in the Venetian archive, over 70 parishes are represented. This supra-parochial quality changed in the later sixteenth century when the *scuole piccole* gave way to the *scuole del Santissimo Sacramento*, expressions of the new piety of the Counter-Reformation and closely tied to the life of the parish. The Visitation of 1581 recorded that all but four Venetian parish churches had an altar to the holy sacrament.[20] According to Francesco Sansovino, each altar represented a confraternity and 'apart from these there were the *scuole* of the trade guilds'.[21] To these we can now turn our attention.

Venetian trade guilds or *arti* had organised devotional confraternities since the thirteenth century. By the end of the sixteenth, a *scuola* was attached to nearly all the city's hundred or so guilds. Unlike the trade brotherhoods of Northern Europe, the devotional

---

[18] ASV, Scuole Piccole, busta 726, Santa Maria della Celestia, Mariegola 1337–1764, fol 3r.

[19] What follows is based on Richard Mackenney, 'Trade Guilds and Devotional Confraternities in the State and Society of Venice to 1620' (University of Cambridge Ph.D. thesis 1982) pp. 94–134.

[20] Silvio Tramontin, 'La visita apostolica del 1581 a Venezia', *Studi Veneziani* 9 (1967) pp. 500–33. See also Hills, 'Piety and Patronage'.

[21] Francesco Sansovino and Giovanni Stringa, *Venetia, città nobilissima et singolare* (Venice 1663: facsimile ed West Germany 1968) p. 290.

confraternities of the Venetian *arti* were not necessarily co-terminous with the craft, and occasionally, the *scuola dell'arte* formed a distinct organisation within the trade guild itself.[22] Nevertheless, the character of such fraternities was strongly influenced by the customary solidarity of those who practised the same trade. In general, craft traditions of mutual aid generated more practical and material help for members than was the case in the *scuole piccole*. Some crafts, for instance, had their own hospitals. At the end of the fifteenth century, the tailors asserted that their hospital was sheltering 50 *poveri* (17 members and their families).[23] The bakers completed a hospital in 1477 and offered shelter for limited periods of time to the 'poor, old and incapacitated' as well as to those without work 'through no fault of their own'.[24]

Some of the corporations selected *poveri* who received recurrent payments. In the 1530s, six poor mercers received 31 *soldi* a month each, five painters were regularly elected as the guild's *poveri* after a sort of means test. The potters were less systematic but as late as 1593 reasserted the principle they had formulated in the fourteenth century that the guild should provide relief for 'any master or assistant who falls into poverty'.[25] However, the very solidarity of a trade guild gave still greater emphasis to the inward looking quality of guild charity. Membership was a prerequisite for any form of support. The bakers made special reference to the fact that their hospital was intended for 'those who have borne the burdens of office in the confraternity'.[26]

Like the *scuole piccole* then, trade guilds were not concerned with poverty as a problem in society as a whole, even though they may have offered help to wage labourers. Moreover, their own charitable activity was often only a part of their devotional life. In 1436, the linen sellers fixed a payment of 4 *soldi* for women

---

[22] Lane, *Ships and Shipbuilders* p. 73; E. Coornaert, 'Des confréries carolingiennes aux gildes marchandes', *Mélanges d'Histoire Sociale* 2 (1942) p. 16.

[23] ASV, index Arti, busta 501, Sartori, Capitoli e parti, 1492–1683, fol 3r.

[24] ASV, Arti, busta 152, Forneri, Atti diversi 1447–1797, petition of 1465, purchase of a site for the hospital 17 November 1471, categories of inmates, document of 1515 marked 'mariegola 35'.

[25] ASV, Arti, busta 314, Marzeri, Capitoli e parti 1508–1608, document of 13 August 1529; busta 103, Dipintori, Mariegola 1517–1682, fol 39r; busta 11, Boccaleri, Mariegola 1300–1804, Capitolo 5.

[26] See above, note 24, document of 1515 marked 'mariegola 35'.

members 'for the souls of the dead and for the well-being of the living of the said guild and for the sustenance of its poor and infirm members'.[27] In the period 1540–54, the goldsmiths gave alms to 16 *poveri* every year. However, the average annual value of what each received was the equivalent of only three days' wages in the building trades. To underline the importance of devotion in the life of the *scuola dell'arte* one should point out that the goldsmiths spent 22 per cent of their total outgoings on candles to light at mass on feast days.[28]

The *scuole delle arti* were, predictably, only loosely attached to a parish church and, unlike the *scuole piccole*, remained so in the sixteenth century. The mercers held a monthly mass at San Daniele, but their weekly service was at San Zulian (much handier for their shops).[29] The glass sellers sought to move from San Polo in the fifteenth century and we know nothing of the outcome, but when they did move (in 1580), it was from San Zuan Novo to Sant'Anzolo.[30]

It was the authority of the state, not that of the Church which changed the shape of the *scuole delle arti* in the later sixteenth century. The guild system was extended and strengthened by the government to provide a supply of oarsmen for the reserve fleet.[31] And as the state sought to exploit the guilds for the fisc, the *arti* themselves were engaged in adjusting to changing economic conditions.[32] In so far as guilds eased the problem of poverty in this period, they did so through the creation of employment opportunities rather than through the distribution of alms.

Some such opportunities arose on the occasion of public festivals in which both the *scuole piccole* and the *scuole delle arti* were – or could be – involved. Of course, public ceremonial had great value

[27] ASV, Arti, busta 182, Linaroli, Ordinazioni per l'arte, 1436, Capitolo 16.
[28] ASV, Arti, busta 425, Orefici, Cassa amministrazione 1541–54. For a full analysis of the figures, see Mackenney, 'Trade Guilds and Devotional Confraternities' pp. 154–92.
[29] ASV, Arti, busta 312, Marzeri, Mariegola 1471–1787, fol 14r.
[30] ASV, Arti, busta 725, Venditori di vetro, Mariegola 1436–1768, fol 7r.
[31] Richard T. Rapp, *Industry and Economic Decline in Seventeenth-Century Venice* (Cambridge, Mass. 1976).
[32] Carlo M. Cipolla, 'The Economic Decline of Italy', in Brian Pullan ed *Crisis and Change in the Venetian Economy in the Sixteenth and Seventeenth Centuries* (London 1968) pp. 127–45; Brian Pullan, 'Wage-Earners and the Venetian Economy, 1550–1630' in the same volume pp. 146–74.

as propaganda. One of the most important aspects of the 'myth of Venice' – the myth of a polity kept stable by a perfectly balanced constitution – was constructed and reconstructed in public spectacle.[33] In the major ceremonies of the Republic, the *scuole* shed their inward looking quality and participated in the public life of the state. On such occasions, the Venetian world was turned inside out rather than upside down.

Displayed in public, the piety of the confraternities and their capacity to unite different sorts of people in the same corporation served to demonstrate that Venetians enjoyed a special relationship with each other in Christian brotherhoods themselves part of a state which enjoyed divine favour. This was emphasised by the overlap between 'religious' and 'state' occasions. The great processions which took place in front of the private chapel of the head of state made a strong impression on all who saw them from Petrarch to Sir Henry Wotton.[34]

There was much more to Venetian ceremonial than propaganda or carnival, the emphasis of the political order or its licensed overthrow. And perhaps a more helpful concept than 'status reversal' is 'status association' which made the principle of brotherhood embodied in the *scuole* part of the public life of the state. The ironmongers, weavers, painters and furriers processed with candles to Saint Mark's on the eve of the Saint's Day, the warden of the fishermen's guild wore ducal robes when a new Doge was elected, the bodyguard of the Doge himself was formed by Arsenal workers.[35] Members of the *scuole* could thereby identify, albeit fleetingly, with the state from which the patriciate otherwise excluded them. When they walked in procession around the Piazza, guildsmen could raise their heads and see columns and architraves

---

[33] On the 'myth of Venice', see Franco Gaeta, 'Alcune considerazioni sul mito di Venezia', *Bibliothèque d'humanisme et renaissance* 23 (1961) pp. 51–76; Edward Muir, *Civic Ritual in Renaissance Venice* (Princeton 1981).

[34] Mackenney, 'Trade Guilds and Devotional Confraternities', pp. 213–14. Petrarch's reaction to Venetian celebrations after victory in Crete in 1364 is recorded in *Letters from Petrarch* ed Maurice Bishop (Indiana 1966) p. 238; Wotton's response to the Corpus Christi procession of 1606 is discussed in Pullan, *Rich and Poor* p. 59.

[35] On the Eve of Saint Mark's Day, see Sanudo, *I Diarii* 27, col 193; on the 'Doge' of the fishermen, Lane, *Venice* p. 12; on the Arsenalotti, Sansovino, *Venetia* p. 298.

decorated with figures of builders, goldsmiths, masons, fishermen, caulkers, sawyers and barbers: permanent symbols of the exaltation of tradesmen in a polity blessed by God.

Their eyes could sometimes turn to more earthly things. Public festivals could provide an opportunity to display goods to the visitors who thronged the city on holidays, often in search of souvenirs. When Henri III visited the city in 1574, the mercers spent 200 ducats on the hire and decoration of a brig which they decked out with expensive cloth.[36] The day after the entertainments, the King made a special visit to the Merceria and specifically asked to inspect the shop of the della Vecchia.[37] Presumably he took his entourage with him. No wonder that Agrippa d'Aubigné wrote in about 1600 that 'when a French gentleman passed through their town [the Venetians] would run to greet him'.[38] In 1597 the mercers spent 500 ducats for the celebration of the Dogaressa's coronation.[39] The description by Sansovino gives the impression that the rooms of the Ducal Palace had been turned into a series of stands at a trade fair.[40] So, even in ceremonies, members of the *scuole* seemed part of the sovereign state and the metropolitan economy.

Venetian confraternities, whether or not they were attached to trade guilds, may well have helped to underpin the city's political stability, but not for predictable reasons. They did not, for example, provide charity on a scale sufficient to vaccinate the city against mass poverty and dealt only in palliatives. And they were not easily marshalled corporate entities entirely subject to the will of a machiavellian state. Instead, they varied in size and seem to have been left to themselves in carrying out their devotions or recruiting members.

The brotherhoods underwent considerable change in the course of the sixteenth century. The growth of the city's population and of the problem of poverty exposed, especially in the terrible famine

[36] ASV, Arti, busta 312, Marzeri, Mariegola 1471–1787, fols 79v–82v.
[37] Tommaso Porcacchi, *Le attioni di Arrigo Terzo* (Venice 1574) fols 32v–33v.
[38] Quoted in Frances A. Yates, *Astraea: the Imperial Theme in the Sixteenth Century* (London 1977) p. 212.
[39] ASV, Arti, busta 312, Marzeri, Mariegola 1471–1787, fols 70r–72r.
[40] The guilds' displays are described in Sansovino, *Venetia* p. 422.

of 1528–29, the inadequacy of traditional institutions which looked after only their own members. Only the *Scuole Grandi* took up the challenge of the new age and expanded their charitable activities.[41] At the same time, the *scuole piccole* were re-shaped by the Counter-Reformation, the *scuole delle arti* by the increasingly absolutist Venetian state.

However, the *scuole* were to retain a vital importance in the social and religious life of the city and they remained the nuclei around which Venetians could cluster for solidarity, though not the solidarity of class, corporation or even neighbourhood.[42] In a curious way only very inadequately explained in this paper, the *scuole* expressed the solidarity of different sorts of people as Christians and Venetians. In this manner, perhaps the *scuole* sublimated some of the tensions which lay in a cosmopolitan community striving for gain in a metropolitan economy under the watchful eye of the ruling caste.

Throughout the discussion, one has emphasised the way in which politics and economics impinged on the life of religious confraternities. To conclude, one should point out that the influence was not all one way. Before about 1550, in Venice at least, confraternities required a positive commitment to identify as an individual with Christ incarnate and to do penance as a poor sinner. What needs far more research is how such commitment influenced the thoughts and actions of the merchants and artisans engaged in commerce who clearly felt an urge to join organisations which reminded them of the transience of the earthly life, and the political attitudes of the subjects of the Venetian state.[43] To begin to make

---

[41] Brian Pullan, 'Le Scuole Grandi e la loro opera nel quadro della controriforma', *Studi Veneziani* 14 (1972) pp. 83–109; idem, *Rich and Poor* pp. 216–422. See also Rheinhold C. Mueller, 'Charitable Institutions, the Jewish Community and Venetian Society: a Discussion of the Recent Volume by Brian Pullan', *Studi Veneziani* 14 (1972) pp. 38–78.

[42] On the neighbourhood, see Denis Romano, 'Charity and Community in Early Renaissance Venice', *Journal of Urban History* 11 (1984) pp. 63–82.

[43] On 'mentalities' in sixteenth-century Venice, see Ugo Tucci, 'The Psychology of the Venetian Merchant in the Sixteenth Century' in J.R. Hale ed *Renaissance Venice* (London 1974) pp. 346–78; Richard Mackenney, 'Guilds and Guildsmen in Sixteenth-Century Venice', *Bulletin of the Society for Renaissance Studies* 2 (1984) pp. 13–14.

sense of such problems, one must be prepared to examine renaissance confraternities on their own terms and not through a distorting lens provided by Protestantism or the Counter Reformation.[44]

University of Edinburgh

[44] On the impact of the Counter-Reformation, see the crucial article by John Bossy, 'The Counter-Reformation and the People of Catholic Europe' *PP* 47 (1970) pp. 51–70.

96

CORPUS CHRISTI FRATERNITIES AND LATE MEDIEVAL PIETY

by MIRI RUBIN

WHILE most scholars agree that fraternities played a major role in the religious and social experiences of late medieval folk in town and village, little has been said about the characteristics which allowed these voluntary associations to fulfil so major a role.[1] Were religious fraternities cherished as venues for more rigorous personal participation in which lay men and women could shoulder duties and tasks beyond those demanded by the Church, or did they act as agents for expression of a vernacular piety which was somewhat removed from Latin liturgy and sacramental ritual? In this paper I shall examine a sub-group of fraternities, those dedicated to Corpus Christi, and through their response to an addition to the calendar shall attempt to assess the aims and means of spiritual expression offered by such groupings.

I wish to thank Miss V. Bainbridge, Professor C.N.L. Brooke, Dr. J.S. Henderson and Dr. D.M. Owen for reading this paper and for offering their helpful comments.

[1] On confraternities see G. Le Bras, 'Les confréries chrétiennes, Problèmes et propositions' *Revue historique de droit français et étranger* 4 ser 19–20 (1940–1) pp. 310–63; on occupational gilds E. Coornaert, 'Les ghildes médiévales (Ve–XIVe siècles)' *Revue historique* 199 (1948) pp. 22–55, 208–43 and on the gild as a form of organisation in secular society see A. Black, *Guilds and Civil Society in European Political Thought from the Twelfth Century to the Present Day* (London 1984) pp. 1–75. On rural religious fraternities see C.-M. de la Roncière, 'La place des confréries dans le contado florentin; l'exemple de la Val d'Elsa' *Mélanges de l'Ecole français de Rome. Serie moyen-âge-temps modernes* 85 (1973) pp. 31–77 and P. Adam, *La vie paroissiale en France au XIVe siècle* (Paris 1964) pp. 15–80; for the sixteenth century A.N. Galpern, *The Religions of the People in Sixteenth Century Champagne* (Cambridge Mass 1976) pp. 52–68. Most work on confraternities has centred on the abundant archives of the Italian towns and has produced such studies as R.F. Weissman, *Ritual Brotherhood in Renaissance Florence* (New York and London 1982), which explores the social and psychological functions of confraternities as well as the doctoral dissertations of R.C. Mackenney, 'Trade Guilds and Devotional Confraternities in the State and

The feast of Corpus Christi was instituted by Urban IV in the bull *Transiturus* in 1264. This marked the formalisation of what had become by the thirteenth century a burgeoning popular devotion to the eucharist, to its reception, contemplation and veneration, a feature of a spirituality rising from the deepening of lay instruction in the Central Middle Ages.[2] The eucharist occupied the minds of theologians and canonists as well as the lives of mystics and monks; the former saw it as a focus for orthodox teaching on sacramental efficacy and clerical authority, the latter as the underpinning of a life devoted to perfection and unity with God.[3] In the Low Countries eucharistic devotion animated a movement of lay women who retired from the world and lived in poverty outside religious houses and orders. The example of women like Mary of Oignies and Eve of St. Martin, Beguines of the diocese of Liège, inspired in churchmen and theologians an appreciation of the didactic value of

Society of Venice to 1620', (Cambridge Ph.D. thesis, 1982) and J.S. Henderson, 'Piety and Charity in Late Medieval Florence' (London, Ph.D. thesis, 1983). All Italian studies owe a great deal of their inspiration and methodology to the magisterial B. Pullan, *Rich and Poor in Renaissance Venice. The Social Institutions of a Catholic State, to 1620* (Oxford 1971). An ambitious and useful attempt at the integration of religious confraternities into the study of medieval mentalities has been made in J. Chiffoleau, *La comptabilité de l'au-delà. Les hommes, la mort et le religion dans la région d'Avignon à la fin du moyen-âge (vers 1320– vers 1480).* Collection de l'Ecole français de Rome 47 (Rome 1980). English confraternities are crying for basic studies to add to the useful survey of gilds based mainly on the returns of 1389 and summarised in H.F. Westlake, *The Parish Gilds of Medieval England* (London 1919). The growing interest in the subject in the recurrence of references to voluntary associations in studies of medieval religion as in D.M. Owen, *Church and Society in Medieval Lincolnshire* (Lincoln 1971) pp. 127–31; J.J. Scarisbrick, *The Reformation and the English People* (Oxford 1984) pp. 19–39 and the intriguing J. Bossy, *Christianity in the West, 1400–1700* (Oxford 1985). Publication of registers and accounts is still in its infancy, but developing interest is manifested in such publications as *Parish Fraternity Register. Fraternity of the Holy Trinity and SS. Fabian and Sebastian in the Parish of St. Botolph without Aldersgate* ed P. Basing, London Record Society 18 (London 1982).

[2] On popular devotion to the eucharist see E. Dumoutet, *Le désir de voir l'hostie et les origines de la dévotion au saint-sacrement* (Paris 1926). On forms and contents of preaching see D.L. D'Avray, *The Preaching of the Friars. Sermons Diffused from Paris before 1300* (Oxford 1985).

[3] On eucharistic theology in the early Middle Ages see J.M. Powers, *Eucharistic Theology* (New York 1967) pp. 11–21; and for a wide and thorough study of the Central Middle Ages G. Macy, *Theologies of the Eucharist in the Scholastic Period* (Oxford 1984).

eucharistic devotion.[4] As the sacraments, and above all the Real Presence, were ridiculed by heretics and doubted by simple believers, examples of devotion to the sacrament and of visions and Host miracles could be useful tools in teaching and defending orthodoxy. Jacques de Vitry, who spent some years in Liège in the early thirteenth century, composed the *Vita* of Mary of Oignies and believed that her eucharistic experiences could aid his preaching campaign against heresy in the South.[5] The visions of another woman, Juliana of Cornillon, spurred discussion within the diocese of Liège on the need to create a eucharistic feast, the absence of which she and others saw as a great deficiency. The idea was seized by ecclesiastical dignitaries such as the archdeacon of Liège, Jacques Pantaleon and the bishop, Robert of Tourhot (1240–6), and was encouraged by the Dominicans, recently established in the diocese.[6] The feast was founded there in 1246, and was instituted throughout the legation of the Holy Roman Empire in 1251. When the erstwhile archdeacon at Liège rose to the Roman See as Urban IV he completed the campaign promoted by him and his friends, raising the feast to universal observance on the Thursday following Trinity Sunday, a moveable feast occurring between the 21 of May and the 24 of June.[7]

Corpus Christi was conceived as a joyous celebration of the institution of the eucharist and of the arrival of grace and the hope

[4] On the world of the beguines see E.W. McDonnell, *Beguines and Beghards in Medieval Culture* (New Brunswick N.J. 1954) *passim*, esp pp. 281–361. On Cistercian mystics S. Roisin, *L'hagiographie cistercienne dans le diocèse de Liège au XIIIe siècle* (Louvain and Brussels 1947).

[5] *The 'Historia Occidentalis' of Jacques de Vitry. A Critical Edition* ed F.J. Hinnebusch, Spicilegium friburgense 17 (Fribourg 1972) pp. 5–12, esp pp. 9–11 and McDonnell, *Beguines and Beghards* pp. 20–39. The dangers of heretical teachings on the eucharist were mentioned in the institution bulls of the feast. On the influence of heretical views on contents of theological discussion and teaching see A.E. Bernstein, 'Theology between Heresy and Folklore: William of Auvergne on Punishment after Death' *Studies in Medieval and Renaissance History* 5 (1982) pp. 5–44.

[6] *Textus antiqui de festo Corporis Christi* ed P. Browe, Opuscula et textus series liturgica 4 (Münster 1934) pp. 1–20. *Acta Sanctorum* I April (5 April) (Antwerp 1675) pp. 437–77. On the background for the foundation of the feast see C. Hontoir, 'St. Julienne et les cisterciens', *Collectanea ordinis cisterciensium reformatorum* 8 (1946) pp. 109–16.

[7] For the Bull *Transiturus* see E. Franceschini, 'Origine e stile della bolla "Transiturus"' *Aevum* 39 (1965) pp. 218–43; pp. 234–43. On the significance of this date see Bossy, *Christianity in the West* p. 71.

of salvation to the world. Seeing that Maundy Thursday, the true anniversary of the eucharist, was dominated by the ensuing commemoration of the crucifixion, and was celebrated in a mournful mood, the propagators of the feast sought a separate occasion on which the salvific aspect of the eucharist could be emphasised.[8] However, the dissemination of the feast and its reception in dioceses and parishes was halted by the death of Urban IV in October 1264.[9] Half a century elapsed before a re-launching of the feast took place in the aftermath of the Council of Vienne when the bull *Transiturus* was repromulgated by John XXII and incorporated in the *Clementines* published in 1317.[10] We witness a process of legislation within dioceses, chapters and religious orders for the observation of the new feast and its integration into existing usages.[11] The first mention of the feast in England occurs in the chronicle of St. Peter's Gloucester, with the entry:

in the year of the lord 1318 the feast of Corpus Christi was first celebrated by the whole of the English church.[12]

---

[8] This distancing from the sacrificial aspect of the eucharist was stressed by all bulls and ordinances on the celebration of the feast, see *Textus antiqui* pp. 21–40.

[9] Not before he commissioned the composition of the Roman liturgy for the feast. The attribution of the liturgy to St. Thomas has recently been argued in P.-M. Gy 'L'office du Corpus Christi et Saint-Thomas d'Aquin' *Revue des sciences philosophiques et théologiques* 64 (1980) pp. 491–507 and 'L'office du Corpus Christi et la théologie des accidents eucharistiques' *Revue des sciences philosophiques et théologiques* 66 (1982) pp. 81–6. For the texts see C. Lambot, 'L'office de la Fête-Dieu. Aperçus nouveaux sur ses origines' *Revue bénédictine* 54 (1942) pp. 61–123. On the liturgy see also J.A. Weisheipl, *Friar Thomas d'Aquino. His Life, Thought and Works* (Oxford 1974) pp. 180–2.

[10] *Corpus iuris canonici* II ed. E. Friedberg, (Leipzig 1881), Clem. lib III, tit XIV, cols. 1173–4. For some speculation on the connection of the repromulgation to the Council of Vienne see E. Müller, *Das Konzil von Vienne 1311–1312, seine Quellen und seine Geschichte*, Vorreformationsgeschichtliche Forschungen 12 (Münster 1934) pp. 644–8. The feast did not take root even in the papal usage before the repromulgation, and is absent from late thirteenth century papal liturgical books such as, *Le cérémonial papal de la fin du moyen-âge à la Renaissance. I. Le cérémonial de Grégoire X (1273)* ed M. Dykmans (Brussels and Rome 1977). John XXII and Clement VI were the first to deal with problems posed by the feast's place in the calendar, *Le cérémonial papal de la fin du moyen-âge à la Renaissance. III Les textes avignonais jusqu'à la fin du Grand Schisme* ed M. Dykmans (Brussels and Rome 1983) pp. 254, 156–8.

[11] For some continental examples see *Textus antiqui* pp. 41–4.

[12] *Historia monasterii Sancti Petri Gloucestriae* I ed W.H. Hart *RS* (London 1863) p. 44. On 4 June 1318 the bishop of Bath and Wells published the feast in his

It was introduced to the province of York by Archbishop Melton in 1322:

> ... we instruct you ... to have the feast of the most precious sacrament of the body of our Lord Jesus Christ celebrated on Thursday after the octaves of Pentecost ... according to the form laid down in the constitution once published on this matter by pope Urban IV.[13]

In their chapter in Northampton in 1325 the Augustinian canons of England undertook:

> to celebrate annually the feast of Corpus Christi, instituted by the apostolic see, as a double or major feast.[14]

Corpus Christi was taken up by the parish in the form of a celebration of the Office of the feast for Vespers and Mass, accompanied by perambulations with the Host around the parish boundaries.[15] Devotion was encouraged by the grant of papal indulgences for attendance at the procession and Mass.[16] As the feast emphasised eucharistic efficacy through the Real Presence of Christ in the elements, it was more of a theological feast than the commemoration of the historical event of the Last Supper. Born out of doctrine and devotion, around an issue so vital for salvation and so given to erroneous interpretation, the feast of Corpus Christi became an occasion for teaching and preaching. In Cambridge it was by the mid-fourteenth century one of the four official *dies*

---

diocese, *Calendar of the Register of John de Drokensford, bishop of Bath and Wells a.d. 1309–1329*, ed E. Hobhouse, Somerset Record Society 1 (1887) p. 13.

[13] York, Borthwick Institute, Register Melton, fol 514 (3 June 1322). I am grateful to Professor Rosalind Hill for pointing out this reference to me and kindly sending me a full transcript of the document.

[14] *Chapters of the Augustinian Canons* ed H.E. Salter, Oxford Historical Society Publications 74 (Oxford 1920) p. 12. By 1332 the feast was established among the major feasts in the list of archbishop Langham, *Wilkins* 2 p. 560.

[15] For a description of such perambulations within a London parish and problems of regulation see *Memorials of London and London Life* ed H.T. Riley (London 1868) p. 509. For a similar custom of perambulation in the village confraternities of Champagne see Galpern, *The Religions of the People* pp. 72–3.

[16] York, Borthwick Institute, Register Melton, fol 514.

praedicabiles of the University.[17] The feast's didactic character was also expressed in the dramatic creation which was inspired by it: the English Corpus Christi drama was neither a Host-miracle play nor a Passion play, it was a cycle, an all-embracing Christian story, of sin, and then penance and salvation. The feast's aspect of universality also inspired municipal interest in its promotion, and many of the larger English towns commissioned celebrations which transcended parish boundaries and which expressed the unity of Christian people in Christian faith.[18]

Within the parishes yet independently of parochial duties, layfolk proceeded to incorporate the new feast into their religious and social life and deemed religious fraternities to be the natural framework for the extension of devotion. The first Corpus Christi fraternity was founded in 1326 in Louth, followed by the Tailors' Corpus Christi gild of Lincoln, founded two years later.[19] A picture of the state of foundations by the late fourteenth century can be gleaned from the returns to the royal enquiry of 1388 into the state of religious gilds;[20] these returns are necessarily an

[17] G.R. Owst, *Preaching in Medieval England* (Cambridge 1926) p. 225. *Documents Relating to the University and Colleges of Cambridge* (London 1853) I p. 398 (*Statuta antiqua* c.168). For examples of indulgences related to attendance at Corpus Christi sermons see *Calendar of Papal Letters* IV p. 165; and a Corpus Christi sermon in *Speculum sacerdotale* ed E.H. Weatherly, EETS 200 (London 1936) pp. 162–3.

[18] On the urban context of the Corpus Christi celebrations see C. Phythian-Adams, 'Ceremony and the Citizen: the Communal Year at Coventry', *Crisis and Order in English Towns, 1500–1700. Essays in Urban History* eds P. Clark and P. Slack (London 1972) pp. 57–85; as well as M. James, 'Ritual, Drama and Social Body in the Late Medieval Town', *PP* 98 (1983) pp. 3–29; esp pp. 10, 13, 18, 24–6. On the development of the feast as a patriotic-civic occasion see E. Muir, *Civic Ritual in Renaissance Venice* (Princeton N.J. 1981) pp. 223–30, esp 223–4, n 28.

[19] The priests' fraternity of Norwich which was founded in 1278 and known as the Corpus Christi gild, seems too early for a dedication to this feast and must have acquired the attribution some time in the fourteenth century. On this gild see N.P. Tanner, *The Church in Late Medieval Norwich, 1370–1532* Pontifical Institute of Medieval Studies. Studies and Texts 66 (Toronto 1984) p. 77.

[20] On the background for the establishment of the enquiry in the Cambridge Parliament see J.A. Tuck, 'The Cambridge Parliament, 1388', *EHR* 84 (1969) pp. 225–43. See also Westlake, *The Parish Gilds* pp. 36–48 and *Parish Fraternity Register* pp. ix–x. The returns are in PRO, C41/38–46; they are geographically

underestimate of such activities as they survive mainly from four counties: Lincolnshire, Norfolk, Suffolk and Cambridgeshire, but they show that 42 of 471 fraternities recorded were dedicated to Corpus Christi (the third most popular dedication, after the Blessed Virgin and the Holy Trinity). The date of foundation of 29 of these associations is known; they were founded in the following sequence: by 1340: 5, between 1341 and 1360: 15, between 1361 and 1380: 9.[21] A surge in the number of foundations in the 1350s and 1360s corresponds to the rapid expansion of fraternities in these decades all over Europe.[22]

What were the particular practices of the Corpus Christi fraternity? The first impression runs contrary to expectations, as only rarely were they dominated by eucharistic devotions. It is more understandable if we remember that religious fraternities were primarily concerned with the treatment of death and its aftermath, and developed social and charitable relations to ensure the efficacy of their efforts. The predominance of the intercessory aim is expressed in one recent description of the medieval fraternity as 'an association of layfolk who, under the patronage of a particular saint, the Trinity, Blessed Virgin Mary, Corpus Christi or similar, undertook to provide the individual member of the brotherhood with a good funeral ... together with regular prayer and a mass-saying thereafter'.[23] Thus, all Corpus Christi fraternities made provisions for commemoration, 32 out of 42 employed a chaplain

unrepresentative as the surviving returns originate for the greater part from the Eastern counties: Norfolk 164, Lincolnshire 123, Cambridgeshire 60, Suffolk 39 and most from urban gilds, Westlake, *The Parish Gilds* pp. 49–58. They obviously reflect norms rather than the reality of behaviour.

[21] Foundations were clustered around the years of the Black Death 1349–1352.

[22] In the Avignon area a later sequence occurred, with concentrated foundation in the last quarter of the century, Chiffoleau, *La comptabilité de l'au-delà* Annexe II pp. 448–53. Italian confraternities dedicated to Corpus Christi appear only very late in the fifteenth century P. Burke, *Culture and Society in Renaissance Italy, 1420–1540* (London 1972) pp. 215–6.

[23] Scarisbrick, *The Reformation and the English People* pp. 19–20. On religious gilds as funerary societies see Chiffoleau, *La comptabilité de l'au-delà, passim*, esp pp. 267, 281–2; W. Monter, *Ritual, Myth and Magic in Early Modern Europe* (Brighton 1983) p. 15. The quest for intercession and commemoration was so widely pervasive that even poor folk endeavoured to provide for themselves, as did the members of the poor men's gild of Norwich, PRO, C47/43/292; see also Owen, *Church and Society* p. 95 and Monter, *Ritual, Myth and Magic* p. 14.

for regular daily or annual celebration of masses for the dead,[24] and half of the fraternities provided for burial of their poor members at the gild's expense. The funerary preoccupation of the late medieval fraternity was predominant, even in those dedicated to Corpus Christi where additional acts were grafted onto the basic routine of cooperative intercession. In Stretham in the Isle of Ely the Corpus Christi fraternity assembled on St. Clement's day, and most of its ordinances were devoted to funerary arrangements, mutual relief and commemoration. However, it also provided 26 candles for the illumination of the Host carried in the Corpus Christi procession and on feast days; and Corpus Christi served as an administrative term for payment of fines.[25] The fraternity at Outwell in Lincolnshire held its principal meeting on Corpus Christi but spent most of its efforts on burial and commemoration of members, and distributions related to intercession.[26] The Holy Trinity fraternity in St. Botolph's church outside Aldersgate, in London, was devoted to the honour of Corpus Christi and assembled on Trinity Sunday when its members heard the mass of the day as well as a Corpus Christi office, which should have occurred four days later.[27] Nine fraternities obliged their members to participate in the Corpus Christi procession and 17 of 42 groups held their assemblies on the feast. At Grantham the fraternity participated in the procession in livery, illuminated its Corpus Christi altar and held an assembly and meal on the day.[28]

Ritual and symbolic acts related to the veneration of the Host, the Lord's Body, were familiar but scattered. The main form of veneration was the maintenance of lights around the Host kept in its case, a ritual stipulated by thirteenth-century diocesan legislation.[29] Of 42 fraternities 19 provided lighting: either perpetually

[24] The Corpus Christi gild of Lincoln employed 9 chaplains for daily masses, Owen, *Church and Society* pp. 129–30.

[25] PRO, C47/38/31.

[26] PRO, C47/44/309.

[27] 'in honorem Corporis Christi et ad sustentandum tresdecim cereos ardentes circa sepulcrum in eadem ecclesia tempore Paschae', *Parish Fraternity Register* pp. 79, 80.

[28] PRO, C47/39/109.

[29] *Councils and Synods and Other Documents Relating to the English Church* 2, eds F.M. Powicke and C.R. Cheney (Oxford 1964) c 2, p. 210 (1224x37 Coventry Council), c 1, p. 345 (1240x66 Statutes for the diocese of Norwich). The account of expenses on the feast day of the Tailors' Corpus Christi fraternity for 1387–

or on feasts and Sundays, spreading their effort of illumination over the whole year. Thus, the fraternity meeting in St. Peter's church, Ely, assembled on the Monday after Easter, but provided two torches for the elevation on every Sunday[30] while the Caistor fraternity concentrated its provision in the period between Holy Week and Corpus Christi when it illuminated the Body of Christ, and also provided 40 candles to be carried by its members at the Corpus Christi procession.[31] The elevation of the host which from the late twelfth century became the supreme moment of eucharistic veneration and union of the believer with God, was favoured by many fraternities which supported the lighting at elevation laid down by canon law.[32] Another interesting example of the absorption of a popular eucharistic devotion occurred in the development of an interest in the *viaticum*, in bringing the Sacrament to the sick and dying.[33] This pastoral duty was elaborated through repeated diocesan legislation in the late twelfth and thirteenth centuries, and sought to ensure not only the reception of communion by ailing believers, but also that the exposed Host be guarded from the elements and from popular abuse.[34] Thus, a ritual of veneration along the route of the parochial procession evolved: the passing

---

8 only mention 12d for carrying the tabernacle from the church to their hall but of the £5 spent that year £2.5 went to on illumination of its tabernacle, *The Making of King's Lynn. A Documentary Survey* ed D.M. Owen, Records of Economic and Social History new ser. 9 (London 1984) pp. 318–9. For an agreement regulating the provision of lights in the Corpus Christi gild of Lynn see B. Mackerell, *The History and Antiquities of the Flourishing Corporation of King's Lynn in the County of Norfolk* (London 1738) pp. 254–5.

[30] PRO, C47/38/21.

[31] PRO, C47/39/92.

[32] On the development and significance of the elevation see G.G. Grant, 'The Elevation of the Host: A Reaction to the Twelfth Century Heresy', *Theological Studies* 1 (1940) pp. 228–50 as well as Macy, *Eucharistic Theologies* pp. 88–9. For examples of provision of illumination by gilds dedicated to Corpus Christi see *Parish Fraternity Register* c 21, p. 4. And for French confraternities see Y. Dossat, 'Les confréries du Corpus Christi dans le monde rural pendant la première moitié du XIVe siècle' *Cahiers de Fanjeaux* 1 (1976) pp. 357–85.

[33] On the development of pastoral work for the sick and dying see J. Avril, 'La pastorale des malades et des mourants aux XIIe et XIIIe siècles' in *Death in the Middle Ages* eds H. Braet and W. Verbeke (Louvain 1983) pp. 88–106.

[34] *Councils and synods* 2 c 15, p. 110 (1222 Oxford Council), c 1, p. 171 (1229 Worcester Council II), c 3, p. 268 (?1239 Lincoln Council). On abuse of the Host and misinterpretation of its powers see P. Browe, 'Die Eukaristie als Zaubermittel im Mittelalter' *Archiv für Kulturgeschichte* 20 (1930) pp. 134–54.

priest and acolytes carrying the Host brought the eucharistic devotion to the streets and allowed layfolk to show their respect by genuflection and recitation of prayers. This practice entered the activities of fraternities in which the charitable act of visiting sick members and the pastoral duty of bringing the Sacrament to them converged. Thus, the Corpus Christi gild of King's Lynn was founded during the Black Death to provide proper illumination for the Host so frequently carried in the streets in those unfortunate years.[35] The Corpus Christi gild of Wisbech illuminated the Sacrament on its journey to the dying, as did the Corpus Christi fraternity at St.-Michael-on-the-Hill in Lincoln.[36] In some French Corpus Christi fraternities the members assisted parish priests on their journeys to the sick, and denied participation in these processions as a form of punishment for infringement of fraternity statutes.[37]

In bigger towns where Corpus Christi was celebrated on a large scale with dramatic cycles and processions, the organisation of the plays was entrusted not to the Corpus Christi gild, but rather to the trade gilds, in which political and economic power was deployed. Where celebration developed in urban processions they were often led by the local Corpus Christi fraternity, as in the case of Bury St. Edmunds.[38] In some towns the Corpus Christi fraternity became a prominent and prestigious group, comprising the whole town patriciate, as in York, Lincoln and Coventry, in which case it led the urban procession of trade gilds, cutting across the purely occupational basis of organisation.[39] In Lincoln too this seems to be the case; the Sailors' gild and the Tailors' gild, both dedicated to Corpus Christi, attended Mass, distributed alms and

---

[35] PRO, C47/42/279.

[36] PRO, C47/38/38 and C47/40/135.

[37] In some Corpus Christi confraternities of Southern France related functions of nursing and patronage of hospitals evolved, Dossat, 'Les confréries de Corpus Christi' pp. 367, 373 and Chiffoleau, *La comptabilité de l'au-delà* p. 284 and p. 282.

[38] R. S. Gottfried, *Bury St. Edmunds and the Urban Crisis, 1290–1539* (Princeton N.J. 1982) p. 188.

[39] On the Corpus Christi procession of Coventry see Phythian-Adams, 'Ceremony and the Citizen' pp. 58–60 and on other towns again James, 'Ritual, Drama and Social Body' *passim*.

led the urban procession.[40] Yet in neither fraternity was devotion restricted or channelled to a particular cult; their ordinances envisaged and supported the undertaking of pilgrimages, charitable distributions, mutual help, burial and commemoration. At Grantham the brethren and sisters were led by priests in a procession, carried candles and attended Mass; they then ate together and later each couple distributed food to poor folk.[41] The accounts of the Corpus Christi fraternity of Cambridge report a large expenditure of 56s.10d. 'circa processionem'.[42]

This short examination of the variety of activities undertaken by Corpus Christi fraternities shows the ways in which these voluntary groupings embraced and at the same time transcended the new feast. At the basis of the coming together of individuals was the wish to sustain each other and benefit from cooperation in search of salvation. This was to be achieved by safeguarding the community, of the quick and the dead, intact; an effort which benefited from para-liturgical activities such as processions and participation in vernacular plays.[43] The absence of rigorous application of a set of symbols connected with the eucharist, the lack of dominance by one spiritual and devotional scheme, the like of which dominated flagellant societies, presents to us a picture of flexibility and openness, free of obsession with form, but preoccupied by substance.[44] Aimed at bringing people together and preparing them for a better life and death, the medieval English fraternity was open to all means of 'increase of worship'. As new feasts were proclaimed, new saints canonised, and as new anxieties

[40] PRO, C47/41/158 and C47/41/159.
[41] Owen, *Church and Society* p. 128.
[42] *Cambridge Gild Records, 1295–1389* ed M. Bateson, Cambridge Antiquarian Society Publications 39 (Cambridge 1903) p. 27.
[43] The Cambridge fraternity owned breviaries, *ibid* pp. 40, 41, the text of a play, *ibid* p. 51 and had a gild reader, *ibid* p. 40.
[44] Corpus Christi gilds developed diverse charitable and liturgical activities; some maintained hospitals, Dossat, 'Les confréries du Corpus Christi' pp. 366–7 and L. Martz, *Poverty and Welfare in Habsburg Spain. The Example of Toledo* (Cambridge 1983) p. 161. For examples of diversification of a gild's activities beyond its original and formal aims and dedication see N. Orme, 'The Kalendar Brethren of the City of Exeter' *Reports and Transactions of the Devonshire Association* 109 (1977) pp. 153–69 and *idem*, 'The Guild of Kalendars, Bristol' *Transactions of the Bristol and Gloucestershire Archaeological Society* 96 (1978) pp. 32–52.

surfaced, they absorbed them into a body which was flexible, responsive and autonomous.[45] These characteristics allowed late medieval town-dwellers to adopt what was practicable and attractive, what was feasible given their organisational and financial restraints, and to apply their findings to the basic quests related to such unchangeable aspects of life as friendship, kinship, sickness, vicissitudes in fortune, and death. These immutables, served by the fraternity's rhythm of charity and commemoration, were highlighted by the annual or occasional eucharistic veneration; the feast and other particular devotions lent coherence to the regular communal salvific effort.

What do their choices, the pattern of absorption of a new feast, teach us about their spirituality?[46] They undoubtedly reflect discretion rather than negligence or incomplete grasp of the feast. Corpus Christi and its doctrinal ramifications were not lost, rather they were seen as a suitable focus for piety in the decades following the institution of the feast. The degree to which fraternities subscribed to eucharistic practice varied, but was never a random choice.[47] In devising their plans these voluntary bodies were assisted by the clergy and friars, in roles which never became so dominant as in Italian confraternities. The clergy and the friars were employed, as they were for the execution of masses and obits, to provide their exclusive services of teaching, exemplification and simplification of dogma, scripture and religious tale.[48] Recognising their special dramatic 'training', towns and fraternities engaged friars in dramatic pageants and processions: in Exeter they led the urban procession of Corpus Christi,[49] and in York a Franciscan, William Melton, composed the final form of the Corpus Christi

---

[45] R. Pfaff, *New Liturgical Feasts in Later Medieval England* (Oxford 1970).

[46] On the voluntary impulse towards liturgical and charitable activities in religious fraternities see Le Bras, 'Les confréries chrétiennes', p. 325 and Chiffoleau, *La comptabilité de l'au-delà* p. 286.

[47] Professor Bossy has suggested that Corpus Christi was espoused so readily because of its message of unity, J. Bossy, 'The Mass as a Social Institution 1200–1700', *PP* 100 (1983) pp. 29–61 at p. 59.

[48] Scarisbrick, *The Reformation and the English People* p. 24. On connections with clergy in rural Italian confraternities see La Roncière, 'La place des confréries dans le contado florentin' pp. 41–2.

[49] A.G. Little and R.C. Easterling, *The Franciscans and Dominicans of Exeter* History of Exeter Research Group Monograph 2 (Exeter 1927) p. 26.

cycle in 1426.[50] But fraternities were based on autonomy and deliberation; this discerning creation of forms of worship which involved personal active participation, group cooperation as well as learning could not but have evolved in the midst of a knowledgeable, partly literate, laity.[51] The products of a century and a half of intensive lay instruction at confession, communion and in the market place, by the mid-fourteenth century the English urban laity had devised forms of spiritual improvement all their own: groupings which were solid in friendship and mutual help, careful in self-regulation and punishment of lapses, regular in adherence to the effort of intercession, and above all, flexible and open to new modes of religious thought and devotion which could assist and promote their search for unity in piety.[52]

Girton College, Cambridge

[50] A.H. Nelson, *The Medieval English Stage: Corpus Christi Pageants and Plays* (Chicago 1974) pp. 39–41; on involvement of friars in the dramatic para-liturgy see L.G. Craddock, 'Franciscan Influences on Early English Drama', *Franciscan Studies* 10 (1950) pp. 383–417, esp p. 387. For some consideration of the clergy's role see Y.-M. Bercé, *Fête et révolte. Des mentalités populaires du XVIe au XVIIIe siècle* (Paris 1976) pp. 136–8.

[51] On lay literacy see J.H. Moran, *Education and Learning in the City of York, 1300–1560*, Borthwick Papers 55 (York 1979) pp. 31–5 and J.H. Moran, *The Growth of English Schooling, 1340–1548: Learning, Literacy and Laicization in Pre-Reformation York Diocese* (Princeton N.J. 1985); as a reminder against overestimation of literacy see P. Heath, 'Piety in Late Medieval Hull', in *The Church, Patronage and Politics in the Fifteenth Century* ed B. Dobson (New York 1985) p. 226. It brings forth the vernacular and personal prayers as a valid source for the study of the religion of a considerable section of the urban population through books such as the *The Lay Folk's Catechism* ed T.P. Simmons and H.E. Nolloth EETS 118 (London 1912), in a direction suggested recently in P. Collinson, *The Religion of Protestants. The Church in English Society 1559–1625* (Oxford 1982) pp. 190–1. For vernacular writings on the eucharist, mass and the feast of Corpus Christi for contemplation and recitation see *The Lay Folk's Mass Book* ed T.F. Simmons EETS 71 (London 1879) pp. 2–60 and *The Minor Poems of the Vernon MS.* ed C. Horstmann EETS 98 (London 1892) pp. 24–5, 168–97, 198–221.

[52] On cooperation and the relation between individual and community in fraternities see J. Bossy, 'Holiness and Society', pp. 75 (1977) pp. 119–37, esp p. 131. A deeper understanding of levels of interpretation of doctrine as well as of commitment can be gained from the study of para-liturgy, festivals, and especially the pageantry and vernacular drama which flourished in connection with Corpus Christi: A.V. Kolve, *The Play Called Corpus Christi* (London 1966); on drama as a source for the study of piety see E.C. Dunn, 'Popular Devotion in the Vernacular Drama of Medieval England' *Mediaevalia et Humanistica* 4 (1973) pp. 55–68.

THE SOCIAL AND ECONOMIC SPREAD
OF RURAL LOLLARDY: A REAPPRAISAL

by DEREK PLUMB

THE evidence given us by John Foxe[1] in his *Book of Martyrs* provides more information about the social and theological standing of Lollards than we know about many later religious dissidents. Recent work has added to our knowledge. Geoffrey Dickens[2] and Claire Cross[3] have reconsidered the place of the Lollards in the development of the English Reformation, especially in theological matters. John Thomson[4] drew our attention to the continuity shown in some areas. Claire Cross[5] and Margaret Aston[6] showed the importance of women Lollards. J.F. Davis[7] has supported the idea of a continuous movement, and stressed the involvement of the remaining Lollard brotherhoods in the Reformation proper. Margaret Aston[8] saw the reformers using Lollard texts to settle the Reformation into a tradition. And John Fines[9] found one group of Lollards definitely not of a low or 'middling sort'. But despite this attention on the part of historians, we still know little of the people labelled Lollards. How did they react to developments locally and nationally? Did they assimilate into their local communities despite their beliefs? What social and economic standing did they have? Was contemporary abuse, which dismissed them as 'lowly sorts', justified?

[1] *The Acts and Monuments of John Foxe* ed S.R. Cattley (London 1837) 8 vols.
[2] A.G. Dickens, *Lollards and Protestants in the diocese of York. 1509–1558* (Oxford 1959).
[3] Claire Cross, *Church and People, 1450–1660* (London 1976).
[4] J.A.F. Thomson, *The Later Lollards, 1414–1520* (Oxford 1965).
[5] Claire Cross, 'The great reasoners in Scripture: the activities of women Lollards, 1380–1530', *Medieval Women: Studies in Church History*, Subsidia I (Oxford 1978).
[6] Margaret Aston, 'Lollard women priests?', *Lollards and Reformers: Images and Literacy in late medieval religion* (London 1984).
[7] John F. Davis, *Heresy and the Reformation in the south-east of England, 1520–1559* (London 1983).
[8] Margaret Aston, 'Lollardy and the Reformation: Survival or Revival?' *History* 49 (London 1964).
[9] John Fines, 'Heresy trials in the diocese of Coventry and Lichfield, 1511–12', *JEH* 14.

Bearing these points in mind, this lack of information, and the prevalence of contemporary abuse, I turn to the particular study I am undertaking: a closer look at the Lollard groups to be found within southern Buckinghamshire; a group well-known through the references in Foxe.[10] I am seeking to put flesh on the bare bones left us by Foxe, and seek to bring to light their standing within their community. Were they really the lowest of the low? Or were they important members of rural society, both economically and socially? Before discussing them perhaps a brief look at the area would be useful.

The chalk escarpment along which runs the Icknield Way divides the county into two.[11] North are large areas of mixed farming; south lie the Chilterns and the Thames and Colne Valleys. In this southern area was a large wooded, sparsely populated area, where smaller fields and isolated farmsteads were normal. Only towards the rivers were nucleated villages more common. Despite this, the proximity of the growing market at London saw growth and development. The valleys were richer than areas just a few miles farther north, on the slopes of the Chilterns themselves. Land values however remained stable, and not surprisingly Wolsey sought to tax goods when these were of more value than land during his reorganisation of the tax system in 1522.

Trade, communication, the family unit, peripatetic preachers and reading groups were important facets in the lives of Lollards. In order to consider the sect better I have, for the purposes of this paper, looked at four parishes and two family groups. By working on the various taxation and probate evidence available I have sought to build up a picture of the Lollards as family units, and as members of Chiltern society during the sixteenth century.

x x x x

Not only does the Great Subsidy of 1524–5[12] provide 'an ideal starting point from which to examine the structure of rural

---

[10] Foxe iv pp. 123–130; pp. 220–240.
[11] Most of my information on the economic conditions in Buckinghamshire at this time is taken from *The Agrarian History of England and Wales, 1500–1640* ed Joan Thirsk (Cambridge 1967); and Michael Reed, *The Buckinghamshire Landscape* (London 1979).
[12] *The Subsidy Roll for the county of Buckinghamshire. Anno. 1524* eds A.C. Chibnall and A. Vere Woodman (Aylesbury 1944).

society',[13] but with the additional bonus of the Certificates of Musters of 1522,[14] historians wishing to trace and categorise those families of particular political or religious propensities stand a good chance of finding much informative data. If probate material is added then, perhaps, much can be written to put flesh on the skeletal knowledge given us by Foxe, of those involved in the trials of 1521–2.

When looking at the overall figures for the 1524–5 Subsidy I am using the statistical breakdown used in her work by Margaret Spufford,[15] although they differ slightly from those used by Julian Cornwall in his study of country towns,[16] and also from those used by Hoskins in his general study of the social and economic developments of the period.[17] However, the variations are unimportant in the context of this study, at least at present.

The breakdown for the four parishes looked at in this paper is seen in Table I below. The table gives a rough guide to individuals who I have identified as Lollards or probable Lollards. It need not be emphasised that there are many questions that are as yet unanswered. Many shadowy areas remain regarding individuals, and many additional factors, such as mobility, which whilst needing caution often adds to our information, can assist in our attempt to build up our knowledge of families and their environment.

My data has come initially by taking the information given us by Foxe: surname, Christian name, parish, trade, and social details. Then I have worked on the Muster Returns and Subsidy Rolls, and archdeaconry court records, to identify persons taxed, or leaving wills, of the same surname, in the same places, as Lollards. There are inevitably many doubts. Most of Foxe's information is based on the trials of 1521–2; the Great Subsidy dates from 1524 (though the Muster Returns, upon which it is based, also date from 1522), so identifying individuals leaves a two-year gap, and we

[13] Margaret Spufford, 'Rural Cambridgeshire, 1520–1680' (unpublished MA thesis, Leicester 1962) p. 58.
[14] *The Certificates of Musters for Buckinghamshire in 1522* ed A.C. Chibnall (London 1973).
[15] M. Spufford, *thesis cit.*, table V p. 80.
[16] Julian Cornwall, 'English Country Towns in the Fifteen Twenties', *ECHR* 2 ser 15 (1962–3) pp. 59–60.
[17] W.G. Hoskins, *The Age of Plunder: The England of Henry VIII, 1500–1547* (London 1976) pp. 36–42.

Table I. Breakdown of Subsidy Roll returns of 1524-5, showing probable Lollards.

	Subsidy totals	adjusted* totals- %	population	Certain Lollards	Probable Lollards	All identified Lollards	percentage identified in Subsidy
Amersham							
30s. and under	51	43	157	nil	5	5	10
+30s.→£4	46	35	142	4	11	15	33
+£4→£9	12	10	37	4	2	6	50
£10 and over	15	12	46	4	4	8	53
Totals	124	100	382	12	22	34	
Denham							
30s. and under	40	68	123	1	6	7	17
+30s.→£4	12	20	37	nil	nil	nil	—
+£4→£9	4	7	12	2	nil	2	50
£10 and over	3	5	9	nil	nil	nil	—
Totals	59	100	181	3	6	9	
Great Marlow							
30s. and under	38	41	117	1	11	12	32
+30s.→£4	33	35	102	3	6	9	27
+£4→£9	11	12	34	1	2	3	27
£10 and over	11	12	34	1	2	3	27
Totals	93	100	287	6	21	27	
Hughenden							
30s. and under	6	30	20	nil	2	2	33
+30s.→£4	8	40	24	1	3	4	50
+£4→£9	3	15	9	1	nil	1	33
£10 and over	3	15	9	1	nil	1	33
Totals	20	100	62	3	5	8	
Grand totals	296	—	912	24	54	78	

* Julian Cornwall, 'English Country Towns in the Fifteen Twenties', *Economic History Review*, Second Series, XV, (Utrecht, 1962-3), pp. 59-60.

know how mobile the population was. However, when an individual is named by Foxe as belonging to a particular parish, and the same name appears in the Subsidy in the same parish, I have taken it that I have found the same individual again. There may be errors; but I have identified enough people as 'certain' or 'probable' Lollards for them to cancel each other out.

Table II: Totals in the Subsidy Roll returns of 1524–5 for the four parishes.

	The two towns and two villages	Total 'Lollards'	approx. percentage
30s. and under	135	26	19
+30s.→£4	99	28	28
+£4→£9	30	12	40
£10 and over	32	12	37
Totals	296	78	

Note: Over one quarter of those eligible to pay taxes in the Great Subsidy of 1524–5 are Lollards (27%).
The social spread can be seen to range throughout all financial levels, with one-fifth at the lower end of the scale and reaching two fifths at the upper levels.

Table I gives the information gleaned from four parishes: two of them being market towns (Amersham and Great Marlow), the other two (Denham and Hughenden) being widespread parishes with non-nucleated settlements. It is apparent that identifiable Lollards were spread through all sections of those eligible to pay taxes in 1524–5, and it is also apparent that the strongest Lollard groups were to be found not at the lowest level of society, financially speaking, but very much towards the middling ranks and indeed into the higher echelons of these basically rural societies. Table II, in which the results from the four parishes are brought together tends to confirm this point. The figures shown there give us a high point of 40% of those taxed in the £4 to £9 group and even at the lowest level one fifth of those listed in the Subsidy are identifiable as Lollards.

Overall, approximately one quarter of nearly three hundred souls in the four parishes can be labelled as Lollards or as having Lollard connections. This makes some nonsense both of the argument that Lollards were of the 'lowly sort' and also that Lollardy was a minority, underground, movement unaffected by, and having little effect on, the society around it.

The need for additional material is met very often by probate records, as the Bartlett family, discussed below, show. And the information provided points to the importance of family connections, the mobility of families, the financial and social spread of Lollard families, if not of Lollardy itself, and the importance, as I see it, of the teaching found in St. James's Gospel, relating to good works.

The probate material itself is producing much information, enabling us to reconsider the place of Lollards within parish and locality. Whilst dedicatory clauses tend to be conservative until the reign of Elizabeth (even those written in Edward's reign show little tendency to protestant formulae) we do find many instances in the wills of south Buckinghamshire of bequests to the poor and for 'public works'. This may be a Lollard phenomenon alone, for certainly Lollard families did this, or it may be an aberration within the archdeaconry, for Margaret Bowker found few such instances in the diocese as a whole.[18] Whichever is the case these Lollard wills do point to one particularly defined Lollard belief being carried out; they followed the teaching of one particular epistle, that of St. James. It was totally alien to Luther's ideas on Justification by Faith Alone of course, and it is interesting that when he spoke to the group at Hughenden Nicholas Field, lately back from Germany, did not mention that particular tenet of protestant belief.[19] The wills suggest to me that the Lollards followed through the teaching of St. James's epistle in their bequests for there are several instances of bequests to the poor. Walter Tredway, a yeoman of Amersham, left 12d. to the poor people of the town.[20] He was of a Lollard family, if not a Lollard himself. Joan Tymberlake

---

[18] Margaret Bowker, *The Henrician Reformation: the diocese of Lincoln under John Longland, 1521–1547* (Cambridge 1981) pp. 48–9.
[19] Foxe, iv p. 584.
[20] Buckinghamshire Record Office (BRO), D/A/We/8/80.

left 6s.8d. for the poor.[21] Edward Littlepage of Little Missenden, left 20s. to be spent on the highways.[22]

These examples, and many others, would tend to throw doubt on the figures given in Margaret Bowker's study of the diocese of Lincoln where she says that the figures for various bequests within the archdeaconry of Buckingham for the years 1521–30 and 1535–6 show little or no such donations. She finds no evidence whatsoever for giving to the poor, to orphans, or to the sick, in either period. As for public works these average out at eight per cent. In the small group of wills I am looking at the evidence is of much higher levels of this type of giving. This now needs to be placed in the context of the particular communities.

x x x x

Firstly, let me take the parish of Hughenden, lying on the slopes of the Chilterns above Wycombe. It was comparatively big, even if sparsely-populated. If Scarisbrick's critical appraisal of Lollardy as a sect mainly of 'deep-rooted, upland, semi-paganism'[23] *is* true, then Hughenden is perhaps the ideal setting. The details given us by the various documents examined relating to the families at Hughenden give a good example of the construction we can make of the community there, and of both the economic and social spread of Lollardy within the community, and also of the widespread family connections involved. The figures given for the parish in Table I indicate that spread only too well.

The parish is mentioned occasionally by Foxe. Widmore Clerk the elder is said to be the cousin of Thomas Africk of Hughenden;[24] Thomas Clerk the elder was detected by Robert Pope,[25] who may have passed through the parish as he fled from the wrath of Bishop Smith in 1511, on his way to East Hendred, Oxfordshire, from Amersham. The Hobbes family were named by some of those

[21] BRO, D/A/Wf/6/163.
[22] BRO, D/A/We/6/197.
[23] J.J. Scarisbrick, *The Reformation and the English People*, (Oxford 1984) p. 6.
[24] Foxe, iv p. 229.
[25] *Ibid.* p. 235.

abjuring at Amersham.[26] There is a whole list of surnames mentioned in Foxe having links with the parish, including that of Widmore.

The Widmore family are a good example of Lollardy at the higher social level. Thomas Widmore was married to a daughter of Roger House,[27] and was known to Thomas Holmes[28] and John Hakker,[29] both preachers of the sect. He was overseer to the will of John Wellysbourne[30] (who, incidentally, had a daughter who was married to one of the Bartletts of Amersham, a Lollard family of impeccable heretical pedigree). The family of Widmore later succeeded the Wellysbourne family at Rockalls Manor. In the Muster Certificate Thomas Widmore had lands at High Wycombe to the value of 10s. and at Hughenden to the value of £4 10s., with goods to the value of £35.[31] Table I gives some indication of the standing within the parish that the family must have had.

Further connections with Lollard families is shown in the will of John Wydmore of Hughenden, made in 1547,[32] when the legatees included his son's wife Christian Herne (of a Lollard family) and the witnesses included Thomas Bernard, of another heretic family.

Lower in the social scale, but according to Foxe related by marriage to the Widmore family,[33] were the Phip family. Both Henry and William, named by Foxe, are found in the Muster Certificate, with goods at £6 and £10 respectively.[34] John, possibly a physician, had lands to the value of £6 at Amersham.[35] He left a conservative will in 1530[36] but left 6s.8d. to the poor, and one of his overseers was Thomas Wydmore the younger.

At the bottom of the social scale was Laurence Hern. He was one of a group attending a sermon given by Nicholas Field at John

[26] *Ibid.* p. 224.
[27] *Ibid.* p. 237.
[28] *Ibid.* p. 226.
[29] *Ibid.* p. 240.
[30] *The Courts of the Archdeaconry of Buckingham, 1483–1523*, ed E.M. Elvey pp. 389–90.
[31] Chibnall, *Musters* pp. 226–274, 282–3.
[32] BRO, D/A/We/6/398.
[33] Foxe, iv p. 237.
[34] Chibnall, *Musters* pp. 282–3.
[35] *Ibid.* p. 230.
[36] BRO, D/A/We/3/318.

Taylor's house in Hughenden in 1530. Hern's will, dated 1556, has Thomas Clerk, Thomas Wydmore, and Frances House as witnesses.[37] All are Lollard surnames, if not Lollards themselves. Laurence Hern left several bequests of sheep to relatives and seems not to be totally without finances, yet in the Muster Returns he is listed as having goods worth only £1 and does not appear in the Subsidy Roll.

The Lollard families at Hughenden encompassed the whole strata of society and were apparently closely connected with each other.

Great Marlow, the second parish, is not only a larger parish in population, but lies on the sandy soil along the Thames; an area of pasture mixed with arable. Once again Foxe mentions several individuals and a few family groups from the parish and adjacent settlements. The socio-economic spread, as indicated in Table I, is similar to that at Hughenden, but if anything it is more widely settled through the parish.

I will mention only a few of those named, as examples. Elenore Godfrey was detected in 1521 by Thomas Collard for speaking against the real presence;[38] John Gray was detected in 1521;[39] the wife of John Simons was both detected and a detector of others;[40] the Sherwood family were detected by John Gardiner, and although neither are said to have come from Marlow other evidence of detections, together with entries in the Muster Certificates and Subsidy Roll, bring one to the conclusion that Great Marlow was their home parish.[41]

In the Subsidy Roll[42] the following are among a long list of those who we might consider as possible Lollards. Thomas Godfrey £9, John Grey £10, Raynold Shyrewode £2, and Richard Ravenyng £20 (Foxe mentions a Richard Rave from Marlow, detected by the Gardiner family. I have been unable to find a single surname Rave in the county, and the evidence would seem to point to Ravenyng as being the person referred to.) It will be seen that the Lollards were well-entrenched within the upper echelons of society,

[37] BRO, D/A/Wf/2/299.
[38] Foxe, v p. 454.
[39] *Ibid.* iv p. 229.
[40] *Ibid.*
[41] *Ibid.*
[42] Chibnall and Vere Woodman, *Subsidy*, p. 23.

although Shyrewode's £2 again points to the economic spread of Lollardy in the parish.

In the Muster Certificates[43] we find several of the same surnames: the Grey family held land to the value of £1 and the two members of the Sherwood family had goods to the value of £10 between them. The archdeaconry court records show the Grey family, not surprisingly, to be widespread throughout the county. There is one entry relating to Great Marlow: Robert Grey is called before the bishop's court for a minor offence. Wills of the family include one of John Grey the elder, who leaves 7d. to the 'brytge at marley magna'.[44]

The only mention of the Sherwood family by Foxe was in connection with a group named by John Gardiner, which had among its number a Mrs J. Simon, and John Grey of Marlow. The wills of two of those named by Foxe, David and Raynolde Sherwood, survive, as does that of Raynolde's wife, Margaret. All three have conservative preambles and show the continued and total connection with parish church life and workings that we have come to expect. David left money for 'amendment of the highways' and also for the 'reparacion of the brigge over the Temys'. Raynolde, who seems to have had a large flock of sheep, left a copyhold within the parish of West Wycombe to his son William. Margaret followed the example of her brother-in-law by leaving 20d. for the repair of the highways leading to Marlow. She also left money for a yearly obit for her soul, and the soul of her husband. William Sherwood, the third member of the family named by Foxe, did not leave a will, but he is mentioned, as the brother and as a beneficiary of both David and Raynolde.[45]

Once again these wills show outward conformity and apparent commitment to the *status quo*. The inner workings of peoples' minds can not be known, but it is difficult to see traces of Lollardy in the words of these wills although they were mentioned by name by Foxe.

There are few references to the parish of Denham although adjacent towns are often alluded to by Foxe. It may however have been of some importance because the manor of Denham Durdants

---

[43] A.C. Chibnall, *Musters* pp. 274–278.
[44] BRO, D/A/We/6/55.
[45] Foxe, iv p. 229; PRO, PROB 11/21 f 19.

was held by the family of Durdant until 1511[46], and the leadership
of the sect in south-east Buckinghamshire seems to have been in
their hands. For our present purposes it is enough to point to the
presence of George Durdant in the Subsidy Roll, rated at £7;[47] in
the Muster Roll he is rated at £1 on land and £10 on goods.[48] Alice
Durdant is rated at £2 on land. Also named is John Clerke, rated
at £5. He may be the John Clerke of Denham said by Foxe to
have abjured in 1521, though the commonness of the name again
calls for caution and his will gives no indication as to his belief or
his connections. The Durdant family will be looked at in greater
detail below. Once again the details given in the Subsidy and
Muster Returns show the wide spread over the economic scale of
Lollardy. It is neither a sect made up of social outcasts and those
of insignificant importance, nor indeed is it an elitist group of
'professors'.

The final, brief, look at parish evidence is that of the centre of
Lollardy in the Buckinghamshire Chilterns: Amersham. Although
larger than Hughenden it was geographically much the same, lying
on the southern slopes of the Chiltern ridge, fostering a mixed
farming economy, but perhaps benefiting from its proximity to the
growing London market. Reference to the entry for Amersham in
Table I yet again shows Lollardy spreading through the social scale
and its strength in the parish is suggested when we note that
something like 20 per cent of those listed in the Subsidy Roll as
eligible for taxation are to some extent or another connected with
Lollardy.

No wonder Alice Saunders could threaten the wavering Thomas
Houre with a loss of employment within the town should he
deviate from his heretical views.[49] He did, and he lost his job with
her husband and his holy-water clerkship within the town – a
strange connection between holding heretical beliefs and being
involved organising local church activities.

Alice's husband Richard was far and away the richest resident
at Amersham, being rated at £200 in the Subsidy, with other

---

[46] R.H. Lathbury, *The History of Denham, Buckinghamshire* (Uxbridge 1904)
p. 189.
[47] Chibnall and Vere Woodman, *Subsidy* p. 17.
[48] Chibnall, *Musters* pp. 218–220.
[49] Foxe, iv p. 231.

members of the family also showing considerable wealth. They are only two of the persons found in Foxe who are discovered in the Subsidy Roll[50] and Muster Certificates.[51] And again the social spread is important and obvious. Robert Tracher with £1 13s. 4d. in goods presumably prayed with Katharine Bartlett with £8 in goods, and with John Penn, gentleman with £40, as well as with Richard Saunders with £200. Similar figures are found in the Muster Certificates.

The Saunders family of Amersham have left no less than six wills. Richard Saunders died in 1524. The preamble to his will was conservative. His religious bequests included 12d. to Lincoln and 3s.4d. to the light before the Rood at Amersham. Additionally he left £6 13s. 4d. for masses to be said 'provided alway that the said priest be able and sufficient to doo service in the quiyer'. He seems to have held the manor of Parmer at Hambleden, as well as several holdings at Amersham. He assumed he would be buried inside the parish church, before the statue of St. Thomas. The conventional nature of the will is supported by the fact that none of those named in the will, in whatever capacity, are among Foxe's Lollards, except his wife Alice.

It was Alice who seems to have been willing to threaten wayward Lollards in Amersham with loss of employment. Her will, made in 1543, had a radical preamble: she left her soul to 'the blessed creator, trusting by my faith that I have in my saviour to be saved and to be parte taker of the kingdom of hevyn' ... but she also left 13s.4d. for masses to be said for her soul. She continued the tendency seen in this area for giving to the poor, leaving 12d. to every couple getting married within a year of her death, and 'four poor men to get a black coat'. And there are connections with others named by Foxe; she left 20s. to Alice the daughter of Roger Benett; 20s. to Thomas Tailor; and one of her witnesses is Robert Andrewe – all Lollards. A third will was that of her grandson Thomas Saunders. Thomas left land at Amersham, Chesham, Hambleden and Ruislip, the last named parish being the home of several Lollards. More than that we cannot say; surnames mentioned are unhelpful, and the preamble, written in 1550, is vague, tending to the conservative.

---

50 Chibnall and Vere Woodman, *Subsidy*, pp. 12–13.
51 Chibnall, *Musters* pp. 230–235.

There is only one entry in Foxe relating to the family and it would be dangerous to assume too much regarding their status within the sect; yet their wealth, their landholding, must have counted for something. It is surely not too fanciful to see them as important cogs in the Lollard organisation in south Bucks. They were deeply involved with the Amersham group, though Thomas Harding's wife felt that Richard Saunders, who was evicted from his land after abjuring, was more interested in commerce than in his beliefs.

The wills of the Harding family, who seem to have lived more in Chesham than Amersham, show geographical and financial variance. The will of John Harding[52] gives, amongst his legatees, members of the Wells family, who were connected by marriage to the Bartletts. He gave a dozen loaves to the poor, and left his soul to God, 'my maker and redeemer'.

It is possible that the Littlepage family, several of whom are named by Foxe as being involved in the Amersham group, fled from Amersham during the great purge of 1521–2. In the Muster Roll we find Thomas Littlepage with goods worth over £13, and John Littlepage had goods of £3.[53] In the Subsidy Roll entry for the parish of Penn, Thomas has goods of £10 and John goods of £1.[54] The will of John Littlepage,[55] proved 7 April 1562, when he is stated to be of Penn, shows him leaving to his brother William lands lying within the parish of Amersham. He also left a sheep each to the three children of Thomas Harding, probably the grandchildren, or great-grandchildren, of the martyr of 1532 and spoke of Thomas Harding, one of his executors, as his cousin.

After this glance at four parishes in southern Buckinghamshire it is time to consider two of the families mentioned above in greater detail.

x x x x

The first of the families is that of the Durdants, based in the Colne valley, on the border with Middlesex and the diocese of London. In 1521 Richard Butler was among those who faced the bishop of

---

[52] PRO, PROB 11/21 f 28; 29, f.29, 33; BRO, D/A/We/9/3.
[53] Chibnall, *Musters* pp. 230–255.
[54] Chibnall and Vere Woodman, *Subsidy* pp. 24–5.
[55] BRO, D/A/We/14/171.

London's chancellor and vicar general, Thomas Bennet, on charges of heresy. The articles against him included the following:

> about the space of three years past, in Robert Durdant's house of Iver-court, near unto Staines, you erroneously and damnably read in a great book of heresy of the said Robert Durdant's, all that same night ... in the presence of the said Robert Durdant, John Butler, Robert Carder, Jenkin Butler, William King, and divers others

Robert Durdant's farm at Iver Court lies within the parish of Staines, in Middlesex. More recently it was called Yeoveney Farm. The manor of Yeoveney was held in 1522 by Robert Durdant, of the Abbey of Westminster. By 1525 Nicholas Durdant had become lessee,[56] and in 1538 he made his will.[57] He left his soul to 'almightie god trustinge emdonbetedly that by the merites of his onlie sonne Jhus criste to be one of his elect'. One of his supervisors was William Grinder and one of the witnesses was Henry Hobbes. Both were Lollard names.

We return to John Foxe, noting both the strategic position of the house and the possible support such a socially-advantaged family might give to poorer fellow-heretics.

There are three entries relating to reading groups in the house at Iver court. Thomas Holmes admitted to the bishop's court that a group had sat all night 'reading all the night in a book of scriptures'.[58] Robert Carver, of nearby Iver, spoke of 'old Durdant' reading from the scriptures 'sitting at dinner'.[59] Among those present were Davy Durdant of Ankerwick and Nicholas Durdant of Staines. Another entry mentions the wedding of Durdant's daughter, when the guests included people from Windsor, Amersham, and London. Meeting in a barn they all listened to readings 'which they liked well'.[60] Another of those attending was Isabel Harding, possibly the wife of Thomas, who would be martyred in 1532. There is yet a further entry relating to a house group at

---

[56] Westminster Abbey Muniments 16905–6, 30501; West. Reg. bks ii, fol 161b, iv, fol 85; WAM 16810; Foxe, iv p. 178.
[57] PRO, Prerogative Court Records, F.4. Spert.
[58] Foxe, iv p. 226.
[59] *Ibid.*
[60] *Ibid.* p. 228.

which Durdant cautioned those attending not to say anything to outsiders lest he be burnt.[61]

This information from Foxe suggests that Iver Court was more than a centre for a reading group. It was a gathering place for what would later be called an underground church or a conventicle. Foxe names twenty-five persons as attending at one time or another. There were probably many more. Also of note is the size of the meeting held after or during the wedding. It seems to have been quite a large affair and would have been difficult to keep secret from the authorities, unless of course Durdant was the local authority!

There is much more work to be done on this branch of the Durdant family. That part of the family living on the other side of the river Colne, at Denham, has been looked at. In the Subsidy Roll[62] George Durdant is listed at Denham, being assessed at £7; at adjacent Iver Nicholas Durdant is assessed at £13 6s. 8d. There are similar entries in the Certificates of Musters. At Wraysbury, about a mile and a half from Iver Court, Davy Durdant is assessed at 4s. in lands. He is said to be living outside the village. At Denham George Durdant has lands to the value of £1 and goods to the value of £10. Another entry relates to Nicholas Durdant at Iver where he has goods to the value of £13 6s. 8d. again.[63]

From the archdeaconry court records we find out that Walter Durdant was given probate for his wife's will, in 1492. He died in 1494,[64] and had been predeceased by two wives, Margaret and Agnes. A brass in the parish church at Denham celebrates the three of them, and their children: three sons and four daughters from the first marriage and nine sons and ten daughters from the second. Being buried within the parish church was itself a sign of social and economic importance; having a commemorative brass placed above the grave was even more significant.

It is probable that Walter died in debt. His son Thomas is known to have begun letting out lands as early as 1498.[65] The decline culminated in the extraordinary confiscation of the manor after

---

[61] *Ibid* p. 230.
[62] A.C. Chibnall and Vere Woodman, *Subsidy* p. 17.
[63] A.C. Chibnall, *Musters* p. 218.
[64] E.M. Elvey, *Archdeaconry Court* p. 112.
[65] R.H. Lathbury, *Denham* p. 189.

Thomas and his son were accused of murder.[66] They fled, leaving George Durdant in the parish. Entries in the court records show George serving as churchwarden and being called 'master'. Thomas Durdant had previously been called before the court of Star Chamber no less than three times. One case, listed as sacrilege, turned out to be a dispute over removal of limestone and materials from the churchyard.[67]

These two family groups, who have so far defied any attempts to unite them, but who were most probably related, were well-off. They held lands, they were the employers of labour, not labourers themselves. We have here a socially-involved, affluent group, and at the same time the apparent makings of a Lollard conventicle, dare we say the makings of a gathered church in south Buckinghamshire and south-west Middlesex? The second family, the Bartletts, was possibly to the fore in the large group of Lollards at Amersham. Foxe suggests that the Church authorities were at pains to secure their conviction; and the subsequent eviction of Robert Bartlett from his farm[68] shows an unusual harshness to those who had abjured.

There are eleven entries within the covers of Foxe during which the Bartlett family are mentioned. The first item goes back to the burning of William Tylsworth in 1511.[69] Among those doing penance were three members of the Bartlett family, Robert, Richard, and John. Foxe expands on the circumstances regarding one of those three. Robert Bartlett was among those who were forced to wear a patch on his sleeve for the space of seven years. But, says Foxe, 'for his profession's sake, (he) was put out of his farm and goods'.

Robert Bartlett of Amersham, and his brother Richard, were subsequently the subject of detection by several 'Amersham men' who spoke of the brothers as 'known men'.[70] The two resisted until their wives, Margaret and Isabel, gave evidence against them. It seems that the two brothers were shortly to detect others, for Foxe quickly turns to the subsequent detections by the brothers

---

[66] *Col LP*, 1 g. 804.
[67] PRO, STAC 1/17/155.
[68] Foxe, iv p. 124.
[69] *Ibid.* p. 123.
[70] *Ibid.* pp. 220–2.

of several heretics, including their sister Agnes, members of the Littlepage family, Elizabeth Dean of West Wycombe, John Scrivener, William Grinder, and several others. The abjurations continued with Agnes Wellis naming her two brothers Robert and Richard Bartlett. Agnes Wellis was in her turn forced to name others outside the family.[71] Isabel Bartlett apparently had contacts with those at Hughenden, for she named the Hobbes and Herne families.[72] Thomas Halfeaker detected Katharine Bartlett, 'the mother of Robert and Richard Bartlett', because, it was claimed, although of good health she seldom went to church, but feigned sickness.[73] William Littlepage later named Robert Bartlett.[74] The family were seemingly associated with several families connected with Lollardy.

The Subsidy Roll[75] confirms this spread, with Bartletts living at Amersham, Eton, Fawley, Upton, and Penn. At Eton Thomas Bartelett is valued at £5; at Fawley Thomas is valued at £1. At Upton and Amersham there are several entries. At Upton William is rated at £5, Raynold at £2, John at £2 and another John at £2. At Amersham Richard Bartlet is rated at £1 13s. 4d. in wages, William at £1 6s. 8d. in goods, and Katharine Bartelet, widow, is rated at £8.

The contrast between the land-owning, apparently affluent, Durdants, and the poorer Bartletts, some of whom were wage-earners, should be emphasised and is confirmed by the details extracted from the Muster Certificates. The Certificates[76] found Thomas Bartlett at Hanslope rated on goods at £1. At Eton Thomas is rated of £1. At Upton and Amersham there are similar groups to those found in the Subsidy Returns. Of particular importance for our purposes is the entry for Katharine Bartlett, widow, assessed on lands at 8s. and goods at £10.

The archdeaconry court records give interesting information as to the family's standing. It was varied. At Upton William Bartlet

[71] *Ibid.* p. 223.
[72] *Ibid.* p. 224.
[73] *Ibid.* p. 225.
[74] *Ibid.* p. 228.
[75] Chibnall and Vere Woodman, *Subsidy* pp. 12–13, 18, 19, 24–5, 26–7.
[76] Chibnall, *Musters* pp. 224, 230, 216.

was churchwarden in 1519,[77] whilst at Amersham John Bartlet and Robert Bonde were having their dispute discussed by the court.[78] The will of John Wellysbourne of Hughenden showed his daughter as having married one of the Bartlett family, and it may be that this connection gave Isabel Bartlett the knowledge to name some Hughenden Lollards in court.

Probate records at Aylesbury add to our knowledge. The will of Katharine Bartlett was made on 24 March 1525,[79] with probate being granted later that same year, on 16 May. The preamble is less than conservative: she left her soul to 'my maker and redeemer Jesus'. Her religious bequests, however, were very conservative: 5d to the mother church at Lincoln, a very high amount; 13s. 4d. for the repair of the church; and a charitable dole of 3s. 4d., to be distributed at a yearly obit. Her lands called Denys, held in fee, went to her son-in-law John Morwyn who had to pay her five children 20s. each. The children were William, Richard, Elizabeth Copland, Agnes Wells, and Mrs J. Morwyn. All were named by Foxe as Lollards. Her fairly large flock of sheep were distributed among her legatees.

The will of John Bartlett, proved in 1546,[80] had a similar preamble. Bequests included 6s. 8d. to be given to the poor. I am inclined to think he is the son of the Robert Bartlett who was evicted from the farm. His son is also called Robert, and his uncle Richard is a witness. Robert Bartlett the elder had a brother named Richard. His station in life, and the probability that he was the son of Robert, is confirmed by his having at least 150 sheep.

A third will, that of Margaret Bartlett, widow, of Woburn, which was proved on 9 November 1558,[81] shows a continued contact with Amersham. She leaves the residue of her goods to Richard Harding the elder, William Hornblowe, and Richard Harding, the son of Simon Harding of Amersham. Certain conclusions can be drawn from this short study of Lollards and Lollardy. Several previously accepted views on their social and economic status can be questioned, and some of the generalisations made by

[77] E.M. Elvey, *Archdeaconry Court* p. 295.
[78] *Ibid.* p. 88.
[79] BRO, D/A/We/2/52.
[80] BRO, D/A/Wf/1/268.
[81] BRO, D/A/We/12/150.

Margaret Bowker can be refined. Her dismissal of Lollards as 'mainly weavers and threshers of comparatively low social status' is wrong.[82] They were to be found at all levels in rural society. And evidence from wills would challenge the idea that attitudes to the poor and needy only changed in the 1550s.

John Fines' study of the social background of those at Coventry showed a group with considerable 'clout' within their society, economically and socially.[83] My brief look at Lollardy would tend to support that view. Although some were wage-labourers and others were of the 'middling sort', many were considerable land-holders and farmers, and one or two were manor-holders. Whilst accepting that throughout the history of heresy and nonconformity the largest group of those so labelled are unknown to us and probably to the authorities it would perhaps be wrong to dismiss them in the generally-scathing terms used by those who are, usually, seeking to denigrate, and dismiss as unimportant, a group they may well have feared. The families I am looking at were neither ostracised from, nor penalised by, the communities they lived in, and sometimes held local office. The student of heresy has much more to do, and indications are there is much more to find.

Corpus Christi College,
Cambridge

---

[82] Bowker, *Lincoln*, p. 58.
[83] J. Fines, 'Heresy Trials' pp. 162–3.

THE 'GODLY COMMUNITY' IN THE THEORY AND PRACTICE OF THE EUROPEAN REFORMATION

by EUAN CAMERON

IT IS now a truism to say that the European Reformation of the sixteenth century brought into being a religion of the word. It arose in literate and learned debate; it was fomented by the printing of written propaganda; it defined itself according to written formulae, including creeds, confessions, and catechisms. It is perhaps almost as generally accepted, and certainly as true, that the 'Word' as envisaged by the Reformers was a doctrine based on reasoning and logic, logically expressed, and meant to be understood in an intellectually coherent way. This trait in the aims of the Reformers emerged most obviously when they set about writing catechisms and pieces of pastoral instruction. In his *Formula Missae seu Communionis* of 1523, Luther required that

> Let [the pastor] not admit the applicants unless they can give a reason for their faith and can answer questions about what the Lord's Supper is, what its benefits are, and what they expect to derive from it.[1]

In the Epistle appended to some editions of his *Shorter Catechism* of 1529, he advised that 'when the simpler sort of people have learnt to repeat well the words of the Catechism, they should then be given an exposition of it, so that they may understand it as well'. Understanding was to be progressive; the pastor was to take his flock steadily through as much as they could take at a time, gradually enlarging the scope of the instruction.[2] In Calvin's *Catechism* of 1542 the intellectual emphasis was even more pronounced; after almost every response which simply repeated a text,

---

[1] *WA* 12, p. 215, as translated in *Luther's Works*, eds J. Pelikan and H.J. Lehmann (Philadelphia 1943–) 53 p. 32.
[2] Latin Epistle to Luther's *Shorter Catechism*, in Luther, *Opera* (Wittenberg 1554) 5 fol 647r.

there was a second answer in which the catechumen was expected to supply the reason, purpose, or ground of his previous reply.[3]

At the same time as imposing this formidable mental task on the laity, the Reformers retained many of the assumptions of the medieval Church regarding uniformity and universality. With the exceptions of Spiritualists, Millenarians, and Anabaptists, the founders of protestantism held that the Church must be a comprehensive society, embracing and supervising both the elect and the reprobate, the zealous and the sluggish.[4] The combination of the two aims of intellectualism and uniformity in sixteenth-century protestantism made the pastoral and didactic work of the Reformers especially difficult. Ministers in town and country parishes continually confronted the problem which reformed theologians only occasionally recognized: try as the pastor might to 'accommodate' his teaching to the level of his audience, there would still be those who could not profit from it, and those who refused to do so. Therefore the issue of doctrinal and moral instruction became bound up with the issue of Church discipline. If the Church had a duty to teach everyone, then it might also have a duty to see that everyone submitted himself to instruction and censure. Moreover, even supposing that the secular power allowed the churches to exercise such a discipline, it was likely to become divisive; congregations might thus be split between the obedient and the refractory, the zealous and the indifferent, or, in short, the 'Godly' and the 'ungodly'.

This essay aspires to shed light on a few aspects of the problem which the incompatible aims of the Reformation created for its leaders. At various interesting points in the history of the movement some of its leading theologians discussed the possibility that, within a universal disciplinary church, there might nevertheless arise an 'inner ring' of devout believers who exceeded the average Christian in evangelical enthusiasm and activity. Moreover, at a number of stages in the so-called 'second Reformation', the period when the protestant churches were being drawn into closer disciplinary control, there are signs that, *de facto*, some such inner

---

[3] *Joannis Calvini Opera quae supersunt omnia*, eds G. Baum, E. Cunitz, and E. Reuss (Braunschweig Berlin 1863–1900) (hereafter *CO*) 6, cols 1–134. See also his *Institution Puérile*, in *CO* 22 cols 101–114, for the same trait.

[4] See for instance W.D.J. Cargill Thompson, *The Political Thought of Martin Luther* (Brighton 1984) pp. 119–30.

rings – though of widely varying characters – did actually arise. An attempt will be made to define the social and religious features of these various manifestations.

It is important at the outset to distinguish the issue of the 'special congregation' or 'inner ring' from two other divisive phenomena in protestantism. Sixteenth-century reformers did not suppose that a visible community of the zealous would be equivalent to those who were elect in the sight of God; they were too aware of the presence in the Church of 'hypocrites' and of those temporarily showing the character of the elect to make any such assumptions.[5] Secondly, those who suggested the creation of such an 'inner ring' in an established church were not, at least in their own eyes, sectaries who believed that a 'gathered' voluntary church was preferable to a universal comprehensive one. Although the charge of sectarianism was often made against them, they repelled it stoutly and repeatedly.[6] Finally, this paper cannot hope or presume to do justice to events in England, which obviously occupied a very special place in Europe as far as this question is concerned.[7] However, a glance at conditions outside England may have useful lessons for those who wish to draw general conclusions.

Luther's doctrine of the Church is one of the most controversial and difficult of the doctrines of that many-faceted and occasionally changeable character, and a generalist is perhaps ill-advised to venture into it. However, it is surely undeniable that Luther helped to commit the magisterial Reformation to maintaining the medieval concepts of church unity and uniformity through his own preference for a territorial rather than a gathered Church. Even in his most 'congregationalist' early phases, for instance in the *To the Christian Nobility* of 1520, he responded to ecclesiastical abuses not by calling for separation, but by urgent pressing for a change of the whole institution, which his 'dear Germans' should bring about acting in concert.[8] While in later years – especially after

[5] Calvin, *Institutes* IV i 7, 8, 13.
[6] As for example by Johann Marbach, in W. Bellardi, *Die Geschichte der 'Christlichen Gemeinschaft' in Strassburg 1546/1550, der Versuch einer 'zweiten Reformation'* (Leipzig 1934) p. 193.
[7] See above all on this P. Collinson, *The Religion of Protestants: The Church in English Society 1559–1625* (Oxford 1982) pp. 189–283.
[8] WA 6, pp. 404 seq.

1525 – he identified these 'Germans' more and more closely with the existing princely and urban aristocracies, the principle of a comprehensive church seems to have been always the same.[9]

Since Luther undoubtedly did envisage a Reformation of the whole Church in any given region, it becomes all the more significant that in several instances he seemed to suggest that some practising Christians might be, so to speak, more equal than others. These remarks arose almost always at a particular point, when Luther was writing about the Eucharist and those who should participate in it. In his Maundy Thursday sermon for 1523, for instance, Luther placed great emphasis on the role of the Eucharist as an occasion where the committed and educated Christians could show their faces in public, in an act of public confession. No-one should be given the Eucharist unless he knew how to declare his faith.[10] Those who did not wish to be so tested and identified were to be excluded from the rite.[11] In the *Formula Missae* of the same year, Luther made clear the process by which this supervision was to work. Prospective communicants were to notify the pastor of their intent, and before communicating were expected to be able to show their understanding of the Lord's Supper and to give a good spiritual reason for wishing to receive it. This examination was to take place once a year, except for the most obviously pious and educated for whom such a test was patently unnecessary. Life and morals of the communicants were also to come under scrutiny, and those who failed on either count were to be excluded. The communicants were to stand apart from the rest of the congregation during Mass, probably in the chancel.[12]

It has been pointed out that Luther did not propose, as the later Pietists did, separating off the communicants altogether and providing special services for them.[13] In fact, the separation of the visible group of communicants during the service and in full view of the rest of the congregation would have provided a more striking visible division of the flock than any private service could have

---

[9] Cargill Thompson, *Political Thought of Martin Luther* pp. 128–54.
[10] *WA* 12 p. 481.
[11] *WA* 12 pp. 485, 491.
[12] *WA* 12 pp. 215–16.
[13] H. Bornkamm, *Luther in mid-career 1521–1530*, trans E.T. Bachmann (London 1983) p. 120.

done. Moreover, three years after writing these passages, Luther was thinking further along the same lines. In the introduction to the *German Mass* of 1526, after proposals for a conservative German Mass and a retained Latin form of service, Luther sketched out a simplified, evangelical ritual for cliques of earnest believers. Such believers were to sign a register of names and appoint a place to meet in a private house, where they would pray, read, baptise, receive the sacraments, and perform other religious works. In this context a Christian discipline could be instituted, and ritual could be simplified to the bare minimum. Catechising could be carried out to the full. However, Luther declined to do more than put this plan forward as a rather remote possibility. There seemed, he felt, no pressing need for its realization, and suitable members of such a society were not to hand. He would only institute it if specifically asked, and would not initiate it for himself. As he added, 'we Germans are a rough, rude, and reckless people, with whom it is hard to do anything except in cases of dire need.'[14]

These passages are well-known to Luther scholars, and the debates around them have already been fought. It is generally agreed that Luther was not urging that a 'true Church' of sectaries be set up.[15] On the other hand, it does seem acceptable to argue that Luther here contemplated in theory ideas which were later worked out in practice in Pietism, and that he felt that an 'ecclesiola in ecclesia' *might* be possible and even desirable.[16] This belief, it should be noted, he expressed at a time when he expected that some exclusiveness in admitting communicants to the Eucharist would be practised in any case. A special spiritual society was not simply a remedy for the absence of uniform discipline (as we shall see it may have been for Martin Bucer) but a way in which discipline might be brought to perfection.

Two concepts touched on here by Luther were to find echoes elsewhere in sixteenth-century protestantism. The notion of a reformed community which would consist of believers known by name to the pastor, imposing discipline on itself, was developed in detail

---

[14] *WA* 19 p. 75.
[15] M. Doerne, 'Gottes Volk und Gottes Wort', *Luther-Jahrbuch* 14 (1932) pp. 89 *seq.*
[16] Cargill Thompson, *Political Thought of Martin Luther* pp. 129–30; Bornkamm, *Luther in mid-career* pp. 478–9.

by François Lambert of Avignon in his proposed constitution for the reformed churches of Hesse, devised for the Synod of Homberg late in 1526. Luther in fact reacted with some hostility to this development of his own ideas, for the same reasons as those which restrained him from putting the project of his *German Mass* into practice.[17] Secondly, in the *Ecclesiastical Discipline* devised for the French Protestant Churches in 1559 tests of doctrine and morality were likewise envisaged for those who wished to participate in the Eucharist (although the reformed churches were to apply this principle very unevenly in practice).[18]

However, it is Martin Bucer who must bear the chief responsibility for developing this strand in Reformation thought to its utmost. In the first place, on several occasions he emphasised the ideal of frequent meeting – more frequent than most whole congregations could be expected to manage – as a sign of truly Christian fellowship. Christians, he observed in his lectures on *Ephesians* of 1550-1, since they had a stronger bond of mutual love than those bound by worldly ties, ought to meet very often to 'teach, exhort, admonish, and inspire' one another; those who abstained from such gatherings were to be accounted schismatics.[19] Bucer had been even more specific in his *Brief Summary* of 1548, where he expressed the view that 'daily gatherings' had been ordained for the more leisured to study the Bible, and to pray and worship.[20]

All Bucer's contributions to the problem, apart from these two very general and rather late comments, were made under the shadow of one particular difficulty: the secular power in Strasbourg consistently refused to allow the reformed clergy to exercise the kind of pastoral discipline which the pastors felt the people required. From about 1535 Bucer renounced in theory the principle

---

[17] G. Anrich, 'Ein Bedacht Bucers über die Einrichtung von "Christlichen Gemeinschaften"' in *Festschrift für Hans von Schubert*, ed O. Scheel (Leipzig 1929) p. 67 and refs; E.G. Léonard, *A History of Protestantism* (London 1965) I pp. 113–15.

[18] J. Garrisson-Estèbe, *Protestants du midi 1559–1598* (Toulouse 1980) p. 142 and refs; compare also *The First Book of Discipline* ed J.K. Cameron (Edinburgh 1972) pp. 165–73 and refs.

[19] M. Bucer, *Praelectiones Doctiss. in Epistolam D.P. ad Ephesios* (Basel 1562) p. 41, trans in D.F. Wright, *Common Places of Martin Bucer* (Abingdon 1972) p. 211.

[20] M. Bucer, *Martin Bucers Deutsche Schriften* ed R. Stupperich (Gütersloh 1981) 17 (hereafter *MBDS* 17), p. 138; trans by Wright, *Common Places* p. 90.

of relying on the support and co-operation of the lay magistrate to enforce discipline.[21] In his *Enarrationes* on the Gospels of 1536 he remarked that the reformed assemblies were then impure, because few were dedicated, and the power of excommunication could not be used; unless then by some special grace the majority of the population and the magistracy could be converted, then those who 'had received Christ more fully' would have to practise fraternal admonition and censure amongst their families, servants, and friends, even to the extent of refusing the Eucharist, 'until the Lord shall restore to us a just polity and true censure in the Church'.[22]

Although Bucer had apparently resigned himself to the unwillingness or inability of secular magistrates to act as disciplinarians of the Church in their own right, he seems in the late 1530s still to have hoped for a universal and yet disciplined church structure. This hope was expressed in his treatise *Von der wahren Seelsorge* of 1538, where he urged that the secular and the spiritual should be rigidly separated in the matter of administering religious and moral discipline, and that the threefold order of pastors, elders, and deacons should be imposed as by divine right.[23] In his ordinances for Hesse promulgated by the Synod of Ziegenhain in 1539 this structure was embodied in a practical piece of legislation.[24] However, the Strasbourg city council gave little or no ground in response to the *wahren Seelsorge* treatise, and the adoption of the Hesse ordinances only made the lack of co-operation from his own city more exasperating.

In response perhaps to these frustrations, in the mid-1540s Bucer brought the theoretical conception of the 'inner ring' as the best way to maintain a voluntary spiritual discipline to its climax. Early

[21] On Strasbourg and Bucer up to this point see F. Wendel, *L'Eglise de Strasbourg, sa constitution et son organisation 1523–1535* (Paris 1942).

[22] M. Bucer, *In Sacra Quatuor Evangelia, Enarrationes perpetuae,* (Geneva 1553) fol 145v; and as cited by Bellardi, *Geschichte der 'Christlichen Gemeinschaft'* p. 26.

[23] Bellardi, *Geschichte der 'Christlichen Gemeinschaft'* p. 20; J. Courvoisier, *La Notion d'Eglise chez Bucer* (Paris 1933) p. 34; Léonard, *Protestantism* I pp. 192–3; R. Bornert, *La Réforme protestante du culte à Strasbourg au xvie siècle (1523–1598)* (Leiden 1981) p. 414.

[24] Bellardi, *Geschichte der 'Christlichen Gemeinschaft'* p. 21; Courvoisier, *Notion d'Eglise chez Bucer* p. 37; Léonard, *Protestantism* I p. 195; see also G.W. Diehl, *Martin Butzers Bedeutung für das kirchliche Leben in Hessen,* (Halle 1904).

in January 1546 Bucer submitted to the council his treatise *Von der Kirchen Mengel und Fähl und wie dieselben zu verbessern*, which set out openly principles and projects for ecclesiastical discipline which Bucer had apparently been advocating discreetly, not to say secretly, for several years.[25] In each parish pastors were to preach on the faults in the Church. They were then to inquire from house to house to find out those who wished to join a 'truly Christian congregation'. The volunteers were to meet and to elect two or three of their number as elders, who would collude with the pastor and possibly also with the state-appointed ecclesiastical supervisors or *Kirchenpfleger* in maintaining discipline and binding members to abide by it. After an initial trial period members of the community were to be examined on the confession of faith and the Catechism. The community would thereafter continue in study and mutual edification, and a register was to be kept of its members. The intention was that the greater parish church would continue in being and function as before, with the exception that parishioners who asked for the Eucharist but refused to take part in these special communities (or *Gemeinschaften*) were to be refused it.[26]

To stay for the moment with the theory rather than the practice of this movement, Bucer made some of his most interesting remarks on the subject in the treatise entitled *Mehrung göttlicher Gnaden* ... , which he wrote defending the special communities in the face of an acrimonious row with the city council in November 1547.[27] Bucer was particularly sensitive to the charge that his project was producing schisms and rifts in the Church comparable to those caused by the sectaries. He had a high estimate of the importance of mutual edification, and was outraged by the suggestion that it could be schismatic for a few zealous Christians to meet together for religious exercises, but not schismatic for the majority to leave off attending church to carouse, go for walks, or to play

---

[25] Full text in *MBDS* 17 pp. 156–95; partial edition in Anrich, 'Ein Bedacht Bucers'; Bellardi, *Geschichte der 'Christlichen Gemeinschaft'* pp. 22 *seq*; Courvoisier, *Notion d'Eglise chez Bucer* pp. 34 *seq*; Bornert, *Réforme protestante du culte* pp. 415–17; see also M.U. Chrisman, *Strasbourg and the Reform* (New Haven 1967) pp. 229–30.

[26] *MBDS* 17 pp. 184–8; Anrich, 'Ein Bedacht Bucers' pp. 53–6; Bellardi, *Geschichte der 'Christlichen Gemeinschaft'* pp. 24–6.

[27] Full text in *MBDS* 17 pp. 317–40.

at sports in service-time.[28] The resonances for later puritanism are obvious. In answer to the objection, 'why do other evangelical churches not have such communities?', Bucer claimed, perhaps spuriously, that in fact *all* truly evangelical churches had such a discipline; he cited the fact that under the Lutheran dispensation strict moral and doctrinal checks were made on those who wished to receive the Eucharist.[29] Finally, replying to the criticism (particularly forceful on that occasion) that the Council had provided all that was necessary for Church discipline in the shape of the *Kirchenpfleger*. Bucer pointed out that many pious Christians had little need of secular social control, but very much wanted spiritual guidance and support.[30] This last point showed, incidentally, how far Bucer had gone from his position in the early 1530s, when he hoped to convert the *Kirchenpfleger* into elders; here they were clearly regarded as a secular institution of very limited spiritual usefulness.[31]

Before considering the practical consequences of Bucer's ideas for a 'truly' Christian fellowship, it is necessary to cast a glance at the form which the Bucerian conception of discipline and community assumed in the thought of Calvin. Calvin, of course, came under Bucer's influence for the first time when the latter prevailed upon him to assume a pastoral charge over the French congregation at Strasbourg following his expulsion from Geneva in 1538.[32] It is to Bucer, moreover, that Calvin is usually assumed to have owed his preoccupation with order and discipline in the Church. However, it is much more doubtful whether Calvin was in any way influenced by Bucer's ideas for the 'special community'. The main element of his thought on Church polity and discipline lay in the direction of an autonomous church disciplinary structure, which could subsist independently of the state, or even where the state was actively hostile. This stage, of course, was precisely that which Bucer's thought had reached by the time of the *wahren*

---

[28] *MBDS* 17 pp. 327–8; Bellardi, *Geschichte der 'Christlichen Gemeinschaft'* pp. 139–40.
[29] *MBDS* 17 pp. 332–4, and n 137 for comparisons with the work of Brenz and Osiander; Bellardi, *Geschichte der 'Christlichen Gemeinschaft'* pp. 144 *seq.*
[30] *MBDS* 17 pp. 335–6; Bellardi, *Geschichte der 'Christlichen Gemeinschaft'* pp. 148 *seq.*
[31] Compare Courvoisier, *Notion d'Eglise chez Bucer* pp. 25–32.
[32] F. Wendel, *Calvin* trans P. Mairet (London 1963) pp. 57–9.

Seelsorge treatise, produced in the year of Calvin's arrival in Strasbourg.[33] Calvin does seem to have agreed with Luther and Bucer that true Christians would be a minority against an indifferent or hostile multitude.[34] However, since the elect were known only to God, Calvin seems not to have favoured a discipline which would be too strict; it was not to be applied with excessive severity, such as would divide the Church; its purpose was chiefly to be as a corrective which should recall the sinner to his senses.[35]

On the other hand, if Calvin in the *Institutes* wrote as though all the members of a congregation should be treated equally, some of the consequences of his thought might have led in a different direction. He wrote that to participate in the Eucharist a communicant should examine himself and beware of receiving the rite unworthily; although he was anxious that those aspiring to take Communion should not try to attain any sort of spiritual perfection.[36] Moreover, during his Strasbourg period Calvin seems to have followed the pastoral practice of the Strasbourg ministers in admitting to Communion only those who had previously presented themselves to the pastor for examination; and the churches under Calvin's influence undoubtedly seem to have attempted to exclude the obviously and publicly sinful and scandalous from the community of Christians.[37]

Evidently these qualifications to the universality of the reformed congregation in Calvin's thought do not add up to anything like an equivalent to what was going on during Bucer's last years in Strasbourg. Those excluded from Communion on moral grounds should have been only a minority of notorious sinners; as many as possible were expected to fulfil the minimum catechetical requirements. Nevertheless, if we combine these intentions with Calvin's expressed preference for frequent Communion,[38] which was to prove very unpopular in ordinary parishes,[39] we have here the

[33] See above, n 23.
[34] Calvin, *Institutes* III xxiv 8; on this see also H. Höpfl, *The Christian Polity of John Calvin* (Cambridge 1982).
[35] Calvin, *Institutes* IV xii 1–13.
[36] Calvin, *Institutes* IV xxvii 40–2.
[37] Wendel, *Calvin* pp. 60–1; below, nn 67–8.
[38] Calvin, *Institutes* IV xxvii 44–6.
[39] B. Vogler, *Vie religieuse en pays rhénan dans la seconde moitié du xvie siècle* (Lille 1974) pp. 713–17.

makings of a scheme under which *in effect* those who subscribed to all the approved teaching and examination for themselves and their families, never fell from the approved moral standard, received Communion and attended worship as often as it was offered, would become a distinct, and even a visible, minority.

Before leaving the theory of the 'inner ring' to consider practice, it may be useful to ponder just why this theme should arise in the Reformers' thought at all. It can, no doubt, be explained simply as a result of a peculiarly intense preoccupation on the part of certain Reformers with discipline and excommunication for its own sake, and can be treated solely as an aspect of the history of moral censure in the protestant tradition. However, it is doubtful whether such a simple explanation does justice to the ideas of either Luther or Bucer. In their different ways both reformers envisaged a close-knit society possibly performing all the characteristically Christian religious exercises – preaching, teaching, catechising, brotherly admonition, ministry of the sacraments, as well as purifying worship and maintaining discipline – within the confines of the zealous brotherhood. Discipline and exclusiveness were not, therefore, ends in themselves, but necessary consequences of the Reformers' profound pessimism about the practicality of realizing their pastoral aims for the congregations of the churches as a whole.[40] This pessimism was quite general and deep-rooted. In 1529 Luther framed his *Catechisms* in the confident certainty that most of the laity were ignorant of and indifferent to religious matters, and that only the young would prove pliable.[41] Twenty-four years later in post-Interim Strasbourg, Johann Marbach, beginning a series of visitations in the rural parishes under the city's jurisdiction, expected widespread shortcomings to emerge; he wrote of the 'shocking scorn and little regard for the Ministry of the Church' shown by the mass of the people.[42] He was not even allowed to conduct visitations in the city itself; its people proved, it seems,

[40] On this see G. Strauss, *Luther's House of Learning* (Baltimore and London 1978) p. 238.
[41] Strauss, *Luther's House of Learning* pp. 160–1; for other similar remarks by Luther see S.C. Karant-Nunn, 'Luther's Pastors: The Reformation in the Ernestine Countryside', *Transactions of the American Philosophical Society* NS 69 pt 8 (1979) pp. 53–4.
[42] J.M. Kittelson, 'Successes and Failures in the German Reformation: the report from Strasbourg', *ARG* 73 (1982) p. 159.

even more recalcitrant in the face of disciplinary efforts than those of the countryside.[43] This attitude from the protestant laity towards the expectations of the pastors produced the so-called 'literature of complaint', where Jeremiads from the protestant clergy about the difficulties of making all or even any of their flock pious and holy became a topos and a cliché.[44] Against this background, the creation of a *de facto* 'special congregation' of rational, dedicated, lay followers of the pastor from amidst the mass of the indifferent would become, not the result of the aberrant exasperation of one frustrated reformer, but a virtually inevitable consequence of the inherent aims of the entire Reformation itself. It is to these practical manifestations of the phenomenon that I now wish to turn.

As with the theory, so with the practice of the 'special congregation', it is the case of Strasbourg which must command the most attention. To set the history of the Christian communities there in context one must cast a glance back over the development of ecclesiastical discipline from the beginnings of the official Reformation in the city. From the first preaching of reformed doctrines there to about 1531 the magistracy took only a fitful interest in regulating religious matters, tending like so many cities at that stage to abdicate responsibility to the various religious groups so long as peace and order were maintained. For some eighteen months from the official abolition of the Mass in February 1529 the pastorate alone were responsible for running the affairs of the Reformed Church. The city magistrates were pressed to issue their first disciplinary orders in May 1531, and in October of the same year created the office of *Kirchenpfleger* or *Kirchspielpfleger*, a class of magistrate of which each parish was to have three, one a patrician, one a member of the council of three hundred, and one a parishioner. These officers, although produced as the result of pressure from the clergy, seem in fact to have been meant more to keep the clergy under lay control, than to subject the laity to the discipline of the pastorate.

In 1534 full Ecclesiastical Ordinances were published for Strasbourg, which laid down procedures for election of pastors, regulation of the sacraments, the instruction of children, the keeping

---

[43] Kittelson, 'Successes and Failures' p. 167; compare Strauss, *Luther's House of Learning* pp. 166–7.
[44] Collinson, *Religion of Protestants* pp. 199 *seq.*

of Sundays, the order for marriages, and the visitations of rural parishes.[45] There has been some dispute over the significance of this move. It has been interpreted as an attempt by Bucer to turn the *Kirchenpfleger*, whose supervision was declared essential to nearly all of the above functions, into church elders, into a spiritual estate. Whether or not this was the case, and whatever the extent of Bucer's influence on the drafting of the Ordinances, it seems agreed that the effect was still further to strengthen the magistracy's hold over church government at the expense of the clergy. It also seems clear that the *Kirchenpfleger* showed little or no interest in acting as the censors of Christian learning and morality which Bucer wished them to be.[46]

The treatises *Von der wahren Seelsorge* and *Von der Kirchen Mengel* must therefore be understood against this background of tension between the clergy and the magistracy over social control. The patricians were clearly concerned about the socially divisive possibilities of strict religious discipline; Münster was near enough to make them acutely sensitive to the risks of sectarianism in a city still notorious for Anabaptism. After promulgating the *Kirchen Mengel* treatise early in 1546 Bucer seems to have waited almost a year before doing anything practical.[47] By February 1547 the city council was receiving reports that two of Bucer's associates among the clergy, Conrad Schnell and Paul Fagius, were inquiring around after those who wished to form a religious community.[48] Schnell's group was based on the parish of St. Thomas's, and Fagius's on New St. Peter's, while other communities were later started by Johann Marbach at St. Nicholas's and by Johann Lenglin at St. Wilhelm's.[49] In April the city council called the pastors before it to answer the charge that their ecclesiastical innovations were causing disorder. The ministers replied with a petition to the council on discipline. Matters came to a head in November 1547 when Fagius's community persisted in meeting on two occasions in defiance of a ban from the council on congregational meetings outside normal

---

[45] Courvoisier, *Notion d'Eglise chez Bucer* pp. 22–32; Bellardi, *Geschichte der 'Christlichen Gemeinschaft'* pp. 16–20.
[46] See Léonard, *Protestantism* I pp. 187–8 and references.
[47] Bellardi, *Geschichte der 'Christlichen Gemeinschaft'* pp. 27 seq.
[48] *Ibid.* p. 30.
[49] *MBDS* 17 p. 256.

services.[50] The row caused a split amongst the city clergy, and the council temporarily cowed Bucer's party by banning any who attended meetings of the communities from attendance at regular church worship. In 1548 the disturbances caused by the imposition of the Interim after the defeat of the Schmalkaldic League at Mühlberg further complicated Strasbourg church politics; as is well-known, it was finally decided that Bucer and Fagius should leave the city, which they did on 6 April 1549. The communities, however, persisted, at least in the case of Fabri at New St. Peter's and Lenglin at St. Wilhelm's. They finally dissolved themselves some time in 1550, in the face of the limitations imposed during the post-Interim phase of the Reformation and further dissension amongst the remaining pastors.[51] No further attempt was made to introduce serious pastoral discipline into Strasbourg until Marbach's attempt in 1572 via the *Kirchenkonvent* or assembly of town ministers.[52]

Thanks to the survival of Lenglin's register of his parochial community at St. Wilhelm's for 1549, we may make some observations about the character of the communities as they functioned during their short life. The participants were very few in number and fairly consistent in their attendance. In ordinary meetings numbers varied between five and ten, all adult males, and presumably most of them heads of households. Their occupations are a matter of conjecture, since many apparently occupational names may have been additional surnames, but they appear to have been small businessmen and artisans: there are references to booksellers, butchers, fish-sellers, and shoemakers. Other than these local laymen only the pastor seems to have been present; Bucer had originally hoped that the *Kirchenpfleger* would attend occasionally, but the council's distrust of the experiment explains their absence.[53]

---

[50] The chronology of this episode is somewhat complicated. See Bellardi, *Geschichte der 'Christlichen Gemeinschaft'* pp. 31–61, and Bellardi's introductions to texts in *MBDS* 17 pp. 207–11, 245–8, 256–60, 291–4, 311–13, 317–19.

[51] Bellardi, *Geschichte der 'Christlichen Gemeinschaft'* pp. 61–79; Léonard, *Protestantism* I p. 198; Chrisman, *Strasbourg and the Reform* pp. 230–2; Bornert, *Réforme protestante du culte* pp. 415–17.

[52] Bornert, *Réforme protestante du culte* p. 417.

[53] For an analysis of the names in the register see Bellardi, *Geschichte der 'Christlichen Gemeinschaft* pp. 199 *seq.*

Normal meetings of the community were meant to take place weekly, although this pattern was not strictly adhered to. Its functions seem to have conformed fairly closely to the pattern envisaged by Bucer. At a meeting on 22 December 1549, for instance, there was an election to a lay office of the community; an agreement on the form to be observed in catechising young and old alike; an exhortation to the laity to meet the pastor more often than on Sundays only, and to pass on news of any moral faults in the parish needing correction; and directions about seeking absolution before receiving communion. Most interesting of all, the traffic in exhortations was not one-way: the laity also petitioned the pastor about convenient times for meeting, asked for more diligent attendance at these meetings by pastors and deacons, and for greater general zeal and diligence amongst ministers, 'so that they should keep their promises'.[54]

Moreover, from the register it is evident that the schism between the party which inaugurated the special communities, that of Bucer, Fagius, Marbach, Lenglin, and Schnell, and those opposed to them, made up of Hedio, Zell, Nigri, and Steinlin, was still a very live and debated issue two years after it opened up in November 1547. A general meeting of the pastors and laity of all the parish communities on 26 November 1549 was the occasion of something like a set-piece debate between the two parties, where their respective principles were set out. Lenglin himself pointed out that his party neither wished to separate themselves from the Church, nor did they regard themselves as better than other men. The purpose of the gatherings was that pastors and people should work together 'to be made better ourselves, to advance in piety as useful members of the rest of the Church'. They were to guard against idolatry, to be conspicuous in religious devotion, to educate their families, and to involve their neighbours in the work as far as possible.[55] Marbach reinforced the point by demonstrating that the communities neither despised the rest of the Church like Anabaptists or Schwenckfeldians, nor abused it like the sectaries at Münster. The community existed to provide an anticipatory version of true discipline, and a

---

[54] *Ibid.* pp. 196–7.
[55] *Ibid.* pp. 192–3.

source of consolation, companionship, and reconciliation.[56] Ludwig Rabus, a somewhat hesitant representative of the opposing faction, acknowledged the need for fraternal correction, and (like nearly everyone in the debate) cited the text of Matthew 18:15–20. However, he felt that such correction was best carried out in the context of the whole parish, and not of a segment of it. He expressed his disapproval of private meetings, and felt that mutual fellowship could adequately be sustained by meetings at regular church services.[57]

One interesting lesson may be drawn from these exchanges. The debate for or against the communities at Strasbourg was not a simple conflict of lay versus ecclesiastical power. No doubt one of the reasons for the hostility of the city council to Bucer's plans for discipline was indeed suspicion of the lengths to which clerical power might aspire in domineering over consciences – a suspicion which one can parallel in Queen Elizabeth or in the Arminian regents of seventeenth-century Holland. However, the most important rift, historically speaking, was between the two factions of the pastors themselves, and was not over ends, but over means. All might acknowledge the need for some protection of doctrine and morality, but they differed in their opinions as to whether or not the parish was a sufficiently manageable structure for the purpose. Moreover, lay desire to supervise the clergy was not confined to members of the patriciate. When lay members of the parish communities pressed for greater diligence from their pastors, they were showing exactly that same desire to get their money's worth from the ministry which may in many cases have prompted their betters to sanction the Reformation in the first place. The conflicting spiritual priorities of laymen and clergymen, and the ways they sought to achieve their aims, cut across the debate over the communities; that debate simply affords an excellent opportunity to observe these perennial conflicts at work.

Although the Strasbourg example is the best-publicised and best-documented instance of a special, exclusive congregation of zealots in sixteenth-century European protestantism outside the sects, there are other instances where a little light is shed on the way in

[56] Ibid. pp. 193–4.
[57] Ibid. p. 195.

which a parish ministry could in practice become exclusive and confined. In the Rhineland in the second half of the sixteenth century exclusivity took a variety of forms. Although the clergy saw their disciplinary power progressively eroded over the region's Lutheran period, ministers could abuse what power they still had. One pastor refused to preach at a poor man's funeral, claiming that his ministry did not include the poor; others became notorious for refusing the rites of the Church to those who had not taken Communion, or giving their blessing very grudgingly.[58] In fairness, these men were often reacting to the hostility and even malice of their parishioners, whom pastors who had been deprived alike of money and dignity were apt to describe as merciless, capricious, grasping, ignorant tyrants.[59] Equally, those who gave the ministrations of the Church indiscriminately were liable to find themselves in trouble with their visitatorial superiors.[60]

However, it was much more common for exclusiveness in church attendance to be the result, not of the clergy restricting those to whom they ministered, but of the mass of the laity abstaining by choice. Such abstention tended to divide church worship into two types: that which the parish as a whole attended, and that in which only a minority participated. The former type comprised the weekly Sunday morning service and sermon, which most people attended, even if they might arrive late, read or sleep as it progressed, or turn up incapably drunk.[61] It might also include the most popular parish communions of the year, at Easter or Christmas.[62] The latter type included the Sunday afternoon service and catechism, weekly services of any kind (at least in most areas), and Holy Communion outside of the great feasts of the old liturgical year.[63] Some services, like vespers, disappeared completely.[64]

The attendance at unpopular services would tend to create a *de facto* inner ring, and attempts have been made to establish its

---

[58] B. Vogler, *Le Clergé protestant rhénan au siècle de la Réforme (1555–1619)* (Paris 1976) pp. 341–2.
[59] *Ibid.* pp. 339–40.
[60] *Ibid.* p. 342.
[61] Vogler, *Vie religieuse* pp. 650–7.
[62] *Ibid.* pp. 715, 733.
[63] *Ibid.* pp. 682 *seq*, 687 *seq*, 731 *seq*.
[64] *Ibid.* pp. 690 *seq*.

membership. Weekday services were mostly attended by women; the same applied to the less popular Eucharists. A minority comprising married women, widows, and the families of some local 'notables' (though by no means all the rural aristocrats) frequented worship more than the mass of the people. Catechism classes frequently contained only children, who once they reached late adolescence tended to be more irregular church-goers than their elders.[65] This voluntary abstention, it should be noted, left the Church's effective censure, which only struck notorious and scandalous sinners, of almost no significance for the issue in hand.[66] One sees here, then, an accidental 'inner ring' of a kind no doubt familiar to ministers at any period: the pious, but usually passive, attendance at unpopular services, to which the pastor's wife might – or might not – give a lead and an example.

Although in the Rhineland the effective disciplinary power of the Church to exclude from the sacraments seems to have been used fairly sparingly, there are reasons to suppose that it may have been more rigorously applied in Calvinist France. Certainly the occasions where pastors provoked a scandal by administering the sacraments without any supervision or restriction of the recipients seem to have been more numerous and more acrimonious in their outcome; this suggests that the norm for a Calvinist pastor was to pre-select his communicants fairly carefully.[67] A few ministers distinguished themselves by an excessive moral severity which one suspects may have alienated almost all, rather than just an indifferent majority, of their parishioners.[68] The violent controversy which erupted after Morelli published his *Traité de la discipline et police chrestienne* in 1562 provides an interesting sidelight. Morelli had proposed that a body of the faithful, consisting of all adult males who were not public sinners, should be invested with the supreme authority over the discipline of the Church. His work, which was so furiously condemned by the French reformed assemblies, rather recalls the lay statism which the Strasbourg oligarchy maintained without difficulty; it also suggests that the

[65] *Ibid.* pp. 685, 688 , 718 *seq*, 732, 743.
[66] *Ibid.* p. 712.
[67] Garrisson-Estèbe, *Protestants du midi* p. 142.
[68] *Ibid.* pp. 148–50.

oligarchy of ministers and consistories had in fact become too obviously exclusive for many laymen to tolerate.[69]

The Rhineland 'inner rings' appear to have been passive in character, of social origins which excluded either extreme, and in general the natural and predictable outcome of a Reformation imposed from above. Different traits appear in two regions of the Alps which I shall now briefly consider. In the Valtelline, a province administered by the Grisons republic from 1512, a religious settlement was arrived at by the 1550s which provided for catholics and protestants to co-exist and not to molest each other.[70] In such a situation one might expect that the 'inner ring' would simply become co-extensive with the protestant population, since protestantism was in any case voluntary; however, there are signs that the communities were far from equal. In the first place, thanks to the Valtelline's position on the natural way of escape for protestants leaving Italy via Milan, a linguistic and cultural ghetto of Italians formed around the parish of Morbegno, with its own pastor.[71] This exclusivism reflected a long-standing tension in the area between the refugee Italians, of dubious orthodoxy and fiery temperaments, and the respectable Zwinglian German-speaking pastors of the indigenous Grisons population.[72] Secondly, to judge by visitation reports, protestantism in the Valtelline seems to have appealed to two social groups: first, a small scattered body of peasants, referred to by the catholics as 'rustic heretics',[73] and besides these an interrelated and intermarried group of local aristocrats from the distinguished families of the region, with names such as Paravicini, Malacrida, Capelli, and Cattanei.[74] It was the Paravicini family which provided the town of Caspano with its first protestant church.[75] Moreover, only the connections between this social group

---

[69] *Ibid.* p. 143.

[70] T. McCrie, *History of the Progress and Suppression of the Reformation in Italy* (Edinburgh 1833) pp. 358–9, 361–8, 393–4; P.D. Rosius a Porta, *Historia Reformationis Ecclesiarum Raeticarum* (Chur 1771–7) I pt 2 pp. 274–6.

[71] F. Ninguarda, *Atti della visita pastorale diocesana.* 2 vols, (Como Società Storica Comense 1892–4) I pp. 268–70.

[72] Rosius a Porta, *Historia Reformationis* I pt 2 pp. 35–7; *Bullingers Korrespondenz mit den Graubündern* ed T. Schiess, 3 vols (Basel 1904–6) I pp. 238, 237, 286; II pp. 542, 544, 552.

[73] Ninguarda, *Atti* I pp. 285–6, 300, 306, 311, 334.

[74] *Ibid.* I pp. 281 *seq*, 330 *seq*, 340 *seq*.

[75] McCrie, *Reformation in Italy* p. 387.

and the family of von Salis, which held the governorship of the region, made it possible for protestant ministers there to receive, or hope to receive, a decent stipend.[76]

In general, where protestantism was voluntary, and where the support of the local rural magistracy was needed to keep it in being, there tended of necessity to be a clique of local aristocrats around the pastor. Pierpaolo Vergerio, the tempestuous and difficult bishop of Capodistria turned minister of the tiny Alpine village of Vicosoprano, admitted in 1551 that the survival of all his work depended upon the re-election of magistrates favourable to the reformed cause.[77] Since this was so essential, it is not surprising that at least one Alpine pastor was tempted to try to force things his way. The protestant church established in the so-called 'Waldensian valleys' of the Duchy of Savoy from 1555 onwards must seem one of the most unlikely regions of all for an 'inner ring'. I have suggested that one of the distinctive features of the former medieval heretics who formed the congregations of this church was their intense communal solidarity, expressed against their catholic neighbours and often against their protestant pastors as well.[78] Scipione Lentolo, however, a highly educated Italian cleric who had imbibed his protestantism during a brief stay in Geneva,[79] contrived to split even this group. His pedagogic method would have been demanding even in a highly-educated free city in Swabia, as it consisted of preaching the same sermon on a part of the Creed twice each Sunday, then holding four assemblies in the week at which he expected each parishioner to come and answer a short catechism of four or five questions on the previous Sunday's sermon.[80] When the elections for the annual officers of his village came round, Lentolo preached to his flock, reminding them of their duty and giving, it would seem, clear indications of where their duty lay as between the candidates. The previous year's syndics then proposed the names of two 'persone da bene' for election; but despite the exhortations the people elected two 'of no value, or at least very

---

[76] Schiess, *Bullingers Korrespondenz* II pp. 107, 128–9.
[77] *Ibid.* I p. 221.
[78] In my *The Reformation of the Heretics* (Oxford 1984) pp. 257–60.
[79] S. Lentolo, *Historia delle grandi e crudeli persecutioni fatti ai tempi nostri ... contro il popolo che chiamano valdese*, ed T. Gay (Torre Pèllice 1906) pp. 4 *seq.*
[80] Oxford Bodleian MS Barlow 8 pp. 513–14, 518, 520.

little worth'. Lentolo recorded his reaction to being thwarted in this way with surprising candour:

> If after all these things the poor pastor is transported with an excessive rage, and calls them devils, ... saying that he would rather he and all his own children were in the fires than amongst those who, under pretence of being the people of God, dishonour him so manifestly, taking no account of the admonitions made to them according to the word of God ... whom would anyone think was to blame?[81]

In this case the 'good people' were the pious ones whom the pastor could countenance; they were also the holders of communal authority. Lentolo was right to try to cultivate them and promote their cause; it seems that shortly after the fiasco of the election he was expelled from his parish and from Piedmont itself.[82]

It will now be obvious that if one is to speak at all of a general tendency of protestantism to generate 'inner rings', at least in the broad European context, one must admit that these informal groups could vary enormously in character. Socially, those of Strasbourg or the Rhineland seem to have been basically middle-class; but concerned with the written word, demanding, and male in Strasbourg, and concerned with liturgy, quiescent, and mostly female in the countryside. In France, where ministers and people alike in protestant congregations seem to have been of rather higher social standing than in Germany, the community could perhaps be socially as well as morally exclusive; and in the Alps it could take on a political character determined by the devolution of lay power over religion to the smallest political units.

It would be in no way unreasonable to claim that these manifestations have almost nothing in common and should not be confused one with another. However, they have perhaps one factor in common: they originated from two unresolved contradictions in the aspirations of both the clergy and the laity who made the protestant Reformation. The clergy, as I have already suggested, aimed at both a universal and all-embracing church settlement, and

---

[81] *Ibid.* pp. 580–1.
[82] T. Gay, 'Scipione Lentolo', *Bulletin de la Société d'Histoire Vaudoise* 23 (1906) pp. 104–7.

at a rational religion free from superstition, where worship was based on hearing, understanding, and responding intelligently. These aims were surely incompatible; and a fair number of ministers recognized that they were so. Hence the pessimism which gave rise to the plans for special communities; the only reason why Luther did not develop such an idea into practice was that he extended his pessimism to include all his immediate circle and himself as well. Secondly, the laity (especially the urban laity) wished to be unencumbered by an ignorant, disreputable, and illiterate priesthood, and to hear 'Godly preachers'; but they wished to hear so much, and only so much, as they thought suitable, and expected to continue to exercise over better-educated and higher-born incumbents the effortless moral and social superiority which they would have enjoyed over the miserable chaplains of the late medieval church.

The question of England having been evaded up to this point, it must be necessary now to give some thought as to why England should have demonstrated in such a widespread and consistent fashion trends which were only partially and occasionally visible over Europe as a whole. One tentative reason may be that in sixteenth-century England the tensions and contradictions which gave rise to the search for a 'special community' were felt more acutely than elsewhere, because the spiritual and political life of the Church there was of such continuous variety and richness. All the ideological passions found in the continental controversies were present; 'prelatists' and 'puritans' expressed the rival views on the identity of the 'godly community' found respectively in the parties of Hedio and Bucer, but expressed them, not over a few years, but over decades. Likewise, the ambitions of the protestant lay authority were articulated in controversies over the scope of lay Governorship of the Church as fully as anywhere. The structures produced by these controversies, of prelacy, magistracy, and patronage, perpetuated the ambivalence and the tension; so, unlike most of Europe, England kept the issues on the boil.

One other lesson may perhaps be drawn from this aspect of the protestant experience. The magisterial protestants repeatedly denied that their desire to create the 'godly community' was sectarian. The insults which they poured on Anabaptists and Schwenck-feldians suggest that this denial had more than token political significance. If we accept that Bucer and Marbach had no ambition to found sectarian congregations antagonistic to the established Church, perhaps we should finally extend the same credence to the English 'puritans', at least in the Elizabethan period; for they undoubtedly worked in the same tradition and with similar motives in mind.

Of course, not all ministers needed to take the road to founding a 'special community' within the Church. The alternative was to accept the limitations of the laity and not try to improve even a section of it. This implied preserving uniformity by sacrificing rationality, and all those higher ambitions with which the 'second Reformation' if not the Reformation itself, began. Marbach's ministry as visitor to the parishes of Strasbourg's rural hinterland after 1553 became less a matter of arousing intense personal commitment, and more a matter of seeing that people arrived at the Sunday service on time, or did not get too drunk when they celebrated baptisms or weddings.[83] 'Success' or 'failure' in the Reformation depended on how high one set one's sights.

All Souls College
Oxford

---

[83] Kittelson, 'Successes and Failures' pp. 160, 165–6.

THE 'PRIVY KIRKS' AND THEIR ANTECEDENTS: THE HIDDEN FACE OF SCOTTISH PROTESTANTISM

by JAMES KIRK

THE history of Scottish protestantism as a clandestine, underground movement can be traced, albeit unevenly, over three decades from parliament's early ban on Lutheran literature in 1525 to the protestant victory of 1560 when, in disregard of the wishes of its absent queen then resident in France, parliament finally proscribed the Latin mass and the whole apparatus of papal jurisdiction in Scotland and adopted instead a protestant Confession of Faith.[1] Out of a loosely-defined body of beliefs in the 1530s, ranging from a profound dissatisfaction at ecclesiastical abuse (shared by those who remained Catholic), to a recognition of the need for a reformation in doctrine (less readily conceded by orthodox Catholics), Scottish protestantism by the 1550s had developed a cellular organisation, enabling it to survive periodic persecution. Early protestants, themselves brought up within the Catholic church as baptised and communicating members, by the 1550s had taken the agonising and momentous step of separating themselves from the fellowship of the established church by forming their own separate communities of believers, worshipping in secret and centred on the privy kirks which arose in the years immediately preceding the Reformation.

Such was the assurance of salvation which one individual, Elizabeth Adamson, experienced from participating in these secret protestant assemblies for scripture study and prayer, fostered in Edinburgh by Knox and others, that on her deathbed this wife of a prominent merchant and magistrate (himself in touch with Knox from Genevan days) rejected all offers of priestly ministration and intercession. 'Depart from me, ye sergeantis of Sathan', she is

[1] *Acts of the Parliaments of Scotland* [hereafter *APS*] ed T. Thomson (London 1814–75) 2 pp. 295, 341–2, 526–34; 3 p. 14.

reported to have uttered, 'for I have refused, and in your awin presence do refuise, all your abominationis. That which ye call your Sacrament and Christes body (as ye have deceaved us to beleve in tymes past) is nothing but ane idole, and hes nothing to do with the rycht institutioun of Jesus Christ; and thairfor, in Goddis name, I command yow nott to truble me'. Extreme unction and the services of a church which hitherto was seen to hold the key to unlock the doors to the kingdom of Heaven were despised by Elizabeth Adamson in Edinburgh. Instead, with simple evangelical piety, she asked those around her to sing the 103rd psalm, because, as she explained, 'at the teaching of this Psalme, begane my trubled soule first effectually to taist of the mercy of my God, which now to me is more sweat and precious then all the kingdomes of the earth war gevin to me to possesse thame a thowsand yearis'.[2]

For Elizabeth Adamson, protestantism, with its emphasis on individual personal faith, had taught her to find a confirmation of her faith in the Bible with a clarity and intensity which the established church seemed less able to provide. Her story also says something about the convictions of those protestants who dissociated themselves from the existing ecclesiastical structure and who sought spiritual nourishment in the company of others who shared their religious preferences in the shadowy underground world of the privy kirks.

The emergence of this tightly-knit cellular structure, in which familial ties afforded both contact and protection, assisted the development of a network of protestant communities, no longer isolated and dispersed, but increasingly organised and militant, so that when the revolution against France and Rome got underway by 1559, protestantism, which had gradually infiltrated local communities for over thirty years, was at last sufficiently responsive to seizing the initiative presented. This it did by wresting control of parish kirks from priests and patrons to ministers and kirk sessions, that is, reformed consistories of elders and deacons, whose immediate antecedents are, again, to be found in the organization of the privy kirks.

The phenomenon of the privy kirk, therefore, marks an intermediate stage between an earlier phase of inchoate, unorganised

---

[2] *The Works of John Knox* ed D. Laing (Edinburgh 1846–64) 1 pp. 246–7.

protestantism and the reformers' concerted bid for power in the revolution of 1559/60 which brought them victory. Although so very little is known about its history, the privy kirk does seem to possess a significance not always adequately appreciated by historians who, by concentrating on the political aspects of the Reformation, have sometimes been insufficiently attentive to the dimension which the religious movement contributed in the highly complex situation which developed at the Reformation-rebellion, and so they have underestimated the strength of attachment to the reformed cause.

That Scottish protestantism acquired and exhibited many of the characteristics of a popular movement, of which the privy kirks were to form only one element, need hardly be doubted. Initially, of course, protestant sympathizers had been confined to articulate and educated but disputatious divines. The first Scottish casualty of the Reformation had been Patrick Hamilton, titular abbot of Fearn, student of Paris, Louvain, St Andrews and Marburg, burned at St Andrews in 1528 for espousing Lutheran heresies. Yet his evangelical theology continued to circulate in the little compilation known as 'Patrick's Places'. Thereafter, Henry Forres, in minor orders, from Linlithgow met a similar fate after conviction for possessing an English New Testament and for approving Hamilton's doctrine.[3]

Others, threatened for their heterodox opinions, chose exile rather than the prospect of the scaffold. Alexander Alane, Augustinian canon of St Andrews and convert to Lutheran doctrines, escaped in 1532 to the safety of Malmö and eventually to Wittenberg where, as an adherent of Melanchthon, he was recommended to Cromwell and Cranmer and lectured in theology at Cambridge, then at Frankfurt on Oder and finally at Leipzig.[4] Another exile from St Andrews, John Fethie, studied at Wittenberg and also taught at Frankfurt.[5] By 1534, two friars, John Macalpine

[3] P. Lorimer, *Patrick Hamilton* (Edinburgh 1857); *Knox* 1 pp. 13–35, 52–3; J. Foxe, *Acts and Monuments* ed J. Cumming (London 1875) 2 pp. 248–63.

[4] J.T. McNeill, 'Alexander Alesius, Scottish Lutheran (1500–1565)', *ARG* 55 (1964) pp. 161–91.

[5] *Album academiae Vitebergensis* ed C.E. Foerstemann (Leipzig 1841) p. 213; *Die Matrikel der Universität Frankfurt an der Oder* (1506–1648) ed G. Liebe and E. Theuner (Leipzig 1887) p. 9.

and John Macdowell, priors at Perth and Wigtown and graduates of Cologne, had fled to England where they preached for Bishop Shaxton in Salisbury. But whereas Macdowell continued to serve in the English church in Dorset and Lincoln for over twenty years, Macalpine by 1540 had left for Wittenberg and then for Copenhagen as theology professor in 1542.[6] Even King James V's confessor, Alexander Seton, prior of the Dominican friary in St Andrews, was suspected of Lutheran heresies and so escaped to Berwick and found service as chaplain to the Duke of Suffolk.[7] A further Dominican friar, John Willock, fled about 1535 from Ayr, where Lutheran doctrines were expounded 'both in private and public', together with other 'blasphemies' against the eucharist. There, too, the English New Testament and other reformed works circulated; instances of iconoclasm occurred in the parish kirk in 1534 and again at the Franciscan friary, where a statue of the Virgin Mary was decapitated. After pursuing a career in the English church which had taken him to Emden as a Marian exile in 1554, Willock returned to Scotland to help organise the privy kirks and establish a Calvinist discipline.[8] To this catalogue of clerical converts in the 1530s, who escaped abroad, may be added Robert Richardson, Augustinian canon of Cambuskenneth, who sought Cromwell's patronage in England.[9]

What all this amounted to in practice may not be readily determined; but it does suggest that Scottish protestantism was already at work making significant converts among the clergy, even though its exponents found it safer to enunciate their beliefs beyond the realm. What is not so readily disclosed is the number of protestant sympathizers who concealed their views from the authorities, the sort of people who might be expected to resort to the privy kirks at a later stage. Yet an indication of the firm foothold which

[6] M.A.F. Bredahl Petersen, 'Dr Johannes Macchabeus: Scotland's contribution to the Reformation in Denmark' (Edinburgh Ph.D. thesis 1935); J. Durkan, 'Some Local Heretics', *Transactions of the Dumfriesshire & Galloway Natural History & Antiquarian Society*, 36 (Dumfries 1959) pp. 66–77.

[7] *Knox* 1 pp. 45–52; Foxe 2 pp. 593–95.

[8] D. Shaw, 'John Willock', *Reformation and Revolution* ed D. Shaw (Edinburgh 1967) pp. 42–69; *St Andrews Formulare, 1514–46* ed G. Donaldson (Edinburgh 1944) 2 no 367; D. Calderwood, *History of the Kirk of Scotland* ed T. Thomson (Edinburgh 1842–49) 1 p. 286.

[9] J. Durkan 'Scottish "Evangelicals" in the Patronage of Thomas Cromwell', *Records of the Scottish Church History Society*, 21 (1982) pp. 127–56 at p. 134.

protestantism had gained in certain towns, later to have implications for the nascent privy kirks, is the series of prosecutions for heresy among laymen in the late 1530s and early '40s.

Nothing like a complete record of these heresy trials has survived; for a start, the proceedings in the ecclesiastical courts are now missing; and evidence is usually forthcoming only in instances where the crown had an interest in disposing of the escheated goods of convicted heretics or in granting heretics remissions for their crimes. Nonetheless, it emerges that, at this date, three inhabitants of Edinburgh, including the schoolmaster, and three more from Leith were convicted of heresy and had their property confiscated;[10] five more were detected in Stirling; some merely had suspect literature, others were more severely punished with forfeiture and at least one was sent to the stake;[11] in Perth, at least seven heretics were convicted at that stage, four of whom were hanged and a fifth drowned; but besides this group, other inhabitants of the burgh including a priest and notary are on record as having fled on account of their heretical inclinations when the periodic searches took place for 'Christers' or protestants.[12] In Dundee, sentences of forfeiture or even death were pronounced in cases involving no fewer than twenty heretics in the burgh; and eighteen more Dundonians were charged with image-breaking and oppressing the friars in the burgh, at a point when Arran as governor of the realm had inclined towards protestantism.[13] Similar

[10] *Registrum Secreti Sigilli Regum Scotorum* [hereafter *RSS*] ed D.H. Fleming *et al.* (Edinburgh 1908 – in progress) 2 nos 2915, 2946, 2988; *Registrum Magni Sigilli Regum Scotorum* [hereafter *RMS*] ed J.M. Thomson *et al.* (Edinburgh 1882–1914) 3 no 2179; *Accounts of the Lord High Treasurer of Scotland* [hereafter *TA*] ed T. Dickson *et al.* (Edinburgh 1877 – in progress) 6 p. 175; 7 pp. 67, 77, 79, 233–34; *Knox* 1 p. 57; *A Diurnal of Remarkable Occurrences in Scotland* ed T. Thomson (Edinburgh 1833) p. 18; *Acts of the Lords of Council in Public Affairs, 1501–1554* ed R.K. Hannay (Edinburgh 1932) p. 486. See also Scottish Record Office, JC1/5, Justiciary Court Book, 21 Feb., 28 Feb., 7 March, 1539 where another individual faced charges of possessing suspect and prohibited literature.

[11] *RMS* 3 no 1955; *RSS* 2 nos 2923, 2975; *TA* 7 pp. 77, 79; *Knox* 1 p. 62; *Criminal Trials in Scotland* ed R. Pitcairn (Edinburgh 1833) 1 p. 216.

[12] *RSS* 2 no 3033; 3 nos 609, 611–613; *TA* 8 pp. 215, 219; *Knox* 1 pp. 117–18; Calderwood 1 pp. 171–75; Foxe 2 pp. 708–709.

[13] *RSS* 2 nos 2644, 2648, 2686, 2704, 2733, 2742, 2962, 3016; 3 no 1635; 4 no 2580; *TA* 6 pp. 307, 376–77; 7 pp. 79, 153; 10 pp. 369–70; A. Maxwell, *Old Dundee* (Edinburgh 1891) appendix B; *The Hamilton Papers* ed J. Bain (Edinburgh 1890–92) 2 no 30.

prosecutions are known to have taken place in the west country, particularly in Ayr; and if the details remain partly obscured, it was Archbishop Hamilton, as primate, who impressed on the pope in 1554 how 'a great part of the diocese of Glasgow' was 'infected with heresies' in the 1540s and how thereafter 'the greatest scandals were perpetrated against the Catholic faith'.[14]

To the problems affecting the south-west may be added those of the north-east. In Angus, the Mearns and Aberdeenshire, thirty members of noble or lairdly families, including the Earl Marischal, the provost of Aberdeen and the parson of Aberdour, were pardoned by the crown in 1544 for activities which included reading suspect books, disputing on scripture and holding opinions forbidden by act of parliament; and by 1547, the bishop of Aberdeen himself acknowledged that heresy was then 'thriving greatly' within his diocese. Elsewhere, details of at least a further sixteen convictions among laymen for heresy have survived for these years.[15]

The incidence of heresy was no longer confined to quiescent family cells of believers. Circumspection, of course, was still essential for survival and few protestants willingly advertised their presence to the authorities. Yet, in Perth, a rather remarkable foursome — a merchant, maltman, flesher [butcher] and skinner — were convicted in 1544 for holding a conventicle, 'an assemblie and conventioun', in St Anne's chapel where they, and no doubt others, conferred and disputed on texts of holy scripture, in defiance of the acts of parliament, to the 'dishonouring of the glorious Virgin Mary and the communioun of sanctis in hevin'. One member of this little company was said merely to have been 'a simple man, and without learning...with no great knowledge in doctrine; yitt because he often used the suspect companie of the rest, he was accused'. The others presumably knew what they were about; the merchant in the group, at any rate, was sufficiently literate to have his copy of the English Bible. What is more, two of the disputants, one with his English Bible in his hand, also had the courage or

[14] *TA* 6 p. 313; *Liber Officialis Sancte Andree* ed C. Innes (Edinburgh 1845) p. 167.
[15] *RSS* 3 no 820; *Registrum Episcopatus Aberdonensis* ed C. Innes (Aberdeen 1845), 2 p. 317; *TA* 6 pp. 8, 176; 7 pp. 78–79; 8 p. 219; *RSS* 2 nos 1302, 1583, 1585, 1611, 1736, 2420, 2797, 2936, 2952, 2976, 2987, 3396; 5 no 1267; *Diurnal of Occurents* p. 19; *Criminal Trials* 1 p. 297; *Acts of the Lords of Council* p. 446.

rashness of their convictions later to interrupt a friar, as he preached from the pulpit, by denouncing his doctrine as false and contrary to scripture. Retaliation, however, was swift; and the heretics were hanged. But greater leniency appears to have been shown to another burgess of Perth, a relative of the burgh's fugitive priest, who received a remission from the crown in 1544 for his crime of holding 'quiet conventions in secret places', disputing on sacred scripture and dishonouring the Virgin Mary.[16]

The problem of conventicles was serious enough to have warranted parliament's attention in 1541 when, in an effort 'to stop the privat congregatioun and conventiculis of heretikis quhair thair erroris ar spred', a reward was offered to any with knowledge of these secret associations; informants who had attended such a gathering, no more than once, were to be free from prosecution; outsiders with information incriminating heretics holding conventicles were to receive a share in the property of the convicted heretic. This act, passed together with a series of statutes requiring the sacraments to be honoured, the Virgin Mary to be worshipped, the statues of saints to be revered, the pope's authority upheld, ecclesiastical abuses reformed, and heretics incapacitated from holding public office, helps to convey an impression of the magnitude of the problem which the ecclesiastical authorities faced. Even two years later, during Arran's governorship, when parliament authorized laymen to read the Bible 'in Inglis or Scottis of ane gude and trew translatioun', disputations on scripture were expressly forbidden by law.[17]

Despite the existence and, in some cases, detection of clandestine gatherings, where literate laymen might read passages from the vernacular Bible to those in their company and discuss controverted texts, there was still a conspicuous absence of protestant-inclined preachers to provide the necessary guidance and leadership. Some sympathetic clerics, of course, had been detected — men like the provost of Roslin, the vicar of Dollar, the priest in Perth, the curates of Lunan and Tullibody, a chaplain in Kirkwall, another in Dunfermline and a third in Stirling, two Franciscans from Aberdeen and Dumfries, two Dominican friars burned at Stirling, a

[16] Calderwood 1 pp. 171–75; *RSS* 3 nos 609, 611–13.
[17] *APS* 2 pp. 370–1, 415.

third who preached in Angus and was murdered at St Andrews, and the wayward chaplain from Brechin diocese whose bishop was instructed to have him punished for heresy. The list is not unimpressive; even more significant is the geographical spread from Kirkwall in the Orkneys to Dumfries in the extreme south west. Even parts of the Highlands were not immune from heresy: the bishop of Ross was empowered by the cardinal to proceed against heretics in his far-distant diocese.[18]

At the same time, the distribution of devotional literature in protestant circles helped to compensate for the shortage of preachers by providing a clear evangelical message.[19] Besides, apart from the personal contact of individual Scots with protestant Europe, the new doctrines were spread at home, as Knox appreciated, 'partlie by reading, partlie by brotherlye conferance, which in those dangerous dayis was used to the comforte of many'.[20] The conventicles thus afforded an element of protection while providing a focus for fellowship and for imparting religious knowledge among the faithful.

A sudden stimulus to protestant preaching came in 1543 from an unexpected quarter with the temporary defection to protestantism, effective for no more than a few months, of the Earl of Arran, then governor during Queen Mary's minority. Not only did he sponsor the heretical preaching at court of a Dominican friar, Thomas Gwilliam, but he also supported as his family's chaplain another unorthodox Dominican, John Rough, from Stirling who also preached in places as far apart as St Andrews and Dumfries and later was burned for heresy at Smithfield in 1557. As governor, Arran supported the heterodox preaching of Robert Richardson,

[18] *RSS* 2 nos 2858, 2903, 3612; 4 no 916; *Calendar of State Papers relating to Scotland and Mary, Queen of Scots* ed J. Bain *et al.* 13 vols (Edinburgh 1898–1969) 1 no 206; *TA* 7 pp. 77, 79–80; *Diurnal of Occurrents* p. 18; *Regality of Dunfermline Court Book, 1531–1538* ed J.M. Webster and A.A.M. Duncan (Dunfermline 1953) pp. 143–44; *Knox* 1 pp. 56–7, 62–5, 118–19; *Criminal Trials* 1 pp. 209–16; *Acts of the Lords in Council* pp. 427, 437, 482; *St Andrews Formulare* 2 no 416.

[19] J. Gau, *The Richt Vay to the Kingdom of Heuine* ed A.F. Mitchell (Edinburgh 1888); *A Compendius Book of Godly and Spiritual Songs* ed A.F. Mitchell (Edinburgh 1897); J.K. Cameron, 'John Johnsone's An Confortable Exhortation of our mooste Holy Christen Faith and her Frutes: an early example of Scots Lutheran Piety', *SCH* Subsidia 2, (Oxford 1979) pp. 133–47; cf *Devotional Pieces in Verse and Prose* ed J.A.W. Bennet (Edinburgh 1955).

[20] *Knox* 1 p. 61.

and even asked the magistrates in Aberdeen to appoint two friars as official preachers of 'the trew Word of God'. One of these friars, the Dominican John Roger, is said by Knox to have 'fructfully preached Christ Jesus to the conforte of many in Anguss and Mearnes'. Yet this 'godly' experiment, promoted as part of the government's programme, proved short-lived. Within three months of their appointment, the two preachers at court had been inhibited from preaching: one left for England, the other for Kyle in Ayrshire, 'a receptakle of Goddis servandis of old'. The renewed repression of heresy ensued; the movement resumed its underground activities; and an act of council in June 1543 depicted heretics as 'Sacramentaris' (or sacramentarians) who held disputations on the effect and essence of the sacraments to the detriment and 'enervatioun of the faith Catholik'.[21]

If the disputations and conventicling activities of protestants in burghs such as Perth are clear enough in outline, it is harder to say with certainty what was happening in the countryside behind the closed doors of a noble's castle or laird's keep, isolated from the prying eyes and ears of informants in the towns. There are indications, however, that private meetings for Bible study and conference similar to those in the towns were features of rural society too. The thirty landowners in the north-east pardoned in 1544 for disputing on scripture and reading forbidden books clearly illustrate the broad tendencies at work; but an earlier episode, narrated by Knox, illuminates the spiritual searching of one laird in Angus who 'delyted in nothing but in reading (albeit him self could not reid)'. His immediate problem was surmounted by having his son read him the English New Testament 'in ane certane qwyet place in the feildis'; and frequently he sought the company of that proto-protestant, Erskine of Dun, near Montrose. Other lairds, too, were thumbing through the pages of their copies of the English Bible in their homes or in small groups, if an expositor like Erskine of Dun could be found. James Kirkcaldy of Grange, later taken

[21] *Ibid.* 1 pp. 95–7, 105, 184; *TA* 8 pp. 168, 170, 183; *Extracts from the Council Register of the Burgh of Aberdeen* ed J. Stuart (Aberdeen 1844) 1 p. 189; *Cal LP* 18 pt 1 no 448; Foxe 3 pp. 957–61; *Concilia Scotiae: Ecclesiae Scoticanae Statuta ...* ed J. Robertson (Edinburgh 1846) p. 294; see further, *Register of the Privy Council of Scotland*, 1st ser. ed J.H. Burton *et al.* (Edinburgh 1877–98) 1 pp. 28–9, 61, 63, 65.

prisoner with his son, William, for their part in Cardinal Beaton's assassination in 1546, was reputed to have been a heretic during his service as treasurer to James V, when, it was noted, 'he had always a New Testament in English in his pouch'; and Sir John Borthwick, well-travelled in England and France and later a visitor to Geneva, was declared a heretic in 1540 not only for denouncing papal authority, the canon law, indulgences, the church's wealth and the religious orders but also for possessing a New Testament in English as well as the works of Oecolampadius, Melanchthon and Erasmus.[22]

Even so, it is really with the preaching mission in 1545 of George Wishart, who helped popularise the views of the Swiss reformers, that the secret network of protestant associations among the lairds begins to be uncovered. A student in Arts at Louvain and later at Cambridge, Wishart was the 'stiff-necked Scot' who had stirred up trouble in Bristol and was obliged to recant some of his more radical tenets. Returning to Edinburgh in 1543, Wishart began to preach in 1545, 'nott in secreat but in the audience of many', first at Montrose and then from the pulpit in Dundee on the Epistle to the Romans before the Earl Marischal and other nobles. His progress to the west country took him to Ayr, where he preached at the market cross after dissuading his followers, the Earl of Glencairn and lairds in Kyle, from taking the kirk by force; so, too, in Mauchline where he resisted Campbell of Kinyeancleuch's offer to storm the church which the sheriff had baracaded. Yet, he did preach in Galston kirk and at the home of the laird of Bar before returning to plague-ridden Dundee, where he visited the sick, preaching from the 107th psalm on healing through the Word; and so to Montrose again 'to salute the Kirk thare' in preaching and 'secreat meditatioun'. Thereafter, he left for Edinburgh, lodging near Dundee at the home of 'a faythfull brother', James Watson in Invergowrie, earlier convicted of Lutheran heresies in 1532, then on to Perth, through Fife to Leith where he remained in secret

---

[22] *Knox* 1 pp. 58–60; *Memoirs of Sir James Melville of Halhill* ed A.F. Steuart (London 1929) p. 15; *Foxe* 2 pp. 695–706; *Register of the Minister, Elders and Deacons of the Christian Congregation of St Andrews* [henceforth *RStAKS*] ed D.H. Fleming (Edinburgh 1889–90) 2 pp. 89–104; *Acts of the Lords of Council* p. 504.

before preaching; but when it proved too dangerous to remain there, Wishart was taken to the homes of East Lothian lairds at Brunstone, Longniddry and Ormiston, and preached in Tranent and in the kirks of Inveresk and Haddington, where he was sheltered by David Forres, later master of the mint and who undertook to 'exhort' the brethren in the privy kirk by 1558. Yet Wishart also found refuge at the home of Maitland of Lethington, who was 'ever civile, albeit not persuaded in religioun'. Captured at Ormiston and condemned to be burned as a heretic, Wishart, in his last prayer 'to conserve, defend and help thy Congregatioun, which thow hast chosen befoir the begynning of the world', helped make more explicit than ever before the belief among Scottish protestants who began to see themselves as forming a congregation of believers, a definition which ultimately led to the gathered church of the radical reformers.[23]

Wishart's translation of the first Swiss Confession of Faith, published in 1548, may also have contributed towards a clearer understanding of church fellowship; but the first attempt to organise a recognisably reformed congregation as such, of which we have direct knowledge, arose as a sequel to Wishart's martyrdom when a group of protestants who occupied St Andrews castle after the cardinal's murder in 1546 invited Knox to become their preacher. After a sermon preached by John Rough on the election of ministers and the power of the congregation to call its minister, Knox was charged to receive the call. At this stage, too, in disputations with Catholic opponents, Knox affirmed: 'we must defyne the Church by the rycht notes gevin to us in Goddis Scriptures of the trew Church'. For Knox, the church malignant must be distinguished from the true church: 'I wilbe of none other church, except of that which hath Christ Jesus to be pastor, which hearis his voce, and will nott hear a strangeir'. In administering the Lord's Supper, Knox extended an invitation to those within the town, as well as the castle, who were willing openly to profess their faith. Yet this attempt at setting up the open face of a reformed church was cut short when French reinforcements stormed the

[23] Foxe 2 pp. 709–17; *The Maire of Bristowe is Kalendar* by Robert Ricart ed L.T. Smith (London 1872) p. 55; *Knox* 1 pp. 125–71.

castle and shipped off to France the members of this revolutionary group.[24]

Even so, as a counterpoise to French influence, English intervention in south-east Scotland from 1547 to 1549 helped sustain the hopes of a party in Scotland anglophile in its outlook and sympathetic to the cause of reform. The destruction caused by English occupying forces may have alienated many; the timid and uncertain may have waited on events; but not only did the provost and bailies of Dundee promise 'to be faithful setters forth of God's word', after which it was said that, in the town, 'most of the honest and substantial men favour the Word of God', but several earls like Glencairn and Lennox also undertook 'to cause the Word of God to be taught and preached'. The inhabitants of Leith were considered 'all good Christians'; and 'Angus and Fife', it was noted, 'greatly desire a good preacher, bibles and testaments and other good English books of Tyndale and Frithe's translation'. The cause of reform, through English aegis, was clearly making further headway. Yet the departure of the English and ascendancy of Mary of Guise meant that Scottish protestantism was again reduced to secret meetings behind closed doors.[25]

Arrested in 1550 at Winton castle, Lord Seton's home, in East Lothian, Adam Wallace, a native of Ayrshire and tutor to Cockburn of Ormiston's children, admitted that 'sometymes at the table and sometymes in other prevey places, he wald reid and had red the Scriptures and had gevin such exhortatioun as God pleaseth to geve to him and to such as pleased to hear him'. He also affirmed that he could find no scriptural warrant for purgatory and prayers to the saints, and appeared to condemn the mass as blasphemy, for which he was burned on castlehill in Edinburgh, despite the Earl of Glencairn's protests.[26]

Nevertheless, from 1555 onwards, freshly recruited preachers 'did sometymes, in severall cumpanyes, assemble the brethrein, who by thare exhortationis begane greatlie to be encoraged, and did schaw that thei had ane earnest thrist of godlines'. In 'privy conference as in doctrin', Knox and others helped impress on

[24] *Miscellany of the Wodrow Society* ed D. Laing (Edinburgh 1844) pp. 1–23; *Knox* I pp. 184–202.

[25] *CSP Scot* I nos 71, 74, 107, 129; *Cal LP* 18, pt I no 974; 19 pt I no 522.

[26] *Knox* I pp. 237–41; Foxe 2 pp. 717–20.

protestant sympathizers the need to refrain from the sacraments of the established church and to organise themselves effectively in their own secret communities; and in his preaching tour in the Mearns, Knox detected a readiness among most of the lairds to refuse 'all societie with idolatrie'. By then, however, the protestants, it was said, 'keapt thare conventionis and held counsallis with such gravitie and closnes that the ennemyes trembled', or so Knox claimed; but the Catholic John Leslie also noted how protestant preaching took place 'in chimlay nuikis, secreit holes and sik priuat places, to truble the hail cuntrie, quench al quyetnes, banise al pease out of the land'. Both seem agreed that the underground organisation among protestants was becoming more effective and that protestants were more defiant and assertive.[27]

Certainly, by December 1557, the lords of the Congregation had bound themselves to renounce the congregation of Satan and to establish the Word of God and his congregation and to sustain faithful ministers. They also committed themselves to provide in every parish each Sunday the reading of scripture and passages from the English prayer book either by the curates, if considered qualified, or by other more suitable parishioners. On the more contentious issues of preaching and interpreting scripture, however, they still planned to meet 'privatlie in qwyet houssis, without great conventionis of the people' until such time as protestant preaching in public was permitted by the prince. Their main aim, however, was for 'Christes religioun to be restored to the originall puritie' by following the example of 'the grave and godlie face of the primitive Churche'.[28]

If protestant prayer-meetings, held intermittently over two decades, were to become authentic churches, they required an authentic structure; hence resort to the congregational eldership, especially so when the church lay under the cross and was subject to persecution. Only evidence for the structure of the privy kirk in Edinburgh has been preserved. There protestants gathered in 'secreit and privie conventiounis' in the large houses of faithful merchants during winter or in the fields by summer. Some were

---

[27] *Knox* 1 pp. 245–57; J. Leslie, *The Historie of Scotland* ed J. Dalrymple (Edinburgh 1895) 2 p. 397; *Statutes of the Scottish Church* ed D. Patrick (Edinburgh 1907) p. 186.
[28] *Knox* 1 pp. 273–76, 299–307.

elected 'to occupie the supreame place of exhortatioun and reading'; others were called as elders to exercise a godly discipline, or as deacons to collect and distribute alms for the poor within the group. The similarities in polity with French protestantism or with the Marian exiles or even the strangers' churches in London are not coincidental: circumstances dictated a primitive government consistent with the example of the early church.[29]

As well as Edinburgh, the towns of Dundee, Perth, Stirling, Ayr, Brechin and Montrose all had reformed congregations with established ministers by 1559; and if, as was claimed at the Reformation, Fife, Angus, Argyll, Strathearn and the Mearns were already largely protestant, it is hard to resist the conclusion that innumerable clusters of privy kirks had taken root in countryside and town alike. But although they might breed a sense of purpose, self-reliance and esteem among the converted, the privy kirks alone could not hope to change society or bring about widespread revolution. The townspeople and countrydwellers who attended their meetings were still accustomed to looking above and beyond their own religious communities for direction and leadership — to preachers and magistrates, to lairds and nobles. Political action was imperative for religious change. Certainly, support for the Reformation from Haliburton, as provost of Dundee, or from Lord Ruthven in Perth helped smooth the transition from privy kirk to parish church. Even an absence of local sanctions could prove helpful: in Dumfries, the magistrates refused the official of Nith's request to have a protestant preacher arrested in 1558.[30] In the end, however, only the aristocratic revolt and the physical presence in leading burghs of the para-military lords of the Congregation signalled decisive change and entrusted the reformers with local power.

[29] Beza, *Histoire ecclésiastique des églises réformées au royaume de France* ed G. Baum and E. Cunitz (Paris 1883–89) 1 pp. 120 *seq*; A.N. Galpern, *The Religions of the People in Sixteenth-Century Champagne* (London 1976) pp. 134–5, 150, 152, 166–7; F.A. Norwood, 'The Stranger's "Model Churches" in Sixteenth-Century England', *Reformation Studies* ed F.H. Littell (Richmond 1962) pp. 181–96; P. Collinson, *Godly People* (London 1983) pp. 213–44.

[30] *Knox* 6 p. 78; *Hamilton Papers* 2 p. 749; cf *Wodrow Society Miscellany* p. 54; R. Keith, *History of the Affairs of Church and State in Scotland* ed J.P. Lawson (Edinburgh 1835–50) 1 pp. 495–6.

In Dundee, the town council in August 1559 assigned the town's preacher a stipend as minister and recognised the work of the kirk session already operating.[31] Perth, too, was reported in June 1559 to have received the 'Order of Commoun Prayers';[32] and thereafter, in April 1560, William Harlaw, a former Canongate tailor turned protestant preacher with a record of service in the Edwardine Church of England, was already installed as 'minister for the tyme', preaching in the parish kirk of St John 'in presens of nobill and rycht honourable men and the haill congregatioun of the burgh' assembled on the 'Sabbith day callit Sounday to the heirying of Goddis name'. There, too, the reforming Alexander Gordon, bishop elect of Galloway and commendator of Inchaffray priory, confessed before the same congregation that he was 'na bischop preist' and had been a married man for 'fourtene yeiris'.[33] Indeed, a measure of the reformation achieved in Perth is again apparent in a petition from the craftsmen to parliament and to the 'haill Congregatioun of this realme' in 1560, remarkable not least for its claim how the merchants and craftsmen, 'sen God sperit up our haill communite of merchandis and craftis be assistance of his Holy Spreit to be jonit in ane congregatioun of Crist being memborris of his misticall body, ressavit his Holy Word and promis amangis us, for the quhilk our persecutioun is notorius ...'[34] The authorities in Ayr dispensed with the services of chaplains in May 1559 and appointed Christopher Goodman as minister and their schoolmaster as assistant minister.[35] Nearby Dalmellington had its own minister in 1559;[36] and in the east, the magistrates in Crail instructed their chaplains 'to apply thameselfis to Goddis Word and lyf godly, conforme to the congregatioun', and specifically ordered one of them to 'renuns the papis lawis and all uther abominatiounis'.[37] Besides, the primatial city of St Andrews, Scotland's ecclesiastical capital, had its reformed congregation and kirk

[31] I.E.F. Flett, 'The Conflict of the Reformation and Democracy in the Geneva of Scotland, 1443–1610' (St Andrews M.Phil. thesis 1981) p. 68.
[32] *Knox* 6 p. 22.
[33] SRO, B59/1/1, Protocol Book of Henry Elder, fol 184.
[34] Perth Museum, MS Original papers and letters of the Convener Court of the Incorporated Trades of Perth, no 34.
[35] SRO, B6/12/3, Ayr Burgh Court Book, 22 May, 6 Nov., 20 Nov., 1559.
[36] *Ibid.* 29 Nov. 1559.
[37] SRO, Crail Town Clerk's Scroll Book, 4 Dec. 1559.

session operating in public by October 1559.[38] The privy kirks had surfaced to assume the rôle of parish churches. Clearly, all this activity was taking place in the localities well before the work of the Reformation parliament got underway in August 1560. Even in a rural parish like Glenholm, near Peebles, the parishioners were accustomed to attending the 'preching and commoun prayaris' in their parish kirk; and they therefore took legal action before the lords of council in February 1561 to recover their stolen church bell, 'quhilk daile rang and warnit the perrochinneris of the said perochin to preching and commoun prayaris'.[39]

Yet to magnify the rôle of the privy kirks, which appeared with deceptive suddenness in the late 1550s, is possibly to underestimate the importance of the earlier conventicling phase in the 1540s, when protestantism was perceived by the authorities as a widespread and formidable problem to combat. The main distinguishing feature of the privy kirks, however, was the emphasis on Calvinist discipline, determination and dedication instilled through the eldership and diaconate. If conventicles were gatherings of the converted, the privy kirks became churches with a mission to convert. All in all, the formation of privy kirks did not by themselves produce the Reformation victory of 1560 but, in the pursuit of that victory, they did provide the mechanism for transferring religious authority from voluntary communities of believers to a Calvinist church, equipped with a congregational structure and intent on becoming the church of a nation.

University of Glasgow

---

[38] *RStAKS* 1 p. 5.
[39] SRO, CS7/20, Register of Acts and Decreets, 20 fols. 330v–331r.

LEAGUES AND ASSOCIATIONS IN SIXTEENTH-CENTURY FRENCH CATHOLICISM

by JOHN BOSSY

Y motives in choosing this subject are: to respond to the invitation of our chairman; to expound the conviction that the persistence of French Catholicism through the crises of the Reformation was largely the result of the voluntary association of French Catholics; and to try to discover whether there was anything in Catholic theological or pastoral teaching of the period which might have given these associations a theoretical perspective, or grounded them in some kind of associative conception of the Church. I add that, despite the very considerable importance of the subject, one might even claim its decisive importance for the outcome of the wars of religion in Europe as a whole, it has (with some shining exceptions) not received very much attention from historians, and that in England essential texts and studies are hard to come by.

On two famous occasions, in the middle of the Peasants' War and at the beginnings of the Schmalkaldic League, Martin Luther said that there could be no such thing as a Christian association. His reasons were that the form of self-help which they embodied revealed a lack of faith in God's providence; that it authorised the cultivation of passions of self-righteousness and aggression which were un-Christian in themselves and incompatible with the doctrine of obedience to the powers that be; and that in practice it would do the devil's work by provoking a state of exterior conflict and chaos in the world.[1] If one were looking for an illustration of the frame of mind which Luther denounced, one would need to look no farther than the history of the Catholic side in the French wars of religion a generation or two later. From the moment, around

---

[1] *Luther's Works* eds J. Pelikan and H.T. Lehmann 54 vols (Philadelphia 1955–75) 46 pp. 23 *seq*; 49 pp. 224 *seq*.

1560, when it suddenly became possible that France might become a Protestant country, the unreformed French, unconvinced of their rulers' capacity or will to prevent that outcome, took to banding together in resistance to it. Their activity took two distinct forms, which I shall call leagues and fraternities.

Leagues were, in the first place, local, sworn associations of Catholics for the purpose of offering forcible resistance to the advance of Protestantism, and (probably) of exterminating it where it had become established.[2] In the first decade of the civil wars they emerged over a large part of the country. The first sign of them seems to have been in the south-west, in the regions of Bordeaux and Toulouse, where they were activated by the presence of the kingdom of Navarre, of Huguenot armies, and of a substantial audience for reformed Christianity among the nobility and others. They also appeared in what seems a highly organised form in Burgundy, and by 1568 are claimed to have dominated a great deal of the countryside of north-central France from the Loire Valley to Champagne. They were usually organised by members of the nobility, and sometimes by regional representatives of royal authority. They were, naturally enough, active at times when the Crown was negotiating with or making concessions to the Protestants, dormant when it seemed to have decided to campaign against them. Settlements with the Huguenots normally contained a clause requiring their suppression, and one hears about them most in the aftermath of such agreements, when Catherine de Médicis was especially anxious to get rid of them, and they were especially anxious not to be got rid of.[3]

On 25 June 1568, for example, the principal clergy of the town of Troyes in Champagne declared their allegiance to a league organised by the royal lieutenant in Champagne and Brie, the terms of which seem fairly standard. They called themselves 'associez de la ligue chrétienne et royale'. They declared themselves as doing

---

[2] I say 'probably' because I do not see much evidence that massacres of Protestants, as in 1572, were actually carried out by Catholic leagues. Bordeaux (see following note) seems to be an exception.

[3] J.H.M. Salmon, *Society in Crisis: France in the Sixteenth Century* (London 1975) pp. 148 seq, 172; R. Boutruche ed *Bordeaux de 1453 à 1715* (*Histoire de Bordeaux*, iv: Paris 1966) p. 244; *Lettres de Catherine de Médicis* eds H. de la Ferrière and G. Baguenault de Puchesse 10 vols (Paris 1880–1909) 1 p. 552 and n. 1.

their Christian duty in defence of the true, historic church of God, Catholic and Roman; defending the house of Valois; and ensuring the performance of their functions in the service of God and the Church. They noted the lieutenant's invitation to join the 'société et ligue royale de la noblesse et états de ce gouvernement', and recited the tenor of the said league. They swore that they would support it by financial assistance in all its enterprises, and acknowledged that in return they would receive its assistance in defending them in arms against those of the contrary party. The terms of the league as recited were that the nobility of Champagne promised to employ their persons, lives and goods in defence of the Church, and of the Crown 'tant et si longuement qu'il plaira à Dieu que nous serons par eux régis en notredite religion apostolique et romaine'; in mutual assistance against all persons, except the king, Queen Mother and family, and without respect of kinship or alliance; and in self-defence against any enterprise against them on the part of enemies 'of the present society and of our said Catholic and Roman religion'. The clergy, who were not competent to join the armed association, were to provide the funds instead.[4]

During the 1570s, when Catholic victories in battle had mysteriously failed to produce the result expected, the political and military situation took a more complicated turn, and though the leagues remained expressions of Catholic solidarity the objects of their hostility became more various. The Crown, and the king's brother François duke of Alençon and Anjou, began to compete with the Huguenots as objects of public detestation. The estates-general of 1576, following another peace favourable to the Protestants, gave them a new push, and the beginning of a national umbrella in the general league organised by the Duke of Guise. King Henri III attempted to head off the movement by imposing a national association under his own authority; this was an intelligent move, but by convinced leaguers regarded as a dishonest gimmick and a scheme of extra taxation. It probably had the effect of encouraging private initiatives of this kind, which were particularly common during the next few years.

[4] *Mémoires de Claude Haton* ed F. Bourquelot 2 vols (Paris 1857) pp. 1152–53.

Thus the town and neighbourhood of Provins in Brie decided in 1578 that it would no longer tolerate the ravaging of the country-side and the demolition of villages and small towns by troops being raised by the Duke of Anjou for his campaign against the Spaniards in the Netherlands. The townsmen assembled at Provins made a league with the 'gens des villages' to massacre any soldiers they could catch, and the clergy agreed to put up the money to pay a militia. Eventually the king consented to send troops to do the job for them, but had to concede the legitimacy of self-defence associations of this kind: a permission, as the diarist of Provins remarked, which was taken advantage of more rudely by the people of Picardy, whither the troops had proceeded, than it had been by themselves.[5]

The south-east of France produced a remarkable crop of such associations at this time, mainly because, after their defeat in Lyon in the 1560s, the Protestants had been waging a patient and suc-cessful war of attrition in the western Alps and the Rhone valley. The movement has been made familiar by Emmanuel le Roy Ladu-rie in his *Carnaval de Romans*, to which dramatic event it forms the background. The leagues which were formed throughout the area during 1579 had the primary object of organising military resistance to the Huguenots on a popular footing; they proceeded from that to suppressing gangs of noble bandits (which was often enough the same thing); to attacking troops of all persuasions, including those being raised by the Duke of Anjou; and to refusing to pay taxes unless the nobility paid them as well. Their objectives were often as attractive to Protestant as to Catholic peasants; parallel leagues were formed, which might act together; in Provence a single league united them against an objectionable faction of Catholic nobility. But I doubt if it is correct to see the leagues in the region of Romans as radically different from those farther south, in the region of Valence, which were ferociously Catholic. Their doings were closely related to the cycle of traditional festivity; in the countryside the meetings from which they arose were usually the patronal feasts or *reinages* of the parishes, and in towns those of the gilds. Of the two leaders who emerged, Jacques Colas at

---

[5] Salmon, *Society in Crisis* pp. 201–3, 207 seq; *Mémoires de Claude Haton* pp. 881–888, 1153–56; pp. 936 seq, 954–961, 1144–45.

Montélimar and Jean Serve *alias* Paumier at Romans, the first was an extreme Catholic who played a notable role in the greater League a decade later; Paumier's was a more complicated case, but he seems perfectly Catholic to me, and if he had not been shot dead at the Carnival of 1580 he might have gone the same way.[6]

The death of Paumier, though not in my view the result of a conspiracy by the upper classes, was certainly a useful contribution to the general dissolution of leagues which Catherine de Médicis had toured the provinces since 1577 to achieve. Her biggest success was in Bordeaux and Guyenne, where there had been a vigorous revival of them in their classic anti-Huguenot form. The peace of 1576 had re-ignited them by handing the province over to the governorship of Henri of Navarre, and they were encouraged by the lieutenant-governor, Biron, who was an enemy of the king. Catherine however seems to have got the support both of the Parlement and of the clergy: here the leagues were effectively dissolved, and the success of the government was surprisingly permanent.[7] In most places the leagues went temporarily underground, to reappear five years later on a tidal wave of popular exasperation in the form of the 'League or Holy Union'. Except that it was a national affair, the great League had the same characteristics as the earlier ones.

The other type of association we need to investigate is the fraternity, or at least a particular type of fraternity. The wars of religion gave a very powerful second wind to a movement, if that is the word, which would otherwise probably have slackened during the sixteenth century. The motives for a revival of fraternal associations were clearly indigenous, the models were mainly Italian, occasionally Spanish; the principal mediator of Italian influence was the papal territory of Avignon. By comparison with older fraternities (or perhaps only with the condition that all such institutions, themselves included, were likely to get into in the

---

[6] Salmon, *Society in Crisis* pp. 208–211; E. le Roy Ladurie, *Carnival: a People's Uprising at Romans, 1579–80* (ET, London, 1980) esp. caps iv and v; Y-M. Bercé, *Fête et Révolte: des mentalités populaires du XVIe au XVIIIe siècle* (Paris 1976) whose interpretation of the Carnival of Romans (pp. 75–78) I find more attractive than Le Roy Ladurie's. *Lettres de Catherine de Médicis* 7 pp. 48, 51, 56.

[7] *Ibid.* pp. 97 seq, 104, 107, 144; Boutruche, *Bordeaux de 1453 à 1715* pp. 249 seq.

course of time), they did not embody the feeling that sociability *per se*, or the performance of a particular charitable work or works, was a sufficient reason for Christian association: they were not, in the traditional sense, 'charities'. They did not, at least in their early days, follow the tradition of organising an annual beanfeast or other convivial pleasures; some of them took a puritanical view of carnival and similar festivities, though others, like Henri III, did not.[8]

Their object was the general reform of the individual life, and the public demonstration of this reform, whence they were generally distinguished as 'pénitents', a term which points to their descent from the Italian flagellant fraternities of *disciplinati* and *battuti*. Their most striking characteristic was the wearing, when on the fraternity's occasions, of a white gown tied at the waist with a rope, and topped by a cowl with a sharp point on top and no opening, except two holes for the eyes: an inquisitorial outfit designed to express anonymity of the most visible kind, and a gift to cartoonists. Their main public performance was the procession, in principle two or three times a year on selected feast days, or *ad lib.* at times of crisis, which meant most times during the years of their foundation. As far as I can see their rules did not actually prescribe the performance of the discipline during processions or otherwise; but self-flagellation with a whip tucked into the rope round the waist at other times, seems to have been fairly common in the years of the League. Other forms of asceticism, like wearing no clothes under the gown or (especially) walking barefoot in processions, were standard practice: the Cardinal of Lorraine, who

---

[8] I have not yet been able to see the essential work of Marc Venard, 'Les confréries de Pénitents du XVIe siècle dans le province ecclésiastique d'Avignon', *Mémoires de l'Académie de Vaucluse*, 6ᵉ série 1 (1967), or his thesis, *L'Eglise d'Avignon au XVIe siècle*. Meanwhile I have drawn upon Philip Benedict, *Rouen during the Wars of Religion* (Cambridge 1981) pp. 190 seq, 246–47; A.L. Martin, *Henri III and the Jesuit Politicians* (Geneva 1973) pp. 60 seq, 86 seq (for Auger); and Philip T. Hofmann, *Church and Community in the Diocese of Lyon, 1500–1789* (New Haven/London 1984) pp. 38–40. Maurice Agulhon, *Pénitents et Franc-maçons de l'ancienne Provence* (Paris 1968), cap, iv, is a mine of relevant knowledge, though it is mainly about the eighteenth century.

did this in a spectacular procession attended by the king in Avignon in 1574, caught a cold and died.[9]

Besides these old-established features, they had two novel ones. First, their members made at entry a specifically Catholic confession of faith, beginning with the Nicene Creed and going on to a long and explicit affirmation of Catholic belief and practice on all controverted points. In the example I have seen it ended:

> I acknowledge and confess the Church of Rome to be the mother of all the churches, and that all supposed particular inspirations contrary to it are suggestions of the devil, prince of dissension, who seeks to disintegrate [séparer] the unity of the mystical body of the Saviour of the world ... I promise strictly to believe and keep all that has been determined and ordained by the holy catholic apostolic and Roman Church, and promise to God and to you [the rector] never to separate from it.

Secondly, they undertook the practice of frequent confession and communion. The rules of the royal congregation of penitents of Paris, which I have been quoting, required monthly communion, admittedly only for those who accepted the stricter of two rules. They also introduced into France the practice of public exposition of, and prayer before, the Sacrament over long periods of time. This was in principle an Italian novelty, though they usually adopted a naturalised version known as the 'oratoire', which entailed a permanent circulating exposition of the Host in parish churches in the larger towns (in Rouen a week each) with processions to carry it from one to the other. This may not sound penitential; yet a large element of expiation was involved, and of making up by adoration

---

[9] I have used as a model the readily accessible *Statuts de la Congrégation des Pénitents de l'Annonciation de Nostre Dame* (Paris 1583) repr. in L. Cimber and F. Danjou, *Archives curieuses de l'histoire de France*, 1ère série 10 (Paris 1836) pp. 435–59, evidently composed by Auger. This was a peculiar example in many ways, but its statutes seem fairly standard; cf., e.g., Hofmann, *Lyon* p. 38. It is worth noting that it had two rules, one laxer and one stricter; the former may be regarded as 'traditional', the latter as 'Counter-Reformation'.

for the dishonour vented upon the Host by Huguenots and others. This is indicated by the mounting of a guard over the Host at each station of the *oratoire*. Besides, apart from such forms of external penance as they might practice, they cultivated the sacrament of penance as much as the Eucharist: the stricter version of the Paris rule required, in addition to confession before the monthly communion, a fortnightly confession in the intervals 'even if communion do not follow'; it recommended a general confession of the whole of members' lives at entry, and a nightly examination of conscience. The cathedral chapter of Rouen covered the city with posters inviting the citizens to save themselves and their Church by penance: the sacrament, they said, 'transforms misery into happiness and changes us from children of wrath to beloved children of God, and in consequence renders us strong and powerful against our enemies'. Philip Benedict seems quite right to speak of the streets of Leaguer cities as 'theatres in which the inhabitants could act out their contrition as a way to avert political calamity', though one should not deduce from this that the contrition was not genuine and personal.[10]

From their origins in Avignon the penitent fraternities began to spread through south-eastern France in the 1560s. They were diffused in a northerly direction mainly by the efforts of the eccentric Jesuit Emond Auger, who brought them to Lyon, Toulouse and the towns of Burgundy during the 1570s. In the Lent of 1583 they made the leap to Paris under the patronage of the king, who invited Auger to come and found there the one already mentioned. For a while they made little progress in the north: a result of the unpopularity of the king, devotional conservatism, a feeling that such exercises were an excuse for failing to fight the Huguenots, and possibly some opposition from the bishops. But from the late 1580s, as the crisis in the state deepened, they were taken up with great enthusiasm in northern towns. In Rouen they were brought in from Spain by a pious merchant of Spanish origins, Jean de Quintanadoines, and will be of special interest to an English audience since they were launched from the convent church of the English émigré community of Bridgettine nuns, and one of them,

---

[10] Benedict, *Rouen* pp. 194, 201.

Elizabeth Sanders, sister of Nicholas, dictated a memorable description of them in 1589:

> The order of Penitents which was brought into this town to reform the people, the first beginning and assembly of it was in our chapel, all being confessed and communyd there upon St. Jerome's day was a twelvemonth [30 September 1588]. And the beginning with processions, upon Maundy Thursday at night to imitate the countries of Italy and Spain, was so disposed of, that it began in our house, from thence going to all the great churches in the town, all returning to our church again, the whole town and streets being in arms during the procession, and the soldiers guarding the procession home to our house ...

Shortly after the foundation, when Henri III had assassinated the Duke and Cardinal of Guise at Blois, the Jesuit Jacques Commolet gave a sensational sermon in the chapel on the highly appropriate feast of St. Thomas à Becket, 29 December 1588. In the summer, when Henri of Navarre came to besiege the town, 'the oratory was commanded to be in our house ... The fear was great, the enemy being at the walls, and infinite traitors within. The concourse of people to our house then was great, and their devotion marvellous, in so much as that (God be thanked) the tenth day after his coming he departed, with much more loss of his side than of ours.'[11]

In northern France the *pénitents* were banned after Henri's final victory, though the impulse continued to find expression in other forms. In the south they continued for another two centuries to provide much of the bony structure of Catholicism, and of social life in general.

Leagues and fraternities were different things, and at times there was hostility between them. Unless one were to take Luther's strict view, one may speak of them both as vehicles of Christianity, associations for the procurement of salvation. The difference was

---

[11] 'Narrative of Elizabeth Sanders', from Archives of the English College, Valladolid: series 2, L.5, no 13; Benedict, *Rouen* pp. 196, 201.

that the leagues proposed to procure salvation by fighting the enemy, the fraternities by fighting the self.

Still, as the state of affairs in Rouen suggests, in the final period of the League it became hard to make a distinction between them. They had had from the beginning a tendency to collapse into one another. Leagues, when looked at closely, are often hard to distinguish from fraternities of the traditional kind. The clergy of Troyes described the association they were joining as a 'ligue, société et fraternité', and themselves as receiving in return from their benevolent contribution the 'société, amitié et fraternité' of all its members. Local leagues in the countryside seem to have been fairly often identical with the *Confréries du Saint-Esprit*, historic institutions of communal sociability in the south; in the towns they were often based on craft-fraternities. Fraternities were behind the operations of the leaguers in Romans in 1580, and possibly behind those of their enemies as well.[12] Even where leagues were organised against something other than the Huguenots, they smacked strongly of the traditional fraternal ethos: its cult of solidarity, penchant for ritual, and pugnacity towards the world outside. On the other side we can find penitential movements whose origins seem very similar to those of the leagues. In the autumn of 1583 the diarist Pierre de l'Estoile noted the arrival in Paris of a series of processions from villages in the countryside, dressed in the manner of the *pénitents*, barefoot, as if on collective pilgrimage. They said they were the offshoot of a movement which had been set off by portentous happenings in the sky, started in the region of the Ardennes, and inspired thousands of countrypeople to make pilgrimages to Reims and other holy places. In doing their best to avert the wrath of God from France they had presumably the Protestants in mind, though they also spoke of plague.[13] Collective

---

[12] *Mémoires de Claude Haton* p. 1153; *Lettres de Catherine de Médicis* 1 p. 552 n. 1; Le Roy Ladurie, *Carnival* pp. 100, 179f; Hofmann, *Lyon* pp. 58–63. Pierre Duparc, 'Confréries du Saint-Esprit et communautés d'habitants au Moyen Age', *Revue historique de droit français et étranger*, 4ème série, 36 (1958) pp. 349–367, 555–585, is the fundamental account.

[13] *Journal de Pierre de l'Estoile: règne de Henri III* ed L.-R. Lefèvre (Paris 1943) pp. 336–7 (September, 1583). I am grateful to J.-L. Flandrin for pointing this passage out to me. Cf. *Mémoires de Claude Haton* pp. 926–28 (numerous pilgrimages, including to Compostela, c.1578); Davis, 'The Sacred and the Body Social in Sixteenth-Century Lyon' *PP* 90 (1981) p. 51.

or delegated pilgrimages seem to have been quite common: depending upon the form which the wrath of God seemed to be taking at the moment, a league or a penitential pilgrimage might seem to be alternative modes of action.

Hence it is not surprising that in the period of the great League, between the death of the Duke of Anjou in 1584 and the conversion of Henri of Navarre in 1593, the distinction between the two tended to disappear. In face of the prospect of a Protestant monarchy, the forces of exterior salvation and those of penitential propitiation were obliged to stand together. These were years of superleagues and superprocessions, the gun in one hand and the discipline in the other. In the sieges of leaguer towns which began in 1589, where hunger added to the general climate of hallucination, purifying the nation and purifying the self became practically the same thing. Indeed, with a glance at Mervyn James,[14] one may feel that the distinction between the self, the community, and the body of Christ in the Host had practically broken down. Naturally the moment did not last: as in the witch-craze, the search for rotten elements proved self-defeating, and earthly deliverers either mortal (like the Duke of Parma) or rotten elements themselves (like the Duke of Mayenne). But while it lasted it had been one of the most extraordinary occasions in French history, and French kings thereafter were wise not to risk a repetition of it.

I should like to spend the rest of my time enquiring what some relevant authorities, ecclesiastical or intellectual, made of all this; and in particular whether this amazing explosion of fraternity had any effect on their notion of Christianity, Catholicism, or the Church. Since Catholicism in France almost certainly owed its survival to these bodies of angry or pious people, you might have expected that the ecclesiastical authorities of the time would have made it their business to encourage them. You would have been wrong. The prelates and churchmen of the League were not totally absorbed in politics: from 1564 to 1590 they held a number of

---

[14] 'Ritual, Drama, and Social Body in the late Mediaeval English Town', *PP* 98 (1983) pp. 1–29.

provincial councils.[15] All of them had something to say about fraternities, most of them quite a lot. Nearly all of what they had to say was hostile.

Their chief preoccupation was the defence of parochial uniformity or integrity against what they saw as a powerful fissiparous and conflictual force. Thus the council of Rouen (1581), with particular reference to the traditional and powerful *charités* of Normandy:

> Though they were originally founded out of piety and devotion, fraternities and fellowships [*societates*] of charity, or under other names, oppress and deform the spiritual ministry of the Church, waste temporal goods, and send people out of their minds [*homines dementant*]. For in every church they erect and oppose altar against altar, sacrifice against sacrifice, priest against priest, and parish against parish.

They went on to concede, with some reluctance, that they ought not to be abolished, because of the good works they did, and because they had a part to play in times of plague and public calamity; but they insisted that they ought to be radically reformed. What reform amounted to was adopting the Tridentine discipline that fraternities ought not to be founded without episcopal licence, and that their rules, activities and funds should be subject to episcopal visitation and supervision. It also meant that their devotional and associative life should be brought within the compass of the parish, and not be allowed to divert Catholics from their primary obligation of parochial observance. The council of Rouen went beyond Trent in saying that, since the parish priest was responsible to God and the bishops for the conduct of his flock, it was he, and not another priest, who should decide what religious activities were to be undertaken by fraternities. All the councils banned fraternity masses during the time of parish Sunday or feast-day Mass, in chapels in the parish church or elsewhere;

---

[15] *Concilia novissima Galliae* ed L. Odespun de la Meschinière (Paris 1646) pp. 169 seq (Rouen, Cardinal Bourbon, 1581: fraternities at pp. 193, 195–6); 225 seq (Reims, Cardinal Guise, 1583: at pp. 229–30); 391 seq (Bourges, 1584: at p. 435); pp. 445 seq (Aix, 1585: at p. 492); pp. 509 seq (Toulouse, Cardinal Joyeuse, 1590: at pp. 536–7). There was also a council at Bordeaux in 1582–3 (*Ibid.* pp. 279 seq): as the *Histoire de Bordeaux* remarks (*Bordeaux de 1453 à 1715* p. 253), it was resolutely Borromean; it did not mention fraternities.

they affirmed that attendance at such masses did not meet the legal obligation. In particular they prohibited the blessing of bread and water by the priest at such masses. What the implications of a distribution of holy water at a fraternity mass would be I am not sure, but those of a consumption of *pain bénit* are obvious enough. Professor Scarisbrick has suggested that the reception of blessed bread was the most important ritual of communion in the everyday traditional mass;[16] the reason for stopping fraternities doing it was evidently to inhibit the fraternity mass from acting as the cement of a closed society alien to the parish community. The councils also said a good deal about other fraternity activities: fraternity feasts, 'either organised separately by brothers in turn or collectively at the expense of the fraternity', were, if not exactly banned, severely frowned on; they were not allowed in fraternity chapels or in connection with fraternity masses; if any officer made an allocution at a fraternity meeting, he was to stick to the virtues and vices and keep off theology; if they wanted a procession with the Sacrament, they would have to get written permission from the bishop; any money they collected above the needs of fraternity masses was to be devoted to pious works (which meant, to be spent under episcopal supervision).

No doubt a lot of this was pretty traditional, and pretty automatic: the picture it suggests of fraternal activities is certainly a traditional one. The interest of the statutes of the last of the series of councils, held in Toulouse in 1590 by François Cardinal de Joyeuse, is both that it was concerned with what was actually going on at the time, and that it was relatively sympathetic and did not simply regard fraternities as a nuisance. It made the usual noises about episcopal permission, supervision or suppression, and about not interfering with parish services; but it cut out the parish priest, and in bringing fraternity officers into direct relationship with the bishop implied that it was concerned to strengthen their authority (as in expelling unsatisfactory members), not to undermine it. Permission and inspection were specifically related to fraternities of *disciplinati* or *pénitents*, and several of their special activities received approval, or at least mention. Bishops were to

---

[16] J.J. Scarisbrick, *The Reformation and the English People* (Oxford 1984) p. 44; cf. Hofmann, *Lyon* pp. 56, 61.

encourage fraternity members to turn up at 'public supplications' — presumably oratories and processions — and might allow them, though *rarissime*, to do this at night, as we have seen being done at Rouen and as had in fact become widespread. Even the statute about preaching at fraternity meetings seems comparatively generous.

Altogether, the clergy of Languedoc showed a fair degree of appreciation of what at least the newer kind of fraternities were doing for the survival of Catholicism in France. They had one explicit piece of common ground in the doctrine of frequent confession and communion, which was propagated by most of the councils. At Toulouse the clergy invited fraternity members to communicate *saepissime*; at Reims they said that frequent communion was the best way to get rid of heresies and revive the apostolic church: people should communicate at least on feast days 'and whenever some pressing necessity, bringing human life into threat and danger, shall suggest'. A group of bishops meeting independently in Paris in 1586, to outline a practical scheme for putting into practice the ideal of episcopacy sketched at Trent, said that the bishop should preach frequent communion to his people. He should invite his whole flock to communicate *en masse* two or three times a year, especially at Carnival time, 'in which time especially the sons of men are prone to indulge in pleasure and luxury', and fraternity members more often, 'by which spiritual food the souls of the faithful will be refreshed and wonderfully inflamed toward Christian piety'.[17] Although they retained some feeling for the social dimension of sacramental rituals, whence their concern with *pain bénit*, their sacramental teaching seems either individualist, or where collectivist simply defensive against heresy or the flesh. They do not seem to have had much idea of the Eucharist as knitting together the body of Christ; and in general their acknowledgement of Catholic fraternity, as such, was extraordinarily tepid.

We may look for something more sympathetic from less official sources, and in particular from the religious orders, which were

---

[17] *Concilia novissima Galliae* pp. 232, 536; *Thesaurus novus anecdotorum* eds E. Martène and U. Durand (5 vols, Paris 1717) 4 cols 1191–1206, at col 1203.

more directly concerned with the promotion of associative Catholicism. In some of her essays Natalie Davis has shown such authorities of the period as the Jesuit Auger and the Franciscan Jean Benedicti expounding in their polemical or devotional writings a sacramental notion of alliance which their opponents could not quite match. So far as I can see (since the writings of Auger and his fellows are not easily available in England), this is fair, though I do not see that any of them offered a systematic exposure of the subject. If one looks at their discussions of the sacraments one will find something of the kind without too much difficulty. On marriage, for example, Auger expounded the fundamental Augustinian point about the incest barrier, the diffusion of charity by marriage, and the 'holy alliance of friendship and peaceful liaison' created among those between whom continence was required. Benedicti, starting from the same point, ended with a Christian version of the submission of childrens' choice of marriage partners to that of their parents which had been a strong theme of French civil thought on the subject. He held that there was a particular obligation of submission when the match was designed for the profit of the 'maison', as in making important alliances, extirpating heresies, and reconciling ancient enmities and quarrels between houses. 'This', he wrote, 'is because of the law of charity, which obliges everyone not to seek his private advantage, but the common good of all'. Professor Davis has pointed to their defence of the mass as performing a number of social functions, most of them posited upon the notion of a communication of spiritual goods which had been denied by reformers since Luther.[18] I would add that, although Auger was a main promoter of the practice of frequent communion, he does not seem to have lost a sense of the social dimension. His exposition of the implications of a corporal as well as spiritual eating of Christ in the Eucharist presented with some particularity the social reality of an organic communion

---

[18] Natalie Z. Davis, 'Ghosts, Kin and Progeny: some Features of Family Life in Early Modern France', *Daedalus* 106 no. 2 (1977) pp. 87–114 (at pp. 101–04); 'The Sacred and the Body Social' pp. 40–70 (at pp. 62–4, 66–7); J.-L. Flandrin, *Les amours paysannes (16e–20e siècles)* (Paris 1975) pp. 27 seq, 40 seq (Benedicti). In the edition of Benedicti which I have consulted, *La somme des pechez et le remede d'iceux* (Paris 2 éd. augmentée, 1595), I can only find (p. 93) a weaker version of the text quoted by Flandrin: had the original been expurgated?

between Christ and the believer, and of the believers among themselves, which was absent from the hierarchy's treatment of the subject.[19]

All this suggests a fairly clear consciousness of Christianity or Catholicism as a social system in what I would call the traditional sense. What it does not suggest, so far as my knowledge goes, is a feeling for the special position of fraternal institutions in this system, or any inkling of envisaging with their help a model of the Church alternative to the hierarchical model illustrated by Trent and the French councils. Perhaps I am being anachronistic in looking for such a model; perhaps, if it is to be found anywhere, late sixteenth-century Catholicism is not the place to look for it. In any event, the French Catholic clergy of the period do not seem to me to have produced one. About the monarchy, they were prepared to be amazingly radical; about the Church, they seem perfectly conventional. No doubt they were anxious not to rock the boat at a critical time; but this motive had not weighed much with them when they were legislating about fraternities.

If it is suggested that it was somehow impossible for people, or Frenchmen, or Catholics to think in this way during the late sixteenth century, I have to report that that is not true. Looming on the edge of our subject, meditating on the extraordinary history of contemporary France from the point of view of a secular lawyer and social philosopher, was the great figure of Jean Bodin. For English-speaking readers, partly because we have depended on a truncated version of the *Six Books of the Commonwealth*, Bodin has been the prophet of inviolable sovereignty and patriarchal *auctoritas* in the state and in the family. Absorbed more fully, he seems to have been saying something more complicated than this. Between the family and the *res publica*, in any commonwealth except the smallest and most primitive, existed a layer of associative bodies variously described as corporations, colleges, gilds, estates or communities. They originated in the expansion of the family beyond its domestic core and in the need for mutual defence; their characteristic was a condition of formal and mutual amity among the members, which Bodin identified as an outward extension of

---

[19] A. du Val, *Sommaire des heresies ... qui sont en la Cène des Calvinistes ... extrait des œuvres de M. Emond Auger* (Paris 1568) nos 6, 8, 20, 21.

family affection, though one might perhaps rather think of it as a new sentiment, the sentiment of fraternity. In a developed commonwealth the sentiment would be promoted, spontaneously by a cultivation of the forms and rituals of social alliance, or authoritatively by the prince. Thus the early princes and legislators of Israel, of the Greek cities and of Rome founded fraternal institutions, *philitia*, *sodalitia*, to replace a condition of conflict among their subjects by a condition of sworn friendship expressed in common eating and the amicable composition of disputes. Even though, in present conditions, such bodies might seem to be mere instruments of faction, conflict, sedition and conspiracy, a wise prince would not wish to abolish them, since they were the chosen vehicle of a fellowship and amity without which a commonwealth could not subsist. In affirming the need for 'unity, intercourse and friendship' for the subsistence of commonwealths, Bodin was not, could not have been, only talking politics. 'The sole end of *all* laws, divine *and* human, is to foster love among men and between men and God, and this is best secured by intercourse and daily association.' In a Christian commonwealth, law creates Christian sociability; conversely religion, or proper worship, provides the cement of the commonwealth. 'Nothing so tends to the preservation of commonwealths as religion', not just (as we have been inclined to assume) because it means reverence and obedience, but because it 'knits each and all in the bonds of friendship'. In Bodin's superb vision, at the end of the *République*, of the intelligently placed dinner as a model of harmonic diversity in the commonwealth and in the universe, we have another falling-together of the political and the sacramental. For 'the foundation of *all* the innumerable multitude of human societies consists in friendship.'[20]

My object is not to present Bodin as the missing ideologist of the League, or as the inventor of an alternative model of the Church inspired by the principle of collegial fraternity. I am not sure that the word 'church' appears in the *Six Livres*. One could of course

---

[20] Jean Bodin, *Six Books of the Commonwealth* abridged, trans and ed M.J. Tooley (Oxford n.d.) pp. 96–107 (Book iii, chap 7), supplemented by *De Republica libri sex* (Lyon/Paris 1586) p. 749. This passage, from Book vi, chap 6, not given by Tooley, is quoted in full in P. Mesnard, *L'essor de la philosophie politique au XVIe siècle* (3 ed Paris 1977) pp. 545–6.

suppose that for Bodin, as for Hooker, the Church and the Commonwealth were the same thing, but it would seem artificial to do so. His principles would seem to imply a degree of approval towards Catholic leagues, and so would his practice: he was, after all, spokesman for the Third Estate at the States-General of 1576 which they dominated, and towards the end of his life a prudently subscribing member. He must also have approved of traditional fraternities, though I am not so clear that he approved of the *pénitents*. He made a number of hostile comments about Anabaptists: first, for erroneously attempting to promote amity and mutual concord by instituting community of property; and second by practising secret rites, something not tolerated in well regulated commonwealths.[21] The first point would not have worried the *pénitents*, rather the reverse; the second might have done, though in truth it would have been more relevant to the seventeenth-century *Compagnie du Saint-Sacrement* than to them.

My aim is to persuade you, and indeed myself, that if we look for any sort of collegial model of the Church in late sixteenth-century French Catholicism we are not looking for an absolute chimaera, but for something which might have been there, and was not. Since it was possible to envisage a collegial model of the state — possible not only to Bodin, but more radically to his Calvinist disciple Johannes Althusius — it must have been possible to envisage a model of the Church as, in Althusius's term, a 'consociatio symbiotica': what Archbishop Laud more pithily described as 'all fellows in the Church'.[22] Of the reasons why it was not envisaged, some seem to me to arise out of the immediate context of the struggle with Protestantism for the soul of France: an obscure feeling, almost certainly incorrect, that 'democracy' was a characteristic of Protestant versions of the Church and, less incorrect, that anything resembling a priesthood of all believers must entail the violation of holy persons and things which was being practised by the Huguenots. Catholics who had banded together in defence of what they thought holy were bound to be sensitive to accusations of profaning the sanctuary themselves. Other reasons seem intrinsic to the history of Catholicism, though

---

[21] *Six Books of the Commonwealth* pp. 8, 105–6.
[22] Mesnard, *L'essor de la philosophie politique* pp. 567–616, esp p. 578.

they were given more or less of a fillip by the immediate religious conflict. Among these I would place the decay of conciliarism, and the revivification of hierarchical claims and responsibilities, papal, episcopal and parochial, by the Council of Trent. Here I would also place what I am inclined to regard as the most fundamental reason of all: the long-term transformation, in the consciousness of lay Catholics, of the notion of a sacrament, or perhaps only of the sacraments of penance and the Eucharist, from a ritual of Christian sociability to a privileged occasion for the transmission of substantive grace to the individual soul. In so far as the fraternities of the League were vehicles of this transformation, I am sure they were, as historians are beginning to recognise, an essential instrument for the revitalisation of French Catholicism in the seventeenth century. By the same token, I do not think they could, despite their collegial form, serve as the model or nucleus of a collegial conception of the Catholic Church. Some may think, with Luther, that that was just as well.

University of York

'A GRACELESSE, AND AUDACIOUS COMPANIE'?[1]
THE FAMILY OF LOVE IN THE PARISH OF BALSHAM, 1550–1630

by CHRISTOPHER MARSH

THE doctrine and membership of the Family of Love in England remain something of a mystery, despite extensive recent work.[2] Why should such an apparently small group have been the specific subject of a royal proclamation?[3] Between June 1575 and November 1580 the sect was referred to a dozen times in Privy Council correspondence, and was clearly the object of considerable anxiety. The Bishops of London, Norwich, Exeter, Ely, Winchester, Lincoln, Salisbury and Worcester were all instructed to conduct investigations.[4] Puritan writers like John Rogers[5] and William Wilkinson[6] published books attacking the sect. The reasons for such sustained persecution over so short a period are hard to establish. One fact which must have contributed to the panic was that there were Familists in the Queen's guard, close to the centre of the political nation.[7] Moreover, reports of the sect in each of the dioceses listed above had presumably been received. It is likely that the Family of Love was much larger

---

[1] Anon, *A Supplication of the Family of Love said to be presented into the King's royall hands* (Cambridge 1606).
[2] Alastair Hamilton, *The Family of Love* (Cambridge 1981); Felicity Heal, 'The Family of Love and the diocese of Ely, Schism, Heresy and Religious Protest' *SCH* 9 (Cambridge 1972) pp. 213–222. Also Margaret Spufford, 'The quest for the heretical laity in the visitation records of Ely in the late sixteenth and early seventeenth centuries' *ibid*. pp. 223–230.
[3] Frederick A. Youngs, *Proclamations of the Tudor Queens* (Cambridge 1976) pp. 212–3.
[4] *APC* 11 pp. 139, 444; 12 pp. 231–2, 317–8.
[5] J. Rogers, *The Displayinge of an Horrible Secte ... naming themselves the Family of Love* (London 1578).
[6] W. Wilkinson, *A Confutation of Certaine Articles Delivered by (H. Nicklaes) unto the Family of Love* (London 1579).
[7] *APC* 10 pp. 332, 344.

191

than the surviving evidence reveals. Familism, as the proclamation suggests, was also thought to involve the threat of social revolution. In a series of letters which Rogers later published,[8] one Familist writer stated that

> I had rather heare an honest poore mans report truly spoken, than a rich credible mans that is a lyer

and quoted Scripture to emphasize the point: 'The Lorde preferueth the simple.' Views like this were dangerously disrespectful, and implied social insubordination.

Such matters were of less concern to Rogers and Wilkinson than the heretical nature of Familist doctrine. Heresy was to be eradicated simply because it was heresy, and not primarily because it implicitly threatened the social structure.

Despite their priorities, Rogers and Wilkinson did make passing attempts to classify the sect's following in terms of social and economic position. Both seem to have believed that the Family of Love's greatest appeal was to the 'poore and simple,' who did not know any better. Rogers, however, knew that the matter was not quite so straightforward. In another of the letters he received a Familist correspondent, rather than refute the claims, admitted that the sect was made up of 'simple men, who can scarcely read English'. In the light of this admission, Rogers reversed the direction of his attack, and argued that many Familists were by no means poor, 'yet to help their weaknesse you call them simple men.'

Such inconsistency urges great caution in interpreting the heated statements of contemporary critics. To call one's enemies poor and simple was to say that they were misguided, uneducated and consequently of little significance except to those who, like oneself, had their best interests at heart. Robert Burton was particularly blunt when, in 1620, he asked 'What are all our Anabaptists, Brownists, Barrowists, Familists, but a company of rude, illiterate, capricious, base fellows?'[9]

Once it was realized that Familists had no violent objections to being called poor and simple, the sect's critics had cause to review

[8] J. Rogers, *The Displayinge* (2 ed London 1579).
[9] Quoted by Julia G. Ebel, 'The Family of Love: Sources of its history in England' *Huntingdon Library Quarterly* 30 (San Marino, California 1967) pp. 336–7.

their tactics. In 1606, a Familist writer claimed that 'We are a people but fewe in number, and yet most of us very poore in worldly wealth.' His unnamed examiner replied that, if the list of members contained in Henry Niclaes's 'Book of Life' could be seen, 'it would appeare, I doubt not, that both the number of them is great, and most of them very rich'.[10]

The current debate over the social and economic status of sixteenth- and seventeenth-century dissenters has given such evidence an additional importance. 'Contrasting communities' have produced contrasting findings. Dr. Margaret Spufford found, in her study of dissent in Cambridgeshire, that the parish of Orwell contained dissenters on all levels of local society, whereas in Willingham dissent was concentrated within the community's wealthier sort. In Cottenham too, dissenters were disproportionately prosperous. The Quakers in Swavesey, however, were predominantly poor. The overall conclusion was that

> dissenting opinions were not confined to the 'wealthy' by village standards, but could also be held by the very poor, even though they made more appeal to the 'wealthy' than the 'poor' in Willingham.[11]

The work of Keith Wrightson and David Levine on the Essex village of Terling produced rather different arguments. The chief impact of puritanism was here felt among the wealthier people in the parish.

The labouring poor were markedly underrepresented in the distribution of non-conformity, which was essentially an affair of the middling sort. In order to explain this, it was suggested that

> Perhaps the matter of the best road to salvation in the next world exercised only a limited appeal over the imagination of those hardest put to keep body and soul together on earth.[12]

It could equally well be argued, however, that those 'hardest put to keep body and soul together' had a greater need for the comfort and hope that religion could bring them. A recent appeal has been

[10] See n. 1.
[11] Margaret Spufford, *Contrasting Communities* (Cambridge 1974) p. 306.
[12] Keith Wrightson and David Levine, *Poverty and Piety in an English Village, Terling, 1525–1700* (London 1979) pp. 166–7.

made for the detailed investigation of the social and economic background of various types of religious radicals throughout the sixteenth and seventeenth centuries.[13] A start has been made with the social spread of the Lollards.[14]

This paper will attempt to set Cambridgeshire Familism in its social and economic context in the single village of Balsham. I shall consider not only the material prosperity of members but their social position within the parish and the manner in which Familist doctrine became established in the area. I hope, later, to present similar evidence for other communities and to expand upon this small contribution to the wider debate.

It would seem at first sight that the available sources had all been fully used. However, the chief list of members contained in Bishop Cox's letter book, omitted some forty-six names, the majority of those investigated in 1580.[15] Some of these missing Familists were certainly from Balsham. I have attempted to retrieve as many of the names as possible by examining the witnesses to wills of known Familists already used by Dr. Heal.[16] Following her example, I traced the wills of these witnesses, where possible, and discovered some that had not previously been studied.[17] These wills were themselves frequently witnessed by other known or suspected Familists, a fact which gave additional credence to the identification of testators as fellow members of the sect.[18] Several of the close relatives of Familists, particularly their fathers and brothers, also

---

[13] Margaret Spufford, 'Puritanism and Social Control?' *Order and Disorder in Early Modern England* eds Anthony Fletcher and John Stevenson (Cambridge 1985) pp. 44–7.

[14] Derek Plumb, 'The Social and Economic Spread of Lollardy: A Reappraisal', see above pp. 111–29.

[15] Cambridge, Gonville and Caius College MS 53/30, fols 72v–3r.

[16] Cambridge University Archives, Ely Consistory Court Will Registers: Bartholomew Tassell (1577), William Cornell (1584), Leonard Dirgeon (1591), John Diss (1596), Henry Marsh (1609), John Taylor (1623).

[17] Camb. Univ. Arch, Ely Cons Court Will Reg: William Lorkin (1597), William Symond (1620). Probable Familists for whom no wills survive were George Woolward, John Smith and John Hasell.

[18] As a rule, I have regarded as additional probable Familists only those witnesses whose names appear twice or more in the wills of other members, or whose own wills are witnessed by two or more definite members.

left wills, which had not been examined before.[19] A number of new members were identified in this way. I have, in addition, read the wills of known Familists from other parishes in the diocese.[20] The same process was followed in identifying new members.[21]

Further, the wills of some members in Balsham and the rest of the Ely diocese have been found in the Prerogative Court of Canterbury,[22] where wills of several Familists from places outside the diocese, including that of William Raven from St. Ives, mentioned by William Wilkinson but never before associated with the Family of Love, also survive.[23] The lay subsidy rolls from 1563 and 1599 contain valuable information on the economic prosperity of Balsham Familists relative to other villagers.[24] The Balsham parish registers were used in order to establish the relationships of Familists to one another, and to other inhabitants of the parish.[25] The visitation records for the period added to the picture by demonstrating that members of the sect held parochial office as churchwardens and questmen,[26] just as convinced puritans later did.[27] They do not seem to have been indifferent to organized religion.

Unfortunately, it is not possible here to undertake an analysis of Familist doctrine. The subject has been thoroughly dealt with by Alastair Hamilton, and discussion in this paper will be restricted to two pieces of intriguing new evidence that have only just come

[19] Camb Univ Arch, Ely Cons Court Will Reg: Richard Cornell (1544), John Taylor (1550), Richard Marsh (1557), Thomas Dirgeon (1558), Richard Rule (1558), William Lawrence (1558), Thomas Diss (1558), Marion Marsh (1560), Robert Diss (1564), John Lawrence (1567), John Rule (1567), John Tassell (1570), William Lawrence (1570), John Smith (1576), Elizabeth Rule (1578), Richard Marsh (1583), John Durgeon (1596).

[20] Camb Univ Arch, Ely Cons Court Will Reg: John Bourn (1593), Thomas Hockley (1601), Thomas Pierson (1613), John Essex (1616).

[21] Camb Univ Arch, Ely Cons Court Will Reg: Henry Barnard (1600).

[22] PCC: Thomas Bridge (1590), Thomas Lawrence (1609), Thomas Diss (1614).

[23] PCC: Lewes Steward (1593), William Raven (1598), John Frend (1608). The wills listed in notes 14–21 form the backbone of this paper. Because they are mentioned so frequently, I will not subsequently repeat the references. The testators' names alone will be adequate for identification.

[24] PRO, E179 82/244; E179 83/307.

[25] Typed transcripts of the Balsham parish registers are available at the Cambridgeshire County Record Office.

[26] Cambridge University Library, Ely Diocesan Records B/2/8, B/2/28.

[27] Spufford, *Contrasting Communities* pp. 268–70.

to light. The first of these concerns the early spread of Familist doctrine. Most of the contemporary critics believe Familism to have begun its spread in England during the 1550s. It was in 1555 that Henry Orinel, a husbandman from Willingham, travelled to Colchester, being anxious 'that my conscience should not be entangled with the Popish pitch.' The story, recited by Wilkinson, is well known:[28] in a tavern, Orinel encountered Christopher Vitells, the foremost disciple of Niclaes in England. It is not certain that Vitells was, at this date, deeply involved with Familist doctrine, but his reference to the man 'who lived beyond the seas in an holy life' seems to imply that he was already committed, if not yet extremely knowledgeable.

We are told also that Vitells later visited Willingham in Cambridgeshire and summoned the husbandmen 'to come and speake with him at an Alehouse'. Orinel, having been thoroughly confused following Vitells' performance in Colchester, preferred not to go and 'sent him word that I would not come at hym nor have to doe with him.'

It seems that Vitells must have noted the names and home towns of those whom he met on his tour of East Anglian inns and alehouses. Attention has hitherto been focussed exclusively upon Orinel and Vitells, and the presence of 'William Raven of St. Ives' at the Colchester meeting has been overlooked. Orinel's bedfellow, 'having likewise fled beying in danger for Religion,' has proved well worth investigating. Raven's will, written in 1598, contains evidence to show that he too was pursued by Vitells. And where Orinel refused to meet his visitor, William Raven was apparently converted to Familism. He leaves twenty pounds to his 'loving frende' Robert Seal of London, 'gent', in recognition of 'divers friendshipps' received at his hands. Seal was one of the yeomen of the guard repeatedly suspected of belonging to the Family.[29] Furthermore, Raven leaves a bequest to, and names as his executor, Thomas Hockley of Clayhithe in Horningsea, who was arrested in 1580, and the will is witnessed by William Bridge, probably the Shudy Camps Familist also imprisoned in the 1580 investigations.[30] Such notorious connections prove beyond all

---

[28] W. Wilkinson, A Confutation.
[29] APC 10 p. 332.
[30] Gon. and Caius Coll MS 53/30, fol 73r.

doubt that William Raven had become a member of the Family of Love.

The Raven evidence casts additional light on the missionary practice of Christopher Vitells. Not only did he pursue the tenuous connection established with Orinel, but he listed the names of others present in Colchester and probably followed up more than two contacts. The Colchester episode seems also to tell us something about the background from which potential Familists came. Raven and Orinel were both present because they were troubled protestants living under a Catholic regime. If they were representative, then attempts by Wilkinson and Rogers to identify Familism with popery fall far short of the truth.

Close study of the Balsham group also reveals clues to indicate that the seedbed for Familist belief was to be found among convinced protestants in the mid-sixteenth century. It is probable that someone from Balsham came into contact with Vitells, or some other elder of the Family, in much the same way as did William Raven. Wilkinson tells us that Vitells stayed with one 'W.H. of B'; quite possibly he is referring to Balsham. It is also possible that there was a conventicle of committed protestants meeting in Balsham, or nearby, in the years preceding Vitells' visit.[31] In a will made in 1550, John Taylor (father of the member arrested in 1580) named as executors Thomas Dys, his brother-in-law, and William Cornell. As witnesses, Thomas Baker and Robert Simonde were present. Without exception the surnames given here were closely linked with the Family of Love thirty years later. These men seem to have been operating as a group within the Balsham community well before Vitells arrived on the scene. That the families involved were associating closely as early as 1550 quite possibly implies shared religious beliefs. Moreover, the next generation adopted heretical religious ideas and the tendency towards such ideas was probably inherited from the parental group. Although nothing can be proved at this stage it does seem plausible to argue that a group of protestants was operating in Balsham under Mary, and prior to the arrival of Familism. If and when Vitells visited Balsham, these

---

[31] I am extremely grateful to Dr. Claire Cross for suggesting to me that the Cambridgeshire Familists could have been connected with Henry Hart and the Free-willers, who were operating in Kent and Essex at this time. Further work is needed, though as yet no link has been established.

would have been the people most interested in dissenting religious doctrine, and the evidence shows conclusively that he successfully converted them.

The second piece of new evidence centres around an inscription which appears on one of the bells in Balsham parish church.[32] Early in the seventeenth century, two of the bells were recast into four, one of which bears the Latin inscription 'non sono *subamina* mortuorun sed *subirua* viventium' and the date 1609. The words are meaningless, until those in italics are read backwards. The translation then runs 'I sound not for the souls of the dead but for the ears of the living.' Two of the other bells, also dated 1609, carry far less interesting inscriptions: 'God save the King' and 'God save thy church.' The latter of these bells also displays the names George Wolard, John Lense and William Taylor. Two of these men were connected to the Family of Love: Wolard or Woolward, had been named, alongside definite Familist John Tailer, as supervisor to the will of Leonard Dirgeon in 1591; and William Tailer, son of John, was actually presented by the 1609 visitation as belonging to the Family, together with his father and Edmund Rule. The Latin inscription then is closely linked with known Familists, and it is possible to see the message not merely as evidence of puritanism, but as a direct reflection of the Family's disbelief in a literal afterlife. If this was the case, then the members were characteristically anxious to disguise their doctrine.

Evidence contained in the wills suggests that Familist belief held its strongest appeal, not for the poor and simple, as John Rogers argued, but for the wealthier members of rural society. The group of men converted to Familism in the 1550s were comfortably provided for both in terms of land-holding and 'worldly goods.' In most cases, a period of some years elapsed between the time of involvement and the date at which a will was written and an individual's economic and social standing could have changed considerably during the interval. However, the majority of Balsham Familists had remained within the parish, and it is probable that their wealth at death was firmly rooted in their inheritance from the previous generation. Men like Henry Marsh followed their

32 My information in this section is taken from the historical notes available in Balsham parish church.

fathers into farming, worked the same land, and passed it on again at the ends of their lives. They were not likely to have undergone any radical transformation in status. Thomas Lawrence died a comfortable yeoman in 1609 and had enjoyed the same status for decades. In 1558, his father William had bequeathed the recently purchased manor of Oxcroft to Thomas and his brother. One prominent Familist at least had not had to claw his way up from the depths of poverty.

From a total of eleven wills that include detailed information on land-holding, seven bequeathed whole yardlands with additional small acreages. One man, Leonard Dirgeon, left a half yardland, also with extras, and another, John Lawrence, held the equivalent of three full yardlands. Within the group, Henry Marsh was fairly typical, bequeathing a whole yardland, a small parcel of waste and 'all my saffron grownds.'

The material possessions listed in Familist wills give the same impression of relative prosperity. Richard Marsh, making his will in 1583, bequeaths many household items, amongst which are found six pewter dishes and two pewter platters. Despite William Harrison's observation that pewter was becoming more common at this time,[33] it almost certainly remained something of a novelty in rural homes. Ten years earlier, William Tassell was still more impressive in leaving 'the cubbard in the hall withall the pewter which useth commonly to be sette upon it.' Harrison also recorded a change in bedding that had taken place during the lifetimes of the older villagers. The previous generation had lain on straw pallets or rough mats, beneath coarse, shaggy coverlets 'with a good round log under their heads instead of a boulster or pillow.' Pillows, in fact, were reserved for women 'in childbed.' Servants had been especially uncomfortable: 'if they had any sheet above them it was well, for seldom had they any under their bodies to keep them from the pricking straws that ran oft through the canvas of the pallet and rased their hardened hides.'

It becomes easier to understand why sixteenth century testators were frequently so precise in bequeathing their bedding. Harrison was presumably exaggerating the changes and it is probable that,

[33] William Harrison, *The Description of England* ed George Edelen (New York 1968) pp. 200–02.

in the late sixteenth century, items like feather beds, linen sheets and joint beds[34] retained a certain prestige value in small agricultural communities. Along with his pewter, Richard Marsh left 'A ioyned beddstedd' and his brother, Henry, bequeathed a feather bed. John Taylor, justifiably proud of his 'hutch of wallnutt tree', was particularly exact in describing his bedding. Taylor's will, written in 1616, shows that the novelty of superior sheets retained some importance. Being approximately eighty at the time, he was clearly old enough to remember the days of 'pricking straws' and 'hardened hides'. Perhaps recalling the 'good round log' he had rested his head upon as a young man, Taylor leaves 'a paire of pillowes' to Margaret his wife. He also mentions two 'flexen pillowbeares' or linen pillowcases. Half of his sheets are of the same material, the others being of 'towinge', a much coarser cloth.

The wills of Balsham Familists suggest that members of the sect were more wealthy than the average villager and analysis of two Elizabethan lay subsidy rolls makes this clearer still (see Tables I and II). There is unfortunately no useful roll for the decade 1570–80.[35] Of those that include names, the closest in time to the period of persecution date from 1563 and 1599.[36] By the later sixteenth century, lay subsidies were only likely to affect the wealthiest section of village society, and the sums at which individuals were valued are relative only; most were probably worth approximately seven times as much.[37]

Bishop Cox estimated that, in 1563, Balsham was made up of eighty households. The twenty names on the first roll therefore represent the parish's upper quarter. In 1599, seven more people were taxed but the proportion of the whole village whose names appeared probably remains roughly the same.

From the earlier roll it is clear that, as their wills suggest, Familism in Balsham drew a striking number of its adherents from the wealthier end of village society. Ten of the twenty men taxed were connected with the Family of Love, and nine of these ten

---

[34] Joint beds were more ornamental and valuable than those made by carpenters.

[35] Most of the Elizabethan subsidies for the Radfield hundred, in which Balsham was situated, recorded only the total sums collected. The 1598 roll includes names, but the list is very faded.

[36] See n. 22 for references.

[37] I am extremely grateful to Dr. Roger Schofield for advising me on this section.

The Family of Love

Table I. Taxable Inhabitants of Balsham: Wealth Distribution in 1563 Lay Subsidy.

Valued at:	£0 £1 £2 £3 £4 £5 £6 £7 £8	
John Woolward	· · · · · · · · · · · ·›	h. in g
Robert Smith	· · · · · · · ·›	l. in l.
William Tassell	─────────────────→	h. in g.
Leonard Woolward	─ ─ ─ ─ ─ ─ ─ ─ ─ ─ ─ ─ ─ →	h. in g.
John Lawrence	───────────────→	h. in g.
William Cornell	────────────→	h. in g.
Thomas Lawrence	─────────→	h. in ld.
William Lawrence	─────────→	singleman in ld.
Edmond Rewle	──────→	h. in ld.
John Tassell	· · · · · · · · · · · ·›	h. in g.
John Cowell	· · · · ·›	l. in ld.
Richard Marsh	───────────────→	h. in g.
John Perne	· · · · · · · · · · · ·›	h. in ld.
Robert Thurgar	· · · · · · · · · · · ·›	h. in g.
John Sters	· · · · · · · ·›	h. in ld.
John Ryche	· · · · · · · · · ·›	l. in ld.
John Rewle	──────→	maester in ld.
William Freman	· · · · · · · · · · · ·›	h. in g.
John Smyth	──────→	h. in ld.
John Smyth	· · · · · · · · · · · ·›	l. in g.

KEY: Probable member of Family of Love ───────────────→
Possible sympathiser ─ ─ ─ ─ ─ ─ ─ ─ ─ ─ →
Not connected with Family of Love ·›
h. = husbandman; g. = goods;
l. = labourer; ld. = lands

Table II. Taxable Inhabitants of Balsham: Wealth Distribution in 1599 Lay Subsidy.

Valued at:	£0	£1	£2	£3	£4	£5	£6	£7	£8	
Thomas Sutton	· ›							(035)		'esq. in terr.'
Richard Hasill	· ›							(£19)		'in bon'
John Linzell	· · · · · · · · · · · · · · · ›									'in terr'
Thomas Lawrence Sen.	———————→									'in terr'
Richard Tassell	· · · · · · · · · · · · ›									'in bon'
Thomas Ballard	· ›									'in bon'
Edmund Rule	——————→									'in terr'
Thomas Teversham	– – – – – →									'in terr'
George Woolward	——→									'in terr'
John Smith Sen	———————→									'in terr'
John Moorden	· · · · · · · ›									'in terr'
Thomas Webbe	– – – – →									'in terr'
John Grigge	· · · · · · · · ›									'in terr'
Alice Larkin	———————→									'vids in terr'
Alex Appleyeard	· · · · · · · · · ›									'in terr'
Richard Mershe	——→									'in terr'
Mathewe Ster	– – – –→									'in terr'
John Smith Jun.	——→									'in terr'
Thomas Smith Jun.	· · · · · ›									'in terr'
William Simond	——→									'in terr'
John Sterr	– — →									'in terr'
Thomas Smith Sen.	· · · · · ›									'in terr'
Richard Ballard	· · · · · · · · · · · · · ›									'in bon'
William Tayler	· ›									'in bon'
Thomas Barker	· · · · · · · · · · · · ›									'in bon'
William Smith	· · · · · · · · · · · · ›									'in bon'
Thomas Lawrence Jun.	· · · · · · · · · ›									'in terr'

Key: Probable member of Family of Love ———————→
Possible sympathiser – – – – – – – — →
Not connected with Family of Love · · · · · · · · · · · · · · · · · · ›
esq. = esquire; terr. = lands;
bon. = goods; vids = widow

were very strongly associated. Moreover, within the quarter of householders taxed, the Familists distribute conclusively towards the top end. Five of them were assessed at a value higher than that of the first householder without a Familist connection. Even within Balsham's wealthiest quarter, the sect's early adherents stood well above the average.

There were, in addition, a small number of Familists who were not taxed in 1563 but were sufficiently well-established to be heads of households by this date. Thomas Diss married in 1563, and his father had died three years earlier. John Taylor was witnessing wills in 1558, and his father had made a will in 1550. Leonard Dirgeon had a son in 1564, and although this does not prove that he was already a householder, the fact that no Dirgeons appear on either rolls suggests that possibly the family was not wealthy enough to be taxed. Similarly, William Simond had married in 1560, and was not taxed in 1563. These four men were, then, probably less wealthy than the ten Familists taxed in the first of the two subsidies, but their wills show that they were at least comfortable. Dirgeon farmed more than half a yardland in 1591, and Simond was taxed in 1599. Taylor bequeathed nearly sixty pounds as well as a long list of household goods. His son William was farming the equivalent of almost two yardlands in the early 1620s.

Three further members were not taxed, but Bartholomew Tassell's father is on the roll, as are the brothers of Henry Marsh and John Lawrence. Clearly, their background was in Balsham's wealthier section, and their future too. All three held more than a whole yardland when they made their wills.

The position in 1563 corresponds closely with the impression given by the wills of known and suspected members. Of fourteen Familists who were sufficiently well established to be heads of households in 1563, no fewer than ten were taxed. The men whose names do not appear were not substantially less wealthy and may well have been taxed in one of the several subsidies collected between 1563 and 1599, which recorded no names.

The second roll presents a similar picture, though Familists no longer fill the top positions, and the proportion of the total number taxed who were also connected to the Family has fallen slightly. Despite the deaths of several prominent members in the 1580s and

1590s, however, the number of people connected with Familism has risen by two. The older members appear to have been passing their beliefs on to the next generation. The Richard Marsh who was taxed in 1599 was, for example, the son of the man who appeared on the earlier roll. Both had strong links with the Family of Love. In 1599, John Taylor was the only Familist old enough to be the head of a household who was not taxed. He may perhaps have settled his land already. The William Taylor who appears towards the bottom of the list may have been John's son, but the parish registers reveal the existence of a second William Taylor, who died in 1600. Because of the doubt, the tax-collector's victim has been treated as a non-Familist. Once again, the firm conclusion must be that the doctrine of the Family of Love appealed to the wealthier members of the Balsham community.

There is little to indicate that the heretical nature of their beliefs precluded Balsham Familists from the parochial offices to which their position entitled them. 'Being of the Family of Love' was not, apparently, something that caused any great offence within the community. If the men who so worried the Privy Council desired to serve in local church offices, there seems to have been nothing to prevent them. The 1573 Visitation Book recorded the names of Balsham's church officers, including as questmen John Taylor and Henry Marshe.[38] The former put his name to the 'confession' of 1574, and both men were arrested as members of the Family six years later. In 1576, questmen included William Symond and Leonard Dirgeon.[39]

Generally non-Familist church officers were willing to co-operate with the followers of Niclaes in the conduct of parish business, but the visitation of 1609 was an exception in this respect.[40] Three men — Edmund Rule, John Taylor the elder and his son, William — were 'named uppon a comon fame to be of the familye of Love.' We are told further 'that the sayd Edmund Rule and John Tayler thelder are ould men of the age of Lxx yeres apeece, and that Edmund Rule is nowe blynde, and Willm [should be John] Tayloure thelder is deaff and cannot here.' It is not easy to see why two old men, one deaf and one blind, should have been

---

[38] Camb Univ Lib, EDR, B/2/8.
[39] Camb Univ Lib, EDR, B/2/8.
[40] Camb Univ Lib, EDR, B/2/28.

presented after decades of visitations had ignored their beliefs. John Taylor (or possibly his son of the same name) had been a warden only two years previously. We can only speculate as to the reasons for the sudden hostility of the other wardens. One of them, Thomas Teversham, later witnessed Taylor's will, and another, William Rule, was himself presented 'for refuseing to sett his hand to the presentments aforesayd.' In other words, he refused to turn against his aged father.

Another item in the 1609 Visitation book orders that the second church bell be taken down and mended. As we have seen, the repair and remoulding that took place ended with one of the bells being inscribed with the name of William Taylor, the same man who had just been presented as a Familist. The whole episode must, for the time being, remain shrouded in mystery. What is clear however is that a proportion of the parochial offices were in the hands of Familists and sympathizers. A similar picture emerges in Shudy Camps and Wisbech, two other centres of Cambridgeshire Familism. With known members of the sect responsible for presenting non-conformists, it is hardly surprising that the Family of Love was so seldom mentioned at visitation.

The Balsham members were then deeply involved in local religious life. The concern for the poor displayed in the wills of many is further evidence that they did not consider themselves an isolated, mysterious group. This impression is reinforced by the wills of Familists from other communities. William Raven of St. Ives made his will in 1598, leaving two pounds to the town's poor, with elaborate instructions relating to the distribution of the money.

> I will that there shalbe fortie poore boyes in the towne of Saint Ives to goe orderlie Two and Two together before my corpes to the buriall thereof And likewise Forty poore wenches to goe in like mannar after my said corpes to the buriall thereof and to have each of them two pence.

The remainder of Raven's two pounds is to be 'distributed amongst the poore of Saint Ives.' In order to call for such treatment, Raven must have been an important figure within his community. It was not the gesture of a man isolated from local society. He cared about the town's poor people and, moreover, he wanted it to be seen that he cared.

In the evidence so far studied, there is nothing to substantiate the allegation, made in the Surrey confession of 1561, that Familists believed 'that they are bound to give alms to none other persons but to those of their sect: and if they do, they give their almes to the divel.'[41] Instead, members of the sect frequently left money to the poor people of their communities, and served regularly in local offices. It was in fact only in the selection of witnesses to wills that the Family appears to have been almost exclusively insular. Testators called to their deathbeds those friends with whom they shared religious beliefs. In a group of committed Christians, this is surely no more than one would expect.

In their marriages too Familists tended towards coreligionists. Little is known of Henry Marsh's first wife, but following her death he married Edmund Rule's sister, who herself died within months. Less than two years later, Henry married again, this time to the daughter of John Taylor. All three men were imprisoned in 1580. Nor is this an isolated example. In the period 1558–1630 Familist surnames came together in marriage more than twice as frequently as did the surnames in a comparable sample of non-Familists.[42] However, marriage within the sect was not a sacred rule. There were many marriages between Familists and apparent non-Familists. Despite the sect's cohesiveness it is clear that Balsham Familists were respected and integrated members of local society.

Extensive discussion of relations between Balsham members and Familists elsewhere is beyond the scope of this paper. The wills and parish registers both contain abundant evidence to show that communications, even across large distances, were good. William Bridge of Shudy Camps, for example, was clearly a very important figure within the Family. Arrested in 1580, he was closely involved with other Familists twenty years later. His presence at a will-making was highly valued: he witnessed wills in St. Ives and Horningsea, as well as being named as executor of a will in London.

[41] A shortened version of this confession was printed in J. Rogers, *The Displayinge*
[42] I am indebted to Dr. Roger Schofield for checking my figures and assuring me that they are conclusive.

Bridge's behaviour has a distinctly itinerant flavour and merits further investigation. Possibly, he was an elder of the Family.

Although Familists preferred their brethren when it came to will-making and marriage, they were by no means isolated within their communities. In other matters, Familists and conformists probably associated freely and without tension. The 'comon fame' that brought Taylor and Rule back into the open, after decades of seemingly peaceful existence in Balsham, was probably not as 'comon' as we are led to believe. The fact that the majority of Familists stayed in Balsham through to their deaths indicates that they were not generally viewed with hostility. The Familist plea, written anonymously in 1575, that 'we might be rightly tryed therein by the voice of the countrey, where we dwell; and by such as know us, or with whom we have had to deal' was a cry from the heart.[43] Without pressure from the Privy Council and Bishop Cox, the Family of Love in Balsham might never have come to light.

The overall picture presented in this paper is of little use to those who seek to show that religious dissent was confined to the bottom of society.[44] It was without doubt the wealthier members of the Balsham community who found themselves attracted to the doctrine of the Family of Love. When Christopher Hill's unnamed source described Familists as 'cow-herds, clothiers and such-like mean people', he had obviously not been to Balsham.[45] A respectable yeomen farmer had much more to lose than the humble cowherd. However, the fact that Balsham Familists were only accused of membership on a couple of occasions implies that, within their own village, they were tolerated. Their economic position at the wealthier end of the community may have given the Family of Love in Balsham a stability and continuity that it would not otherwise have enjoyed. To the members of the sect in Balsham,

[43] Anon, *A Brief Rehersal of the Belief of the Good Willing in England, which are named the Family of Love ...* (London 1656).

[44] I am deeply indebted to Dr. Margaret Spufford for the great encouragement she has offered me in the research for, and writing of, this paper. Her tremendous enthusiasm has not been inhibited in the slightest by the fact that one of her main concerns has been to show that dissent was not restricted to the more comfortable members of local communities.

[45] Christopher Hill, *The World Turned Upside Down* (1972 repr Harmondsworth 1975) p. 27.

comfortable on their featherbeds, the socially subversive aspect of Familism, highlighted both by Leonard Romsye[46] and by Christopher Hill, can have had little appeal.

Corpus Christi College, Cambridge

---

[46] A Coppy of the voluntary confession of Leonard Romsie ... some time of the familye of Love, PRO, SP 12 133.

THE GENESIS OF A GODLY
COMMUNITY: TWO YORK PARISHES
1590–1640

by CLAIRE CROSS

THE inside cover of the Elizabethan register of St John's, Ousebridge, York contains the following entry:

> Memorandum that John Stoddart, clerk, began to serve in this parish of St John's at Ousebridge end in August 1591 and doth still serve the same, who also did rule this same parchment book in such form and sort as it is, of his own proper cost, after that it was bought by James Cristalson, being churchwarden, in the year of the reign of Queen Elizabeth etc. 41, anno domini 1599 ... price vii s.

The corresponding register of the adjoining parish of All Saints, North Street, where Stoddart became the pluralist rector in March 1594, begins very similarly. These (at least for York) uniquely full registers, supplemented by a set of churchwardens' accounts from St John's and the eighty or so wills which can now be traced for the two parishes make it possible to chart the development of a loosely associated group of committed protestants in an area of central York which the arrival of a resident minister stimulated in both a positive and, less predictably, negative way. The story of voluntary religion which emerges is not one of high drama, faction-fighting, or even separation between the godly and the rest, but rather of a sustained and ultimately triumphant attempt of a minority to enrich the spiritual life of their parishes.[1]

Throughout almost the entire course of the sixteenth century the clerical work force manning the more than twenty, very poor parish churches of the city of York had been predominantly local,

---

[1] Borthwick Institute, York PRY/J1 inside parchment cover; PRY/ASN1 fol 1v (all spelling has been modernised throughout); and see P. Collinson, *The Religion of Protestants: the Church in English Society 1559–1625* (Oxford 1982) esp chapter 6.

but matters were beginning to change around 1590, and John Stoddart was very much a harbinger of an increasing professionalism among the lower clergy. A Cumbrian, and so very much an outsider, he had also broken with York tradition, where the parish clergy at best had usually only received a grammar school education, by matriculating at Cambridge as a sizar from Jesus in the Michaelmas term of 1573, though he did not spend enough time there to proceed to a first degree. By 1580 at the latest he had returned to Cumberland where, on 7 August, described as 'literatus', he was ordained deacon in Rose Castle; eighteen months later, then said to be of Warwick, a small settlement a few miles from Carlisle, he was made priest in Carlisle cathedral. In August 1586 he obtained his first living, the rectory of Castle Carrock, a village to the south east of Carlisle on the edge of the fells. Valued at a mere £5 12s. 10d. in 1536 Castle Carrock can have possessed few material attractions for a young man at the start of his career and Stoddart stayed there for less than three years before resigning the cure in readiness, apparently, to seek his fortune on the other side of the Pennines. Before he left his native county, however, he took a wife.[2]

Stoddart's marriage in fact suggests that he may have come from a rather higher level of Cumberland society than his quasi servile status at Cambridge might indicate and that he had means of his own apart from his exiguous clerical income, for otherwise Clement Skelton of Barwickfield Hall, esquire, land sargeant of Gilsland and deputy warden of Carlisle Castle under the right honourable William Dacres would have been scarcely likely to have permitted him to wed his daughter, Joan. It may indeed be this marriage which precipitated Stoddart's removal from Castle Carrock: at all events by the summer of 1591 he, his pregnant wife and his elderly mother, Marion Stoddart, had established their household at All Saints, North Street in York, where his son, Christopher, was born in November. In August Stoddart began his thirty-five years

---

[2] C. Cross, 'Priests into Ministers: the Establishment of Protestant Practice in the City of York, 1530–1630', in P.N. Brooks ed *Reformation Principle and Practice: Essays in Honour of A.G. Dickens* (London 1980) pp. 203–225; C. Cross ed *York Clergy Wills 1520–1600: 2 The City Clergy* (Borthwick Texts and Calendars; Records of the Northern Province) forthcoming; *Al. Cant.* pt 1, 4 p. 165; Carlisle Episcopal Registers, Barnes pp. 107, 117–18, 148, 165–6; *Valor Ecclesiasticus* Record Commissioners (London 1825) 5 p. 279.

of ministry in the neighbouring parish of St John's, Ousebridge to which he added the rectory of All Saints in March 1594.[3]

Financially Stoddart's transfer proved just about worthwhile, but he certainly had not achieved any glittering prizes. The revenues of St John's, Ousebridge, appropriated to the York Dean and Chapter, had it seems been considered too irregular even to feature in the *Valor Ecclesiasticus* and by the end of the sixteenth century had fallen entirely under parish control, the churchwardens collecting the Easter offerings and paying the minister a regular £8, soon rising to £9, in two half-yearly instalments to which they referred without any attempt at equivocation as his 'wages'. At All Saints Stoddart seems to have been in a little more control of his income, though this may well have been even lower than that at St John's, since in the *Valor* All Saints' rectory had been assessed at only £7 7s. 6d. per annum. Despite his pluralism Stoddart can only have enjoyed an income of around £16 a year.[4]

The poverty of the livings of St John's and All Saints in no sense reflects the relative importance of these two small parishes on the west bank of the Ouse. Taking in a sizeable stretch of Micklegate, one of the chief arteries of the city, St John's numbered among its inhabitants some very wealthy merchant families such as the Beckwiths, Mosleys and Breareys while All Saints, though somewhat less prosperous, still had its rich tanners in the Fawcets, Lobleys, Lishmans, Yates and Atkinsons some of whom also held high civic office. At the other end of the spectrum St John's housed a *maison dieu* and the two city prisons, the Kidcotes, on Ousebridge, so that Stoddart could count almswomen, criminals and debtors among his parishioners. If not much better remunerated life for a cleric in St John's and All Saints must at least have been much more varied than the rural round at Castle Carrock.

Until Stoddart's appointment neither St John's nor All Saints had retained a resident incumbent for any length of time since Elizabeth's accession. Indeed, for different periods both livings had been used to augment the stipends of clergy beneficed elsewhere. In 1575 Simon Blunt, the rector of All Saints, did not live in the city and the parish had to manage with the assistance of a reader.

[3] Borthwick PRY/ASN1 fols iir, 3v, 64r, 65r; PRY/J1 inside parchment cover.
[4] Borthwick PRY/J17 fols 9v–57v; PRY/ASN1 fol iir; York Minster Library J. Torre ms City Volume p. 601.

Two years later the archbishop's visitors discovered that the still nonresident rector had leased the parsonage house to three tenants and was holding services 'out of time', that is before seven o'clock in the morning. In 1586 matters had not improved though George Cawood had replaced Blunt in the cure. Not surprisingly under the circumstances protestantism seems to have been rather slow in taking root. In 1568 Thomas Stiddy, a churchwarden of All Saints, had had to answer certain charges before the ecclesiastical authorities of disturbing the minister, abusing the suffragan bishop of Nottingham, and keeping two popish priests in secret. Outright catholic recusancy, nevertheless, does not seem subsequently to have presented a particular problem. In All Saints in the 1570s and 1580s the male parishioners had all become outward conformists, though Richard Lobley and John Gamble had recusant wives. In St John's Thomas Hewitt's wife and daughters seem to have been strong catholics, but there, too, by 1590 catholic recusancy seems to have all but disappeared.[5]

Despite the undoubted neglect the two parishes had suffered, a lively form of protestantism had begun to manifest itself well before Stoddart came into residence. As early as 1572 John Warriner, a dyer from St John's, selected a very protestant preamble for his will in which he surrendered 'into the hands of my Lord God my soul and spirit ... nothing doubting but firmly believing that even for his mercy's sake set forth in the death and precious blood shedding of his dear son, Jesus Christ, mine only saviour and redeemer, he will receive my soul into his glorious kingdom and place it amongst the company of his heavenly angels and saints'. At the end of this same decade two other deaths occurred which Stoddart took particular pains to commemorate for posterity. When Margaret Metcalfe died in October 1579 she was reputed to be a hundred years old: the widow of Anthony Metcalfe of Wensleydale, by whom she had borne twelve children, (though eleven had predeceased her,) she had at some stage come to York to live near her son-in-law, Francis Bayne, merchant of St John's. When

---

[5] Borthwick V 1575 CB1 fols 6r–7v; V 1577 CB1 fol 12v; V 1586 CB1 fol 6r; J.C.H. Aveling, *Catholic Recusancy in the City of York, 1558–1791* Catholic Record Society (1970) pp. 70, 168, 184–5, 189, 190, 199, 200–1, 205, 206, 210, 211, 212, 225, 227, 232.

copying out his new register in 1599 Stoddart inserted a particularly revealing account of her character and religious disposition.

> This woman in her youth was well brought up; after she was married [she] sustained sundry troubles diversly; all mischiefs she bare patiently; in an ill matter she had a good stomach. She was gentle, courteous, fair spoken, friendly, very desirous of peace, a lover of good company, and for all companies when she was young and lusty meet, and continued so still till she was well stricken in years: she was very pleasant, merrily conceited, and as the company served, so she would frame her talk. She used to use sundry pretty taunts and nips, and had her answer ready at every objection. She was religious, devout and godly and sore repented of her former life, idly spent and evil, and called to God for mercy and grace, and was heartily sorry that she was so superstitiously and popishly bent in times past, and desired God to forgive her therefore, and wholly and fully reposed her whole confidence and trust in the death and passion of Jesus Christ and in that faith departed hence. Wherefore now I trust she resteth with Abraham, Isaac and Jacob in the kingdom of heaven.

A butcher, Robert Harrison, though clearly a less vivid personality, Stoddart also determined should be similarly remembered for his christian virtues.

> He was true hearted and faithful to his friend, upright and just in his dealings, friendly to his friend, and to his enemy not revengeful, as it appeared by that he sent for some of his adversaries who, when they were come unto him, he was very well content to forgive, which was a manifest token that he was a man of peace, and that he was governed by God's spirit: he lived in God's fear and died in the true faith of Jesus Christ, unto whom he commended his soul and in whom he reposed his whole confidence.[6]

Among the stalwarts of the faith still alive when Stoddart began his ministry the most exotic and perhaps the most intimidating must have been Ferdinando Phawghney, a naturalised French

[6] Borthwick Prob. Reg. 19 fols 296v–297r; PRY/J1 fol 27v.

Huguenot. By the 1590s Phawghney had spent long enough in Yorkshire to have acquired an English wife, at least one locally born godchild, Ferdinando Robinson, and, much more significantly, a thorough knowledge of the religious inclinations of the ministers in the vicinity of York. Having singled out in his will two other fellow compatriots for small gifts of money, Peter the Frenchman dwelling within Bootham Bar and another Frenchman, Anthony, who had been Mr Gilming's man, Phawghney particularly favoured James Grainger, minister of Castlegate parish in York, upon whom he bestowed 40s. and a copy of Tremellius' version of the Bible. To Mr Thomas Wood, preacher at St Michael's, Ousebridge, he left four angels and a New Testament translated from the Greek by Beza and Englished by Laurence Tomson. In addition to bequests to the poor of All Saints and St Michael's he gave £6 'for the maintenance of the preaching of God's word at my parish of All Hallows ... for four several sermons to be made yearly for the space of three years at the appointment of Mr Thomas Wood, minister'. Although Stoddart received 20s. from Phawghney and featured as one of the witnesses of his will he obviously did not stand sufficiently high in the foreigner's esteem to be entrusted with the oversight of a preaching fund in his own parish.[7]

With others among the spiritual and social elite of his parishioners, however, Stoddart did succeed in establishing much closer relations. On the birth of his son only four months after his appointment to St John's the new minister persuaded Christopher Beckwith, a wealthy merchant and a future lord mayor who had already served the city as chamberlain and sheriff, to name the child: the baby's other sponsors were another merchant and former chamberlain, Henry Banister, and Mistress Anne Boughton, wife of John Boughton, chamberlain in 1597. Stoddart's next child, a daughter, Mary, born in 1593 received equally eminent godparents in Mr John Bousfield, draper and a former chamberlain and master of the Merchant Taylors' Company, Lady Herbert, widow of Alderman Christopher Herbert, lord mayor in 1573 who had died in 1590, and Mistress Anne Bayne, wife of Edward Bayne, a substantial merchant of All Saints.[8]

[7] Borthwick Prob. Reg. 26 fol 354v.
[8] Borthwick PRY/ASN1 fol 3v; Prob. Reg. 37 fol 432v; York City Library R.H. Skaife, ms 'Civic Officials of York' I pp. 40, 62–3, 102–3, 125; 2 pp. 360–1.

In the matter of godparents the condescension inevitably went in one direction towards the young cleric's family, but from early in his ministry there was one sphere, that of will making, in which those of his parishioners who did not wish, or could not afford, to have recourse to a lawyer sought Stoddart's aid. Of the fifty-two wills which survive for his incumbency he certainly wrote at least twenty and to all but two of these gave an identical, and, for the two parishes, novel Calvinist preamble by which the testator bequeathed his soul to 'Almighty God, my creator, redeemer and saviour, trusting through the effusion of Christ's most precious blood to be one of God's chosen and elect company in heaven'. Alongside this activity Stoddart continued to record especially edifying deathbed scenes, such as that in 1597 of the octogenarian Andrew Watson

> who was religious in his knowledge and frequented the church very diligently, charitable towards all people, pleasant and merrily conceited, being fit for any company, and so made a zealous, virtuous, yea, and though some did think a sudden, yet I hope a godly end, calling on the Lord, 'Come, Lord Jesu, come quickly and receive my spirit, into whose hands I commit the same, for thou hast redeemed me.'

Similarly in January, 1598 Stoddart set down in St John's register that Edward Wilcock, late servant of Mr John Moore, the lawyer, had made 'a godly, faithful and a christian end.'[9]

Death struck Stoddart's own family three times within this same decade, carrying off first in 1595 his mother, Marion Stoddart, 'of the age of lxxx and odd years', then in 1597 his second son, John, within a few hours of his birth, and lastly his much lamented wife, Joan, 'who in her life time was religious and godly, and so, making a christian and a charitable end, was buried in the chancel [of All Saints] on the south side of the table the xix[th] of February 1599 [/1600].' At a period when the marriage of the clergy could still meet with opposition in conservative circles in York, Stoddart

---

[9] Borthwick Prob. Reg. 26 fols 310v–311r; Prob. Reg. 27 fols 98v–99r; Prob. Reg. 29 fols 499v, 504v–505r, 609r; Prob. Reg. 30 fols 13r, 488r–v; Prob. Reg. 31 fols 667r–v, 796v; Prob. Reg. 33 fols 694v–695r, 736v; Prob. Reg. 34 fols 267r–v, f 606r–v; Prob. Reg. 36 fols 350r–v, 655v–656r; Prob. Reg. 37 fols 61r–v, 116v, 296r–297r, 555v–556r; Prob. Reg. 38 fols 377v–378r; PRY/J1 fol 29r.

seems deliberately to have used the occasion of his wife's funeral to reinforce protestant teaching. Having invited in Anthony Hartford, MA and rector of the nearby parish of St Martin's, Micklegate, to preach the funeral sermon, he entered in his register how he 'did observe and note ... in her commendation three things ...'

> First, in her youth, in her middle age and period of time, she was religious. Secondly, married into the state of the holy ministry, and now eternally to Christ Jesus, the true bridegroom of the holy church. Thirdly, buried amongst the sepulchres of her ancient and most holy fathers and prophets, and therefore in hope expecteth a joyful resurrection. And thus according to the saying of Bildad unto Job, as Job chapter 8 verses 5, 6 and 7, she early sought God and prayed continually unto the Almighty, was pure and upright in life and conversation, therefore surely God in mercy did awake up unto her both in her life time, and at the day of her death made the habitation of her righteousness prosperous, and with Job crowned her latter end with eternal happiness, and so resteth with Abraham, Isaac and Jacob in the kingdom of heaven.[10]

The death of Joan Stoddart left her husband to cope alone with the needs of a young family, and he understandably soon sought a second wife, marrying Frances, late daughter of John Browne of Topcliffe at St Lawrence's church without Walmgate Bar on 10 November 1601. Ten months later their first child, Elizabeth, was born. This respite from suffering proved to be of all too short duration, however, before in the early years of James I's reign Stoddart had to face his most severe time of trial, both as a pastor and as a father, when first in May 1603 his nine year old daughter, Mary, died and then, less than a year later, the great plague hit York and destroyed something like a third of the city's population. Throughout the plague's ravages Stoddart remained at his post, listing 105 victims in St John's and 80 in the rather smaller parish of All Saints: his own family had to pay as high a cost as any of his parishioners. On 3 August 1603 his twenty month old daughter,

---

[10] Aveling, *Catholic Recusancy in the City of York* p. 194; Borthwick PRY/ASN1 fols 4r, 64r–v, 65r.

Elizabeth, died, though he did not think she had caught the infection. His wife was pregnant for the second time and on 28 August gave birth to a son, Joseph, by which date the plague had certainly taken its hold on the household for on 5 September two of Stoddart's servants, Margaret Lonsdale and Jane Barnes, died, being buried in the same grave, to be accompanied two days later by twelve year old Christopher Stoddart, by then the only remaining child of the minister's first marriage: on 17 September the Stoddarts lost their last child, three week old Joseph.[11]

Both Stoddart and his wife, however, survived the tragedy, Mrs Stoddart to live on as a widow in All Saints until at least 1646, and they were in fact subsequently blessed with children to succour them in their old age. In October 1605 a new son was born and named John, for whom John Stable, then city chamberlain, Miles Fawcet, tanner of All Saints, and Mistress Mary Cartwright, wife of Reginald Cartwright, dyer, stood sponsors. Five years later they had their last child, Jane, who had as her godparents Reginald Cartwright, chamberlain in 1607, Mistress Jane Lobley, probably the wife of one of the churchwardens of All Saints in 1611, and, the most prestigious of all, Mistress Jane Atkinson, wife of Thomas Atkinson, a very wealthy tanner who ended his life a sheriff of the city. Both these children lived to maturity, John following closely in his father's footsteps by studying for a time as a sizar at Cambridge before being ordained in York in 1626 and going on to become vicar of Wilberfoss in the East Riding.[12]

As the years passed John Stoddart senior must have realised that he would not achieve further promotion in the church. Periodically he reckoned up the time he had spent in his two York parishes, reflecting with some pride on the fact that August 1621 marked the thirtieth anniversary of his institution to St John's. He did not die until 16 January 1627 and so in all accomplished thirty-five years of service. The financial rewards for his faithfulness do not seem to have been great. Whereas in the large and rich parish of Holy Trinity, Hull popular preachers like Thomas Wincop or the

[11] D.M. Palliser, 'Epidemics in Tudor York', *Northern History* 8 (1973) pp. 45–63; Borthwick PRY/ASN1 fols 5r, 43v, 66r–67r; PRY/J1 fols 30r–31r.
[12] Borthwick Orig. Wills Sept 1646–7 (Harrison); PRY/ASN1 f 5v; J.S. Purvis, 'Stuart Crockford' sub Stoddart; York City Library Skaife, 'Civic Officials' I pp. 28–9, 148–9, 264, 2 p.705; Venn, *Al Cant* pt I, 4 p. 165.

poet's father, Andrew Marvell, gained between £50 and £60 each from funeral bequests from grateful auditors, Stoddart had to count his gratuities in shillings, not pounds. Of the twelve parishioners who mentioned him at all in their wills, most gave him a mere token of from 2s. to 5s.: of the more generous Percival Barnes, who died during the plague, bequeathed him 10s.; John Stable, his son's godfather, £1 and his widow, Mrs Elizabeth Stable a wine bowl marked with the initials J.S. or its money equivalent of 26s. 8d.[13]

The cause of Stoddart's ultimate failure, despite all his assiduity, to move the hearts or at least the purse strings of his parishioners seems to have lain in his inability to preach. From the time of Ferdinando Phawghney onwards the godly in the two parishes had increasingly been calling for more sermons and had begun to make funds available for supplying the need, but demonstrably did not consider Stoddard capable of that duty. In 1599 Alderman Christopher Beckwith, the godfather of Stoddart's eldest son, having asked in his will to be buried near his wife in the middle choir aisle of St John's, went on to leave 20s. to the civic lecturer, Richard Harwood, 'praying [him] to preach at my funeral if he conveniently may.' Harwood also preached the funeral sermon in All Saints in 1610 of Miles Fawcet, young John Stoddart's godfather. When in March 1618 Mary Spence, 'who was modest, courteous, sober and religious died about the age of xx[ty] years after she had borne four children' her husband, Thomas Spence, tanner, chose Henry Rogers, an Oxford graduate and vicar of St Denys and St Mary, Bishophill Senior in plurality to commemorate her passing. Rogers preached again at the young man's particular request on the death of his stepson, James Fawcet, son of Miles Fawcet. The supervisors of Mistress Elizabeth Stable, of whom Stoddart was one, procured William Foster of Whenby in the North Riding to deliver her funeral oration in 1620. Two years later James Conyers, MA, the civic preacher, performed the same service for John Wildon, gentleman. In August 1622 on the death of Edward Bayne, merchant, and again in February 1623 on the

[13] Borthwick PRY/J1 inside parchment cover; PRY/ASN1 fol 72r; Prob. Reg. 30 fol 488r–v; Prob. Reg. 33 fols 763v–764r; Prob. Reg. 36 fol 350r–v; C. Cross, *Urban Magistrates and Ministers: Religion in Hull and Leeds from the Reformation to the Civil War* Borthwick Paper 67 (York 1985) p. 23.

death of Bridget, wife of John Buckle, another of the civic lecturers, Marmaduke Gibbons, MA, vicar of both St Martin's, Micklegate and St Mary, Bishophill Junior came into All Saints to preach.[14]

Exactly the same sort of commemorations were taking place in Stoddart's other church of St John's, Ousebridge. In 1623 Marmaduke Gibbons officiated at the funeral of Mr John Chomley, son of Sir Henry Chomley, while on the death of his sister, Mistress Jane Chomley, five years previously Richard Whittington, vicar of St Mary, Bishophill Senior had preached. Also in 1623 Roger Bellwood, the graduate rector of St Crux conducted the funeral of Mr William Banister, merchant and vintner and the Mosley family had recourse to the rector of St Michael's, Spurriergate and another civic preacher, Miles White, no less than three times in 1623 and 1624 to deliver sermons on the deaths of Mrs Mary Thorndike, daughter of Alderman Thomas Mosley, of John Mosley, the alderman's son and heir, and of Alderman Mosley himself. The other cleric Stoddart noted as preaching a funeral sermon in St John's was John Whittacres, rector of St Saviour's, commended years later by the Commonwealth Commissioners for being 'a constant preaching minister'. How much this sort of preaching meant to the godly is revealed in the will of Alderman Mosley who in 1624 left an annuity of £4 charged on his house in Upper Ousegate to Miles White so long as he continued rector of St Michael's and thereafter to the minister of that church in perpetuity 'towards the furtherance of holy and sacramental sermons and religious exercises.'[15]

After Stoddart's death in 1627 the supply of sermons improved immeasurably in the two parishes which reverted once more to having separate ministers of their own, both now graduates, Thomas Clarke at John's and Ralph Vincent at All Saints. When Clarke died prematurely in 1643 the chief men of the parish, Samuel Brearey, Christopher Brearey, Henry Brearey, Thomas Herbert and others organised a petition to the earl of Newcastle to obtain a pension for his widow and young family, stressing how in his life time their minister had been 'a constant, diligent preacher and

---

[14] Borthwick Prob. Reg. 27 fol 722r–v; PRY/ASN1 fols 68r, 69v, 70v–71r; York City Archives Housebook 1626–1637 fol 156.
[15] Borthwick PRY/J1 fols 33v–34v; Prob. Reg. 38 fols 238v–240r; Lambeth Palace Library Ms 919 fol 574.

very zealous in exhorting his parishioners and auditors to their obedience to God and the king and ... a man of marvellous honest and religious conversation.' At All Saints, similarly, Ralph Vincent provided regular preaching for his congregation which included the godly Thomas Atkinson, one time sheriff of the city, 'who said often upon his death bed, "Although I shall die, yet I trust my life is hid with Christ in God, for when Christ, who is my life, shall appear, then I shall also appear with him in glory."' In his will Atkinson took particular pains that these sermons should continue unabated, not only requiring 'Mr Ralph Vincent to make a sermon at the time of my burial, wherein the people may be admonished of their mortality and how they should dispose of themselves in this life that when the time cometh they may yield up a living soul into the hands of the everliving God' but also bequeathing him 'six pounds for the preaching of twelve sermons in my parish church within three years next after my death. And I do intreat him to take his text all that time out of the third chapter of the proverbs of Solomon.'[16]

This same desire for constant preaching in 1649 moved Richard Hartforth, gentleman, to make a grant in his own life time of a rent charge of 20s. in perpetuity for two sermons to be preached, one at St John's, Ousebridge on Michaelmas day and the other at St Sampson's on 20 March each year for ever. By far the most munificent benefaction, however, came to St John's on the death of that 'worthy and well affected gentlewoman, Mrs Elizabeth Mosley, widow, sometime wife to John Mosley of the city, esquire, one of the daughters and coheirs of Thomas Trigott of South Kirby, esquire.' In 1640 she left to 'the curate of the parish church of St John's ... being an able, constant preaching minister of God's word, and not otherwise ... forty pounds per annum for ever for and towards his maintenance' issuing out of lands and tenements in South Kirby. By this one act she altogether transformed the value of the living: whereas Stoddart had received a mere £9 annually, the churchwardens now had the means to pay Vincent and his successors a far more realistic £50 each year. Well might the parish in

---

[16] Borthwick DR/CWP; Orig. Wills June 1642–3 (Atkinson); M. Stephenson, 'Monumental Brasses in the City of York' *Yorkshire Archaeological Society* 18 (1905) pp. 9–10.

its commemoration of Mrs Mosley's charitable institution declare that by this 'pious work, being dead, she yet speaketh.'[17]

How representative of parish opinion in St John's or All Saints the demand for frequent preaching had become by the time of the Civil War must remain a matter for conjecture and perhaps never more than a minority of the parishioners experienced this craving. Very occasionally hints at discontent with the religious developments surfaced in the two parishes. Percival Banks, of All Saints, for example, appeared before the archiepiscopal visitors in 1613 'for saying that the Magnificat in the Book of Common Prayer was not worthy to be read in the church, and for disturbing the minister in time of prayer in many speeches ... : he said Mr Stoddart did behave himself like a stage player when he went to the communion table to read the commandments.' In 1615 the churchwardens of All Saints found themselves charged with 'not assisting the minister in calling the youth of the parish to be catechised'; years later in 1640 in St John's Robert Beckwith and his wife had transgressed 'for keeping a company of troopers drinking in their house in service time upon a Sunday.'[18]

Voluntary religion, nevertheless, seems to have exerted a pretty wide appeal in the two parishes of All Saints and St John's, attracting men and women, young and old, rich and relatively poor. Only in a very nebulous sense did these committed protestants form a community and yet in a more fundamental way they proved to be the 'little leaven' that 'leaveneth the whole lump.' Because of Stoddart's superior record keeping more can be known about the inhabitants of All Saints and St John's than about those of most other York parishes in the same period, but there is no reason to think that the godly there differed from the godly elsewhere in the city while the religious complexion of York as a whole seems to have mirrored that of many other English towns in the first part of the seventeenth century. The appetite of these zealots over the years for 'sacramental sermons and religious exercises' subtly altered the balance of the Prayer Book services authorised by the 1559 Settlement, but it was only when churchmen of the stature

[17] Borthwick PRY/J17 fol 235v; Orig. Wills Ap 1640 (Elizabeth Mosley); York City Library Skaife, 'Civic Officials', 2 p. 519.
[18] P. Collinson, *The Religion of Protestants* esp pp. 189–241; Borthwick V 1613 CB2 fol 48v; V 1615 CB2 fol 22v; V 1640 CB1 fol 2a.

of Archbishop Neile in the 1630s began attacking these practices in an attempt to restore the equilibrium that a self-conscious 'puritan party' emerged.[19]

University of York

[19] 1 Cor. 5 v 6; R.A. Marchant, *The Puritans and the Church Courts in the Diocese of York, 1560–1642* (London 1960) p. 277.

THE ENGLISH CONVENTICLE

by PATRICK COLLINSON

IN the midst of the nervous excitement of the autumn of 1640 a Londoner called Roger Quatermayne, a puritan and, as we might say, barrackroom lawyer, was investigated by Archbishop Laud and other Privy Councillors for the offence of holding religious meetings in circumstances which were politically as well as ecclesiastically suspect, since it was thought that Quatermayne and his friends had made treasonable contact with the Scottish army, then at war with its king and in occupation of English soil.[1] Quatermayne, charged with holding a *conventicle*, asked the archbishop to inform him 'what a Conventicle is.' Laud replied: 'Why, this is a Conventicle, ... when ten or twelve or more or lesse meet together to pray, reade, preach, expound, this is a conventicle.' Laud's definition may appear uncontroversial, particularly if to his 'ten or twelve or more or less' is added the formula of the 1664 Conventicle Act, 'over and above those of the same Household'.[2] But Quatermayne objected: 'My Lord, I do not so understand it.'

Quatermayne's point was that private meetings held in a domestic setting for mutual edification were 'nothing but godly conference', not properly conventicles at all. He would have found many to agree with him, including the consistory of the Dutch church in London which in 1621 judged that by the laws of England members of their congregation who met with the pious purpose of bettering their religious knowledge did not constitute a conventicle, since a conventicle was an unlawful gathering openly defiant of the doctrine and government of the Church of England.[3] Many years later, Richard Baxter agreed in refuting the suggestion that such

---

[1] Roger Quatermayne, *Quatermayns conquest over Canterburies court* (London 1641) pp. 28–31. See Murray Tolmie, *The Triumph of the Saints: the Separate Churches of London 1616–1649* (Cambridge 1977) pp. 30–1.
[2] 16 Car. II c.4.
[3] Guildhall Library MS 7411/2 fol 42r. I owe this reference to Dr O.P. Grell.

223

private meetings were schismatic. If held not 'in distaste' of the public meeting nor in opposition to it, but at a different hour and 'in subordination to the publique', they represented 'not a separated Church but as a part of the Church more diligent then the rest ... '[4] However, Laud seems to have considered any private meeting as at least potentially schismatic, a doctrine to which Quatermayne took strong exception: 'I did alwayes thinke that publick duties did not make voyd private, but that both might stand with a Christian.'[5] The difference between public and private duties was a familiar commonplace, and not only in the metropolis. As far away as Westmorland, and half a century before Quatermayne's appearance before the Privy Council, a preacher distinguished between 'two temples', both requiring the Christian's attention: 'publike assemblies' and 'godly societies': that is, 'ordinary assemblies and meetings together at the house of prayer', and 'godly societies and assemblies of the righteous'.[6]

The contention between Quatermayne and Laud – as to whether any small unauthorised religious meeting constituted a conventicle and whether it stood *ipso facto* condemned by that label – remained unresolved. Laud appealed to the Lord Chief Justice to confirm his definition but judges are better at asking learnedly naive questions about terms and entities than responding to them and the Lord Chief Justice 'answered nothing', or so Quatermayne alleged.[7] This was wise, and the wisdom was shared by the Restoration Conventicle Acts, which nowhere define what a conventicle is. The ambiguity underlying the Quatermayne–Laud exchange was rooted in English usage of the sixteenth and seventeenth centuries and has persisted in the vocabulary of historians. On the one hand, we encounter the neutral, non-pejorative definition of 'conventicle' offered in a glossary of 'hard English words' published in 1604: 'a little assemblie', evidently a little *religious* assembly since this was a religious glossary.[8] On the other hand a conventicle could mean an unlawful assembly, involving conspiracy, not necessarily

[4] Richard Baxter, *The saints everlasting rest* (London 1650) pp. 290–1. I owe this reference to Dr Eamon Duffy.
[5] Quatermayne, *Quatermayns conquest* pp. 28–9.
[6] Richard Leake, *Foure sermons* (London 1599) p. 8.
[7] Quatermayne, *Quatermayns conquest* p. 29.
[8] Robert Cawdrey, *A table alphabeticall, conteyning and teaching the true writing and understanding of hard usuall English wordes* (London 1604).

religious at all. One might have a conventicle of highwaymen or of pickpockets. Holdsworth found in a late fourteenth-century source a conventicle of tenants banded together to resist certain demands of their lords, which suggests a medieval usage in the context of agrarian bargaining more or less equivalent to the early nineteenth-century 'combination': a conspiracy to deflect the laws of economics.[9] There is potential here for absurd errors. In the Staffordshire Quarter Sessions Rolls for 1586 we find the indictments of four individuals, three of them gentlemen, 'for unlawful and riotous assembly in conventicle in the highway at Fowtherley', leading to an assault on two individuals and battery upon a third. The same phrase, 'unlawful assembly in a conventicle' was used in conjunction with two other Staffordshire cases of assault and battery in 1587. The editor of these proceedings chose to detect in such cases what he called 'glimpses of the puritan movement' and he classified them under the heading of protestant dissent.[10]

This bizarre confusion need not detain us. It is not my purpose to argue that associations hitherto regarded as religious were in fact criminal conspiracies in disguise, still less to suggest that covens of criminals, denizens of the late Gamini Salgado's Elizabethan Underworld, were really prayer meetings which have received a bad press. All reference in what follows will be to conventicles in the common and religious sense. Dr. Jim Sharpe, in his study of the Essex parish of Kelvedon Easterford, can demonstrate that not all the members of a particular conventicle were necessarily impeccable. Even visible saints could be guilty of sexual misdemeanours, drunkenness, theft and other offences against God and man.[11] But that is neither here nor there. Let us assume that these assemblies held for a conventionally religious purpose by persons who desired to appear conventionally religious were, in a conventional sense, religious assemblies. Were they as innocuous as Quatermayne insisted and were they generally so regarded, except in the perception of hardline prelates? If so, then pre-revolutionary England (as Dr. Christopher Hill has characterized

[9] W.S. Holdsworth, *A History of English Law* (3 ed London 1923) 3 p. 204.
[10] *The Staffordshire Quarter Sessions Rolls* I *1581–1589*, ed S.A.H. Burne, William Salt Socy (Kendal 1931) pp. xxxvi, 145, 153, 155.
[11] J.A. Sharpe, 'Crime and Delinquency in an Essex Parish 1600–1640', in *Crime in England 1550–1800* ed J.S. Cockburn (London 1977) pp. 106–7.

it), or at least pre-Laudian England, was a more open society than some historians have allowed.

The issue between Quatermayne and Laud cannot be resolved on a narrowly legal basis, although that is how we shall deal with it in the first instance. If we ask whether 'conventiclers' like Quatermayne intended to take part in activities which they knew to be incompatible with their responsibilities as baptized members of the established Church and subjects of its discipline the question moves publicly away from the law of the land and towards ecclesiology, and privately, for the individual, it adds to the matter of legal liability a further consideration of conscience. Either Quatermayne was in good faith or he was not. Some 'conventicles' were separatist, others not. A group meeting at Balsham and Strethall in north-east Essex in the 1570s persuaded first the Elizabethan Master of Peterhouse, Andrew Perne, and then, a little later, myself that their meetings were innocent. In fact we now know the men at Balsham to have been members of a radical sect of professional dissemblers, the Family of Love.[12] However, I shall argue that a historiographical bias has operated in favour of paying too much attention to conventicles the implications of which were schismatical and sectarian and too little to conventicles which were free of such connotations: which is as much as to say that the conventicle, as distinct from the gathered church to which it occasionally tended, has not been much studied. For this bias two explanations offer themselves: first, the dependence of historians on the record of various kinds of criminal procedure which would be wasting time on innocent, non-separatist conventicles; second, the preponderance (until recently) of denominational history which has quite naturally focussed on the emergence from the conventicle, or from whatever other historical circumstances, of the fully gathered and separated Church. So the annals of Broadmead Church Bristol, while preserving precious evidence of the origins of that society in more or less spontaneous and casual conventicles, encourage us to regard it as a natural progression for the conventicle

[12] For Perne's mistake, see Inner Temple Library MS Petyt 538.47 vols 492–3; for mine, *The Elizabethan Puritan Movement* (London 1967) p. 379, *Godly People: Essays on English Protestantism and Puritanism* (London 1983) p. 10. The record is put straight by Felicity Heal, 'The Family of Love and the Diocese of Ely' *SCH* 9 pp. 217–18; see also pp. 191–208 above.

to grow into a church, and diverts attention away from those conventicles – perhaps, though this can never be verified, the majority – which obstinately remained pumpkins and were never transformed by the magic wands of Mrs Dorothy Hazard of Broadmead or Archbishop Laud into Cinderella's coaches.[13] Conventicles, like other voluntary and relatively unstructured and discontinuous religious societies, lack the direct historiographical posterity which churches enjoy. That is some justification for this volume: to redress the balance.

However, the historian who confines himself to the conscious and deliberate levels of human motivation and action is tying one hand behind his back. I shall also argue that beyond intentionality the English conventicle of the sixteenth and seventeenth centuries always had the potential to become, or give birth to a separated and gathered church. At many points in the proceedings of this conference the reader encounters the difficulty, for contemporary actors and historians alike, of distinguishing clearly between voluntary societies within or alongside the Church and alternative or rival churches taking shape outside it and in total rejection of it. To claim an exclusivity in certain respects and for certain purposes, which self-selecting groups must do, devoting themselves to ends which are not those of mankind or even of the Church in general, may imply a claim to the general, absolute and ultimate exclusivity of the Church itself, especially where the ends in question are of an exalted moral and spiritual character and pursued in the context of a larger society which itself claims to be christian and is suspicious of minority groups and hostile to the exclusive. Nevertheless it is not, I submit, a piece of pedantry but recognition of a debt which the historian owes to the past to insist that the rudderless drift of many a conventicle into separation was without deliberate intent, indeed directly contrary to intention, and principle. Edmund Wilson wrote a book called, *Apologies to the Iroquois*, the allbut extinct Indian tribe which had once inhabited New York City. Although I have never been a Presbyterian and am unlikely now to become one, what follows could be called 'Apologies to the Presbyterians', or to the long defunct aspirations

---

[13] *The Records of a Church of Christ in Bristol, 1640–1687*, ed Roger Hayden, Bristol Record Society's Pubns 27 (Bristol 1974).

of the Presbyterians of the first half of the seventeenth century, a world of human and religious experience and aspiration which we have lost.

II

The question must now be faced: were conventicles at risk under common law, a law which might have endangered a Jacobean association of, as it might be, anglers or bird-watchers? Or were they made illegal by particular statutes or canons? It would be a rash man who laid down the law of public assembly in England before the nineteenth century, if his life depended upon it.[14] Tudor and Stuart magistrates and constables were empowered to arrest and imprison anyone who presumed to play bowls, likewise those playing a variety of other unlawful games, 'already invented or hereafter to be invented'.[15] Bowls was a sociable game requiring the assembly of a number of players. But wherein lay the unlawfulness of unlawful games? Perhaps in the principle of playing for money,[16] perhaps in their attractiveness to the lower orders or in their lack of athletic and martial utility, not in the principle of assembly. William Hawkins, in his *Treatise of the Pleas of the Crown*, argued that such sporting diversions as bull-baiting, wrestling and the like were not unlawful: or at least the assemblies associated with them were not unlawful since they implied no intention to riot.[17] (Nowadays he would have to revise his opinion.) And what about assemblies for a religious purpose, commonly and significantly called religious *exercises*? When subjected to harrassment, religious people complained of a double standard. It was no crime for ten or twenty men to meet together in an alehouse

[14] I have followed William Hawkins, *A Treatise of the Pleas of the Crown* (5 ed 1771), Sir Matthew Hale, *Pleas of the Crown* (1707) and Holdsworth, *History of English Law* with some guidance from Dr John Stevenson.

[15] William Lambarde, *Eirenarcha: or of the office of the Iustice of Peace* (London 1592) p. 197. Cf William Lambarde, *The duties of constables* (London 1604) pp. 49–50, Michael Dalton, *The countrey Iustice* (London 1619) p. 341.

[16] James Balmford in *A short and plaine dialogue concerning the unlawfulnesse of playing at cards or tables, or any other game consisting in chance* (London 1593) argues that these games 'must needes be somwhat evill, because they somewhat depend upon chance.' To win money at play was a kind of theft. (Sigs A4ᵛ–6).

[17] Hawkins, *Pleas of the Crown* p. 157.

and there lewdly misspend their time. 'All this is no harme: it is but good neighbourhood, it is no conventicle.' It was said on behalf of some Kentish ministers in 1584: 'If all manner of meetings for the bellie and pastimes ... have their tolleration and allowance, must the meeting of mynisters at a sermon ... be judged a conventicle?' While denying that he was a conventicler, Roger Quatermayne denounced a sporting assembly attended by a great crowd on the Sabbath as 'a fearfull conventicle'.[18] Here was a tension not so much in the law as in the interpretation of the law within the moral economy of the time, amounting to a contradiction. The classification of unlawful games was an exact, if arcane science. To repress those sociable offences which went with a pot of ale accorded with social mores which if not popular were increasingly dominant in provincial society. But it was the religious sociability of those godly persons who in their own eyes were the staunchest upholders of law and order which in the time of Archbishop Whitgift or Archbishop Laud seemed most at risk.[19] In 1639 a Cambridge shoemaker and his wife were told by the Court of High Commission that when a householder received a minister 'together with any company of men and women of other families' for the purpose of repeating a sermon, all those involved were to be accounted 'conventiclers and breakers of His Majesties Lawes Ecclesiasticale and the Constitution and Canons of the Church of England.' Like Quatermayne, the shoemaker's wife stoutly denied it. She had not heard and did not believe that such activities were unlawful. John Winthrop noted in his Diary for 1624 that many were 'unjustly traduced for Conventicles'.[20]

There was no law which in the sixteenth and seventeenth centuries positively protected and in so doing defined a right of common assembly. Legally, no such right existed. But on the other hand the legal principle of *un*lawful assembly was very narrowly

[18] John Udall, *Two sermons of obedience to the gospell* (London 1596) Sig I iiiij; *A Seconde Parte of a Register* ed A. Peel (Cambridge 1915) 1 p. 231; Quatermayne, *Quatermayns conquest* p. 27.
[19] Compare the argument of 'Magistracy and Ministry' in my *The Religion of Protestants: the Church in English Society 1559–1625* (Oxford 1982) pp. 141–88.
[20] Bodleian Library Ms Tanner 65 no 35 fols 67–76; Winthrop quoted in D.G. Allen, *In English Ways: the Movement and the Transformation of English Local Custom to Massachusetts Bay in the Seventeenth Century* (Chapel Hill 1981) p. 181.

defined and glossed and would not be extended before the nine-teenth century.[21] In defining unlawful assembly, legal com-mentators concerned themselves with motives and actions which were a potential extrapolation beyond the assembly: which is to say that the concept of unlawful assembly was connected with the concept of conspiracy and that in its turn to the twin principles of rout and riot. An unlawful assembly, by definition, was one which conspired to cause a riot. Those who were able to prove that this was not their intention were neither conspirators nor unlawfully assembled. For, according to Coke, the act of unlawful assembly cannot be perpetrated unless the purpose of assembly is illegal, while the action of a man to assemble his friends for the purpose of defending his property is specifically indulged by law: for, says Hawkins, following Sir Matthew Hale, 'a Man's House is looked upon as his Castle.'[22] Similarly, William Lambarde, while noting that statute law recognised a variety of 'conventicles', observed that they were all definable as such by virtue of a conspiracy to commit an indictable offence, whether to kill a man, or to corrupt the course of justice. '*Champeries*, also *Maintenances*, *Conspiracies*, *Confederacies* and giving of *Liveries* ... be contained under the worde *Conventicles*', even if they contained no 'apparent shewe of Assembly against the Peace.'[23]

Until the later years of Elizabeth I it was not apparent that a private assembly of a man's friends held in his house for a religious purpose was unlawful, but nor was it positively lawful. It is sig-nificant that the succession of Conventicle Acts, beginning in 1593 and taken up in 1664 and 1670, are consistent with the common law of unlawful assembly in that they all allege some conspiratorial motive without which, or so it appears, there would have been no conventicle within the meaning of these acts. The Elizabethan statute 'to retain the Queen's subjects in obedience', came closest of all the conventicle acts to defining the religious motive of the conventicle as constituting an offence in itself, since the 'unlawful assemblies, conventicles or meetings' against which it legislated were said to be frequented by persons who obstinately refused to

---

[21] Holdsworth, *History of English Law* 8 p. 327.
[22] Hawkins, *Pleas of the Crown* pp. 155–8; Hale, *Pleas of the Crown* p. 137; Holdsworth, *History of English Law* 8 pp. 324–7.
[23] Lambarde, *Eirenarcha* pp. 177–8.

repair to church or who persuaded others to absent themselves. In 1664 and 1670 there is no mention of recusancy. However even in the 1593 statute the connection between a species of recusancy and conventicling is no more than an inference.[24]

In the eighteenth century it was said that 'the preamble of acts of parliament is the great window by which light is let in upon the sense of them',[25] and from the preamble to the 1593 Act and its parliamentary and wider context we know that the act was provoked by the discovery of the overtly schismatic and separatist congregation associated with the names of Henry Barrow, John Greenwood and John Penry, who all suffered execution on somewhat dubious grounds while the statute was in passage.[26] Similarly, those ecclesiastical canons of 1604 which addressed themselves to the subject of conventicles (nos. 11, 71, 72 and 73) are capable of a specific and relatively narrow historical gloss in each case. Canon 11 intends to condemn outright Brownist and Barrowist separation. Canon 72, which outlaws solemn fasts held publicly or in private, together with 'prophecies or exercises in market towns or other places', also speaks of fasting and prayer to drive out devils, which suggests that the canon in its entirety arose from particular anxieties surrounding the case of John Darrell, the puritan exorcist.[27] Canon 73 speaks of 'conventicles and secret meetings of priests and ministers', which makes it an echo of the Elizabethan classical movement. And by this canon such meetings are only judged unlawful if they 'tend to the impeaching or depraving of the doctrine of the Church of England or of the Book of Common Prayer', or of any part of the established government and discipline of the English Church. So it is by no means as clear as Holdsworth supposed that by 1604 the holding of a conventicle, by which, according to Holdsworth, was meant any assembly for the exercise of religion in another manner than is allowed by the liturgy or practice of the Church of England, was made punishable. Nevertheless, there is evidence that in the perception of the architect of

---

[24] 35 Eliz. I c. 1.
[25] Richard Burn, *Ecclesiastical Law* (London 1781) 2 p. 159.
[26] J.E. Neale, *Elizabeth I and her Parliaments 1584–1601* (London 1957) pp. 280–97.
[27] Collinson, *Elizabethan Puritan Movement* pp. 437–8; Keith Thomas, *Religion and the Decline of Magic* (London 1971) pp. 483–5.

the Canons, Archbishop Bancroft, any privately conducted meetings for 'extraordinary expositions of Scripture or conferences together' stood condemned as 'schismatical conventicles'.[28]

When we reach the Conventicle Acts of the Restoration, 1664 and 1670, we find reference not to 'the exercise of religion in other manner than is allowed' but to 'any Assembly, Conventicle or Meeting under colour or pretence of any exercise of religion in other manner than is allowed ... '[29] a phrase borrowed directly from the Elizabethan Act of 1593. Somewhat may hang upon what we understand by 'under colour or pretence of any exercise of Religion'. If 'exercise of Religion' is an expression properly attributed only to the authorized rites and ceremonies of the Established Church (and *religio* had properly carried that limited sense for centuries) then any other, irregular practice of what was not properly religion at all could amount to a 'colour or pretence of religion', and the intention of these acts may have been simply to outlaw any religious exercise conducted outside the terms of the Act of Uniformity. A Cambridgeshire J.P. seems to have thought that this was the intention of the statute when he asked: 'If the liturgy bee said, question if itt bee a conventicle?'[30] Yet it appears more consistent with the internal logic of the statutes and of what we know of their context and origins to suppose that the phrase 'colour and pretence' hints at other illegal activities for which the religious exercises conducted in conventicles were thought to be a mere pretext and cover. For the title of the 1664 Act speaks of 'seditious conventicles' and it is aimed at 'seditious sectaries and other disloyal persons', who 'under pretence of Tender Consciences do at their Meetings contrive Insurrections, as late Experience hath shewed.' It would be hard indeed to exaggerate the impact of 'late Experience' on the post-1649 perception of religious dissent.

[28] Holdsworth, *History of English Law* 6 p. 198; *Elizabethan Episcopal Administration* ed W.P.M. Kennedy Alcuin Club Collections 27 (London 1925) 3 p. 350.
[29] 16 Car. II c. 4; 22 Car. II c. 1. It would be useful to trace the origin of this phrase. See Bishop Aylmer's visitation articles for London diocese of 1586: 'Whether any schoolmasters under pretence of catechising their scholars ... do keep lectures, readings, or expositions in their houses ...?' (*Elizabethan Episcopal Administration* 3 p. 205).
[30] Bodleian Library MS Rawlinson D 1136 p. 145. I am grateful to Mr Anthony Fletcher for supplying the reference and to Dr Kenneth Fincham for securing a transcript of Sir Thomas Schlater's 'Doubts in the Act for Conventicles'.

Admittedly, the mentality of the legislators may have found it difficult, unnecessary and even meaningless to distinguish between sedition and insurrection in a religious and in a civil sense. Nor do I suggest that local magistrates adhered to the strict terms of the Conventicle Acts, still less to what might appear to be their motivating spirit, in their summary and even arbitrary proceedings against all kinds of private religious meeting, even before the 1664 Act was passed. Nevertheless it is significant that in Parliament at least it was thought inappropriate to make conventicles criminal without connecting them in the public mind, however loosely, with such events as the regicide or Venner's Rising of 1661. In the two years intervening between the implementation of the Uniformity Act and the first Conventicle Act, the steps already being taken against dissenters in Lancashire seem to have been motivated by fear of a presbyterian rebellion, Booth's Rising in reverse. This alarm and the rumours which fuelled it are reflected in the correspondence of Sir Roger Bradshaigh, whose vigilance was desired by three other justices 'to prevent all future dangers which may accrew by the Presbyterians or other factions which tends to the disturbance of the peace and quiet of the Kingdom and the subvertion of his Majesties present Governement.' As the Quaker Act of 1661 and its implementation suggest, Quakers were feared more than Presbyterians as insurrectionaries, and for reasons only indirectly 'religious': above all for their refusal to take the Oath of Allegiance and other oaths, refusing and inciting to refuse inferentially constituting the conspiratorial purpose for which Quaker 'conventicles' were assembled.[31] So it was as 'factious persons' that the frequenters of conventicles were targetted by the cavalier magistracy.

Knowing himself to be no 'factious person', the Lancashire minister, Adam Martindale, was resistant, before the passing of the first Conventicle Act, to any imputation that private religious gatherings were necessarily 'conventicles'. 'For I knew they were not unlawfull by the law of God, ... and some particulars comprehended within their generall terms were confessedly neither against statute, common law, or the canons.' The statute of 1664

---

[31] 'Sir Roger Bradshaigh's Letter-Book' (absit author) *Transactions of the Historic Society for Lancashire and Cheshire* 63 (1912) pp. 120–73; William C. Braithwaite, *The Second Period of Quakerism* (2nd ed Cambridge 1961) pp. 22–3.

left the conscience of this doughty preacher of lawyer-like yeoman stock equally undisturbed. A posse of officers outside the locked doors of a private house in 'a dark corner of Bury parish' was ignored while Martindale calmly concluded an exercise of preaching and prayer. The reverend magistrate before whom he was taken expressed surprise that he should expose himself to the lash of the law for conventicling. 'I told him he was mistaken; it was no conventicle, either by statute, common, or canon law.' As for the first, there was no statute in form which defined it; and for the second, a conventicle, by common law had been defined by the lord chief justice as a meeting together to plot against the King and the state. 'And as for the canons, I told him there was only two cases that were made conventicles by them, and this was neither, as I clearly proved.'[32] So far as I can tell, Martindale was substantially correct. But these things were almost as uncertain as they had been in the days of the Laud-Quatermayne encounter. In September 1662 Henry Newcome desisted from preaching but thought the domestic exercise of repeating sermons no offence. 'But the Justice told me it was.'[33]

III

Let us cease to pretend to be lawyers, or legal historians. What, leaving aside the tinctures of 'faction', 'sedition' or 'insurrection', was a conventicle? Of what did it consist, in content and proceedings and in the perceptions of the participants? As I have already suggested, the subject has not been much explored phenomonologically. Even sources which are among the most familiar to seventeenth-century ecclesiastical historians have not been read with an eye to practice, or to terms and idioms; otherwise the historical literature would display a better sense of the language defining the religious culture of, for example, protestant Lancashire in the time of Newcome and Martindale. Newcome maps out his spiritual odyssey and that of his people in such significant terms

---

[32] *The Life of Adam Martindale Written by Himself* ed R. Parkinson, Chetham Society 4 (Manchester 1845) pp. 145, 194–5.

[33] *The Diary of the Rev. Henry Newcome* ed T. Heywood, Chetham Society 17 (Manchester 1849) p. 126n.

as the distinction between 'private days' and 'public days': that is, private or public days of preaching, prayer and fasting. Note these phrases: 'We had a day in public'; 'Oh what days were these!' 'We kept a private day in the house of Benjamin Brooke in Broughton.' Public is also used substantively of public worship, always called 'the public'. Compare the use of 'the public place' in the annals of Broadmead, Bristol, where the splendid fane of St Mary Redcliffe becomes simply 'Redclif publique place'. The ordinary and daily private devotion of the household or of the individuals who make it up are described by Newcome as 'duty' – 'family duty': 'Wee had sweet family duty'; 'Wee had pretty lively dutyes.' 'Duty' or 'duties' was supplemented by conference and 'repetition', of which more anon. Compare Oliver Heywood's account of his father's religious habits: 'Ever after that he associated himself with gods people, maintained days and dutys of fasting and prayer, conference, and other christian exercises'; 'many days of that nature in my fathers house'.[34] Such was the rhythm and shape of the life pursued by those 'notable christians', known for an 'eminent profession of religion' in the North-West. It was made up of regular 'exercises', together with monthly 'lectures by combination' or 'running exercises', and the less predictable funerals, always marked by two sermons punctuated by dinner.[35] It is in this cultural setting, and according to the authenticity of its own language of identification, that the so-called conventicle must be understood: as a species of religious activity associated by those undertaking it with the private domain: Quatermayne's 'private duties' which were not made void by 'public duties'.

Since the English conventicle was not an invention of the mid-seventeenth century, let us carry this kind of sensitivity back to what I take to be its earliest discernible origins, in the religious gatherings held in private houses in the fifteenth and early sixteenth centuries, uncovered by the ecclesiastical authorities and incriminated by association with Wycliffite heresies held and propagated

---

[34] *The Autobiography of Henry Newcome M.A.* ed R. Parkinson Chetham Society 26 (Manchester 1852) 1 pp. 27, 34, 94; *Diary of Henry Newcome, passim; Records of a Church of Christ* p. 85; *The Rev. Oliver Heywood B.A. 1630–1702; His Autobiography, Diaries (etc.)* ed J. Horsfall Turner (Brighouse) (1882) 1 p. 20.
[35] Collinson, *Godly People* pp. 486–7, 521 n98, 538–9.

by so-called 'Lollards'. 'To encapsulate the history of the conventicle in terms of a continuity with its roots in Lollardy may seem to subscribe to Dr. Christopher Hill's theory of a more or less continuous and coherent tradition of radical dissent, 'from Lollards to Levellers'.[36] That is possible rather than proven or even proveable but it is not something which I wish to argue for on this occasion: rather that at the level of a somewhat low lowest common denominator there is a consistency of habit in the meeting together of a considerable number of 'friends' (in the sense of that word current in the period, that is, embracing kindred as well as unrelated neighbours) for a purpose both sociable and religious. The religious purpose which we happen to know about from the sources available to us was one of dissenting more or less radically from the received doctrine of the Church and orthodox religious practice, and of drawing spiritual sustenance from an alternative source, the Bible or parts of the Bible in the vernacular. It is possible that this tincture of heretical dissent is exaggerated in our sources, even planted there in some cases by the inquisitorial mind:[37] although it could be argued that it was only the critical edge of the heretical or semi-heretical mind which was capable of introducing an element of religious indoctrination and controversy into the idle gossip which might otherwise have accompanied the eating and drinking which was perhaps the chief business on such occasions. Not only their heterodoxy but the structural informality and wholly domestic setting of these gatherings distinguished them from more formal religious fraternities.

The question of Lollard belief enters the present argument only indirectly, for the subject of Lollardy has been discussed too exclusively in terms of belief, as if the thing consisted of a bundle or series of bundles of doctrine, carried about by obscure and in

---

[36] Christopher Hill, 'From Lollards to Levellers', in *Rebels and their Causes: Essays in Honour of A.L. Morton* ed Maurice Cornforth (London 1978) pp. 49–67. In a later essay 'A Bourgeois Revolution?', Dr Hill appears to hold a more open mind on 'whether or not there was a continuity underground from Lollards via Anabaptists and Familists to the sectaries of the 1640s.' (*Three British Revolutions, 1641, 1688, 1776* ed J.G.A. Pocock (Princeton 1980) p. 114). Dr Hill's readers will detect in what follows critical refractions not only of this argument but of his brilliant essays 'The Spiritualization of the Household' and 'Individuals and Communities' in his *Society and Puritanism in Pre-Revolutionary England* (1964).

[37] Anne Hudson, 'The Examination of Lollards', *BIHR* 46 (1973) pp. 145–59; J.A.F. Thompson, *The Later Lollards* (Oxford 1965) p. 229.

themselves unimportant human vectors. The basic *res* of Lollardy, what is available to handle, is not so much a body of beliefs as a corpus, or rather scattered detritus of texts.[38] But what can be said about Lollardy as a social institution? It is important to insist that when Lollards met together, they met as a kind of conventicle, not as some kind of church.[39] It is more profitable to consider what Mrs. Hawisia Moone of Loddon in Norfolk may have meant when, in the late 1420s, she confessed to having been 'right hoomly and prive' with nineteen named persons, four of them priests, 'and many others',[40] than to ask whether the Lollards celebrated the sacraments among themselves. Indeed the latter is probably a question badly put in respect of the later Lollards, since there is hardly enough evidence one way or the other to justify putting it, and to pose it at all is to imply that Lollardy constituted a counter-church with ministers, and that its meetings were 'church' occasions, perhaps conducted vaguely along the lines of a later nonconformist 'service'. Dr. J.A.F. Thompson came close to implying as much when he wrote of 'the Lollard congregations' and 'the Lollard sect'.[41] We may well heed Dr. Euan Cameron's warning about the lesson 'which the late medieval clergy could not learn, that heretics were not like another kind of public church, mirroring the official institution in every detail.'[42] These 'known men' and women comprised not a separate sect but a tendency within a Church so comprehensive that it defied imagination to put oneself wholly outside it.[43] Mistress Alice Rowley of Coventry might boast that 'my beleve is bettur than thirs', but the self-defining elite of which she was part still went to church and behaved themselves there

---

[38] Anne Hudson ed, *Selections from English Wycliffite Writings* (Cambridge 1978); Anne Hudson ed, *English Wyliffite Sermons*, (Oxford 1983); Anne Hudson, *Lollards and their Books* (London 1985). Compare Margaret Aston's 'cultural' rather than textual approach in various essays in *Lollards and Reformers: Images and Literacy in Late Medieval Religion* (London 1984).

[39] But note also the contemporary term 'Lollardorum familia'; Hudson, *Selections* p. 9.

[40] *Heresy Trials in the Diocese of Norwich, 1428–31* ed Norman P. Tanner, Camden 4 ser 20 (1977) p. 140.

[41] Thompson, *Later Lollards* pp. 5, 72, 81, 241.

[42] Euan Cameron, *The Reformation of the Heretics: the Waldenses of the Alps, 1480–1580* (Oxford 1984) p. 261.

[43] See above, pp. 131–53.

with exaggerated devotion.[44] At Amersham the local heretics were so dominant as to dare to demonstrate their contempt for the consecrated host. But it was in church that they conducted themselves in this fashion, and only after mass was over did they go off to their own conventicles.[45] This resembles Elizabethan Puritanism more than Elizabethan Separatism. There are elements of Wycliffite ecclesiology which point in the same direction, the *Lantern of Lizt* distinguishing between the Church as 'a litil flok' of truly faithful souls and as a 'comyng togiddir of good and yvel in a place that is halowid' for sacraments, prayer and preaching; while denouncing the religious orders as 'private religion', 'our new fayned sectis', insisting that 'peple schulde drawe to parische churchis and here her service there.'[46]

If Lollardy was a kind of conventicle, it was also a kind of school, or a conventicle which functioned as a school, and the documents echo to the phrase 'schools of heresy'. Sir Thomas More complained of 'night schools', while a hundred years earlier Hawisia Moone had confessed to the frequent holding of 'scoles of heresie yn prive chambres and prive places of oures', in which she had 'herd, conceyved, learned and reported' errors and heresies.[47] The plurality of 'chambres and prive places' may be significant, for there is no need to suppose that the whole attention of those present in a house on such an occasion would have been concentrated on a single discourse or action. From later generations, Marian, Elizabethan, Jacobean, Caroline, it is possible to collect examples of religious sociability which is distinctly fragmented (to borrow a phrase and concept from Dr Keith Wrightson[48]). It was reported of those present in a house in Ash in East Kent in 1625, where a religious conference between separatists and

---

[44] John Fines, 'Heresy Trials in the Diocese of Coventry and Lichfield, 1511–12' *JEH* 13 (1962) p. 162; *The Acts and Monuments of John Foxe* ed S.R. Cattley (London 1837) 4 p. 558.

[45] Ibid. pp. 224–5.

[46] Hudson, *Selections* pp. 116–17.

[47] *Heresy Trials* p. 140. Cf. Thomas More, *A Dialogue Concerning Heretics, The Complete Works of St Thomas More*, 6 eds T.M.C. Lawler, G. Marc'hadour & R.C. Marius (New Haven 1981) p. 240.

[48] K.E. Wrightson, 'The Puritan Reformation of Manners, With Special Reference to the Counties of Lancashire and Essex, 1640–1660', (Cambridge Ph.D. thesis 1974) p. 38.

non-separatists continued for two whole days, that many said nothing at all and 'some took not any notice at all.'[49]

What were the modes of instruction in a 'school of heresy'? We can distinguish between reading aloud and the recitation of passages of scripture, and the teaching of certain 'lessons', although some of the early sixteenth-century sources suggest that the latter was often a one-to-one tutorial exercise, not necessarily occurring in the context of a well-attended conventicle, or proceeding on its periphery. Of these two elements we can be confident. What is less clear is how far there may also have been religious conference, whether in the sense of the free exploration of religious topics or of the disputation of questions, and whether discussion would have proceeded syllogistically, or by means of biblical texts and precedents, or according to still more primitive mental and rhetorical principles. 'Questions' may have belonged to the realm not of idle curiosity but of conscience. In Mary's days it was conscience which drove the husbandman Henry Orinel from Willingham in Cambridgeshire to a brief and disturbing encounter with the Familist joiner Christopher Vittels in a Colchester inn and sent him on his way again to the more reliable counsel of the protestant bishops imprisoned in Oxford.[50] 'Lessons' taught in Lollard and early protestant circles seem to have been encapsulated in the memorable, aphoristic forms, whether scriptural in origin or 'popular', which Dr Cameron has described as the typical expression of the minds of the heretical mountaineers of the Vaudois in the same period.[51] John Foxe carefully described the prodigious evangelical learning of the cloth-workers of early protestant Hadleigh according to a threefold formula. They had read the whole Bible through. They could recite many of Paul's Epistles by heart. And they were

---

[49] Canterbury Cathedral Archives and Library MS Z.4.4 fols 67^v–9^r. Other examples will be found in Miles Huggarde, *The displaying of the Protestantes* (London 1556) fols 121–5 (Marian); Sir Julius Caesar to Lord Burghley, 18 May 1584, BL MS Lansdowne 157 no 74 fol 186 (Elizabethan); the High Commission case of James and Elizabeth Andrews of Cambridge, Bodleian Library MS Tanner 65 no 35 fols 67–76 (Caroline).

[50] William Wilkinson, *A confutation of certaine articles delivered unto the Family of Love* (London 1579) Sigs ☞ iiii, Ai^r.

[51] Cameron, *Reformation of the Heretics* pp. 68–9.

well able to supply 'a godly learned sentence in any matter of controversy'.[52]

That was a degree of erudition beyond anything attainable before the days of regular protestant preaching and widespread literacy and bible ownership, but one which may have grown out of earlier traditions, especially with respect to 'godly learned sentences', such as the sixty-nine *mala dogmata* listed by the Lower House of Convocation in 1541.[53] Assuming that we are justified in positing some continuity between pre-Reformation 'schools of heresy' and post-Reformation conventicles, a major difference would appear to lie in the greater dependence of the latter on the public sermon and, indeed, on the person and authority of the preacher, whether physically present or represented by the notes of his sermons carried and deployed by the hearers. There were other probable differences between the agenda of a typical early seventeenth-century conventicle and its precursor: notably in the use of vocal prayer, condemned in some Lollard sources as mere 'lip-labour',[54] and in psalm-singing. But these seem to have been concomitants to the main function of the domestic meetings of early protestant generations which was repetition: that is, repetition of sermons.

'Repetition' is among the more neglected words in the religious glossary of the seventeenth century. Among the Elizabethan godly, neighbours met to pray, or to listen to the New Testament or to readings from Foxe's Book of Martyrs, but primarily to engage in repetition.[55] So it was in Lady Margaret Hoby's model household at Hackness[56] and in countless humbler households. It was said of the Norwich M.P. Sir John Hobart that he was unwilling to let a sermon pass without also hearing it repeated.[57] The 'supposed

---

[52] *Acts and Monuments of Foxe* 6 (London 1838) p. 677.

[53] BL MS Harleian MS 419 fols 117–22. Compare William Perkins's list of 'common opinions' (old-fashioned and popish) which his late Elizabethan catechism was designed to replace with acceptable and godly opinions. (*The foundation of Christian religion* (London 1641), Preface 'to all ignorant people'.)

[54] I owe this point to Dr Susan Brigden.

[55] See my 'The Godly: Aspects of Popular Protestantism' in *Godly People* pp. 1–17. The *locus classicus* for this type of religious culture is Sir Julius Caesar's description of a 'conventicle' in the Essex parish of Aythorp Roding, BL MS Lansdowne 157 no 74 fol 186.

[56] *The Diary of Lady Margaret Hoby 1599–1605* ed Dorothy M. Meads (London 1930).

[57] John Collings, *A memorial for posteritie* (London 1647) p. 21.

conventicle' against which the puritan lawyer Nicholas Fuller defended his clients Lord and Maunsell in a *cause célèbre* of 1607 was a regular exercise of repetition. For it was the practice of these Yarmouth shopkeepers on Sunday evenings to join with their minister 'in repeating of the substance and heads of the sermons that day made in the church.'[58] John Udall of Kingston on Thames supplies a rationale for the practice: 'If one have missed the observation of this or that point, another hath marked it, so that among them they may bring away the whole, and so be edefied one by another.'[59] Such was the practice around Manchester and generally in South-East Lancashire and neighbouring parts of Cheshire in the mid-seventeenth century.[60] In Baxter's Kidderminster, 'you might hear a hundred families singing psalms or repeating sermons as you passed through them.'[61] In John Angier's Denton there was repetition of the morning sermon both in Angier's house and in the church 'to many people that stayed there', with psalms sung before and after. This occupied the time until the afternoon sermon, which in its turn was immediately repeated. On Monday nights Angier's family repeated the sermon of the preceding Sunday morning, on Saturday nights the same day's afternoon sermon.[62]

The fact that the principal activity in 'meetings of the godly' was to repeat sermons heard in public earlier in the day is important in itself, the implications of the fact even more so. Repetition was akin to the process of catechizing, in that sermons having been reduced in summary form to their 'heads' (it seems to have been a rare gift to memorise an entire sermon, verbatim[63]) were by repetition impressed, perhaps permanently, on the minds of the hearers. The Fifth Monarchist John Rogers later recorded the consequences of his adolescent exposure to this discipline in his

[58] *The argument of Master Nicholas Fuller in the case of Thomas Lord and Maunsell, his clients* (London 1607) p. 1.

[59] Udall, *Two sermons*, Sig I iiiij.

[60] See the narratives of Thomas Newcome, Adam Martindale and Oliver Heywood, cited elsewhere in this essay.

[61] Quoted, G.R. Cragg, *Puritanism in the Period of the Great Persecution, 1660–1688* (Cambridge 1957) p. 140.

[62] *Oliver Heywood's Life of John Angier of Denton* ed E. Axon, Chetham Society n.s. 97 (Manchester 1937) p. 85.

[63] But see Oliver Heywood's vignette of his brother-in-law Thomas Crampton, 'a man of stupendious memory, that I have heard him repeat a sermon almost verbatim, memoriter ...' (*Oliver Heywood* 1 p. 36).

superstitious habit of repeating sermons to himself in bed, as a kind of talisman to protect himself against the Devil while he slept, and according to a set plan. On Sunday night he would repeat the sermon heard that afternoon, on Monday a sermon heard the previous Sunday, on other nights sermons heard as much as ten years before.[64]

This was how that famous edifice 'the puritan mind' was erected and furnished. We may apply to repetition what has been said of the mental effects of catechisms: that those who listened to sermons and read the Bible did so with faculties trained by catechisms[65] – trained, that is, to arrange what they heard in formal rhetorical structures, a much more advanced facility than the tendency of earlier heretics and protestants to reduce a sermon to one or two strikingly memorable and even scandalous pronouncements, prefaced by 'he hath heard it said that ...' or 'that there was a saying in the country that ...'[66] Mentally and rhetorically this was the very essence of what Dr. Cameron has called 'the reformation of the heretics'.[67]

The gratification offered by the catechetical method may seem to us somewhat elusive, and our prejudice against a stultifying exercise tends to be reinforced by the accounts given by the radical spiritual autobiographers of the age – Quaker, Ranter, Muggletonian – of their subsequent emancipation from the truly vain repetitions of this religious culture. Richard Farnworth, for one, described a youth spent writing and repeating sermons 'and all this while I was but carnall and earthly, knowing nothing ...'[68] However we should not ignore the fact that Henry Newcome employs

---

[64] John Rogers, *Obel or Beth-shemesh* (London 1653) p. 421. Oliver Heywood's mother related to him 'many passages' of sermons she had heard preached before she was married. (*Oliver Heywood* 1 p. 53).

[65] Peter F. Jensen, 'The Life of Faith in the Teaching of Elizabethan Protestants' (Oxford D.Phil. thesis 1979) p. 182.

[66] A.G. Dickens gives examples in 'Heresy and the Origins of English Protestantism' in Dickens, *Reformation Studies* (London 1982) pp. 378–9. See two collections of scandalous and heretical sayings culled from sermons in PRO S P 1/113 fols 106–9, BL MS Cotton Cleopatra E.V fol 397.

[67] In the title of his study of the Waldenses of the Alps, already cited.

[68] *The heart opened by Christ* (London 1654) pp. 1–2. 'Forms of Religion without Life do not profit', we read in *The invisible power of God known in weakness with a Christian testimony of the experience and sufferings of Edward Brush aged ninety-one years* (London 1695) p. 6.

a spiritually emotive language to describe the experiences of his own household as they perfected this art: 'Wee had repetition pretty lively' – 'very comfortable repetition and prayer' – 'after supper wee had repetition pretty sweet'. In his diary for Sunday 11 May 1662, Newcome wrote: 'Now for mee comfort may come in at repetition, and to them that partake of it.' As for whole 'private days', Newcome noted that they were called by some 'soule fatning dayes', while Oliver Heywood wrote of 'a sweet melting heart-inlarging day'.[69]

But for the present purpose the importance of repetition lies chiefly in the link, the umbilical cord as it were, which it served to symbolise between the public assemblies and doctrine of the Church and the exploration of religious knowledge and experience at a private and domestic level; and also between the trained and qualified professional, the minister, and his people. So long as lay participation in conventicles, whether or not a minister was present, was confined to the derivative exercise of repeating what had been uttered authoritatively from the pulpit, stopping short of an original exposition of the text, then there was no separatist implication, no claim that God was communicating in a directly inspirational manner with and through the minds and tongues of those gathered in private. This was the case even when the doctrine was carried back from other parishes by those who 'gadded' to sermons elsewhere for want of preaching at home or in pursuit of 'edification', a practice typical of Elizabethan lay puritanism and yet not schismatic, neither in the perception of the gadders themselves nor according to some ecclesiastical lawyers.[70] And even within the separated world of the gathered sect, the same principle of dependence might prevail. In the Weald of Kent in 1627 we come across Margaret Adams, an old woman who trudged around with 'notes in papers' of the sermons of the separatist tallow chandler John Turner 'and where she commeth there she sheweth them.'[71] When

---

[69] *Diary of Henry Newcome* pp. 14, 36, 41, 83; *Oliver Heywood* 1 p. 199. Cf. Humphrey Mills's recollection of Richard Sibbes's 'sweet soul-melting Gospel-sermons.' (Rogers, *Obel* p. 410).

[70] Collinson, *Religion of Protestants* pp. 248–9.

[71] Canterbury Cathedral Archives and Library MS Z.4.4 fol 208. For Turner, see R.J. Acheson, 'Sion's Saint: John Turner of Sutton Valence,' *Archaeologia Cantiana* 99 (1983) pp. 183–97.

defenders of the godly way of life spoke of their meetings as 'honest and lawful conventions'[72] and denied that they were conventicles in any pejorative sense, they meant that those participating were regular attenders at public worship who did not presume to utter original doctrine in their more private meetings.

By the same token, the moment at which a conventicle or private 'society' of christians ceased (in these terms) to be an innocent and legally defensible annexe to the public assembly and became, in its own eyes, a separated and gathered church in its own right might coincide with the point at which the leaders of the group cast aside their sermon notes and depended upon their own relatively unaided capacity to expound directly from the biblical text. The *locus classicus* for this process of emancipation is the Baptist William Kiffen's *Remarkable Passages*, where we encounter a group of London apprentices (which included the future Leveller John Lilburne) which met at five in the morning, an hour before the lecture at one of their preferred London churches, to pray, communicate to one another what they had received from the Lord, 'or else to repeat some sermon which we had heard before.' But in the course of time they began to read a portion of Scripture and to speak from it 'what it pleased God to enable us.'[73] The annals of Broadmead, Bristol, record a similar progression, from informal meetings for repetition, 'repeating their notes to one another, whetting it on their hearts', to separation from the 'public places', with gifted 'brethren of the Church' taking on the ministry and 'carrying on the Meetings'. Significantly it was at this point that the separatist presumption of the group attracted public hostility with a riotous mob attacking their meeting place and complaining of the novelty of 'a Church with a Chimney in it.'[74]

This was a very thin line to cross, a tiny ditch, but a Rubicon nevertheless. Participants in a late Elizabethan Dover 'conventicle' protested that their meetings implied no intention 'to become singular' but were undertaken 'in the way of simplicitie'. Yet, with the best will in the world, and in all simplicity, 'singularity' could

---

[72] The defensive phrase was used of meetings gathered in the Wealden town of Cranbrook in the mid-1570s by John Strowd. (Collinson, *Godly People* p. 418).

[73] *Remarkable Passages in the Life of William Kiffin Written by Himself* ed William Orme (London 1823) pp. 11–14.

[74] *Records of a Church of Christ* pp. 82, 85–6, 97.

not always be avoided.[75] It was said of the early Bristol Separatists that in 1640 there were no more than five of them, and that like Abraham they went out 'not knowing where they went.'[76] No doubt in many cases the first steps into schism were taken blindfold, and as a series of more or less instinctive reactions to circumstances, although we should not underestimate the charismatic role in initiating a decisive separation of leaders like Dorothy Hazzard in Bristol, or Katherine Chidley in Bury St Edmunds, with her tiny nucleus of eight covenanting members.[77] Some of these emigrations into separatist dissent are well-documented and provide familiar paradigms in the history of nonconformity. Others are a matter of inference. We do not know who or what turned the godly of Cranbrook whose persons and 'private communion' their minister Robert Abbot had 'loved' and approved into incorrigible Brownists who rejected his ministry outright. Probably it was no single heresiarch, or Abbot would surely have named him in his book *A Trial of our Church Forsakers*, or in his correspondence with Sir Edward Dering.[78] But it is a reasonable inference that a large number of dissenting churches of late seventeenth-century Kent had come into being before 1662, many of them in the 1640s, and by some process which had transformed non-separated conventicles into fully gathered churches.[79]

IV

The argument of the remainder of this paper proceeds along intentionally different lines from the time-honoured exercise of tracing the origins and development of 'The English Separatist Tradition',

[75] Canterbury Cathedral Archives and Library MS X.9.1, fol 5. I owe this reference to Dr. R.J. Acheson.
[76] *Records of a Church of Christ* pp. 88–9.
[77] John Browne, *History of Congregationalism and the Memorials of the Churches in Norfolk and Suffolk* (London 1877) pp. 393–5; G.F. Nuttall, *Visible Saints: The Congregational Way 1640–1660* (Oxford 1957) pp. 27–9, 52. Katherine Chidley was the author of *The iustification of the Independent Churches of Christ* (London 1641).
[78] Collinson, 'Cranbrook and the Fletchers: Popular and Unpopular Religion in the Kentish Weald', in *Godly People* pp. 427–8.
[79] G.F. Nuttall, 'Dissenting Churches in Kent before 1700' *JEH* 14 (1963) pp. 175–89.

and establishing the proper genealogy of English, or American, Congregationalism.[80] There was, in the exceptional circumstances of the mid-seventeenth century political and ecclesiastical crisis, as, somewhat earlier, in the even more unusual environment of New England, a convergence of religious experience and practice upon elements and even the core and essence of the tradition of radical and exclusive dissent with which the argument *is* concerned, although it is fundamental to my purpose to insist that that convergence was as circumstantial and fortuitous as any great departures in human affairs can be. I refer to the coalescence of the 'Independency' of 'the Congregational Way'. At the heart of that emergent tradition was an ecclesiology, a settled and developed conviction that the national corporation calling itself the Church of England was not, as a body, a true Church of Christ, a title restricted to gathered and covenanted societies of 'visible saints'; although (according to all but the most far out of sectaries) the national parochial church might contain true Christians within it. We are not concerned with the theoretical formulation and elaboration of that proposition either, but only with some of the personal and collective circumstances and experiences which contributed to it.

Those who look for the beginnings of Separatism, as a principled and 'ideological' application of certain strongly discriminatory scriptural texts, rightly begin with the most drastic separation in all English religious history: the conviction of the first generation of lay protestants, in all probability planted in their consciences by highly educated preachers, and subsequently brought to white heat in the Marian persecution, that they and they alone constituted the elect of Christ's little flock, the two or three gathered in his name.[81] 'Wherefore', wrote the Essex curate William Tyms 'to all God's

---

[80] Most recently, B.R. White, *The English Separatist Tradition: from the Marian Martyrs to the Pilgrim Fathers* (Oxford 1971) and Michael R. Watts, *The Dissenters: from the Reformation to the French Revolution* (Oxford 1978). For a fuller exploration and exposition of the contentious issues hinted at in this paragraph, see my essay 'Towards a Broader Understanding of the Early Dissenting Tradition', in *Godly People* pp. 527–62.

[81] See examples in *Acts and Monuments of Foxe* (London 1839) 8 p. 330, 499. It was not some Lollard hedge-priest but Bishop William Barlow who in November 1536 preached that 'where so ever ii or iii simple persons as ii coblers or wevers were in company and elected in the name of God, that ther was the trewe Churches of God.' (BL MS Cotton Cleopatra E.V fol 415).

faithfull servants', 'come out from among them and separate your-selves ... and touch no unclean thing.' When the Londoner Ger-trude Crockhay was told on her deathbed that unless she recanted and received the sacrament she could not be given christian burial she exalted: 'Oh how happy am I that I shall not rise with them but against them!'[82] But here we are concerned with the post-1559 protestant establishment, and with those situations in which a conscientious testimony was sustained against 'Anabaptist' Sepa-ratism and where there was no deliberate intention to contract the universality of the Church into the petty sectarian particularity of the conventicle; and yet where this nevertheless tended, against all intentionality, to happen. In the broader context of christian history, seen through Troeltschian spectacles, this was a poignant chapter in English seventeenth-century religious history, and one contained broadly within what was emergent as the presbyterian wing of the puritan tradition, or close to the indeterminate frontier dividing Presbyterianism from the Independency of the Con-gregational Way.

That we are able to observe this chapter in some intimate detail we owe to the habit of those ministers of the time who kept diaries or made autobiographies out of their experience. I refer to the first-person narratives of the Lancastrians, Thomas Newcome, Adam Martindale, Thomas Jolly and Oliver Heywood.[83] But the roots of this self-monitoring introspection grew in East Anglia and Essex, where Richard Rogers wrote his diary in the Armada years and afterwards. For Oliver Heywood wrote the life of John Angier who came out of Dedham where Rogers's formidable kinsman John Rogers ruled the Jacobean pulpit and was trained by John Cotton of Boston who was himself in debt to this tradition.[84] Newcome tells us that it was the diary of Samuel Ward of Sidney Sussex with its many frank disclosures which first inspired him: 'I thought it was a very brave thing ...'[85]

---

[82] *Acts and Monuments of Foxe* 8 pp. 118, 728.
[83] References to Newcome, Martindale and Heywood earlier in this essay; add *The Note Book of the Rev. Thomas Jolly ... Extracts from the Church Book of Altham and Wymondhouses*, ed Henry Fishwick, Chetham Society n.s. 33 (Manchester 1895) pp. 120–1.
[84] *Two Elizabethan Puritan Diaries by Richard Rogers and Samuel Ward* ed M.M. Knappen (Chicago 1933); *Heywood's Life of Angier*.
[85] *Autobiography of Newcome* I p. 14.

The fullest as well as the bravest record of the puritan conscience in action in this uncertain time, pitched somewhat between Presbyterianism and Independency, established church and gathered church, is the Diary of Ralph Josselin, vicar of Earls Colne near Colchester:[86] the Josselin who recalled how he was first drawn to the awesome challenge of the ministerial office: 'I confesse my childhood was taken with ministers and I heard with delight and admiration and desire to imitate them from my youth, and would be acting in corners': words which are echoed in Newcome's Lancashire autobiography where we find a childhood 'attempting making English discourses sermonwise at vacant times ... it being my ordinary play and office to act the minister among my playfellows.'[87]

These narratives bring us into close contact with the professional christian, striving through a lifetime of pastoral endeavour to retain and strengthen a sense of obligation to all God's people, to those afar off as well as those that were nigh. 'Have a care of the whole flock', Cromwell told Barebone's Parliament.[88] In the perception of ministers and preachers like these, voyaging together in a broad-bottomed and by now securely established puritan tradition, the conventicle and its membership constituted that portion of a large and fluctuating parochial flock which was responsive to the gospel and willingly subject to its discipline, the kind of christians described as 'conscionable', 'eminent', 'serious', 'the regenerate and truely religious christians', 'renowned christians'.[89] When Rogers of Wethersfield entered into a special covenant with a score of his people in 1588 he remarked that they did 'as farre exceed the common sort of them that professe the Gospell as the common professors do exceed them in religion which know not the

---

[86] *The Diary of Ralph Josselin 1616–1683* ed Alan Macfarlane, Records of Social and Economic History 3 (Oxford 1976). See also Alan Macfarlane, *The Family Life of Ralph Josselin A Seventeenth-Century Clergyman: An Essay in Historical Anthropology* (Cambridge 1970).

[87] *Diary of Josselin* p. 1; *Autobiography of Newcome* p. 7. And cf. Heywood: 'When I was a little child I delighted in imitating preachers and acting that part among my playfellows.' (*Oliver Heywood* 1 p. 157).

[88] W.C. Abbott, *The Writings and Speeches of Oliver Cromwell* (Cambridge Mass. 1947) 3 p. 62.

[89] Richard Bernard, *The ready way to good works* (London 1635) pp. 281, 311.

Gospell',[90] those whose practice of religion was prodigious. In many of these little societies there seems to have been a female preponderance, explicable in terms of the special relationship often forged between preachers and anxious, self-deprecating Calvinist women, enduring what Oliver Heywood, describing his own mother, called their 'soul troubles'.[91] Whether they chose to or not, ministers in this tradition found that they had an exclusive relationship with these super-christians which may have threatened their more general pastoral success. Adam Martindale, wrestling in conscience with the issues dividing the Presbyterian and Congregational tendencies in what he called 'that bustling year' of 1646, when both struggled in the womb like Jacob and Esau, wrote: 'I made no doubt of the truth of our English Churches, and consequently I thought they needed onely reformation, no new constitution, and that the congregationall way of gathering churches was the way to spoile many churches for the new making of one.' Yet Martindale was unable to fulfil his pastoral obligation to the entire parochial congregation, including the profane majority, especially since he lacked the power of discipline over those who stayed away from his ministrations. Of these he wrote that he was unlikely to see the faces of the tenth part of them.[92]

One way of defining a conventicle of the mid-seventeenth century would be to say that it consisted of faces which ministers like Martindale saw rather frequently, the inner fold of a scattered flock. And yet this little flock, with its intricate fabric of special intimacies, maintained a deeply conscientious abhorrence of separation and separatism. That abhorrence is deeply imprinted in the biographies of the famous ministers and eminent 'private christians' of this generation, which were derived from funeral sermons and built into substantial bodies of hagiographical ecclesiastical history

---

[90] Richard Rogers, *Seaven treatises* (London 1605) fol 478[r]. Rogers insisted that their meetings were not conventicles 'for the disturbance of the state of the Church and peace thereof.'

[91] *Oliver Heywood* 1 p. 42. See my 'The Role of Women in the English Reformation Illustrated by the Life and Friendships of Anne Locke', in *Godly People* pp. 273–87. I hope to write more extensively elsewhere on the implications of women's 'soul troubles'.

[92] *Life of Martindale* pp. 61, 66–7.

by Samuel Clark, minister of St Bennet Fink.[93] In the post-Restoration situation for which these 'lives' were adapted, anti-separatism served an obvious polemical purpose, yet there is not reason to doubt the authenticity of these convictions in their original, Jacobean context. Witness the anti-separatist polemics of Richard Bernard, John Darrell, William Bradshaw and many other ministers. Bradshaw wrote of the 'mistake' of supposing that non-conformists were 'all Brownists in heart', recalling 'how many Non-Conformists have written against Brownisme, as Maister Cartwright, Gifford, Hildersham, Darrell, Brightman, Ames, Paget etc.'[94] So John Staunton was said to have declaimed against Separatism as England's 'incurable wound': 'It will never be well within the Church of God in this Nation so long as Christians are so prone to division and separation.' Arthur Hildersham was called 'the hammer of schismatics' and Thomas Taylor was credited with mightily confuting and reclaiming Brownists.[95] Thomas Gataker's life of Bradshaw ('and indeed to separatists he was ever very adverse') quotes him as declaiming in a public sermon: 'It is the great mercy of God toward us that we have no cause to seek the word in deserts and wildernesses, in woods and caves and desolate

---

[93] Patrick Collinson, '"A Magazine of Religious Patterns" An Erasmian Topic Transposed in English Protestantism', in *Godly People* pp. 499–525.

[94] William Bradshaw, *The unreasonablenesse of the separation* (London 1614) Preface. See also Richard Bernard, *Christian advertisements and counsels of peace: also disswasions from the Separatists schisme, commonly called Brownisme* (London 1608), *Plaine evidences* (London 1610); Henoch Clapham, *The syn against the Holy Ghost* (Amsterdam 1598), *Antidoton: or a soveraigne remedie against schisme and heresie* (London 1600), *Errour on the right hand, through a preposterous zeale* (London 1608); John Darrell, *A treatise of the Church, written against them of the separation, commonly called Brownists* (London 1617); Peter Fairlambe, *The recantation of a Brownist* (London 1606); Henry Jacob, *A defence of the churches and ministery of Englande* (Middleburg 1599), *A declaration and plaine opening of certaine points* (Middelburg 1611); John Paget, *An arrow against the separation of the Brownists* (London 1618). Particular interest attaches to the writings of the reverted Separatists, Clapham, Fairlambe and White, and to the polemics of Bernard, Bradshaw and Darrell, who had all spent time on the Separatist frontier. Jacob was a *complexio oppositorum*. But see the pronouncement in *A declaration and plaine opening* p. 5: 'Howsoever, as to the point of separation, for my part I never was, nor am separated from all publike communion with the congregations of England.'

[95] Samuel Clarke, *The lives of sundry eminent persons in this latter age* (London 1683) p. 170; Samuel Clarke, *A general martyrologie* (London 1677) pp. 120, 126, 56–7; Samuel Clarke, *The Lives of two and twenty English divines* (London 1660) p. 73.

mountains, but such worthy edifices as these to assemble in, dedicated only to this use.' Even among puritans more deeply alienated from the establishment than ministers of the mainstream we find the same aversion from what the radical Scot Alexander Leighton called the 'quicksands of Separation'.[96] Far from cherishing the parish churches as 'worthy edifices', Randall Bate, who died in a London prison in 1613, demanded their total destruction, as temples dedicated to idols. Yet no Jacobean puritan denounced separatism more vehemently than Bate, insisting that the communion of the godly in private meetings must never lead to neglect of 'public meanes'. 'Men must not separate till the Lord separate.' 'This kind of separation obscures the good providence of God towards the land.' 'Make not the Church weak by your renting from it.'[97] When Archbishop Laud charged Roger Quatermayne with being 'the ring-leader of all the separatists', Quatermayne retorted that he was 'one of their greatest opposites'.[98]

We may find this insistence hard to understand, even incredible, and difficult to penetrate. Was the attitude of a puritan like Bate to 'the public' comparable to our own rectitude in respect of civic duty, tax-paying, jury service and the like, and thus a *political* sentiment? Did the warmer feelings aroused in private meetings where there existed, in principle, no barriers or differences, no scandals not sought out and cauterised by mutual discipline, represent the substance of church fellowship, attendance on public duties and means their formal and empty shell? Perhaps, although twentieth century christians are almost disqualified from answering such a difficult question.

However, there was more than one form of separation. Jeremy Corderoy, no 'Separatist', in his *Warning for Worldlings* (1608) addressed himself to you, 'most deerely beloved brethren ... who have separated your selves from other men, to set forth the glory of God.'[99] The Gloucestershire minister John Sprint wrote of

[96] Quoted, Stephen Foster, *Notes from the Caroline Underground* Studies in British History and Culture 6 (Hamden Conn. 1978) p. 27.

[97] *Certaine observations of that reverend religious and faithfull servant of God and glorious martyr of Iesus Christ, M. Randal Bate* (Amsterdam 1624?) pp. 177, 183–9. For Bate, see Foster, *Notes*, p. 89 n37.

[98] Quatermayne, *Quatermayns conquest* p. 18.

[99] Jeremy Corderoy, *Warning for worldlings* (London 1608) Sig A 10.

separating *in the Church*, that is, from its corruptions; and John Paget, minister of the unseparated English congregation in Amsterdam, recommended 'separation from known evils, but not from the Churches of Christ for evilles among them.' It was a commonplace among the unseparated that this kind of separation was more costly than the way taken by the Brownists. One such puritan wrote to a friend in John Robinson's Leiden congregation and reproached him for not choosing to share 'the sharpe scourge of persecution' among 'our poor afflicted brethren'. Sprint wrote: 'We suffer for separating in the Church.'[100]

Whether this language referred to real persecution or was simply the metaphorical rhetoric of spiritual travail, unseparated puritans practised, or at least preached, a drastic separation not only from 'known evils' and corrupt practices but from purportedly evil and corrupt persons, their neighbours. And here we confront three paradoxes which will complete the argument. As the popular Reformation progressed and put down social roots, as preaching became more prevalent and instructed Protestants more numerous, the conviction that true christians – the 'better part' – were a mere remnant, 'the fewer part', whereas christians 'in name only' comprised 'the greater part', seems to have grown in intensity and practical application. Jeremy Corderoy took it for granted that he lived in 'the last times', when 'corruption of manners shal most abound.'[101] John Darrell thought that nineteen parts out of twenty might prove to be 'naught', 'but the twentieth part good'.[102] This deeply pessimistic diagnosis was shared with the Separatists, for whom the scandal of promiscuous church membership was the strongest of all imperatives to separate.[103] Yet antiseparatists or semi-separatists like Darrell or Richard Bernard (and this was the key to their ecclesiology) professed not to doubt that a little leaven

---

[100] Collinson, *Religion of Protestants* p. 277.
[101] Jeremy Corderoy, *A short dialogue wherein is proved that no man can be saved without good works* (Oxford 1604), Epistle.
[102] Darrell, *Treatise of the Church* pp. 28–9.
[103] Or so I would argue. But strictly speaking, the Separatist platform was laid by Henry Barrow in the form of a quadrilateral, of which the second plank was 'the profane and ungodlie people receved into and retayned in the bozom and bodie of ther churches.' (Henry Barrow, 'Foure Causes of Separation', in *The Writings of Henry Barrow 1587–1590* ed Leland H. Carlson, Elizabethan Nonconformist Texts 3 (London 1962) p. 54).

entitled the whole lump to the title of 'churches of the saints' 'in the respect of the better part, though the fewer by many.' 'So we speake, calling a heape of chaffe and wheate wheate onely, not naming the chaffe ...' In the parable of the tares, the field signified not the world but the visible Church, 'a mixt companie of good and bad' for which the primitive church at Corinth was an apt model.[104]

The second paradox is that the semi-separatism or merely social separatism advocated and, to an extent hard to measure, practised by Jacobean puritans was more starkly divisive in its consequences, more prejudicial to consensual community values, than strict ecclesiastical separatism. The separatist elder and ideologue Henry Ainsworth taught that the saints were to have no communion with the wicked in matters of religion, whereas his advice in respect of all other occasions of life was relaxed and permissive. In civil affairs such as eating and drinking, buying and selling, the saints were taught of God to converse with the wicked in peace.[105] How else could the separated live in the foreign environment of Amsterdam? But even in England a separatist might conduct himself with tact and circumspection. The Wealden tallow chandler John Turner was accounted by his neighbours 'a separatist from the Church of England' but 'yet in his dealinges was taken and reputed for an honest man.'[106] With the non-separated puritans, still living in the English parishes, the position was exactly reversed. It was necessary to gather and even communicate with the wicked and promiscuous multitude in the public exercises of religion. The law required it. St Paul writing to the Corinthians positively commended it. Those who had the authority to do so ought to separate out the ungodly, as Hagar and Ishmael were put out of the tent and into the wilderness. But if the magistrate failed to do this – the only act of

---

[104] Bernard, *Christian advertisements* p. 86; Stephen Bredwell, *The rasing of the foundation of Brownisme* (London 1588) p. 20. See also Richard Alison, *A plaine confutation of a treatise of Brownisme* (London 1590): 'In the visible Church of God there will be tares, yea untill the harvest: chaffe among the wheat, goates among the sheep, hypocrites among the true professors: nay to go further, Antichrist for a time sitting in the temple of God, and other monstrous men abiding in the Church, turning the grace of God into wantonnesse.' (pp. 12–13).

[105] Henry Ainsworth, *The communion of saints* (Amsterdam 1607) p. 137.

[106] Canterbury Cathedral Archives and Library MS X.II.16 fol 103ᵛ.

separation which could be justified – there was no obvious remedy for the private christian. Thomas Hooker taught: 'Suppose they that are in authority will not separate them ... yet the saints of God should not abstain from the congregation. It is pitiful indeed and the thing is troublesome and tedious to a gracious heart (and we must mourn for it) but being [so], it is not in my power; I must not abstain.' However, in all private respects, 'familiar accompanying in private conversation', the godly man not only could but must cut himself off. This too was Paul's doctrine. 1 Corinthians 5:9–10. As a Carlisle preacher put it in 1614: 'Though a corporall separation cannot be had, yet in spirit thou must separate thyselfe.' 'Keepe thy selfe in the fresh aire.' 'Be no common companie keeper', wrote Richard Kilby of Derby. At Paul's Cross, William Crashawe's advice was the same: 'Wee must separate our selves from the wicked mans companie and societie, as far as lawfully and conveniently we may.' That was the true application of Jeremiah 51:11, forsaking Babel. Thomas Hooker's Chelmsford hearers were told: 'I can keep a man out of my house, but I cannot fling him out of the open congregation.'[107] As early as 1588 Stephen Bredwell had asked whether this principle undermined such fundamental social and political obligations as marriage, parenthood, civil obedience and commercial bargains. The answer was no. We must not be unnatural. But such necessary duties, when performed towards the carnal or wicked, must be undertaken with a 'kind of mourning and affliction for their sakes.'[108] In other words, a wife must not refuse her ungodly husband his conjugal rights. But she must not appear to enjoy it.

The conventicle, into which the godly withdrew from the 'company keeping' of what has been called the 'festive community',[109] no longer seems as innocuous as it did when we set out on this enquiry. Given the expectations and necessary conditions of a harmonious social existence in seventeenth-century England, it now

[107] *Thomas Hooker: Writings in England and Holland, 1626–1633* ed George H. Williams et al., Harvard Theological Studies 28 (Cambridge Mass. 1975) 110–11; Bernard, *Christian advertisements* p. 108; Lancelot Dawes, *Two sermons preached at the Assise holden at Carlisle* (Oxford 1614) pp. 33–5, 38; Richard Kilby, *The burthen of a loaden conscience* (Cambridge 1608) p. 95; William Crashawe, *The sermon preached at the Crosse Feb. xiiij 1607* (1608).

[108] Bredwell, *The rasing of the foundations* p. 39.

[109] Wrightson, 'The Puritan Reformation of Manners' pp. 24–5.

looks thoroughly obnoxious. So we come to our third and final paradox, a familiar one which is so central to the traditional historiography of the puritan revolution that there will be no need to labour it. Just when the deep contradictions of Jacobean Puritanism should have been resolved in an all-embracing reformation, and when the spiritual resources built up in the conventicle ought to have been generally released to the Church at large, almost the reverse happened. In the 1640s the Church in the puritan parish – or in some parishes known to us – effectively contracted to the limits of the conventicle which now came closer than ever before to detaching itself from the nominal christianity of those outside its narrow walls. That is far from adequate as an account of the great diversity of ecclesiastical history in the period of the Civil Wars and Commonwealth. It also ignores the origins of powerful sectarian movements in the opportunities and opportunism of the time, which actively and willingly liberated forces and tendencies previously suppressed. I should not want to argue that the Quakers happened in a fit of absence of mind. But so far as the puritan mainstream is concerned, the analogy of a great glacier advancing to engulf a whole landscape but then surprising itself by disintegrating and calving icebergs into a chilly sea seems apt.

Or so the precious autobiographical narratives suggest. Here we find on the one hand the imperialistic puritan imperative, looking for nothing less than a general and national reformation, on the other the sense of a certain number, all too few, of 'serious Christians', those who are known for 'an eminent profession of religion', 'substantiall Christians of our societie'. Adam Martindale was attracted to a parish 'where there was a knot of good people'. 'Our society', whether in Martindale's Gorton or Jolly's Altham or Josselin's Colne was a choice but tiny fragment, almost lost to sight among the vastly more numerous ignorant and profane, Martindale remarking of his own large parish that 'the multitudes of the people would be dead, in all probability, ere we could goe once over them.'[110]

The crossroads was reached with the power now in principle within the grasp of many such ministers to apply stringent pastoral discipline, excluding from the sacrament all but the visibly worthy.

[110] *Life of Martindale* pp. 133, 79, 122.

In one direction the road led up from this crux to the sunny uplands of an effective discipline on Scottish lines, something far from impossible in some parts of South-East Lancashire. But in the other it ran steeply down into a cosy but insecure sectarian hollow. Mainstream Puritanism, having fought its way to the cross-roads, hoped to find the high road but more often than not missed its way. Martindale's conditions of admission to the sacrament effectively restricted what in the north of England were called 'rightings' to 'serious christians', for he required communicants to use prayer and instruction in their families, to read the Bible and to sanctify the Lord's Day 'according to which rule (since the Reformation) we conceive we have walked and (God assisting) do intend to continue so.'[111] But who, in Lancashire, were 'we'? In Jolly's Altham, where this was called 'good order', the Lord's Supper was reserved for those who were worthy, that is, 'saints visible to the eye of rational charity'. These comprised 'the society of God's people', and baptism was made available only to the children of those who were now designated *members*, persons who had subscribed a church covenant. These were just twenty-nine persons, including fourteen women, representing only twenty of the 150 families which made up the parish. This gathered church within the Church never numbered more than two or three dozen, and yet it retained the ambition of imposing a general reformation on the whole community, at the time of the major-generals offering to search out in their houses the nineteen out of twenty who never went to church. But in 1656 it was noted: 'No conversion work at Altham.' After St Bartholomew Day 1662 the little 'society' withdrew altogether from public worship and reverted to meeting in an alehouse, where, in 1667, Jolly preached to two women only.[112]

Josselin's diary tells a similar story of sectarian defeat snatched from the jaws of puritan triumph, but with a less drastic and tidy conclusion. In Earls Colne the involuntary drift in a sectarian direction is first perceptible in 1645, when Josselin refers to household meetings with those in spiritual affinity as 'conference with divers of my people', 'the society of divers loving friends' and 'the

[111] *Ibid.* p. 129.
[112] *Note Book of Thomas Jolly* pp. 120–1, 128, 133–4; Wrightson, 'The Puritan Reformation of Manners' p. 281.

society of my friends', but when 'the society' had yet to become, as at Jolly's Altham, a formalised, covenanted membership. But in December 1646 Josselin and his intimates pitched upon a method and order for their meetings and met for the first time in Josselin's house.[113] On the face of it, these were 'lawful conventions' of a traditional type, and no threat or alternative to public church assemblies. But in the absence of the ecclesiastical courts and without any alternative form of credible parochial discipline, the assemblies were no longer very public. The sacrament of the Lord's Supper was already suspended (and remained in suspense for nine years), while in May 1647 Josselin noted that his congregation had grown 'very thinne ... people seldom frequent hearing the word.'[114]

Meanwhile the small circle of 'the society', itself attended in August 1647 by 'very few', was threatened on the one hand by backwardness and indifference, on the other by the 'opinionative' who were insisting that only 'real saints ... so farr as we can discerne' were to remain in fellowship. Although Josselin from time to time recorded 'comfortable' meetings and 'sweet' discourse, by the summer of 1648 (and with 'the Puritans' ostensibly triumphant what irony in this dating!) he doubted whether there was still work in Colne for him to do.[115] Sometimes it seemed that his 'friend of friends' and benefactor Mistress Mary Church, the source of 'loving and plentiful entertainment' for the society, was his only support. 'The Lord thins our town of christian people.' Moreover he had difficulty in securing his tithe income and probably doubted his right in conscience to collect it from parishioners who failed to come within his restrictive definition of 'christian people'. But the crisis passed thanks paradoxically to the death of Mistress Church, from whose estate Josselin benefitted.[116]

In February 1651 the Lord's Supper was administered for the first time for many years, but only to 'such as in charity wee reckon to be disciples', some thirty-four persons. Although there was no covenanting, or none which Josselin recorded, it was on this deeply moving occasion that 'our society', now with formal

---

[113] *Diary of Josselin* pp. 31, 33, 77–9, 81.
[114] *Ibid.* pp. 77, 230, 516, 83.
[115] *Ibid.* pp. 102, 105, 124, 126, 132, 235, 137–8.
[116] *Ibid.* pp. 197, 127, 140, 134–5, 204–5, 210.

procedures for admission, became, in effect, the Church in Earls Colne. A few weeks later the subject of conference was 'the practice of love mutually one to another', and in May there was another conference 'about the Saints mutually praying for one another.'[117] Yet in the 1650s Josselin continued to preach to 'sleepy hearers' and anyone else who cared to attend the larger, open and more diffuse congregation in church, where parishioners were still liable to insist in noisily disruptive fashion that their tithes and rates entitled them to a place.[118] Let us drop, for a moment, the convention which made such church attenders 'carnal' and irreligious. The population of Earls Colne was not far short of 900.[119] Large numbers of now nameless christian people continued to claim their baptismal rights and to perform some of their duties, however vestigial, more or less regardless of developments which, in the eyes of a dominant but tiny minority, denied them all or most interest in it.

The Restoration found Josselin still secure as vicar of Colne, as, more surprisingly, did the Sundays following 24 August 1662, when 'great droves of people' flocked to hear him preach, doubtless attracted by the curiosity of the last beneficed nonconformist in that part of the country. Subsequently, congregations fell back to eighty or ninety.[120] But when the Lord's Supper was revived on Easter Day 1665 (the first Easter administration since the early 1640s) there were only twelve communicants, in 1669 twenty, in 1670 fourteen. On Easter Day 1674, Josselin wrote: 'Christs number at this sacrament. 6 men and 6 women and my selfe.' In 1679 'wee had 4 men. 12 women at sacrament.' As for conventicles, or meetings of 'the society' they had ceased, or at least are no longer mentioned by Josselin.[121]

It would make for a tidy conclusion to be able to say that by now roles were reversed. The conventicle had become the church, in the form of a tiny group of less than twenty communicants; whereas it was the open assembly of the parish church building which had become a peripheral and more or less casual audience

---

[117] *Ibid.* pp. 235, 238, 244, 313.
[118] *Ibid.* pp. 376–7.
[119] Wrightson, 'The Puritan Reformation of Manners' p. 273.
[120] Diary of Josselin pp. 492, 505.
[121] *Ibid.* pp. 516, 546, 553, 574, 621.

of 'sleepy hearers'. Dissent was fully institutionalized, to endure for three centuries. But there is no neatly severed end to the strands of this rope, only a mass of loose and straggly threads. Josselin died in 1683, still vicar of Colne and so still charged with the cure of all its many souls. One loose end is old Henry Newcome, deprived of his living and denied a public ministry but still taking himself off to 'the public' in the first years of James II 'out of conscience of the duty of public worship: and I bless God I met with something that did me good.'[122] Another frayed thread is Adam Martindale, scrupulously and 'constantly' attending the sermons of the conformist who had supplanted him and then following the old custom of repeating the sermons to 'an house full of parishioners of the devoutest sort' – who were kind enough to say that they liked the sermons better in the repetition than in the preaching.[123] The interacting themes of voluntary and involuntary religion are an endless and never resolved counterpoint. Here we have heard no more than a few bars of a theme explored elsewhere in this volume through more variations than Diabelli inspired in Beethoven.

University of Sheffield

---

[122] *Autobiography of Newcome* ed Richard Parkinson, Chetham Society 27 (Manchester 1862) 2 p. 257.
[123] *Life of Martindale* p. 173.

OLIVER HEYWOOD AND HIS CONGREGATION

by W.J. SHEILS

THE ministerial career of the presbyterian divine Oliver Heywood, spanning as it did the years from 1650, when as a young man still technically too young for ordination he first accepted the call of the congregation at Coley chapelry in the parish of Halifax, until 1702 when on 4 May he died there, a patriarchal figure respected and admired by fellow ministers and congregation alike, was considered by contemporaries and has subsequently been thought of by historians as an exemplary study of the pastoral tradition within old Dissent. His career illustrates how one man could lie at the centre of a network of nonconformist divines, patrons and adherents scattered throughout West Yorkshire, South Lancashire and Cheshire and also demonstrates the ambivalent and shifting relationship between Dissent and the Established Church in the latter half of the seventeenth century.[1] These insights into both the internal and external relationships of Dissenters depend mainly on the corpus of Heywood's writings, not his published works but his autobiographical notes, diaries and memoranda books published just over a century ago, and it is these writings which form the basis of this paper.[2] To begin with though we can turn to the diary of the antiquary Ralph Thoresby who

---

[1] There have been a number of biographies of Heywood. J. Fawcett, *The Life of the Rev. Oliver Heywood, with Historical Sketches of the Times in which he lived; and Anecdotes of some other Eminent Ministers ...* (2 ed Halifax 1809); R. Slate, *Select Nonconformist Remains* (Bury 1814) and J. Hunter, *The Rise of the Old Dissent, exemplified in the Life of Oliver Heywood, one of the Founders of the Presbyterian Congregations in the County of York, 1630–1702* (London 1842) are the fullest accounts. The collected works of Heywood were published by W. Vint ed *The Collected Works of the Rev. Oliver Heywood* (5 vols Idle 1825–7).
[2] J. Horsfall Turner ed *The Rev. Oliver Heywood B.A. 1630–1702; His Autobiography, Diaries, Anecdote and Event Books* (4 vols Bingley 1881–5) and also idem, *The Nonconformist Register ... generally known as the Northowram or Coley Register* (Brighouse 1881). This and Vint above print many of the manuscripts in BL.Add.Mss.45963–81.

attended Heywood's funeral on the 7 May 1702 and recorded the event as follows:

> rode with Mr Peter's to North Owram to the funeral of good old Mr O. Heywood. He was afterwards interred with great lamentations in the parish church of Halifax. [I] was surprised at the following arvill, or treat of cold possets, stewed prunes, and cheese, prepared for the company, which had several conformist and non-conformist ministers and old acquaintances.[3]

The funeral as recorded by Thoresby was an occasion which transcended denominational loyalties and the sometimes bitter conflicts of the previous half century, which had seen Heywood successively called to the ministry, ejected from it, granted a licence for a meeting-house, having that withdrawn, imprisoned for much of 1685, and eventually on 8 July 1688 preaching his first sermon in the newly-erected chapel for his congregation at North Owram. The funeral also provided the opportunity for that relaxed but serious minded sociability which often formed as essential a part of worship and of voluntary religion as did those intense spiritual encounters of which we read so much in puritan literature.[4]

Heywood's writings have made his personal story well-known to successive generations and have also thrown light on what was truly a voluntary association sustaining the life of the Church, that network of nonconformist ministers, teachers, gentlefolk, farmers and tradesmen who, scattered throughout the north of England, provided hospitality and sustenance, and sometimes physical protection to visiting clergy on preaching tours. Their homes in time of persecution were often the venues for fasts, both public and private, and sometimes served as a chapel for a day or two for public preaching and administration of the eucharist. Thus in the latter half of 1668 we can follow Heywood from the beginning of July when he was staying at Knaresborough, uncharacteristically at an inn rather than a private house, to Ripon and back to Knaresborough where, on the Sabbath he and his brother preached at a house near the spa, moving on then to lodge at Mr Cholmeley's

---

[3] J. Hunter ed *The Diary of Ralph Thoresby (1677–1724)* (2 vols London 1830) 1 p. 362.
[4] Discussed by W. Haller, *The Rise of Puritanism* (2 ed New York 1957).

of Bream where he preached and from there to a private occasion at Leeds at which the house of Robert Hilton was dedicated. On this occasion Oliver and his wife lodged with Elkanah Wales who, as curate of Pudsey, had served as secretary to the Halifax exercise held some sixty years before. From there he preached at another house in Leeds before making private visits in Wakefield to Lady Hoyle and Mistress Riddlesden, a former member of his congregation at Coley. He then returned to North Owram remaining there for a month and receiving other ministers, his brother included, for the conduct of fasts and services. On 9 August he preached at a public fast at Pudsey 'before a multitude of people out of all parts, the gentleman of the place Mr Milner invited me to preach, entertained me, and I returned home safely upon Monday, blessed be my God!'. Nine days later he returned to Wakefield, staying at Flamsill Hall, and from there made his way to York where he visited 'many friends', and on the Sunday preached '3 times at 3 severall places in the city' as well as on the following evening. Heywood returned home by Leeds and Bramley, preaching at both places, and on the last Sunday of the month he preached all day before a 'mighty congregation' at Idle chapel. For the first half of September he remained at Coley, leaving only for the funeral of Mistress Riddlesden at Wakefield, before setting out on the fifteenth for Lancashire and Cheshire. In six weeks there he journeyed about on social and spiritual engagements among his extensive Aungier and Heywood cousinage at Denton, Gorton, Uckington, Chester, Tarvin and Warrington. His activities in Lancashire were exhausting and the first week of October found him preaching or conducting fasts on every day except Tuesday and at six different venues.

In all, the visits made during this stay comprised a mixture of public occasions, helping in the 'public work' at Denton and at 'a great meeting' at Chester, and private fasts, such as that at Little Bolton for his cousin John Godwin who was 'sensible of his miscarriages, oh what a good day it was'.[5] Professor Collinson has reminded us of the importance of the distinction which the early puritans made between the public and the private and we can be confident that many of these private occasions had the character

---

[5] Horsfall Turner, *Heywood* 1 pp. 256–9.

of family or household worship with a minister present, the small and exclusive attendance owing as much to a sense of kinship and social relationship as to any spiritual exclusivity, though of course the two were never entirely separate.[6]

At the end of October Heywood returned home and on 3 November, with two other ministers, conducted a fast at the house of Lady Rhodes. The following Sunday he addressed a great assembly in his own home and on the Wednesday renewed 'that solemn duty of conference', presumably with the young men of his congregation who met regularly for study and prayer.[7] A short series of sermons at Farsley, Bramley and Kirkstall ended on 19 November and the following five weeks were given over by Heywood to his studies, punctuated only by the occasional private fast in a follower's house. The final week of 1668 saw him once again on his travels preaching.[8]

These energetic six months were typical of Heywood's activities in the years between 1662 and 1684 and, to that extent are unexceptional. This pattern of activity must have been repeated by many of the nonconformist clergy in the north, such as Thomas Jollie of Altham,[9] and to this extent it was unexceptional save in the detail we have. At a conference with a presidential address on the English Conventicle mention of such activity is almost otiose for the story is typical of what has become known as the conventincling tradition, whether rightly or wrongly understood, which produced those meetings of the godly or most forward in religion in private gatherings apart from the world at large.[10] As such, of course, that story belongs properly to the history of voluntary association, and all of Heywood's writings are permeated by his sense of belonging to an extensive spiritual (and often familial) cousinage throughout West Yorkshire and the north-west which made for a mutually supportive community. The diary entries referred to above illustrate that sense of mutual support,

[6] Collinson, 'The English Conventicle' see above pp. 249–54.
[7] Horsfall Turner, *Heywood* 3 pp. 145–6 mentions the monthly conference and other 'private meetings' among his 'constant hearers' in 1676.
[8] *Ibid.* 2 p. 260.
[9] H. Fisher ed *The Note Book of the Rev. Thomas Jolly 1671–1693, extracts from the Church Book of Altham and Wymond houses 1649–1725* (Chetham Society NS 33, 1894). Jolly was a close friend and frequent visitor to Heywood.
[10] Collinson, 'English Conventicle' pp. 223–60.

and that sense of belonging to an extensive association is further revealed in Heywood's own compilation of births, marriages and deaths of friends, acquaintances, and some notables living throughout the area.[11] Further consideration of this far-flung cousinage is proper to our theme and could be profitably explored further but is not my chief purpose. Beyond noting its existence and acknowledging the important part it played in Heywood's ministry it is not my intention to examine the network of northern nonconformity in these years. In the light of that network I wish now to focus on the congregation which Heywood drew to himself and to each other within the chapelry of Coley and which he served for fifty-two years despite invitations to prestigious pulpits at Manchester, London and Halifax itself in the years following the Act of Toleration. Throughout his time at Coley he endeavoured to spend the greater part of the year there and, as a presbyterian, Heywood's ministry was founded on the twin pillars of the call he received from that particular congregation in 1650 and on his subsequent ordination by the Second Bolton classis in 1652.[12]

Coley chapelry comprised the townships of Shelf, North Owram and Hipperholme in the north east corner of Halifax parish, one of the largest in the country. Pastoral provision at Coley and in most of the other outlying townships of the parish had, from the late fifteenth century, depended on voluntary initiative if not association. A chapel had been established at Coley Hall about 1500 but by 1513 increasing population meant that a new chapel was required. This was supported by endowments and legacies from the inhabitants of the chapelry, who also appointed feoffees to administer the funds. Patronage, however, was vested in the vicar of Halifax. The revenues of this chapelry were confiscated by the Crown in 1546,[13] but pastoral needs were such that voluntary contributions were again supporting a minister in 1569. Provision remained fitful and by the time of Heywood's arrival these voluntary contributions, by then amounting to £20 a year, still formed the greater part of the minister's salary, although bequests had also

---

[11] Horsfall Turner, *North Owram Register* pp. 17–106; *Heywood* 2 pp. 129–82.
[12] J. Hunter, *The Rise of the Old Dissent* pp. 69–70, 94, 389, 391.
[13] S. Sheils, 'Aspects of the history of Halifax 1480–1557 (Unpub. York MA thesis 1982) p. 60.

by this time guaranteed a further £10 a year.[14] Coley, like other chapelries in large northern parishes, represented therefore a mission field in the late sixteenth and seventeenth centuries which the structures of the Established Church could only cater for with the support of the voluntary endeavour of the parishioners.[15] This voluntary endeavour could only be successful in a place like Coley, which had no single great benefactor, if it involved cooperation ,and, in this respect, the parochial structure of the place required that a tradition of voluntary association should exist. This association meant that, within the ten chapelries of Halifax, a tradition of congregational independence had developed early and created a reputation for religious radicalism known to archbishop Grindal in the 1570s[16] and which, under the benign supervision of the vicar John Favour, had developed in the early seventeenth century so that, in the 1620s, Halifax became the location for the most celebrated exercise in the north of England[17] and its chapelries an expression of that church 'consolidated by local loyalties' which was an essential element of the early seventeenth-century Church.[18]

Heywood arrived in Coley in 1650 as the established minister of the chapelry but, in the light of his subsequent ejection in 1662, his inheritance of this voluntary tradition was important. In other respects too Coley was likely to foster independency; proto-industrial but scattered settlements from which most of the coal required for Halifax came[19] and without a resident squire, the townships clearly fall into the pattern discussed by Professor Everitt and Dr Hey in their studies on rural Dissent.[20] After his ejection from the living in 1662 it was as a dissenting minister that Heywood served his congregation at Coley and, in those circumstances, membership

[14] J. Hunter, *Old Dissent* p. 70.
[15] C.J. Kitching, 'Church and chapelry in sixteenth century England' *SCH* 16 pp. 279–90.
[16] Strype, *Grindal* p. 281.
[17] J.A. Newton, 'Puritanism in the diocese of York (excluding Nottinghamshire) 1603–40' (Unpub. Ph.D. London 1955) pp. 218–38.
[18] P. Collinson, 'Lectures by Combination: structures and characteristics of church life in seventeenth-century England' *BIHR* 48 (1975) p. 212.
[19] M.E. Francois, 'The Social and Economic Development of Halifax 1558–1640' *Proceedings of the Leeds Philosophical and Literary Society* 11 pt. 8 p. 257.
[20] A. Everitt, *The Pattern of Rural Dissent: the Nineteenth Century* (Leicester 1972) p. 45; D. Hey, 'The Pattern of Nonconformity in South Yorkshire, 1660–1851' *Northern History* 8 pp. 92–4.

of that congregation required a decision to associate with like-minded neighbours. It is to this local voluntary association within a particular congregation rather than to the wider contacts of Dissent that we must now turn.

We know the particulars of Heywood's congregation from six listings surviving among his papers, five of them were drawn up by him for various purposes during his lifetime and the sixth is a list of those members of the congregation, or rather the communicants, on 25 January 1703, eight months after Heywood's death. The five lists compiled by Heywood provide us with 449 names covering the years from 1655 to 1702 and allowing for duplication within the listings, refer to 345 individuals who gained admittance to full membership of the church, the sixth list contains a further 51 names, only eight of which are not mentioned in the earlier lists. In total we know the names of 353 members of the Coley chapel between 1655 and 1702, but both Heywood's position within the chapelry and his reasons for compiling the different lists were subject to change and before assessing the completeness of the listings we should look further at these.[21]

The earliest listing referred to 1655 when Heywood was the incumbent of the chapelry and does not relate to his time as a dissenting minister, it is therefore of a different order than the others but nevertheless remains useful for us. The reasons for the compilation refer to Heywood's attempt to place his church under a covenant and the listing, of 73 names, contains those who subscribed to the covenant. It represents therefore those willing to associate with the covenant, which proved a divisive issue in the chapelry and which many refused,[22] and as such records a situation which resulted in that separation of some from the multitude so characteristic of the conventicling tradition. The list we have was not drawn up at the time, but some years later, and contains principally the names of those members who had either died or otherwise removed from the Coley congregation since 1655, it is therefore incomplete and other sources suggest that about another fifty people signed the original covenant. Some of those missing

---

[21] The lists are found in Hensall Turner, *Heywood* 2 pp. 17–36.
[22] Hunter, *Old Dissent* pp. 99–105, his brother attempted the same at nearby Illingworth chapelry with similar difficulties.

names will almost certainly be on the second listing made by Heywood, again a listing of signatories to a covenant made in 1672 following the Toleration Act of that year[23] but also one made some years after the event. From 1672 until 1702 however, we have what appears to be a register of admission to membership of the presbyterian church at Coley, complete except for a gap covering the years between 1684, the year of Heywood's imprisonment at York, and 1688, the year when his chapel was opened. This register exists in two sections separated by the final, and shortest, listing giving the names of those members of a nearby chapel at 'Sowerby' who joined with Heywood's church after the death of their minister, Henry Root, despite the fact that their's had previously been a 'gathered society in the Congregational way'.[24] The evidence of the lists suggests that we have a comprehensive if not a complete listing of the members of the dissenting church at Coley but, as Heywood's diary suggests, attendance at the chapel was not limited to members but also included some who were hearers, and may also have attended the Established Church, and occasionally others who were affiliated to other dissenting churches in the area. The evidence of the listings and of the 51 members noted in 1703 suggest that membership of the chapel comprised about 10 per cent of the adult population with an unknown further percentage of attenders.[25]

A first examination of these lists confirms one of our expectations about such church membership, namely what Patrick Collinson and Keith Thomas have reminded us of, the importance of women in these churches.[26] In all lists except that referring to the members of Henry Root's congregational church, women predominate, 44 as against 29 men in 1655, 74 to 44 in 1672 and in more or less

---

[23] Horsfall Turner, *Heywood* 2 pp. 22–4.

[24] *Ibid.* p. 31, 3 p. 109.

[25] This size makes the membership similar to that of other early eighteenth-century churches such as that of Philip Doddridge at Northampton, Everitt, *Rural Dissent* p. 13 n. 1; the numbers of hearers could often be much greater, see G. Nuttall, 'Dissenting Churches in Kent before 1700' *JEH* 14 (1963) pp. 175–89. The proportion is based on the hearth tax returns and accords with the Compton Census figures for the whole of Halifax parish, Bodl.Lib. Tanner Ms.150, fol.

[26] P. Collinson, 'The Role of Women in the English Reformation illustrated by the life and friendship of Anne Locke' *SCH* 2 pp. 258–72; K. Thomas 'Women and the Civil War Sects' in T. Aston ed. *Crisis in Europe 1560–1660* (London 1965) pp. 317–40.

the same ratio in the two registers of admissions. Within families we see the same pattern; Susan, Alice, Rachel and Grace Gill were joined by Thomas and by Grace's husband Daniel whilst Joseph Learoyd was joined by Mary, Grace, Esther, Sarah and, among the next generation, another Sarah Learoyd. The close association between dissenting ministers and these godly women, often referred to by Heywood as 'gracious women', can be seen throughout Heywood's record of visits and ministrations and one week, in October 1699, can serve as an illustration. Sunday was given over to the public worship in his chapel and to a private dinner with a fellow minister and his wife, on Monday Heywood in company with his wife, visited 'Ann Northen, I prayed and discoursed with her, heard AW's daughter for a catechism'. Tuesday was a day of prayer and study punctuated by a visit from Jeremiah Batley, but on the following day Heywood and some of his congregation conducted a private fast at John Robinson's house, Heywood preaching on Psalm 25 verse 16 'a text his [Robinson's] wife gave me, having buryed 4 sons and a daughter in a year before'. Thursday was a day of public thanksgiving and preaching and after a day of study on Friday Heywood visited Susan Butler. On Saturday, after dinner and some time spent with his wife 'sweetly in prayer' Heywood paid another call on Ann Northen for prayer and discourse. In this round of visiting and errands of spiritual comfort and mercy it was Heywood's female followers who were most often mentioned, and the assistance of his wife was a valued asset on many of these occasions. In pointing out the preponderance of women among church members it is perhaps worth recalling that civil restrictions might have discouraged some men from formal membership of a dissenting church, but if this produces an image of a congregation dominated by godly widows, matrons, and spinsters then that needs to be dispelled. Women members never achieved any formal role, even a minor one, in ministry in the way that some of the sectaries discussed by Thomas permitted. The fast at Robinson's house showed that, whilst Mrs Robinson might choose the text, the female members of the congregation played no part in the conduct of the fast, prayers being led by Samuel Holdsworth, William Clay and John Ramsden.[27]

[27] Horsfall Turner, *Heywood* 2 pp. 17–36; 4 p. 185.

The obvious importance of women in sustaining numbers in the church and, like Mistress Oates, as patrons and supporters, was not reflected in a comparable role within the public worship of the community, and the evidence of their private works and virtues remains elusive. The cumulative evidence of the diary and the visits and counselling recorded suggests however that these works and virtues were a considerable if largely hidden part of church life at Coley. Possibly another illustration of the distinction between the public and the private work of the church and the relative importance of the sexes within each sphere.

If the preponderance of women among his followers is to be expected we might be more surprised by the relatively small numbers of married couples recorded in the listings, especially as the tradition of the godly household was so potent elsewhere.[28] Among the 73 names referring to 1655 there are only eight married couples and only ten are found among the 117 noted for 1672. Between that date and 1684 another seventeen couples are recorded among the 159 new members. To some extent these low figures can be attributed to the way in which the lists were compiled, but that cannot explain all.[29] Nor can the penal legislation be used to suggest that the menfolk did not seek admission in order to avoid penalties under the law. The number of married couples seeking admission does not increase after 1688 and whilst Joseph Hollins and his wife Mary were first 'entertained' together on 27 December 1691 it was more usual for partners to be admitted on separate dates, so in 1696 Samuel Drake followed his wife Mary into membership after a period of six months.[30] In the listing of 1703 only six married couples are identified among the 51 members, though there are a

---

[28] See A. MacFarlane, *The Family Life of Ralph Josselin a 17th-century clergyman* (Cambridge 1970); C. Hill, 'The Spiritualization of the Household' in *Society and Puritanism in Pre-Revolutionary England* (London 1964) pp. 443–81; R.A. Houlbrooke, *The English Family 1450–1750* (London 1984) pp. 147–9 for Heywood's own mother.

[29] The list of those members signing the covenant of 1655, for example, refers to those members who had died or had removed from the congregation in the 21 years since the covenant. Other sources suggest that about 40 names are missing and some of these clearly are likely to include spouses of named members, Horsfall Turner, *Heywood* 1 p. 171.

[30] *Ibid.* 2 pp. 34–5.

few other possible instances.[31] The evidence suggests, therefore, that the church at Coley was not founded on several godly households with husband and wife sharing the same commitments, but that membership of the church was a decision of the individual. When partners joined the church together, or when two members, such as Abraham Illingworth and Lydia Clough, decided to get married then it was of course a day for rejoicing, but there is no sense in which the marriages contracted by members of the Coley chapel were exclusive to fellow members at Coley or at any other presbyterian community.[32] Church membership was not restrictive in this way and, indeed, it was a marriage within the congregation which caused Heywood most anxiety. When James Brooksbank married the daughter of Anthony Lea in 1692 litigation was threatened over the terms of the settlement and the case brought before the York assizes despite Heywood's endeavours at reconciliation. On 8 March Heywood, desperate that at a court hearing 'they would in many things contradict one another in open court, which would turn to great scandal, being professors and my hearers, I set myself solemnly to seek God about it', God answered and, happily, the parties agreed to arbitration and the marriage appears to have been a successful one.[33] Heywood was regularly called in, as above, to settle 'sad cases of difference among good people',[34] but we have very few instances of Heywood intervening in disputes between spouses, whether over religion or any other matter, although on 24 February 1679 we find him and others keeping a fast 'on behalf of a woman unequally yooked' and at other times interceding in times of family distress.[35] Disputes in general sometimes arose within the congregation but more often than not involved individuals who were not members, and so bring us to consideration of the relationship between the congregation and those neighbours not associated with it. To understand something of this we need to look beyond the records of the church itself to

---

[31] *Ibid.* p.36, there are nine others who have the same surname and some of these were certainly brother and sister.
[32] *Ibid.* p. 34.
[33] *Ibid.* 4 pp. 142–3.
[34] *Ibid.* 2 p. 108.
[35] *Ibid.* p. 86.

those relating to the economic and political life of the neighbourhood.

As with Margaret Spufford's dissenting peasantry in Cambridgeshire the membership of Heywood's congregation cut through all ranks of local society from Abraham Lockwood of Bleak House, who styled himself gentleman and was able to leave £500 each to his daughter Ann and his younger son, also Abraham, in addition to land to his eldest son John, to Edward Brook described by Heywood as 'a godly poor man'.[36] Evidence from the hearth tax of 1666 is fragmentary, perhaps due to the preponderance of women in the first listing, but the few positive identifications that can be made reflect this range of wealth, with Jeremy Brigge being assessed for 3 hearths, a few others at two hearths and Simeon Lord at one hearth. Too much reliance on these figures is dangerous but, if anything, the members of the congregation seem to be more fully represented in the middle ranks of society than among its poorer members.[37] This measure of prosperity among the leading layfolk made possible the erection of a chapel in 1688, followed by a school in 1693 in which a master taught 27 scholars.[38]

Rather more surprising, however, is the fact that while the modest prosperity is confirmed by the probate valuations of those members of the congregation who made wills, it was not translated into bequests for the chapel or its works.[39] Perhaps the precarious nature of the congregation precluded any endowment by a cautious clothier in the years before 1688 but even after that date the situation did not change. However generous his followers were during their lifetimes they rarely remembered Heywood or the church on their deathbed and only one will leaves a bequest to a minister or to a charitable work associated with the church.[40]

---

[36] Borthwick Institute, York, orig. wills July 1696; Horsfall Turner, *Heywood* 2 p. 18. M. Spufford, *Contrasting Communities* (Cambridge 1969) pp. 300–06.

[37] PRO, E179/210/394A, I am grateful to Mr Ronan Bennett for supplying me with this information and for discussion of the Halifax material.

[38] Hunter, *Old Dissent* pp. 356–8.

[39] These are all deposited at the Borthwick Institute of Historical Research, York.

[40] There is some problem with the sources here as in 1678 Heywood gives an account of his income showing that he received from 'my hearers at my house' £34 11s. 6d. and that he had a further £34 13s. 5d. by way of legacies and 'others

Further, Heywood himself, despite his role as arbitrator in other affairs, does not appear once as executor or even as witness to any of these wills, and among the church membership the choice of executors and witnesses by clothiers like John Mellin or yeomen like John Bentley was arbitrary and just as likely to include other friends as fellow presbyterians.[41] This is unexceptional but is in stark contrast to the self-conscious awareness of each other and of their ministers exhibited in the will making of the godly townsmen of early Stuart England who so often provide us with our model.[42]

We come finally to local government where of course there were restrictions on nonconformists. In Coley, however, where manorial government within the manor of Wakefield remained vigorous, participation in office-holding was not only possible but often required of members of the congregation. As occupiers of land many of them had to serve as reeve in the sub-manor of Hipperholme and in 1686 the lot fell to Joseph and Jonathan Priestley. The jury appointed for that year reads like a list of church members and included Heywood himself. The office of constable within the three townships that made up the sub-manor carried more responsibility for law enforcement and in 1695, when John Ramsden and John Bentley served the townships of North Owram and Shelf respectively, fellow members of the congregation were presented for failure to maintain the highway. One of those presented was James Brooksbank who was himself constable in 1699. Throughout the period their numbers and their social standing meant that, within the manor at least, the presbyterians played an

---

abroad', Horsfall Turner, *Heywood* 2 p. 189. It may be that what he terms legacies come from sums left by the greater patrons for the generality of nonconformist ministers, sums which Heywood was often entrusted with distributing, and that most of the amount came by way of gifts from individual supporters; *ibid.* 3 pp. 275–6.

[41] BIHR, Probate Register 48 fols. 499v–500; orig. will, October 1696.

[42] See for example M.C. Cross, *Urban Magistrates and Ministers; Religion in Hull and Leeds from the Reformation to the Civil War* (Borthwick Papers 67 1985) pp. 22–5; and P. Clark, 'The Ramoth-Gilead of the Good: urban change and political radicalism at Gloucester 1540–1640', P. Clark, A.G.R. Smith and N. Tyacke eds *The English Commonwealth 1547–1640* (London 1979) pp. 181–4.

active part in local government.[43] Thus when we are able to move beyond the records of the church itself and to glimpse the dissenters in their daily lives the distinctive nature of their life-style is less obvious, but before it disappears from view entirely we should return to the question of voluntary association and what it meant for the godly.

Clearly it was of central importance in the lives of those who took a covenant or sought admission to the church and, in many ways, it did separate them off from their neighbours. This separation, however, may well have been less important to them than the spiritual bonds of the fellowship they were joining and, in the covenant of 1672, the continuing if residual commitment to the whole of humanity as well as to each other was recognized by the signatories who 'inhabitants of Coley chapelry and others, being professours of religion' gave themselves to the Lord accepting the leadership of Heywood and promising 'to believe and practice what truthes and duty he shall make manifest to us in the mind of God, desirous to maintain communion with God and one another in God's worship, and to discharge what mutual dutyes God requires of us in his word as members of the same body ... in all good conscience towards God, one another, and to all others to the end of our days'.[44] The reference to 'all others' if taken seriously ensured that the divisive force of such covenants, and divisions there were at Coley, not only between the congregation and the unregenerate but also within the congregation itself between those who were admitted to full membership and those who hung back,[45] was never overwhelming.

The sources most often cited in the history of the godly, the spiritual autobiography, the clerical diary, the exemplary life preached as a sermon, and the stories of harassment and persecution by authority concentrate on the internal life of the individual or congregation and thereby serve to further that sense of separation

[43] Leeds, Yorkshire Archaeological Society, MD 225, e.g. 1674, 1676, 1686, 1687, 1696, 1699.
[44] Horsfall Turner, *Heywood* 2 p. 22.
[45] *Ibid* 1 pp. 171–3 discusses the division of 1655, characteristically Heywood claimed to have had more trouble at this time from the over zealous than from the lukewarm and was critical of those who sought 'an unwarrantable groundless separation'.

from the world which members of the gathered churches experienced.[46] In this, Heywood's diary is no exception, and gatherings like the day of thankfulness held on 14 December 1691 'wherein we had near 20 young men and women, John Learoyd, William Naylor, James Oates prayd, praised God, were much inlardged, then we dined, and after that Mr Jeremy Bairstow and I prayed, God made it a very good day'; were central to the life of the congregation at Coley just as much as elsewhere.[47] It was through such meetings that the members acted in good conscience towards one another and supported their spiritual lives. The covenant also, however, required them to act in good conscience to all others, and the experience of the members suggests that, although their spiritual association might distinguish them from other people it did not set them entirely apart. Their association remained an open one admitting of the normal neighbourly niceties and drawing strength from them. This openness was reciprocated by at least part of the conformist community at Coley and in 1677 there was an attempt to allow Heywood to preach again in the parish chapel, supported by some 'that have neither heard nor owned me for almost twice seven years', but who clearly remembered him with respect from the days before his ejection.[48]

---

[46] The literature is extensive and the best guide to the shortcomings of these sources and the approach they encourage is P. Collinson, 'Towards a Broader Understanding of the Early Dissenting Tradition' reprinted in his *Godly People: Essays on English Protestantism and Puritanism* (London 1983) pp. 527–62. For a nice contrast between a local study based on those sources and one based on a wider range of material see the same author's 'Magistracy and Ministry: a Suffolk Miniature' and 'Cranbrook and the Fletchers: Popular and Unpopular Religion in the Kentish Weald', reprinted in the same collection.

[47] Horsfall Turner, *Heywood* 4 p. 141.

[48] *Ibid.* 3 p. 170. See M. Spufford 'Can we count the "Godly" and the "Conformable" in the Seventeenth Century' *JEH* 36 (1985) pp. 428–38 for some pertinent remarks on the relationship between these two groups. It would be foolish to deny that there was periodically considerable friction between Heywood and his conformist neighbours, particularly in the years immediately after 1662 and around 1684, Horsfall Turner, *Heywood* 1 pp. 179–87; Hunter, *Old Dissent* pp. 320–6. He did however attribute the undisturbed nature of his ministry, at least in part, to the leniency of the local magistrates and constables, Horsfall Turner, *Heywood* 4 pp. 70, 72. He was often in trouble with the church courts but, at visitation, only isolated presentments were made against his followers and it was more often the wardens of Coley who were prosecuted for not making presentments of non-communicants, BIHR, V.1667/CB.1 fol. 76; V.1682/CB. fols. 110v–111v; V.1684–5/CB.1, fols 55v–56v.

Heywood's church at Coley illustrates an important feature of the godly, or those who covenant for religion, which is not often stated. Firstly the godly within the community were not necessarily exclusive and the members could have close contacts with respectable folk of other traditions, if not with the multitude at large. The godly, therefore, cannot be defined in terms of a particular denominational grouping, and, despite official persecution, bridges were kept open between presbyterians, independants and conformists. It was in this sort of context that, in later years, the practice of occasional conformity could be seen not just as a cynical circumvention of the constraints of the law but as a realistic and legitimate political response to a law which did not appear to recognize the large measure of agreement that could exist within some of the protestant churches.[49] That response was just as common as was the sectarianism and withdrawal about which we hear so much. The church at Coley, and Heywood himself, certainly suffered persecution in this period but its history reflects the humane as well as the heroic tradition within Dissent. In his autobiography Heywood expressed this well:

> I would always be in company of them that fear God that I might get some good to my soul by soul-raising, grace-exercising, heart-quickening dutys and discourses, and a day in such company is better than a thousand in the tents of wickedness, I desire to embrace all opportunities in public ordinances and private exercises for the furthering of my poor soul in the way to heaven: nor would I limit my love or complacency to those who are of the same judgement with myself, or who for other carnal ends may seem to attract it, but those that are of other judgements and opinions in lesser points and circumstantial things, yea though in greater if I can see their souls are within the covenant of grace, and I love them purely for their relation to Christ.[50]

This attitude also had practical application. In 1682 when the chapelry at Coley was without an incumbent for many months Heywood was troubled by the consequences he observed, 'sabbaths

---

[49] See C. Hill, 'Occasional Conformity' in R.B. Knox ed *Reformation, Conformity and Dissent* (London 1977) pp. 199–220.
[50] Horsfall Turner, *Heywood* 1 pp. 141–2.

were prophaned, ordinances slighted, souls ruined, people grew barbarous' and prayed for the provision of an honest minister. 'At last (I hope I may truly say) in answer to prayer, God graciously sent in an honest conformist (one Mr Ellison of Linfit by Slaithwaite) who liveth soberly preacheth zealously against sin, orthodoxly, a moderate man. I hope gracious people acquiesce in him, flock to hear him – blessed be God'.[51] The gathered community remained open to the good in the wider world at least and, without that openness, Heywood's funeral would hardly have been the sociable and inter-denominational occasion that it clearly was. Conventicling and voluntary association did not always lead to sectarianism and withdrawal even though it is those features which the traditional sources most often highlight.

University of York

---

[51] *Ibid.* 4, pp. 80–1. After 1688, if not before, this good will was reciprocated. Thoresby records a visit made to Heywood's chapel by the vicar of Halifax who 'with fervency, uttered these words "the Good Lord bless the word preached in this place"'. Hunter, *Thoresby's Diary* 1 p. 256.

RELIGIOUS SOCIETIES: METHODIST AND EVANGELICAL 1738–1800

by JOHN WALSH

ONE does not have to believe in free trade to recognize that in religion as well as economic life the erosion of a monopoly can provoke an uprush of private enterprise. It must be more than coincidental that two modern 'church in danger' crises which accompanied an erosion of Anglican hegemony – the Revolution of 1688 and the constitutional crises of 1828–32 – were followed by bursts of voluntary activity. Clusters of private societies were formed to fill up part of the space vacated by the state, as it withdrew itself further from active support of the establishment. After the Toleration Act perceptive churchmen felt even more acutely the realities of religious pluralism and competition. Anglicanism was now approaching what looked uncomfortably like a market situation; needing to be promoted; actively sold.[1] Despite the political and social advantages still enjoyed by the Church, the confessional state in its plenitude of power had gone, and Anglican pre-eminence had to be preserved by other means. One means was through voluntary societies. The Society for the Reformation of Manners hoped by private prosecutions to exert some of the social controls once more properly exercised by the Church courts. The S.P.G. sought to encourage Anglican piety in the plantations and the S.P.C.K. to extend it at home by promoting charity schools and disseminating godly tracts. It was a task of voluntarism to reassert, as far as possible, what authority remained to a church which, because it could not effectively coerce, had to persuade.[2]

---

[1] See A.D. Gilbert, *Religion and Society in Industrial England* (London 1976) pp. 8–12.

[2] See G.V. Bennett, 'Conflict in the Church' in G.S. Holmes ed *Britain after the Glorious Revolution* (London 1980) p. 165; G.V. Bennett, *The Tory Crisis in Church and State* (Oxford 1975) pp. 20–1.

JOHN WALSH

While the larger societies looked to extend Anglican influence in
the external world, the little devotional cells known as the 'religious
societies' aimed quietly to revitalize it from within. Though these
dated back to about 1678, when small groups of young men
organized weekly meetings under the direction of Anthony Horneck who gave them a rule, they enjoyed their full flowering after
the Revolution, and by 1700 there were some 40 of them in London
and a number of others in cities and market towns.[3] Their spread
owed a good deal to the little tract of the Rev. Josiah Woodward,
*An Account of the Rise and Progress of the Religious Societies in
the City of London*, which appeared in 1699, reaching a fifth
edition in 1724. Much of the attraction of Woodward's *Account*
lay in its provision of specimen rules – those of his own society in
Poplar – which gave a model that was to be applied, with local
adaptation, for a century. Religious society members appear to
have been mostly young (between 16 and 30), mostly tradesmen
'of the middling sort' and of 'sober education'.[4] Their aim was the
pursuit of 'real holiness of heart and life' by a regimen of self-
examination, fasting, attendance at church and sacrament, and
weekly meetings for 'pious conference', often in church vestries.
Confined strictly to members of the Church of England, their
religious exercises were based firmly on the Liturgy and were
normally presided over by a clerical spiritual director.

In the optimistic vision of those who promoted them the societies
had a multiple role to play in the work of national reformation.
They would allow an immobile church to mobilize its resources
against competitors who were already confederated; infidel clubs,
Roman orders and associations of Dissenters. If politicians banded
together in parties and investors in joint-stock companies, why
should churchmen not combine? The obstacles to piety would not
be 'removed by a few single, private reformations. There must
be ... publick confederacies in virtue, to balance and counterpoise

---

[3] For the religious societies see G.V. Portus, *Caritas Anglicana* (London 1912);
J.S. Simon, *John Wesley and the Religious Societies* (London 1921);
D.W.R. Bahlman, *The Moral Revolution of 1688* (New Haven 1957);
F.W.B. Bullock, *Voluntary Religious Societies, 1520–1799* (St. Leonard's-on-Sea
1966).
[4] J. Woodward, *An Account of the Rise and Progress of the Religious Societies in
the City of London* (5 ed 1724) p. 32. A 7th ed appeared in 1800.

those of vice'.[5] Living by pious rule, the society members would provide voluntaristic models of that ancient corporate discipline which the Church so deplorably lacked and seemed unable to impose.[6] By their moderate communal asceticism, and a quasi-monastic 'voluntary retirement', they might partly fill a devotional gap which, despite the brief experiment of Little Gidding, had remained tragically void since the Reformation had destroyed the 'exemplary piety of the old British monks'.[7] Samuel Wesley, senior, in a rhapsodic *Letter concerning the Religious Societies* (1700) hoped to transpose them into a rural context and use their members as a virtual diaconate on the primitive model to help parsons in huge, straggling parishes – like the Isle of Axholme with its 7000 souls – where population growth had overwhelmed the pastoral machinery of the Church.[8] In sum, here appeared one way to restore to practicality that elusive vision of a pristine 'primitive Christianity' which mesmerized so many post-Restoration Anglicans.[9]

To those who joined them they offered what contemporary Anglicanism did not really offer; a close-knit 'Fellowship of Christian Brotherhood'. Whatever clergymen assumed, the familiar forms of public liturgical worship, coupled with closet devotions, were not enough for some sin-sick souls in search of spiritual growth and collective moral support. To anxious youths the societies offered a counter-cultural alternative to the rackety life of apprentices and other bachelor tradesmen, similar to that provided by early Methodism in metropolitan centres, and by the Y.M.C.A. in the nineteenth century. The members of this 'fraternity' Woodward explained, 'admonish and watch over one another ... and fortify each other against those temptations which assault

---

[5] S. Wesley, *A Letter concerning the Religious Societies* (London 1724) pp. 51-2, quoting ch 20 of *The Whole Duty of Man*. The *Letter* was first published as a 16 page Appendix to Wesley's *The Pious Communicant Rightly Prepar'd* (London 1700).

[6] See E.A. Duffy, 'Primitive Christianity revived; religious Renewal in Augustan England', *SCH* 14 (Oxford 1977) pp. 287-300.

[7] S. Wesley, *Letter* pp. 37-9. Wesley was not alone in his nostalgia for the religious communities of the past; see J.W. Legg, *English Church Life from the Restoration to the Tractarian Movement* (London 1914) pp. 281-6.

[8] S. Wesley, *Letter* pp. 39-45; W.O.B. Allen and E. McClure, *Two Hundred Years: the History of the S.P.C.K.* (London 1898) pp. 89-93.

[9] Duffy, 'Primitive Christianity' pp. 292-7; T. Isaacs, 'The Anglican Hierarchy and the Reformation of Manners; 1688-1738', *JEH* 33 (Cambridge 1982) pp. 408-11.

them ... Knowing each other's manner of life [they] ... can much better inspect, admonish and guard each other than the most careful minister can'. The societies allowed an openness in discussion impossible among strangers and social superiors.[10]

In their prime, the societies basked in the sunshine of much official approval. They were praised by Archbishop Tenison, blessed by Queen Mary and eulogized by the saintly Nonjuror Robert Nelson as impeccably 'primitive'.[11] All the same, their proceedings and their very existence aroused undercurrents of suspicion. The conception of a voluntary society within a national church was too novel, too redolent of gathered churches, sectarianism and separatism, to be assimilated by churchmen distanced by only a few decades from the Commonwealth. 'Things of that kind had been formerly practised only among the Puritans and the Dissenters', noted Burnet.[12] If the confessional state seemed remote from present reality, the Hookerian theory of the organic union of church and state, which underpinned it, still retained great potency, reinforced by nostalgia and sharpened up by Tory party polemics. Private societies could well be viewed not as strengthening the institutional Church but weakening it; their presence symbolised the perception of some inadequacy in the organism, an implication that the Church of England – most pure and reformed of all Reformed Churches – was still somehow imperfect and its liturgy unsatisfying. What need was there for such societies, asked George Stanhope, dean of Canterbury, when young men already possessed 'opportunities for learning [their] duty in public' and had 'ready access ... to good books, good ministers and good friends in private'?[13] Behind the associational principle lay barely concealed the suggestion that the national Church did not possess a natural, divinely ordained claim to the allegiance of all citizens, but might perhaps be a covenant community of freely acting adults.

---

[10] Woodward, *Account* pp. 82–3.

[11] Bahlman, *Moral Revolution* p. 72; R. Nelson, *A Companion for the Festivals and Fasts of the Church of England* (3 ed London 1705) Preface p. x.

[12] G. Burnet, *History of his own Time* 6 vols (Oxford 1833) 5 p. 18; see too R. Kidder, *The Life of the Rev. A. Horneck* (London 1698) p. 17; Bahlman, *Moral Revolution* p. 90.

[13] G. Stanhope, *Advice to the Religious Societies* (London 1730) p. 6, first published as *The Duty of Rebuking; a Sermon ... to which is added a Post-script to the Religious Societies* (London 1703).

It was hardly surprising therefore that Woodward devoted a nervous chapter of his *Account* to fending off 'the most considerable objections' to the societies: that they were potentially schismatic, 'a society within a society, refining upon a reformed church'; that their members usurped the pastoral office of the clergy by charitable visiting and the reproof of evil doers.[14] Where Woodward found himself on more delicate ground was over the space allowed among his young laymen for 'pious conference' – free discussion of issues relating to the spiritual life and, by implication, Christian dogma. The sharp-eyed reader must have observed that Woodward merely deemed it 'expedient' to have a clerical director present at weekly meetings and envisaged situations in which lay stewards might conduct the proceedings.[15] Here lay openings for mischief; an opportunity for youthful self-assertiveness and the usurpation by laymen of priestly authority. Casting a fearful eye back to the Civil War, Dean Stanhope reminded the societies how rank enthusiasm could 'grow out of methods ... piously intended and innocently begun'. These suspicions were not forgotten. They were to break out more vehemently at the rise of Methodism in the late 1730s.[16]

By this time the religious society movement had lost much of its freshness and the expectation of Augustan churchmen that the societies might prove the vanguard of a national reformation had dimmed. To High Church suspicions about separatism were added Whiggish fears that the societies were potential cells of Jacobitism. In an updated version of Woodward's rules in 1724 was the significant insertion that members must 'bear true allegiance to his Majesty King GEORGE'. By the late 1730s, though new societies were still being formed, many had died and others were moribund.[17]

The Evangelical Revival represented a new wave of voluntarism. Noticeably, it too followed on from a 'church in danger' crisis, that of the mid 1730s when a conjunction of Deist propagandism, Old Whig anti-clericalism and Dissenting restlessness under the Test Acts appeared to some gloomy Churchmen to threaten the

---

[14] Woodward, *Account* ch 7, 'The chief objections against them answered'.
[15] Woodward, *Account* p. 133.
[16] Stanhope, *Advice* pp. 88–9.
[17] *Orders belonging to a Religious Society* (London 1724) p. 3; J.W. Legg, *English Church Life* p. 297.

future of established religion.[18] Hopes that reformation might still be carried out by state agency were by no means dead, but it seemed highly unlikely that they would emanate from an anticlerical like Sunderland or a sceptic like Walpole. Many of the functions of the older societies – moral reformation, the propagation of the faith, the provision of para-institutional fellowship – were taken over by the evangelical movement and energetically promoted by fresh tactics and a new theological rationale. This is not surprising since a number of early evangelical leaders had been nurtured in the voluntary society movement. In 1737 the young Whitefield was in demand among the London societies as a preacher and did much to ginger them up. John Wesley, son of an energetic exponent of societies, had been elected a corresponding member of the S.P.C.K. in 1732, and sailed as a missionary for Georgia under the auspices of the S.P.G.[19] It is not surprising that in 1733 we see him noting with warm approval a passage in *The Country Parson's Advice*; that religious societies were 'the most effectual means for restoring our decaying Christianity'.[20] It is noteworthy that when, in a retrospect of Methodist history, he singled out the three most crucial early stages in the 'rise' of the movement, each was linked to the formation of a voluntary society: the Holy Club in 1729; his religious societies in Georgia in 1736; and the Fetter Lane religious society in 1738.[21] His famous conversion experience took place at 'a society in Aldersgate Street'.[22]

The rapidity with which early Methodism established itself owed a great deal to its ability to cannibalize the religious societies of London, Bristol and elsewhere. Methodists used to the full the personal links with them which had been built up in previous

---

[18] For the crisis of the 1730s see N. Sykes, *Edmund Gibson, Bishop of London 1669–1748* (London 1926) pp. 148–75; S. Taylor, 'Sir Robert Walpole, the Church of England and the Quakers Tithe Bill of 1736' *HJ* 28 (1985).

[19] G. Whitefield, *Works* 6 vols (London 1771–2) 5 pp. 107–22, 159–69; A.A. Dallimore, *George Whitefield* 2 vols (London 1970, 1980) 1 p. 120. For the connection of Whitefield and Wesley with the SPCK see *The Diary of Thomas Wilson* ed C.L.S. Linnell (London 1964) p. 173; L.W. Cowie, *Henry Newman. An American in London* (London 1956) pp. 237–9; J. Wesley, *Journal* ed N. Curnock, 8 vols (London 1909–16) 1 pp. 159, 322, 343; Simon, *Wesley and Religious Societies* p. 113.

[20] J. Wesley, *Letters* ed J. Telford 8 vols (London 1931) 4 p. 119.

[21] J. Wesley, *Works* 14 vols (London 1872) 13 p. 307.

[22] Wesley, *Journal* 1 p. 475.

years, and exploited the sense of stagnation which had overtaken
some of the societies, a number of which seem to have been bereft
of any firm clerical control.[23] To society members like James
Hutton the new Gospel of immediate justification by faith and the
instant assurance of it came as a revelation: 'this was to us all
something so new, unexpected, joyful, penetrating; for the most
of us had sorely striven ... against sin ... without profit or result'.[24]
To the London clergymen who had supported the societies,
however, they seemed to have gone mad. Replacing the old 'private'
societies were new ones which were virtually 'public congregations'
or 'conventicles', packed with strangers and cranks.[25] The new
practice of extempore prayer in societies infiltrated by Methodism
seemed particularly shocking to High Church leaders like William
Berriman. Instead of 'a stated, pre-composed form, appointed by
authority and known beforehand' was the cult of immediately
inspired utterance; 'sudden and unpremeditated excursions'.[26] For
a High Churchman like Berriman forms and liturgies were more
than mere modes of worship; they were deeply symbolic of the
Tory social ideal of a static, hierarchical, orderly community
governed by prescription.[27] Methodism, like Commonwealth sectarianism, represented the intrusion of a religious individualism,
the 'private spirit', into communal worship in a way which might
shatter the old unities beyond repair. In the sharp struggle between

---

[23] See J.D. Walsh, 'Origins of the Evangelical Revival' in *Essays in Modern English Church History* ed G.V. Bennett and J.D. Walsh (London 1966) pp. 144–8. In addition to some of those in London and Bristol, religious societies in Cardiff, Badsey, St. Ives (Cornwall), Colne, Nottingham, Bunbury, Alpraham and Leominster seem to have been taken over by 'Methodism' in its various forms. Other examples can probably be disinterred.

[24] *Proceedings of the Wesley Historical Society* 15 (Burnley 1926) p. 208; D. Benham, *Memoirs of James Hutton* (London 1856) p. 9.

[25] H. Stebbing, *A Caution against Religious Delusion* (London 1739) pp. 18–19; T. Land, *A Letter to the Rev. G. Whitefield. With a previous Letter addressed to the Religious Societies* (London 1739) p. 20; T. Church, *A Serious and Expostu-latory Letter to the Rev. Mr. Whitefield* (London 1744) pp. 38–9; [E. Gibson], *Observations upon the Conduct and Behaviour of a certain Sect* (n d London) p. 8.

[26] W. Berriman, *A Sermon preached to the Religious Societies in London* 3 ed (London 1739) pp. 21–2. For earlier defence of liturgical forms see J. Spurr, 'Anglican Apologetic and the Restoration Church' (unpub Oxford D.Phil. thesis 1985).

[27] For the social implications of liturgical worship see Rhys Isaac, *The Trans-formation of Virginia 1740–1790* (Chapel Hill 1982) pp. 64–5, 121–4.

those who wished the societies to proceed in what Bishop Gibson called their 'inoffensive way', and those who vehemently tried to rescue them from what they held to be a 'dead formality', the traditionalists came out clear losers.[28] Though some city societies continued for decades, many disintegrated, their members often reabsorbed into Methodism or Moravianism.[29] Wesley's elder brother, Samuel, complained in 1739 of his brothers' Methodists, 'their societies are sufficient to dissolve all other societies but their own'.[30] The religious society movement, once the rising hope of High Churchmen, was largely discredited in their eyes and, with some historical irony, was largely appropriated by evangelicalism.

Yet it was to flow in two divergent streams. On the one hand Methodism opened it out and transformed it into something dramatically different from the Horneck-Woodwardian model. On the other hand, among 'regular' Evangelical parish clergy, who stood apart from Wesleyan irregularity, the Woodward plan was consciously perpetuated, with local variations, for the remainder of the century. It is with these sharply divergent adaptations that the rest of this paper is concerned.

When in 1744 Wesley's 'United Societies' published their *Rules* in the style of Dr. Woodward, they showed elements of continuity with their predecessors – weekly meetings, monthly fasting communion, personal asceticism – but these only masked the degree to which the older models had been radicalized.[31] First, the parameters of association had been stretched to the utmost. Since 1739, when Whitefield and Wesley began outdoor preaching to the colliers of Kingswood, recruitment to the societies had been aimed not only at the urban, literate and respectable of Dr. Woodward's social milieu, but at the 'outcasts', 'the forlorn ones'; the marginalized who squatted on the edges and in the gaps of the parochial

---

[28] [Gibson] *Observations* p. 8; Whitefield, *Works* 4 p. 31.
[29] There were still 12 religious societies in the London area in 1759, listed in W. Dodd, *Unity Recommended in a Sermon, preached before the Religious Societies in and about London* (London 1759) Appendix p. 24. The society at St. Giles, Cripplegate lasted till 1762; J.W. Legg, *English Church Life* p. 313.
[30] L. Tyerman, *The Life of the Rev. J. Wesley*, 3 vols (London 1870–1) 1 pp. 286–7.
[31] F. Baker, *John Wesley and the Church of England* (London 1970) pp. 74–79. Compare J. Lawson, 'The People called Methodist: our Discipline' in R.E. Davies and E.G. Rupp ed, *A History of the Methodist Church in Great Britain* 3 vols (London 1965–85) 1 p. 196.

system; the street poor of the cities whom Bishop Gibson dismissively termed 'the rabble'.[32] The society retained its inward focus as a private association of those in search of personal holiness, but onto this had been grafted a very different function, that of the evangelistic society looking outwards at large social groups of the unchurched which were viewed as living in a veritable *pays de mission*.

The chorus of disapproval which greeted the Methodist movement in its early phase convinced Wesley that the only way forward lay through an irregular mission: those beyond the parochial system could only be reached by extra-parochial methods and without the leave of most of the parish clergy. Wesley had already been educated out of his Holy Club strictness by pastoral experience of a 200 mile 'parish' on the American frontier and the pragmatic missionary proved stronger than the rubrical High churchman as he crashed through a succession of canonical barriers, picking up evangelistic expedients which had hitherto been accepted as being distinctive marks of sectarian Nonconformity; extempore prayer, itinerant field preaching, the authorization of lay preachers, the building of 'preaching houses'.[33] 'We have heard of field conventicles in Scotland', wrote Joseph Trapp disgustedly, '... We have ... had something of this nature in England, as practised by Brownists, Anabaptists, Quakers, Ranters or such like. But for a clergyman of the Church of England to pray and preach in the fields, in the country, or in the streets in the city, is perfectly new'.[34]

Compounding the novelty of all this was the articulation of societies into a new organizational form; the connexion. While the Woodwardian societies had been virtually independent cells circumscribed by the localisms of parish life, the Methodist societies were affiliated into a network which stretched from Cornwall to North-east Scotland, spanned the Irish Channel and soon crossed the Atlantic. Here was a new form of religious polity, corresponding, as Frank Baker has observed, 'neither to congregationalism nor presbyterianism, nor diocesan episcopalianism ... but ... perhaps nearer to the formative formlessness

---

[32] [Gibson] *Observations* p. 4.
[33] J. Wesley, *Letters* 1 p. 229.
[34] J. Trapp, *The Nature, Folly, Sin and Danger of being Righteous overmuch* 2 ed (London 1739) p. 57.

of the primitive church with its dominant notes of evangelism and pastoral care, and its loose affiliation of varied groups linked by apostolic labours'.[35] From an early stage therefore, the Methodist societies were something more than simple *ecclesiolae in ecclesia*; they were the 'United Societies' of 'the people called Methodists'; part of 'one body firmly united together' in 'a general union'.[36] To Hanoverian churchmen uneasily aware of the decentralized locus of authority in church and state this development was alarming: Methodism seemed 'the most powerful affiliated society in existence'.[37]

In the new Methodist societies the area for lay participation and leadership was extended far beyond that envisaged by their predecessors. Save for the distant control of Wesley and his few clerical coadjutors, the Methodist cadres were entirely in lay and often plebeian hands. As class leaders, band leaders, stewards, trustees, local preachers and itinerants, members were encouraged to actualize in service to the society the sense of power and freedom – key words in Methodist spiritual autobiography – which accompanied the experience of conversion. The societies departed sharply from the precedent of the older societies by not only recruiting women but encouraging them to lead classes and bands, and permitting a few to preach, a step redolent of Quakerism. The devotional space allowed by Woodward for 'pious conference' was greatly enlarged, especially in the intimate sub-groupings of class and band, whose members reported on their spiritual growth and sustained their mutuality by comfort and reproof. Among the most successful of Wesley's innovations was the love feast (curiously neglected by historians of Methodism); an adaptation of the primitive *Agape* at which a simple meal of cake and water was communally shared, and the two-handled porcelain loving-cup handed round from mouth to mouth in a domesticated, democratised folk-Eucharist which aimed, in Wesley's words, 'to encourage free and familiar conversation in which every man, yea and every woman,

---

[35] Baker, *Wesley and the Church* p. 117.
[36] See F. Baker, 'The People called Methodists: Polity' in Davies and Rupp, *Methodist Church* 1 p. 242.
[37] 'Cursitor', *A Letter to the Lord Bishop of Lincoln, respecting the 'Report from the Clergy of a District of the Diocese of Lincoln'* (London 1800) p. 20.

has liberty to speak whatever may be to the glory of God'.[38] Such shifts of emphasis from the liturgical to the charismatic were essential to a mission aimed at the semi-literate or the entirely analphabetic. If Wesley was to leap the cultural as well as the spatial gap separating the Church from the unchurched he had to make large allowance for plebeian spontaneity and for orality as well as literacy in the life of the societies; rather less room for the mediation of grace through the set forms of the Liturgy and the printed Word, rather more for the 'freedom of the spirit'. For, as a simple Methodist poet observed of the work of the Holy Ghost:

> Were *books* His constant residence indeed
> What must the millions do who cannot read?[39]

In extempore prayer and preaching, in the sporadic emotional release of revivals, generous allowance was made for popular 'enthusiasm', for this had to be engaged and encouraged, even though it was ultimately to be contained and canalized. The centrality of the hymn in early Methodism symbolized the dual requirements of emotional spontaneity and control in Wesley's system. Hymn singing combined the expression of individual with communal religious feeling; it aroused lyrical sincerity and fervour while also confining it within formulaic limits. Hymns, 'the sung creeds of Methodism', possessed a pedagogic function, imparting dogma to the unlettered in ways which had emotional resonance and also mnemonic durability, for they were customarily 'lined-out' (read out line by line) for the illiterate.

For discipline as well as freedom was built into the Wesleyan societies. If Arminian Methodism offered free grace it did not offer cheap grace, but subjected members to a regimen more exacting than that of the old religious societies. Its cellular organization allowed the close scrutiny of conduct, benignly termed 'watching over one another in love', and were expressly intended by Wesley to remedy the lack of a primitive 'true Christian discipline' in the

---

[38] J. Wesley, *Journal* 4 p. 471. Little has been written on this subject save for Frank Baker's useful pamphlet *Methodism and the Love-Feast* (London 1957).
[39] *The Arminian Magazine* 4 (London 1781) p. 227.

contemporary Church.[40] If the societies recruited they also expelled; in 1748, for example, we see Wesley reducing the Bristol society from 900 to 730 almost at a stroke.[41] Wesley's societies were not intended as modern free-expression psychotherapy groups but as disciplined pilgrim companies pressing along a strenuous path to perfection.

The ecclesiological status of Wesley's societies was far more perplexing to contemporaries (and to modern historians) than those of Dr. Woodward. From the outset, Methodism possessed built-in anomalies of theory and practice, which rendered it taxonomically hard to place. While the old religious societies were exclusively confined to sacrament-taking Anglicans, Wesley's were denominationally inclusive; open to all who possessed the desire to be saved from their sins. They had no credal test for entry. They purported to exemplify not a strictly Anglican but an open 'Catholic' spirit. 'They do not impose in order to their admission, any opinions whatever', claimed Wesley. 'Let them be Churchmen or Dissenters, Presbyterians or Independents, it is no obstacle . . .They ask only, "Is thy heart herein as my heart? If it be, give me thy hand"'.[42] Members were expected regularly to attend their normal place of worship, be it meeting house or parish church. Methodism was to be no tumour feeding on the tissues of other bodies, but a regenerative cell renewing the life of all communions. Its 'original design' was not to create new sects but to 'stir up all parties, Christians and heathens, to worship God in spirit and truth, but the Church of England in particular', an ideal which has echoes of Zinzendorf's early ideal for the Moravians as a unifying 'leaven' in all churches.[43] At the same time, however, in many of his public statements Wesley spoke of the societies as though they were entirely Anglican. But how could loyalty to the ecumenical idea be held in tandem with loyalty to the Church of England? Wesley's perplexed critics saw in his profession of the 'catholic

[40] J. Wesley, *Journal* 6 p. 353 and *Works* 8 p. 225–6. See too R.A. Knox *Enthusiasm* (Oxford 1950) p. 429; H.A. Snyder, *The Radical Wesley* (Downers Grove, Illinois 1980) pp. 54–63.
[41] J. Wesley, *Journal* 3 p. 380.
[42] J. Wesley, *Works* 13 p. 266, echoing his sermon on the 'Catholic Spirit' in *Works* 5 pp. 492–504.
[43] J. Wesley, *Journal* 7 p. 486; A.J. Lewis, *Zinzendorf the Ecumenical Pioneer* (London 1962) pp. 98–160.

spirit' not brotherly love but an exercise in sheep-stealing, by which society members could be recruited from all denominations under the cloak of a spurious interdenominationalism. The widespread image of Wesley as a 'Jesuit in disguise' fed on the suspicion that the ambivalences of Methodist ecclesiology were highly calculated. Moreover, the results of this promiscuous recruitment of Dissenters and the unchurched poor were rightly seen to be dangerous for the long-term attachment of Methodism to the Church of England.

Wesley moved on from one devotional and evangelistic expedient to another, regarding himself as a man guided as with pillars of cloud and fire by clear leadings of Providence. He was not concerned with the future effects of his irregularity on the order of the Church; God would look after that. 'My part', he wrote, 'is to improve the present moment.'[44] Always the experimentalist, he had a simple criterion for the evaluation of each providential call to a new, irregular 'prudential help'. Did it win souls and build them up? If it was 'owned', it could be assumed to be divinely sanctioned. 'His blessing my work is abundant proof', he wrote in 1747.[45] A conviction, buoyed up by *frissons* of pre-millenial hope, that this was an 'extraordinary', almost Pentecostal outpouring of the Spirit, enabled him to justify the use of lay preachers ('*extraordinary* messengers, raised up by God to provoke the *ordinary* ones to jealousy') and to sanction women preachers on the same grounds, assuring one of these, Mary Bosanquet, that since Methodism was 'an extraordinary dispensation of His providence, therefore I do not wonder if several things occur therein which do not fall under the ordinary rules of discipline'.[46] Church order he regarded in severely functional terms. Ultimately, the terrestrial church was an organisation for saving souls and its legal and administrative apparatus subservient to that purpose. 'What is the end of all ecclesiastical order?' he asked. 'Is is not to bring souls from the power of Satan to God ...? ... Order, then, is so far valuable if it answers these ends; and if it answers them not, it is nothing worth.'[47] What would it profit a man who could have

[44] J. Wesley, *Letters* 2 p. 94.
[45] J. Wesley, *Letters* 2 p. 97.
[46] J. Wesley, *Works* 7 p. 277; *Letters* 5 p. 257.
[47] J. Wesley, *Letters* 2 pp. 77–8.

snatched souls from hell, to plead at the Judgement Seat, 'Lord, he was not of my parish'?[48]

What inspired Wesley's resolution to keep Methodism as far as possible within the Church was not only inbred affection but a pragmatic awareness that separatism might weaken the missionary effectiveness of the Methodist societies. If the 'godly ones' hived off into gathered churches they could no longer make use of the apparatus of establishment or tap the massive latent institutional loyalty which accrued to a national church.[49] The failure of Puritanism to achieve a national reformation was, he thought, the direct result of its fissiparousness and its encouragement of separatism.[50] The biblical injunction to 'come out and be separate' was no justification for schism but was intended as a general call to Christians to avoid close contact with worldly society.[51] Wesley did not intend the Methodist connexion to go the way of the forlorn Nonjurors of his youth, nor to become like the inward-looking early eighteenth-century Dissent of which Isaac Watts sang,

> We are a garden walled around
> Chosen and made peculiar ground.[52]

In Wesley's view the societies remained an evangelical order within a Church whose surrounding environment of catholicity – apostolic order, liturgy, sacramental life – was largely taken for granted and assumed to be readily available.[53] While Methodism gathered to itself some additional 'prudential' means of grace, it relied on the Church for the traditional institutional means. Societies held their own preaching services, love-feasts, watch nights, covenant services at New Year, but – at least in Wesley's optimistic view – these were not substitutes for but supplements to the liturgical public worship of the parish church. Only 'in a sense' did all this constitute 'public worship', Wesley considered, for it was defective in the four grand parts of public prayer; deprecation, petition, intercession and

---

[48] J. Wesley, *Letters* 2 p. 137.
[49] J. Wesley, *Works* 7 p. 278.
[50] J. Wesley, *Works* 7 pp. 427–8.
[51] J. Wesley, *Works* 6 pp. 465–6.
[52] Isaac Watts, *Works* (7 vols Leeds n.d.) 7 p. 137.
[53] See A. Outler, 'Do Methodists have a Doctrine of the Church?' in Dow Kirkpatrick ed *The Doctrine of the Church* (London 1964) pp. 26–7.

thanksgiving, which it seldom employed.[54] Society worship, like university sermons, presupposed full public worship elsewhere. Society prayers were to be kept short; society meetings were scheduled outside church hours, even though this meant in some cases before 5 a.m. or after 5 p.m.[55] Above all, the societies were deliberately stinted of the administration of the sacraments, which Wesley saw as the crucial line dividing a voluntary society from the Church itself. He clung tenaciously to his conviction that the lay preachers had inherited the role of evangelists in the New Testament; they were commissioned, albeit by an inward call, to preach and spread the Gospel, but *not* possessed of the priestly status of pastors who presided over the whole life of a flock and administered the sacramental ordinances to it.[56] 'Do the work of evangelists' he told his preachers. 'I earnestly advise you, abide in your place; keep your own station.'[57] The preachers were no more 'ministers' than the societies were 'churches'.

Holding this line against pressure from below was not easy, and ultimately impossible, but Wesley maintained it, more or less, at least until his highly anomalous ordinations in 1784. It was a task made somewhat lighter by the itinerant life of the preachers and the annual changes of circuit which kept them conveniently on the move. It was also helped by Wesley's astonishing longevity which gave him patriarchal authority as a latter-day Abraham; without this it would have been harder for him to maintain the convenient fiction that the societies were his own private army – a kind of religious equivalent of the Atholl Highlanders – possessed of no corporate being apart from their leader, with whom they were in a private and voluntary association.

Though fighting a spirited rearguard action against the steady drift of his societies into separatism, Wesley expended little energy in trying to weld them back more firmly into the parish system. It is noticeable that while he might move forward only reluctantly, he never moved back. At an early stage it became clear to Charles Wesley and others that the societies could only be reintegrated into the Church by sacrificing lay preaching and the itinerant principle,

---

[54] *Minutes of the Methodist Conferences* 2 vols (London 1862) 1 p. 59.
[55] *Minutes* 1 p. 59.
[56] J. Wesley, *Works* 7 pp. 273–81, sermon on 'The Ministerial Office'.
[57] *Arminian Magazine* 13 (London 1790) pp. 288–9.

and unscrambling the connexion in such a way that local societies were effectively parochialized. Accordingly, in 1756 Charles Wesley and Walker of Truro evolved a plan by which the more presentable preachers should be ordained and the remainder anchored firmly to their parishes as lay 'readers' or 'inspectors' of a particular society.[58] Wesley brushed this scheme aside, for it would involve handing over the great majority of societies to hireling shepherds.[59] But what if the parish minister should be a *Gospel* minister? As the number of Evangelical clergy grew and more and more 'faithful' ministers took over parishes containing Methodists, they pressed for Wesley's societies to be handed over to their control. There was trouble over this issue in Cornwall in the 1750s, and again in Henry Venn's parish of Huddersfield between 1761 and 1765, when Wesley first agreed to suspend Methodist preaching for some years and then rather shamefacedly restored it.[60] In 1764 a dozen Evangelical clergymen appeared at the Bristol Conference to press the point, but in vain. Wesley was locked on to his irregular course; he would not dismember his connexion and give his people over to clergymen who, though godly, would contaminate Methodist teaching by Calvinist 'poison'.[61] He would not abandon the itinerant irregular preaching; by what other way would the church reach those otherwise 'utterly inaccessible'?[62] He must have known that the likelihood of any large-scale ordination of preachers was highly improbable, given the professional and class barriers which had to be overcome. The Roman Catholic churches of Ireland or France with their seminary-trained peasant priests and their lay orders might absorb plebeians with ease; not so the Hanoverian Church of England whose clergy were increasingly expected to be not only genteel, but graduates of a university. Some of Wesley's preachers who gained ordination were significantly appointed not to English parishes but relegated to outposts of empire like Newfoundland or the West Indies.

---

[58] E. Sidney, *The Life and Ministry of the Rev. S. Walker* 2 ed (London 1838) pp. 201–7. The correspondence is brought together in G.C.B. Davies, *The Early Cornish Evangelicals 1735–1760* (London 1951) pp. 88–129.
[59] J. Wesley, *Letters* 3 pp. 192–6.
[60] J. Wesley, *Letters* 3 pp. 221–6; 4 pp. 160–1, 216; *Journal* 4 p. 161; J. Pawson *An Affectionate Address* (Liverpool? 1795) pp. 10–11.
[61] J. Wesley, *Letters* 3 p. 144.
[62] J. Wesley, *Works* 8 p. 230.

By the mid-century, long before the 'grand climacterical year' of 1784 which saw Wesley's ordinations and the Deed of Declaration, his societies were set on course for secession.[63] There is no bettering the lapidary description of the process by the Victorian Wesleyan, Dr. Beaumont: 'Mr. Wesley, like a strong and skilful oarsman, looked one way while every stroke of his own oar took him in the opposite direction'.[64]

But the societies of Wesley and other Methodist leaders like Whitefield and Harris were not the only societies in the Evangelical Revival. The need to form them was recognized among the growing band of 'regular' Evangelical parish clergy, slowly coalescing into what became a definable grouping in the Church of England.

The Evangelical parish clergy were well aware that the piety they aroused could not easily be contained within the liturgical framework of the Church, even when its Sunday services were enlivened by sermons and augmented by family prayers. 'We want something more than preaching among us', said John Clayton. 'We want a nearer approach, a faster hold on our people.'[65] 'The interval from Sabbath to Sabbath is a good while, and affords time for the world and Satan to creep in', observed John Newton.[66] If the parish priest did not meet the demand for fellowship and fervour beyond that provided by public worship, Dissenters and Methodists would. New converts 'must … *will* seek that light and instruction of which they feel the want', wrote William Richardson of York. 'To obtain it, they will break through every barrier and cast aside prejudices against … unauthorised teachers of every sect and name. Like persons … parched with thirst, they will be ready to … drink water out of the dirtiest ditch.'[67] To meet this need, Evangelical parish clergy picked up the idea of the religious society when other Churchmen had virtually dropped it. 'Of all the methods that have ever been tried to keep up the power of godliness among our flocks', one wrote in 1802, 'to preserve them from

[63] J. Whitehead, *Life of the Rev. J. Wesley* 2 Vols (London 1793, 1796) 2 p. 404.
[64] B. Gregory, *Sidelights on the Conflict of Methodism* (London 1898) p. 161.
[65] *Eclectic Notes* ed J.H. Pratt (London 1856) p. 186.
[66] J. Newton, *Works* 6 vols (London 1816) 2 p. 103.
[67] *A Brief Memoir of the Rev. W. Richardson*, 2 ed (London 1822) p. 25.

being scattered, seduced, corrupted, or tossed about with every wind of doctrine, none has been found so efficacious as this'.[68]

The form taken by societies was shaped by a number of variables; local circumstance, size of parish, style of churchmanship. At one extreme stood the elite society which James Hervey attended in the Northampton area, whose members had to appear with copies of the New Testament in Greek.[69] At the other were the society or prayer meetings which evolved naturally out of family worship in the parsonage kitchen, thrown open to outsiders.[70] In several parishes, like that of Thomas Vivian at Cornwood, Evangelicals organized class meetings – even in some instances using Wesleyan hymns – to beat the Methodists at their own game.[71] The degree of pastoral control which could be extended to formally constituted societies varied according to the compactness of a parish. In a small nucleated village supervision might be easy; not so in large upland parishes like those of the North country. In the corners of Henry Venn's rambling parish of Huddersfield where converts travelled miles to parish services from scattered settlements and homesteads, societies sprang up among the bands who trudged home to their hamlets discussing the sermon. Their remoteness meant that Venn could only visit them monthly and had to recognise their self-governing autonomy; when he left Yorkshire, replaced by a stiff anti-evangelical of whom a disgusted convert remarked 'they might as well have put a poker in't pulpit', these groups slipped easily into Methodism and Dissent.[72]

From the start, Dr. Woodward's prescription for the religious societies had admirers among the 'regular' Evangelical parish clergy. The old Holy Club member, James Hervey, whose Bideford society, founded in the early 1740s, ran for a decade, was an

---

[68] *The Christian Observer* 1 (London 1802) p. 565.

[69] J. Hervey, *A Collection of Letters* 2 vols (London 1760) 1 pp. xxxi–xliii, 2 p. 198.

[70] See C. Smyth, *Simeon and Church Order* (Cambridge 1940) pp. 25–7.

[71] *Arminian Magazine* 1 (London 1778) p. 587; A. Watmough, *History of Methodism in Lincoln* (London 1829) pp. 60–2.

[72] C.M.S. archives Venn MSS, Henry Venn (of C.M.S.) Diary of a Visit to Yorkshire in 1824; J. Venn, *Life and Letters of the Rev. H. Venn* ed H. Venn (ed 5 1837) p. 44; *Memoirs of the Rev. J. Cockin* 2 ed (London 1841) p. 24; J.G. Miall, *Congregationalism in Yorkshire* (London 1868) pp. 277–8; J. Horsfall Turner, *Independency at Brighouse* (Brighouse 1878) pp. 15–17.

early propagandist for Woodward.[73] The most influential example, however, was Samuel Walker's Truro society, founded in 1754, which suggested to later generations that Woodward's plan could be safely and successfully put to the service of 'vital religion', as an Anglican alternative to the irregular societies of John Wesley. Walker's rules were closely based on Woodward's *Account*, which he prudently disseminated among his flock to counteract charges of novelty.[74] Only regular communicants were admitted, and these by Walker personally. Applicants who belonged to other societies – like the Methodists – were excluded. For the most part proceedings were strictly formalized, consisting of extracts from the liturgy, bible readings and set prayers. There was no extempore prayer and no 'private person' was allowed to contravene Walker's instruction *'no one is to be talking there but myself'.*[75]

The success of the Truro model comforted many late eighteenth century Evangelicals who knew by observing Wesley at work that societies could promote growth, but were fearful of the enthusiasm and separatism of the Methodist example. Yet the pros and cons of societies were the subject of vigorous debate, especially when Evangelical clergymen gathered in their clerical clubs like the Elland Society in Yorkshire or the Eclectic in London. Were they really worthwhile? At their best they deepened the spiritual life of the parish. They forged closer links between pastor and people: 'how could I know my sheep if I did not see them in private?' asked Simeon.[76] They encouraged spiritual development; 'growth in grace'. They prevented waverers from falling away. They withdrew souls from irreligious company, chalking out a demarcation line between the Church and the World. By instituting them, a minister could separate out 'the spiritual from the visible Church', and gain some of the advantages of tending to a 'gathered church' while still

[73] *Herveiana; Sketches of the Life and Writings of the Rev. J. Hervey* 2 pts (Scarborough 1822) 1 p. 43.

[74] E. Sidney, *Life of the Rev. S. Walker* 1 ed (London 1835) pp. 63–8; S. Walker, *Fifty-two Sermons on the Baptismal Covenant* 2 vols (London 1763) 1 Preface p. xxix.

[75] E. Sidney, *Life of Walker* 1 ed (1835) p. 63. See too pp. 63–8 for the smaller groups which Walker organized among his converts, resembling Wesley's bands, to allow more freedom and intimacy in conversation.

[76] W. Carus, *Memoirs of the Rev. C. Simeon* (Cambridge 1847) p. 138.

operating the normal parochial system of the Church of England.[77] Above all, they offered a fellowship and communion unprovided by the public services of the Church.

At the same time, there were formidable problems involved in running societies. While they bonded 'serious' Christians together, they might do so at the cost of alienating non-members. John Venn admitted that gathering an elite into a society might encourage people to 'consider the Church as divided' and create a party mentality in the parish.[78] It was not easy to adjust the thermostatic control on the heat of their piety. If societies were too tightly constricted and too liturgical, their aridity might drive their members into the easy fraternities of Dissent; if too laxly supervised, they became anarchic and heatedly disputatious and ended up at exactly the same destination. In a small country parish they might wither for lack of support; in a metropolis they might be easily infiltrated by sectarian predators.[79] It is noticeable that their negative effects – as a prophylactic against Dissent – were often more strongly emphasised than their positive benefits. Thus Charles Simeon urged 'the absolute necessity of such meetings, not merely for the edification of the people, but *chiefly for the preservation of the Established Church*'.[80]

Simeon was one of many who felt that when societies were not formed 'the clergyman beats the bush but the Dissenters catch the game'.[81] Others were more hesitant. Though admitting their benefits, the Revd. J. Davies told the Eclectic Society in 1800 'as religious societies are at present formed, the evil generally preponderates'.[82] If started and then stopped, 'the consequences are worse than if they had not been undertaken'.[83]

On one point at least there came to be a general consensus. If they *were* set up it was essential to follow Woodward and Walker by drawing up rules and keeping to them. At an Elland Society meeting in 1787 it was minuted 'gentlemen are requested to read

---

[77] C. Bridges, *The Christian System* (London 1830) p. 597; *Eclectic Notes* p. 188; J. Pearson, *The Life of W. Hey* 2 pts in 1 vol (London 1822) pt 2 pp. 73–7.
[78] *Eclectic Notes* p. 186.
[79] *Eclectic Notes* pp. 189, 191.
[80] Carus, *Simeon* p. 138.
[81] Carus, *Simeon* p. 139.
[82] *Eclectic Notes* p. 185.
[83] *Eclectic Notes* p. 187.

Woodward with a view to the regulation of religious societies'.[84]
Doctrine apart, the Evangelicals saw much to admire in the orderly
life of the old post-Restoration societies. It was agreed that it was
vital to keep clerical control over them. At all costs the elevated
position of the pastor should be maintained. He 'should not meet
his people in these societies as on an equal footing' argued Josiah
Pratt.[85] Robinson of Leicester, who had been forced to abandon
his own fractious group, insisted that 'there must be no meeting
without the minister presiding, no prayer in his presence which
does not proceed from his lips'.[86] 'The pastor should be gener-
alissimo' agreed Thomas Scott, whose view of societies was permanently soured by bad memories of the unruly gathering he had
inherited from John Newton in the Dissenter-ridden town of
Olney.[87] For this reason small and manageable societies were better
than large ones, in which some delegation of authority was often
unavoidable. It was deemed unwise to allow opportunities for
unrestrained expression of personal experiences, or Methodist-style
'testimony'. 'I have great objection to "experience meetings"', said
Scott, 'they are a short sermon upon the little word "I"'.[88] Even
Woodward's classical model with its space for 'pious conference'
was deemed too lax on this vital point, at least for some late
eighteenth-century readers. A correspondent to the *Christian
Observer* in 1806, though admiring of Woodward, considered his
willingness to allow 'extempore discussion' in societies permissible
in former times but inadvisable now in a more sectary-ridden age.
'Extempore prayers, exhortations and expositions of the Scriptures
are generally productive of evil', he thought, for if they were
encouraged, laymen might become addicted to them and migrate
to the Dissenting chapel where they were practised more wholeheartedly, an especial danger when an Evangelical incumbent was
succeeded by an 'unconverted' one, who reverted to a strict use of
the Liturgy. It was far safer to use some carefully selected form of

---

[84] West Yorks C.R.O., Minutes of Elland Clerical Society, meeting of 1 March
1787.
[85] *Eclectic Notes* p. 188.
[86] E.T. Vaughan, *Some Account of the Rev. T. Robinson* (London 1815) pp. 85–8.
See too E. Sidney, *The Life of the Rev. R. Hill* (London 1834) p. 147.
[87] J. Scott, *The Life of the Rev. T. Scott* 6 ed (London 1824) pp. 503–4; *Eclectic
Notes* p. 189.
[88] *Eclectic Notes* p. 191.

prayer, accompanied by a chapter or sermon read aloud from some 'judicious publication of our *own* divines'.[89]

The idea, axiomatic in Wesley's movement, that societies should act as a training school for lay religious leadership and for the promotion of lay spiritual 'gifts', was treated with great caution. Evangelical ministers were all too conscious of what might be called 'the problem of the eloquent convert' – what to do with the scantily educated layman who felt a call to preach, found the road to Anglican orders blocked, and ended up – like thirteen or more of Henry Venn's converts – in the Nonconformist ministry.[90] Clerical funds like that of the Elland Society existed to send a few such aspirants to the universities and into orders.[91] But the religious societies of the late eighteenth century do not seem to have been regarded as agencies to encourage such upward mobility, or to provide large creative outlets for the spiritual energy of ordinary lay people. 'They *may* be a means of bringing out modest young men, who might afterward be useful ministers', admitted Scott, but they were more likely to be '*hotbeds*, on which superficial and discreditable preachers were hastily raised up' – youths like those who had issued from the turbulent Olney society to contradict John Newton, having picked up 'a little bit and scrap of Christianity ... – something about grace and Christ – but little which enters deeply into Christian truth and the Christian life'.[92] In 1800 the devotional role cast for the simple layman in an Evangelical religious society was still a restricted one.

Behind these attitudes there no doubt lay a good deal of conventional social conservatism. There is a wealth of class significance packed into Walker of Truro's terse rebuke to Wesley for his use of lay preachers: 'It has been a great fault all along, to have made

---

[89] *Christian Observer* 5 (1806) pp. 150–3. T.S. Grimshawe, *A Memoir of the Rev. Legh Richmond* 3 ed (London 1828) pp. 41–2 describes a society run on these lines.

[90] H. Venn (of C.M.S.) Diary of a Visit; *An Account of the Rev. J. Fawcett* (London 1818) p. 29.

[91] For clerical education societies see F.W.B. Bullock, *A History of Training for the Ministry of the Church of England from 1800 to 1874* (St. Leonard's-on-sea 1959) p. 25; J.D. Walsh, 'The Yorkshire Evangelicals in the Eighteenth Century' (unpub Cambridge Ph.D. thesis 1956) pp. 233–73; A. Haig, *The Victorian Clergy* (London 1984) pp. 63–72.

[92] *Life of T. Scott* p. 504; *Eclectic Notes* p. 188.

the low people of your counsel'.[93] But the cautious Evangelical approach to religious societies also reflected a traditionally 'high' view of the dignity of the pastoral office, to which many Puritans and Dissenters would no doubt have subscribed in principle (as would some later Buntingite Wesleyans). 'Ministers must diligently dispense the word and the people must meekly receive it', Walker assured his people.[94] The minister alone, agreed Richard Cecil, 'is the man whose office and profession, in all their parts, are raised into dignity and importance by their direct reference to eternity'. 'He must stand as with wings on his shoulders'.[95] If it was the prophetical more than the priestly office that was here being extolled, it still left little room for the devotional activism of the layman, especially the plebeian layman, who was held to have a dangerous proclivity towards 'enthusiasm' which needed to be firmly held in check. 'The common people ... readily receive the doctrine of a divine influence, and quickly pervert it', one Evangelical clergyman complained.[96] The Evangelical religious society was not usually intended to engage popular religious culture on its own terms.

Not that the Evangelical clergy rejected the use of lay activism in the service of 'vital religion' and the Established Church; the astonishing proliferation of Evangelical-dominated voluntary societies in the age of Wilberforce – from the Church Missionary Society to the City of London Truss Society for the Relief of the Ruptured Poor – was evidence enough to the contrary.[97] Yet though Evangelical clergymen welcomed the leadership of laymen in a host of philanthropic causes, and, increasingly, in parochial education,[98] they were unwilling to engage 'lay-agency' in roles which appeared to undermine ministerial authority, above all in

---

[93] Sidney, *Life of Walker* 2 ed (1838) p. 216.
[94] Walker, *Fifty-two Sermons* 2 p. 194. For the pastoral office in Methodism see W.R. Ward, 'The Legacy of John Wesley: the Pastoral office in Britain and America' in A. Whiteman, J.S. Bromley and P.G.M. Dickson eds *Statesmen, Scholars and Merchants* (Oxford 1973) pp. 323–50; J.S. Kent, *The Age of Disunity* (London 1966) pp. 44–85.
[95] *The Works of the Rev. R. Cecil* 3 ed 2 vols (London 1827) 1 pp. 107–8, 2 p. 483.
[96] *Christian Observer* 7 (1808) p. 317.
[97] The fullest account of the Evangelical societies is that of F.K. Brown, *Fathers of the Victorians* (Cambridge 1961).
[98] *Christian Observer* 7 (1808) pp. 739–40.

worship. The layman could speak freely on the platform, in the committee room, or in the school room, but not on devotional occasions in public. There was indeed a large space assigned to the layman to develop his spiritual gifts of extempore exposition and prayer, but it was not in the sanctuary or in the religious society – it was in the domestic seclusion of the home; in the household prayers so central to the spirituality of the Evangelicals.[99] Here, in the delimited but vital familial sphere, the layman was encouraged to consider himself 'to be what Noah, Abraham and the Patriarchs of old were – the priest of his own household'.[100]

Jesus College, Oxford

[99] Useful recent studies of Evangelical family piety are E. Jay, *The Religion of the Heart. Anglican Evangelicalism and the Nineteenth Century Novel* (Oxford 1979) pp. 131–48 and C. Tolley, 'The Legacy of Evangelicalism in the Lives and Writings of certain Descendants of the Clapham Sect' (unpub Oxford D.Phil. thesis 1980).
[100] C. Bridges, *An Essay on Family Prayer* (London 1847) p. 27.

IDEALISM AND ASSOCIATION IN EARLY NINETEENTH CENTURY DISSENT

by DERYCK LOVEGROVE

I N April 1799 Francis Wollaston, rector of Chislehurst, published a pamphlet warning his parishioners and the public at
large of the activities of certain seditious societies whose
purpose was that of disseminating Jacobin principles; ideas already
responsible for plunging France into chaos. His enquiries, he
announced, had confirmed his worst suspicions:

> The parties who so kindly, and out of pretended benevolence
> undertake to instruct my people for me, are members of a
> society, calling itself the Union Society of Greenwich: the
> same, as I am informed, which under the name of an Itinerant
> Society, had been driven from a public-house in that neigh-
> bourhood some little time since.[1]

Wollaston's message, an ecclesiastical variant of the more general
concern to engage in active defence of the established order,
received its definitive form the following year at the hands of
Bishop Samuel Horsley. In an important passage in his second
visitation charge to the clergy of Rochester diocese the bishop
referred to the emergence of an ecclesiastical subculture consisting
of religious conventicles, Sunday schools and itinerant preachers.
In Horsley's eyes these ecclesiastical excrescences were merely the
outward manifestations of a more sinister and worrying development, the appearance of associations designed to defray the costs
of the current spate of unauthorized 'religious' activity.[2]

[1] F. Wollaston, *A country parson's address to his flock, to caution them against
being misled by the wolf in sheep's cloathing, or receiving Jacobin teachers of
sedition, who intrude themselves under the specious pretense of instructing youth
and preaching Christianity* (London 1799) p. 30.
[2] S. Horsley, *The charges of Samuel Horsley LL.D., F.R.S., F.A.S., late Lord
Bishop of St Asaph, delivered at his several visitations of the dioceses of St David's,
Rochester and St Asaph* (London 1830) p. 104.

Both Wollaston and Horsley were pointing to one of the remarkable phenomena of the late 1790s, the sudden proliferation of religious societies and associations within a sector of the Christian community not previously known for its emphasis upon co-operative activity; evangelical Calvinistic Dissent.[3] On every side voluntary bodies were springing up, providing a visible measure of the quickening pace of religious revival.

The new age of the voluntary religious society has been carefully studied in relation to the Established Church,[4] but its extension to the traditional rivals of the Church of England, to the autonomous congregations of Baptists and Congregationalists, has received little attention.[5] Yet it was that development rather than the efforts of the Clapham Sect which alarmed the High Church contemporaries of William Wilberforce. The new Dissenting societies and associations seemed to be multiplying like cancerous growths in the ecclesiastical body politic. Their shadowy origins and obscure leadership, rendered even less distinct by congregational autonomy and by the absence of hierarchy, gave them a peculiarly malevolent and uncontrollable appearance. Their intentions towards the Established Church appeared subversive and hostile. To cap it all their success in attracting a large measure of popular support was undeniable.

Apart from the stimulus given to Establishment fears the new bodies were remarkable in a number of ways. Their existence marked a watershed in Dissenting thought: the appearance of a new and more positive approach to society epitomizing the fusion of evangelical zeal with Enlightenment optimism and humanitarian concern. They signified a radical departure from the traditional veneration for the principle of independency. Despite protestations

---

[3] For the purposes of classification this paper will include Calvinistic Methodist bodies under this heading.

[4] See F.K. Brown, *Fathers of the Victorians. The Age of Wilberforce* (London 1961) cap. 9; K. Heasman, *Evangelicals in Action. An Appraisal of their Social Work in the Victorian Era* (London 1962); I. Bradley, *The Call to Seriousness. The Evangelical Impact on the Victorians* (London 1976) cap 7.

[5] Useful comments are made by: G.F. Nuttall, 'Assembly and Association in Dissent, 1689–1831', *SCH* 7 (1971) pp. 289–309; W.R. Ward, *Religion and Society in England 1790–1850* (London 1972) pp. 48–50; A.D. Gilbert, *Religion and Society in Industrial England. Church, Chapel and Social Change, 1740–1914* (London 1976) pp. 55, 59, 117 & 190; and I. Sellers, *Nineteenth-Century Nonconformity* (London 1977) pp. 4–5.

in favour of congregational self-government the era of religious societies marked the adoption of an unacknowledged connexionalism. In the realm of doctrine the strict logic of the age of reason had begun to give way to more questioning views, yet the new religious bodies represented graphically the potency and stability of the emerging moderate form of traditional Calvinism. At an important historical juncture Protestant Dissenters found themselves for the first time with the means of exerting a significant impact upon national life; with an instrument which at the same time propelled them irresistibly towards the new age.

The primary impulse towards association stemmed from a renewed interest in evangelism. Clear statements of evangelistic intent appeared in the foundation plans of a host of county associations, societies for the support of itinerant preaching and organizations for the promotion and maintenance of Sunday schools. Yet care is necessary, for studies concerned with early Protestant missionary activity have demonstrated the complexity that existed in this period in the matter of personal motivation.[6] A similar diversity in ideals may lie behind the growth of Dissenting societies in spite of the tendency of most historical commentators to accept the foundation statements uncritically.

A number of societies incorporated the idea of evangelism in their title. Societas Evangelica (founded in 1776 and refounded twenty years later), the Baptist Society in London for the Encouragement and Support of Itinerant and Village Preaching (1797), the Congregational Society in London for spreading the Gospel in England (1797) and the Evangelical Association for spreading the Gospel of Salvation in the Villages of the Four Northern Counties (1798) were four of the more prominent bodies to follow this practice.[7] But even where the title was less revealing, as in the case of some of the county unions and seminaries, the evangelistic intention was clearly stated. At its opening meeting the Bedfordshire Union of Christians declared its object to be 'to promote the

---

[6] See J. Van Den Berg, *Constrained by Jesus' Love. An Inquiry into the motives of the missionary awakening in Great Britain in the period between 1698 and 1815* (Kampen 1956); M. Warren, *The Missionary Movement from Britain in Modern History* (London 1965) caps 1 & 2.
[7] The three latter societies are hereafter referred to as the Baptist Society, the Congregational Society and the Northern Evangelical Association.

knowledge of the Gospel'.[8] Similarly, many of the new generation of evangelical academies, institutions such as Hoxton and Hackney, each with its own supporting committee, arose with the stated intention of preparing suitable young men for a full-time evangelistic ministry. All would have identified with the plan of the Baptist Society when it stated: 'It is with peculiar pleasure that we contemplate the recent formation of Societies in the Country, not only among the Particular Baptists, but also among our Congregational Brethren, for the spread of the gospel in this land by Village Preaching.'

For many of the architects of the movement towards association the impetus towards evangelism derived from a powerful sense of obligation. As David Bogue pointed out to his fellow members of the Hampshire Congregational Association in 1797 the Christian ought to be zealous for the propagation of the gospel. It was a duty owed both 'to the Lord Jesus, and to the souls of men.'[9] Within this emphasis upon obligation the element of compassion is clearly visible especially in conjunction with a sense of remorse for past years of inactivity, but at times this idea is subordinated to a sterner note of command. In a number of writings the primary theme seems to be the unquestioning loyalty of the individual Christian to the sovereign God. According to the plan of the Baptist Society:

> Preaching the Gospel, or publishing salvation by Jesus Christ, is the ordinance of God; and the grand mean of converting sinners, in order to their present peace, their greater usefulness, and their final happiness. *Preach the Gospel to every creature*, was the high command of our sovereign Lord, to his disciples, just before he ascended the throne of universal dominion. This divine order is yet in force; and its obligation extends to [all ministers and private Christians].

References to the theme of duty in response to divine command are found most frequently in material connected with Baptist organizations, and while this may be merely a matter of chance, it may also reflect the more explicit Calvinism found in that quarter with

[8] Bedford County Record Office (CRO) MS Z 206/1 fol 1ᵛ.
[9] *A Circular Letter, from the associated ministers of the Gospel, in Hampshire, Convened at Andover, June 7, 1797* p. 5.

its emphasis upon the divine will and initiative. Indeed to many Calvinists in the 1790s the twin notions of an obligation to engage in evangelism and the duty of sinners to believe the gospel were anathema, undermining everything for which the concept of the sovereignty of God stood. In the Northamptonshire Association William Carey fought against such prejudice to launch the Baptist Missionary Society in 1792, while in the Baptist Western Association his counterpart in domestic evangelism, William Steadman, attacked the same doctrinally-inspired complacency, arguing that election and reprobation though 'sublime doctrines' were being insisted upon 'to the neglect of other more plain and useful doctrines of the Gospel.'[10]

Possessing the same theological motivation and subject to the same sense of heightened millennial urgency it is scarcely surprising that concern for home and overseas evangelism arose in the same quarters in close chronological proximity. A number of domestic associations including the Baptist Society and the Essex Congregational Union acknowledged the connection openly. On 5 May 1795 having resolved to support the committee in London formed to launch a mission to 'the unenlightened parts of the world' (the genesis of the London Missionary Society) the Essex association of Congregational ministers decided to turn its attention to the question of domestic evangelism, a move which led to the formation of a county union of churches three years later.[11] In subsequent years the attitude of some domestic societies seemed to enshrine the belief that too much attention had been given to overseas matters in comparison with the need at home. This objection, issuing from Idle Academy in 1806 and from the Yorkshire and Lancashire Baptist Association in 1825 reflected the convictions of William Vint and William Steadman respectively, contemporary presidents of two of the most prominent Yorkshire seminaries.[12]

---

[10] T. Steadman, *Memoir of the Rev. William Steadman, D.D.* (London 1838) p. 200.
[11] R. Burls, *A Brief Review of the Plan and Operations of the Essex Congregational Union for Promoting the Knowledge of the Gospel in the County of Essex and its Vicinity* (Maldon 1848) pp. 9–10.
[12] *Idle Academy Report for 1802–1806* pp. 3–4; *Circular Letter from the Elders and Messengers of the several Baptist Churches of the Yorkshire and Lancashire Association assembled in Westgate, Bradford, May 24th and 25th, 1825* (Bradford 1825) p. 7.

Implicit in the sense of duty attached to the task of evangelism may have been an expectation of success, of an influx of converts to the churches bringing with it expansion, stability and perhaps even a greater sense of financial security, yet the command was not necessarily construed in terms of cause and effect. In 1821 the official itinerant supported by the Essex Baptist churches commented in his annual report to the county association that the continuance of evangelistic effort should not depend upon results. Quoting Alexander Waugh he argued:

> Had there been no success at all in your efforts, I contend that our duty would remain the same; it is the command of Him that made us – of Him that redeemed us – that his blessed Gospel should be sent to the ends of the earth, and much more that it should be sent to our neighbours and fellow subjects. From this obligation nothing can release so long as there is an open door and sinners disposed to hear.[13]

Yet this spirited defence of principle is at variance with other evidence which points to the emergence of a more pragmatic approach. Whereas the Village Itinerancy was prepared in 1820 to decline an offer to convey a chapel to its trusts saying that it had no wish to engage in that process 'merely to plant [its] own students about the country', the decade ended with an evident concern on the part of the committee to extend the society's control to as many properties and, therefore, congregations as possible.[14] Much earlier the Baptist Society had reported with evident approval that one of the local ministers receiving support from its funds had begun to concentrate his preaching in those villages from which people might be expected to attend his church, and that this policy had 'had its desired effect as the congregation [was] thereby kept up'.[15] Most societies concerned to promote evangelism found themselves confronted with the kind of dilemma acknowledged by the North Bucks Independent Association. The choice seemed to be between a true itinerant ministry, genuinely mobile but requiring indefinite external funding, and concentration upon those places

[13] London Baptist Union, Essex Baptist Association minutes 29 May 1821.
[14] London Dr Williams's Library (DWL), New College MS 58/1 minutes 15 Nov 1820. Compare with MS 60/1 minutes for 1828 *passim*.
[15] London Baptist Missionary Society, MS Ue minutes 22 Oct 1807.

where the prospects were greatest of raising a new, self-supporting congregation to act as a base for further evangelism.[16]

A great deal of effort expended by the new societies and associations was taken up with education. The majority reported the establishment in their area of simple facilities for the achievement of basic literacy. The earliest work of the Essex Congregational Union concerned the provision of day schools in two villages in the county each with places for twenty children aged eight years or over.[17] Equally typical was the lay initiative in the village of Great Horwood which commenced with a Sunday school for 100 children 'many of them almost at maturity'. Within two years the original enterprise had grown into a range of related activities including a week-night school for older children, a sewing school for girls and a village reading society.[18] It was these uncontrolled forays into popular education as much as the phenomenon of itinerant preaching which prompted Bishop Horsley to warn of the growth of Dissenting associations during the 1790s.

The difficulty lies in judging the extent to which these efforts represented a genuine commitment to education. The Northamptonshire Association letter for 1792 spoke of doing good to the rising generation 'by encouraging Sunday Schools, and other charity schools' with the subscribers offering personal oversight and occasional assistance.[19] Literacy was the necessary prerequisite for personal study of the Bible and, therefore, for comprehension of the message of those who preached. In many cases schools were closely connected with evangelism, the work with children leading to the establishment of regular meetings for biblical exposition and preaching. The prevailing utilitarian attitude to education was not often admitted but the committee of the Essex Congregational Union was more open than most. From the outset the union was aware of the usefulness of the school as a device for gaining access to communities where difficulties might otherwise have been

---

[16] *North Bucks Association of Independent Ministers and Churches Report for 1826* p. 11.
[17] Essex CRO MS D/NC 9/1 minutes 7 Aug & 23 Oct 1798, 19 Mar 1799.
[18] *North Bucks Independent Association Reports for 1820* p. 14 & *1821* p. 20.
[19] J. Rippon ed *Baptist Annual Register* 4 vols (London 1790–1802) 1 p. 430.

encountered.[20] Writing in 1848 the historian of the union acknowledged that once the early day schools had ceased to have this expedience value they had normally been relinquished in favour of Sunday schools with their more obvious religious purpose.[21] Schools of any kind were seen primarily as aids to evangelism.

This judgment does not mean that the general attitude to education was hostile. The architects of the new academies were in many cases leading supporters of the county associations and itinerant societies. The most prominent advocates of the new evangelicalism, men such as William Roby, Charles Whitfield, William Vint and William Steadman, were concerned to maintain satisfactory levels of intellectual attainment among those who offered themselves for ministry. Whitfield's presence at the founding of the Northern Education Society[22] at Hebden Bridge was merely the logical extension of his earlier advocacy of Christian learning expressed both in his published sermon of 1792 entitled *The obligations to mental improvement stated, and the use of books recommended, especially to youth*, and in his establishment of a remarkable subscription library at his church at Hamsterley, County Durham. In the educational regimes instituted by Roby, Vint and Steadman in the academies at Manchester, Idle and Bradford the same conviction concerning the essential compatibility between evangelical activism and sound learning is readily apparent.

Though the institutions which followed the pattern of Trevecca laid less emphasis upon the academic ingredient of ministerial preparation than their eighteenth century predecessors, the change of emphasis was almost inevitable in the face of the practical demands upon student time made by itinerant preaching. But by the second decade of the nineteenth century signs of a reviving interest in academic excellence began to reappear. The growth in the size and prestige of the leading seminaries when taken in conjunction with the introduction of preliminary courses of instruction, increasing course length, curriculum development, better qualified tutors and the progression of some of the most able students to university, leaves little doubt concerning the resurgence of the academic ideal within evangelical Dissent.

[20] Essex CRO MS D/NC 9/1 minutes 23 Oct 1798.
[21] Burls, *Brief Review* p. 23.
[22] The parent society of the Baptist academy which opened at Bradford in 1806.

In the light of the large amount of Sunday school work among poor children and the later social concern displayed by Anglican Evangelicalism it might be reasonable to presume a degree of interest in charitable activity. Yet the plan of the Bedfordshire Union of Christians compiled in 1797 warns against such presumption. In pursuit of their primary aims of Christian unity and evangelism the authors of the plan stated that the objects of such an association were 'not of a civil, but of a religious kind; not of a formal, but of a spiritual nature'. The plan went on to say that as far as the capacity of the union allowed 'every object of general usefulness, that is of a purely religious nature, and tending to the everlasting salvation of fellow sinners, should be embraced in its progress'.[23]

In spite of the considerable sums spent by Dissenting associations in support of village preaching, in the erection and repair of premises, and in the purchase of books and other materials used in Sunday schools, evidence of a wider charitable concern is extremely sparse. The offer to scholars of small sums of money or an annual pair of shoes, which seems to have been the practice of a number of London-based societies, appears to have been more in the nature of an inducement than a spontaneous response to material need. Rowland Hill admitted in his defence of the Southwark Sunday schools that, 'the sight of a *penny-piece* ha[d] a wonderful charm on a poor child's mind'. The one possible exception to the idea of inducement is found in his statement that the Southwark teachers were in the habit of giving relief to sick children out of their own pockets.[24]

If the Sunday schools and the paucity of further examples are not sufficiently convincing the early work of the Village Itinerancy merely confirms the picture of material disregard. The manuscript which records the society's foundation notes that a room was taken 'near Brick Lane, Spitalfields, among poor weavers, whose outward appearance indicated the greatest poverty and wretchedness. Here some good effects were soon discovered in the conversion of a few individuals to God, the reality of which appears by the consistency

---

[23] S. Greatheed, *General Union Recommended to Real Christians* (London 1798) p. 17.
[24] R. Hill, *An Apology for Sunday Schools* (London [1801]) pp. 42–43.

of their conduct ever since'.[25] No indication is given of any consideration of the need to give material assistance to these recipients of evangelical preaching.

A few rare examples of charitable action can be found which at first sight appear to be cases of disinterested benevolence, yet in every case careful investigation seems to indicate more practical considerations. A lying-in charity providing linen for the poorer women of King's Sutton in Northamptonshire was launched with obvious apologetic intentions, and a similar reason can be advanced for an apparently gratuitous collection made by a branch of the Village Itinerancy in Hampshire on behalf of the county hospital at Winchester.[26] Donations to local charities were frequently part of the price exacted by the Dissenting Deputies for dropping legal proceedings against rioters, yet the motive appears to have had less to do with the need of the beneficiaries than with the desire of the Dissenters not to be seen to be profiting from recourse to law.[27] Even the response of certain members of the Baptist Midland Association to economic distress in the Black Country by setting up soup kitchens and dispensing clothing was at best in-house charity, being directed at the worst affected members of the particular church concerned.[28]

In spite of the multiplicity of records it is difficult to point to any evidence of a significant attachment to the principle of charitable activity. Evangelical Calvinism appears to have engendered in the minds of its adherents either a fatalistic disregard for material need or, more likely, a pervasive distrust of anything capable of being construed as good works. The latter undoubtedly derived its force from two considerations: from the likely effect upon the recipient in distorting the impact of evangelism, and upon the donor in diverting energy from the divine imperative to preach the gospel.

One of the most noticeable features of the late 1790s was the prevalence among Dissenters of a spirit of co-operation and common purpose which transcended denominational boundaries, the

[25] London DWL, New College MS 44 fol 2ʳ.
[26] *North Bucks Independent Association Report for 1827* p. 30; London DWL, New College MS 41/72.
[27] London Guildhall MS 3083 minutes 27 Dec 1805, 27 Feb 1807 & 25 Nov 1808.
[28] Gilbert, *Religion and Society* p. 91.

mood which David Bogue regarded as marking the 'funeral of bigotry'. One of the earliest bodies, Societas Evangelica, linked Congregationalists with Calvinistic Methodists, but others went even further. The Bedfordshire Union of Christians, though limited in practice by those who wished to join, expressed itself desirous of uniting 'serious Christians of every denomination'. At the end of 1797 Samuel Greatheed stated that the union included members from six religious denominations.[29] One of these, George Livius, was a prominent member of Bedford's Moravian congregation.[30] Similar bodies appeared in other counties, while at the national level the Baptist Society expressed its willingness to allow its itinerants to join forces with evangelical paedobaptist ministers.[31] The most remarkable example of the new spirit of unity was the Independent seminary at Newport Pagnell which under its new title as the Newport Pagnell Evangelical Institution produced with complete equanimity young men bound both for Congregational and Baptist pastorates.[32]

In practice certain clear limits to the undenominational ideal existed. The strong distaste felt by most clergymen for every form of irregularity and the fear of incurring the taint of disloyalty precluded all but the most insignificant level of Anglican co-operation. Moderate Calvinism, in spite of its reduced emphasis upon doctrine, still had theological reservations concerning close co-operation with those who held Arminian views. Neither Wesleyans nor Dissenters showed much inclination to unite with one another, except in the case of Lord Sidmouth's bill in order to defend essential freedoms. Tensions also existed at times between Calvinistic Methodist bodies and those of their preachers who expressed a preference for the independent form of church government.[33] But most serious and pervasive of all was the deep division which existed between fellow Dissenters over the issue of baptism. Almost every example of tolerance in this area can be matched by instances

---

[29] Greatheed, *General Union Recommended* pp. 2 & 79.
[30] Bedford CRO MS Z 206/1 fol 2ʳ.
[31] Baptist Society Plan p. 3. A copy of the plan is preserved in the society's minutes, London BMS MS Ue.
[32] F.W. Bull, 'The Newport Pagnell Academy' *Transactions of the Congregational Historical Society* 4 (1909–10) pp. 305–319.
[33] London DWL, New College MS 57 Village Itinerancy minutes 4 Aug 1806.

of intolerance: by strained relationships, declarations of non-eligibility and even formal exclusion. Societas Evangelica on more than one occasion refused financial help to local Baptist ministers.[34] The rules of Hoxton Academy in 1797 stipulated that no anti-paedobaptist applications could be considered.[35] In 1798 the London Itinerant Society informed several applicants for membership that 'pedobaptists and antipedobaptists [could] best serve the general interests of ... Jesus Christ by preaching and teaching among the societies of their own persuasion'.[36] Eighteen years later a minor scandal erupted within the Village Itinerancy when the society dismissed one of its preachers for having adopted anti-paedobaptist views.[37] In the majority of cases the bitterness stemmed from the paedobaptist side. Even though a genuine change of convictions had taken place the natural feeling of betrayal all too easily degenerated into allegations of secrecy and subversion.

At the same time practical help, approval and support was given on a considerable scale with little regard for denominational differences. The Independent academy at Hoxton benefited from a range of donors including Henry Thornton, William Wilberforce and Admiral Gambier.[38] Similarly, in 1815 the names of Wilberforce, Joseph Hardcastle and Lord Holland could be found gracing the subscription list of the building fund launched by the Baptist academy at Bristol.[39] For many years Congregational ministers from the south western counties took part in the devotions held at the annual meetings of the Baptist Western Association, and this clear sign of friendship and respect was repeated and reciprocated in other regional bodies.[40] It was not unknown for applicants to evangelical academies to give as referees the names of local ministers from other denominations. In 1808 the committee of the Bristol

[34] London DWL, New College MS 122/1 minutes 25 Jan 1799; MS 124/1 minutes 30 May 1806 & 28 Aug 1807.
[35] London DWL, New College MS 126/1 minutes 9 Jun 1797.
[36] London Congregational Library MS Ii 35 minutes 16 Mar 1798.
[37] London DWL, New College MS 56/1 minutes Oct 1816–May 1817.
[38] London DWL, New College MS 126/1 minutes 6 Apr 1787, 12 Apr 1799 & 18 Apr 1800.
[39] *Bristol Education Society Report for 1815* pp. 62, 53 & 54.
[40] *Baptist Western Association Circular Letters 1797–1830, passim; Buckinghamshire Association of Baptist Churches Circular Letters for 1822* p. 13 & *1828* p.13; *North Bucks Independent Association Reports for 1821 & 1822.*

Education Society, the body which supported Bristol Baptist Academy, admitted as a student John Vernon on the recommendation of his own pastor, Joseph Kinghorn of Norwich, and the Congregational minister at Yarmouth.[41] The close and harmonious working relationship which often existed between Dissenting bodies was epitomized by the adjacent academies at Idle and Bradford. On those occasions when William Vint found himself with insufficient students to service his weekly network of village preaching he employed men from the Baptist seminary at Bradford whose president, William Steadman, was always ready to oblige.[42]

A number of conclusions concerning the extent of undenominationalism are possible. As long as close practical identification was avoided a great deal of mutual respect could be shown. To judge by the contents of association letters and reports, which can always be misleading, the willingness to co-operate bore an inverse relationship to the degree of emphasis laid upon doctrine. Those societies which showed the greatest disregard for denominational differences concentrated upon the practicalities of evangelism. As a general rule local associations exhibited more harmonious relationships than those which functioned at the national level. It is also possible that regional factors played a part. The associations which operated in the south midland counties of Bedfordshire and Hertfordshire displayed a greater degree of common effort than their counterparts in Essex. Bedfordshire in particular had a long tradition of Dissenting harmony dating back to the time of Bunyan and manifesting itself in congregations which practised both forms of baptism. Jealousy and distrust were never confined to relationships between societies of differing denominational complexion. Similar tensions can be traced between bodies with the same ecclesiastical derivation.

At the root of the new idealism lay the fundamental conviction that the task entered upon was one which had the best interests of the nation at heart. In spite of Horsley's scaremongering evangelical associations without exception espoused the ideal of model citizenship. With the spread of evangelicalism overt sympathy for

---

[41] *Bristol Education Society Report for 1808* p. 11. The report erroneously ascribes the Christian name David to Kinghorn.
[42] *Idle Academy Reports for 1817* p. 6, *1818* p. 11, *1825* pp. 6–7 & *1829* p. 11.

political causes including the easing of religious and civil disabilities gave way to a markedly loyalist and apolitical stance. Hill's early denial of political intent received a powerful restatement in 1812 from the Northamptonshire Association:

> In explaining the nature, and stating the objects of our associ-ation, we desire it may be remembered, that they are not political. We are not, and never have been, a disloyal or revolutionary faction ... we have neither cherished nor incul-cated hostility against the civil and ecclesiastical polity of the nation ... and we take this opportunity of again declaring, that we are sincerely attached to our excellent constitution, and to the family on the throne, by whom we are protected in the enjoyment of our civil and religious liberty.[43]

The actions of Dissenting organizations gave no reason for ques-tioning any part of this statement. Societies concerned with village preaching for the most part took great care to ensure that the requirements for the registration of meeting-houses and the licens-ing of preachers were scrupulously observed. Every effort was taken to avoid any form of confrontation with those responsible for administering the law, and while the attitude adopted towards the Established Church was more complex, it invariably aimed at preventing rivalry. Deference to the parish clergyman was especially obvious where the incumbent or curate was of Evangelical persuasion,[44] but even where that was not the case most societies favoured a policy of holding village meetings at times which did not conflict with the services of the parish church.[45] Generally clerical hostility encountered a policy of non-resistance. Two excep-tions to this approach stand out, both involving participation in riot. In the first instance in 1798 though the case proceeded to trial the committee of the Deputies with typical caution refused to lend any assistance.[46] In the second case the clergyman at Ansty in Wiltshire was prosecuted successfully by the Protestant Society for the Protection of Religious Liberty.[47]

[43] *Northamptonshire Association Circular Letter 1812* pp. 3–4.
[44] London DWL, New College MS 124/1 minutes 27 Jan 1804.
[45] *Hoxton Academy Report for 1823* p. 5; *North Bucks Independent Association Report for 1822* p. 20.
[46] London Guildhall MS 3083 minutes 25 Jan 1799.
[47] *Baptist Magazine* 10 (1818) pp. 157–8.

On a more positive note several associations emphasized the importance of their work to the stability and prosperity of the English people. The Baptist Society and the Essex Baptist Association both treated the contemporary spate of village preaching as a necessary antidote to the rationalist principles seeping across the Channel, ideas subversive 'both of true religion, and civil government'. The imagery used in the apologetic passages depicted the members of societies as divinely appointed watchmen sounding the alarm to the people of God and going out as Christian soldiers to contend against the common foe of infidelity.[48] At the same time the apologists argued the constructive nature of the work, pointing to the change in moral standards which had taken place in many communities, since the inception of regular gospel preaching. Village evangelism had become the means, societies the agents, of a remarkable return to spiritual and social health.

St Mary's College,
University of St Andrews

---

[48] Baptist Society Plan p. 2; London Baptist Union, Essex Baptist Association minute book 1805–64, introductory notes.

FROM RANTERS TO CHAPEL BUILDERS: PRIMITIVE METHODISM IN THE SOUTH LINCOLNSHIRE FENLAND c.1820–1875

by R.W. AMBLER

ON 26 October 1832 Jonathan Gibbons of the parish of Lutton, some twelve miles east of Spalding, wrote to John Kaye, bishop of Lincoln, describing how 'A great proportion of the lower orders are now supporting a sect called ranters and attending their meetings as the only resource for religious instruction.' The reasons for this, he argued, lay with 'lax government and want of proper attention to services and duties' in the Church, but in addition to these problems the Church of England also had the difficult task of extending its ministrations into the scattered communities of the newly drained and cultivated south Lincolnshire fenland. In Lutton the people were left 'open to all the evils attendant upon unrestrained ignorance' and the voluntary religious bodies, including the Primitive Methodists or Ranters, were often quicker to respond to their needs than the Established Church.[1]

The area with which this paper will be concerned, the fenland of south Lincolnshire, stretches from the latitude of Boston in the north to the county boundaries of Cambridgeshire and Norfolk in the south and from the shores of the Wash in the east to the fen edge villages of Kesteven in the west, an area largely, but not entirely covered by the Holbeach, Spalding and part of the Boston civil registration districts. By the beginning of the nineteenth century the landscape of the area had been completely changed by drainage and enclosure. A way of life based largely on pastoral husbandry in the undrained lowlands was replaced by one in which arable farming increased in importance. The large number of common grazing rights of the undrained fens were exchanged for

[1] Lincolnshire Archives Office, Correspondence of Bishop Kaye 1827–53 Cor B 5/4/75/5.

freehold farms, so that the area developed a distinctive social structure with considerable division of land and numerous small farmers,
many of whom owned their holdings. New settlement patterns
developed as people left the old village centres to move on to the
newly-drained lands, accentuating a process of dispersal which had
begun with small scale attempts at drainage in the middle ages.
Some large farms were however also created at enclosure.[2]

The ancient parishes of the area were often very large and in its
southern part most were twelve or thirteen, and some sixteen,
miles long. Holbeach with 26,666 acres was one of the largest
parishes in England.[3] The Revd J.C. Lowe of Whaplode Drove,
writing in 1849 of his efforts to establish a place of worship in
the fenland settlement of Dowsdale, said that its 'considerable
population' who lived three miles from the nearest Anglican place
of worship were 'almost totally neglected' during nearly nine months of the year when, he said, the roads were 'almost impassable.'[4]
The problems he faced, after making allowance for what may have
been special pleading, were not peculiar to Dowsdale and in 1845
the Revd W. Wayet, patron and incumbent of Pinchbeck, described
his parish:

> nine miles in length, by four in breadth, and the church being
> nearly at one end of it, renders it a matter of great difficulty
> for the inhabitants of the distant parts to attend it, particularly
> as those inhabitants are generally speaking of the poorer class,
> who have no means of conveyance. The most populous district
> too lies at the distance of between two and three miles from

---

[2] For the development of the fens see David Grigg, *The Agricultural Revolution in South Lincolnshire* (Cambridge 1966) and H.C. Darby, *The Draining of the Fens* (Cambridge repr 1968) *passim*. For settlement patterns see also H.E. Hallam, *Settlement and Society: a study of the early agrarian history of south Lincolnshire* (Cambridge 1965) pp. 4–5, 40, 72; Dorothy M. Owen, *Church and Society in Medieval Lincolnshire* (Lincoln 1971) pp. 10–12; G. Joan Fuller, 'Development of Drainage, Agriculture and Settlement in the Fens of South-East Lincs. during the 19th Century', *East Midland Geographer* 1 (1957) pp. 6–7, 11–12. Joan Thirsk, *English Peasant Farming: the agrarian history of Lincolnshire from Tudor to recent times* (London 1957) pp. 220–50, 232–6 describes changes in fenland agriculture. For a map of the registration districts of the area see *Lincolnshire Returns of the Census of Religious Worship 1851* R.W. Ambler ed (LRS 1979) p. xxxvii.

[3] Hallam, *Settlement and Society* p. 3.

[4] LAO, Cor B5/4/3/13.

the church so that dissent has obtained a footing there, for which state of things we can hardly blame the people.[5]

In 1851 the amount of accommodation provided for public worship by the Church of England in the Holbeach, Spalding and Boston registration districts was, at 29.6, 32.2 and 34 per cent of the population respectively, the lowest in Lincolnshire.[6] The result was that in remote settlements voluntary religious bodies created, in the absence of any alternative provision, a religious establishment of their own. When attempts were being made to establish an Anglican presence in the newly established ecclesiastical district of Gedney Drove End in 1855 its first minister the Revd W.G. Patchell noted in his journal 'Methodism or nothing has been the order of things ... so that I rather like to meet with people calling themselves Wesleyans or Ranters – It is some slight proof that they have the fear of God before their eyes.'[7]

The Primitive Methodists had first arrived in south Lincolnshire in 1817 moving out from Nottinghamshire as the connexion spread eastwards from Cheshire and Staffordshire where it originated.[8] By 1820 there were travelling preachers, as the Primitive Methodist connexion's full time ministers were known, based at Boston and working in the fenland area.[9] Their work appears to have been relatively uncoordinated and they may well have been preceded by other revivalists who had little or no formal contact with the connexion. The diaries of Francis Birch indicate that he was not

---

[5] LAO, Cor B5/4/77/4.
[6] Parliamentary Papers 1852–53 LXXXIX (1690) Religious Worship (England and Wales) 1851, p. cclxxxix.
[7] Kenneth Healey, '"Methodism or Nothing ..." (in Gedney Marsh, 1856)', *Epworth Witness and Journal of the Lincolnshire Methodist History Society* 2 (1974) pp. 120–2.
[8] John Petty, *The History of the Primitive Methodist Connexion from its Origin to the Conference of 1860, the First Jubilee Year of the Connexion* rev by James Macpherson (London 1880) pp. 72–4.
[9] *Ibid* pp. 119, 149, 158; H.B. Kendall, *The Origin and History of the Primitive Methodist Church* 2 (London c 1905) pp. 558–9.

the first Primitive Methodist preacher to visit either Spalding or Holbeach when he preached in the towns in October 1820.[10]

The activities of these early Primitive Methodist preachers moved the stipendiary curate of an unidentified place near Spalding to write to *The Christian Remembrancer* early in 1821 to complain of 'the proceedings of the Ranters, and of other itinerants' in the neighbourhood who 'with good words and fair speeches, [were] deceiving the hearts of the simple'. This 'organized banditti of strolling Methodists, vociferating Ranters, and all that impious train of *et cæteras* [*sic*]' were said to openly denounce the clergy, coming into the writer's parish 'as the dusk of evening approaches, being designedly met by people from neighbouring parishes, parading our streets with turbulence and uproar.'[11]

The expansion of Primitive Methodism in the early 1820s was too rapid for the connexion's organisation to assimilate and a period of 'depression and crisis' followed between 1824 and 1828.[12] The situation was such that Hugh Bourne, one of the founding fathers of Primitive Methodism, had his confidence in the connexion's continued existence shaken. The reasons for this collapse were analysed by John Petty who wrote in the 1850s in his history of the connexion how the 'amazingly rapid' growth of Primitive Methodism had meant that societies which had been created had been 'composed of members whose experience in church affairs was small, and whose view of ecclesiastical discipline was necessarily limited and imperfect.'[13] Travelling preachers had been recruited rapidly and this had meant that

> sufficient numbers possessing the requisite qualifications could not be obtained, and too little care was exercised in the selection. Unsuitable persons were thus introduced into the regular ministry, who proved to be a burden, and in some instances,

[10] *Primitive Methodist Magazine* 2 Mar. 1821 pp. 58–60. For the activities of some of the revivalists who preceded Primitive Methodist preachers in Lincolnshire see George Herod, *Biographical Sketches of Some of those Preachers whose Labours Contributed to the Origination and Early Extension of the Primitive Methodist Connexion* (London n.d.) p. 479; George Shaw *The Life of John Oxtoby, ('Praying Johnny')* (Hull 1894) pp. 14–15, 21–26; Kendall, *Origin and History* 1 pp. 365–7.

[11] *Christian Remembrancer* 3, Mar. 1821 pp. 136–8.

[12] Kendall, *Origin and History* 1 p. 434.

[13] Petty, *History of the Primitive Methodist Connexion* pp. 250–1.

a curse rather than a blessing. The societies languished under their inefficient labours, and even once flourishing circuits became feeble.[14]

Petty did not describe his ideal minister, but the qualities of a man like Edward Vaughan, a travelling preacher on the Boston circuit who died in 1828, were apparently less appropriate to the new phase of more carefully planned and securely based expansion which began in 1829 than to the earlier period of the connexion's growth. It was said of Vaughan that although 'in the converting line the Lord put great honour upon him' he was a man 'of slender abilities in regard to management.'[15]

The new period of growth was based on a stronger institutional structure and a tighter organisation so that, for example, the 'healthy and flourishing condition' of the Wisbech circuit, which extended into south Lincolnshire at this date could be said in 1835 to be due to 'the Divine blessing accompanying the preaching and a regular adherence to the discipline of the connexion.'[16]

An important aspect of this more disciplined approach was the building of chapels. As well as providing tangible evidence to the wider world of the connexion's progress and development buildings gave it greater status and a more secure place in the local community. The outward characteristics of a chapel were seen as reflecting the attributes of the community who worshipped in it. The Donington Primitive Methodists became, in the eyes of outsiders, as solidly prosperous in spiritual terms as the 'very commodious building greatly admired by the public for strength and neatness' which was opened in 1834 and which was said to reflect great credit upon them.[17] Chapel building 'for the accommodation of those persons who feel disposed to attend the ministry of the Primitive Methodists' was adopted as an official policy of the Wisbech circuit in 1836.[18]

[14] *Ibid* p. 251.
[15] *Prim Meth Mag* 6 new series Nov. 1836 p. 438.
[16] *Ibid* 5 new series June 1835 p. 233.
[17] *Ibid* Oct. 1835 p. 392.
[18] *Ibid* 6 new series Feb. 1836 pp. 62–3.

When Donington chapel was opened it was seen as a source of spiritual strength for the village's Primitive Methodists: 'The presence of the Lord was felt in a very peculiar manner; yea, the divine glory overshadowed us, and the shout of triumph ascended to the skies.'[19] Visits by Primitive Methodist preachers in 1833 to Holbeach Bank 'a small benighted hamlet situate about two miles from Holbeach town' brought success and the future prosperity of Primitive Methodism in the place was seen as directly related to the need for a chapel.

> In 1835 we found that the cause had suffered, and was likely to suffer for want of a convenient place to rest the ark of the Lord. The cry of the people was, 'Give us room that we may dwell.' We decided upon building a chapel. The Lord made our way plain before us; the building was completed.[20]

A local newspaper report emphasised the way in which the acquisition of a building could mark the turning point between the Ranter past and an increasingly institutionalized future when a correspondent referred to what he thought was the assumed name of Primitive Methodist, which was probably used on Donington chapel in 1834, and the more general usage of Ranter.[21] However, not all Ranter patterns of behaviour disappeared once a Primitive Methodist congregation had a purpose-built place of worship and in August 1842, a few months before Donington Primitive Methodists were to further improve their chapel by adding a gallery to it, they were still capable of shocking an Anglican sympathiser with their 'prayers, singing, shouting, and preaching' at an open air meeting in the village.[22]

Signs of divine favour often marked chapel openings, thus sanctioning the step the local community had taken. Holbeach Bank 'was crowded to excess. A gracious influence rested upon the congregations, and the collections exceeded our most sanguine expectations.'[23] Gosberton Clough chapel opening was marked as being 'a powerful time' at which, 'Many tears were shed ... and

---

[19] *Ibid* 5 new series Oct. 1835 p. 392.
[20] *Ibid* 6 new series Sept. 1836 pp. 346–7.
[21] *Lincoln, Rutland and Stamford Mercury* 5 June 1835.
[22] *Ibid* 19 August 1842, 16 June 1843.
[23] *Prim Meth Mag* 6 new series Sept. 1836 p. 347.

the glory of God filled the place. Halleluia! Halleluia! for the Lord God Omnipotent reigneth.'[24] Chapel openings marked by conversions were taken as a sign that 'the spirit of God accompanied the word of his grace'.[25]

The number of small freeholds in the fens meant that voluntary religious bodies could acquire land on which to build chapels relatively easily. In 1851 the Primitive Methodists had 26 congregations in the Boston, Holbeach and Spalding registration districts. The Church of England had 55, the Wesleyan Methodists 60 and the Baptists 25. Twenty-two of the Primitive Methodist congregations met in separate buildings set aside for religious worship and the connexion's success in establishing itself in the outlying fenland communities can be seen by the fact that 12 of these were away from the centres of the main villages of the area.[26]

Further evidence on which to base an assessment of the place of Primitive Methodism in the south Lincolnshire fenlands comes from an analysis of the occupations of trustees in chapel title deeds and the occupations of parents given in baptism registers. Twelve deeds for 8 chapels in the area survive for the period 1826 to 1874. These have details of the occupations of 113 trustees.[27] There are registers of baptisms for the Boston and Spalding circuits for various dates from 1823 although alterations to circuit boundaries mean that they do not give a uniform coverage of the area over the whole period. However, after the baptisms of more than one child belonging to the same parents have been eliminated the registers contain information to 1874 on 1087 children brought

[24] *Ibid* 5 new series Oct 1835 p. 393.
[25] *Ibid* 7 new series Dec 1837 p. 473.
[26] Parl Papers, Religious Worship 1851, p. 82; *Lincolnshire Returns of Census of Religious Worship* pp. 18–54. The official report gives 27 Primitive Methodist congregations, but two returns were made for the chapel at Moulton Seas End and these were both included in the final total.
[27] Boston Centenary Methodist Church Circuit Chapel Deeds Packet Nos 3, 31 and 33: Fosdyke (1826 and 1874); Hubberts Bridge (1871). Spalding Methodist Church Circuit Chapel Deeds: Moulton Seas End (1835 and 1854); Little London (1842 and 1866); Pinchbeck West (1842 and 1873); Weston Hills (1853); Bicker (1854); Spalding (1870).

for baptism to Primitive Methodist ministers. No information on parents' occupations is given in 62 cases.[28]

There was a marked contrast between the social composition of the trustees and the parents who brought children for baptism. Whereas 44 (38.9 per cent) of the trustees were farmers and 21 (18.6 per cent) labourers, 579 (53.3 per cent) of the baptisms were of labourers' children compared with 114 (10.5 per cent) of farmers'. The proportion of craftsmen and tradesmen who acted as trustees and those who had children baptized was much closer, whereas this group comprised one quarter of the trustees 206, exactly one-fifth, had children baptized. Compared with the population of the area as a whole farmers were over-represented on chapel trusts while labourers were under-represented. There was probably a slightly higher proportion of trades and craftsmen acting as trustees than in the whole population. However, the proportion of farmers having their children baptized by the Primitive Methodists was less than in the population as a whole, but the number of labourers was significantly higher, while there were probably proportionately less tradesmen and craftsmen.[29]

An analysis of the places from which the children who were baptized came provides a further indication of the connexion's place in the local communities of the fenland. In the Spalding circuit they came from 95 places, a considerable proportion of which were out in the fens, the largest number of baptisms from any one place being 49 from Sutterton Fen. Other important centres were Little London with 36 and Gedney Drove End with 34. Spalding, which had 41 baptisms, and Donington with 37 are exceptional in being town or village centres from which there were a large number of baptisms. Otherwise the villages of the area such as Gosberton or Pinchbeck had very few baptisms while outlying Gosberton Fen had 21, Gosberton Clough 22, Pinchbeck Fen 21 and Pinchbeck West 25.

[28] PRO, Non-Parochial Registers RG4/1930 Boston Primitive Methodist Baptismal Register 1823–37; LAO, Meth B/Boston Circuit/33/1 Register of Baptisms 1844–89; Spalding Gentlemens' Society, Methodist Archives Primitive Methodist Church Baptismal Register for Spalding, Little London and other chapels 9 May 1844–26 June 1881; Baptismal Register Donington Circuit 24 Dec. 1843–10 Dec. 1893.

[29] Parl Papers 1852–53 LXXXVIII part II (1691–II) Population, Ages, Civil Condition, Occupations, &c. Tables II ... pp. 576, 578.

The relative success of the Primitives among the workers of the fenlands, measured in terms of baptisms, may only be a tentative indication of the strength of the commitment to the connexion of groups of people whose allegiance might otherwise have been slight. In so far as the Primitives provided what was regarded as a necessary rite of passage by performing baptisms in the outlying areas of the fens they may have been regarded as an alternative voluntary religious establishment. The connexion's attitude to baptism was not at this period well-defined and when its first service book was drawn up in 1861 the form for the administration of baptism was for voluntary and not obligatory use, nor is there any evidence that the Primitives sought to confine baptism only to the children of fully committed members.[30]

On the other hand, even in those areas where it was most difficult, the pull of the Church of England for parents seeking baptism for their children still seems to have been strong. The Revd J. Tunstall Smith of Whaplode said in 1845 that he frequently performed private baptisms on a weekday in the parsonage to accommodate parents who had brought their children, 'generally on or about the third day' after birth, from remote parts of the parish.[31] The attitude of a labourer from Weston who was, according to the local clergyman writing in 1846, 'captivated by the mode of worship among the Ranters', is a further indication of the attraction the Church of England could still exert. He

> had two or three children baptized by the superintendent of that sect, in his neighbourhood. Now, however, without any change in his general religious views, he wishes, as he says, to have these children christened ... Thus he wishes to fulfil *all* righteousness, taking the conventicle as his guide, as far as it goes and superadding, from the church, what he *fancies*, without understanding its nature.[32]

The fact that proportionately fewer farmers had their children baptized by the Primitives than acted as trustees may suggest that among the farmers of the area as a whole the Church of England

---

[30] Horton Davies, *Worship and Theology in England IV: from Newman to Martineau 1850–1900* (London 1962) pp. 141, 143.
[31] LAO, Cor B5/4/54/1.
[32] LAO, Cor B5/4/87/2.

had a relatively stronger hold over them than the labourers. Since Primitive Methodist chapel trustees were among the people signing the petition for a church to be built at Gedney Drove End in 1855 this may indicate that chapel trustees, among whom farmers were prominent, might have taken on this role in order to support voluntary religious provision where there would otherwise have been nothing.[33] It is also important not to over emphasize the distinction between farmers and labourers in the fens. The 'very numerous' small freeholders of the area were described in 1867 as 'a class in many cases very little raised above the hired labourer, and more hardly worked and less well fed and housed.'[34]

The building and maintenance of a chapel as well as support of the work of the Primitive Methodist connexion placed heavy burdens on the fenland communities. They were largely dependent on their own efforts, although middle and even upper class patronage could be exploited occasionally, particularly to support a building project. At Frieston Shore, a bathing resort near Boston, the ground for the chapel which was opened there in 1838 was given by 'a gentleman bather', a member of the Church of England, who was also a contributor to the building fund and helped to beg contributions for it. Despite his generosity and efforts £50 of the total cost of the chapel of £70 remained to be paid off by the thirteen members of the local society.[35]

The usual method of meeting any deficit in chapel building costs was to borrow money on a mortgage using the chapel and land on which it stood as security. In 1842 the land purchased to build a chapel at Pinchbeck Northgate, together with the two houses which stood on it was mortgaged for £150. Similarly, at Bicker in 1854 land with a cottage and buildings was mortgaged, with the chapel that was to be built on it, for £100. The trustees of the chapel at Moulton Seas End, which had been opened in 1835, borrowed £100 in 1854, probably to replace or add to the older building. The loan had still not been repaid in 1870. Similarly, the £200 needed to meet the cost of what seems to have been a rebuilding

[33] Healey, "'Methodism or Nothing ...'" pp. 120–1.
[34] Parl Papers 1867–68 XVII (4068) Agriculture (Employment of Women and Children). First Report of the Commissioners on the Employment of Children, Young Persons and Women in Agriculture, with Appendix, part I, p. 74.
[35] *Prim Meth Mag* 9 new series Dec 1839 p. 459.

of Little London chapel was raised by a mortgage with the new building as security.[36] There do not seem in either of these cases to have been debts carried over from earlier buildings, but in other places the burden was made worse by replacing a chapel before the debt on the older building had been extinguished. This was the case at Fosdyke where a £25 debt from the old chapel building was carried over to make a total mortgage of £90 on the new building when it was opened in 1861.[37]

Chapel debts in the Donington circuit in June 1868 included £220 at Donington, £175 at Sutterton Fen, £110 at Quadring, £117 at Bicker, £30 at Wigtoft Bank and £290 at Gosberton Clough. There was no apparent relationship between the size of the debt and the strength of the local Primitive Methodist society. The 1853 report of the connexion's General Chapel Fund, itself a body with limited resources, noted that 'suitable chapels, on good sites, and in workable circumstances, are among the most effective secondary agencies for promoting the welfare of old societies and congregations, and for giving permanency and extension to new ones' but the need to reach these objectives might lead smaller and poorer societies to incur greater debts in proportion to their size than larger bodies.[38]

Local Primitive Methodist societies in the south Lincolnshire fenland also had difficulty in meeting their financial obligations to the connexion to the extent that their preoccupation with this aspect of their lives meant that spiritual needs were often subordinated to financial and administrative imperatives. Revivals were planned and promoted by committee, often with the object of improving the local organisation's viability rather than saving souls for their own sakes. The Donington circuit regularly failed to raise enough money to finance its activities between 1858 and 1875, and from 1860 onwards it usually had a deficit. In the 1850s these deficits were made up by borrowing money while an economy measure which might also be adopted was not to pay the travelling preachers'

---

[36] Spalding Methodist Church, Circuit Chapel Deeds: Pinchbeck West, Moulton Seas End, Bicker, Little London.
[37] LAO, Meth B/Boston Circuit /55/1 Correspondence File 1861–94.
[38] Quoted in Kendall, *Origin and History* 2 p. 455 and p. 458 for the General Chapel Fund.

salaries in full.[39] In December 1860 a Mrs. Sanderson was asked to come 'to assist in holding a few revival services' on the Spalding and Holbeach branch of Donington circuit. If she accepted she was to be asked to preach at Holbeach on 16 December 'and make collections for lighting and cleaning.'[40] When in June 1872 the members of Spalding and Holbeach mission were asked to 'pray for an increase of piety' it was with the aim of bringing 'such an increase of members and money that the station may become self-supporting.'[41]

The need to increase income also meant that social activities which attracted support because of their entertainment value became an important element in chapel life. Some of these had no obvious religious content beyond their endorsement through speeches and recitations of morally uplifting sentiments and there was a danger that chapel events would lose any of their distinctive qualities and be completely absorbed into the social calendar of the local community. In 1863 a special committee of Donington circuit discussed the prices of teas at chapel and Sunday school events. It was noted that:

> Several persons who are decidedly not the friends of either the chapel or school, and ought not to be encouraged, have declined to buy tickets for the chapel tea, making it a boast that they could have a 'Blow out' at the school for less money. We are expecting to lose the custom of these gormondizers but we shall try to do without them.[42]

Boston circuit quarterly meeting found it necessary in 1865 to pass a resolution disapproving of 'the system of drinking ale and certain games practised' during the time of Sunday school anniversary services. They also asked that the 'bands of music' should cease to play then. In 1873 the same body passed a resolution regretting 'that proceedings of a questionable character are indulged in at our various school feasts, and hopes that steps will be taken by the

[39] SGS, Donington Circuit Account Book 1853–78.
[40] SGS, Donington Circuit Spalding and Holbeach Quarterly Meeting Minute Book 1860–62 6 Dec. 1860.
[41] SGS, Spalding and Holbeach Mission Quarterly Meeting Minute Book 1862–83 3 June 1872.
[42] SGS, Donington Quarterly Meeting Minute Book 1856–73 23 June 1863.

various school authorities to prevent any irregularities by clearing the fields not later than 7.30 and holding a special religious service.'[43]

The rhetoric of the Ranter past could still have a strong hold in a period of organized revivalism and preoccupation with balance sheets. This can be seen in an account of a revival which began in the Holbeach area in 1851. It had

> been going on, more or less, in various parts of this branch since last July. Several courses of special services have been held which, under the blessing of Jehovah have been very effective, and showers of saving grace have been vouchsafed. The consciences of the guilty have been grappled with; a free, full and great salvation has been urged; and though we have had some dreadful conflicts with the powers of darkness, the hosts of Israel have been more than victorious. Satan's right to the souls of those whom he has long held as his slaves, has been courageously disputed by the servants of the living God; and the grand adversary has, in many cases, been defeated. Jesus has come to our help; the prey has been taken from the mighty; and upwards of 60 souls have professed to obtain the blessing of sin forgiven, and united into the Church of Christ.[44]

However, the act of moving Ranterism on to a more secure institutional base changed its nature, bringing responsibilities and burdens which the fenland Primitive Methodist communities of south Lincolnshire, with their comparatively lowly social base, could only meet with difficulty. As a voluntary organisation the Primitive Methodists had responded quickly to the religious needs of the settlements of the newly drained fens, but their comparative success in these areas ultimately brought problems for the connexion's local societies.

University of Hull

[43] LAO, Meth B/Boston Circuit /41/1 Quarterly Meeting Minutes 1855–67 12 June 1865; 41/3/ Quarterly Meeting Minutes 1869–83 10 Mar. 1873.
[44] *Prim Meth Mag* 10 third series April 1852 p. 239.

THE EVANGELICAL ALLIANCE IN THE 1840s: AN ATTEMPT TO INSTITUTIONALISE CHRISTIAN UNITY

by JOHN WOLFFE

IN 1844 Baptist Wriothesley Noel, minister of the Anglican proprietary chapel of St. John's Bedford Row since 1827, published a book of verse, with a piece on 'Schism' containing the following stanzas:

> For man-made discipline let bigots fight
> Canons and rules old fathers have approved;
> By us may those whose faith and life are right,
> Be owned as brothers and as brothers loved.

> All true believers are the ransomed church,
> Children of God by Jesus owned and loved;
> And in the day when God the heart shall search
> Will they who part them be schismatics proved.[1]

In the 1820s Noel had been an enthusiastic sympathiser with the pan-evangelicalism then prevalent in London and had remained loyal to these views during the period of stormier relations between Church and Dissent in the 1830s.[2] In the slightly calmer waters of the 1840s Noel's sentiments again came to represent the views of a small number of Anglican Evangelicals and a rather larger proportion of moderate Dissenters whose efforts to promote Christian unity were to culminate in the formation of the Evangelical Alliance in 1846.

---

[1] B.W. Noel, *Protestant Thoughts in Rhyme* (London 1844) p. 73. On Noel see *DNB*; D.W. Bebbington, 'The Life of Baptist Noel: Its Setting and Significance, *The Baptist Quarterly* 24 (1972) pp. 389–411.
[2] *Ibid.* pp. 391–2; B.W. Noel, *The Unity of the Church, Another Tract for the Times, Addressed particularly to Members of the Establishment* (London 1837).

The only modern account of the Evangelical Alliance[3] is rather slight in character and general accounts of the religious history of the period have tended to dismiss it somewhat misleadingly as a primarily defensive and anti-Catholic appendage to the anti-Maynooth agitation of 1845.[4] The neglect of the Alliance by scholars is scarcely justified as it provides important insights into interdenominational relationships and, in the context of this volume, provides a revealing case study of the problems faced by a voluntary religious organisation as it sought to give institutional focus to the abstract ideal of Christian unity. This paper will first consider the events leading up to the formation of the Evangelical Alliance, which have hitherto been imperfectly understood, and will then turn to consider the motives prompting the supporters of the organisation. Finally the problems and limitations evident from an early stage will be considered.

In the 1830s only a few brave spirits were prepared to make efforts for Christian union. Baptist Noel's call to his fellow Anglicans to show toleration in minor matters 'not inconsistent with the love of the Gospel' was paralleled on the Dissenting side by George Radford, a Worcester Independent minister, who, in 1834, wrote to John Blackburn, the editor of *The Congregational Magazine*, suggesting the holding of a general convention of all the orthodox protestant Churches of Great Britain, Europe and America.[5] Nothing seems to have come of this proposal and in general eirenical gestures were restricted to the platforms of a few interdenominational religious associations, notably the London City Mission, founded in 1835, and the Bible Society.[6] However,

---

[3] J.B.A. Kessler, *A Study of the Evangelical Alliance in Great Britain* (Goes, Netherlands 1968). The problem of slavery in relation to the Alliance is considered by J.F. MacLear, 'The Evangelical Alliance and the Anti-slavery Crusade', *The Huntington Library Quarterly* 42 (1978–9) pp. 141–164.

[4] *cf.* E.R. Norman, *Anti-Catholicism in Victorian England* (London 1968) pp. 50–1; G.I.T. Machin, *Politics and the Churches in Great Britain, 1832–1868* (Oxford 1977) p. 176; R.H. Martin, *Evangelicals United: Ecumenical Stirrings in Pre-Victorian Britain* (Metuchen, New Jersey and London 1983) pp. 200–1.

[5] Noel, *The Unity of the Church* p. 9; London, Dr. Williams's Library Blackburn MSS L52/2/101, Radford to Blackburn, 16 April 1834.

[6] On the London City Mission see D.M. Lewis, 'The Evangelical Mission to the British Working Class: A Study of Anglican Support for a Pan-evangelical Approach to Evangelism, with Special Reference to London, 1828–1860' (unpublished Oxford D.Phil. thesis 1981) pp. 81–124.

the Baptist Francis Cox complained, after fulsome speeches professing brotherly love ' ... they separate, it is to be feared, generally with undiminished prejudices, jealousies and dislikes, with scarcely a shake of the hand, never to meet again till another anniversary ...'[7] The prominent Evangelical Anglican, Edward Bickersteth, had hopes that the Bible Society might serve as a focus for Christian union but he was pessimistic regarding its future prospects.[8]

In May 1842 John Angell James, since 1806 minister of Carr's Lane Independent Chapel in Birmingham, in an address to the Congregational Union, expressed his conviction that there was a hidden yearning for extensive union and that the Congregational Union was the body best placed to take steps to make this a reality, thus raising up a defence against 'Infidelity, Popery, Puseyism, and Plymouth Brethrenism'.[9] In this speech James suggested that union would encompass only Voluntaries but in a letter to *The Congregational Magazine* in July he envisaged that the bonds of fellowship might tentatively be further extended:

> The following may be expected:- the whole body of Congregationalists in England, Scotland, Wales and Ireland, the Baptists, Lady Huntingdon's Connexion, the Calvinistic Methodists, the Moravians, perhaps the Synod of Ulster; and should a new secession take place from the Church of Scotland, these also would probably join. Gladly should I see the Wesleyan body in such a union, and the pious clergy of the Churches of England and Scotland.[10]

One of James's major concerns was to refute the assertion of the Brethren that other Protestant groups were devoid of brotherly feeling but this particular motive did not persist.[11] In the autumn

---

[7] F.A. Cox, *On Christian Union: being a Brief Inquiry into the Causes of Disunion among Christians and the Reasons of Failure in the Efforts at Union hitherto made* (London 1845) p. 7.

[8] T.R. Birks, *Memoir of the Rev. Edward Bickersteth* (2 vols London 1850) 2 p. 236.

[9] R.W. Dale, *The Life and Letters of John Angell James: including an Unfinished Autobiography* (2 ed London 1861) pp. 397–8.

[10] *Ibid.* pp. 399–402; *The Congregational Magazine* new series 6 (1842) pp. 458–62.

[11] Dale p. 399; *cf.* Kessler p. 17.

James was able to report to the Congregational Union that individual members of various Churches had expressed interest, but it was clear that his own denomination was wary of taking hasty action.[12] Nevertheless on 2 January 1843 a meeting for Christian Union was held in London, at which the Baptists, Congregationalists, Moravians, Presbyterians and Wesleyans were represented.[13] After a second meeting in February, a committee was set up which issued an invitation to a gathering at Exeter Hall in June, which attracted so much interest that two overflow meetings had to be held. A few Anglicans, including Baptist Noel, now became involved but the movement was overwhelmingly dominated by Dissent.[14] Against the background of conflict over the educational clauses of Graham's Factory Bill most of the Anglicans who had been approached, including Edward Bickersteth, felt unable to go beyond general expressions of interest and sympathy.[15]

An important stimulus was provided in 1843 by the Scottish Disruption. The Free Church leaders were anxious to gain support in England and had been careful to prepare the ground before their formal act of secession. Robert Smith Candlish, the most prominent among the younger generation of Free Churchmen, had attended the London meeting in February and expressed, according to Jabez Bunting, ' ... a strong desire for a close and affectionate union of all Protestant Christians ...'[16] Some English Nonconformists responded warmly. Sir Culling Eardley Smith, a prominent Congregationalist layman, wrote to Chalmers hailing the Disruption as a potential catalyst for general Christian union.[17] The Wesleyans,

---

[12] Dale pp. 404–7; *The Congregational Magazine* new series 6 (1842) pp. 905–11.

[13] *Ibid.* 7 (1843) pp. 140–52.

[14] *Ibid.* pp. 376–8, 542–4.

[15] Cox pp. 11–14; Birks 2 pp. 229–31.

[16] *The Congregational Magazine* 7 (1843) p. 230; A.J. Hayes and D.A. Gowland eds *Scottish Methodism in the Early Victorian Period, The Scottish Correspondence of the Rev. Jabez Bunting* (Edinburgh 1981) pp. 88–9, Bunting to Chalmers, 5 April 1843. Hayes and Gowland date this letter to 1840 but, from internal evidence, it quite clearly belongs to 1843. I have been unable to trace the original: Hayes and Gowland state that it is in the Thomas Chalmers Collection at New College, Edinburgh, but, despite considerable efforts, the Library staff there have been unable to find it.

[17] New College, Edinburgh, Thomas Chalmers Collection, CHA.4.311.23–4, Smith to Chalmers, 9 May 1843.

sandwiched between the Church of England and Voluntaryist Dissent, were especially sympathetic to the desire of the Scottish seceders for a purified but still national church. Thus in April 1843 Bunting urged Thomas Chalmers to attend the Exeter Hall meeting in June in order ' ... to declare in the metropolis of Britain the Catholicity of the Scotch Free Church.'[18] In the event Chalmers was unable to attend, but he took a prominent part in a meeting held in Edinburgh in July 1843 to commemorate the bicentenary of the Westminster Confession.[19] This had been arranged with a view to furthering friendly relations with other churches, but in the wake of the Disruption it inevitably assumed the character of a demonstration in support of the Free Church. James Massie, the Manchester Independent minister who was later to serve as chronicler of the Evangelical Alliance, gave testimony to the denominational character of the meeting while acknowledging the warm reception he had received himself. In his speech Massie expressed a desire for ' ... a bold and resistless confederacy ... against popery, prelacy and *all* Erastianism'.[20] Defenders of the Established Churches were even less likely to be reassured by a resolution of the Relief Synod in May 1843 which, after expressing support in general terms for Christian union, went on to interpret the attack on patronage in the Church of Scotland as a hopeful sign of a developing congruence among evangelicals, and derided the recent 'arrogant assumptions' of the Church of England clergy 'to be the exclusive teachers of the whole community', while anticipating that such 'ecclesiastical usurpation' would serve to promote unity among those opposed to it.[21]

Inspired by the Edinburgh gathering, John Henderson, a lay member of the United Secession Church, sponsored the writing of a collection of essays on Christian union. The contributors were all Scottish Free Church and Dissenting Presbyterians, with the exception of James, the only Englishman to participate, and the

---

[18] Hayes and Gowland pp. 14–17, 88–9, Bunting to Chalmers, 5 April 1843.

[19] W. Hanna, *Memoirs of the Life and Writings of Thomas Chalmers, D.D.* (4 vols Edinburgh 1849–52) 4 pp. 378–9.

[20] J.W. Massie, *The Evangelical Alliance: its Origins and Development containing Personal Notices of its Distinguished Friends in Europe and America* (London 1847) pp. 91–8; *The Congregational Magazine* new series 7 (1843) pp. 74–6.

[21] *Ibid.* 7 (1843) pp. 617–9.

Glasgow Congregationalist, Ralph Wardlaw.[22] Coincidentally the volume appeared in 1845 when the evangelical world, both Anglican and Dissenting, was joining in opposition to Peel's Bill to provide for the perpetual endowment from public funds of the Irish Roman Catholic seminary at Maynooth. The great inter-denominational Anti-Maynooth Conference, held from 30 April to 3 May 1845, gave an important boost to the movement for unity and it was especially significant in giving rise to greater Anglican involvement and in strengthening an anti-Roman Catholic stance. Nevertheless, the significance of Maynooth appeared greater from an English and Anglican perspective than from a Scottish and Dissenting one and, in his account of the formation of the Alliance, David King, the minister of Greyfriars Secession Church in Glasgow, did not even mention it.[23]

The Anti-Maynooth Committee was called upon to arrange for the setting up of a Protestant confederation, but declined to do so on the grounds that an initiative taken by them would have an unduly political character.[24] The field was therefore clear for a group of Scots, led by Chalmers, Candlish and King and receiving financial backing from Henderson, acting independently of the Anti-Maynooth Committee, to issue on 5 August 1845 an invitation to a preliminary meeting in Liverpool in October in order to prepare the ground for a subsequent larger scale international meeting in London ' ... to associate and concentrate the strength of an enlightened Protestantism against the encroachments of Popery and Puseyism, and to promote the interests of scriptural Christianity.' They apparently acted at the instigation of James who felt that no English group could appear sufficiently independent to take an initiative.[25] However the Scots were themselves treading on dangerously thin denominational ice as they did not include any Church of Scotland men among their number and thus could be readily regarded as a Free Church and Voluntaryist lobby. Sir Culling

---

[22] Dale pp. 408–11; Massie p. 383; *Essays on Christian Union* (London 1845).

[23] Dale pp. 408–11. The best account of the anti-Maynooth agitation, though unreliable in details, is given in Norman pp. 23–51.

[24] *The Congregational Magazine* new series 9 (1845) p. 767.

[25] Massie p. 109; Dale p. 412; Hanna, 4, p. 385; A.S. Thelwall, *Proceedings of the Anti-Maynooth Conference* (London 1845) pp. clxxxvi–clxxxvii; *Conference on Christian Union – Narrative of the Proceedings of the Meeting held in Liverpool, October 1845* (London 1845) p. 59.

Eardley Smith, now chairman of the Anti-Maynooth Committee, was worried by the allusion to 'Puseyism' in the invitation as he felt that it was not fair to expect Evangelical Anglicans to associate with Dissenters in an assault on an evil confined to their own communion.[26] Edward Bickersteth, although he was himself currently advocating Christian union in a series of letters to *The Record* newspaper, hesitated for a month before replying to the Scottish invitation during which time he consulted other Anglicans who in general proved too suspicious of the movement to commit themselves to it. He considered requiring as a precondition for cooperation with Dissenters the suspension of the Church and State controversy, but abandoned this idea as impracticable. Ultimately, in 'fear and trembling' he agreed to go to Liverpool.[27]

The support of an Anglican of Bickersteth's stature was a great gain for the Alliance, but of the 216 men who assembled at Liverpool on 1 October 1845 only fifteen were members of the Church of England, with four coming from the Church of Ireland. The Church of Scotland was represented only by a layman and a minister resident in Liverpool.[28] Speaking on behalf of the Scottish requisitionists King acknowledged that, 'Some may think that ... unless we could have acted with more catholicity ... we should have wholly declined the undertaking', but emphasised that the current proceedings were purely preliminary.[29] A.S. Thelwall, an active Anglican member of the Protestant Association and the Anti-Maynooth Committee, complained at the tardiness of any attempt to involve the Church of Scotland, but King and Candlish gave an explanation which appeared to satisfy the meeting, while Bickersteth later expressed his belief that they had been cleared of any intention to slight the Kirk. Nevertheless it was clear that the issue had threatened to disrupt the conference before it had properly started.[30] The difficulty was overcome in a spirit of forbearance

---

[26] *The Congregational Magazine* new series 9 (1845) pp. 769–72.

[27] Birks 2 pp. 303–8; C.E. Eardley, *A Brief Notice of the Life of the Rev. Edward Bickersteth* (London 1850) p. 13.

[28] *Conference on Christian Union held in Liverpool on Wednesday the 1st of October 1845 and Subsequent Days* (Liverpool 1845) pp. 6–13.

[29] *The Congregational Magazine* new series 9 (1845) pp. 775–6.

[30] *Narrative of the Proceedings of the Meetings held in Liverpool* pp. 8, 34, 37. The printed record is, probably deliberately, vague regarding the details of this incident. Press reporters had been excluded from the meeting.

and readiness to differ in non-essentials which surprised and grati-
fied the participants. The three days of the Liverpool conference
thus ended in an atmosphere of euphoria, and further steps to
develop the movement, leading up to an international meeting in
August 1846, quickly followed.[31]

T.R. Birks, Edward Bickersteth's son-in-law and biographer,
saw the Evangelical Alliance as the product of two main causes,
'the growing conviction, in the minds of sincere Christians, belonging to different bodies, that their real union of heart and judgement
was far greater than the outward appearance' and 'the progress of
Popery'.[32] Certainly considerable reference was made to the second
of these factors. In 1828 Baptist Noel had devoted his sermon in
a course of lectures against Roman Catholicism to arguing that
Protestants were in agreement in fundamental doctrines.[33] Massie
similarly related the essential unity of the sixteenth-century
Reformers to their protest against Rome and suggested that their
continuing divisions were due to the traces of 'Romanism' which
continued to leaven the Reformed Churches.[34] Edward Bickersteth
emphasised the call for united action against 'that great apostasy',
while Thomas Chalmers felt that the organisation should be first
a 'great anti-Popish Association' and suggested that it would be
better to name it the 'Protestant' rather than the 'Evangelical'
Alliance.[35] However, James Hamilton, Free Church minister of
the Scotch Church at Regent Square, appeared to strike a chord in
the Liverpool conference when he said that he should regret '... that
this were, even chiefly or principally, an Anti-papal movement, or
even an Anti-infidel movement, or that it took any mere *anti*
form.'[36] Subsequently the Alliance adopted a stance towards Rome
which was noticeably milder than that of other contemporary anti-
Catholic societies and was only willing to commit itself collectively

---

[31] Birks 2 pp. 311–2; Dale pp. 413–5; Massie pp. 169, 198–210.
[32] Birks 2 p. 303.
[33] B.W. Noel, *On Protestant Unity in Fundamental Doctrines* (London 1828).
[34] Massie pp. 10–17.
[35] Birks 2 p. 308; Hanna 4 pp. 386–7; T. Chalmers, *On the Evangelical Alliance; its Design, its Difficulties, its Proceedings and its Prospects: with Practical Suggestions* (Edinburgh 1846).
[36] *Narrative of the Proceedings of the Meetings held in Liverpool* p. 16; William Arnot, *Life of James Hamilton, D.D.* (London 1870) pp. 188, 203, 231; Massie p. 149.

to the limited measure of collecting relevant information. This failure to take vigorous action meant that those concerned to promote an inter-denominational anti-Catholic campaign formed a new society, the Protestant Alliance, in 1851.[37]

Thus, in considering the motivation for the formation of the Alliance, equal weight has to be given to the first factor adduced by Birks, the positive desire for unity.[38] Evangelicals of all denominations, sharing a high view of the inspiration of Scripture, felt that they had to take seriously the command and prayer of Christ that his followers should be one, as being as much an obligation upon them as the texts which they felt buttressed their denominational peculiarities.[39] It was also pointed out that the Early Church had not been particularly doctrinally scrupulous and had enjoined forbearance on its members.[40] Millenial expectation also played a part: Massie saw the Alliance as potentially ushering in the restoration of Zion, while Bickersteth's support for it in the face of the lack of enthusiasm of his fellow Anglicans is largely attributable to his conviction that it was a fulfilment of prophecy.[41] Linked with this was excitement at the contemporary wave of revivals associated with itinerant American evangelists in Britain, which also served as a spur to the internationalist aspirations of the Alliance.[42] The experience of the early meetings fortified this yearning for unity, as warm personal relationships developed and shared acts of worship and prayer proved emotionally and spiritually satisfying.[43]

---

[37] J.R. Wolffe, 'Protestant Societies and Anti-Catholic Agitation in Great Britain, 1829–1860' (unpublished Oxford D.Phil. thesis 1984) pp. 279–81, 303–7.

[38] This is against Martin who contrasts (pp. 200–1) the Evangelical Alliance unfavourably with early nineteenth century pan-evangelicalism, as being predominantly negative and anti-Catholic.

[39] Massie pp. 137–8, 205, 231–3 and *passim*; John 15. 9–17; 17.21.

[40] *Essays on Christian Union* pp. 38–48.

[41] Massie p. ii; Birks 2 p. 356. Lewis (p. 162) relates Anglican Evangelical differences over the Alliance to differing views of eschatology. This is an ingenious argument which sheds light on the respective positions of McNeile and Bickersteth, but should be regarded with some caution, if only in the light of Birks's statement (2 p. 480) that those Christians who concurred most with Bickersteth's views of prophecy disagreed with him over the Alliance.

[42] R. Carwardine, *Transatlantic Revivalism: Popular Evangelicalism in Britain and America 1790–1865* (Westport 1978) pp. 71–83, 94–100, 102 seq.

[43] Massie pp. 201–5; Birks 2 pp. 233–4, 327–50.

The task facing the Alliance in the autumn and winter of 1845 was to give institutional form to this strong but essentially intangible desire for unity. There was general agreement that this was a nettle which had to be grasped. Baptist Noel urged that the union should become a permanent one not just a 'holiday' or 'platform' affair,[44] while Alfred Barrett, a Wesleyan preacher on the Islington circuit, in a long letter to Jabez Bunting, an enthusiastic advocate of the Alliance, argued that annual conventions would not produce a sufficiently close union nor exhibit Christian union adequately to the world. Barrett felt that 'The generous excitement of susceptible minds in a great meeting leads to an expression of mutual charity and love which is not afterwards realized.' Both Barrett and Noel felt that some kind of religious or doctrinal test for membership was necessary. If it were possible for those who were not truly Christians to be admitted to the Alliance they would become a source of disunion within it and try to divert it to their own unsanctified purposes.[45] Barrett suggested that the basis for admission should be simply the possessing of a communicant status within one's own denomination while Chalmers felt that the only requirement should be acknowledgement of Scripture as the sole repository of truth.[46]

The Liverpool meeting shared James's feeling that a specific statement was required and proceeded to draw up a basis of fundamental doctrines associated with an agreement to differ in matters not covered therein.[47] This task was not accomplished without some disagreement, particularly in relation to the successful insistence of some members that an article be included upholding 'the divine institution of the Christian ministry'. Others opposed this as it would exclude Quakers and possibly Brethren who were now regarded with greater favour than in 1843.[48] Some were unhappy that no commitment to Sabbath observance was included although this was mentioned in an accompanying statement of the objects

---

[44] Massie p. 153.
[45] W.R. Ward ed *Early Victorian Methodism – The Correspondence of Jabez Bunting, 1830–1858* (Oxford 1976) pp. 333–4, Barrett to Bunting, nd (Oct. or Nov. 1845).
[46] *Ibid.* p. 335; Chalmers pp. 33, 36.
[47] Massie pp. 126, 173.
[48] *Narrative of the Proceedings of the Meetings held in Liverpool* pp. 34–5.

of the Alliance.[49] Outside the conference the basis was attacked by a Wesleyan who felt that it should contain a specific disavowal of antinomianism and, conversely, by a group of Free Churchmen who found it insufficiently Calvinist.[50] The Alliance attempted to meet such criticism by stating that the omission of certain tenets should not be held as implying that they were unimportant, but this served to make their position seem still more equivocal.[51] At the international conference in August 1846 the British and Americans found that they could not in practice agree to differ on the issue of communion with slaveholders, not covered in the basis, because the former felt their position would be disastrously compromised by any concession on this issue while the Americans were concerned to maintain a distinction between the system of slavery and those individuals trapped by it. Thus the various national movements were obliged to go their separate ways.[52]

The Establishment issue exposed the Alliance to attack on two fronts. Militant Voluntaryists would have nothing to do with an organisation which admitted Churchmen, thus, in the eyes of *The Eclectic Review*, degrading itself into a farce.[53] An anonymous Free Church Presbyterian felt that association on such terms would imply that nothing of real value had been at stake in the Disruption. The Alliance was a subject of lengthy debate at the Free Church Assembly in 1846. While the freedom of individual ministers to participate was upheld, the Church as a whole did not commit itself.[54] On the other hand the Alliance enjoyed the active support of such strong Voluntaryists as Cox and Wardlaw, which taken in conjunction with an unfortunate speech at Liverpool by Thomas

---

[49] *Ibid.* p. 35.

[50] Ward pp. 343–4, John Wesley Thomas to Bunting, 20 August 1846; James Gibson, *Speeches of the Rev. James Gibson, A.M. and Rev. Andrew King, A.M. in the Synod of Glasgow and Ayr with a Review of the Principles Maintained in the Speeches of the Rev. Dr. Candlish and others on Christian Union Delivered in Glasgow, on the 28th October 1845; also Remarks on the "Narrative" and "Address" of the Liverpool Conference* (Glasgow 1846) p. 13.

[51] Massie p. 304.

[52] MacLear pp. 156–60.

[53] *The Eclectic Review* 4 series 19 (1846) p. 500.

[54] *The Evangelical Alliance the Embodiment of the Spirit of Christendom* (Edinburgh 1847) pp. 35–43; *The Free Church of Scotland. A Report of the Proceeding in the General Assembly on Wednesday, May 27, 1846 on the Subject of Christian Union. Revised* (Edinburgh 1846).

McCrie maintaining that it had substantially the same objectives as the Solemn League and Covenant,[55] caused many Anglicans to view it as a Trojan horse. Opposition was headed by the fiery leaders of Lancashire Evangelicalism, Hugh McNeile and Hugh Stowell, together with *The Christian Observer* magazine.[56] Common antagonism to 'Popery' was an insufficiently cohesive force, especially as Voluntaryists united the attack on 'Puseyism' with that on Establishments while Anglicans were conscious of the tendency of Nonconformity to align politically with Catholicism.[57]

Even advocates of Christian union were not willing to abandon the assumption that they themselves possessed a monopoly of truth. *The Record* was willing to support the Alliance but did so with an analogy which was scarcely flattering to Nonconformists. To stand aloof from it because of the prevalence of political Dissent was like refusing to join '... an Institution for the amelioration or suppression of immorality, because immorality dreadfully abounded, and was even exhibited by some of those who talked of joining the Society.'[58] A Scottish Methodist similarly revealed denominational preoccupations in suggesting that support for the Alliance would give the Wesleyans increased power and influence and even an augmentation of numbers.[59]

A further problem was the difficulty of finding a clear role and means of procedure, beyond a vague general commitment to the advance of Christian unity. Meetings for worship and prayer were regarded with much enthusiasm but they were liable to give credence to the charge that the Alliance was assuming the character of a Church and thus promoting schism rather than healing it.[60] The undertaking of specific tasks such as the promotion of missions or Sabbath observance was liable to appear supererogatory as other organisations already existed for such purposes, while even the taking of preliminary steps could open up differences among the membership.[61] James was particularly critical of the Alliance's

[55] Massie p. 190.
[56] Wolffe p. 278.
[57] *Ibid.* pp. 146–51.
[58] *The Record* 18 Dec. 1845.
[59] Hayes and Gowland p. 119, George Scott to Bunting, 4 June 1846.
[60] *Eclectic Review* 4 series 19 (1846) pp. 493–502.
[61] *Evangelical Alliance, British Organization. Report of the Proceedings of the Conference of British Members held at Manchester, from November 4th to the 9th inclusive 1846* (London 1847) pp. 151–66.

failure to take practical action, feeling that it had 'too refined' a principle and observing that it was called a 'Do-nothing society'.[62] Inherent difficulties were compounded by misfortune. Chalmers's death in 1847 and Bickersteth's early in 1850 were losses that could be ill afforded. James lived on until 1859, but was too frail in the last years of his life to take an active part.[63] In 1848 Noel left the Church of England to become a Baptist, thus seeming to confirm the suspicions of Anglicans that the Alliance's supporters were unsound on the Establishment.[64] There were also tactical mistakes, particularly the premature courting of wide publicity, which caused judgements to be based on initial arrangements never intended to be other than provisional in character, while the printed word proved unable to convey convincingly the subjective spirit of brotherhood and unity evident at Liverpool.[65]

The wide-ranging vision evident in the early days of the Alliance could not but make the relatively modest level of its actual achievement appear to be failure. In 1848 the Council, unable to bring into operation the extensive network of local branches which had initially been envisaged, recorded that they could not 'reflect without deep regret on the comparatively contracted sphere over which the Alliance has extended its operations.'[66] The annual conference in Glasgow in 1849 attracted only a disappointingly small attendance while in the same year there was a serious financial crisis.[67] The 'Papal Aggression' of 1850 did something to improve the Alliance's fortunes, particularly in enabling it to retain a modicum of Anglican sympathy and in attracting to it the influential support of John Campbell, the Congregationalist editor of *The Christian*

---

[62] Dale p. 418.
[63] *Ibid.* pp. 520–1.
[64] Birks 2 pp. 406–7; Bebbington p. 396.
[65] Massie pp. 164–6; Dale p. 417.
[66] *Evangelical Alliance, British Organization. Abstract of the Proceedings of the Second Annual Conference, held in Bristol, June 1848 with the Annual Report presented to the Conference and Lists of Members and Contributors* (London 1848) p. 46.
[67] *Evangelical Alliance, British Organization. The Annual Report Presented to the Conference held in Glasgow, October 1849 with an Abstract of the Proceedings of the Conference* (London 1849) pp. 18–21; Hayes and Gowland p. 126, Farmer to Bunting, 15 Oct. 1849.

Witness.[68] However the net gain from the 'No Popery' outcry of 1850 and 1851 was small, because it led to the creaming off of anti-Catholic enthusiasm into the Protestant Alliance. In the year 1851–2 the Evangelical Alliance's income was £1,324 against £1,486 received by the Protestant Alliance.[69]

The Evangelical Alliance had its roots in the general striving for greater spiritual and ecclesiastical purity evident in early Victorian Britain which produced such diverse fruits as the Oxford Movement and the Scottish Disruption. The centrality of the Disruption for the religious history of England as well as Scotland is all too seldom appreciated and it was crucial for the development of the Evangelical Alliance which was remarkable for its endeavour to transcend the bounds of nationality as well as those of denomination. The linking of the Alliance with protest against Erastianism meant that its appeal to members of the Establishment was limited, although the obstacle was one which could be negotiated by those who acknowledged the existence of a deeper spiritual idealism behind the movement. Success in achieving widespread support led, however, to near paralysis in respect of further practical action and the limitations of the Alliance seemed at times in danger of discrediting the very cause it sought to promote. Nevertheless the vision remained, as was evident in James's conviction, expressed two days before his death, 'that the one only *indispensable* condition for Christian fellowship was mutual acknowledgement of Christ as Son of God and Saviour of the world.'[70]

Wolfson College, Oxford

[68] *Evangelical Alliance, British Organization. Abstract of the Proceedings of the Fourth Annual Conference, held in Liverpool, October 1850 with the Annual Report presented to the Conference and a List of Members* (London 1850) pp. 17–23; *Evangelical Protestantism: Report of a Meeting Convened by the Evangelical Alliance but Open to all Christians holding the Doctrines of the Protestant Reformation, held in the Large Room, Exeter Hall on Thursday, February 27 1851* (London 1851); Lewis p. 257.

[69] *Evangelical Alliance, British Organization. Abstract of the Proceedings of the Sixth Annual Conference, held in Dublin, August 1852, with the Annual Report presented to the Conference; and a List of Members and Subscribers* (London 1852) p. 62; *The Bulwark* 2 (1852–3) p. 15.

[70] Dale p. 524 (italics in the original).

VOLUNTARYISM WITHIN THE ESTABLISHED CHURCH IN NINETEENTH CENTURY BELFAST

by S. PETER KERR

'THE Irish need to be governed and controlled as well as excited.'[1] So wrote Daniel Wilson, a young English clergyman later to be bishop of Calcutta, after visiting Armagh in June 1814 to discuss with local clergy the possibility of setting up a branch of the Church Missionary Society. An Irish (Hibernian) Church Missionary Society, he argued, would

> ... have a tendency both to revive and regulate the piety of members of the Church, fostering whatever is holy and energetic, and yet directing both in ... orderly submission to the Church ...[2]

In this observation, Wilson focuses the nature of the tension to which the existence and growth of voluntary societies, within an established Church, inevitably gives rise. It is the tension between 'fostering what is holy and energetic' and the 'governing' of the consequent upsurge of religious excitement by ecclesiastical authority, a tension as old as the New Testament Church at Corinth.

In Ireland, as in England and Scotland throughout the nineteenth century, the existence of voluntary religious societies granted church members the permission to indulge their particular enthusiasms for anything from education to 'penitent females'. In this respect, the growth of such societies was a major factor in the revitalisation of an Anglican Establishment which had traditionally recoiled in horror at the mere mention of the word 'enthusiasm'. Even James Godkin, one of the more hostile critics of the Established Church in Ireland, writing in 1867, felt impelled to comment

[1] F.E. Brand, *How the Church Missionary Society Came to Ireland* (1935 Dublin) p. 149.
[2] *Ibid.*

347

on 'the great increase of life in the Irish Church', which he attributed to 'the formation within the establishment of a voluntary church based on the religious societies and proprietary chapels.'[3] That these societies posed problems of control and regulation is hinted at in a modern historian's account of The Irish Church Mission. This society was founded by an English evangelical clergyman and former soldier, Alexander Dallas, mainly for the purpose of converting Roman Catholics in the west of Ireland. Bowen suggests that Dallas's achievement was to have built up 'a small establishment which did not supplement but was in some ways a rival to the Church of Ireland.'[4] An establishment within The Establishment! Dallas's achievement then had posited, in its starkest form, the tension between the revival and the regulation of enthusiasm. The effect of such tension on the Established Church in nineteenth-century Belfast and the growth and impact of the spirit of voluntaryism which gave rise to it are the central subjects of this study.

Societies, ecclesiastical and secular, abounded in nineteenth-century Belfast. By 1870, the first year of Disestablishment, when there were nineteen Anglican churches in Belfast,[5] serving a population of about 174,000, there were at least twenty societies being supported or run by the clergy and laity of the Established Church, as well as many local parochial voluntary societies concerned with such things as basic education and money-lending. The former larger societies represented a myriad of interests: Church Accommodation, Church Architecture, Amelioration of the Working Classes, Discountenancing of Vice, Unfortunate Females, Protestant Clanship, Education and many more.

Membership of the societies often overlapped and seemed to centre on an extremely energetic group of laity and incumbents. The laity included M.P.'s and prominent businessmen amongst their number,[6] while the clergy were mainly the perpetual curates

---

[3] Quoted by R.B. McDowell, *The Church of Ireland 1869–1969* (London 1975) p. 23. See also James Godkin, *Ireland and Her Churches* (London 1867) p. 501.
[4] D. Bowen, *The Protestant Crusade in Ireland* (London 1977) p. 235.
[5] Population and denominational statistics from D.J. Owen, *History of Belfast* (Belfast 1921). Statistics on Anglican Church buildings from J. MacNeice, *The Church of Ireland in Belfast* (Belfast 1931).
[6] Robert Bateson M.P., Emmerson Tennant M.P., Andrew Mulholland and William Ewart.

of technically non-parochial churches or 'proprietary churches' usually maintained by voluntary rather than Establishment support.[7] The most influential member of the group and the motivating force behind much of the voluntaryism within the Established Church in Belfast was undoubtedly the Reverend Thomas Drew, perpetual curate of Christ Church, who combined an energetic social concern with a fiery evangelicalism and a staunch political conservatism. He was a founder member of the Church Accommodation and Clergy Aid Societies and heavily involved in the Ulster Protestant Association, the Belfast Parochial Mission and the Orange Order – the latter three, all being groups with heavily sectarian overtones.[8] The Church Education Society also enjoyed his active support, while in his own parish he organised parochial associations, sunday schools, an asylum and had built, what he called, 'Houses of Prayer' in the outlying areas. Drew had several able and equally energetic lieutenants in the Reverend Charles Seaver of St. John's Laganbank, the Reverend William McIlwaine of St. George's, High Street and the Reverend Theophilus Campbell of Holy Trinity, Trinity Street off the Crumlin Road.

There is a lack of evidence about the active role of the bishops in these societies which, in itself, may not be insignificant. They tended, at least initially, to view such manifestations of voluntary enthusiasm with a wary eye, especially those with overtly sectarian tendencies. Bishop Knox forbade the open-air preaching of the Belfast Parochial Mission in 'localities where it is calculated to excite an outbreak',[9] while Richard Mant banned any members of the Church Home Mission from operating in his diocese.[10] Some societies, like the Church Education Society and the Union Prayer Meeting, did eventually gain some measured episcopal support.

The reasons for the emergence of voluntary societies can be divided into two categories. First, those arising from the inadequacy or insufficiency of the Church's traditional pastoral ministrations and evangelical outreach, and second, those arising from the restrictive character of the Establishment.

---

[7] *Report of His Majesty's Commissioners of Inquiry into Ecclesiastical Revenues and Patronage in Ireland* (1836) p. 244.
[8] A. Dawson, *The Annals of Christ Church Belfast from Its Foundation in 1831*. Unpublished papers, Northern Ireland Public Records Office, T1075/11.
[9] R. Knox, *A Charge delivered at the Ordinary Visitation of the United Diocese of Down, Connor and Dromore* (Belfast 1858) p. 20.
[10] R. Mant, *Episcopal Jurisdiction Asserted* (Dublin 1834) p. 36.

The insufficiency of Church resources in the face of a growing city and diocese contributed directly to the founding of an important cluster of societies within the Church. They promoted various causes: church building, additional curates and the beautification of existing church buildings. However, societies existing for these sort of purposes, though often involving laity,[11] tended to operate under the episcopal imprimatur and for that reason cannot really be considered voluntary. For the purposes of this paper, I want to deal with some of those societies, which, while being founded to supplement the work of the Church, nevertheless had their origins in what might, in contemporary parlance be labelled the 'voluntaryistic tendency'.

One such society was the Clergy Aid Society. Though later to become episcopally acceptable, it had doubtful parentage! In the *Christian Examiner and Church of Ireland Magazine* of December 1828, there appeared a leading article commenting on what the writer considered to be 'a peculiar deficiency in the operative machinery of the Established Church'.[12] What the writer was referring to was the Church's failure to preach to Roman Catholics 'the great truths of the Gospel of Christ', and his comments led to the formation of what was to become known as The Home Mission. Despite the fact that the membership of this society contained many with ecclesiastical titles, it was rather a freelance organisation as far as episcopal discipline went. The Home Mission resolved, in the spirit of Wesley, to see the world as its parish. Parish boundaries were irrelevant. Members must be 'prepared to address their Roman Catholic brethren', not only in 'such pulpits of the establishment as shall be opened to them', but 'in such other places as it shall be found possible to collect them'.[13] Once representatives of the society started turning up in dioceses and parishes without the bishops' prior permission, the inevitable happened and the Home Mission was banned in some dioceses. One of the diocesans who imposed a ban was Richard Mant of Down

---

[11] L.M. Ewart, *Handbook of the United Diocese of Down, Connor and Dromore* (Dublin 1886) p. 34.
[12] W. Mant, *The Memoirs of the Right Reverend Richard Mant* (Dublin 1857) p. 306.
[13] *Ibid.* p. 307.

and Connor. In a charge of 1834, he claimed, not only that 'the order of the Church was broken and her discipline abrogated', but also that 'the formularies of public worship were mutilated or abandoned'[14] by these maverick Home Missioners. Roman Catholics may have been brought to the light, but even that was not good enough reason, for a high churchman like Mant, to mutilate public worship and ignore church discipline. Voluntaryism must be immediately discouraged!

A number of the Belfast clergy who sympathised with the aims of the Home Mission were of the opinion that the bishop's pronouncement should not be the end of the matter and two of their number, R.W. Bland and Thomas Drew, approached Mant with the idea of initiating a Diocesan Mission. But the bishop, again suspecting the spirit of voluntaryism to be behind this petition, refused it, stating that 'the whole proposal appeared ... an uncalled for and unauthorised interference with his jurisdiction.'[15]

Despite this rebuff, Mr. Drew persevered, and after a decent interval, with the concurrence of the bishop and the archdeacons, The Down and Connor Clergy-Aid Society was inaugurated in January 1837[16] with the purpose of providing additional clerical help in areas where the need for such help had been expressed by the local incumbent. Diocesan discipline was to be observed.

But it was not simply a matter of providing extra manpower. For it would seem that the society spawned a nineteenth-century version of the House-Church movement. What were called 'preaching stations' were set up at nine locations – usually private houses throughout Belfast:

> Whiterock, Springfield, Ardoyne and Lepper's Mill stations are (said the report) in a very cheering state; the only thing complained of is want of a room: the first three stations being private houses are crowded to suffocation ... the station of Upper Falls is doing very well. The average attendance is stated to be about 100.[17]

---

[14] R. Mant, *Episcopal Jurisdiction* p. 36
[15] W. Mant, *Memoirs* p. 350.
[16] *Account of the Proceedings of the Down and Connor Clergy-Aid Society* (Belfast 1838) p. 13.
[17] *Ibid.*

So, the Clergy-Aid Society, which had its origins in the unofficial voluntaryist Home Mission and which had been opposed by the bishop, retained some of the Mission's extra-mural character. Further, the whole process through which it came into being illustrates the tension which inevitably arises when voluntarist energy and enthusiasm is confronted by the episcopal need to have things done 'decently and in order'.

Many, perhaps the majority of churchmen, would have agreed that the Great Revival of 1859 provided the Protestant Churches of nineteenth-century Belfast with the most dramatic supplement to their work of evangelistic outreach. Most would have concurred with the assessment that, on balance, 1859 was indeed 'The Year of Grace',[18] though, it must be said, there was some support for the title 'The Year of Delusion'![19] Whatever the assessment of its final outcome, it was an emphatically voluntaryist movement:

> It originated not with the clergy, it arose among the people; they came together in prayer; they invited their minister to pray for and with them.[20]

Its movement from America to the small County Antrim parish of Connor and from thence to Belfast was imperceptible, but its impact instant and dramatic. It 'struck'[21] from nowhere – rather like the great potato blight of 1845.

Did it make good the pastoral and evangelical deficiencies of the Church in Belfast? It is difficult to produce any hard statistical evidence from disinterested parties about the impact of the Revival, though it was reported that the number of prisoners brought to trial at the County Antrim Quarterly Sessions in October 1859, the height of the Revival, was only half the number of the previous year.[22] But there are certainly many reports from clergy of a

---

[18] This was the title that the Reverend W.G. Gibson gave to his account of the Revival. W.G. Gibson, *The Year of Grace* (Belfast 1860).
[19] The title of Isaac Nelson's rather hostile account of the Revival. I. Nelson, *The Year of Delusion* (Belfast 1860).
[20] C. Seaver, *Religious Revivals: Two Sermons preached in St. John's Laganbank on Sunday July 10th 1859* (Belfast 1859) p. 9.
[21] 'Struck' was the term most often used to indicate that someone had been physically affected by revival-inspired conversion. See Edward Stopford, *The Work and the Counterwork. The Religious Revival in Belfast with an Explanation of the Physical Phenomena* (Dublin 1859).
[22] W.D. Killen, *Ecclesiastical History of Ireland* (London 1875) p. 529.

dramatically increased tempo in church life, and of a general change
for the better in the 'outward face of society':

> Millowners and managers, magistrates and policemen, men
> sceptical as to the causes, indifferent to the movement or hostile
> to it, have all concurred in bearing witness to the change on
> the face of society: to the almost entire disappearance of certain
> vices, to the sobriety and honesty that characterises all classes.[23]

Trinity Church experienced an 'increased seriousness' at public
worship and larger congregations, though only sixteen 'stricken
cases' were recorded;[24] in Christ Church the 'physical manifestations' were few but '... two hundred more partook the Communion on last Christmas Day than on the previous'. St. Paul's,
St. Mary Magdalene's and St. John's Laganbank were also 'largely
visited'. Even the bishop was impressed. Commenting on the two
hundred percent rise in confirmation figures over the previous year
he observed:

> ... never since I have administered that rite of my Church,
> have I witnessed such solemnity of manner and deep feeling,
> as was exhibited by all whom I then confirmed.[25]

Inevitably the Revival spawned other instances of voluntary
religious association, involving both clergy and laity. Charles
Seaver, incumbent of St. John's, helped organise a weekly inter-
denominational prayer meeting called 'The Union Prayer Meeting'
which seemed to be very popular amongst the clergy and laity of
all the Protestant denominations, including the Mayor and prominent linen barons like Charles Ewart. Though the meetings were
held in the Music Hall in Belfast and in no way conformed to the
liturgy of the Established Church, Bishop Knox presided over at
least one of them. In favouring this particular voluntary association
with the presence of the supreme symbol of the ecclesiastical establishment, Bishop Knox incurred the displeasure of a rather caustic
Presbyterian commentator, who accused him of degrading his order
and of forfeiting the respect of intelligent men. He continued:

---

[23] C. Seaver, *Religious Revivals* p. 7.
[24] W. Gibson, *The Year* p. 408.
[25] *Irish Ecclesiastical Gazette* July 1859.

> If in future, he does not choose to lend the weight of his great intellect to the support of some Gospel truth, we recommend him to select rather the House of Lords, than the Lord's House; and to advocate Sunday Sports rather than Revival pretense.[26]

Perhaps more important to the impact of the Revival were the small local prayer meetings, conducted, significantly not by the clergy, but, as Seaver reports 'laymen of an humbler rank in society'.[27] This assumption by the laity of some of, what Seaver calls, the 'ministerial functions' may have provided the impetus for the recommendation at a diocesan conference in 1862 that each of the clergy in Belfast should organise a 'parochial association'[28] in his parish. The theological principle behind this proposal was the priesthood of all believers or, perhaps more accurately, every-member ministry; '... every member has his vocation and ministry', argued the Reverend J.A. Kerr, the initiator of the scheme; 'the work we have to do is not individual but relative (sic), for the chief object of the Church is to build up men into one family'.[29] The chief purpose of these associations was the pastoral support of the clergy in their parochial ministry.

But just as Bishop Mant had been extremely wary, if not initially hostile, to the voluntaryistic spirit of his Belfast clergy in their proposal for a diocesan mission, so the clergy themselves had their doubts about the voluntaryism of this revival-inspired lay ministry. Even committed revivalists like Seaver admitted that where there had been lay involvement there had been 'mistakes and indis-cretions',[30] while McIlwaine of St. George's questioned the depth of the commitment of some of the actively involved lay people who,

> ... in 1859 were exercising the offices of preachers, teachers and evangelists and who have in 1860 returned to all the

[26] I. Nelson, *The Year* p. 208.
[27] C. Seaver, *Religious Revivals*.
[28] A. Lee, *Report of the Proceedings of the Conference of the Clergy and Laity of the United Diocese of Down, Connor and Dromore* (Belfast 1862) p. 57.
[29] *Ibid.*
[30] C. Seaver, *Religious Revivals* p. 8.

carelessness and godlessness of the most barren profession or even to the ranks of the scoffer and the profane.[31]

Even the proposal about parochial associations, though supported in principle, was only implemented by Thomas Drew in Christ Church and he dissolved his association because of a bitter disagreement between the ladies' and the gentlemen's committees. Seaver of St. John's Laganbank may have put his finger on the reason for the clergy's reticence in trying to harness this enthusiasm of the laity when, in supporting lay participation, he asked only that they should co-operate 'according to some fixed rule'.[32] The enthusiasm and vitality of the laity must be regulated, 'the Irish need to be governed and controlled as well as excited'.

Voluntaryism – the organising of societies or loose associations to complement the work and resources of the Established Church – arose, therefore, amongst clergy and laity because of perceived deficiencies in the Church's pastoral and preaching ministries. But other areas, in which the Establishment was actually perceived as being restrictive, were also a powerful impetus towards voluntary movements.

One such area was the patronage system. Though not on as major a scale as in Scotland, the working of the patronage system was the cause of definite voluntaryist aspirations in Belfast. According to reports and correspondence in *The Newsletter* of 12 January 1821, a group from St. Anne's, the parish church of Belfast, with a Mr. Wright, one of the churchwardens, as spokesman had proposed the building of a new church in Belfast in addition to St. Anne's and St. George's. The reason put forward for such a building had been lack of accommodation at the other two churches. However, the empty pews at both these churches, as was pointed out by a correspondent to the newspaper, certainly cast doubt on the group's stated intent. Suspicions of a hidden agenda were confirmed at a vestry meeting called to discuss the proposal, when it transpired that some of the parishioners considered that they had been deprived of the services of a favoured curate, Mr. Brown, by the action of the patron, the Marquis of Donegal and did not want it to happen again. They were,

[31] W. McIlwaine, *Ulster Revivalism 1859* p. 11.
[32] A. Lee, *Report of the Proceedings of the Conference* p. 69.

... anxious, as far as possible to avoid future mortification and disappointment ... or being subject therein to the caprice or whim of the patron of the benefice.[33]

Discussion was heated. Thomas Verner, the Sovereign of the city, accused the churchwarden, Mr. Wright, of removing a set of chandeliers from St. Anne's, an establishment red herring. It was a prominent layman, Sir S. May, who accurately focused the real issue:

The true motive of this proposal was to embody a sect under the protection of the Established Church though differing in principles and doctrines.[34]

In short, it was voluntaryism within the Establishment. Though the vote went in the voluntaryists' favour by a majority of 138, the vicar, Arthur Chichester MacCartney (the patron was also from the Chichester family!) defused the situation by calling for an official scrutiny of the voters at the meeting and at this point the issue seems to have disappeared from the columns of *The Newsletter*, though it was later reported that the charges against the churchwarden for removing the chandeliers had been dropped. Doubtless the vicar did not want the publicity of the court proceedings to revive voluntaryist feeling.

In the face of growing Catholic militancy, many of the clergy and laity in Belfast also felt that the Establishment, State as well as Church, was by the late 1830s restricting their prosletysing amongst the Roman Catholic population. Their consequent frustration was the driving force behind the Church Education Society. It was founded in Belfast in 1839 to protest against a state system of National Schools, proposed in 1831, which would not have the actual text of Holy Scripture as its core curriculum. This proposal was interpreted by the supporters of the Church Education Society in Belfast as keeping the Bible from Catholic children. It was not only declared to be an impediment to the clergy from keeping their ordination vow 'to banish away all erroneous and strange doctrines' but also to be in direct opposition to the principles of the Established Church whereby clergy were 'bound by the law of the State

[33] *Belfast Newsletter* 19 Jan 1821. The report of the meeting was 'from memory'.
[34] *Ibid.*

as well as of the Church, to teach the people committed to their charge out of the Scriptures'.[35] The State was accused of 'binding' the clergy to 'assist the oppressor'.[36] Thomas Drew considered the National System to be a case of blatant bias toward Rome, describing the decision of the Dublin administration to agree to such a system in these colourful terms: 'then amidst the midnight festivity of Dublin Castle, the impulsive Viceroy drank deep of Jesuit potions.'[37]

Despite the support of Bishop Mant, the Society was strongly opposed by his more liberal successor, Robert Knox, who considered the National System to be 'the only system suited to the want and requirements of this country'.[38] In 1849 he very courageously forbade two members of the Society from preaching in Christ Church Belfast despite a threat by the clergy and laity of the diocese to withdraw their cooperation.[39] In 1862, with the support of some of his clergy and laity, he proposed a compromise formula but it was rejected outright by the Commissioners of National Education. His efforts at regulation and 'government' of the Society's enthusiasm were unsuccessful.

As we have seen, many members of the Church Education Society in Belfast considered the State's education policy not just to be restrictive, but to be representative of a bias towards Rome. They were not alone in their views. The Catholic Emancipation Act of 1829 and the Irish Church Temporalities Act of 1833 were certainly seen in Ireland, and England, as representing a policy of conciliation towards Rome. Thomas Drew even went so far as to accuse the government of discrimination in favour of Roman Catholics in its appointments, so that 'Rome's sycophants receive what belongs to the true Protestant's birthright.'[40] It was inevitable

---

[35] C. Seaver, 'The Case of the Church Education Society for Ireland' as published in *Problems of a Growing City, Belfast 1780–1870* (Belfast 1973) p. 210.

[36] The Commissioners of the Ulster National Education Association, *The National System and Board: a Reply to the Explanatory Paper of the Commissioners of National Education of Ireland* (1864) p. 5.

[37] Thomas Drew, *State Education considered: The Church, the State, the Parent, the Child, (a sermon)* (Belfast 1862) p. 6.

[38] *Dublin Evening Mail* 29 Apr. 1862, Quoted in the *Irish Ecclesiastical Gazette* 15 June 1862.

[39] A. Dawson, *Annals.*

[40] *Commission of Inquiry into the Riots in Belfast, 1857* (1864) Appendix 1 p. 250.

that this Protestant paranoia would manifest itself in the formation of some very militant anti-Catholic societies, most of them closely connected with the Established Church.

The most well-known of these was, of course, the Orange Order. The Order had originated in the eighteenth century supposedly for the protection of Protestant farms against the incursions of Roman Catholic groups like the 'Defenders'. It soon developed a quasi-religious character with one of its avowed aims being the maintenance of the Established Church. The fortunes of the Order were directly related to the level of Catholic confidence in the community and, conversely, to Protestant insecurity. The 1830s and 1840s were a period of Catholic militancy both in Ireland and England, so it comes as no surprise to discover that the Grand Lodge of Ulster was formed on 12 February 1844 'to give mutual support and defense in these perilous times', and because the Grand Lodge of Ireland had dissolved itself in response to government pressure in 1836. By the middle of the century it was growing apace. Clergy, yeomanry and gentry were enrolling 'convinced that the time has come for their uniting in a powerful and defensive phalanx'.[41] Just how potent and influential a force the Orange Society had become in Belfast was made very clear by one James McGouran in a letter to *The Ulsterman* in August 1857. He described 'Orangeism' as having all the 'characteristics of a secret society'; complained of its immunity from government investigation or prosecution; and suggested that Lord Derby and Mr. Disraeli would choke the Orangeman 'without compunction if he were not the outwork of two institutions rather strong for even their hands – Landlordism and the Church Establishment.'[42] He castigated the authorities for relying on the 'fanaticism of a Drew or the cant of a McIlwaine ... backed up by the bloodthirsty scum and rabble of a low Protestantism to ensure the stability of the executive.'[43]

Less well known than the Orange Order, but with a similar purpose, was the Ulster Protestant Association, formed in 1849 'to combine still more closely the various bodies of Protestants'[44] with

[41] *Protestant Defender* 13 Dec. 1848.
[42] Letter to *Ulsterman* quoted in *Commission of Inquiry* p. 257.
[43] *Ibid.*
[44] *Protestant Defender* 20 Jan. 1849.

the, by now expected, clergy deeply involved: Thomas Drew, Theophilus Campbell and William McIlwaine. The flavour of this Association is well communicated by a quote from the speech of the Reverend Richard Oulton who addressed the society in April 1849: 'Popery' was the cause of 'that degradation of character which leads to habits of carelessness and filth that would disgrace the African Hottentot or the uncivilised savage of the forest.'[45] A similar sort of provocation of the Catholic community was provided by the activities of the Belfast Parochial Mission, founded by clergy and laity in 1857,[46] with the worthy object of providing opportunities for worship in unchurched parts of the city. However, its polemical preachers and its open air services in politically sensitive areas, according to a not unfriendly critic,[47] provided at least 'a pretext for disgraceful excesses', in the form of the most bloody sectarian riots that Belfast had seen. The preachers were William McIlwaine and Thomas Drew!

This kind of enthusiasm could not be easily regulated or governed by the Establishment. It was not just religious vitality. These societies and associations were an expression of the historic political identity of a community, a community that once again saw itself as under siege. Indeed, this question of political identity surfaced in most of the disputed issues in Belfast church life during this period. The comment of Robert Hamilton, claiming to represent the 'hard-fisted artisans' of the city, on the proposed state-enforced voluntaryism of disestablishment epitomises the thinking behind the formation of these militantly anti-Catholic societies:

> it is the cause of the truth of God and the house of God and the religion of God ... We were loyal, and we are loyal; and if need were, we would shut the gates again.[48]

---

[45] *Ibid.* 14 Apr. 1849.
[46] A. Dawson, *Annals.*
[47] *Ibid.* The not unfriendly critic was Dawson himself, curate of Christ Church.
[48] *Report of the Conference of Archbishops and Bishops, Clergy and Laity of the Irish Branch of the United Church of England and Ireland* (1869) p. 62. 'The gates' referred to were the gates of the walled city of Londonderry which were shut against the Catholic King James in 1689, an event which had become part of Protestant folk-lore.

The bishops made their token attempts to regulate and govern. Mant did not attend a 'Great Meeting of Protestants'[49] in 1834 at Hillsborough when the Presbyterian leader, Dr Henry Cooke, proposed 'marriage' between the Established Church and his own in an effort to create a united front against resurgent Catholicism. Bishop Knox, as we have seen, stood out against the sectarianism of the Church Education Society; he also banned the provocative open-air preaching of the Belfast Parochial Mission.[50] But in the face of what was rapidly approaching community hysteria these actions were as mere straws in the sectarian wind.

A final motive for the formation of at least some of the associations within the Church, was concern about the influence of the increasing number of societies being founded outside the Church for the purpose of improving the lot of the working classes, particularly those, like the Belfast Mechanics Institute (1825) and the Belfast Working Classes Association for General Improvement (1847) which believed that 'such institutions are likely to be most stable and useful when chiefly supported and managed by mechanics themselves.'[51] It was doubtless these sorts of societies which Thomas Drew had in mind when he condemned 'Literary Societies' for making 'many dissatisfied with their proper station in life, querulous of imaginary wants, and insubordinate to their employers.'[52]

The impression is given that the Church of Ireland Young Men's Society (1850) was founded to counteract the subversive influence of such societies. The annual report of 1856 pointed out for the 'fiftieth time' that the Society 'had nothing to do with politics', but that its purpose was 'to exalt the moral and religious tone of young men in our town',[53] and to disabuse those same young men of any such idea as that '... the working classes are the only true and proper owners of property.'[54] Such aims are unsurprising when

---

[49] *Irish Protestant* (1834–35) 1 p. 137.
[50] Robert Knox, *A Charge delivered at the Ordinary Visitation of the United Dioceses of Down, Connor and Dromore* (Dublin 1858) p. 20.
[51] 'Constitutions and Laws of the Belfast Mechanics Institute' in *Problems of a Growing City* p. 80.
[52] *The Irish Pulpit* (collections of sermons) p. 259.
[53] *The Sixth Annual Report of the Church of Ireland Young Men's Society* (Belfast 1856) p. 9.
[54] *The Fourth Annual Report of the Church of Ireland Young* (1854) p. 9.

the impeccable pedigree of the society's committee is recognised. Amongst its number it included the perpetual curates of Trinity Church (Campbell), St. George's (McIlwaine) and St. John's Laganbank (Seaver).

What impact did this growth of voluntary societies and associations have on the Established Church in Belfast? Did it indicate a change from a pastoral communal church, seen primarily as an agency of social cohesion, to an associational church more responsive, for good or evil, to the social needs, the theological emphases and political aspirations of particular groups of enthusiasts? Does this mushrooming of associational life within the Establishment suggest the emergence of a church whose vitality and identity no longer depended on the patronage of the Establishment but on the energy and exclusiveness of voluntaryism? In short, are we witnessing in this upsurge of voluntaryism the birth of a new sort of church more appropriate to a pluralist and socially fragmented urban society?

There is certainly some support for such a thesis in this study. There is implied criticism of the traditional parochial system in the very organisation of so many voluntary auxiliary societies like the Church Accommodation Society and the Clergy Aid Society to make up for the 'peculiar deficiency in the operative machinery of the Established Church'. There is impatience with the constraints imposed by Establishment both, with regard to the education of children, and the Church's relationship with the Catholic community. The clergy who appear again and again in this study – Drew, Seaver, McIlwaine and Campbell, all incumbents of proprietary or 'voluntary' churches – along with some influential laymen like Robert Bateson M.P. represent a powerful and energetic interest group constantly seeking to impose their admittedly narrow evangelical identity and social concern on the Church at large. And that constant pressure, certainly until the end of the 1850s, meant that the Establishment was contended with, rather than its patronage sought. The change in the Church's self-understanding is perhaps signalled by a growing maturity in dealing with, and a success in channelling this contentious energy of the societies. From the blank refusal of the vicar of Belfast to accede to the voluntaryist demands of the group seeking an independent church in 1821, there is movement towards the more irenic position of

Bishop Knox and his proposal of a compromise formula in the conflict over education in 1862. In the same year there is further evidence of a growing maturity with regard to the Church's attempts to govern the enthusiasm of voluntaryism. For it was in that year that Bishop Knox inaugurated the first of his annual diocesan conferences for clergy and laity through which

> opportunities have been ... afforded of considering what additional agencies are most needed for carrying on the Church's work and for increasing the practical efficiency of those in present use.[55]

So, by the 1860s it was being accepted that Establishment was not enough. The need for voluntary societies to complement the work of the Established Church in Belfast was recognised and machinery set up to monitor their work. Thus, James Godkin's argument for disestablishment, that the strength of the Irish Church was due to an 'invasion of voluntaryism' rather than its established status[56] seemed to bear close relation to the evidence, a realisation which may well have influenced Bishop Knox in his lone – amongst the bishops – support for Gladstone's bill in 1869. By that time voluntaryism had given the Church in Belfast a distinctive identity and released sources of previously untapped lay energy. On the local pastoral level at least, the Act of Disestablishment simply recognised and legitimated what was already happening.

However, the final testament to the voluntaryistic vigour of the Established Church in Belfast comes from the lips of some English 'gentlemen' who, on leaving the Diocesan Conference in 1862, told the bishop

> that they left more deeply impressed than ever with the importance of the Church in this country, ... and that they would not be at all surprised to see meetings of the same kind established in England.[57]

Lincoln Theological College

[55] A. Lee, *Report of the Proceedings* preface.
[56] James Godkin, *Ireland* p. 501.
[57] A. Lee, *Report of the Proceedings* p. 103.

VOLUNTARY ABSOLUTISM: BRITISH MISSIONARY SOCIETIES IN THE NINETEENTH CENTURY

by PETER HINCHLIFF

I N 1818 Dr John Philip was sent out to supervise the London Missionary Society stations at the Cape of Good Hope. His first letter to the Society's headquarters is dated from Liverpool on 5 December of that year and contains the statement, 'We have been at sea for seventeen days and are still in the Mersey River.'[1] Philip went on to ask for various items, including – significantly perhaps – a barometer! And there was time for the barometer to reach him before he left the Mersey: it was a further five days before the winds changed.

In broad terms this paper is about the organizational aspects of missionary societies as voluntary associations. The story about Philip is relevant because it is a reminder that the development of missionary societies as organizations and the development of the technology necessary for the efficient *running* of an international organization, went on more or less simultaneously. Enthusiasm for missions began in the late eighteenth century: the missionary *movement* did not become really significant until the 1840s.

In the strictly constitutional and legal context 'voluntary association' is usually contrasted with 'coercive jurisdiction'. The crucial question, in that context, is whether one is subject to ecclesiastical discipline because one has *chosen* to be so or because the church authorities can claim jurisdiction over anyone or everyone. In practice – at least in modern times – coercive jurisdiction only exists where it has the sanction of the state and that, in turn, implies some form of establishment. There were some surprising attempts to claim a coercive authority on the part of nineteenth-century missionaries, chiefly in the context of what Roland Oliver

---

[1] London University School of Oriental and African Studies, LMS Incoming Correspondence South Africa Box 7 Folder 5 Jacket C.

has called 'mission states'.[2] Sometimes there was even an attempt to undergird them with positive theological or constitutional theory of an eccentric kind – such as Dr John MacRae's contention that missions of the Church of Scotland were sovereign and independent colonies.[3] But the jurisdiction exercised in such cases as these was exercised in the field rather than within the structures of the sending bodies.

Every modern British organization to which we conventionally attach the label 'missionary society' was a voluntary association in the strict sense. But within that formal homogeneity, the societies varied enormously. In the Church of England the CMS was almost militantly a body of individual volunteers; while the SPG tried very hard to seem like an official arm of the Church. The Wesleyan Missionary Society *was* a part of the formal church structure, just as the Foreign Mission Committee of the Church of Scotland was. The members of the interdenominational London Missionary Society were so fiercely opposed to the least suggestion of state support that they even protested against the Society's accepting financial assistance from government for rehabilitating emancipated slaves.[4] But the Society's interdenominational character caused it to leave the thorny decisions about emerging ecclesiastical structures to the new churches it was creating in the mission field. And so it found itself opting for independency in an ecclesiological sense, too. In terms of their relationship to any existing denomination, some societies were much more voluntary than others.

This is important because of the tendency of some historians to talk about 'the missionaries' as if they were a homogeneous group. It ought to be perfectly obvious to anyone that a Tory high churchman would have ideas about the nature of the Church's mission and of its political implications, quite different from those of a conscientious free churchman. Thus Joshua Watson could suggest that, if the government could not afford to bring Ceylon under the wing of Britain, the Society for the Propagation of the

[2] R. Oliver, *The Missionary Factor in East Africa* 2 ed (London 1965) pp. 50–66 and 74.
[3] P. Hinchliff, 'The Blantyre Scandal: Scottish Missionaries and Colonialism', *Journal of Theology for Southern Africa* 46 (1984) pp. 29–38.
[4] LMS Home Letters 1795–1875 A (1) Box 6 File 6 Jacket A.

Gospel might do so instead.[5] One could not conceivably imagine such a suggestion being made by the radically republican William Carey, founder of the Baptist Missionary Society, though in some respects he was an admirer of the SPG.

But, though the missionaries were far from homogeneous in their background and outlook, and though their societies differed considerably in their degree of independence from both state and parent church, there were – at the same time – some ways in which none of this made for significant differences. For instance, alongside considerable variations in the voluntariness of missionary societies, there could exist a surprising degree of similarity in organization. Though serious scholarly work on the missionary societies as organizations is relatively recent, a comparative study of the Church Missionary Society and the Mill Hill Fathers shows just this combination of sameness and variation – and not always precisely where one would expect each to be.[6]

Indeed, if one is to understand the nature of the voluntary societies, one has to remember that the term 'voluntary' applied not to the missionaries but to the people in England who had *chosen* to support the society. The missionaries were *employed* by the society and, by the terms of their contracts, were required to do what the society told them to do. Therefore, it may make a vast difference to the *constitution* of a society whether it was an official ecclesiastical organ or a body composed of individual and volunteer members. But it may not make the least difference to the authoritarian way in which it treated its agents in the field. So it was possible for Bishop Blomfield, of all people, to describe the reign of Dandeson Coates, secretary of the very voluntary CMS, as 'a virtual tyranny', adding 'he *is* the Society'.[7]

It was, moreover, very rare for those who ran the societies to have had any direct missionary experience or even to have visited

---

[5] Rhodes House Oxford, USPG Archives C/IND/Gen 4: Watson to Archbishop Manners Sutton, December 1817. As from May 1985 the USPG archives are being transferred to Rhodes House. The references given here are to the classification used before the transfer but will enable documents to be found without difficulty in the new location.

[6] L. Nemer, *Anglican and Roman Catholic Attitudes on Missions: An Historical Study of two English Missionary Societies in the late Nineteenth Century (1865–1885), Studia Instituti Missiologici Societatis Verbi Divini* 29, (St Augustin 1981).

[7] USPG Archives Home Box – to 1840: letter dated 24 August 1847.

a mission station. William Carey was exceptional in being both a founder of a society and one of its missionaries. And his missionary experience came after he had launched the Society. The organizers were often quite ignorant about the circumstances in which their employees worked.

This ignorance was relative, of course. Missionary societies were often, for instance, better informed than the colonial office – where the administrators were equally innocent of first-hand experience[8] – but one has always to bear their ignorance in mind. In 1813 the LMS sent a commission of enquiry to visit its stations at the Cape and the commissioners' reports show how inaccurate some of the Society's previous information had been.[9] Societies sometimes confused different place names; or made mistakes about the distances between places; or failed to take into account the fact that there might be deserts, mountains or rivers in the way. Part of Livingstone's importance in the history of African missions is that he enabled maps to be more accurate and more realistic. But in the first half of the century, particularly, missionaries were constantly complaining that they were being given impractical instructions because societies were muddled about basic facts. The Wesleyans even, who were used to obeying the dictates of Conference, were frequently driven to argue with their superiors. Sometimes they did not seem to know in which of the mission districts a particular station actually was.[10]

This important difference between administrators and missionaries originated in the way in which most of the societies came into existence in the late eighteenth or early nineteenth centuries. They were originally simply small groups of people who believed that it was important for the Christian gospel to be preached outside Europe and who met to pray together; to try to learn about what was or was not being done; and what the needs were. They had no offices, no structure, no regular income. They actually knew very little of the magnitude of the undertaking upon which

---

[8] See e.g. CMS Archives CA1/E1, No 21; now transferred to Selly Oak College, Birmingham.

[9] LMS Archives Incoming South Africa Box 5 Folder 1 Jacket F and Folders 2 and 3: letters from G. Thom and J. Campbell.

[10] E.g. London University School of Oriental and African Studies, MMS Archives Correspondence – South Africa: Cape Box 6 File 1829–34: B. Shaw, 31 August 1830 which implies this kind of ignorance.

they were launching themselves. In a sense they might as well have been meeting to discuss and pray about atrocities in Armenia or the education of the poor.

On 23 February 1796, for instance, the *Glasgow Mercury* carried a notice announcing that a missionary society was to be formed in that city (like the societies that had recently come into being in other parts of Britain), which would procure funds, devise means and discover fit persons for missionary work. Even that, perhaps, suggests something too much like a modern missionary society. As the standard history of Scottish missions points out, almost every town of any size in Scotland was to have 'praying societies on the missionary plan'.[11] The Glasgow Society, though it eventually became a small independent missionary society in the stricter sense, was not essentially different from these others. Even the Edinburgh society, which arrogated to itself the title of 'The Scottish Missionary Society' was really just such a local body.

So one has to imagine these societies, and not in Scotland alone, as originating in groups of people who had other jobs to do, many of whom held pastoral charges in British churches. They met occasionally because they were concerned about the need for missions abroad. They prayed about them and tried to raise some money for them. If they discovered someone who wanted – or could be encouraged – to go and work anywhere in the 'heathen' world they would try to satisfy themselves that he was suitable. And they might then undertake to support him with their money and prayers and interest. They were totally different from the later missionary societies proper, with offices and officials, a systematic selection procedure and an international network of stations. And even when those organizational developments had begun to occur – about the second quarter of the nineteenth century – the distinction between the senders and the sent survived for a long time. The voluntary members of the societies were, so to speak, amateurs with a hobby. The missionaries themselves were professional, full-time employees bound – in varying degrees – to obedience.

On the whole the missionary societies, whatever their constitutional character, were remarkably authoritarian. They exercised a direct and often absolute control over the lives of their employees

---

[11] E.G.K. Hewat, *Vision and Achievement* (London 1960) pp. 8–9.

and in matters of minute and almost trivial detail as well as in the broader issues of policy. It is well known that, in some parts of Africa to this day, Christians who are asked their denomination, will respond with the name of the missionary society which evangelized the area. This may partly be because some missionary societies are undenominational. But it may also partly be explained by the fact that many missionary societies exercised the kind of authority that is proper to a church. And it was an authority which largely sprang from a pastoral concern.

In December 1817, really very early in the history of missionary organization, a young man called Edwards arrived in Cape Town. Before the end of that month he had taken up his appointment as an assistant on a Wesleyan station in Namaqualand, to the south of what is now Namibia. In the course of his few days in Cape Town he had written to his Society in London to say that he thought he ought to get married. A year later – for three months was then an average time for a passage to the Cape – headquarters replied. Their necessary ignorance is revealed in their letter for they said that Edwards might go ahead if he could find some 'suitable young female' at the Cape. As the mission was some hundreds of miles from the nearest settlement and the missionaries only visited a town perhaps once a year, this was hardly as generous as it might have seemed. Edwards wrote several further letters to the Committee, frankly explaining the difficulties of an unmarried missionary. One of them was actually sent in duplicate as though he feared that the letters were simply not reaching England. He was plainly becoming desperate. The superintendent missionary also joined in the correspondence, reporting to the Society that Edwards was very unsettled and that something had better be done about him. After two more years the Committee managed to find a bride for the young man and on 12 June 1820 he wrote to tell them that she had arrived safely.[12]

Because this was the Wesleyan Society, the degree of oversight implied in Edwards's story is not surprising: the authority of Conference hung over the whole Missionary Society. Another young assistant missionary who was making trouble with the colonial authorities by insisting on his 'right' to visit native prisoners

[12] MMS Archives C – South Africa General Box 1 File 1819 and File 1820.

in jail, was told by his superintendent that 'preachers have been tried before Conference for saying so much ...'[13]

The LMS, as one would have expected, exercised a less direct and detailed control, certainly so far as the personal lives of their missionaries were concerned. LMS missionaries had some room for manœuvre denied to others. But even this Society exercised a good deal of supervision. Each station had to submit a careful annual report. A watchful control was exercised over expenditure. The Society's Foreign Secretary kept up a regular correspondence with most of the men in the field, though there were sometimes holes in his net. It was possible for one missionary to delay his first official report to headquarters for two years and to wait a further eighteen months beyond that before the Society recognised his existence.[14] But, on average, most LMS missionaries wrote to the Society, with a fairly full account of their doings, several times a year.

What is less attractive is that they also wrote fairly fully to headquarters about the inadequacies of their colleagues. Whether the Society actually encouraged this tale-telling or whether it was the product of sheer *invidia*, I do not know. But a good deal of LMS correspondence from the Cape in the first half of the nineteenth century contains complaints from one missionary about another and the rejoinders of those complained about. And the very fact that they felt an *apologia* to be necessary was a recognition of the Society's authority. Moreover, though they seem to have been given some latitude about where they set up their stations, the Society maintained the right to direct missionaries to certain areas upon occasion. Indeed the relationship between its agents and the LMS – a mixture of obedience and independence – is very well illustrated by the case of a man called Calderwood who wrote to the Society in 1842 acknowledging the Board's decision to send him back to what was then called 'Caffreland' and undertaking to go at the 'year's end'.[15] As his letter is dated in May this was hardly instant obedience. But, in fact, he was like the son in the parable who, after telling his father that he would not go, went all

[13] P. Hinchliff ed, *The Journal of John Ayliff* (Cape Town 1971) p. 55.
[14] LMS Archives Incoming South Africa Box 13 Folder 1 Jacket D and Box 14 Folder 1 Jacket B: T. Edwards, 6 November 1832 and 28 March 1834.
[15] LMS Archives Incoming South Africa Box 18 Folder 3 Jacket C.

the same. Calderwood's next letter is dated 10 October and contains an account of his journey to the mission to which he had been appointed.[16]

The two main Anglican missionary societies developed rather different patterns of control. CMS was much more like the Methodist Society, maintaining a direct and fairly strict control over its agents. SPG, by the 1840s, had adopted a consistent policy of working through the local bishop, where there was one, and largely leaving it to him to exercise authority over individual missionaries. This reflects a deeper difference between the two societies than even their different relationships with the official structures of the Church of England. SPG had been initially created in the seventeenth century as much to ensure that the English Church took root among colonists abroad as for any strictly missionary motive. CMS was always, in the classical sense, a missionary society and, though it required its men to hold a bishop's licence, did not tend to restrict its operations within the colonial framework as the SPG did.

Perhaps the most surprising thing about the authority exercised by the societies is that the missionaries were prepared to accept it as tamely as they did. They were, on the whole, strong personalities; tough, independent men; mavericks even. Otherwise they would not have gone where they did. Societies often chose and admired them for those very qualities. At an Anglican missionary conference at the very end of the nineteenth century the principal of the CMS college at Islington said, 'The missionary ought to be a "ready" man ... One of my predecessors ... told us ... that this was the description of the character and gifts of one of the students: "He is a man who can build a stone wall, or go through it."' It is clear that this was intended as praise, for the principal added, 'That student became an archdeacon.'[17] But a man chosen for his ability to go through stone walls is not a man designed by nature to take orders from a distant headquarters.

In part, I think, the willingness of societies to give orders and of missionaries to take them is to be explained by the fact that the administrators were often older, better educated and from a higher

[16] LMS Archives Incoming South Africa Box 18 Folder 4 Jacket B.
[17] *Missionary Conference of the Anglican Communion, Official Report* (London 1894) p. 54.

social class than the missionaries. A.F. Walls reminded an earlier meeting of this Society that it is now the accepted view that the early nineteenth century missionary was a fairly homespun character without much formal education but that, by the end of the century, his successor came typically from the same sort of social and educational background as an ordained man at home. And he pointed out that the missionary was always regarded, first and foremost, as a minister who was not – so far as his training went – thought to be at all different from those in the ministry in England.[18]

In general that picture is a true one but it is important to remember that the change was very gradual rather than something that happened suddenly somewhere in mid-century. Missionary societies did sometimes recruit university graduates, even in the earlier part of the century. Soon after the middle of the century the Universities Mission to Central Africa adopted a deliberate policy of staffing its stations with unmarried products of public school and university, who would work in Africa in much the same spirit as their contemporaries were serving in east end curacies. CMS seems to have begun to encourage rather than discourage graduates some time in the 1860s.[19] But even at the end of the century there remained a publicly expressed fear that a man might get himself ordained for the mission field as a means of advancing his social position in Britain.[20]

Nor was it the Church of England alone which might accept a candidate whose 'social and educational attainments were not such as would have brought him ordination to the home ministry'.[21] Anglicans might take on a shop assistant with some secondary education: Methodists a weaver who could read and write: the LMS an artisan who was not really literate at all.[22] Though it may seem trite and trendy to use class as an explanation of the relationship between the senders and the sent, it may yet be an accurate if only partial one. One has to imagine the average missionary

---

[18] A.F. Walls, '"The Best Thinking of the Best Heathen": Humane Learning and the Missionary Movement' *SCH* 17 (1981) pp. 341 and 351–352.
[19] Nemer p. 78.
[20] *Missionary Conference Report* p. 39.
[21] Walls p. 341.
[22] P. Hinchliff, 'The Selection and Training of Missionaries in the Early Nineteenth Century' *SCH* 6 (1970) pp. 132–133.

candidate as a fairly young man, without a great deal of formal education or any real pastoral experience even in this country. He might even not have been acceptable for ordination at home. The leaders of his society would be middle aged or elderly *gentlemen*, often with university degrees and ministerial experience and would therefore seem to be greatly superior to him. The very fact that he and they were both essentially thought of as *ministers* – and they had the greater pastoral experience – would help to disguise the fact that the directors' were not really experts on missions.

In 1817 a woman who lived in Cape Town and was a great friend of missions and missionaries wrote to the directors of LMS. She was distressed by many things that were happening in the Society's stations at the Cape. She did not approve of the radical political stance taken by some of the missionaries; she was saddened by quarrels among the missionaries themselves; and she was opposed to an attempt that had been recently made to set up a council of local missionaries to exercise corporate control. She told the Board very firmly that the only way to reimpose discipline and unity was to send out a 'Father in Christ' – and she uses the actual term – from headquarters. Though she may have been quite mistaken in this, she seems to have believed that such a man would have been received with near episcopal reverence even by the very independent LMS men.[23]

Class differences between administrators and missionaries during most of the century could, I believe, be demonstrated statistically. I prefer to try and convey the flavour of it by quoting a letter, dating from the 1860s, which is in the archives of CMS. Though the letter is from an African ruler, one can detect the hand of a missionary in its phrasing – and this is presumably why the document has come to be in the Society's files. The letter is addressed 'To all the Ballogun or War Chiefs in the Camp at Makun or elsewhere.' It begins, 'Sirs, I hasten to drop you these few lines …' and ends, 'I remain Sirs, Yours very truly, The Basorun of Abeokuta'.[24] The hoping-this-finds-you-as-it-leaves-me style of this letter is not the kind of thing that would emanate from one of Jane Austen's clergymen.

[23] LMS Archives Incoming South Africa Box 7 Folder 3 Jacket C: Mrs Smith 12 November 1817.
[24] CMS Archives C A2/06 Bound volume of Correspondence between Missionaries and Native Chiefs and Authorities: copy dated 28 November 1862.

But, perhaps even more important than class differences were the very needs of the missionaries which made them desperately dependent on the societies and therefore predisposed them to accept the directions which were issued by headquarters. They asked for an almost infinite range of things – copies of the New Testament; books on sheep breeding and crop growing; money to manumit slaves or to buy intending missionaries out of the army; handkerchiefs; machinery for making bricks, pumping water or printing books; help in coping with good-for-nothing sons shipped back to England; garden implements; schoolbooks; seeds for planting; new or second hand clothes; church bells; pious magazines; help in providing education for missionary children; the odd wife or two; medicines; help, encouragement and concern.

The variety of the things they asked for must not be allowed to obscure the fact that each of them was a symptom of the loneliness of the men in the field. Again and again the administrators at headquarters were told that what mattered most was that the missionaries should receive letters.[25] It is not surprising that even the most independent of missionaries was willing to put up with a good deal of direction from headquarters, in return for knowing that there was someone, somewhere, who actually cared what happened to him.

In response to this flood of demands for care and direction, the societies built up a complex and sophisticated office structure. In one sense this is not surprising. Some of the best administrative minds of the nineteenth-century church shared in the work – Jabez Bunting, who was for eighteen years secretary of the Wesleyan Missionary Society; Joshua Watson who helped to rationalize the activities of SPG and SPCK; the younger Henry Venn who was the real architect of the CMS system; even Charles James Blomfield, the apostle of ecclesiastical efficiency, whose willingness as bishop of London to take his responsibilities for the church in the colonies seriously led to the creation of the Colonial Bishopricks Fund.

There were two particular reasons, perhaps, why societies felt compelled to deal efficiently with all the paper that came flooding

---

[25] E.g. LMS Archives Incoming South Africa Box 6 Folder 2 Jacket E: report to the Society from G. Thom dated 23 December 1814.

in from the field. One was the obvious legal importance of some of it. Documents relating to missionaries' pension rights, for instance, or arrangements made about paying for the education of their children, would have to be carefully kept so that the society's contractual obligations were clear. For instance, although the bulk of the correspondence addressed to the Glasgow and Edinburgh Societies has completely disappeared – and was probably lost or destroyed after the societies ceased to have an independent existence in the 1840s – a small collection of letters and papers relating precisely to matters of this kind have survived.[26]

More important even than this factor, however, was the societies' need for publicity. Since they were all – whether voluntary societies or official ecclesiastical structures – very largely dependent on the giving of individuals, each society tended to launch its own magazine and other publications soon after coming into existence. By as early as 1821 the Wesleyan *Missionary Notices* were receiving widespread circulation and serving as a kind of house journal for missionaries.[27]

The need for publicity, in turn, created further material requiring methodical organization. By the 1840s the LMS, for instance, employed a miniaturist to take the likenesses of those being sent out to the mission field. The Society was creating something very like a newspaper 'morgue' so as to have pictures in stock to accompany published articles and reports.

For much the same reason the Wesleyan Society required all its agents to keep a journal and send summaries back to London at the end of each quarter. Not only was this a check on what the missionary was doing: it was also a source of material for publication. Keeping a journal was so much the mark of a Methodist missionary that an aspiring candidate could practise writing one, much as an Anglo-Catholic ordinand might dress himself in a priest's soutane.[28]

One is bound to say that the portraits as well the written accounts were sometimes romanticised: Livingstone's miniature might as

[26] National Library of Scotland Acc. 7548 – D.1.
[27] *Journal of John Ayliff* pp. 11 and 105: for a succinct description of the range of publications produced by CMS in the second half of the century, see Nemer pp. 65–67.
[28] *Journal of John Ayliff* p. 6.

well be that of the young Keats. And it is to the eternal credit of the missionaries that they often protested against exaggerated accounts of their successes.[29] On the other hand, the administrators are not to be greatly blamed for their concern for publicity. Financing missions was difficult, not only because large and regular commitments had to be met from an income composed of small and irregular donations. The very fact that the enterprise was international made for complications. Missionaries lived a long way from the nearest outposts of commercial activity. They had to obtain their money through bills drawn on headquarters and often discounted at a punitive rate. Keeping track of all this must, in itself, have been an organizational feat. Of the forty odd surviving letters received by LMS from the Cape colony during 1826, seven are notifications of bills drawn by missionaries, amounting to several thousand pounds.

To control all this – publicity, pastoral direction, policy, placing and finance – an elaborate organization was required. Part-time officials were reinforced or replaced by full-time executives. Committee structures were created to take policy decisions. In the 1860s CMS, for instance, normally had five secretaries in addition to the Honorary Secretary who was the Society's chief executive and whose office, as its title suggests, was a survival from older less institutional days. (It also, it has to be said, accurately reflected the fact: the secretary was unpaid.) To these officials were added in the 1870s two further posts at managerial level.[30]

The final authority of CMS was the General Committee, a vast and somewhat indeterminate body which nevertheless took decisions in such matters as the selection, placing and other detailed personal affairs of missionaries. In other matters it worked through four main Committees – Patronage, Correspondence, Funds and Accounts. In the 1880s the Correspondence Committee – which was really the executive committee – spawned three Area Committees, each dealing with different parts of the world so that, for instance, Africa, Palestine and New Zealand were allocated to the

---

[29] E.g. LMS Archives Incoming South Africa Box 9 Folder 1 Jacket B: J. Melvill 28 May 1823.
[30] Nemer pp. 46–48.

third of them.[31] There were also subcommittees for specific purposes such as the oversight of the Society's training college or the screening of candidates.

The records of the Area Committees are a researcher's dream. Letters and reports from missionaries were summarized in a printed agenda paper for the Committee. These have been pasted into the minute book and the Committee's decision or recommendation – and, in matters of crucial importance, the decision of the Committee of Correspondence – is recorded on the page opposite. It is possible, therefore, to see at a glance how the missionaries on the spot saw their problems and how the administrators at home reacted to them. In some cases – as, for instance, in the desperate and dangerous situation in Buganda in the 1880s and 1890s[32] – this can be vital for understanding the policy and behaviour of CMS.

Perhaps the most important decision any society had to take was about the relationship between themselves and the new church they were creating in the mission field. In theory– though not always in practice – this was easiest in those organizations, like the Church of Scotland or the Wesleyan Methodists, which were part of an official church structure. All they needed to do was to extend the system of government which already existed at home. For 'voluntary' societies the problem was more difficult. The LMS policy of leaving the decision to the emerging 'native' church represented one solution. Others were devised by missionary thinkers seeking a theoretical or theological basis for practical action. The best known of these is Henry Venn's doctrine of the 'euthanasia' of missions and their replacement by self-supporting, self-governing, self-propagating churches.[33] Another, arguing for episcopal missions, was advanced by Anthony Grant in his Bampton Lectures of 1843 and was developed and put into practice by Bishop Robert Gray of Cape Town with the help of Samuel Wilberforce of Oxford.[34]

[31] Nemer pp. 44–46.

[32] CMS Archives: G3/A5/P3.

[33] M. Warren ed *To Apply the Gospel: Selections from the writings of Henry Venn* (Grand Rapids 1971) pp. 25–26, 51–52, 74–78: T.E. Yates, *Venn and the Victorian Bishops Abroad* (London and Uppsala 1978) pp. 16–17.

[34] M.M. Goedhals, *Nathaniel James Merriman: A Study in Church Life and Government* (Rhodes University, South Africa, Ph.D. thesis 1982) pp. 87–88: P.Hinchliff, *The Anglican Church in South Africa* (London 1963) pp. 69–72.

For Anglicans the problem was complicated by the establishment and by the existence of a colonists' church alongside the mission. Colonial establishment has never been easy to understand – then or now. Some scholars have assumed that establishment and financial support from the colonial budget were virtually the same thing. Edward Norman seems to do this, for instance when he speaks of the ending of government subsidies as 'a pattern of disestablishment'.[35] But this is to confuse establishment proper with what was essentially a Whig view of the right relationship between religion and the State in the colonies, as is made clear in Lord Grey's defence of Russell's colonial policy between 1846 and 1852.[36] Finances and establishment were often connected, as the case of the clergy reserves in Canada clearly shows. But in that, as in other cases, financial support from government was specifically intended as an alternative to establishment.[37]

The crucial issue was always that, in the absence of establishment, a bishop's automatic coercive jurisdiction was doubtful. And financial need often led to its being called in question. Bishops sometimes sought to create synodical government in order to set diocesan finances on a sound footing[38] and synodical government frequently led to the substitution of voluntary association for establishment.

Ecclesiastical establishment existed in the colonies as a facet of the royal supremacy and the prerogative power of the *English* Crown. It was a consequence of a personal nexus between the supreme governor of the English Church and his or her Anglican subjects. No other hypothesis will account for the many apparent anomalies which accompanied colonial establishment, not least the fact that the Church of England, but not the Church of Scotland, was always assumed to be established in British colonies. The

---

[35] E.R. Norman, *Christianity in the Southern Hemisphere: the Churches in Latin America and South Africa* (Oxford 1981) p. 109 and cf p. 191 (where 'fiendly' is presumably a misprint for 'friendly').

[36] (3rd) Earl Grey, *The Colonial Policy of Lord John Russell's Administration* 2 vols (London 1853) I pp. 13–14.

[37] P. Burroughs, 'Lord Howick and Colonial Church Establishment' *JEH* 25 (1974), pp. 381–405 (Lord Howick was later the Earl Grey referred to in the previous footnote).

[38] P. Hinchliff, 'Laymen in Synod' *SCH* 7 (1971) pp. 322–3.

Scottish religious settlement gave no such personal authority to the sovereign.

The 'Eton College' judgement of 1857 first raised doubts about the existence of the establishment – and therefore of coercive jurisdiction – in those colonies where the Crown, by granting the right to legislate to the colony, had limited its own prerogative powers. By this time some parts of the church overseas had already begun to experiment with synodical government. And there followed a period in which even those overseas dioceses which had no reasons of their own for desiring it, were virtually compelled to devise a form of organization and discipline for themselves. The first Lambeth Conference drew up a prototype constitution, which was one of three models upon which the emerging Anglican provinces based their own proposals.[39]

These new provinces differed from the Church of England in two ways. One was the obvious one; that they were not established but regarded in law as based upon a voluntary compact, so that the secular courts – if appealed to – would regard their disciplinary procedures as being analogous to those of, for instance, the Jockey Club. The other was a seemingly surprising accompaniment to the substitution of a voluntary for a coercive system. Almost invariably the provinces created a very much tighter and more authoritarian ecclesiastical discipline than that of the Church of England with its parson's freehold, independent episcopal baronies and almost total absence of central administrative structure. Indeed, when the English Church came to construct such structures it sometimes looked to colonial experience to provide it with a model.[40]

Although there were problems, and sometimes serious ones,[41] the new system of government was usually accepted with surprisingly little resistance, given its revolutionary character. Part of the explanation for this may be that so many of the key personalities

---

[39] The other two were a draft bill which had been agreed by the House of Lords but rejected by the Commons in 1853, and the constitution of the American church; see P. Hinchliff, *The One-Sided Reciprocity* (London 1966) pp. 184–185.

[40] E.g. K.W. Orr, *Changes in the Methods of Financing of the Church of England, c.1870–1914, with special reference to the Parochial Clergy* (Oxford D.Phil. thesis 1983) pp. 283–285 and 307–308.

[41] For an account of the constitutional problems as they affected one province, see Hinchliff, *Anglican Church in South Africa* pp. 48–53, 87–103, and 111–129.

were already accustomed to a similar blend of voluntary association and strict disciplinary control within the missionary societies themselves.

Balliol College, Oxford

THE VOLUNTARY PRINCIPLE IN THE COLONIAL SITUATION: THEORY AND PRACTICE

by MARGARET DONALDSON

W HEN the London Missionary Society (LMS) came into being in 1795 two principles formed the twin pillars of its existence: the Fundamental Principle, which declared that the Society existed to preach the gospel to the heathen and not to promote any particular form of church polity: and the voluntary principle, which declared that financial responsibility for a church devolved upon its members, and not upon the government or, in the long term, upon the missionary society. This paper examines the problems of applying the voluntary principle in a colonial situation. The investigation focuses on the work of the Revd Richard Birt, LMS missionary in South Africa from 1838 to 1892. Birt was a supporter of the voluntary principle by conviction, by background and by commitment to the LMS. In practice, however, his life's work was to show the difficulty of maintaining the voluntary principle in a pioneering missionary situation.

Birt offered his services to the LMS in 1835. At the time he was a member of the King's Weigh House Chapel in London. His minister, the Revd Thomas Binney, was London's most outspoken advocate of the voluntary principle. A sermon of Binney's published in 1834 caused a furore because of its assertion that the Established Church was 'a great national evil; an obstacle to the progress of truth and godliness in the land'.[1] Some of Binney's fierce loyalty to the voluntary principle no doubt rubbed off onto the young men in his congregation, including Richard Birt. Binney was also a staunch supporter of the LMS and served periodically as a Director. His influence for the voluntary principle would be felt there too.

---

* Abbreviations: CWM Council for World Mission; CA Cape Archives
[1] E. Kaye, *The King's Weigh House Chapel* (London 1968) p. 67.

Richard Birt was sent to South Africa in 1838. His first mission was at Umxelo, near Fort Beaufort, on the eastern frontier of the Cape Colony. He laboured here from 1838 to 1846. When war broke out that year he and other missionaries had to leave. On his flight into the colony Birt took with him some fifty families from the mission. They formed the nucleus of the second station Birt founded when the war ended in 1848.

As early as April 1847 Birt wrote to the LMS that he had selected a new site, some twelve miles beyond the Society's station at Kingwilliamstown. He had chosen the position because of its economic possibilities. He hoped that those who lived on the mission would grow crops to sell at Kingwilliamstown or become wagon owners and transport drivers. He expected 'that in three years your Society may possess there a self-supporting Station – a Station supported by the voluntary contributions of an industrious people'.[2]

The community moved to their new station, Peelton, in 1848. The first years were hard, mainly because of drought and a shortage of food. Birt offered to supply millet and Indian corn for the people until they had their own crops. In return they offered to build the church and mission house. Birt obtained the money and materials for the church from friends in the colony. It pleased him that the church was 'presented to the Society free of any expense whatever'.[3] When Revd J. Freeman toured the colony in 1850 he described the church as a 'noble monument of the voluntary principle'.[4] But the move to Peelton signalled a subtle shift away from the principle as well.

Peelton was in the newly-annexed territory of British Kaffraria. In establishing British rule here the governor, Sir Harry Smith, sought the cooperation of missionaries returning to their work.[5] He offered material aid to mission stations. Birt, like others, accepted, asking for seed, a plough and yokes for the oxen. Later he applied for other tools.[6] Birt showed no concern that the voluntary principle was being infringed.

---

[2] Birt to Directors, 14 Apr. 1847, CWM SAI Box 21 FI 5D.
[3] Birt to Directors, October 1849, CWM SAI Box 24 F2 JD.
[4] J.J. Freeman, *A Tour in South Africa* (London 1851) p. 106.
[5] Southey, Circular to Missionaries, 17 Apr. 1848, CA BK 437.
[6] Birt to McKinnon, 26 July 1848 and 28 Aug. 1848, CA BK 433.

But in England the watchdogs of the voluntary principle were alert. Members of the LMS Auxiliary Society of the West Riding of Yorkshire spotted in government schedules a number of small grants to the Society's missions in South Africa, some pre-dating the peace settlement. The Auxiliary asked the Directors for an explanation and threatened to withdraw their financial support if the voluntary principle were abrogated. It took all the diplomacy the Directors could muster to pacify the Auxiliary. The Directors reaffirmed the voluntary principle and declared that as a society they had never received state aid for their missions. However, individual missionaries, in exercising the freedom that the Fundamental Principle gave them, might have accepted such grants.[7] The depth of feeling on the question may be gauged from a letter of Edward Baines on behalf of the Auxiliary.

> My own opinion would be decidedly against accepting government money for any of our Missionary schools. If we accept State aid for religious teaching, it matters little whether the teaching is in schools or in chapels; the principle is the same; and we shall soon go on to accept and crave State aid for our Missions, and, if for them, also for our Home Missions, and for our own Chapels. This is entirely to destroy the leading principle of Nonconformity ...[8]

In the colony Smith's grants had marked a small beginning of government aid. In 1855 a new governor, Sir George Grey, offered large subsidies to missionary institutions. Grey's offer came at a time of crisis for missionaries in Kaffraria, who were once again rebuilding after war. Part of Grey's frontier policy was to promote missionary and educational work to prepare the tribesmen for fuller participation in the life of the colony. The imperial government voted £40,000 per annum for this work. Most missionary societies eagerly accepted government subsidies; they used them to establish new educational institutions, particularly the industrial schools that were an important feature of Grey's programme.

But the LMS faced a dilemma. In London they had given an assurance that they stood by the voluntary principle. In the colony

---

[7] Board Minutes, 24 Oct. 1849, CWM Box 31.
[8] Baines to Freeman, 27 Sept. 1847 CWM Home Box 9 F5 JB.

the Society had taken a similar stand. In 1848 Union Chapel, Cape Town, the mother church of the LMS, had petitioned the government against increasing ecclesiastical grants. And in 1855, the very year that Grey offered his subsidies, Union Chapel again submitted a petition, asking for an end to ecclesiastical grants and the acceptance of the voluntary principle on the grounds that,

> Government grants in aid of religion have proved, and ever will prove, a fertile source of political disaffection and disorder, a constant ground for sectarian jealousy and distraction, and a serious obstacle to the progress of the gospel.[9]

Here is the colonial echo of Binney's and Baines's sentiments.

Grey's mission subsidies were primarily but not exclusively for education. Even this nice distinction made it no easier for the LMS to bend its principle. In England in the 1840s and 1850s Nonconformists had vehemently resisted government aid for their schools. Thus LMS policy could lead only to a refusal of aid from the government. But what of the missionaries on the spot?

The temptation to forego the principle and accept help was strong, especially in British Kaffraria where war had taken its toll. Indeed, in 1853 the LMS had been reluctant to reopen its Kaffrarian missions because of the costs involved, but had yielded to the pleading of Birt and others.[10] Birt's own resources were exhausted. Yet he still cherished dreams of a flourishing evangelical and educational work. The mission residents could offer little help. They had been struggling even before the war. When it ended and they returned to Peelton they had to start from scratch. The Society in London had a current deficit of £12,000 and was under severe financial strain. In these circumstances it is not surprising that even Birt should have greeted Grey's proposals with hope and enthusiasm. Without waiting for guidance from London Birt applied for a few small grants: £45 for wood for wagon making; £50 for a shoemaking business; £150 for constructing a dam on the Yellow-woods river; and a supply of school stationery.[11]

---

[9] Union Chapel, Minutes of Church Meetings, 31 May 1848 and 30 Mar. 1855, CA ACC 1697.
[10] Peelton Report 1850, CW, SAI Box 25 F5 JC.
[11] Grey to Maclean, 27 Aug. 1855, CA BK 1; Rawson to Maclean, 19 May 1855, CA BK 437; Birt to Maclean, 15 Sept. 1855, CA BK 91.

In the colony and in London the problem of the grants was aggravated by the fact that from 1853 the LMS Directors had urged the South African missions to become self-supporting. The Society could not continue supporting its missions indefinitely. In 1855 the Directors sent the Revd William Ellis to the colony to investigate how the missions could become financially independent. On the basis of his report they drew up proposals to this end.[12] Ellis also carried back to London details of Grey's new scheme for subsidies, which required a decision by the Directors.

The Kaffrarian missionaries awaited this decision with some anxiety. In August 1855 Birt wrote to the Directors on the question. His own views were ambivalent.

> If the substantial assistance can be accepted without prejudice to those high Gospel principles in which our venerable Society's operations are mainly based, and to which I do most firmly adhere, I shall of course be glad, for our necessities are urgent. But if the proposition made by His Excellency through the Rev'd. W. Ellis to your Board, be such as may not be accepted by the Society, I for one shall not have unmingled regret.[13]

The only ground for regret that he stated was that as a missionary 'enjoying the confidence of the Gaika Kafirs' he risked losing this trust if he became involved with the government.[14] On the other hand he wrote in detail of many ways that the mission could benefit from government aid. He wanted to extend the boys' school and to provide boarding facilities. He was already caring for eleven boys, five of them orphans, in his own household and received private help for only one of them. He wanted to build a larger church, to hold the Peelton members and the many neighbouring heathen who attended services. He needed an extra £200 for this and had appealed directly to Thomas Binney.

Birt told of a teacher who had moved from an LMS mission to a Free Church mission because the salary was better – £50 per annum, £40 of which came from the government. Not only were

---

[12] R. Lovett, *The History of the London Missionary Society* 2 vols. (London 1899) I p. 575.
[13] Birt to Directors, 8 Aug. 1855, CWM SAI Box 29 F4 JA.
[14] *Ibid.*

teachers' salaries inadequate at the LMS stations. Birt pointed out the inadequacy of the missionaries' allowances; 'You must be prepared for your missionaries turning traders or farmers, or else to save them from bankruptcy and disgrace every now and then.'[15]

Birt received support for his work from another missionary agency in England. From 1838 he had had the help of a teacher supplied by the Female Education Society. This society cooperated with the LMS and other missionary organisations, but was independently constituted. The Female Education Society had now offered to provide teachers for the infant and girls' schools and these teachers could care for about forty boarders. If Birt could build the school and the teachers' accommodation, the Female Education Society would furnish and equip the buildings as well as recruit the teachers. Birt estimated building costs to be about £500. He told the LMS, 'I applied to Sir George Grey for that amount and he at once granted it. I am now commencing that large building'.[16] Birt had anticipated and sidestepped any restrictions the LMS might impose on him.

These were some of the projects that Birt wrote about in August 1855. In January 1856 the Directors responded to the question of government aid for missions. Mindful of their recent unequivocal stand for the voluntary principle, mindful too of the needs of the missions, they tried to find a way to accommodate these incompatibilities. They explained that they did not see their way clear to accepting subsidies from the government. Any mission schools which did receive such subsidies would not be regarded as belonging to the Society,

> but the Missionaries are quite at liberty, in the exercise of their discretion, to avail themselves of Government grants for the promotion of the more secular objects of the Missions, or in aid of Schools, provided they are not regarded or reported as Mission schools.[17]

[15] *Ibid.*

[16] *Ibid.* This estimate was too low. By 1858 the government had provided £916. Pilkington to Maclean, Estimate for finishing Peelton Schools, 29 Jan. 1858, CA BK 91.

[17] Tidman to Birt, 23 Jan. 1856, CWM Africa Europe and Madagascar Outgoing Box 8.

Obviously the Directors found the question difficult. They stood by the voluntary principle in theory but made a loophole in practice. Birt duly informed the governor of this reply. Grey discerned a problem. Government grants were available for institutions not individuals. He referred the matter to the Chief Commissioner of British Kaffraria. Col. Maclean did not mince matters.

> I cannot realize the honesty of the theory which refuses all state support yet sanctions a particular institution accepting a grant of Government money for a water course, or other local improvement – the society won't receive it – the missionary does, and expends it, who benefits? the natives whose improvement is supposed to be the result of Voluntary contributions ... it is worse than nonsense – I can't take your money myself but my friend here will, and will apply it just as I would myself, in fact he is my agent in all other matters, and this he will also expend in my service, but I cannot receive your money, it's against my principle.[18]

Maclean's words exposed the hypocrisy of pretending that the voluntary principle was still in operation. In fact it had been abrogated. The practice no longer tallied with the theory.

Not surprisingly problems about the support for the missions remained contentious issues between the Directors and the missionaries. A brief survey will indicate a few of the problems that Birt experienced.

Although it was against government policy to make personal grants to missionaries, Grey accepted the Directors' suggestion. He gave Birt a farm, to be registered in Birt's name but used to support educational work at Peelton. This condition was written in to the grant of the land. Birt tried to make the farm profitable. He built a dam on it and ordered a watermill from England. The Female Education Society paid £200 for the machinery. Birt was convinced that a well-operated mill could bring great profits to the mission.[19] He might have been right, but the vagaries of the climate were against him. Two years of drought followed and then

---

[18] Maclean Memorandum, enclosed with Maclean to Grey, 17 July 1856, CA GH 8/29.
[19] Birt to Tidman, 8 June 1860, CWM SAI Box 32 F1 D.

devastating floods that cut a new watercourse and destroyed the immense dam structure. Birt salvaged something from the disaster by selling the mill for its original price.

In 1869 Birt visited Cape Town because of his health. He learned of a flourishing silk industry and decided to branch out into this line. He studied silk manufacture and wrote enthusiastically to the LMS about his new project to make the mission self-supporting. The Directors' response was cool, to say the least. They warned against the snares of secular pursuits. While they recognised that Birt's motives were good, they nevertheless expressed 'grave objections to their missionaries being brought into intimate personal connection with such matters as silk culture, farming or anything of a trading character'.[20] Did Birt at this time recall the warning he had previously given to the Directors that if their missionaries did not receive an adequate allowance they would be driven to become farmers or traders? Birt had poured his own money into the mission and had also received liberal support from friends and churches in England and in the colony. But this was not enough. Entrepreneurship was needed to create profits. The LMS wanted the stations to be self-supporting. Yet they discouraged initiative. In fairness it should be noted that the Directors' anxiety was in part due to a recent problem they had had with another of the Kaffrarian missionaries, who had been involved in rather shady personal profiteering.

Birt's farm schemes had failed. Peelton was still not self-supporting. Birt therefore decided to sell the farm. In 1874 he obtained £1,000 for it. Part of this he used to meet existing debts, and part he appropriated as a temporary loan towards the cost of the new church he was building. To Birt's great indignation when the Directors learned this, they admonished him for borrowing the capital for use at Peelton. They claimed the right to allocate funds from the sale of the farm for other missionary work. Birt sent a stinging reply.

> ... the said farm was given *not* for the Society's use to be employed in any other portion of the Mission field – but alone at Peelton ... surely the Board might have spared the feelings of an old man who has worked 37 years in the Mission Field

---

[20] Whitehouse to Birt, 6 Oct. 1870, CWM Africa Outgoing Box 12.

and not used language so exceedingly severe as the following: 'They deeply regret ... to find that without consulting them you have appropriated the large sum of £360 ... as a loan to your Church. Did it never occur to you that this money belonged to the Board?' Why stronger language could scarcely have been used if I had taken the sum and appropriated it to my own use!!!²¹

'Did it never occur to you that this money belonged to the Board?' No wonder Birt blazed with righteous indignation. The money did *not* belong to the Board. They had expressly chosen in 1856 *not* to accept government subsidies. The farm had been in lieu of a grant of money. In making such a claim the Directors were repudiating their former decision. Maclean's caricature of 1856 had become a reality. Birt nevertheless agreed to the Directors controlling the use of the money, provided it were spent at Peelton. From 1875 the Board allocated the funds from the sale of the farm, using them for projects at Peelton, particularly the girls' school.

When Richard Birt died in 1892 Peelton was not yet self-supporting. Birt still received his salary from the LMS, though it was channelled through the Congregational Union of South Africa, which had come into being in 1877. What had hindered Peelton from attaining financial independence? A strong case can be made out that it was the Directors' insistence on the voluntary principle, together with their strictures against commercial enterprise, that prevented the Kaffrarian missions from developing into institutions of major significance. The voluntary principle demanded an end to support from the LMS as well as the rejection of state aid for missions. But the mission communities needed training, capital and initiative to provide a point of economic take-off. Schools, industrial training centres, agricultural projects, and in some places hospitals, were part of the Christian witness and care for a people moving from one way of life to another. Young churches could not sustain the full financial burden of these enterprises. The paradox was that only through training and economic development could the members of mission communities become financially independent themselves. And this was a prerequisite to the mission church becoming financially independent.

²¹ Birt to Mullens, 13 July 1875, CWM SAI Box 38 F2 JI.

When Birt wrote in 1855 to the Directors about the possibility of receiving state aid he stated that although he still accepted the voluntary principle, he would have 'no conscientious objection to receiving government aid in the erection of schools, nor to Government donations in any way for *Education* with non inter-ference and control'.[22] This might have been a better guideline for the wider work of the gospel than the views of men like Binney and Baines, the Directors of the LMS or the deacons of Union Chapel, Cape Town. What was needed was a *modus operandi* that would allow the Society to accept financial help from outside, but would protect the Society's control over its missionary and educational work.

The voluntary principle was appropriate for a settled, econ-omically viable community. It was not necessarily suitable for a developing mission community, struggling with unstable frontier conditions, imperial expansion and social and economic transition. Flexibility was needed rather than fixed principles. A com-prehensive approach that could include farming, trading and even silk culture rather than one that separated the spiritual and secular aspects of life. In their attempt to adhere rigidly to the voluntary principle the Directors of the LMS imposed heavy burdens on their missionaries and curbed rather than encouraged the wider work of the gospel.

Rhodes University, Grahamstown

[22] Birt to Directors, 8 Aug. 1855, CWM SAI Box 29 F4 JA.

FROM CHURCH TO MISSION: AN EXAMINATION OF THE OFFICIAL MISSIONARY STRATEGY OF THE CHURCH MISSIONARY SOCIETY ON THE NIGER, 1887–93

by C. PETER WILLIAMS

CROWTHER'S consecration in 1864 did not produce a church on the Niger which was entirely independent of the CMS.[1] It remained financially dependent. Nonetheless, though technically still a mission, it had a very great deal of independence and, in some respects, it seemed to symbolize the Venn ideal – a self-governing native church. That the events of the nineties in the Niger represented a major disenchantment with Henry Venn's vision of an independent church under African administration cannot be questioned. The curtailment of Bishop Crowther's powers, the appointment of European missionaries on the Niger, the public criticism and dismissal of African ministers, and the replacement of Crowther by a European all made the point eloquently.

Considerable attention has been given to the reasons for the change. Webster, Ayandele and Ajayi have urged that it came about because of heightened racialist feelings within the society.[2] Tasie puts more emphasis on the real problems arising from Crowther's over-indulgent episcopate.[3] Porter is sceptical about the concentration on racialism and points rather to the intense missionary

---

[1] Church Missionary Society (MS, London, CMS and Birmingham, University of Birmingham). All MS references are to CMS archives unless otherwise specified.
[2] E.A. Ayandele, *Holy Johnson: Pioneer of African Nationalism, 1836–1917* (London 1970) p. 230; *The Missionary Impact on Modern Nigeria, 1842–1914: A Political and Social Analysis* (London 1966) p. 213; J.F.A. Ajayi, *Christian Missions in Nigeria, 1841–1891: The Making of a New Elite* (London 1965) pp. 263–4; J.B. Webster, *The African Churches among the Yoruba, 1888–1922* (Oxford 1964) p. 8.
[3] G.O.M. Tasie, 'The Story of Samuel Ajayi Crowther and the CMS Niger Mission Crisis of the 1880s: A Re-Assessment', *Ghana Bulletin of Theology* 4 (1974) pp. 47–60.

convictions of a new breed of young missionaries nurtured on Keswick holiness teaching and looking to Hudson Taylor-like ideals of a missionary society.[4] These ideals were of missionaries largely freed from the trammels of a London based missionary bureaucracy, living by faith and practising a simple, ascetic lifestyle.

What none of these studies have done is to examine in detail the official policy of the society. Ayandele is satisfied that the behaviour of the new young missionaries 'was fully and unblushingly endorsed by the directors of the Church Missionary Society'.[5] This paper, while agreeing with Porter in his analysis of the rationale behind the new breed of missionaries, seeks to examine how committed the society was to their perspective. It argues that the conversion of the CMS from a vision of an Africanized church to a more Europeanized mission was no more straightforward and unhesitating than that of the politicians of the period from economic to territorial imperialism.[6] It did not accept the underlying theories of its missionaries but it thought that it could control them to its own advantage. It failed. It sought to minimize the failure by distancing itself from its missionaries. While it did adopt a policy of Europeanization, initially at the behest of its missionaries, it soon became part of a strategy designed not only to assert its authority over the African church but also to reassert it over its European missionaries.

There had been moves to improve Crowther's administration as early as 1878 and these had led to an agreement in 1881 that a European secretary should be appointed.[7] Though this limited Crowther's power and was personally hurtful,[8] it was not a defeat for Venn's indigenous policy. That had always allowed for the

---

[4] A. Porter, 'Evangelical Enthusiasm, Missionary Motivation and West Africa in the Later Nineteenth Century: The Career of G.W. Brooke', *The Journal of Imperial and Commonwealth History* 6 (1977) pp. 23–46 and 'Cambridge, Keswick and Late Nineteenth Century Attitudes to Africa', *The Journal of Imperial and Commonwealth History* 5 (1976) pp. 5–34. Hudson Taylor was the founder of the China Inland Mission (hereafter CIM).

[5] Ayandele, *Holy Johnson* p. 227.

[6] C.C. Eldridge, *Victorian Imperialism* (London 1978) p. 173.

[7] G/C 1, vol 46, pp. 568–9, 5 April 1881, Committee of Correspondence Minutes (hereafter CCM).

[8] G/AZ 1/4, no. 158, 'Report of the Deputation Appointed by the Committee of the CMS to Confer with Bishop Crowther and Others ...', 1881, p. 2.

possibility of Europeans working under Africans. It is significant that the main figure behind the 1881 recommendations was J.B. Whiting, acknowledged on all sides as an ardent supporter of Venn and the African cause.[9] His recommendations were seen at the time,[10] and later[11] as being a pro-African rejection of much more hostile reports. Meanwhile wider CMS policy remained committed to creating an indigenous episcopate and there were serious efforts in this direction in Yoruba in the later eighties.[12] In brief, problems on the Niger in the eighties had shaken but had not destroyed its commitment to Crowther.[13]

J.A. Robinson was appointed as the CMS secretary on the Niger in 1887. With Wilmot Brooke he was to become the leader of the reforming group and it is therefore important to ascertain how far the CMS sent him out with instructions to carry out the policies with which he later became associated. The instructions he received were entirely compatible with Venn's objectives. He was to work in the closest possible co-operation with the bishop. The Niger mission was 'a Native mission' and the committee had no desire 'to alter its general character in this respect'. The few Europeans involved were required to work 'outside the general pastoral and evangelistic work of the Mission which still remains wholly under the charge of the African Bishop and Archdeacons'. The instructions continued:

> It is in strengthening his administration – in supporting his authority – in encouraging him by your influence and counsel – in paying the fullest possible respect to his position and office, that your support will be most wisely and effectually rendered.[14]

There was moreover no reason to think that Robinson would be an advocate of dangerous Hudson Taylor-like principles which

[9] Ayandele, *Holy Johnson* p. 157; G.O.M. Tasie, *Christian Missionary Enterprise in the Niger Delta, 1864–1918* (Leiden 1978) p. 92.
[10] Ajayi, *Christian Missions* p. 247.
[11] Lambeth Palace Archives (hereafter LPA), Benson Papers (hereafter BP) vol 166 fols 177–9 Memorandum of the Rev. J.A. Robinson, September 1890.
[12] Ayandele, *Holy Johnson* pp. 147–8, 156–7.
[13] J.P. Loiello, 'Samuel Ajayi Crowther, the Church Missionary Society and the Niger Mission, 1857–1891' (University of London PhD) pp. 273, 299, 323.
[14] G3/A3/L3, p. 35, 18 January 1887, Instructions, R. Lang and W. Gray.

would challenge the traditional basis of missionary work. One mark of the holiness enthusiast was fear of theology.[15] Robinson had a first class Cambridge degree in theology and was to cause disquiet amongst his conservative missionary colleagues because of his more advanced views of the Bible.[16] The enthusiasm for missionary work generated by Hudson Taylor was at its peak in the university world in 1884–5. Robinson left Cambridge in 1882 and had been in Germany since 1884.[17] Indeed he seems to have known little or nothing about Keswick or the CIM. When Brooke met him in 1889 he instructed him concerning 'the absolute claim of Christ on his servants, and their absolute possession of him'. He went on to explain the principles and practice of the CIM and he recorded in his diary: 'He was much impressed thereby: he had heard nothing before.'[18]

It is consistent with this that Lang, the home secretary with particular responsibility for Africa, was concerned in his correspondence with Robinson to encourage the development of a truly indigenous ministry. The problem was that nearly all the native ministers were in fact from Sierra Leone and seemed to be highly Europeanized. He constantly stressed to Robinson the need to encourage a more simple life-style for the church leaders and identification with the people amongst whom they worked.[19] There is little doubt that this impatience with Europeanized Africans and habits was a by-product of the ascetic emphasis of the period.[20] European missionaries should also live more simply. The thinking was symbolized in the 'Missionary Controversy' within the Wesleyan Methodist Missionary Society,[21] and in the attacks on extravagant missionary life-style by Canon Isaac Taylor.[22] Though it was

---

[15] C.P. Williams, 'The Recruitment and Training of Overseas Missionaries in England between 1850 and 1900' (University of Bristol MLitt 1976) pp. 182–3.

[16] Acc 82 F 4/7, Pt. 2, pp. 42 and 182, 17 April 1889 and 5 March 1890, G.W. Brooke's diary.

[17] *Register of Missionaries (Clerical, Lay and Female) and Native Clergy, 1804–1904* (private circulation nd) no. 1044.

[18] Acc 82, F 4/7, Pt. 2, p. 52, 23 April 1889, Brooke's diary.

[19] G3/A3/L3, p. 61, 20 July 1887, Lang and Gray to Robinson and p. 76, 5 August 1887, Lang to Robinson.

[20] Williams, 'Recruitment and Training', p. 176; E. Stock, *History of the Church Missionary Society* 3 vols (London 1899) 3 pp. 356, 361, 433; Porter, 'Evangelical Enthusiasm' p. 28.

[21] Wesleyan Methodist Missionary Society, *The Missionary Controversy: Discussion, Evidence and Report* (London 1890).

[22] Isaac Taylor, 'The Great Missionary Failure' *Fortnightly Review* 44 (1888) pp. 488–500.

influential on Keswick, it had roots which were quite separate and indeed with its emphasis on developing a truly indigenous church it seemed entirely congenial with Venn. It is significant that though Robinson shared the analysis,[23] he was, in contrast to his position after he had come under the influence of Brooke, far from being 'utterly pessimistic' in his assessment of the native church.[24] Consequently his ideas about reform in no sense excluded Africans and he suggested, for example, that Archdeacon Crowther, who a few years later was regarded as typifying all that was most unacceptable about the Niger church, should be made a suffragan bishop.[25] Meanwhile Bishop Crowther's influence at Salisbury Square remained considerable enough to secure the rejection of some of Robinson's reforming proposals.[26] In brief, though Robinson had radical ideas, they were consistent with past policy and, in any case, there was no certainty that the society would accept them.

What changed the direction irrevocably was the appointment of Brooke. He had a strong, impatient personality. His holiness convictions made him intolerant of any spirituality which appeared to fall below his own rather narrow and extremely intense ideal. He believed that he was part of a process called to do for African missions what Hudson Taylor had accomplished in China.[27] Why did the CMS, normally extremely cautious, appoint him and allow him to become an independent missionary and consequently somewhat less under its control?[28] He had not been to its training institution at Islington. He was not ordained. His Anglicanism was in some question as he had reservations about infant baptism and the necessity of ordained presidency at the Lord's Supper.[29] He was not qualified in any profession. He had however two advantages likely to appeal to selectors. He was prepared to pay for himself and, much more significantly, he was a symbol of precisely that committed enthusiasm emanating from holiness circles which

[23] G3/A3/1887/68, 26 May 1887, Robinson to Lang.
[24] G/Y/A3/1/1J, 7 May 1888, Robinson to Lang.
[25] G3/A3/1888/108, 17 October 1888, Robinson to Lang.
[26] G3/A3/L3, p. 142, 27 July 1888, Lang to Robinson.
[27] Porter, 'Evangelical Enthusiasm' pp. 34–5.
[28] G/C 1, vol 53, pp. 269–71, 8 January 1889, CCM.
[29] G3/A3/1888/115, 17 December 1888, Brooke to Lang.

the CMS wanted to tap.[30] Within the CMS power-structure Eugene Stock, by far the longest serving secretary, had emerged as in many ways the most forceful personality,[31] and as editorial secretary his interests were primarily in developing the society in England. He had clear links with Keswick spirituality.[32] He greatly admired Brooke[33] who in turn regarded him as the man in CMS closest to his own thinking and 'a cautious reformer'.[34] There is no doubt that he played a key role in Brooke's appointment.[35] The honorary secretary, F.R. Wigram, who significantly, and unlike any other holder of the most important post in the CMS hierarchy, had had day to day dealings with the foreign field excluded from his brief,[36] had consequently a primary interest in promoting the society's image in England[37] and was close to Stock and involved in the attempts to identify the society more closely with holiness spirituality.[38]

The decision to appoint Brooke was, from the society's point of view, deeply dangerous. The signals were there from the very beginning. His farewell meeting was organized, not by the CMS, but by those noted for their radical application of holiness theology to missionary strategy.[39] The proceedings shocked the society's representative, Whiting, because of the explicit criticism of the CMS.[40] The society had however in the past demonstrated an ability to appeal to radicalism and, at the same time, to dull its effect through its complex institutional committee and secretarial mechanisms.[41] It evidently hoped to do the same with Brooke by keeping a watchful eye on him. Consequently Lang wrote to Robinson indicating 'our anxiety regarding our dear friend. Indiscreet language on his part may be the occasion of difficulty and mischief. He is so devoted that unless he is under control he may

---

[30] Stock, *History* 3 pp. 361, 433.

[31] G/AC 4/7/1360a, 31 May 1891, R.N. Cust to F.E. Wigram.

[32] E. Stock, *My Recollections* (London 1909) pp. 200–3.

[33] *Ibid.* p. 162.

[34] Acc 82 F 4/7, Pt. 2 p. 148, 10 October 1889, Brooke's diary.

[35] Stock, *Recollections* pp. 161–2.

[36] Stock, *History* 3 pp. 260–1.

[37] G/AC 2/32, pp. 7–10, 2 November 1889, Wigram to H. Moule.

[38] Stock, *Recollections* pp. 142, 143–4, 203, 250–1.

[39] Porter, 'Evangelical Enthusiasm' p. 34.

[40] G3/A3/L3, p. 192, 22 March 1889, Lang to Robinson.

[41] Williams, 'Recruitment and Training' p. 279.

run off in any direction, and, with the most single purpose in his own mind act very unwisely.'[42] In brief, the society was fully aware of the dangers which Brooke posed but equally confident of its own capacity to tame him. That policy was doomed to failure because Brooke, who could have a mesmeric influence,[43] quickly brought Robinson to share his convictions.[44] Its existence does however once again show how far the CMS was from simply underwriting Brooke's radicalism. The society was certainly foolish to employ a man likely to challenge its own *raison d'être*. That is very different from saying that it employed him because it subscribed to the challenge which he was to bring.

The directions which the society sent to the field as Brooke was preparing to go to the Niger indicate no change of policy. The inappropriateness of grandiose buildings, the risk of 'denationalizing' the 'natives' and the need for a more simple life-style were all emphasized.[45] Robinson, now home, had however, under the influence of Brooke, a new theme. He concentrated not only on the failure to produce 'an indigenous form of Christianity', not only on the unsatisfactory 'black Englishmen' but on 'the negro' incapacity to rule. He went on to propose the retirement of Bishop Crowther and the introduction of a European head and a greater number of European missionaries.[46] In the first real sign of change the society accepted part of his case, but essentially using arguments within a Venn-like framework. It agreed that more European missionaries were needed, but it did so because the work was not being undertaken on sufficiently spiritual grounds nor by indigenous 'natives' 'but by Africans who are strangers, not only in race, but also in training and association, to the people amongst whom they work.' What, significantly, it did not agree to was the retirement of Crowther, rather he was to be invited to England for a conference on the changes proposed.[47] He returned, as did

---

[42] Lang to Robinson, 22 March 1889, loc. cit.

[43] G/AC 2/38, p. 289, 30 November 1891, Wigram to S. Gedge.

[44] Stock, *History* 3 p. 363.

[45] G3/A3/L3, pp. 181–183, 15 February 1889, Lang to Archdeacon Crowther and pp. 190–1, 21 March 1889, Lang to G.F. Packer.

[46] G/Y/A3/1/1A/16, 20 June 1889, Robinson Memorandum; G/Y/A3/1/1/J, 20 June 1889, Robinson to Lang; G3/A3/1889/86, 9 July 1889, Robinson to Lang.

[47] G3/A3/P3/1889, 12 August 1889, General Committee Minutes (hereafter GCM).

Brooke, and there were frequent conferences involving the bishop, Brooke, Robinson and Lang.[48] The result was an acceptance of resolutions which agreed not only to more European missionaries and to fairly sweeping changes in the conditions of the African agents, but to Brooke's 'simple and more economical' methods being tried in the Upper Niger. Most ominously it was also resolved that Brooke's unique experience qualified him 'in a peculiar measure for a prominent share in the conduct of the Mission'. He was to be a joint leader with Robinson.[49]

That the CMS gave such an endorsement to its European missionaries at this stage was partly because of the cumulative evidence of problems on the Niger, partly because Europeans were available but largely because of the evident impact on finance and personnel of a cause as exciting as the conversion of 'Mohammedans' on the Upper Niger and Sudan, particularly when presented by a figure both as charismatic and as close to the missionary commitment of holiness spirituality as Brooke. He was very well aware of this factor. He began almost immediately a constant barrage of threats to reveal his findings about the Niger church to the British public. As early as July he was speaking not only of laying the true state of affairs before the committee but also before 'friends of the Committee at Cambridge'. Cambridge was the centre of the new missionary enthusiasm. It represented precisely the constituency which the CMS had envied for years and was now beginning to penetrate.[50] The unusual underlining in blue pencil of 'and friends at Cambridge' by a reader at Salisbury Square is an indication that the threat was not lost.[51] It is revealing of the atmosphere that in the same month as the resolutions were passed six Cambridge men, along with Brooke now as a full missionary, were accepted for Africa. Stock comments that the committee meeting which accepted them was 'one of the most memorable on record'.[52] Indeed far more graduates, and most of them from Cambridge, were sent out by the CMS in the following year than in any other through the

---

[48] G3/A3/L3, p. 225a, 10 January 1890, Lang and Wigram to native clergy and lay agents.

[49] G/C 1, vol 54 pp. 224–33, 9 December 1889, GCM.

[50] Williams, 'Recruitment and Training' pp. 8–9.

[51] G3/A3/1889/118, 16 July 1889, Brooke to Lang.

[52] Stock, *History* 3 p. 364.

whole century.[53] Stock's observation is illuminating: '... when men saw that the Church Missionary Society could accept a Graham Brooke and a Barclay Buxton and look kindly on the plans of Heywood Horsburgh, they were more ready to join a body which some regarded as stiff and old-fashioned.'[54] It even took the very unusual step of agreeing to a separate committee to handle support and funds for the Sudan and Upper Niger.

Despite the undoubted retreat from Venn's orthodoxy, close examination reveals that the support of the committee, even at this stage, was much less than total. Bishop Crowther remained as the ultimate spiritual authority and even gave his blessing to the new proposals if the European missionaries would come 'as *fellow labourers, with Christian sympathy and brotherly love, as servants of the same Master*'.[55] The society pointedly underlined these qualities to both Brooke and Robinson.[56] The bishop, even with his power largely gone, was likely to be a barrier to change and this Robinson saw and said very clearly.[57] If the society had been committed to the precise policies of its new missionaries, it should have been prepared to adopt the more ruthless methods which they urged. It did not because it was trying to gain all the advantages of the new spirituality while still holding to some of the central ingredients of the old. The fact that this objective was unrealistic does explain why it got the worst of all possible worlds. It explains also why later it could be thought by both European and African missionaries to have sold out to the other. It does not justify the historian agreeing with either assessment when the evidence is of a much more complex and less logically clear-cut commitment.

Brooke and Robinson returned to the Niger with a new party of like-minded missionaries and began the task of reform with a fearsome and intolerant energy. Everything had to be rooted up.[58] Soon, however, the attack was turned on the society and the secretaries. They were guilty of concealing the awful reality of the

---

[53] Williams, 'Recruitment and Training', tables 1A–E. Thirty-five graduates became missionaries in 1890, 24 from Cambridge (CMS, *Register*).

[54] Stock, *History* 3 p. 433.

[55] G3/A3/1889/166, 9 December 1889, Bishop Crowther's Observations.

[56] G3/A3/L3, pp. 245–7, 21 January 1890, Lang and Wigram's instructions to Brooke and pp. 229–33, 13 January 1890, instructions to Robinson.

[57] G3/A3/1889/86, 9 July 1889, Robinson to Lang.

[58] G3/A3/1890/93, 5 June 1890, Brooke to General Touch.

mission. They did not allow missionaries the sort of independence which Brooke, with his eyes on the CIM, regarded as necessary. There must be a purge, not only in the Niger, but in all the society's African fields.[59] Matters came to a head at the meeting of the local governing body, the Finance Committee at Onitsha, in August 1890. Though Bishop Crowther was chairman, African representation had been reduced and the old man was humiliated and his archdeacon son was suspended along with several other African clergy.[60] Civilized, let alone Christian, relationships broke down completely between European and African. The attack had been carefully planned[61] and it was linked to a long and bitterly harsh memorandum on the Niger with carefully tabulated details of African misdemeanour particularly designed for the home committee. The church was 'a seething mass of corruption not mere wickedness and decay, but active and virulent evil'. For this the society was to blame because in its commitment to Venn's policies it had 'grossly deceived' the Christian public for years. Again there came the threat to reveal all and the consequences would shake the society 'more than a dozen Canon Taylors, or trouble with Bishops in Ceylon or Reredos' at home.'[62] The action of the Finance Committee and the language of the memorandum together reveal men driven by a passionate and narrow vision to something disturbingly close to hatred. What is notable for our purposes is that the critique was directed so powerfully at the society. From the perspective of the missionaries, the society, far from supporting them, carried the ultimate responsibility for the real state of affairs on the Niger.

The administration at home was taken aback by the ferocity of the passion engendered on the Niger. Its actions reveal shocked, cautious, frightened, and rather divided men. It is not surprising that it dissented from the analysis and methods of its missionaries, but its dissent emerged slowly and somewhat in code. Typically

---

[59] *Ibid.* /124, 6 August 1890, Brooke to Lang and /122, 5 August, Robinson to Lang.
[60] *Ibid.* /165, 18–28 August 1890, Minutes of Finance Committee.
[61] *Ibid.* /122, 5 August 1890, Robinson to Lang.
[62] LPA, BP, vol 166, fols 102, 184, September 1890, Robinson's Memorandum. His references were to controversial events in CMS's recent history, Stock, *History* 3 pp. 203–16, 333–9, 343–8.

the first decision was to set up 'a select and influential Sub-Committee' to deal with all the issues relating to the Niger.[63] At the same time there was an attempt to deal with the participants and to soothe or to warn as appropriate. Here divisions within the secretariat began to appear. Wigram wrote rather vaguely to Brooke about the need for reorganization in the society,[64] and sympathetically to Crowther.[65] He remained however more committed to his missionaries,[66] no doubt very aware of their importance in the appeal for a thousand extra missionaries which was being urged on the society by its supporters.[67] The African secretary, Lang, who was closer to the realities in West Africa and who was not as Webster contends a supporter of Wigram,[68] was much more critical of the missionaries. He argued that their evidence did not amount to very much. It was legally flimsy. Opportunity must be given to the accused to exculpate themselves.[69] Bishop Crowther must be respected and given an important place in decision making. Neither did Lang hide his distaste for the events at the Onitsha Finance Committee. 'We cannot conceal the profound sadness which the reading of these minutes has produced upon our minds.'[70] He also made a characteristically Venn-like point that standards of judgement for an infant church in a 'heathen' country had to be different, and that as well as denunciation there must be 'loving consideration for the offender, and a patient effort to recover him and lead him on into true light.'[71] He wrote to Bishop Crowther sympathizing with him for 'the very real pain and sorrow' he had been caused and hinting that the society's views might be rather different from those of either European or African on the Niger.[72]

The sub-committee appointed included leading Afrophiles such as R.N. Cust, Whiting and Sidney Gedge. Their influence was

[63] G3/A3/L3, p. 316, 18 October 1890, Lang to Robinson.
[64] G3/A3/L3, pp. 323–4, 22 October 1890, Wigram to Brooke.
[65] *Ibid.* pp. 321–2, 22 October 1890, Wigram to Bishop Crowther.
[66] G/Y/A3/1/1J, 21 November 1890, 'Rough Notes' of Niger Sub-Committee.
[67] Stock, *History* 3 pp. 669–71.
[68] Webster, *African Churches* pp. 27–8, 31.
[69] G3/A3/L3, pp. 316–8, 18 October 1890, Lang to Robinson.
[70] *Ibid.* pp. 348–50, 18 November 1890, Lang and Gray to Dobinson.
[71] *Ibid.* pp. 336–7, 7 November 1890, Lang to Dobinson.
[72] *Ibid.* pp. 319–20, 24 October 1890.

considerable and certainly the missionaries who brought the accusations judged its mood to be hostile to them. Eden, the secretary of the Lower Niger, complained that its members felt 'that their European agents used frequently very unparliamentary language during the sitting of the Finance Committee and failed to treat the aged bishop with that respect which was due to him'.[73] He was consequently convinced that its conclusions were biased against him.[74] Brooke was aggrieved that he was only allowed to see the committee once and then only after threatening, in characteristic fashion, to go to the press. When he met it he was asked no questions and had to make a statement to which two or three leading members objected.[75] He considered, almost certainly correctly, that some members of the committee were seeking his disconnection.[76]

There is no doubt that the committee was very divided.[77] One faction wanted reform.[78] Its leader was Stock and its chief organ was the influential and prestigious *Church Missionary Intelligencer*.[79] Within the society Wigram supported Stock, while Lang wanted 'to do as little as possible', going on '*quietly, faithfully, circumspectly*', sympathizing with and encouraging the missionaries but 'urging all due care and proper loyalty to the powers that be.'[80] The Stock/Wigram group was not dominant. Stock, for example, in the course of the discussions proposed a motion 'expressing the regret of the Committee at the evident tendency of the African members of the Finance Committee to oppose honest efforts to relieve the Mission of men of doubtful character.'[81] It did not appear in the report. Though the Afrophiles were not a majority, they did possess sufficient knowledge and legal skills to make them

---

[73] G3/A3/1890/214, received December 1890, F.N. Eden Memorandum.

[74] G/Y/A3/1/1A/32, 22 January 1891, Eden to Wigram.

[75] G3/A3/1891/169, 28 May 1891, Brooke to Lang.

[76] *Ibid.* /208, 17 July 1891, Brooke to Lang.

[77] *Ibid.* and Eden to Wigram, loc. cit.; Stock, *History* 3 p. 393.

[78] Acc 82 F 4/7, Pt. 2 pp. 147–8, 10 October 1889, Brooke's diary.

[79] G/AC 4/7/1360a, 31 May 1891, Cust to Wigram.

[80] G/AC 4/7/1257, 29 December 1890, Lang to Wigram.

[81] G3/CS 1, pp. 49–50, 8 December 1890, Minutes of the Special Niger Sub-Committee. Stock's name has been crossed through in the minute book but his general stance makes it probable that this was a decision about the detail of the minutes rather than their accuracy. No other name was substituted.

powerful.[82] Between the two groups there were those with less knowledge[83] or clear-cut opinions. They were concerned about the ecclesiastical implications of the missionaries' treatment of the Crowthers[84] and their inclination was therefore to support something akin to the *status quo*. Among these there would, certainly in the General Committee, have been some committed to voting against anything which appeared to be a departure from the Venn orthodoxy.[85] Consequently the eventual resolutions which were produced in a report form were something of a compromise.[86] The claim that it upheld all that the Europeans had been fighting for except the removal of Crowther[87] can scarcely be sustained if any attention is given either to its detail or to the reactions of the missionaries.

Certainly the report was far from satisfactory from an African perspective. It called for even more European missionaries; it suspended some African agents; it appended a tendentious account of Crowther's episcopate and it failed to apologize for Onitsha. However, from the missionaries' view-point it was also highly defective. It appeared to be motivated by personal animus against them.[88] It declared the suspension of Archdeacon Crowther to be null and void; it reinstated other deposed Africans, albeit under European supervision; it acknowledged the services of its European missionaries but abstained 'from discussing certain matters of detail which might otherwise be regarded as fairly open to criticism'; it hoped that on calmer reflection Eden, Brooke and Robinson would 'feel that the strong language used was not justified by the circumstances of the case, and that the tone adopted towards the Bishop and Archdeacon was not such as was due to their age and office' and, to their evident humiliation, it freed Robinson and Brooke from their seats on the Finance Committee. The major role

---

[82] G3/A3/1891/208, 17 July 1891, Brooke to Lang; for Whiting's considerable role see G3/CS 1, pp. 43–4, 5 December 1890, Special Niger Sub-Committee Minutes.
[83] G/Y/A3/1/1A/32, 22 January 1891, Eden to Wigram.
[84] G3/A3/L3, pp. 336–7, 7 November 1890, Lang to Dobinson.
[85] R.N. Cust, 'The Committee of the Church Missionary Society: A Retrospect', *Church Missionary Intelligencer* (hereafter *CMI*) ns 25 (1900) p. 733.
[86] G/C 1, vol 55 pp. 208–13, 20 January 1891, Special GCM.
[87] Ayandele, *Missionary Impact* p. 220.
[88] G3/A3/1891/208, 17 July 1891, Brooke to Lang.

of the Afrophiles on the sub-committee had not been without effect.

Brooke at first accepted the report, though in a martyred sort of fashion. 'It is far better that we should have been wronged than the Africans'.[89] He very soon however began to react angrily against it because it obscured, in typical CMS fashion, he maintained, the reality.[90] Eden was convinced that a wrong impression had been given and that the sympathetic elements on the committee had been over-ruled.[91] To Robinson it was first 'a terrible disappointment' and then a 'grave injustice'.[92] Even the mild and generous Dobinson, later to be so positive in his assessment of Africans and so ashamed of his involvement at Onitsha, complained that the report had passed a vote of no confidence in the leaders of the mission.[93] The consequence was a remarkable joint-letter from all the missionaries declaring that the report was dishonest, that key documents had been withheld from the General Committee by the sub-committee and that if action were not taken then the resignation of all the missionaries with all the consequent publicity and effect on funds must ensue.[94] It was a rare, perhaps unprecedented, event for CMS missionaries to threaten mass mutiny and it effectively demonstrates that whatever may be true of CMS policy, its missionaries were very far from perceiving it as a mirror-image of their objectives.

The anger which the report produced in West Africa has been well chronicled.[95] What has not been noticed is the effect of the crisis on the secretarial nerve and therefore on CMS policy. Both Wigram and Lang were indisposed for long periods.[96] With a reduced leadership the society lost whatever sensitivity and cohesion it had had. It was, commented one observer, in a 'panic

---

[89] *Ibid.* /31, 24 January 1891, Brooke to Lang.
[90] *Ibid.* /169, 28 May 1891, Brooke to Lang.
[91] G/Y/A3/1/1A/32, 22 January 1891, Eden to Wigram.
[92] G3/A3/1891/112, 27 March 1891, Robinson to Lang and /122, 8 April 1891.
[93] G3/A3/1891/142, 23 April 1891, H.H. Dobinson to Lang. Cf. Webster, *African Churches*, p. 17 for his later position.
[94] G3/A3/1891/175, June 1891, Joint Letter from the Niger Missionaries.
[95] Ayandele, *Holy Johnson* cap. 9.
[96] G3/A3/L3, p. 419, 20 February 1891, B. Baring-Gould to Bishop Crowther. From the letter-books it appears that Wigram returned in May and Lang in the autumn.

altogether unworthy of it'.[97] It was sufficiently insensitive to suggest to Bishop Crowther that he should accept Eden, one of the principal actors at Onitsha, as his archdeacon.[98] Crowther's proposal that an independent Niger Delta Pastorate be established[99] revealed the deep uncertainty. It was, from one perspective, mutiny. From another it was the completion of a goal to which the society had always aspired. There were still forces sufficiently supportive of the traditional aspirations in the influential Group Committee responsible for Africa for the proposal to be accepted provided Crowther's power was limited to the Delta.[100] It was subsequently rejected,[101] but its initial acceptance is an indication that, though driven to compromise, the Afrophiles were not without influence.[102]

By the autumn of 1891 the society had mutiny threatened by the African church in the Delta and by its missionaries. As far as the missionaries were concerned its response was at first aggressively negative. The secretaries played on the inappropriateness of young missionaries questioning the judgements of committees whose leading members had had twenty or thirty years experience. They declared that Robinson had 'painfully exaggerated' and asserted that they were glad for his sake that his exaggerations were not widely known.[103] The missionaries were in no mood to succumb to such blustering, particularly as Robinson had died and they saw their attack as being sacred to his name.[104] One of them, Harford-Battersby, was allowed to put their case in October. His position was uncompromising. Africans should not be chosen for the higher positions in the West African church at present and the plans which had allowed them so to do had 'allowed zeal to outrun discretion, and sentiment to have greater weight than sober facts.' The missionaries had been mistreated by the sub-committee. Much of the

[97] G3/A3/1891/41, 21 January 1891, J. Milner to Cust.
[98] Baring-Gould to Crowther, 20 February 1891, loc. cit. pp. 417–9.
[99] G3/A3/1891/131, 8 May 1891, Crowther to CMS.
[100] G3/A3/P3/1891, 15 July 1891, Group 3 Sub-Committee.
[101] G/C 1, vol 55 pp. 586–7, 21 July 1891, CCM.
[102] G/AC 4/8/1410, 25 July 1891, Whiting to Wigram.
[103] G3/A3/L3, pp. 485–9, 31 July 1891, secretaries to the European missionaries of the Lower and Upper Niger.
[104] G3/A3/1891/233A, 1 October 1891, Preface to the joint letter.

administration of the society was 'radically unsound'.[105] Under this pressure and the threat of a public scandal[106] the society capitulated. Wigram in particular was desperately worried at the prospect of a break with the missionaries and felt it crucially important that they should not have 'the shadow of a grievance' against the committee.[107] Three committee members were appointed to re-examine the missionaries' case.[108] They recommended that the sub-committee's report be accepted but that a letter be sent 'expressive of their solemn sense of the need that exists for a higher moral and spiritual tone on the part of the West African Churches.'[109] This was not to the liking of either all the secretariat or all the committee,[110] but was accepted by Wigram as part of the price of getting the sub-committee report accepted, of in other words buying off the missionaries.

The letter which was sent to West Africa was a pusillanimous piece of work which well justifies Ayandele's judgement that it was the language of the Scramble Era in the corridors of Salisbury Square.[111] It argued the case for a European presence on the grounds of African weakness and it defended the actions of the missionaries.[112] The sense of balance which was, in measure, still retained in the report was now lost. The society had apparently come close to its missionaries. That it changed its position at this juncture is not in doubt. It did so partly because of fear of the damage the missionaries might inflict on its image, partly because Wigram and Stock had sympathy with their aspirations – Stock went off on a European holiday with the objectionable Harford-Battersby shortly after he had given his evidence[113] – partly because the Afrophiles had gradually been effectively silenced or manœu-

---

[105] G/Y/A3/1/1A/37, 13 October 1891, C.F. Harford-Battersby to the General Committee.
[106] G3/A3/1891/263, 17 September 1891, Brooke to secretaries.
[107] G/AC 2/38, pp. 287–90, 30 November 1891, Wigram to Gedge.
[108] G/C 1, vol 55 pp. 668–70, 13 Oct. 1891, GCM.
[109] G3/CS 1, p. 83 23 October 1891, Special Conference on the Niger Mission.
[110] Wigram to Gedge, loc. cit.
[111] Ayandele, Holy Johnson p. 241.
[112] G3/A3/P3/1891, 4 November 1891, Statement and letter from Wigram and C.C. Fenn to the West African Christians connected with the Church Missionary Society.
[113] G3/A3/1891/269, 10 November 1891, Harford-Battersby to Lang.

vred off the most important committees,[114] and partly because the imperialistic attraction of being a 'Governing Body' with responsibilities over 'the governed' had begun to counter the traditional commitment to working for independence.[115] That the society moved in the way that it did was a considerable triumph for the unrelenting pressure and blackmail of its missionaries. They were however far from satisfied[116] for though the society had moved away from its confidence in African leadership, it had not given Brooke the independence which he wanted nor had it endorsed his methods of evangelism.

What the following years reveal is a sustained effort to secure CMS 'direction and control'.[117] Trusted supporters of the traditional policy such as Cust and Lang felt compelled to resign.[118] They were part of the substantial minority who wanted Crowther replaced by another African.[119] Whiting was so at odds with the society that he refused to write the *Intelligencer* obituary for his great friend Bishop Crowther.[120] The Afrophiles were driven to working through Archbishop Benson.[121] The CMS seemed determined to make no concessions to the Niger Delta Pastorate because amongst other reasons it had not evolved according to the pattern preordained by the CMS.[122] It was the voice of institutionalized paternalism.

It is however important to see in closing that its voice was also raised, though more discreetly, against the European missionaries.

---

[114] Whiting was obliged to resign from the Group Sub-Committee (G/AC 4/8/1406, 23 July 1891 Whiting to Wigram). Cust agreed not to speak on Niger matters (ibid. /1439a, 28 September 1891, Cust to Wigram).

[115] G/AC 2/36 p. 987, 10 July 1891, Wigram to Whiting and p. 949, 9 July 1891, Wigram to Cust.

[116] G3/A3/1892/81, 21 January 1892, Brooke to Lang and /237, 6 December 1892, E. Lewis to CMS.

[117] G3/A3/L3, p. 501, 17 November 1891, Instructions to Archdeacon J. Hamilton and Rev. W. Allan.

[118] LPA, BP vol 165 fols 49–50, 24 May 1892, Cust to Archbishop Benson. This resignation was from the Committee of Correspondence. G/AC 4/8/1572a, 8 February 1892, Lang to Wigram.

[119] *CMI* ns 17 (1892) pp. 546–8 and G3/A3/L4, p. 66, 26 February 1892, Lang to Hamilton for Lang's mind on the matter.

[120] G/AC 4/8/1522, 11 January 1892, Whiting to Lang.

[121] LPA, BP vol 165 fols 85–90, 8 June 1892, Whiting to Benson and fols 102–3, 28 June 1892, Cust to Benson.

[122] *Ibid.* fols 79–84, 3 June 1892, Wigram to Benson.

Hill, the CMS choice to succeed Crowther, though very sym-pathetic to Keswick spirituality,[123] was also a long serving CMS missionary. He was not a university man but had been trained at Islington and was rather looked down on by some because of his humble background.[124] He was, in other words, a classic old-style CMS missionary. He had no sympathy with 'the rush to the mission field of untrained, inexperienced workers, acting on the mere cry that "the heathen are perishing"'.[125] He was not afraid to be critical of the inexperienced Brooke and Robinson.[126] In particular he did not like Brooke's CIM model[127] and therefore concluded that the principles of the Sudan Mission were impossible and should be abandoned.[128] The society, despite Brooke-like complaints and resignation from his successor Lewis,[129] meanwhile opened up the possibility of volunteers being accepted, even for the pioneer Sudan, on a more normal basis.[130] It allowed the separate organization which Brooke had established to be dissolved.[131] It marked the end, though the society never officially admitted it, and indeed Stock asserted the opposite,[132] of an unsuc-cessful experiment.

The CMS, not surprisingly given the very wide spectrum of evangelicalism which it represented, was never a mere reflection of Brooke and Robinson. It was influenced nonetheless. It caught some of their defensive intolerance. It began to exhibit a little less the generosity of the age of philanthropy and a little more the hard dynamism of the age of expansion. It cannot be said however that it ever committed itself to one simple ideology and certainly neither

---

[123] G/AC 4/8/1514, 7 January 1892, J.S. Hill to Wigram. Crowther died in Dec. 1891, Stock, *History* 3 p. 396.

[124] LPA, BP vol 165 fols 417–8, 25 June 1893, Cust to Benson; P.E.H. Hair, 'Archdeacon Crowther and the Delta Pastorate, 1892–9' *Sierra Leone Bulletin of Religion* 5 (1963) p. 23.

[125] R.E. Faulkner, *Joseph Sidney Hill: First Bishop of Western Equatorial Africa* (London 1895) p. 116.

[126] LPA, BP vol 165 fols 244–265, 20 December 1892, Hill's Memorandum to Benson.

[127] G3/A3/1892/224, 30 September 1892, Hill to Harford-Battersby.

[128] *Ibid.* /1893/41, 31 January 1893, Hill to F. Baylis.

[129] *Ibid.* /1892/237, received 6 December 1892, Lewis to CMS. Brooke died in March 1892, Stock, *History* 3 p. 394.

[130] G3/A3/L4, pp. 167–171, 6 December 1892, CCM.

[131] *Ibid.* pp. 198, 24 February 1893, Baylis to Hill.

[132] *CMI* ns 19 (1894) p. 146.

to racialism nor to the missionary principles of the CIM. The point is of some importance. It explains why the society first feted and then tolerated Brooke while eventually rejecting his principles, why it never entirely abandoned confidence in the African capacity to lead and why it therefore, and the point is a considerable puzzle to Ayandele,[133] continued to be admired by African church leaders such as James Johnson. The traumatic events of the early nineties caused it to depart from its original principles without ever abandoning them totally. It moved from a firm commitment to the development of an independent church, which had never quite excluded its own role as a mission, to a firm determination to emphasize its role as a mission, which was never however quite to exclude the goal of the independent self-governing church. If it learned from Brooke and Robinson to distrust African leadership in the church, it learned also the danger of relaxing central control over its own missionaries. Both lessons underlined the importance of a well organized mission and made more distant the prospect of an independent church.

Trinity College, Bristol

[133] Ayandele, *Holy Johnson* pp. 32, 79, 331–2.

BUILDING THE "CATHOLIC GHETTO": CATHOLIC ORGANISATIONS 1870–1914*

by HUGH McLEOD

'IT was a ghetto, undeniably,' concluded the American political journalist, Garry Wills, when recalling from the safe distance of 1971 his 'Catholic Boyhood'. 'But not a bad ghetto to grow up in.'[1] Wills's ghetto was defined by the great body of shared experiences, rituals, relationships, which gave Catholics a strongly felt common identity, and separated them from their Protestant and Jewish neighbours who knew none of these things. Wills talked about priests and nuns, incense and rosary beads, cards of saints and statues of the Virgin, but in this essay said very little about Catholic organisations (apart from a brief reference to the Legion of Decency). In many European countries, by contrast, any reference to the 'ghetto' from which many Catholics were seeking to escape in the 1960s and '70s inevitably focused on the network of specifically Catholic organisations which was so characteristic of central and north-west European societies in the first half of the twentieth century. The Germans even have a pair of words to describe this phenomenon, *Vereins-* or *Verbandskatholizismus*, which can be defined as the multiplication of organisations intended to champion the interests of Catholics as a body, and to meet the special needs, spiritual, economic or recreational, of every identifiable group within the Catholic population. So when in 1972 the Swiss historian Urs Altermatt wrote a book on the origins of the highly self-conscious and disciplined Swiss Catholic sub-culture, the result was an organisational history, as stolid and as soberly objective as Wills's book was whimsical and partisan. Its purpose was to determine how it came about that so many a Catholic 'was born in a Catholic

* I wish to thank the British Academy and Social Science Research Council for research grants, and Elizabeth Roberts for permission to quote from oral history interviews.
[1] G. Wills, *Bare Ruined Choirs* (New York 1974) p. 37.

hospital, went to Catholic schools (from kindergarten to university), read Catholic periodicals and newspapers, later voted for candidates of the Catholic Party and took part as an active member in numerous Catholic societies', being also 'insured against accident and illness with a Catholic benefit organisation, and placing his money in a Catholic savings bank'.[2]

The most important of the organisations described by Altermatt were founded between about 1890 and 1914, though many of them had a pre-history dating back to the aftermath of the Swiss civil war of 1847. A number of recent studies of American Catholicism have also established the significance of the years around the turn of the century, when the advocates of a fortress-like and Roman-oriented Church decisively defeated those who advocated a more liberal and distinctively 'American' Catholicism.[3] This paper will try to place the Swiss and American examples in a broader context by providing an overview of the development of Catholic subcultures in the United States and in the relatively industrialised countries of central and north-western Europe between about 1870 and 1914. Besides Switzerland and the United States, the other countries to be included will be Belgium, the Netherlands, Great Britain, Germany, Austria and France. Detailed examples will be taken mainly from Germany, Britain and the U.S.A. The paper will begin by assessing the extent and forms of the highly organised Catholicism described by Altermatt, will then go on to ask how and why this situation came about and what implications it had for the lives of Catholics, and it will conclude by looking at some of the strengths and weaknesses of these organisations.

I

Vereinskatholizismus reached its fullest extent in the Netherlands, and it was there that support for specifically Catholic organisations

[2] U. Altermatt, *Der Weg der Schweizer Katholiken ins Ghetto* (Zurich 1972) p. 21.
[3] R.E. Curran, *Michael Augustine Corrigan and the Shaping of Conservative Catholicism in America* (New York 1978); D. Merwick, *Boston Priests, 1848–1910* (Cambridge, Mass. 1973); H.B. Leonard, 'Ethnic Tensions, Episcopal Leadership and the Emergence of the Twentieth-Century American Catholic Church,' *Catholic Historical Review* 71 (1985) pp. 394–412.

was highest. A series of surveys in the 1950s showed just how far this process had gone. Ninety-five per cent of the Catholics belonging to organisations for women, youth or farmers belonged to specifically Catholic organisations; 90 per cent of Catholic primary school children went to a Catholic school; 84 per cent of Catholic voters chose the Catholic People's Party at the 1959 elections; 79 per cent of newspaper-reading Catholics subscribed to a Catholic daily paper; and 61 per cent of Catholics belonging to sports clubs were members of the Catholic federation. The great majority of Catholic trade unionists belonged to the Catholic union, though here precise figures do not seem to be available. One of the few areas of Dutch life where the tendency to confessionalisation was relatively weak was higher education: only about a quarter of Catholic students attended a Catholic university. But the central importance of sectarian sub-cultures was reflected in two other statistics: 91 per cent of Catholics marrying in 1957 married a fellow-Catholic; a study of friendship networks showed that 85 per cent of practising Catholics included fellow-Catholics among their closest friends, and a majority of them had no non-Catholics on their list.[4]

Most of these institutions had been founded between about 1870 and 1914. The main development of Roman Catholic primary schools came after the joint pastoral letter of the Dutch bishops in 1868, and especially after the school law of 1889, providing state aid for denominational schools. In the same period the Catholic political party gradually took shape. The first Catholic trade union was formed in 1888 (a national federation following in 1909), and the first peasant league in 1896. The first Catholic daily paper had been founded as early as 1846, but spoke to a relatively limited educated readership, and was also noted for its liberal standpoint. Mass Catholic journalism began with *De Maasbode*, established as a weekly in 1868 and a daily in 1885, and distinguished by its popular style, strident tone, conservative view of ecclesiastical issues, and sometimes radical standpoint on economic and social issues.[5]

[4] J.A. Coleman, *The Evolution of Dutch Catholicism, 1958–74* (Los Angeles 1978) pp. 69–71, 75–7.
[5] L.-J. Rogier and P. Brachin, *Histoire du catholicisme hollandais depuis le XVIe siècle* (French trans Paris 1974) pp. 84–5, 105–34.

A similar range of organisations existed by 1914 in France, Belgium, Germany and Austria, as well as in Switzerland.[6] Among these countries only France did not have an explicitly Catholic political party during this period. Germany lacked a separate system of Catholic elementary schools, because the general availability of Catholic teaching for Catholic children in state schools made this unnecessary, though the Catholic authorities were unhappy about the system of 'simultaneous schools' established in the later nineteenth century in many German states, whereby children of all confessions attended the same school, separating only for religious instruction;[7] in Austria a movement to establish private Catholic schools was initiated in 1886, but the resulting system was very small compared with those established in this period in France and Belgium, and it was largely limited to the areas (Vienna and Lower Austria) where Catholics were dissatisfied with the arrangements for religious teaching in state schools.[8] In all of these countries Christian trade unions were formed, though in Germany these took an inter-confessional rather than an exclusively Catholic form, and in Switzerland these were mainly concentrated on German-speaking areas: the French-speaking Catholic workers' associations encouraged their members to join 'neutral' unions also supported by many socialists.[9] In all these countries the period from about 1870 to 1914 was especially significant in the history of Catholic organisations.

Two countries stand out from the general pattern: Britain and the United States had no Catholic political party or trade unions, and relatively few other national Catholic organisations. This has led Whyte to contrast the 'closed' Catholicism developing in continental Europe between 1870 and 1920 with the relatively 'open' Catholicism of North America, Britain and Australasia.[10] Mean-

---

[6] For a useful summary, see the relevant sections of H. Jedin ed *Handbuch der Kirchengeschichte* 7 vols (Freiburg im Breisgau 1962–77) 6 part 2, 'Die Kirche zwischen Anpassung und Widerstand, 1878 bis 1914'.

[7] See for instance A. Wahl, 'Confession et comportement dans les campagnes d'Alsace et de Bade, 1871–1939', Metz University doctoral thesis 2 vols (1980) 2 pp. 794–5.

[8] A. Wandruszka and P. Urbanitsch eds, *Die Habsburgermonarchie 1848–1918* 4 vols (Vienna 1973–85) 4 pp. 179–80.

[9] Altermatt, *Der Weg der Schweizer Katholiken* pp. 254–75.

[10] J.H. Whyte, *Catholics in Western Democracies* (Dublin 1981) pp. 45–6 and *passim*.

while, Coleman, in his study of Dutch Catholicism, also compared the English-speaking countries with continental Europe, but came to different conclusions: he contrasted the Dutch system of 'pillarisation', whereby none of the four major ideological groupings was dominant, and each had a share of power in society, with the situation in the English-speaking world, where Catholics tended 'to become isolated in ghettos cut off from the dominant culture'.[11] These arguments seem to me to overstate the differences between the forms of Catholicism found in the two areas. In both there was a strong tendency towards the formation of a Catholic 'ghetto' in this period, though the types of organisation that this entailed were not precisely the same.

In two respects, Britain was closer to the continental pattern than is generally realised. First, Catholic elementary schools had already in this period achieved attendance by the great majority of Catholic children.[12] Second, although there was never to be a national organisation of Catholics, there were many occasions in the later nineteenth and early twentieth centuries when local Catholic political organisations were formed. Catholic candidates stood for election to School Boards and to Boards of Guardians, and there were Catholic parties on certain local councils, including Bermondsey in the 1900s and Liverpool in the 1920s.[13] However, there were important differences between the nature of Catholic organisations in Britain and the United States on the one hand and continental Europe on the other. One important factor was the relationship between Catholicism and ethnicity in the former countries. The concentration of Catholics within certain ethnic communities assisted the Church in its endeavours to isolate them from anti-Catholic influences. Furthermore the mutual reinforcement of

[11] Coleman, *Dutch Catholicism* p. 64. M.E. Marty, 'The Catholic Ghetto and all the Other Ghettos,' *Catholic Historical Review* 68 (1982) pp. 185–205, convincingly challenges this type of argument, so far as the U.S.A. is concerned. For a lively overview of Catholicism in Britain, Australia and the U.S.A., see S. Gilley, 'The Roman Catholic Church and the Nineteenth-Century Irish Diaspora' *JEH* 35 (1984) pp. 188–207.

[12] See for instance H. McLeod, *Class and Religion in the Late Victorian City* (London 1974) pp. 40–1.

[13] See for instance P.J. Waller, *Democracy and Sectarianism: A Political and Social History of Liverpool 1868–1939* (Liverpool 1981) pp. 123–4, 299–304; P. Thompson, *Socialists, Liberals and Labour: The Struggle for London 1885–1914* (London 1967) p. 313.

religion and nationalism made it less likely that Catholics would give up their faith entirely. But the possibility of mobilising Catholics as Catholics was limited by the fact that ethnic loyalties were as strong as sectarian loyalties, and when the two came into conflict, ethnic loyalty often received a higher priority than explicitly Catholic concerns. Thus in pre-war Britain, preoccupation with Ireland meant that Catholics voted overwhelmingly for Liberal candidates in most elections, in spite of the insistence by many of the clergy that Catholic schools would fare better with the Conservatives.[14] In the United States at this time Catholics were deeply divided along ethnic lines, which made it difficult to organise Catholics as a body even at diocesan, let alone at national level.[15]

Perhaps for these reasons, the 'ghetto' tendency in British and American Catholicism was reflected in the proliferation of parish-based organisations, sometimes loosely linked to a wider chain, as with the numerous Holy Name men's societies, rather than in the more centralised national federations characteristic of continental European Catholicism. Take the example of sport: in the early twentieth century, Germany and France had national Catholic sporting federations, whereas Britain and the United States did not. Yet within their parishes, sporting Catholics were under strong pressure to box or to play football in Catholic institutions, and nowhere else. Thus, in New York's Sacred Heart parish, on the West Side of Manhattan, the Ozanam gym was built around 1910 to enable Catholic boys to box in Catholic surroundings, and excommunication was threatened to those boxing at the neighbouring Hartley House Settlement; in inner south London around the same time Catholics were boxing at the Fisher Club, while Protestants boxed at the Oxford and Bermondsey Club.[16] The only important difference between this situation, and that in continental European countries lay in the fact that in Britain and America teams and individual athletes acted as standard-bearers for their community, whereas in Germany, for instance, leaders of the rival

[14] E.D. Steele, 'The Irish Presence in the North of England, 1850–1914' *Northern History* 12 (1976) pp. 239–40.

[15] See for instance S.M. Tomasi, *Piety and Power: The Role of the Italian Parishes in the New York Metropolitan Area 1880–1930* (Staten Island 1975) pp. 74–105.

[16] H.J. Browne, *One Stop above Hell's Kitchen: Sacred Heart Parish in Clinton* (New York 1977) p. 58; H. Gibbs, *Box On* (London 1981) p. 23.

sporting federations tried to ensure that sport was only practised within an ideologically sealed-off world, within which a good Catholic or socialist was not permitted even to kick or punch a person adhering to a different world-view.[17] By contrast, the participation of Celtic in the Scottish League from 1890 onwards enabled Glasgow Catholics to witness their triumphs with the same sense of vindication that black Americans later derived from the victories of Joe Louis.[18]

2

The building of Catholic 'ghettos' in the later nineteenth century marked the culmination of a process which had its roots in the Church's reaction to the French Revolution. Whereas the eighteenth-century Enlightenment had seen some degree of convergence between Protestant and Catholic Europe, at least so far as the religious thinking of the educated classes, including many of the clergy, was concerned, the nineteenth century saw the revival of specifically Catholic forms of piety, quite foreign both to Protestants and to many liberals. Meanwhile, the distance between educated and uneducated Catholics, between clergy and laity within the Catholic Church was narrowing, as an ultramontane orthodoxy was establishing its hold over the great majority of Catholics in the second half of the century. The various schisms that followed the Vatican Council of 1869–70 brought about the departure of the more committed opponents of this trend. Among the great majority who remained, even those least enthusiastic about papal claims felt constrained to put Catholic unity above all other considerations in the crisis of the 1870s. Loyalty to the Pope and deference to Roman authority thus became integral parts of the form of Catholicism dominant in the last quarter of the nineteenth century and the first half of the twentieth. Two other important developments beginning in the first half of the nineteenth century served to widen the gulf between Catholics and those outside the Church: the great revival

---

[17] See S. Gehrmann, 'Fussball in einer Industrieregion', J. Reulecke and W. Weber eds *Fabrik Familie Feierabend* (Wuppertal 1978) pp. 382, 395–7.
[18] J.E. Handley, *The Celtic Story* (London 1960) pp. 28–9, 80–2, 168–80, discusses the relationship between Celtic and its Catholic supporters.

of the religious orders, whose members had always provoked far more hostility on the part of Protestants and anti-clericals than did the secular clergy; and the series of appearances by the Virgin Mary, starting in Paris in 1830, which led to the establishment of a number of national and international shrines, highly attractive to Catholics of all classes in our period. One further precondition for the 'ghetto' should be noted: the doctrine of 'no salvation outside the Church'. Even though priests might hope that loopholes were available for the many outsiders 'invincibly ignorant' of the Church and its teachings, the belief that the apostate or non-practising Catholic was in necessary danger of hell provided a very powerful motive for isolating parishioners from any potentially dangerous influence.

However, an explanation of the 'ghetto' solely in terms of Catholic history is incomplete, since there was a general tendency in late nineteenth-century Europe for the various political and religious communities to form highly organised, discrete sub-cultures. Socialists, in particular, tended to be as highly organised and as exclusive as the Catholics. And a variety of other groups developed in the same way in particular countries. In Austria, for instance, the so-called *Lager* system comprised three main blocs – Catholics, socialists and nationalists.[19] In the Netherlands, it was the militant Calvinists who initiated the process of 'pillarisation', and the Catholics and socialists who followed.[20] Certainly the members of these various groups were in conscious competition with one another: for instance, the proliferation of socialist organisations was a major reason for the formation of Catholic organisations, and vice-versa. Yet the 'ghetto'-builders whether they were socialists, Catholics or (in the Netherlands) conservative Protestants, faced some of the same problems and the same enemies, and were responding to the same opportunities.

Each of these groups felt itself under threat from the most powerful social force in the industrialising nations of western Europe and north America, the industrial, commercial and professional elite. In most continental European countries this group was in the 1870s and '80s Liberal in politics, and its members,

[19] See for instance A. Diamant, *Austrian Catholics and the First Republic* (Princeton 1960) pp. 73–80.
[20] E.H. Kossmann, *The Low Countries 1780–1940* (Oxford 1978) pp. 302–7.

whether they were Protestants, Jews or anti-clerical Catholics, were generally hostile to ultramontane Catholicism. In Britain and the United States, the urban elite, though less likely to adhere to the kind of liberal ideology prevalent in continental countries, was overwhelmingly Protestant.[21] France was somewhat outside the general pattern, since the period following the revolutions of 1848 had seen a 'return to the Church' on the part of significant sections of the bourgeoisie;[22] however, the growth of anti-clericalism in the lower middle class and the political dominance of the republicans from the later 1870s onwards meant that Catholicism, after a period of exceptional prosperity in the 1850s and '60s, was under more severe attack in France than anywhere else. In Germany and Switzerland too, in the 1870s, and in Belgium between 1878 and 1884, Catholicism had come under direct attack from the government, while in Austria in the later 1860s and early '70s the government introduced a set of more modest measures designed to control and to limit the influence of the Church. But even where no such direct assault was attempted or even contemplated, the clergy believed that the hostility to the Church of those in positions of power posed a threat to the faith of Catholics. In particular, the development of the press and the general introduction of systems of universal compulsory education in the second half of the nineteenth century meant that the dominant class had unprecedented facilities for indoctrinating the people. Governments, employers and wealthy Liberals also tried to sponsor and organise popular leisure, at a time when sport in particular was becoming of obsessive interest to large sections of the population, especially to young males. In the minds of Catholics and socialists, every apparently harmless club for cyclists or gymnasts was a tool of the Liberals or the bourgeoisie, and needed an ideologically pure counterpart.[23] The 'ghetto' was a means of creating space free from the encroachment

[21] For discussion of the religious affiliations and attitudes of the bourgeoisie, see for instance, Wandruszka and Urbanitsch, *Habsburgermonarchie* 4 pp. 128–31; J. Sperber, *Popular Catholicism in Nineteenth Century Germany* (Princeton 1984) pp. 44–7; R. Jensen, 'Metropolitan Elites in the Midwest 1907–29.' F. Jaher ed *The Rich, The Well-Born and the Powerful* (Urbana 1973) p. 292.

[22] See for instance G. Cholvy, *Religion et société au XIXe siècle: Le diocèse de Montpellier* 2 vols (Lille 1973) pp. 1441–6.

[23] For examples of youth or sports clubs sponsored by government or employers around the end of the nineteenth century, see T. Margadant, 'Primary Schools and Youth Groups in Pre-War Paris: Les 'Petites A's' *Journal of Contemporary*

of these pervasive anti-Catholic and anti-socialist forces.

Catholics, socialists and Protestants also faced a series of more intangible problems in the cities of later nineteenth-century Europe and America: the difficulty of keeping their members at a high level of commitment when innumerable drinking places offered relaxation and companionship after the long hours of work; the weakening of social controls in the city, and the facilities for prostitution, gambling and crime; and the development of commercialised leisure, which promised to create an ideologically neutral world within which politics and religion were irrelevant.[24] Many Catholic organisations of this period arose out of concern for the dangerous attractions of 'city life', and especially fears for the well-being of young men, who seemed to be the group most at risk. Indeed, among the first of the many national and international chains of organisations established during the nineteenth century for specific sections of the Catholic community were the Kolping associations for young artisans, the first of which was formed in Elberfeld in 1846. In London in the early twentieth century, drunkenness and apathy seem to have caused Catholic priests considerably more anxiety than the possibility of apostasy or of involvement in socialist organisations. All south London parishes had some kind of special organisation for teenage boys and young men, including one or more confraternities, and sometimes a boys' brigade and a social club; many parishes had a branch of the Catholic temperance organisation, the League of the Cross. But membership of confraternities tended to be low, and there was a good deal of despondency among priests about this age-group.[25]

History 13 (1978) pp. 323–36; C. Korr, 'West Ham United Football Club 1895– 1914' *Ibid.* pp. 211–32.

For the hostility of German socialists and Catholics to the 'liberal-Protestant-bourgeois' *Turnvereine*, see W. Eichel ed *Die Körperkultur in Deutschland* 3 vols (East Berlin 1964–5) 2 p. 421 and *passim*; W. Schwank, *Kirche und Sport in Deutschland von 1848 bis 1920* (Hochheim-am-Main 1979) pp. 32–4.

[24] See for instance G. Barth, *City People: The Rise of Modern City Culture in Nineteenth-Century America* (New York 1980).

[25] See Visitation Returns in parish files at the Archives of the Roman Catholic Archdiocese of Southwark. In 1897 the Bishop's questionnaire asked for an estimate of the percentage of boys aged 14–21 who were 'satisfactory Catholics'; in 1912 pastors were asked 'Have secret societies, spiritualism or socialism obtained any footing among your people?' The answer to the latter question was invariably (in the returns I have seen) 'No'. Answers to the former question included estimates varying between 10% and 50%; comments were frequently pessimistic.

'Building the "Catholic Ghetto"'

Though the development of Catholic (as also of socialist) organisations in the later nineteenth century was partly a form of self-defence, it was in some respects an attempt to take advantage of the opportunities offered by the democratisation of politics. Catholic and socialist parties (and also the ultra-Calvinist Anti-Revolutionary Party in the Netherlands) had in common the fact that they appealed mainly to industrial workers, peasants and the lower middle class, whereas continental Liberal parties had their greatest strength in the educated middle class. The broadening of the franchise in many European countries in the later nineteenth and early twentieth century usually increased the proportion of Catholics in the electorate, and the Church with its ready-made national network of parish priests had organisational advantages over its rivals, especially in rural areas.[26]

While the most violent hostility to the Church was found in traditionally Catholic countries, there was in predominantly Protestant countries a pervasive prejudice against Catholics which gave them strong reasons for isolating themselves and for organising. There was, of course, nothing new about these anti-Catholic prejudices; but the massive migration of Catholic peasants to live in Protestant-dominated cities and to work in Protestant-owned mines and factories meant that members of the two communities were increasingly coming into direct contact with one another. Moreover, the concentration of Catholics in cities like Dortmund and Glasgow, Amsterdam and Geneva, made the formation of an extensive network of Catholic organisations possible. The hostile stereotyping of Catholics by Protestants in this period has been discussed particularly thoroughly by Alfred Wahl in a study of relationships between Protestants, Catholics and Jews in rural Alsace and Baden. He showed that the three communities were divided by very marked cultural differences, by membership of opposing parties, and by a strong sense of their separate identities. Protestants regarded Catholics as lazy, as primitive and superstitious in their religion, as slavishly submissive to pope and priests; they believed that Catholicism was associated with economic and technological backwardness; Protestant youths delighted in par-

---

[26] On the role of the clergy in elections, see G. Lewis, *Kirche und Partei im Politischen Katholizismus* (Vienna 1977) cap 4; M.L. Anderson, *Windthorst: A Political Biography* (Oxford 1981) cap 9; Wahl, 'Confession et comportement' 2 pp. 1002–4.

odying Catholic ceremonies; and the main National Liberal newspaper in Baden presented the German Reich as a Protestant state and regarded Catholics as being generally unpatriotic. In similar vein, a dictionary of German superstition published in the 1930s referred in the entry *'Konfession'* to the usage current among Protestants whereby 'Catholic' was synonymous with 'stupid'.[27]

Of course, Catholics were equally uncomplimentary about Protestants, but the concentration of economic, and often political, power in Protestant hands in so many countries meant that Protestants were far more often in a position to put their prejudices into practice. In Frankfurt-am-Main in the early twentieth century, Catholics complained that their children were being ridiculed by teachers in the city's non-denominational 'simultaneous' schools, and that it was impossible for a Catholic to become a headmaster; they also objected to the constant attacks on Catholic teaching, the clergy and the pope in the city's press.[28] In the Glasgow area Catholics were heavily concentrated in unskilled jobs, because discrimination by foremen and by the skilled workers' unions made it difficult for them to obtain apprenticeships.[29] In both Lancashire and Scotland some employers gave preference to workers of their own denomination, and since far more employers were Protestants than Catholics, this worked to the overall disadvantage of Catholics.[30] In both Britain and the United States well-financed Protestant charities were a source of constant anxiety to Catholic priests, who feared they could be a means of seducing their poorer parishioners. For instance, the founding in 1889 of the famous Hull House Settlement in Chicago led to a prolonged feud between local clergy and the Settlement's foundress, Jane Addams. The Catholics argued that Addams's charitable and recreational activities were undermining the Catholic home, and were an implicit slur on Catholic parents. They also particularly objected to the fact that a

---

[27] Wahl, 'Confession et comportement' 1 pp. 388, 614–53 2 pp. 958, 1254–70; E. Hoffmann-Krayer ed *Handwörterbuch des deutschen Aberglaubens* 9 vols (Berlin 1927–38) 5 p.180, referring to 'die Redensart "du bist katholisch" = "du bist verrückt, dumm"'.

[28] H. Blankenberg, *Politischer Katholizismus in Frankfurt am Main 1918–33* (Mainz 1981) pp. 7, 13–4.

[29] I. MacLean, *The Myth of Red Clydeside* (Edinburgh 1983) p. 181; A.B. Campbell, *The Lanarkshire Miners: A Social History of their Trade Unions, 1775–1874* (Edinburgh 1979) p. 157.

[30] *Ibid.* p. 223; P. Joyce, *Work, Society and Politics* (Brighton 1980) pp. 172–7.

group of anti-clerical Italians was allowed to meet at the House and to perform a play about Giordano Bruno.[31]

The fears and hopes which encouraged the multiplication of Catholic organisations in predominantly Protestant countries during the later nineteenth century are usefully summarised in the prospectus for the Catholic Order of Oddfellows, founded by a group of Nottingham Catholics in 1871:

> Disunited in everything except our Holy Faith, we have been deprived of our legitimate influence in all public matters – social, educational and political. For want of union we have been exposed to defeat in every movement which affects our poor, our schools, or the interests of our Holy Religion. ... Thousands of our young men have been driven by necessity to join one or other of the great Orders or Friendly Societies in which for the sake of peace and concord, every allusion to religious subjects is strictly prohibited. Here the young Catholic, at the most critical period of his life, naturally selects his companions from among his fellow members, the great majority of whom are either Protestants or Infidels, and in too many cases Religion gradually loses her influence over him until he becomes indifferent, or is entirely lost to the Church. For the purpose of remedying these evils the Catholic Order of Oddfellows has been established – to draw the Catholics of the whole kingdom into closer union with each other and with the Pastors of the Church; to teach them to know their strength when united, and to use it when necessary; to make it no longer compulsory for our young men to join societies the members of which seldom or never mention our Holy Religion, except as an object of hatred or impious ridicule; but to place within their reach benefits at least equal to those available elsewhere, in lodges composed entirely of Catholics with laws and ceremonials essentially Catholic, and under the spiritual supervision of the Pastors of the Church.[32]

---

[31] C. Shanabruch, *Chicago's Catholics* (Notre Dame 1981) pp. 132–7.
[32] Prospectus in 'Societies pre-1900' file, Archives of the Roman Catholic Archdiocese of Southwark.

3

The age of *Vereinskatholizismus* was first and most obviously a time when the identity of large sections of the population was defined most clearly by the organisations they belonged to. It was a time of flags and parades through the street; a time when funerals were attended by members of all the organisations to which the deceased had belonged – the listing of these organisations in death notices provides a good indication of the importance attached to membership.[33] It was a time when membership of certain organisations precluded membership of many others, so that organisations helped to define clear boundary lines within the local community. Admittedly there always were some people who tried to maintain a dual identity – to be, for instance, a Catholic *and* a socialist – or who tried to enjoy the sport or the singing that a Catholic or socialist organisation provided and to ignore the associated ideology. But leaders and rank and file militants made life difficult for such people. Catholic organisations were consistently and often loudly anti-socialist during this period; socialist organisations were more flexible in their policy towards the Churches, alternating between periods of total opposition and times when they tried to maintain neutrality – but even in the latter phases, rank and file members were often openly and bitterly scornful of anyone who had any connection with organised religion.[34] Catholic sports and singing societies frequently faced during the later nineteenth century the problem of members who also belonged to socialist or liberal organisations; in Germany, at least, the answer usually was that such members should be expelled. Socialists were

---

[33] See for instance the death notices column of the *New Yorker Staatszeitung*, the city's leading German-language newspaper. In a sample of forty notices from April 1888, sixteen included invitations to fellow-members of organisations to which the deceased or his/her spouse had belonged to attend the funeral. A sample of sixty from March 1910 included twenty-three such invitations. Sometimes the organisation itself published an instruction to members to attend the funeral of 'our dead brother'.

[34] See for instance J. Loreck, *Wie man früher Sozialdemokrat wurde* (Bonn 1977) pp. 145–56.

equally resentful of comrades who 'sang with the bourgeoisie'.[35]
By the early twentieth century the politicisation of all areas of life
had gone so far that France had two rival national football teams,
one Catholic and the other secularist; and in the 1920s and '30s
socialist and communist workers' olympiads were organised in
opposition both to the 'bourgeois' olympiads, and (until the Popular Front era) to one another.[36]

This was also a time of pilgrimages and of regional, national
and international congresses, when thousands of Catholics would
converge on a favourite shrine or on a chosen city, to demonstrate
their numbers, discuss common problems, and gather strength
for future struggles. In German-speaking countries, national mass
gatherings of Catholics, known as *Katholikentage*, were held at
frequent intervals. The first of these was held at Mainz in 1848;
by the 1880s and '90s they were being held annually in Germany,
slightly less often in Austria and Switzerland, the venues changing
from year to year. They frequently resulted in the formation of
yet more Catholic organisations. These in turn would usually have
a variety of national gatherings, which inevitably included some
provision for public flag-waving. If the city chosen were a stronghold of anti-clericalism, the necessity for establishing the Catholic
presence was all the greater, and there was a good chance that the
local authorities or sections of the local population would assist by
staging a confrontation – as in Calais in 1908, where the mayor
tried unsuccessfully to stop the 1800 delegates to a congress of the
Catholic youth federation marching through the streets.[37] But the
most effective public display of Catholic strength, and the form
most characteristic of this period, was the political pilgrimage. The
1870s, in particular, was a decade of mass pilgrimages, whereby
German and Swiss Catholics demonstrated their refusal to be
intimidated by the *Kulturkampf*, and French Catholics their sup-

---

[35] Schwank, *Kirche und Sport*, p. 35; D. Dowe, 'The Working Men's Choral
Movement in Germany before the First World War' *Journal of Contemporary
History* 13 (1978) p. 275.

[36] R. Holt, *Sport and Society in Modern France* (London 1981) p. 201;
R.F. Wheeler, 'Organised Sport and Organised Labour' *Journal of Contemporary
History* 13 (1978) pp. 200–2.

[37] Y.-M. Hilaire, *Une chrétienté au XIXe siècle? La vie religieuse des populations
du diocèse d'Arras, 1840–1914* 2 vols (Lille 1977) 2 p. 773.

port for the restoration of the Bourbons.[38] While many of the shrines of local saints were in decline, a select group of regional and national shrines, most of them associated with the Virgin Mary, benefited from the new respectability of pilgrimages in the eyes of the bishops and of educated Catholics, and also from the railway. They became the ideal focus of Catholic identity in the face of attacks from anti-clericals, Protestants and rationalists.[39]

If marches, demonstrations and pilgrimages provided one kind of expression of unity and display of strength, equally important was a local headquarters, large enough both to proclaim the presence of the organisation, and to contain a wide range of facilities and activities. An account of the opening in October 1898 of the *Vereinshaus* of the Catholic workers' association in south Cologne conveys something both of the symbolic significance attached to such buildings, and of the spirit of the organised Catholicism of the time. The celebrations began with a church service, after which an 'imposing festive procession' moved through the southern part of the city, with members of 34 Catholic workers' associations taking part, 38 flags flying and three bands playing. When they got to the *Vereinshaus* the crush was so great that not everyone could crowd in to hear the numerous speeches. Those who squeezed in found that two very familiar themes predominated: loyalty to the Pope, and attacks on Social Democracy. The opening speaker described the house as 'a stronghold against Social Democracy. At the threshold of this house, Social Democracy has to stop. It shall not propagate its subversive teachings in here ...'. Another called on Catholics to work together, and stressed the importance of such institutions in strengthening the Catholic worker, who had

---

[38] Sperber, *Popular Catholicism* pp. 224–5; I. Baumer, 'Kulturkampf und Katholizismus im Berner Jura' G. Wiegelmann ed *Kultureller Wandel im 19. Jahrhundert* (Göttingen 1973) pp. 88–101; A. Dansette, *Histoire religieuse de la France contemporaine* 2 vols (Paris 1948–51) 1 pp. 442–4, 454–5.

[39] The best general discussion of pilgrimages in this period is M. Marrus, 'Pilger auf dem Weg: Wallfahrten im Frankreich des 19. Jahrhunderts' *Geschichte und Gesellschaft* 3 (1977) pp. 324–51; also relevant are G. Korff, 'Formierung der Frömmigkeit: Zur sozial-politischen Intention der Trierer Rockwallfahrten 1891' *Geschichte und Gesellschaft* 3 (1977) pp. 352–83; W.K. Blessing, *Staat und Kirche in der Gesellschaft* (Göttingen 1982) p. 241; Wandruszka and Urbanitsch, *Habsburgermonarchie* 4 pp. 134–6.

to face 'scorn and ridicule from his Social Democratic workmates' and 'many kinds of injustice from certain employers'.[40]

The imagery of struggle pervaded the Catholic literature of this period. In American cities, for instance, Catholic priests saw themselves as fighting a three-sided battle: against the entrenched power of an arrogant and bigoted Protestantism; against the socialism that was competing strongly for the loyalty of their working class parishioners; and against the spirit of paganism, which was less clearly defined, but seemed to be gaining ground rapidly by the first decade of the twentieth century. The exclusivism and the polemical tone of the Catholicism of the time is well illustrated in the bulletins issued by New York parishes between 1890 and 1914. Our Lady of Good Counsel, a working class Irish parish on the Upper East Side of Manhattan, represented the more intransigent wing of contemporary Catholicism. A typical article of 1910 tried to hit the two favourite targets with one shot: it began by fiercely attacking socialism, and then went on to claim that Protestants came into conflict with socialists less often than Catholics did, because they were not true Christians. Two articles from 1905 reflected two aspects of the oft-repeated message that Catholics had nothing to learn from those outside the Church, and that they should keep their distance from them. The first, entitled 'Courageous Catholics', included criticism of Catholics who 'cringe to those outside the Church' and 'cater to Protestant prejudices'. The second defined various categories of non-Catholic, 'heretic', 'agnostic', etc., the greatest condemnation being reserved for 'apostate' – 'God abandons them that abandon Him'. The conclusion was that 'the source of all this unbelief is in the proud mind and sensual heart of man'.[41] The most liberal of the bulletins I have seen was the organ of Saint Paul's, a socially mixed Irish parish on the West Side of Manhattan, staffed by the Paulists. They too were critical of Protestants and socialists, but they were more moderate in their attacks, and they took the criticisms of the Church by these outsiders more seriously. They also appeared to be more serious than the priests of many other parishes in urging Catholics

---

[40] E.-D. Broch, *Katholische Arbeitervereine in der Stadt Köln 1890–1901* (Hamburg 1977) pp. 98–102.
[41] *The Parish Monthly* of Our Lady of Good Counsel Roman Catholic church, New York, Dec. 1910, Feb. 1905. (Copies in New York Public Library).

to fight for social justice. But they too made sure that their readers were aware of the doctrine of 'No salvation outside the Church'. Thus an article on 'Why become and why remain a Catholic' stated:

> If in our belief the Catholic religion were only equal to other religions; if it were not alone true and absolutely necessary, we would renounce it, because it brings many sacrifices and not a few bits of unpleasantness. We are persuaded that invincible ignorance of the Catholic faith, and unconquerable prejudice, will be satisfactorily pleaded by many at the throne of God's Judgement; but in setting aside these two excuses, the Catholic faith as set forth in the Catholic Church must be embraced under pain of eternal separation from the Kingdom of Christ.[42]

Besides such explicit teaching, the Catholic clergy strengthened the sense of separate identity among the Catholics of religiously mixed nations by their stress on loyalty to the pope, and devotion to Mary and the saints. In the second half of the nineteenth century, and especially after 1870, these became not so much distinctively ultramontane emphases as generally accepted tokens of orthodoxy. In Germany, for instance, where the proceedings at the Vatican Council had caused great unease among many of the bishops and leading laymen, the launching of the *Kulturkampf* turned Pius IX into a symbol of Catholic defiance: 16 June (anniversary of the Pope's accession) came to be generally celebrated in Catholic areas, while the officially fostered celebrations on 2 September (anniversary of the battle of Sedan) were ignored.[43] In Switzerland the main national organisation of Catholics in the second half of the nineteenth century was called the *Piusverein*. And in London in the 1920s the banners carried by Catholics or hanging above Catholic streets during processions, typically carried two messages: 'Hail, Queen of Heaven', and 'God bless our Pope'.[44]

A set of documents from a slightly later period embodies in a striking way this tendency for the Catholic clergy of the early

---

[42] *Calendar of the Church of Saint Paul the Apostle*, New York, Dec. 1895. (Copy in the Archives of the Paulist Fathers, Saint Paul's rectory, New York.)

[43] Sperber, *Popular Catholicism* pp. 225–7. See also the account of the 'pope-cult' in 1890s Bavarian Catholicism in Blessing, *Staat und Kirche* pp. 239–40.

[44] See the collections of photographs of Roman Catholic processions in Southwark and Tower Hamlets local history libraries.

twentieth century to place the greatest stress on those aspects of Catholic belief and practice that set Catholics apart from other Christians. These were the Visitation Returns from the Diocese of Southwark in the 1920s and '30s, on the back of which the bishop made what appear to be notes for the sermon to be delivered when he visited that parish. Here, for instance, are the subjects he proposed to cover at Corpus Christi, Brixton, in 1930: a Plenary Indulgence issued by Pius X; praying for the pope; persecution of the Church in Russia, Mexico, France and Malta; prayer for benefactors and past parishioners; the failure of Brixton to contribute to the diocesan seminary fund; frequent Communion and attendance at mass; devotion to Mary; a forthcoming pilgrimage to Lourdes; the threat to Catholic schools; prayer for the canonisation of the English martyrs, which could have a big influence on the conversion of England.[45]

A history of St Monica's, a mainly Irish New York parish, refers to 'the rise' in the late nineteenth and early twentieth centuries 'of that family spirit for which the parish is justly remembered best by those who now live beyond its limits'. While this remembered 'family spirit' is no doubt in part a product of nostalgia, the term nonetheless epitomises some of the strengths and limitations of the organised Catholicism of this period. The author of this history referred to the help given to poorer parishioners by the St Vincent de Paul Society, to the pastoral work of the clergy, and to the numerous fairs, festivals, socials, dramatics and sports events – 'Christian sociability at its best enjoyed in union with the parish and its priests'.[46] But the 'family' metaphor is perhaps relevant in other ways too. For instance, the Catholic parish, which made such great claims on the loyalty of its members, was something that the great majority of them had been born into, and grew up in, without ever having had any choice in the matter. There was a real contrast here with the situation in the Protestant Churches where, in Britain and the U.S.A. particularly, but to a lesser extent in other countries too, many people were born into one denomination and converted as teenagers or as adults into another;

---

[45] In parish file for Corpus Christi, Brixton, Archives of the Roman Catholic Archdiocese of Southwark.

[46] G.A. Kelly, *The Story of St Monica's Parish, New York City, 1879–1954* (New York 1954) pp. 3, 25.

indeed it was quite common for a Protestant to have belonged to several different denominations.[47] This often meant that Catholics had a much deeper sense than Protestants of sectarian identity, but more ambivalent feelings about the teachings and ethos of their Church. The 'family' metaphor is also relevant to the relations between the 'fathers' and their 'children'. Intense relationships developed, in which affection and pride often played big parts,[48] but also some element of mutual resentment. The priests had a life that was often lonely, and they envied the laity their freedom; they also tended to have a feeling of being used – the laity had no hesitation about calling out a priest in the middle of the night, but when it came to supporting their church they were always too busy or too hard up.[49] The people, meanwhile were apt to feel that it was the priests who had an easy life, and they were also very sensitive to any slight by the clergy, any sign that they were not loved as they deserved to be. These relationships had considerable bearing on the character of Catholic organisations in this period. Parish societies were usually under the supervision of one of the clergy – which could lead to conflict where an active priest clashed with an active laity, or it could lead to nothing at

[47] As one example, the parish registers of Holy Trinity Protestant Episcopal church, in the Yorkville section of New York, for 1897–1920 record the denomination in which confirmees had been baptised. No more than 40–50% had been baptised as Episcopalians or Anglicans. (Registers at the Church Office.) During the same period the Protestant journal, *Federation*, undertook surveys of the religious affiliations of New Yorkers. These showed great diversity among immigrants from predominantly Protestant countries, such as England, Scotland and Sweden, whereas immigrants from Ireland and Italy, and gentile immigrants from Poland were overwhelmingly Catholic.

[48] Parish histories often contain a lot of information about priest-people relations and the distinctive qualities of particular priests, most commonly in the form of testimonials from satisfied customers, though sometimes in terms of veiled criticism. As one example, L.E. Whatmore, *The Story of Dockhead Parish* (London 1960) pp. 72–9 includes an interesting attempt to define the influence of Fr Murnane, a formidable Irish-born priest, with a reputation as a saint, who dominated Bermondsey Catholicism from the 1890s to the 1920s. 'His influence over the people was phenomenal (it is hardly an overstatement to say they "worshipped" him) but was never obtained, as has been known, by bullying. He ruled it has been said, by revealed love and concealed discipline.'

[49] London School of Economics Library, Booth Collection, B274 pp. 63–5, B280 pp. 3–5. The interviews with London priests by Charles Booth and his assistants in the 1890s include many comments about their relations with their parishioners. Recent oral history projects have provided a lot of new evidence about Catholic views of their clergy in this period. See below, footnotes 67 and 84.

all happening if a deferential laity waited for an inactive priest to give the lead. A lot therefore depended on the personality of the clergy.[50] In Germany, the Catholic workers' associations were limited as a means of working class self-expression by the fact that each branch had a priest as a president, with a right of veto. Admittedly, many of these were younger priests, some of whom gained reputations as 'red curates' (*rote Kaplane*); but they in turn were answerable to their bishops, who had no hesitation about transferring any who gained too radical a reputation.[51] Meanwhile, organisations like Germany's Christian trade unions, which had a mainly Catholic membership, but were independent of priestly control, were subject to constant harassment from certain members of the hierarchy.[52] The extreme unevenness of support for Catholic organisations in this period can partly be understood in terms of this very hierarchical power structure. Where priestly leadership was both popular and effective the system could work very well; where it was not, the results were disastrous.

4

Catholic organisations gained their highest level of support in areas where a homogeneously Catholic rural population lived in close proximity to, but seldom in close contact with non-Catholics or anti-Catholics. A good example would be the rural areas of Alsace

[50] W.M. Walker, *Juteopolis: Dundee's Textile Workers 1885–1923* (Edinburgh 1979) pp. 130–3, 137, provides a useful account of the role of the priest in Catholic parish organisations, and brief comments on priest-people relations in general. The latter have been studied mainly in situations where open conflict is endemic, as for instance in T. Zeldin ed *Conflicts in French Society* (London 1970), or where hostile stereotypes of the clergy are widespread, as among the first and second generations of Italian immigrants in the U.S.A., whose religion has been interpreted in a fascinating study by R.A. Orsi, 'The Madonna of 115th Street: Faith and Community in Italian Harlem, 1880–1950,' (Yale University Ph.D. thesis 1982) see esp. pp. 150–1. For our period there has been little attempt to unravel the potentially more interesting situations where attitudes to the clergy were more varied and less clear cut.

[51] Broch, *Katholische Arbeitervereine* p. 15. For the 1860s and '70s see E.D. Brose, *Christian Labor and the Politics of Frustration in Imperial Germany* (Washington D.C. 1985) pp. 46–60.

[52] *Ibid.* cap 10 and *passim*.

and Baden, in both of which Catholics were a numerical majority in the period 1871–1914, yet saw themselves as economically and politically subordinate. The majority of villages were religiously homogeneous, but sectarian consciousness was kept at a high level by the frequent proximity of Protestants and Jews, whether as employers, state officials and money-lenders, or as inhabitants of neighbouring villages; in Baden the Catholic sense of grievance was exacerbated by the fact that the Archdukes were Protestants and Liberal governments had been pursuing their own *Kulturkampf* for some years before the establishment of the Reich. The rural areas of these states were marked by very high levels of Catholic practice in the later nineteenth century, by frequent sectarian conflicts, and by the proliferation, especially from 1884 onwards, of Catholic organisations.[53] Analysis of early twentieth-century German elections showed that the proportion of Catholics supporting the Centre Party reached maximum levels in areas of a similar kind (Oldenburg and rural districts of Westphalia and Württemberg), where there was a concentrated Catholic population living in villages and small towns in a Protestant-dominated state.[54] A similar situation existed in the 1950s in the Netherlands: support for the Catholic People's Party reached maximum levels in rural areas of the Catholic south, and in Catholic enclaves in the Protestant north.[55] Catholic organisations also achieved very high levels of rural support in certain regions of such Catholic countries as France, Belgium and Austria. For instance Flanders and Lower Austria became strongholds of the Catholic peasant movement.[56] Here it may be that antagonism towards the more secularised French-speaking Belgians or towards Vienna with its socialist working class and Jewish bourgeoisie may have underpinned a strong sense of Catholic identity in the same way that hostility to Protestant power did in Germany.

While maximum levels of involvement by Catholics in Catholic institutions were achieved in heavily Catholic rural areas; it was

[53] Wahl, 'Confession et comportement' 1 pp. 31–3, 623–39, 2 pp. 861–87.
[54] J. Schauff, *Das Wahlverhalten der deutschen Katholiken im Kaiserreich und in der Weimarer Republik* (Mainz 1975) pp. 80–9.
[55] H. Bakvis, *Catholic Power in the Netherlands* (Kingston, Ont. 1981) p. 151.
[56] G. Lewis, 'The Peasantry, Rural Change and Conservative Agrarianism: Lower Austria at the Turn of the Century,' *PP* 81 (1978) pp. 119–43; Kossmann, *The Low Countries* pp. 421, 467–8.

also in such areas – for instance, the 'dechristianised' Limousin of central France, that the level sometimes sank almost to nothing.[57] In religiously mixed rural areas, and in towns, such extremes were not reached, and the influences bearing on Catholic organisational involvement were more complex. Participation tended to be fairly high where religious identity was reinforced by ethnicity, as in New York, where in 1901, about 50 per cent of Catholic adults attended church on a single Sunday, a remarkably high figure by European urban standards.[58] Catholic organisations also developed strongly in such areas as the Rhine/Ruhr industrial zone of western Germany, where Catholics were locally in a majority, yet subject both to the Protestant Prussian state and to an employing class which was predominantly Protestant. The Rhine and Ruhr became by far the most important centre of organised Catholicism in Germany, noted for the strength of the Centre Party, Christian trade unions and Catholic workers' associations, and the Rhineland textile town of Mönchengladbach was the headquarters of the *Volksverein für das Katholische Deutschland*.[59]

There were two kinds of area in Germany where support for the Centre Party and for the Catholic *Volksverein* was relatively weak. One was heavily Catholic Bavaria, the only state in the German *Reich* where both the ruling house and the majority of the population was Catholic; the other example is that of areas, including many of the major cities of northern and central Germany, where Catholics were dispersed in a heavily Protestant population. In the former area, it would seem that Catholic identity was less strongly developed than in states and provinces accustomed to Protestant rule, and social conflicts within the Catholic population were more deeply divisive. In the latter areas, Catholic

[57] See A. Corbin, *Archaïsme et modernité en Limousin au XIXe siècle 1845–1880* 2 vols (Paris 1975) 1 pp. 688–90.

[58] See H. McLeod, 'Catholicism and the New York Irish' J. Obelkevich, L. Roper, R. Samuel eds *Disciplines of Faith* to be published in 1986.

[59] S. Hickey, 'Class Conflict and Class Consciousness: Coal Miners in the Bochum Area of the Ruhr, 1870–1914,' (Oxford University D.Phil. thesis 1978) pp. 103–42; Sperber, *Popular Catholicism* pp. 277–97 and *passim*; H. Heitzer, *Der Volksverein für das Katholische Deutschland im Kaiserreich 1890–1914* (Mainz 1979) pp. 54–7, 313–7; M. Schneider, 'Religion and Labour Organisation: The Christian Trade Unions in the Wilhelmine Empire' *European Studies Review* 12 (1982) p. 351.

organisations were slow to develop, and many Catholic workers were absorbed into the powerful socialist sub-culture.[60]

There have been few studies of the differential appeal of Catholic organisations to the two sexes and to different age-groups. However, there is some evidence that throughout our period parish organisations for women attracted more members than those for men,[61] and that in the early twentieth century women's organisations were playing an increasingly significant role in Catholic life both at parish and at diocesan level. In the face of the growing influence of anti-clerical left-wing parties on nominally Catholic men, and the consequent difficulty in many parishes of forming vigorous lay organisations of men, the clergy came to rely on the greater piety of Catholic women. In the diocese of Arras in northern France, women's and youth organisations were given key roles in the diocesan strategy for Catholic revival in the period following the Separation of Church and State in 1905.[62] Kaufmann has shown the importance of Catholic women's organisations in Weimar Germany, where, with $1\frac{1}{2}$ million members, they continued to lead the field at a time when the Centre Party was losing ground, and the Christian trade unions were still a long way behind their secular rivals. At the same time Catholic propaganda was exalting the role of women, on whom the revival of Christian family life was seen to depend, and women were being given important positions within the parish as collectors and visitors. As Kaufmann states: 'The women's organisation created for women a religiously

---

[60] Schauff, *Das Wahlverhalten* pp. 137–42, 200–1; Blankenberg, *Politischer Katholizismus* pp. 250, 273.

[61] H.J. Brand, 'Kirchliche Vereinswesen und Freizeitgestaltungen in einer Arbeitergemeinde: Das Beispiel Schalke, 1872–1933' G. Huck ed *Sozialgeschichte der Freizeit* (Wuppertal 1980) pp. 208–11 provides membership figures for parish societies between 1909 and 1927 in a working class suburb of Gelsenkirchen, where nearly half the Catholic population attended mass regularly and about half belonged to Catholic organisations. These showed that the *Frauen- und Mutterverein* always had at least twice as many members as the male *Arbeiterverein*, and that the organisation for young women always had considerably more members than that for young men. In south London where both mass attendance and membership of organisations was lower, the Bishop of Southwark asked in the Visitation Returns for 1897 and 1912 for the membership of confraternities. In the five parishes for which I have seen figures organisations for women always had more members than those for men, though the difference was sometimes fairly narrow.

[62] Hilaire, *Une chrétienté?* 2 pp. 763–79.

legitimated "counter-identity" to the "privatising" demands of the men.'[63] Similarly, young women, a group whose involvement in parish activities was often particularly high, could find in charitable work an approved sphere of action outside the home that even normally highly protective parents might accept. In New York, for instance, young women's sodalities were responsible for 'Island Work', which meant visiting Catholic inmates of the various city institutions sited on Blackwell's Island in the East River.[64]

5

For Catholic shopkeepers, small businessmen and politicians, the 'ghetto' made obvious sense, as it provided a ready-made clientele. There were also a great many other Catholics who found in the church-based sub-culture a strongly supportive community, with which they could fully identify. But there were always some sections of the Catholic population whose essential needs this sub-culture could not meet. The final section of the paper will look at some of these discontented groups.

One set of problems arose out of the relative poverty of the Catholic minorities in such countries as Britain, the United States, or the Netherlands. This meant that the Catholic community often had difficulty in supporting its poorest members, and that the very poor were strongly tempted to seek charity from non-Catholic sources. Even in New York, where the Church's links with the Democratic machine meant that it might pay to be a good Catholic,[65] some poor families seem to have adopted a fluid religious identity which could be adapted to take advantage of whatever offers of help might be available. The New York branches of the Charity Organisation Society and the Association for

[63] D. Kaufmann, 'Vom Vaterland zum Mutterland: Frauen im katholischen Milieu der Weimarer Republik' K. Hausen ed *Frauen suchen ihre Geschichte* (Munich 1983) p. 263. Similar comments on Catholic organisations for women workers in Bavaria are made by W.K. Blessing in *Staat und Kirche* p. 242.

[64] *The Year Book and Book of Customs of Our Lady of Lourdes, Washington Heights* (New York 1916) p. 106; interviews with Miss Caroline Kolb, New York City, 21 Nov. and 5 Dec. 1983.

[65] See replies to questionnaire on history of Sacred Heart parish, New York, at Sacred Heart rectory. One reply stated that in the inter-war years the church was 'hand in glove with the McManus Democratic Club, which could furnish jobs at the drop of a hat'. A priest who was assistant from 1947–57 stated that the McManus club gave food baskets on the church's recommendation.

Improving the Condition of the Poor kept files on families applying for aid, in which they recorded the family's religion. In some cases, however, they found it hard to determine what that religion was, as the family retained links simultaneously with a number of different denominations. In the 1890s the German-born Storm family, who had earlier belonged to a Reformed church, were attending both a Lutheran and a Roman Catholic church, and receiving help from the St Vincent de Paul society at the latter. The Irish-born Tighe and Sweeney families had links with Catholic and Baptist, and with Catholic, Baptist and Episcopalian churches respectively, and the Irish-born Berry family had recently converted from Catholicism to Methodism for reasons that their new church regarded as suspect. Meanwhile, Mrs Buckley, an Irish-born Catholic with a largely absent husband, was successfully applying for help from the local Episcopalian church, saying 'she could not apply to priest for assistance as she never goes to church'.[66]

In nineteenth- and early twentieth-century Lancashire, where power was emphatically in Protestant hands, there could be strong material inducements for the many very poor Catholics not to take the exclusivist demands of their Church too literally; considerable tensions within the Catholic community resulted. A Preston woman, born in 1898, who has always had a somewhat ambivalent attitude to her Church, recalls that her earliest happy memory was of the Shepherd Street Protestant mission, which provided lantern slide shows, outings and free breakfasts for poor children. At the Catholic school the children got into trouble for going to 'Protestant places', 'So you had to hide a lot of these things'. When her parents separated, her mother sent her to live with another family, and she went to a Protestant school. Her father was furious, but 'My mother didn't crack on, because they were doing her a good turn. Religion won't keep you when all's said and done.'[67]

The relative poverty of Catholics was also reflected in the fact that they often lacked the cash to build the schools that their bishops demanded, and that when they built the schools the facilities tended to be inferior. Thus in the Netherlands, only 20 per

[66] New York, Archives of the Community Service Society, case-files of the AICP and COS, R-127, 130, 133, 136, 138.
[67] Centre for North-West Regional Studies, University of Lancaster, Oral History Archive: Interview by Elizabeth Roberts with Mrs P1P, p. 30.

cent of Catholic children were attending Catholic primary schools before public money was made available to them in 1889.[68] Thereafter, attendance at Catholic schools gradually rose, to reach very high levels by the 1950s. In the United States, however, there continued to be a considerable proportion of Catholic parents who preferred the public schools, even when parochial schools were available. Priests and nuns were continually having to justify the Church's insistence on attendance at Catholic schools, in the face of complaints that the teachers were less well qualified, that religious instruction occupied too large a place in the curriculum, and that public schools offered the children a better chance of getting ahead. Moreover, some parents used the existence of the two rival systems as a bargaining counter, threatening, if they failed to gain satisfaction from one kind of school, to transfer their children to the other.[69] So that sectarian loyalty was only one consideration among many in determining where Catholic children went to school. In early twentieth-century New York most of them went to public school, with only those of Irish descent having a parochial school majority.[70]

Another major problem faced by the leaders of the Catholic community in this period was the often very severe tension between Catholics of different classes. During the period 1870–1914 the social group in which alienation from the Catholic community was most likely to take place was the industrial working class. Earlier in the century it had often been the professional and commercial middle class that was most distant from the Church. But by the

[68] Rogier and Brachin, *Histoire du catholicisme hollandais* p. 143.

[69] Parish bulletins and other parish publications gave a lot of space to explaining the necessity for Catholic schools and answering criticisms. See the *Calendar* of Saint Paul's parish, September 1908; *Parish Monthly* of Our Lady of Good Counsel, April 1908; *Year Book and Book of Customs of Our Lady of Lourdes* pp. 41–4. For examples of the more flexible views of some parents see M.J. Oates, 'Organised Voluntaryism: The Catholic Sisters in Massachussets 1870–1940,' J.W. James ed *Women in American Religion* (Philadelphia 1980) p. 161; J.J. Bukowczyk, 'Steeples and Smokestacks: Class, Religion and Ideology in the Polish Immigrant Settlements of Brooklyn 1880–1929' (Harvard University Ph.D. thesis 1980) pp. 108–11.

[70] *Reports of the Immigration Commission* 41 vols (Washington D.C. 1911) 32 p. 619. For statistics of school attendance in New York from 1800 to 1970, see D. Ravitch, *The Great School Wars* (New York 1974) p. 405. Attendance at Catholic schools peaked at about 25 per cent of the total in 1960.

1890s the attractions of socialism and the frequent opposition of the clergy to strikes and to labour organisations were bringing class-conscious Catholic workers into conflict with their Church in many parts of Europe and America. It was also generally in working class districts of cities and in new industrial communities that the shortage of priests and of religious facilities was most serious, and as a result many working class people largely lost touch with the Church. These tendencies were weakest in the Netherlands, where right into the 1950s and '60s, Catholic organisations continued to enjoy strong support from Catholics of all classes; even so, precisely the processes described above were being reported in early twentieth-century Rotterdam.[71] At the other end of the spectrum, the tendency towards working class alienation was very marked in France, Austria, and French-speaking areas of Belgium.[72] In Austria, according to Boyer, in his study of the rise of the Christian Social Party, 'the more the priests became politicians, the less they could sustain the pretense of service to all society'; the alliance formed in the 1880s and '90s between lower clergy, peasantry and urban lower middle class meant that the Church had made 'an informal decision to abandon the Austrian working class'. These alignments were reflected in the immense strength of Catholic peasant organisations, especially in Lower Austria and the Tyrol, and the weakness of Catholic workers' organisations.[73] Somewhat similar contrasts were evident in France, though the very pronounced regional differences meant that both peasant and working class attitudes to Catholic organisations varied greatly; for instance, the militant anti-clericalism of Parisian workers contrasted with the relative strength of Catholic organisations in the northern textile region.[74]

Boyer's analysis gains support from the fact that in the 1920s those Vienna priests who were trying to establish closer links with

[71] Rogier and Brachin, *Histoire du catholicisme hollandais* pp. 116–8.
[72] For a general discussion see H. McLeod, 'The Dechristianisation of the Working Class in Western Europe (1850–1900)' *Social Compass* 27 (1980) pp. 191–214.
[73] J.W. Boyer, *Political Radicalism in Late Imperial Vienna: Origins of the Christian Social Movement 1848–1897* (Chicago 1981) pp. 181–2; Lewis, *Kirche und Partei* pp. 217–56.
[74] See two contributions to the outstanding collection. F. Bédarida and J. Maitron eds *Christianisme et monde ouvrier* (Paris 1975): J. Bruhat, 'Anti-cléricalisme et mouvement ouvrier en France avant 1914' pp. 79–115, and Y.-M. Hilaire, 'Les ouvriers de la région du Nord devant l'Eglise catholique' pp. 230–3, 241–3.

the working class were agreed in condemning the Church's ties to the Christian Social Party.[75] Political Catholicism had a polarising effect: it greatly strengthened the Church's hold on certain sections of society, while tending to alienate others. In Britain, however, where the Church was politically neutral, there were a great many Catholics who seldom attended mass, and did not belong to any Catholic organisation, but there was nothing at all comparable to the mass alienation of working class Catholics that took place in some continental countries. In the years before 1914 the Catholic clergy were strongly critical of socialism in Britain, as elsewhere, and some Catholic members of the Independent Labour Party left the Church as a result; but at this stage Irish issues had a higher priority than class issues with the majority of Catholic voters. In the 1920s, when there was a widespread movement of Catholics into support for the Labour Party, the clergy did not attempt to oppose this trend, but concentrated their fire on the small Communist Party.[76] In the United States, the Church's ties were with the Democratic Party. Throughout our period, and for many years afterwards the majority of working class Catholics shared this loyalty, though there were periods in which more radical politics won widespread support. One was the 1880s when many Irish Catholics were strongly involved in the Knights of Labor and in Henry George's campaign to be mayor of New York. At this time a mass revolt of working class Catholics seemed possible, especially after the ex-communication in 1887 of the radical New York priest, Edward McGlynn. However, the attempts by conservative bishops to obtain a papal condemnation of the Knights of Labor failed; McGlynn was readmitted to the Church in 1892, but shunted off to an obscure upstate parish; and the great majority of Irish Catholics remained within the Church, and returned to supporting the Democratic Party.[77] In the years immediately before World War I, the Socialist Party began to attract voters in some areas, in spite of fierce opposition from the Catholic clergy. But a very high proportion of

[75] Lewis, *Kirche und Partei* p. 255.
[76] W.M. Walker, 'Irish Immigrants in Scotland: Their Priests, Politics and Social Life' *HJ* 15 (1972) pp. 665–7; W. Knox ed *Scottish Labour Leaders 1918–39; A Biographical Dictionary* (Edinburgh 1984) pp. 30–3, 94, 176, 275–7.
[77] H.J. Browne, *The Catholic Church and the Knights of Labor* (Washington D.C. 1949); Curran, *Michael Augustine Corrigan*.

Socialist Party supporters came from only three ethnic groups (the Jews, Germans and Finns),[78] and in the 1930s the New Deal turned the former Socialist strongholds such as the Jewish areas of New York, into strongholds of the Democratic Party. In both Britain and the United States the Church's relationship with its mainly urban working class membership was also eased by the absence of the ties to agrarian interests or to industrialists which severely limited the clergy's political options in many continental countries. They were thus better able to identify themselves with the needs of their own parishioners, which in some parts of the U.S.A. seems to have meant a cautious support for labour organisations and strikes.[79]

In Germany the Centre Party did succeed in gaining and holding the support of the majority of Catholics of all social classes during the 1870s and '80s. But by the mid-'90s it was finding it increasingly difficult to hold together the various mutually incompatible groups within its ranks. In Düsseldorf, for instance, a generational split among working class Catholics appeared about that time. While older Catholic workers remained loyal to the Centre and strongly represented in Catholic workers' associations, younger Catholics, especially those born outside the city, were switching to the Social Democrats, 'pushed' by the Centre deputies' support for tariffs and opposition to franchise reform, 'pulled' by such factors as the attractions of the socialist unions. In 1911, the Social Democrats won the city's Reichstag seat for the first time, though even in 1906 more than two-thirds of the leaders of Düsseldorf Social Democracy were still Protestants, and it is quite possible that many Catholics *voted* socialist, without becoming drawn into active membership of socialist organisations, with their non-religious or anti-religious atmosphere.[80]

---

[78] C. Leinenweber, 'The Class and Ethnic Bases of New York City Socialism, 1904–1915' *Labor History* 22 (1981) pp. 29–56.

[79] E. Foner, 'Class, Ethnicity and Radicalism in the Gilded Age: the Land League and Irish America' *Marxist Perspectives* (1978) pp. 37–8; Shanabruch, *Chicago's Catholics* pp. 149–151. Bukowczyk, 'Steeples and Smokestacks' pp. 173–80 tries to disentangle the role of Fr William Farrell of Saints Peter and Paul, Brooklyn, in the 1910 sugar strike: he declared his support for the strikers, but was suspected by many of them because he urged them to make concessions.

[80] M. Nolan, *Social Democracy and Society: Working Class Radicalism in Düsseldorf 1890–1920* (Cambridge 1981) pp. 44–7, 72–5, 118, 132, 160–4, 221–3; for statistics of decline in Centre voting, and of Catholic support for other parties, see Schauff, *Das Wahlverhalten* pp. 74, 112–5, 132.

But perhaps the most intractable of all the problems faced by the 'ghetto'-builders was that of mixed marriages. Wherever Catholic and non-Catholic came into close contact, whether at work, at school or in the neighbourhood, some romantic attachments ensued, in spite of all the discouragements offered not only by priests, but often by parents and siblings as well. The result was traffic between religious communities, children with a foot in both camps, and sometimes the alienation from their Church of those who resented the heavy-handed attempts of their elders to make them put sectarian loyalty before love.

Mixed marriages were a major concern of the clergy in the early twentieth century, wherever the population was to any significant degree religiously mixed. Sometimes precise figures are available. For instance, in the south London working class parish of Holy Trinity, Dockhead, there was a slow but remorseless rise in the proportion of mixed marriages among all those recorded by the priest, from a quarter in 1881, to just over a quarter in 1895, to just over a half in 1928, and three-quarters in 1963.[81] In Baden the proportion of all marriages that were religiously mixed rose steadily from 9 per cent in 1869–73 to 22 per cent in 1934. But the averages concealed considerable variations: the percentage was very low in peasant families, but much higher among the rural proletariat, and also in the cities.[82] It is less clear, however, how far mixed marriages resulted in net losses to the Catholic community. It is interesting to note, for instance, that in south London the large number of mixed marriages did not lead to the spectacular decline in Catholic practice that Victorian bishops would have predicted: at Dockhead a higher percentage of Catholics were attending mass in 1963 than had done so in the 1890s. It may be that mixed marriages were removing a section of the Catholic population who were already luke-warm towards their Church, while more strongly committed Catholics were both more likely to marry a co-religionist, and, if they married a Protestant, quite likely to secure their partner's conversion. The net effect of mixed marriages may therefore have been slightly to reduce the total number of Catholics, while increasing the proportion who were actively committed. In Baden and Alsace, where the issue has been carefully studied by Wahl, mixed

---

[81] See parish file in Archives of the Roman Catholic Archdiocese of Southwark.
[82] Wahl, 'Confession et comportement' 2 pp. 764–5.

marriages clearly worked to the benefit of Protestantism, though probably only slightly so.[83] In Lancashire, where a lot of evidence is available from the oral history surveys by Roberts (covering the period 1890–1939) and Thompson and Vigne (c1880–1918),[84] the picture is less clear. Out of twenty-one cases I have seen where the respondent or the respondent's parent married someone of the other religion, eleven of the marriages benefitted the Protestants, in that the Catholic partner either converted or allowed the children to be brought up as Protestants, nine benefitted the Catholics, and in one case a decision was made that one child would be brought up as a Catholic and the other as a Protestant.

What stands out from many of the Lancashire interviews and from some of the evidence from Baden and Alsace is the tremendous bitterness often associated with mixed marriages. 'Both communities,' notes Wahl, 'regarded mixed marriages as treason.'[85] On the Protestant side the pressure came mainly from parents and other relatives. On the Catholic side, however, priests played a major part in seeking to dissuade potential 'traitors'.[86] The clergy were encouraged by their bishops to preach against mixed marriages, and many did so. In Alsace some clergy also refused absolution to those intending to marry Protestants, and denounced individuals from the pulpit. Private appeals were of course used more generally. Such tactics helped to ensure that the great majority of Catholics did marry Catholics, and that many of them retained a horror of mixed marriages, and joined readily in the persecution of those who stepped out of line. But these efforts were to some degree counter-productive. Those who did persist in marrying a member of a different Church remained scarred by the resulting conflicts for years afterwards. The resentment they felt led some Catholics to break entirely with their Church, and others to go through a long period in which their loyalty ran very thin.[87] The fact that the clergy were able to mount such pressures against the

[83] *Ibid.* 2 pp. 761–85.
[84] Transcripts of interviews in Thompson and Vigne's project are kept at the Department of Sociology, University of Essex.
[85] Wahl, 'Confession et comportement', 2 p. 784.
[86] *Ibid.* 2 pp. 718–84. The same contrast is apparent in the Lancashire interviews.
[87] Essex Oral History Archive, tape no. 68, pp. 47–9, informant born Manchester 1883; Elizabeth Roberts, interview with Mr E1P, pp. 6, 31, informant born Preston 1895, and interview with Mrs D1P, p. 33, informant born Preston 1908.

deviant, and that so many Catholics were ready to assist was a testimony to the strength of Catholic identity and to the powerful hold of the sub-culture which the clergy had worked so hard to build up. Yet coercion was a double-edged weapon. The means used to enforce Catholic unity produced strong under-currents of resentment even among many of those who remained Catholics. An interview by Elizabeth Roberts with an elderly Preston woman, who had been Catholic all her life, and was at the time waiting for a visit by a priest, provides an interesting illustration of this. She was unusual among practising Catholics in the volume of criticism that she was prepared to direct at her Church. But many of the individual points that she made were repeated in other interviews.[88] She criticised the Catholic Church for being bigoted in its attitude to other Churches, for being obsessed with money, and for hell-fire preaching in its schools. She was also resentful of the harassment she had received from the clergy for non-attendance at mass following her marriage to a husband who had insisted on her staying at home on Sunday mornings. Towards the end of the interview she delivered a concentrated attack on various aspects of Catholicism, claiming that her Church had done a lot of harm:

> I have Communion and he comes here every month. I thought, I am nearly at the end of my tether and I will have to repent for my sins, but I still don't believe in a lot of things. I don't believe in Confession. Why should an old woman go to a young priest, and say 'Please father, forgive me?' He hasn't been living when the temptation was there for you to do wrong or tell lies or whatever you did. We never did anything wrong, but I could have done to steal some clothes for my children when they were little. ... There's been many a couple parted through not being the same religion and the Church telling them they were living in sin, and all things like that. ... There's many a woman in her grave to-day through having a houseful of kids through religion being forced down their necks.[89]

[88] See for instance, Essex Oral History Archive, tape no. 72, informant born Bolton 1891, (she left the Catholic Church after being told by a nun that her dead brother was in hell or purgatory); Roberts, interview with Mr F1P, informant born Cumberland 1906 (gave up going to mass because of various slights received at church; claimed priests were only interested in his money).

[89] Roberts, interview with Mrs P1P, pp. 32–6, 64.

High levels of Catholic practice and of involvement in Catholic organisations were thus consistent with high levels of resentment against the all-encroaching authority of the Church. Here perhaps we have one explanation for the sometimes drastic reduction in the level of Catholic practice that followed the slackening of the controls in the late 1960s and 1970s.[90]

University of Birmingham

---

[90] The most spectacular drop was in the Netherlands, where weekly mass attendance fell from 64 per cent to 26 per cent between 1966 and 1979: see Bakvis, *Catholic Power* p. 117. In many other countries there was a sharp fall within a short period in the late '60s and early '70s. See, for instance, F. Lebrun ed, *Histoire des catholiques en France* (Toulouse 1980) p. 488; and for Belgium, R.E.M. Irving, *The Christian Democratic Parties of Western Europe* (London 1979) p. 167.

THE WELFARE STATE WITHIN THE STATE: THE SAINT VINCENT DE PAUL SOCIETY IN GLASGOW, 1848–1920

by BERNARD ASPINWALL

A T a great protest meeting in Glasgow against Ultra-montanism in 1874, the Jesuits, those wily chameleons, were acccused of masquerading as members of the St. Vincent de Paul Society. That body was

> ostensibly to benefit the poor but it is in fact a religio-political organisation. It has local, central and general councils; quarterly meetings, conferences, fetes, pilgrimages; it has passports and circular letters to its members. It adapts itself to all classes and conditions – addresses itself to the scholar, the soldier, the mechanic, the apprentice, the labourer – to the mother and the daughter, for all of whom it issues a suitable publication.[1]

As another speaker, the redoubtable Charles Newdegate, M.P., said these 'subtle energies' were part of the impenetrable strength of Romanism.[2] Forty years later, G.K. Chesterton's convert friend, Professor John S. Phillimore, the first Catholic professor in the University of Glasgow since the Reformation, stressed the strength and importance of the St. Vincent de Paul Society in sustaining the Catholic community, staving off revolution and undermining bigotry in the west of Scotland.[3] The society, as Archbishop Eyre, the architect and organiser of Glasgow Catholicism observed, should have been named the 'General Purposes Society'.[4] Like a

---

[1] Rev. Dr. Duff of Edinburgh in *Ultramontanism: A Full Report of the Great Public Meeting in the Interests of Civil and Religious Freedom, Glasgow, 7 October 1874* (Glasgow 1874) p. 46.

[2] *Ultramontanism* p. 24. He enjoyed his most enthusiastic support in Scotland. W.L. Arnstein, *Protestant versus Catholic in Mid-Victorian England: Mr. Newdegate and the Nuns.* (Columbia, Mo. 1982) pp. 7, 52.

[3] *Annual Report of the St. Vincent de Paul Society* (Glasgow 1914) pp. 13–14. Hereafter cited as *A.R.S.V.P.*

[4] *A.R.S.V.P.* (1897) p. 7.

great department store it met and provided for every conceivable need.

These compliments to a voluntary association of laymen suggest something of its importance, its influence, and its contribution to the protection, consolidation and improvement of the new and largely immigrant church in Glasgow. Founded by Frederic Ozanam in Paris in 1833 it offered spiritual and material succour and support to the poor. Through alms, instruction, visits and general assistance it hoped to improve their lot. Thirteen years later the S.V.P. arrived in Scotland. The francophile Bishop Gillis built upon the existing Holy Gild of St. Joseph in Edinburgh. The original members of the gild and their offices were absorbed into the S.V.P. The first president was significantly a distinguished convert, James Augustine Stothert. Educated at Edinburgh and Cambridge, Stothert was a poet, antiquarian and later, for a time, a priest. Two years later the society came to Glasgow.[5]

The first president was the solicitor, James B. Bryson, who had been responsible for the foundation of the Scottish Catholic Temperance Association in 1839.[6] After spending two years in Edinburgh where he joined the S.V.P., he returned to Glasgow. With seven other gentlemen he founded the St. Andrews's conference under the guidance of Revd. William Gordon. Among those original members who are known were three prosperous businessmen, a coal merchant, a commission agent, an ironmonger and painter; an artisan; a shopkeeper; and a former teacher and religious repository keeper. Within ten years Glasgow had fourteen conferences with 131 active members. In 1898 there were forty-one conferences

[5] This paragraph is based on *Report of the Second Festival of the Holy Gild of St. Joseph Friendly Society* (Edinburgh 1843); *Tablet*, 18 April, 23 May, 1 Aug 1846. It continued to function until the 1850s. A brief account in English of the S.V.P. is in A.J. Dunn, *Frederic Ozanam and the Establishment of the S.V.P.* (London 1913) and Daniel T. McColgan, *A Century of Charity: The First One Hundred Years of the S.V.P. in the United States* (Milwaukee 1951) pp. 1–52. J.B. Duroselle. *Les Débuts du Catholicisme Social en France, 1822–70* (Paris 1951) remains the classic study.

[6] *The Scottish Temperance Journal* March, 1840, pp. 177–89 and *Souvenir of the Golden Jubilee of the S.V.P. in the archdiocese of Glasgow* (Glasgow 1898) which gives a summary. The originals and early printed reports, 1848–52 are lost. Rev. Peter Forbes, St. Mary's, Glasgow had wanted a similar organisation for the poor a few years earlier. See *Grand Soirée and Presentation to Rev. Peter Forbes, 27 April 1846* (Glasgow 1846). The only copy is in the Glasgow archdiocesan archives.

and 569 members. By the First World War sixty-nine conferences with 1052 members were dealing with some 13,000 individuals.[7] That means that one in thirty of the estimated Catholic population were sufficiently hard pressed to require some kind of support from the S.V.P. by that time.

The original complaint about the society which opened this paper may seem to have been justified. The S.V.P. demonstrated the strength and resilience of the Catholic laity. Ironically it also reflected the clericalism of the Presbyterian Church; a point noted earlier by Combe and Buckle.[8] The S.V.P. prevented any significant penetration of the Catholic body by proselytism: colporteurs were invariably rebuffed. Its social work reinforced the ethnic and class resistance to patronising Scottish middle class enterprises.[9] As in the United States and Ireland the Protestant crusade floundered in the face of communal cynicism about selective consciences. Liberal outrage about European Catholic excesses failed to disturb poor Irish reinforced in their folk religion by petty Scottish discrimination and social prejudice. The local priest shared the community culture and accent which the welfare services of the S.V.P. further defended. At the same time its endeavours contributed to the conversion of men of wealth and influence, and in turn their Tory social romanticism and cash were to assist the society.[10]

Within the Catholic community the S.V.P. offered men opportunities for the exercise of significant apostolic spiritual roles and social functions in the parish. They were enabled to transmit, albeit

[7] *Glasgow City Directories* 1848–53; *Souvenir* pp. 14–17; J. Darragh's population figures are in D. MacRoberts ed *Modern Scottish Catholicism, 1878–1978* (Glasgow 1979) p. 229.

[8] George Combe, *Notes on a Visit to the U.S.A. during a Phrenological Visit*, 3 vols (Edinburgh 1841) 1 pp. 135–39 and 3 pp. 227–35 and T.H. Buckle, *History of Civilisation in England* quoted in James T. Young, *The Rousing of the Scottish Working Class* (London 1979) p. 98.

[9] See the examples in 'Shadow', *Midnight Scenes and Social Photographs (1858)* ed John F. McCaffrey (Glasgow 1976) pp. 136–41. On similar strains and tensions see R.A. Billington, *The Protestant Crusade, 1800–1860: A Study of the Origins of American Nativism* (New York 1938) and D. Bowen, *The Protestant Crusade in Ireland, 1800–1870* (London 1978).

[10] See John Davies, *Cardiff and the Marquesses of Bute* (Cardiff 1981) pp. 22–27; D. Hunter Blair, *John Patrick 3rd Marquess of Bute, 1847–1900* (London 1921). Monteith usually claimed to have been converted by the Irish poor. See also W.G. Ward, *Ideal of the Christian Church* (London 1844).

unwittingly, the significant values of the host society to their co-religionists: thrift, sobriety, self-help, and community. To that extent they were conservatives, conveying accommodating attitudes. Yet by sharply contrasting a romantic view of the middle ages with the dominant competitive capitalism of the day they were presenting alternative visions of society. To the poor they offered the riches of a superior, older ethnic culture. Significantly the S.V.P. developed against the background of many Scottish aristocratic conversions such as that of the Marquess of Bute. Even more decisive was the convert of 'new' wealth, Robert Monteith. A friend of Tennyson, Manning and Newman, he and David Urquhart, the Russophobe, were the architects of modern Catholic social thought with their ideal of a cohesive community. Like the Scottish Free Church, Scottish Catholics briefly might envisage a new model order in New Zealand; but the development of roots in Glasgow was more practical. The convert had a role in a welfare state within the existing order.[11]

The S.V.P. met the immediate needs of the local poor Catholics: like a political machine it provided a safety net. Decentralised and local its primary concern was moral regeneration of the group. With its main emphasis upon stability and compassionate community support from cradle to grave, it merely reproached the existing order. At the same time, by sustaining the group within the normative values of the church, the S.V.P. strengthened 'traditional' family networks of support and service. As a recent study has shown, Irish immigrants had few state bureaucratic supports.[12] The S.V.P. gave vital personal aid at critical times: birth, illness, education, unemployment and bereavement. In the process it contributed to the formation of a mentality which welcomed a gradualist programme of social reform, a moral critique of competitive capitalism and a somewhat diffuse egalitarian rhetoric. The S.V.P.

---

[11] See my articles 'David Urquhart, Robert Monteith and the Catholic Church' *Innes Review* 31 (1980) pp. 57–70 and 'The Formation of the Catholic Community in the West of Scotland' *Innes Review* 33 (1982) pp. 44–57. The Urquhart Papers, Balliol College, Oxford contain some correspondence regarding Monteith and W. Cargill who seems to be the same man as the founder of Otago, New Zealand. See Tom Bowling, *And Captain of their Souls: An Interpretative Essay on the Life and Times of Captain William Cargill* (Dunedin N.Z. 1984).

[12] See Michael Anderson, *Family Structure in Nineteenth Century Lancashire* (Cambridge 1971) esp pp. 87–8, 108, 178.

was a microcosm of a social welfare state. In association with other organisations it encouraged healthy recreational pursuits, preferably in a temperance atmosphere. It provided training in organisational skills, contributed to community policing, and mobilised the community family system to safeguard unfortunate individuals. And arguably, it laid the emotional foundations for the Labour Party in Scotland.[13]

The S.V.P. arrived in Glasgow at an opportune moment. The famine immigration was at its height. Bishop Murdoch, embarrassed, overwhelmed and uncomprehending, hoped that the Irish nationalists of 1848 would have a 'skinful of bullets'.[14] Robert Monteith with his wealth was beginning to build the institutional infrastructure through his aid to religious orders. The Scottish Poor Law Amendment Act (1845) had set a five year residence restriction on settlement claims. Even then relief was not available to the ablebodied. Not infrequently immigrants were sent back to Ireland to prevent them becoming a charge. Crammed into a city with a population density of 5,000 per acre the Irish sometimes lived twenty to a room in the worst housing in Europe. In 1870 thirty per cent of the population lived in single rooms; even twenty years later almost one-fifth lived in such conditions.[15] The S.V.P. served these areas, by maintaining a link with the folk religion and by making a sectarian point by offering social salvation. They were reaching those whose problems, as a recent historian has claimed, a smug middle class had hardly begun to solve.[16]

With the alternative attractions of city life in the saloons and streets, the secular threat of Chartism, followed by Fenianism and then Socialism, the pressures from Orange societies and anti-Catholic press and lecturers like Gavazzi and 'Angel Gabriel' Orr,

---

[13] See J.F. McCaffrey, 'Politics and the Catholic Community Since 1878' in D. MacRoberts pp. 140–155 and Ian S. Wood, 'John Wheatley, the Irish and the Labour Movement in Scotland' *Innes Review* 31 (1980) pp. 71–85.

[14] Edinburgh, Scottish Catholic Archives, Blairs Papers, Bishop Murdoch to Rev. Dr. Kyle, 21 April and 20 Aug. 1848.

[15] On this aspect see Audrey Patterson, 'The Poor Law in Nineteenth Century Scotland' in Derek Fraser ed *The New Poor Law in the Nineteenth Century* (London 1976) pp. 171–193; Thomas Ferguson, *The Dawn of Scottish Social Welfare* (London 1948) and his *Scottish Social Welfare* (Edinburgh 1958); J.H. Treble, *Urban Poverty in Britain, 1830–1914* (London 1979).

[16] James D. Young, *The Rousing of the Scottish Working Class* pp. 33–36.

the pastoral problems were immense. As in America tensions not infrequently resulted in street clashes and violence, but as the city slowly developed suburbs the tensions and opportunities for crude sectarianism diminished. The Catholic social problem remained. Where there had been three families in 1779, by 1851 there were 100,000 and by 1914 there would be almost half a million souls.[17]

The number of Catholic churches increased dramatically to twenty four by 1900, but they were still unable to match the population increase. Poverty, fear and ethnic suspicion may have caused Archbishop Eyre's predecessors to tread warily before 1868 and only twelve more churches were built before World War Two. In this period then Catholicism was an inner city faith. Hitherto historians have emphasised new devotional attitudes as decisive in building the renewed Catholicism, a view reassuring to those convinced of Catholic anti-intellectualism.[18] The explanation may partly rest elsewhere. Organisations of laymen have received little attention. In that network of bodies related to the S.V.P. clericalism rested on lay initiatives. In the early days S.V.P. members frequently complained at the lack of clerical support from overworked priests.[19]

In general the S.V.P. developed a constructive, conciliatory manner. Only during the brief episcopacy of bishop Lynch was there any militantly Irish attack on 'souperism' among the poor.[20] Such allegations only encouraged greater lay activity. Under the aristocratic Archbishop Eyre, a more confident, quietly assertive and bridge building attitude emerged. He regretted that Catholics did

---

[17] *Scottish Catholic Directory*, hereafter cited as *S.C.D.* (1853) p. 94; Darragh p. 229; James E. Handley, *The Irish in Scotland* (Glasgow nd) remains the standard authority. On the containment of Irish radical sympathies in Scotland see James Epstein, *The Lion of Freedom: Feargus O'Connor and the Chartist Movement, 1832–1842* (London 1982); A. Plummer, *Bronterre: A Political Biography of Bronterre O'Brien, 1804–1864* (London 1971); P. Quinlivan and P. Rose, *The Fenians in England, 1865–1872* (London, 1982); K.R.M. Short, *The Dynamite War: Irish-American Bombers in Victorian Britain* (Dublin 1979).

[18] The classic statement is Emmet Larkin, 'The Devotional Revolution in Ireland, 1850–1875' *AHR* 77 (1982). I have derived these figures from an analysis of the opening dates of churches in the *Western Catholic Calendar* (Glasgow 1984).

[19] For example *A.R.S.V.P.* (1863) pp. 8–9; (1864) pp. 8–9, (1866) pp. 6–7; (1869) p. 9.

[20] *A.R.S.V.P.* (1867) p.8. Catholic soup kitchens were established.

not make their needs known to their fellow Protestant citizens,[21] some of whom, like the businessman, Sir Daniel Macaulay Stevenson, did occasionally give support. Some coal dealers sent coal for distribution to the poor: W.L. Dunn, Daldowie collieries and others invariably gave fourteen loads for many years. Others supported the elderly in the care of the Little Sisters.[22] The overwhelming burden, however, was carried by the local Catholic community already overtaxing itself in providing schools, churches and other institutions.

The S.V.P. remained very much a local democracy in that its funds were raised and largely distributed in the local parish. In the first four years in Glasgow, 1848–52, it distributed some £881 and dealt with 746 people each week. By 1914 it was spending almost £10,000 on some 13,000 clients.[23] Funds were also received from benefactors like the Marquess of Bute and Robert Monteith or from former parishioners settled in America, Canada or New Zealand.[24] The S.V.P. reinforced the sense of parish identity even before the Catholic revivals. Parish bazaars, oratorios and concerts all contributed fair sums. The League of the Cross, the temperance organisation, often raised £50 from concerts in the late nineteenth century.[25] Charity sermons, which became parish occasions, also raised funds with star preachers. In 1864 Ignatius Spencer, the Passionist, made over £25 but significantly in the heated Irish-Scottish Catholic ethnic rivalry of the time, two Irish preachers raised over £37 and over £44 respectively.[26] In 1901 the Revd. Lord Archibald Douglas raised over £61 on one occasion.[27] One parish, St. Patrick's even raised money from the sale of photographs of the clergy,[28] whilst another important contributor was

[21] A.R.S.V.P. (1872) p. 8. He invariably took greater interest in the society than his predecessors and tried to attend the a.g.m. each year.
[22] For example Sir D.M. Stevenson in A.R.S.V.P. (1892), list of contributors. Coal in A.R.S.V.P. (1891) p. 41: numerous other examples could be cited.
[23] See A.R.S.V.P. (1848–52) a composite version in the Jubilee volume cited above; A.R.S.V.P. (1914), financial statement.
[24] See A.R.S.V.P. (1899); (1905); (1880).
[25] See A.R.S.V.P. (1903); (1848–52) for oratorios and bazaars from the earliest days.
[26] A.R.S.V.P. (1864) p. 35 and (1865) p. 38.
[27] A.R.S.V.P. (1901) p. 8.
[28] A.R.S.V.P. (1905) p. 16.

Celtic Football Club.[29] Founded originally to help feed the children of the east end of the city, the club and its supporters clubs were regular donors to parochial societies. But the Marquess of Bute remained the most generous benefactor by establishing the Bute Fund, which the S.V.P. might use in emergencies. That was not his only subsidy as we shall see. The origins and means by which funds were raised reflected the growing sense of communal identity, parochial strength and individual concern: the S.V.P. greased the wheels of Catholic progress.

Stability and defence went together: loyalty and amelioration followed. The appeal to the folk memory of the Catholic poor was irresistible. The Irish step-father of the great temperance advocate, J. Dawson Burn, whatever his many failings, 'never forgot to pray, morning or evening'.[30] As recent historians have suggested there was more contact in Roman Catholic norms than attendance figures reveal. Even so attendance was fair.[31] According to the 1851 religious census about 12,000 attended Mass.[32]

Although only one in twenty of the poor might attend church their residual Catholic loyalty might be enkindled by compassion: 'Whatever can be done to assimilate the condition of the Catholic rich and poor ... is so much positive aid to the spiritual advancement of the church ... the true spirit of Christian self-sacrificing charity leavens all classes alike and civilisation and conversion proceed hand in hand'.[33] The most convincing sign of the Church was a commitment to the poor: controversy over scripture and history meant nothing to the mass of the population. Better housing, education and general uplift would ensure a future for

---

[29] James E. Handley, *The Celtic Story: a history of Celtic F.C.* (London 1960) remains the standard account. Nearly every *A.R.S.V.P.* gives details of gifts. Bute's considerable generosity also appears in virtually every issue.

[30] J. Dawson Burn, *Autobiography of a Beggar Boy* (London 1855) p. 19.

[31] For example, Lynn Hollin Lees, *Exiles of Erin: Irish Immigrants in Victorian London* (Manchester 1979) pp. 165–69, 184. Also 'Shadow' cited above and R. Howie, *The Churches and the Churchless in Scotland* (Glasgow 1893) especially p. xxviii on Catholic success with the working classes.

[32] *The Census of Religious Worship 1851 – Glasgow.*

[33] J.M. Capes, 'The Wants of the Times' *Rambler* 5 (1850) pp. 485–504 esp p. 502. Capes who had been corresponding with Scottish Catholic figures wrote a remarkable commentary on the Scottish condition in *Rambler* 3 (1849) pp. 597–99 in which he said 'If ever there was a principle and a body of men existing *in* a kingdom and not *of* it, it is Catholicism and Catholics in Calvinistic and Puritan Scotland.'

the Church and, in marked contrast to philanthropy, that distant do-gooding, all classes participated.[34]

To converts like Monteith and his friends, the S.V.P. fulfilled these demands. The Church had neither caste nor party. Like his friend Urquhart, he wanted a compassionate cohesive order deeply rooted in the locality; 'where a community is united *there cannot be destitution.*'[35] That was an understandable notion, since his father had been partly responsible for the arrival of Thomas Chalmers in Glasgow, and it echoed the idea of parochial visitation:

> a parochial economy is not less effectual; for this purpose that the jurisdictions it institutes, instead of being of a legal, are of a moral and charitable character. The kindly intercourse that is promoted between the various classes, under such an arrangement as this, is the best possible of all possible emollients in every season of political restlessness.[36]

Monteith had been involved with other Protestants in the Holy Gild of St. Joseph in Edinburgh through its concern for public health and morality.[37] Its ceremonial occasions particularly appealed since they showed the unity of all classes: 'This holy levelling of rank and station without lowering either; this mingling of classes without confusion of grade or detriment to social order is preeminently the secret of the Catholic church.'[38] Monteith was also the driving force behind the voluntary Association of St. Margaret. Established in 1848, it directed its efforts towards the protection of the orphan poor, to grants to teachers in training, to assisting emigration through Mrs. Chisholm's schemes, to life assurance, the provision of cheap improving Catholic literature, the encouragement of congregational singing and the demonstration

---

[34] J.M. Capes in *Rambler* 4 (1849) pp. 473–82.

[35] D. Urquhart, *Wealth and Want, or Taxation as Influencing Private Riches and Public Liberty* (London 1845) p. 6. Also see his *The Spirit of the East* 2 vols (London 1839) 2 p. 201; *Turkey and Its Resources* (London 1833) pp. 254–55. Henry Formby, *A Visit to the East* (London 1843) betrays similar Urquhartite sentiments throughout.

[36] T. Chalmers, *The Right Christian and Civic Economy for a Nation with a more special reference to its large towns* 3 vols (London 1848 ed) 1 pp. 387–88 also p. 405.

[37] *Tablet*, 28 April 1848; see also 22 Feb. 1845, Monteith gave the toast; 18 Sept. 1847, 28 June 1851, 12 Feb. 1853.

[38] *Tablet*, 3 May 1851.

of Catholic loyalty to priests and papacy.

Monteith wanted patriotism and ultramontanism: 'We shall have something independent alike of O'Connell and Lord Shrewsbury – and something to unite the poor cotton spinner of Glasgow with the chief and clansman of the north. We shall have a little Catholic government and parliament in the land without the folly of and squabbling of factions.'[39] His ambition was for an extended democracy, extended rights, extended duties and extended abilities. Hymn singing was a means of inculcating new ideas of a Catholic community: Robert Skerrington, Edward Caswall and Henry Formby seem to have been influenced by him.[40] The Association however foundered and the S.V.P. continued as the only available vehicle to achieve such ends.

The society was very concerned with children. The operation of the Scottish poor law allowed too much proselytism of orphans. Only slowly did the S.V.P. win the right to inspect the poor house register for Catholic children: the Catholic orphanage established in 1832 proved too small until Smyllum was established on land given by Monteith in 1866. Only then were their concerns quieted. Even so Mgr. Munro told the annual general meeting in 1872 that children should be given far greater priority than the elderly: the poor house remained a real threat to their faith.[41] That distrust of the secular state threw the community back upon its own institutions.

In the early days the S.V.P. had been involved with the Bootblack Brigade children providing shelter and moral uplift.[42] That

---

[39] Edinburgh, Scottish Catholic Archives, Blairs Papers, R. Monteith to Rev. P. McLachlan, 20 Aug. 1848.

[40] His convert lawyer friend, R. Skerrington and Edward Caswall spent some time writing hymns in Edinburgh while as noted above Formby expressed very Urquhartite views. See J.M. Stone, *Eleanor Leslie, A Memoir* (London 1898) pp. 162–64.

[41] *A.R.S.V.P.* (1871) p. 7. See R. Skerrington, *Petition to the Lords and Commons to appoint a Superintendent of Roman Catholic Pauper Children in Scotland* (Edinburgh 1861). Robert Hay, *Catholicity in Glasgow Thirty Years Ago* (Glasgow 1868) gives details of the problems of Catholic orphans. No Catholic became a Scottish M.P. before 1914 and before 1881 at least no Catholic served on Glasgow city council.

[42] *A.R.S.V.P.* p. 10 and (1866) p. 43. These developments are summarised in the *Souvenir Jubilee* cited above pp. 20–1. See also *The Childrens Refuge Annual Report* (1897) and (1905). According to the *Catholic Directory* there were almost 60,000 children in the archdiocesan schools.

initiative developed into the Day Feeding School (1883) and later the Newsboys Shelter (1887), an institution offering some limited accommodation and a far more considerable food service to young working children. Six years later thirty children had accommodation and had been found jobs, while 177 had been aided in the year. In addition almost 32,000 meals had been provided at low or no cost. The shelter also ran a savings bank, seaside trips and Christmas parties. As early as 1897 it was providing free cinema shows. Unlike the city model lodgings to which priests were denied access, the Marists maintained a presence. New accommodation was built later and the S.V.P. contributed over £250 a year towards the cost. But with the Education Acts of 1872 and later, the raising of the school leaving age and the massive expansion of the Catholic schools system pressure on these facilities diminished.

Another initiative supported by the S.V.P. was the Children's Refuge, founded by Archbishop Eyre in 1887. A founder of the Scottish Society for the Prevention of Cruelty to Children, Eyre won the practical and financial support of the society to the extent of around £400 a year. By 1905 the home had dealt with some 3200 children.[43] The majority were invariably the children of widows; some seventy to eighty were admitted each year but many were deserted or orphans. The S.V.P. helped with adoption, placement with guardians, apprenticeships or education.

The Catholic Industrial School begun in 1862 was another concern. Children found to be destitute or known to be petty criminals could be committed to these institutions. Twenty-five years later it was dealing with almost 600 youths. Behind these figures lay appalling tales. In 1879, half of the 142 admitted could neither read nor write; 133 had never been to confession and 115 had never been to communion.[44] However, prevention was far more important than cure. To that end the Glasgow conference underook a massive programme of underwriting Catholic parochial schools. Nearly every parish had a clothing scheme for children: hundreds of pairs of boots and outfits were provided. School fees were paid: 690 children were kept in school in 1870.[45] Meals were

[43] *Tablet*, 1 Aug. 1884 and the reports included in *A.R.S.V.P.*
[44] *Annual Report of the Industrial School* (Glasgow 1869). 1879, 1880 and 1889 all have similar figures. Also see *Jubilee Souvenir*.
[45] *A.R.S.V.P.* (1870) p. 8.

provided: St. Mary's conference gave almost 73,000 free dinners in 1895.[46] Schoolbooks were paid for; sometimes for as many as 300 children. When they left school some pupils were found jobs.

The S.V.P. had attempted to develop some youth programme from the start. A central hall with recreational and cultural facilities had been a constant if unfulfilled dream. The Catholic Youngmen's Society (C.Y.M.S.) had emerged in Glasgow during the 1850s aided by visits by its founder and other speakers.[47] The League of the Cross had arrived after 1872 to promote temperance and cultivation.[48] Archbishop Eyre extended it to every parish in the diocese. By 1900 there were more than 15,000 members in the archdiocese. Numerous recreation halls were built but some puritanical Catholics were outraged by the introduction of billiard tables. Proposals to enlist schoolchildren in the League's temperance band seem to have faded rapidly following the death of Eyre.

The S.V.P. still tried to encourage some cultivation through the provision of small parish libraries. Either occasionally, weekly, or during parish missions the S.V.P. manned the library as an antidote to non-Catholic culture. Its members might also sell prayer books, religious objects and distribute pamphlets published by the Scottish Catholic Truth Society (1894): one parish gave out more than 2000 of its booklets as well as other literature.[49] Such enterprises however were limited by the social and educational level of the community. A more substantial voluntary body later overtook these efforts. The founding of the Catholic Institute (1912) was a watershed. Professor J.S. Phillimore and Dr., later Revd. W. Eric Brown of Glasgow University, encouraged by archbishop Maguire, began an ambitious social and intellectual group. Within a year it had some 525 members devoted to the study of social issues, lectures and

---

[46] A.R.S.V.P. (1895) St. Mary's return. See the annual figures for example in (1892) p. 8, (1893) p. 20.

[47] Rev. Fr. O'Brien, Limerick and T.E. Bradley, editor of the *Lamp* came. *Tablet* 8, 22 July 1854, 12 July, 15 Dec. 1855.

[48] See Glasgow Archdiocesan Archives, League of the Cross Returns, 1901. In addition there were nearly 7,300 women and children members. Two years later the grand total was 25,178 members: Mackintosh Papers, J. Brady to Archbishop Mackintosh 3 Nov. 1913; Eyre Papers, Rev. O'Reilly S.J. to Archbishop Eyre, 24. Sept. 1888. There is also a full census of the archdiocese in 1888.

[49] A.R.S.V.P. (1864); (1869) p. 12; (1892) p. 57.

other meetings. By its nature and subscription charge, it remained an elite group.[50] After the First World War amid the conflicts over Ireland and Socialism the Catholic Workers Educational League emerged from these beginnings.

The S.V.P. concentrated on more immediate concerns. Many Catholic doctors freely provided services to the Catholic community, Dr. Thomas Colvin of the Gorbals becoming something of a legend.[51] In addition the S.V.P. often paid for hospital, convalescent or sanitoria care. From the 1890s it sought to provide holidays for the poor in Ayrshire and thirty years later provided a holiday home at Langbank on the Clyde. By 1926 over 2200 had been given holidays there.[52] In addition to the various religious orders of women devoted to the poor, the society also supported St. Elizabeth's House (1893), and provided the services of forty home nurses for an average 2,500 cases a year. The service was available free or funded by the S.V.P.[53] Although the Marquess of Bute massively subsidised the home up to £1000 a year, the scheme eventually ended in 1915. If illness proved fatal to the poor, the S.V.P. often covered funeral expenses and in Airdrie even provided a burial plot.[54]

Unfortunate adults were not neglected. From 1896 the Discharged Prisoners' Aid Society, supported by the S.V.P., took a particular interest in women, finding them accommodation or jobs away from Glasgow, or providing street traders' goods. From 1902 men came under its wing and six years later 2000 were being assisted,[55] some being helped to emigrate to America and Canada.

---

[50] Glasgow Archdiocesan Archives, Miscellaneous, J.M. McGlinchey to Mgr. J. Ritchie, 13 Nov. 1920; *Reports of the Catholic Institute, 1913–22*. The father of Sir Denis Brogan served on the committee. Dr. W.E. Brown, a lecturer in History, Glasgow University, became a Catholic priest after his conversion and later served as chaplain to the Catholic undergraduates. I am indebted to Dr. John Durkan for this and information on Rev. P.J. Flood. Also see J.M. Cleary, *Catholic Social Action in Britain 1909–1959* (Oxfore 1961) p. 84.

[51] See the numerous annual tributes to Dr. Colvin and many fellow doctors in the *A.R.S.V.P.* 1890–1920.

[52] Glasgow, A. Arch., Miscellaneous, D. Mullen to Archbishop Mackintosh 10 Oct. 1924; *A.R.S.V.P.* (1926) p. 13; (1927) pp. 88–9.

[53] *St. Elizabeth's Home Annual Reports* (1897–1916) and Glasgow, A. Arch., Misc., Memorandum, 3 Feb. 1903.

[54] *A.R.S.V.P.* (1866) p. 26. Funeral payments will be found in virtually every report.

[55] *A.R.S.V.P.* (1895–1914) include appendices with *Discharged Catholic Prisoners Aid Society Reports*. Rev. Cornelius's obituary is in (1907).

In addition, the society helped the Passionist, Fr. Cornelius campaign for the Immoral Traffic Act (Scotland). Seafarers were also provided with the comforts of home through the Apostleship of the Sea, which effectively began in Glasgow in the 1890s. With the support of the S.V.P. a lively religious centre with accommodation and entertainment was established and by 1928 over 15,000 a year were using its facilities.[56]

Drink was usually considered the fastest way out of Glasgow. Emigration was the other. As we have suggested earlier, Mrs. Caroline Chisholm's schemes had won support among Catholics.[57] The S.V.P. had helped children emigrate to join their families, or others to begin better lives elsewhere. But these enterprises faded until, in the late nineteenth century, assisted emigration for children attracted wide support. Some Catholics welcomed this idea as it gave opportunities abroad without social dislocation at home. Archbishop Maguire initially opposed the idea on practical and pastoral grounds.[58] However on the eve of the First World War a scheme did get under way. Through S.V.P. patronage between five and ten children a year were sent to Canada and Australia,[59] but by 1926 the end of government subsidised child emigration and considerable difficulties in placing children with Canadian Catholic families seems to have brought the scheme to a halt.[60] However in the depressed post-war period many Catholics were emigrating. The S.V.P. tried to provide an information service for intending immigrants through its contacts overseas and a special

---

[56] Glasgow, A. Arch., Misc., D. Shields to Archbishop Maguire, 1 Mar. 1904, 13 Mar. 1905; *Annual reports Apostleship of the Sea* (1925–29).

[57] Margaret Keddle, *Caroline Chisholm* (Melbourne 1951); *Rambler* 3 (1848) pp. 30–33; Many *A.R.S.V.P.* mention children and others helped.

[58] See the differences between the then Bishop Maguire and J. Brand J.P. at the a.g.m. *A.R.S.V.P.* (1895) which presents a classic difference of attitude.

[59] Glasgow, A. Arch., Misc., D. Mullen to Canon Ritchie, 12 Feb. 1912.

[60] *A.R.S.V.P.* (1912–1914) and (1926) p. 12. Glasgow, A. Arch, Misc., Mgr. Geo.V. Hudson, Birmingham to J.F. Higgins, 13 July 1925; J.F. Higgins to Mgr. J. Ritchie, 12 Aug. 1925. Abbe P. Casgrain to Abp. of Glasgow 3 Feb. 1925; on the background see H.L. Malchow, *Population Pressures: Emigration and Government in Late Nineteenth Century Britain* (Palo Alto, Cal, 1979).

emigrant supervisory chaplain was appointed.[61] But by then Glasgow Catholicism had entered a new era.

Any consideration of the work of the S.V.P. raises several questions about Catholic social thought. The movement traditionally attributed to Manning and continental figures would seem to have drawn heavily on local attitudes and responses. Although there were many Dutch, Belgian and French clergy in late nineteenth-century Glasgow who were presumably influenced by continental thinking, Scottish voluntary thought would seem far more decisive. Thomas Chalmers, Scottish Social Romanticism, class and ethnic solidarity contributed to a united voluntary enterprise. In the process the Irish Catholic immigrant was allegedly transformed into a conservative, archetypically a shopkeeper. Averse to Chartism, Fenianism or Socialism, he would strive towards self-improvement within the existing order. He was saving for the future; his faith, his property, his children. His central demand would be equality before the law. The reality was to be somewhat different. The majority of Catholics who remained in Glasgow existed on the margin of poverty and dependence. From their voluntary society experience they had learned to take pride in the achievements of the group: the churches, schools and other institutions; in Celtic football club; in the ancient cultural achievements of their past. Their roots were in an ethnic and class tradition. They saw what the group might achieve in future within a more caring social order.[62] They would seek after the Labour Party. The voluntarist legacy of the S.V.P. was varied, but undeniably its achievements were remarkable.

Glasgow University

---

[61] Glasgow, A. Arch, Misc., F. Higgins to Archbishop Mackintosh, 29 June 1925, and Circular regarding Rev. Alfred Gallacher, appointed as emigrants supervisory priest.

[62] My conclusions differ somewhat from W.M. Walker, 'Irish Immigrants in Scotland: Their Priests, Politics and Parochial Life' *HJ* 15 (1972) pp. 649–66 and agree more with R.J. Morris, 'Voluntary Societies and British Urban Elites, 1780–1850: An Analysis' *HJ* 26 (1983) pp. 95–113.

THE CATHOLIC FEDERATION 1906–1929

by PETER DOYLE

BISHOP Casartelli of Salford wrote in his diary for 13 October 1906, '*Deo Gratias*! The magnificent Catholic Demonstration ... organised by our new Catholic Federation, has been a wonderful success ... 40,000 or more from every part of the Diocese. Extraordinary enthusiasm.'[1] His joy was understandable, for the Catholic Federation had been founded only a few months before. The aim had been to start something altogether different from the many specific Catholic societies already in existence. It was to be a

> powerful Catholic organisation knit together in unity and solidarity, with the spirit of the Maccabees and the spirit of faith sending an electric current of living and vital Catholicity into the soul of every unit, and calling them to action against the growing hosts of enemies of God, Religion and Social Democracy.[2]

Its organisation was based on the parish as the basic unit. Each parish, or branch, sent delegates to a District, or Deanery, Committee. At branch level, other parish societies could affiliate to the Federation, so that the branch meeting would become a common meeting ground for individuals and associations, and a 'great centre of unity and source of support'.[3] There was an overall Executive Committee for the diocese, and a number of sub-committees, for example, for education, trade unions and electoral registration. The movement spread quickly to Westminster, Leeds, Portsmouth and Hull. By 1910 the original Salford Federation was able to launch

---

[1] Bishop's House, Salford, Diocesan Archives, Bishop Casartelli's diaries. On Casartelli, see *DNB* and *The Catholic Who's Who and Year Book 1923* (London 1923) p. 411. I would like to thank the 27 Foundation for a grant towards the cost of this research.
[2] *The Federationist* Feb. 1910 p. 3.
[3] T. Sharrock and T. Burns, 'The Salford Diocesan Catholic Federation', *The Month* 113 pp. 465–76.

a monthly journal, *The Federationist*, which it published until 1929.[4] While it failed to become the mass movement which the initial enthusiasm seemed to presage, it remained active and influential for some years. This paper deals almost entirely with the Salford Federation, which was apparently the most active and popular of the diocesan bodies and which, for many people inside and outside the movement, *was* the Catholic Federation.

The occasion for its foundation was the 1906 Education Bill and the threat which it posed to religious schooling. There was, therefore, a large element of defensiveness in the motivation behind the movement, and this was to remain very strong throughout its existence. Defence was necessary for various reasons: while the immediate enemy might be the Liberal government, the long-term battle was against the onslaughts of modern society. Here the movement was far more ambitious and, while still undoubtedly defensive in outlook, it also exhibited an aggressiveness born of a new confidence. The only antidote to society's ills, it claimed, was in the application of catholic principles to every sphere of public life. Parallels with the 'Nonconformist Conscience' are obvious, though, not surprisingly, they were not acknowledged at the time. One of the movement's aims was to 'create a catholic mentality' in Catholics who were unthinking about their faith, to 'marshal the forces of the Catholic Church in the great battles of the future against the rising tides of Freemasonry, Socialism and an anti-Christian democracy'.[5]

These forces could only be mobilised through careful organisation. Much was made of comparisons with the situation abroad. While Catholics in Germany and Belgium had organised themselves and were flourishing, in France this had not been done. As a result, French Catholics had failed to prevent the progress of Freemasonry and anti-clericalism, and had awoken to find their position undermined, their schools closed and everything lost. It is interesting to find French writers supporting this idea by holding up the Salford Federation as a model to French Catholics.[6] If such disasters could

---

[4] It soon became *The Catholic Federationist*. Sets in BL, Colindale, and Bishop's House, Salford.

[5] *Federationist* Nov. 1910 p. 2.

[6] For example, see 'L'Organisation Des Catholiques Anglais', *Bulletin Religieux du Diocèse de Beauvais* (1910) pp. 408-12.

happen in a country where Catholics were in the majority, how much more easily in England could the hard-won gains of the nineteenth century be swept away. As one writer put it,

> How long shall we sleep and content ourselves with singing Faith of our Fathers, whilst the enemy is undermining the foundations of Christian civilisation of which we are, or ought to be, the real guardians?[7]

The organisation was to be largely lay in its composition. Indeed, the original initiative to start the movement came from some Catholic laymen in Salford. They had met on a number of occasions before writing to the bishop for his support.[8] The Federation was to remain strongly lay in character, and its journal frequently stressed the importance of the laity: the movement had 'to destroy that false principle that the Church and her interests are the monopoly of the priest'.[9] The paper argued that too many Catholics stood aloof, 'watching the battle between the priests and the enemies of the Church, whereas the layman should have his part in the fray'.[10] In practice, the organisers of the movement tried to keep the clerical presence small; for example, it was the rule that in any representation of a branch at district level the laity had to outnumber the clergy by three to one.[11]

This stress on the role of the laity reflected closely Casartelli's own views. In his first pastoral letter he had urged Catholics to take a fuller part in public life, to accept the duties of citizenship as well as its fruits and not to be content with merely Catholic activities. They should be active in local politics, in trade unions and in social work, and should stand for office at every level. This would be of service both to the Church and to the commonwealth.[12] In another entry in his diary he had rejoiced that at a great Catholic demonstration on the schools question, he had

---

[7] *Federationist* Nov. 1912 p. 2; see also June 1910 p. 2.
[8] Bishop's House, Federation papers, letter from J.P. Dunne to Bishop, 26 Jan. 1906. Later references to Fed. papers will be to this largely unsorted material.
[9] *Federationist* June 1910 p. 2.
[10] *Ibid.* Nov. 1912 p. 2.
[11] Fed. papers, 'Proposals for the Diocesan Executive Council' (1906) p. 3.
[12] Louis Charles, Bishop of Salford, *The Signs of the Times* (Salford 1903) pp. 9–11.

been the only clerical speaker on the platform.[13] Another Catholic movement which he strongly supported, the middle-class Catenian Association, was unique among Catholic societies in not having even a clerical chaplain at any of its meetings.[14] There was a connection here with his interest in education: it was not just a struggle for Catholic rights, but a realisation of the need for good Catholic secondary schools to enable Catholics to be good citizens; without them the Catholic would become 'the helot of the social system'.[15]

At the same time, he was faced by the situation in his diocese. While some Catholics were experienced in local politics and trade unions, most of his mainly working class flock would, he felt, need careful instruction and guidance from the clergy to start with.[16] This, however, immediately raised some difficult questions. With their long tradition of firm control, would the clergy ever be willing to allow their lay people the initiative envisaged by the movement's founders? Could any Catholic association survive in a parish if the local priests were antagonistic? These problems were evident from the very beginning. When the bishop sent the initial, lay, proposals to his vicar general for comment, the reply was brief: 'much ado about nothing ... ignores the Clergy and every existing society'.[17] Even some of the priests who were in favour had doubts. One parish priest reported that the initial meeting had been a success: the Canon had been elected to the chair and only 28 out of 260 had voted for a layman.[18] The Reverend Sharrock, who was to become very actively involved as General Secretary, wrote to the bishop of the '*great* (sic) distrust' of the clergy among the people, because the clergy exercised 'their veto-ing of all such movements with great arbitrariness'. He went on to say that as in 99 per cent of the parishes the labouring or artisan class predominated, they would need 'very judicious leading', yet they were 'sufficiently filled with socialist principles to object to the high-handed methods of some of the clergy.'[19]

[13] Diaries, 5 Mar. 1906.
[14] P. Lane, *The Catenian Association 1908–1983* (London 1982).
[15] *Federationist* Jan. 1910 p. 3.
[16] *Signs of the Times* p. 10.
[17] Fed. papers, letter from Mgr. Boulaye VG to Bishop, 28 Jan. 1906.
[18] *Ibid*. letter from The Presbytery, Alexandra Rd, to Bishop, 3 July 1906.
[19] *Ibid*. letter from Rev. T. Sharrock to Bishop, 17 June 1906.

In addition to any mistrust between priests and people, there was the strong parochial spirit that had been deliberately fostered among Catholics. Some saw the Federation as destructive of that spirit, although supporters of the movement pointed out that it had not always worked to the good of the Church as a whole: 'unity and the forces which make for unity had been hampered ... (where necessary) parochial idols should be overthrown and narrow parochial ideas exploded'.[20]

Whatever the reasons, and despite frequent exhortations from the bishop, a number of clergy remained hostile. A list of branches in the diocese, drawn up probably in 1910, is instructive here, and may be summarised as follows.[21]

District	Parishes	Parishes with no Branch	No returns	Hostile	Attitude of Clergy: Indifferent/ Unsatis factory	Loyal and Favourable
Manchester and Salford	46	4	1	11	13	21
Blackburn	27	11	14	2	1	10
Rossendale Valley	5	0	0	2	0	3
Bolton	13	5	0	0	11	2
Oldham	11	3	0	0	5	6
Rochdale	7	2	2	0	1	4
Burnley	13	1	0	1	0	12
Bury	6	1	0	0	0	6
Totals	128	27	17	16	31	64

Clearly, branches could exist where the parish priest was hostile or indifferent, but some clergy took their opposition further and refused to allow a branch to be established.[22] One was described as 'secretly hostile and wily', tolerating the existence of a branch only because of the tact of the lay secretaries; another had been

[20] *Federationist* Aug. 1913 p. 4.
[21] Fed. papers, membership list in Sharrock's hand; there are some discrepancies in the original.
[22] Sharrock to Bishop, 17 June 1906.

hostile but had become more sympathetic 'since the Synod', though he was inclined to flippancy; another, unfavourable, was in fact secretary of the branch but refused to pay any levies. A number of branches had become extinct because of clerical opposition. It is difficult even to estimate the membership of the branches, as returns were not made carefully enough except for the Manchester and Salford district. There were a few large branches, for example 750 at Holy Name, Manchester, and 850 at the Cathedral, Salford; in these cases the clergy were obviously behind the movement. Even where the priest was said to be 'loyal and favourable', however, some of the branches were very small, with figures of 19, 34 and 40, for example. If the two exceptionally large branches are excluded, the average branch membership was 55, which must have been a small percentage of the members of these Manchester and Salford parishes. The 42 branches in this district totalled about 3,800; total membership throughout the diocese was at most twice that figure. It is clear that the Bishop's original 40,000 did not refer to members of the Federation.

At the beginning of the movement Fr. Sharrock had insisted that the 'clergy would have to take their coats off' if it was to succeed. The high numbers at the Cathedral, he went on, had been achieved by 'hard work and house to house visitation, which will have to be repeated'.[23] The attitude of the clergy in general, however, did not improve. By 1917 the number of branches had declined: from 42 in the Manchester and Salford district to about 30; from 16 in Blackburn to 10, and from 12 in Burnley to 8. Again there were very unfavourable comments about some of the clergy. A number were listed as 'impossible'; one Dean was said to 'fear the influential layman'; one had not paid for copies of the journal for three years, and so on.[24] To expect a strong lay response in such a situation was unreasonable.

Yet there was much about the movement which should have been attractive. Its leaders were passionately committed to the cause of social justice. The capitalist system, with its gross individualism, was attacked regularly by clerical and lay writers. *The*

---

[23] *Ibid.*
[24] Fed. papers, Memo from T. Burns, 'On the condition of the Federation', 4 Jan. 1917.

Federationist supported the miners in their 1912 strike,[25] and argued in favour of the closed shop: it was outrageous that workers 'who do not share the cost of self-protection should have the impudence to work side-by-side with those who levy themselves to maintain a living wage and abolish sweating'.[26] It supported the right to picket, arguing that the cards in any industrial dispute were so heavily stacked in favour of the employer that the worker had to retain the right to strike and to picket.[27] The paper argued against a minimum wage, wanting instead a just, living wage for all. It carried a regular section headed Labour Notes, and it was here that many of these views were put forward. In addition, it wanted votes for women, and urged Catholic women to play active roles in the trade union movement.[28] It urged the abolition of the Poor Law, and ran a series of articles on the scandal of youth unemployment.[29] Occasionally, it is true, it struck a conservative note in its attitude to strikes, stressing the damage they did and that they must only be used as a last resort.[30] But the general commitment to trade union activity and to the labour question was total.

The Federation also offered its members a range of facilities both social and religious: debating societies, lectures, rambling clubs, libraries, Social Guild study classes and retreats. It organised visits to London, and pilgrimages to Oberammergau, Lourdes and the Eucharistic Congress at Cologne. On a broader plane, it encouraged Catholics to be involved beyond narrowly parochial interests and to look outside the Catholic institution with its traditionally introverted character.[31] It is possible to see here the vision of Bishop Casartelli, who has been described as a man of fully cosmopolitan mind, a bishop to whom the activities and problems of the

---

[25] *Federationist* July 1912 p. 8.
[26] *Ibid.* Feb. 1912 p. 8.
[27] *Ibid.*
[28] *Ibid.* May 1910 p. 2.
[29] *Ibid.* Mar.-April 1910 p. 8.
[30] *Ibid.* Mar. 1913 p. 3.
[31] See G.P. Connolly, 'The Transubstantiation of Myth: towards a New Popular History of Nineteenth-Century Catholicism in England' *JEH* 35 (1984) pp. 78–104.

continental churches were as familiar as those of his own diocese.[32] In particular, he was especially interested in Italian Catholic social ideas, and in the German *Volksverein*, and no doubt this was why *The Federationist* from time to time carried a section headed German Notes, biographies of people like Windhorst and extracts from the social writings of Bishop Bonomelli of Cremona.

Great stress was, indeed, laid on the position of the bishop in the movement. One finds statements like, 'nothing matters if the bishop approves',[33] and, in answer to the charge that the movement was not representative, 'I will tell you whom you represent. You represent your Bishop'.[34] A later apologist, when asked how the Federation was to know whether an election issue was vital to Catholic interests or not, wrote that they could tell an essential question was at stake when the bishop 'in his wisdom directs that it is'.[35] This insistence on episcopal authority (strong in both Salford and Westminster) was one way of counteracting the opposition and indifference of the parochial clergy. To have been effective, however, episcopal leadership would have had to have been very active. There is no doubt that Casartelli was wholeheartedly behind the movement, and he wrote a 'Bishop's Message' for the front page of every issue of the journal until his death in 1925. His support, however, was that of the scholar not that of the actively involved pastor; he was somewhat retiring by disposition, and seems to have lacked the 'common touch' that might have been able to overcome the tensions and prejudices which the movement faced.

One of these difficulties arose as early as 1908, in connection with the by-election resulting from Churchill's promotion to the Liberal cabinet. The Irish Nationalists supported him because of a Liberal commitment to Home Rule, but the Federation recommended Catholics to vote for his Tory opponent because Churchill supported the Liberal policy on education. The ensuing campaign was bitter, and some Federation branch meetings ended in

---

[32] P. Hughes, 'The Coming Century' in G.A. Beck ed *The English Catholics 1850–1950* (London 1950) pp. 1–41, at p. 38.

[33] *Federationist* May 1910 p. 4.

[34] *Ibid.* p. 5.

[35] Sir Charles Russell, *The Catholic Federation: Principles upon which it Should Act* (London 1909, rev ed 1922) p. 12.

brawls.[36] Churchill was defeated, and the Irish immediately blamed the Federation, calling it the Tory Party in disguise and accusing it of being anti-Irish.[37] At the annual meeting in 1910 Casartelli was at pains to defend the Federation's actions, on the grounds that it had only done what he had asked it to do in seeking from candidates their views on the education issue and in publishing the results.[38] Even supporters of the movement felt uneasy; the 'loyal and favourable' priest at St. Patrick's, Oldham, thought that the Federation should abstain from all interference in parliamentary elections, while having a free hand in municipal ones.[39] But the harm had been done, and an area in which the movement had been very active through its registration and canvassing work became one where it frequently had to defend itself. Attempts to explain that it was not linked to any one political party occur so often that the accusation must have been common. Here was a major obstacle to the desired unity of action, and a reason why it did not appeal to larger numbers of Catholic working-men. With the strength of Irish Nationalist sympathy in Manchester, the damage must have been long-term and may have been irreparable.

The problems which have been dealt with so far might have been avoided or overcome, but the final one to be looked at was more fundamental. It was, essentially, ideological, and the stance taken by the Federation was so doctrinaire that it alienated many people from the movement and cut it off from some fruitful developments in English Catholic social thinking. As it found itself increasingly unable to win its case, it turned more stridently to other causes which might win it support in some Catholic circles, though they would increase its alienation from society at large. The issue was that of the correct Catholic attitude to Socialism, and, linked to this, the question of Catholic membership of the Labour Party.

For a movement as involved in the 'social question' as the Federation was, and which was trying to get a largely working-class body to become more involved in politics and the trade unions, it was essential to tackle this problem. It loomed large in

---

[36] Lane, *Catenians* p. 14.
[37] *Federationist* May 1910 p. 2.
[38] *Ibid.* p. 5.
[39] Fed. papers, 1910 (?) membership list.

English Catholic thinking of the day.[40] The issue was clouded by the ambiguities in the term Socialism: did it mean extreme Socialism, associated on the Continent with anti-clericalism and revolutionary excesses, and condemned by the papacy; or did it mean the milder, English versions, which called for greater state involvement in order to end the evils of unbridled laissez-faire? While most English Catholic writers still condemned Socialism, and the Catholic Socialist Society of Leeds got short shrift from the local bishop,[41] some new approaches were being worked out. The new Catholic Social Guild was taking the lead here, with Fr. Vincent McNabb OP willing to go further along the collectivist road than most other Catholics. It is interesting in this context that, in 1913, Archbishop Whiteside of Liverpool could find acceptable some of the ideas in Snowden's *Socialism and Syndicalism*, and even talk of Catholics 'shaking hands with him' on some issues.[42]

From the start the Federation adopted an uncompromising attitude towards Socialism. It may even be that fear of the spread of socialist ideas among Catholic workers was a key motive in its foundation, at least among the clergy. Fr. Sharrock, writing in 1906, thought that the movement had come just in time, for Socialism had penetrated deeply in Blackburn, and when he had attended the early meetings before the Federation had been formally set up, he had been struck by the fact that the content of the speeches had been 'inoculated with Socialist principles pure and simple'.[43]

Certainly *The Federationist* was insistent in warning its readers against those principles. In some instances the language used was emotive and the arguments simplistic. For example, an article by a Blackburn priest warned working men against being taken in by Socialism: 'Don't swallow Socialism. It is poison, not medicine. It poisons a man's faith with its materialism. It poisons a man's life with discontent. It would poison society with its revolutionary

---

[40] Articles appeared regularly in *The Month*, *The Tablet* and other periodicals. For a useful summary, G.P. McEntee, *The Social Catholic Movement in Great Britain* (New York 1927).
[41] McEntee pp. 109–110.
[42] *Ibid*. p. 99.
[43] Sharrock to Bishop, 17 June 1906.

ideas'.[44] In its third number it reprinted an article attacking International Socialism. The voice of Socialism, it claimed, was

> the voice of a real aggressor, striking where and when he feels he can safely do so ... (in England) its batteries are masked, it flies the Union Jack, its propagandists fraternise with ordinary decent citizens ... the gullible Christian is asked to believe that Socialism is merely ... to redress economic wrongs.[45]

Workers who failed to see Socialism in its totality, it went on, were endangering their eternal salvation; 'satanic forces' were behind it, and it was 'an undoubted fact' even in England that Catholics who dabbled in Socialism soon abandoned all religious practice. A later article argued that it was up to the Federation to unmask the attempt to 'cloak Socialism in a little mantle of Christianity in order to masquerade as Christian'.[46]

While keeping a generally watchful eye on any developments which might help to spread Socialist principles, two areas came in for particular scrutiny. First of all, there were those Catholics who claimed that it was possible for them to be Socialists without incurring any condemnation. Among these was Larkin, the leader of the great Dublin strike in 1913, who merited a whole editorial to himself.[47] He had visited Manchester to appeal for help, and in his typically outspoken way had said, 'The man who tells you it is impossible to be a Socialist and a Catholic is a liar'. It was easy to warn readers against the danger of 'little Larkins' in the movement and to accuse him of having forgotten all his principles. More difficult was to know how to deal with the Catholic Social Guild, which was, basically, saying the same thing. The Federation had originally given a warm welcome to the Guild, praising especially its study circles for working men. But then came the doubts. By 1914 Thomas Burns, the Organising Secretary of the Federation, was quarrelling openly with McNabb, condemning him for a favourable review of Snowden's book, and accusing him of confused thinking when he said that the Pope had not condemned all

---

[44] *Federationist* Feb. 1910 p. 5.
[45] *Ibid.* Mar.-April 1910 p. 6.
[46] *Ibid.* Nov. 1912 p. 2.
[47] *Ibid.* Oct. 1913 p. 2.

forms of Socialism.[48] Two years later *The Federationist* was attacking the 'shilly-shallying' of the Guild, which was, it claimed, strangely shy about condemning Socialism. It was doing no good service to Catholics, the writer continued, to talk of different kinds of Socialism; one might just as well talk about 'forms of Protestantism' or 'kinds of Modernism'.[49] A few years later Burns wrote to Casartelli that the Church was now reaping the full benefit of the loose thinking of 'the Guild, Prior McNabb and the remainder, and I'm afraid that things will become worse'.[50]

The second area where danger was sensed was that of the Labour Party and the way it was attracting Catholics. In 1912 *The Federationist* warned its readers against being too wholehearted in their support of the Party, for both Secularism and Socialism vitiated its platform.[51] The movement was already known for its dislike of some Labour policies, as Burns had been running a campaign in the TUC and at party conferences since 1906; his aim was to stop the Party adopting secular education and nationalisation as official policies. No doubt that was why the right wing British Labour Party had made overtures to the Federation in 1911.[52] While the campaign on secular education was successful, that on nationalisation finally failed when the Labour Party adopted it into its constitution in 1918.[53] Once this had happened, the Federation claimed, the Labour Party had ceased to exist, and had been replaced by the Socialist Party of Great Britain.

An article in 1918 made the movement's position clear. It had long been taught that the fight of the future would be between the two irreconcilable forces of the Church and Socialism. Some people seemed incapable of recognising Socialism unless it was accompanied by 'flag-flying, gun-shooting and blood running'. The writer quoted Leo XIII, Belloc and Cardinal Mercier to show that collectivism equalled Socialism which was what had been condemned and which was what the Labour Party had now

---

[48] *Ibid.* Feb. 1914 p.3; Mar. 1914 p. 3. The controversy first appeared in *The Tablet.*
[49] *Ibid.* Dec. 1915 p. 2.
[50] Fed. papers, letter from Burns to Bishop, 23 Sept. 1918.
[51] *Federationist* Mar. 1912 p. 2.
[52] P.J. Doyle, 'Religion, Politics and the Catholic Working Class', *New Blackfriars* 54 (1973) pp. 218–25.
[53] McEntee p. 132. See also *Federationist* May 1914 p. 1.

become. The result was that the organised workers of the country were now organised within the Socialist Party, and were financing it through their trade union levies. The policy of permeation was finished, since Catholics could no more permeate a Socialist party than they could permeate Protestantism.[54]

The subsequent, intransigent opposition to the Labour Party seriously damaged the Federation in two ways. First of all it split the movement internally, and, secondly, it cut it off almost completely from the rest of the Catholic body. When Burns spoke in Leeds in 1918, half of the Catholic trade unionists who attended walked out, claiming to be both Socialists and Catholics.[55] A few years later, at the annual conference of the various diocesan organisations affiliated to the Federation, he persuaded the delegates to adopt an anti-Labour Party resolution.[56] The Westminster delegates objected, and later at an executive meeting tried to get the resolution toned down, apparently with the full support of Cardinal Bourne. When this failed there was a move to expel Salford from the movement![57] It is clear from later statements in *The Federationist* that members of the movement were not prepared to leave the Labour Party.[58]

The effects on the relations between the movement and other Catholics were equally serious. Burns tried very hard in 1918–19, on behalf of the movement, to get the English hierarchy to pronounce against the Labour Party, but without success.[59] Indeed, the attempt so annoyed Cardinal Bourne that he wrote to Casartelli to complain about Burns and the journal.[60] Burns, he felt, seemed to expect the hierarchy to make pronouncements as and when he wished, whereas none of the bishops had been impressed by his arguments. *The Federationist*, he added, had developed a deplorable tone, suggesting that only Salford had the truth. A few months later, Archbishop Whiteside stated publicly that Catholics were free to join the Labour Party as it had not been explicitly condemned by

---

[54] *Federationist* April 1918 pp. 2–3, 'The Extinction of the Labour Party'.
[55] Fed. papers, Burns to Bishop, 23 Sept. 1918.
[56] *Federationist* Nov. 1921 carries a full report of the meeting in Sheffield.
[57] Fed. papers, Burns to Bishop, 31 Mar. 1922.
[58] For example, *Federationist* Jan. 1921 p. 7.
[59] Fed. papers, Burns to Bishop, 15 May 1919.
[60] *Ibid.* Cardinal Bourne to Bishop, 20 May 1919.

Rome.[61] Some of the catholic press went further: the *Catholic Times* openly and very strongly supported the Party in the 1918 election as the only hope for a just society,[62] and an editorial in the *Universe* stated clearly that a man could be a collectivist and a good Catholic.[63]

The question arises as to how far the Federation had the support of Bishop Casartelli in all this. Burns was careful to disassociate the bishop from his hare-brained launch of an alternative political party in 1918, called the Centre Labour Party, which would fight for Christian Democracy as opposed to Social Democracy.[64] He always claimed, however, that the bishop supported him in the anti-Socialist stand and had actually forbidden Catholics to join the Labour Party after 1918.[65] Certainly, Casartelli cannot have opposed the line, for the Federation would not have adopted so definite a policy against his wishes. There is some evidence that he did support the extreme view. In 1924 the Cardinal stated publicly that there was nothing in the Labour Party which threatened religion, and that it even 'approached in certain aspects to Catholic social doctrine'.[66] Casartelli ordered *The Federationist* not to comment on the statement, as a public quarrel between himself or the paper and the Cardinal would only cause scandal. The 'extra-ordinary statement' was unfortunate, but they had better 'lie low till the squall had passed over'.[67]

There is, perhaps, evidence here of the debit side of what may be called Casartelli's continentalism. His links with the Continent and his interest in its concerns put him in touch with the latest developments in Catholic social thought, and gave him a wider vision than most of his fellow bishops. But they also brought him into contact with the routine refrain of anti-clericalism in continental Socialism. It is clear that by this time some leading Socialists

---

[61] McEntee p. 133.

[62] *The Catholic Times* 23 Nov. 1918 p. 6.

[63] *Universe* 1 Mar 1918, Editorial.

[64] Fed. papers, Burns to Bishop, 23 Sept. 1918; also, printed prospectus, *The Centre Labour Party*. The Party organised three or four branches around Manchester, and put up a candidate for the municipal elections; it folded about a year later.

[65] *Federationist* Feb. 1921 p. 7.

[66] McEntee p. 136.

[67] Fed. papers, Bishop to Sharrock, 22 and 23 Aug. 1924.

were themselves tiring of, and even embarrassed by, the old nine-teenth-century brand of obnoxious anti-clericalism. A number of interesting developments were taking place within Socialist thinking which were unfortunately masked from Catholic eyes by the cloud of abuse which the subject of religion could still cause to rise in Socialist circles.[68] Socialism, therefore, remained for those Catholics what had been condemned in the nineteenth century. Other English Catholics were more pragmatic in approach; the Labour Party was not anti-religious in practice and so there was no point in alienating Catholic workers by saying they could not belong to it.

Despite splits and disagreements the movement carried on for some years. Initially membership figures stayed stable, and even picked up by 1921: in that year there were still 25 branches in the Manchester and Salford district, six of them founded in the previous twelve months, with a membership of 7,000.[69] By 1926, however, the number of branches had fallen to 13, and membership was down to 4,000.[70] Early in 1929 *The Federationist* suddenly ceased publication. There is not space here to give a full analysis of the journal in the 1920s, but it can be said that its emphasis changed. Much less space was devoted to labour news and the social question; instead the emphasis seemed to be laid increasingly on two other aspects of the movement. One of these, which we have seen already, was Catholic education; the other, not mentioned so far, was what may be called public morality.

It was not a new concern. As early as 1910 the bishop had urged Catholics to support the National Vigilance Association in its fight against immoral literature, and in 1912 there was an article on the necessity of supporting the Pernicious Literature Committee.[71] Divorce was a recurring topic, and the censorship of films and plays featured fairly regularly.[72] What the 1920s saw was an intensification of the emphasis on these issues, with the addition of a

---

[68] See the interesting discussion in A.C. Jemolo, *Church and State in Italy, 1850–1950* (Oxford 1960) pp. 143–5.
[69] *Federationist* June 1921 p. 6.
[70] *Ibid*. April 1926 p. 4.
[71] *Ibid*. Nov. 1910 p. 1, and Jan. 1912 p. 3.
[72] *Ibid*. issues of 1914–15, *passim*, and Jan. 1917 p. 7; April 1918 pp. 6–7.

new one, birth-control and family-planning clinics.[73] There was, as one would expect, much about the threat to family life, and a reactionary note was struck over the proposed Care of Infants Bill (1922): both Salford and Westminster Federations objected on the grounds that it would undermine the authority of the father by making the mother joint head of the family.[74]

Clearly, the move away from labour questions to those affecting public morality was not due just to the troubles after 1918; the outspoken Labour Notes, for example, had gone by 1916, and one of the original aims of the movement had been to resist the evils of modern society. But the new emphasis was connected with those troubles, and was an attempt to unite Catholics on issues which they would find non-controversial. At times the journal gives the impression that political bogeys were being manufactured to win extra support. Certainly there is an air of desperation about it; Casartelli criticised the amount of large, heavy type in the paper which, he thought, produced the effect of 'too much shouting or even yelling' and which tended to discredit much of the writing.[75]

The Federation had set out to mobilise the strength of English Catholicism in a novel way. It failed for a number of reasons, some accidental, some fundamental to its approach. It was both too ambitious and too defensive. Mass Catholic support could only be mobilised successfully when a recognisably specific threat to Catholics seemed imminent, as in 1906. Issues of public morality, or of ideological difference, were not seen in that light by the Catholic worker whose support was essential to the Federation's existence.

Bedford College of Higher Education

[73] *Ibid.* issues of Feb., Mar., May, 1926.
[74] *Ibid.* June 1921 p. 5; Archives of the Archbishop of Westminster, Cardinal Bourne papers, 5/43d, 1922.
[75] Fed. papers, Bishop to Sharrock, 22 Aug. 1924.

476

FINDING A SPACE FOR EVANGELICALISM: EVANGELICAL YOUTH MOVEMENTS IN NEW ZEALAND

by PETER J. LINEHAM

VOLUNTARY religious societies may be viewed either as powerful instruments for mobilising the Christian community, or as bodies which divert its energies from their proper function. They tend to be enclaves where distinctive values and activities are encouraged and confirmed. They have been marked by a greater degree of internationalism than the broader church, no doubt because their narrowness and specificity make their transfer outside their home context less problematic. Evangelical voluntary organisations provide good illustrations of these features. It is the intention of this paper to examine the establishment of two evangelical movements which appeared in the distinctive environment of New Zealand. One of them, the Inter-Varsity Fellowship, is a well-known force in twentieth-century voluntarism in the western world. The other ultimately became a branch of the Children's Special Service Mission, now known as Scripture Union, but it began as a movement unique to New Zealand, as its original name, the Crusader Movement, suggests. The origins of these two evangelical voluntary societies in New Zealand give some indication of the potential and problems of new evangelical movements.

Voluntary movements which see themselves as complementary to the Church and not substitutes for it (hence the term 'parachurch agencies') by definition cannot exist apart from the Church. Consequently in an environment where the Church itself is weak, voluntary movements struggle to survive. In the English context voluntary movements, despite their various theological, denominational and social environments, took the Church for granted. They justified their own existence, sometimes in a specious manner, by arguing that their task was to complement what the Church

477

(by which they meant the denominational organisations) was under-taking. In addition they reacted adversely to the structures, formal procedures and hierarchy of the churches, and set people free to take initiatives for themselves.

Their activities presuppose not only a denominationalised Prot-estant community but also a high level of denominational organ-isation. It was because this was absent in the colony of New Zealand's newly settled European communities that evangelical voluntarism was slow to emerge there. It flowered only after a century of colonial development, in the nineteen-thirties. Inevitably this affected the character of evangelicalism as a social phenomenon. Voluntary movements had indeed played a crucial role in the birth of the Church in New Zealand. The Church Missionary Society, the Wesley Methodist Missionary Society and the Society of Mary had each participated in the extensive mission to the Maori people before 1850. As an organised European Church began to emerge these missions found themselves identified as a threat to the emerg-ing local structures, and the C.M.S., for example, concluded a rather unsatisfactory agreement with the bishop of New Zealand, George Augustus Selwyn. For the next fifty years voluntary move-ments were comparatively few in number, a feature the more remarkable considering the plethora of religious organisations in the British homelands of the immigrants. Not until 1895 was a New Zealand auxiliary of the Church Missionary Society estab-lished within the Anglican Church.[1] It was in the eighteen-nineties that New Zealand churchpeople began to play a part in the wider world, for in 1896 the Presbyterian Women's Missionary Union was founded, and in 1894 committees of the China Inland Mission were established in the North and South Islands.[2]

At a local level a diverse range of voluntary societies had developed by this stage, but they were not co-ordinated within national organizations, instead functioning as small branches of British bodies. The earliest national society was, not surprisingly, the British and Foreign Bible Society, the London committee of

[1] Ken Gregory, *Stretching out continually: a history of the New Zealand Church Missionary Society 1892–1972* (Christchurch 1972) pp. 16–19.
[2] J.S. Murray, *A Century of Growth: Presbyterian Overseas Mission Work 1869–1969* (Christchurch 1969) p. 24; M.L. Loane, *The Story of the China Inland Mission in Australia and New Zealand 1890–1964* (Sydney 1965) p. 13.

which had sponsored the preparation of the Maori Bible. Having welcomed the auxiliary formed in Sydney in 1817, they were pleased at the formation of a New Zealand auxiliary in 1846. Effectively this auxiliary was only an Auckland branch, and the branches subsequently established in Wellington and Christchurch had no links with it. In Dunedin the Scottish settlers formed an independent Bible Society of Otago in 1864, just as the Presbyterian Church in that province refused to amalgamate with the Presbyterian Church of New Zealand. The other Bible Society auxiliaries united in an autonomous dominion organisation in 1925.[3] Colonial society was slow to establish bodies which had a national identity.

One reason for this was the absence in New Zealand of the middle class approach to leisure and enthusiasms which was so important a factor in the world of English voluntary movements. Although the Young Men's Christian Association arrived in Auckland as early as 1855, it attracted little support, and sometimes its New Zealand branches were criticized for a 'spirit of exclusive pietism'.[4] Interdenominational movements in particular did not seem to appeal. New Zealanders had sometimes protested about the introduction of denominational barriers and the spirit of clericalism into the colony. Yet they were unenthusiastic towards voluntary organisations, preferring to invest their limited resources in bodies more obviously relevant to the colony. The New Zealand Tract and Book Society founded in 1873 was quite active,[5] but an attempt to form a local branch of the Scripture Union failed when no-one attended the meetings held to publicize its work.[6] Although Sunday School Unions were commenced in the larger towns, they were never organised into a national body.[7]

[3] J.G. Laughton & P.R. Thomas, *New Zealand and the World's Book* (London and Wellington 1964) pp. 63–4.
[4] See *Encyclopedia of New Zealand* ed A. McLintock (Wellington 1964) 3 p. 701; *Freethought Review* 3 (October 1884) p. 5.
[5] See *Cyclopedia of New Zealand* (Christchurch 1905) 4, *Otago and Southland Provincial Districts* p. 356.
[6] P.J. Lineham, *No Ordinary Union: The story of the Scripture Union Children's Special Service Mission and Crusader Movement of New Zealand 1880–1980* (Wellington 1980) p. 12.
[7] See A.R. Jaimeson, 'The contribution of the Auckland Sunday School Union to religious education during the years 1865–1940' (University of Auckland M.Ed. thesis 1967) pp. 22–32.

New Zealanders evidently required strong incentives to attract them into voluntary bodies. Because there was a widespread and deep fear that society was threatened from within by the demon drink, Bands of Hope and other temperance bodies flourished from the time of the foundation of the Women's Christian Temperance Alliance in 1885. Youth organisations also attracted support when European settlers realised their responsibility to train the first locally born generation. Boys Brigades made a brief appearance between 1886 and 1910, although the Brigades were not recommenced until 1926.[8] In the 1890s Christian Endeavour Societies were more successful.[9] John R. Mott's visit in 1896 led to the formation of the Student Christian Movement, which organised school as well as university branches. It was a relatively weak body until 1911, when it became independent from the Australian S.C.M.[10]

The largest of the voluntary youth movements in New Zealand represented a singular adaptation of the voluntary principle. In 1880 George Troup reorganized the Bible Class at St. John's Presbyterian church in Wellington on the 'co-operative principle', in which the young men took responsibility for the conduct of the class and supplemented it with other social activities. Similar classes were soon established in congregations of various denominations, and they co-operated with each other in sporting activities and inspirational camps. In 1902 the Presbyterian Young Men's Bible Class Union was formed, and its organisation was soon duplicated by Bible Classes of the other sex and the other denominations.[11] The movement had a powerful cohesion and dynamic.

The success it enjoyed paradoxically clarifies our understanding of the problems which plagued many other voluntary movements in the dominion. Not only did they lack a sufficient social justification; they also lacked a close link with congregational life. In

---

[8] M.E. Hoare, 'Training in "Manliness": some historical and contemporary participants perspectives on Boys Brigade work in Australia and New Zealand' (Massey University Dip. Ed. thesis 1979) pp. 7–10.

[9] See for example Wellington Provincial Christian Endeavour Union, *Souvenir: Tenth Annual Convention* (Wellington 1903) pp. 5–6.

[10] See P.E. Sutton, 'The New Zealand Student Christian Movement, 1896–1936' (University of Canterbury M.A. thesis 1946) pp. 1–35.

[11] See E.P. Blamires, *Youth Movement. The story of the rise and development of the Christian Youth Work in the Churches of New Zealand – as seen by a Methodist* (Auckland 1952) pp. 14–15.

the town of Dunedin where Scottish settlers predominated, and in Nelson, where evangelical Anglicanism was the major religious force, inter-denominational societies could work within congregations without denominational suspicions arising about their activities. In other towns this was not so easy. It was not that the community as a whole was hostile to evangelical protestantism. On the contrary the churches and the community as a whole were suffused with a simple revivalist piety.[12] Perhaps in consequence of this, voluntary groups seemed unnecessary. A branch of the Evangelical Alliance had been formed in Wellington as early as 1848, but it soon faded away, never to be successfully revived,[13] because its 'catholic principles' did not prove useful in the commencement and maintenance of community religion and the basic structures of church life. In the close-knit colonial society, voluntary organisations rarely served such ends efficiently. United revivalist missions had their place, but they were subservient to the congregations and denominations. If inter-denominational activity did not serve the urgent needs of the congregation it was thought to be sectarian.

In the nineteen-twenties and thirties these assumptions were undermined. The denominations were now so securely established and their structures seemed so institutionally-minded that some church members were alienated by them. Also theological shifts in the Anglo-American world finally became apparent in New Zealand. It was no longer difficult to place local clergy, theological colleges, denominations and societies on the theological spectrum. A small organisational and theological space opened up, and inter-denominational evangelicalism swiftly filled it. These inter-war years saw the Student Christian Movement and the denominational Bible Class Unions at the height of their strength and influence. For the same reasons evangelical voluntarism was established in these very decades.

The English Inter-Varsity Fellowship was founded in 1928 after a long buildup of tensions within the Student Christian Movement,

---

[12] See my article, 'How institutionalised was Protestant Piety in Nineteenth-Century New Zealand?' *JRH* (1985).
[13] See *New Zealand Evangelist* 1 (1848–9) pp. 256–7.

especially within the Cambridge and London colleges.[14] One of the incentives for its foundation was the concern of the conservative evangelical voluntary societies about the deleterious influence of the S.C.M. on the potential future leadership of the evangelical community. The I.V.F. was a student movement, characterised by student enthusiasms and a self-confidence instilled into public school pupils. At its first meeting the I.V.F. decided to send a representative to Canada to promote evangelical secession there also. This representative, Howard Guinness, who was the grandson of a famous Irish evangelist, had just completed his medical training at St. Bartholomew's hospital. After a period in Canada he accepted an invitation from laymen in the evangelical Anglican diocese of Sydney to bring his message to Australia. Then he was persuaded to make a very brief tour of New Zealand, from 22 September until 18 November 1930, before his return home.[15] Rarely had a voluntary organisation spread so rapidly. Yet Guinness's achievement was not simply the establishment of replicas of the I.V.F. in the dominions. In each of the three countries a different structure evolved. Alike in their commitment to conservative evangelical theology, their structure as voluntary societies reflected their unique settings.

It was the era of fundamentalism.[16] And fundamentalism had awakened some responsive chords in New Zealand. The New Zealand churches had generally been theologically conservative, although liberal movements had gained victories within the Presbyterian Church in disputes in 1888 and 1908, and in the Methodist Church in 1893 and 1912. But in none of these cases had the liberalism been particularly extreme. The New Zealand churches did little by way of theological education, and the level of theological awareness was low. Consequently such issues rarely troubled the ordinary congregation.[17] Moreover heresy debates within

---

[14] See D. Johnson, *Contending for the Faith: A History of the Evangelical Movement in the Universities and Colleges* (Leicester 1979) pp. 87–148.

[15] See Lineham, *No Ordinary Union* pp. 35–51; H. Guinness, *Journey among Students* (Sydney 1978) pp. 42–73.

[16] See George M. Marsden, *Fundamentalism and American Culture: the shaping of twentieth-century Evangelicalism* (New York 1980).

[17] See Ross M. Anderson, 'New Zealand Methodism and World War I; crisis in a liberal church' (University of Canterbury M.A. thesis 1983).

the denominational courts seem to have ceased almost entirely in the inter-war years.

Nevertheless in those years some currents of 'modernism' made their appearance. Their vocal supporters were concentrated in the various youth movements, which were the most advanced and anti-traditional bodies within the Church. The youth movements vigorously supported internationalism and the application of the gospel to modern social problems. The General Secretary of the S.C.M. from 1926 to 1929, Donald Grant, ably argued the liberal case, and renamed the Movement's magazine *Open Windows*.[18] The S.C.M. was a very influential group in the universities and the protestant churches, and many students were involved in its cultural, literary and religious activities.

In contrast fundamentalism in New Zealand was essentially a backwoods movement. In the Methodist Church its stronghold was the Lay Preachers Association; in the Presbyterian and Anglican Churches the smaller and more rural presbyteries and dioceses. Then in the inter-war period there emerged a group of preachers and churches strongly committed to the defence of the traditional faith in the town of Auckland, which had just become the largest town in New Zealand. At Beresford St. Congregational church an Australian preacher, Lionel Fletcher, drew very large congregations. A Presbyterian minister, A.W. Murray, after a visit to Princeton seceded to form a United Evangelical Church. The Baptist Tabernacle made an even greater impact, for its pastor in the twenties had previously ministered at Charlotte Chapel in Edinburgh and the Metropolitan Tabernacle in New York, and was well able to stir up evangelistic and fundamentalist fervour in the dominion. His institutional achievements were of no mean order. He established the first Keswick-style annual inter-denominational convention in the North Island. Like D.L. Moody he established an interdenominational Bible Training Institute next door to his church. He encouraged the formation of inter-denominational missionary societies. The B.T.I. published a monthly magazine, *The Reaper*, which informed its denominationally

---

[18] Sutton, 'Student Christian Movement' pp. 54–88.

widespread readership about the international modernist/ fundamentalist controversy, and instructed them about dispensational eschatology and biblical inerrancy.[19] Although it took some time for Kemp's approach to gain acceptance, it laid possible foundations for populist fundamentalism.

There was a distinctly defensive note about this party. It was also a divisive note, and even the Baptist leader and campaigner for protestantism J.J. North disliked it.[20] Inevitably it led to tensions within the Student Christian Movement. An Auckland medical doctor, William H. Pettit, who had once been inspired by the S.C.M. to serve as a missionary, was inspired by the new fundamentalism to lead a protest against the theological trends in his beloved organisation. Pettit had hoped that John R. Mott's visit to the dominion in 1926 would reverse the modernist trend which he had witnessed at the conferences he regularly attended, but Mott had disappointed him.[21] Pettit appears not to have known about the tensions in the English S.C.M., but perhaps Kemp and A.A. Murray had informed him about J. Gresham Machen's establishment of a League of Evangelical Students,[22] for he persuaded a group of university students attending evangelical congregations in Auckland to commence a Bible study group which on 15 August 1927 formally organized itself as the Auckland College Student Bible League. The name suggests Machen's influence. So does the requirement that all members accept the Bible 'as the Word of the living God', and affirm 'the foundation truths of the Christian Faith, such as the Deity, Virgin birth, the true and sinless humanity of the Lord Jesus Christ, his substitutionary atonement,

[19] See G.R. Pound, 'Reverend J.W. Kemp and the Baptist Tabernacle' (University of Auckland M.A. thesis 1978); R.L. Roberts, 'The Growth of Inter-denominational Mission Societies in New Zealand' (University of Auckland M.A. thesis 1977).

[20] Wellington, Tertiary Students Christian Fellowship Archives, A3d/5, J.J. North to J.M. Laird, 9 November 1943.

[21] See W.H. Pettit, 'Experiences in Christian Work among New Zealand Students' in *N.Z. Inter-Varsity Papers No. 2: The Inter-Varsity Fellowship of Evangelical Unions (N.Z.), A Sketch of its Origins, Doctine and Practice* (Wellington c.1940) pp. 22–36.

[22] C. Stacey Woods, *The Growth of a Work of God. The story of the early days of the Inter-Varsity Christian Fellowship of the United States of America* (Downers Grove 1978) pp. 16–18. There is a specific reference to the League in Auckland E.S.F. records, TSCF Archives, A2c/003, A.W. Morton to B. Williams, 31 May 1932.

His bodily resurrection, and his personal return'.[23]

Pettit found support for his concerns from a Dunedin engineer, R.S. Cree Brown, but despite this southern support the initial schism was confined to Auckland. Cree Brown however had learnt from English magazines and Australian friends about the tour of the I.V.F. representative Howard Guinness, and he hoped that a visit to New Zealand by Guinness might be a means of cautioning the S.C.M. to reform its ways. Guinness himself like Pettit hoped that his visit would lead to the foundation of a separate evangelical student movement in the dominion. The visit which lasted from September to November in 1930 was too short and came too late in the university year to achieve much of significance in the universities. Guinness was a master of Irish oratory, and he was able to impress upon a large evangelical audience in Auckland the importance of the Evangelical Students Fellowship, as it then decided to rename itself. At Otago University in Dunedin an Evangelical Union separated from the S.C.M., and at Canterbury College in Christchurch evangelical students agreed to meet together. Yet the great achievement of Guinness was in a realm which formed no part of the vision of the English I.V.F.; the secondary schools.

Guinness had been gradually realising during his tour of the new dominions that the I.V.F. in England owed some of its inherent strength to the quality of evangelical work among public and grammar school pupils. Various organisations worked to inculcate evangelical principles and develop relationships which then continued at university. In the dominions the lack of any early training in evangelical belief coupled with the secular character of state education meant that most university students were deeply influenced by the liberal tone of higher education.

The S.C.M. in the antipodes had groups in many of the state girls' secondary schools. This may have inspired Guinness to formulate a new strategy while he was in Australia. Since there were so few interdenominational evangelical bodies working among young people, he decided that the work of the future I.V.F. must begin in the schools. He explained his plan to Cree Brown:

to get an entrance into the important schools of N.Z. and

[23] Wellington, TSCF Archives, D. Penman, Notes on Auckland.

speak to them, stay one or two days and form definite C.U.s 'run by the boys for the boys', thus starting a witness for Christ where it is 100 per cent easier to get results. In this way the Varsities will find themselves being *fed by Christian boys* instead of heathen. ... I am convinced that the secret to the Varsity work lies in the schools! Let the evangelical Varsity men make their main field of evangelism *the schools* and they [will] reflexly more than double the effectiveness of their own witness at the University.[24]

Guinness misunderstood the New Zealand educational system. Less elitist than the English system, the schools were not receptive to evangelism by university students, and the schoolboys and girls of the dominion lacked the self-confidence bred into the English public school pupils, which equipped them to organize their own christian societies. Yet Guinness made a stir in many schools, and although this proved counter-productive in private schools, it led to the formation of christian groups in many state schools. These groups he called Crusader Unions. The name he borrowed from the Boys Crusader Union in England, to which he had once belonged. This English evangelical body conducted inter-denominational Sunday afternoon Bible classes for grammar school pupils. This was not the role Guinness envisaged for his New Zealand Crusader Unions, but without consultation he borrowed an appealing name and also the badge of the English Unions (although to its motif he added the southern cross). The Boys Crusader Union was not at all impressed at his initiative; it demanded the abandonment of its name and its badge. After Guinness's departure the New Zealand movement was persuaded by another British visitor, Dr. John Laird, to link up instead with another English body, the Children's Special Service Mission (also known as Scripture Union). Four years later it was reluctantly persuaded to change its name to the Crusader *Movement* for the sake of good relations between the two English organisations, but it was not prepared to abandon the badge.[25]

[24] Wellington, Scripture Union Archives, H. Guinness to R.S. Cree Brown, 11 April 1930, cited in Lineham, *No Ordinary Union* p. 42.
[25] Wellington, SU Archives, Crusader Movement Minutes, vol 1 (1930–35) pp. 226–231 (meeting of 17 July 1934).

The broader dimensions of these developments deserve reflection. In England each evangelical voluntary body kept its distance from other bodies, and had its own loyal body of supporters. In New Zealand these infrastructures and loyalties were absent. The only significant loyalty was denominational. In the city of Auckland there was emerging a new fellowship of fundamentalists suspicious of their denominations, and this spirit influenced the new student movement. Yet a movement which wanted to make an impact in the secular schools and universities of the dominion could not flourish if its tone was simply the doctrinal defensiveness characteristic among conservative theological groups. To inspire young people an outward-looking fellowship was needed, and the Crusader Movement and the Crusader Unions in the university colleges proved to have exactly this character. Consequently around them a different sort of evangelical community emerged than what existed in England, or indeed what was beginning to emerge in Auckland. After the death of Joseph Kemp in 1933, the mood of Auckland fundamentalism itself began to move the Crusader way. Thus because evangelical witness in both the schools and the university colleges was established at the same time, a national evangelical community of unusual character emerged. In it the various interdenominational bodies were closely interconnected. To be an evangelical was less a matter of theology than of participation in the various interdenominational organisations. Evangelical students usually spent part of their summer vacations assisting at Crusader camps or C.S.S.M. beach missions. School pupils who belonged to the Crusader Movement automatically joined the Evangelical Unions at university.

Dr. John Laird, the representative of the English Scripture Union and first General Secretary of the Crusader Movement and first chairman of the Executive of the Inter-Varsity Fellowship, nevertheless resisted proposals to merge the two movements into one body. Laird explained his reasons to the Crusader Council:

> On paper and in the minds of the public the two movements must be kept entirely separate as they are in Great Britain. The children's work must necessarily be of a general and simple nature. The work in the University needs special treatment on account of its peculiar difficulties. ... The bond between the

two would be no less real though officially they would be entirely disassociated. This will need emphasis, reiteration and discretion.[26]

New Zealand evangelicals plainly regarded this division as somewhat artificial. Conscious as they were of the common goals of the two organisations, their common genesis and their common fellowship, they could not see the need for multiplication of organisations. Although they formally accepted Laird's strategy, the travelling secretaries of the Crusader Movement kept in close contact with the students in the Evangelical Unions, and when the I.V.F. was formed, its office was in the headquarters of the Crusader Movement.

Nevertheless there were certain advantages in maintaining some distinction between the two bodies. The Crusader Movement came into existence more smoothly than did a national Inter-Varsity Fellowship of Evangelical Unions. There were many Christians with sufficient local influence who were willing to unite to gain entry for the Crusader Movement into state secondary schools. There were fewer evangelical Christians with sufficient standing to lend respectability to university societies which might be crushed by accusations that they were sectarian and demeaning to the character of the university. A national organisation of Evangelical Unions would inevitably heighten the criticism. When an Auckland student, Archie Morton, tried to induce the birth of the I.V.F., the Otago University Evangelical Union expressed its fears about this.[27]

Equally, while it was easy to agree upon a simple syllabus of basic Bible instruction for the Crusader Movement, theological and denominational questions inevitably arose with the organisation of a national Inter-Varsity Fellowship. Some of the evangelical university students were deeply influenced by the Calvinist theology of traditional Presbyterians. In Scottish Dunedin there was a concentration of such people. Evangelical Anglicanism was a major force in Christchurch, where the Vicar of Sumner,

---

[26] Wellington, SU Archives, Report of J.M. Laird to Crusader Council, 8 June 1931, cited in Lineham, *No Ordinary Union* pp. 163–4.
[27] Wellington, TSCF Archives, A2c/010, Graham Miller to Basil Williams, 30 September 1935.

W.A. Orange, had a profound effect on a large group of ordinands, the 'orange-pips'. In contrast a lecturer in classics at Auckland University College influenced students there towards a more academic apologetic. Furthermore the denominations most supportive of the Crusader Movement and the Evangelical Unions were rather sectarian bodies, and were as insistent on their particular ecclesiological views – the nature of baptism, or the rejection of an ordained clergy – as they were about the nature of the atonement. The Baptist students were one such group. A larger group of students in the E.U.s came from the Plymouth Brethren, which had become a very strong body among the middle class in New Zealand. Students from this background tended to think that Anglicanism, even of the evangelical variety, was abhorrent.

It was a critical problem. As Dr. Laird, himself a member of the Brethren, explained to the Crusader Council, opinion in the major churches would not look sympathetically on a movement with close links with 'two bodies of Christians in the Dominion, neither of which are popularly supposed to be such as would be able to contribute helpfully, to say the least, to the spiritual needs of Secondary Schoolboys and Varsity students'.[28] The first chairman of the Crusader Council, Dr. Pettit, did not easily recognise that his reputation as a critic of all churches other than the Brethren tended to bring the new movement into disrepute. Pettit was swift to criticise others in the movement who erred in this area. In 1931 when the Rev. W.A. Orange first addresssed an Evangelical Union, he had concluded the houseparty by conducting a Communion Service, no doubt using the Anglican liturgy.[29] In 1946 after a bitter complaint from Dr. Pettit that Brethren had a conscientious objection to the use of liturgy, celebration of the sacrament was prohibited at I.V.F. functions.[30]

It was not only the Brethren who caused difficulties. The I.V.F. sought to unite conservatives from all the Protestant denominations, but many potential supporters were confessionalists in their denominations and opponents of ecumenism. They sometimes

---

[28] Report of Laird, cited in Lineham, *No Ordinary Union* p. 163.
[29] Wellington, TSCF Archives, P.J. Lineham, 'Evangelical Witness at Canterbury University: a history of the EU/CU 1930–1974' (1974) p. 7.
[30] Wellington, TSCF Archives, A2a/021, W.H. Pettit to IVF, 27 September 1946 and reply, 18 October 1946.

could not comprehend the concept of interdenominational evangelicalism, which distinguished between the doctrines of substitutionary atonement and biblical infallibility which were regarded as fundamental, and 'ecclesiastical' doctrines, which were regarded as *adiaphora*. The formation of a national Inter-Varsity Fellowship was not possible until a significant number of evangelicals were prepared to accept a demarcation between movement and church, in which the non-essential matters varied depending on the context.

Before this moment arrived the Evangelical Unions regarded themselves as distant members of the British I.V.F., and tried to maintain regular contact with it.[31] They also contributed to a termly Prayer Bulletin of an informal 'Fellowship of Evangelical Unions in the Universities of Australia and New Zealand'.[32] In May 1932 the nascent Canterbury College Evangelical Union wrote to existing E.U.s and to 'senior friends' proposing the formation of an 'Inter-Collegiate Fellowship for Evangelical Study' as an appropriate local institutional framework for the E.U.s, which would provide a relationship between the Unions with an aura of academic respectability ensured by a council of senior supporters.[33] But this proposal received little support.

Eventually, despite the policy of the Crusader Council that the Evangelical Unions should develop separately, it was at its initiative that the Inter-Varsity Fellowship was formed. The General Secretary of the Crusader Movement, John Laird, had assisted in the formation of an Evangelical Union in Wellington in 1933, and on his regular visits to other parts of the dominion he helped the existing Unions and encouraged moves to establish Unions at the two agricultural colleges, which would complete the national network of Evangelical Unions in every tertiary college. The Crusader Council was troubled by the diversionary effect that this involvement had on Laird's workload, and felt that it would be fairer to appoint a colleges' travelling secretary. But which body

---

[31] Wellington, TSCF Archives, A2c/002, J.S. Burt to B. Williams, [1932]; See also Leicester, Universities and Colleges Christian Fellowship Archives, J.S. Burt to D. Johnson, 7 October 1933.

[32] Fellowship of Evangelical Unions in the Universities of Australia and New Zealand, *Prayer Letter*, third term 1933; *ibid*, first term 1934. Copies held in UCCF Archives.

[33] Wellington, TSCF Archives, A2c/001 B.H. Williams to Mr. Moore and other correspondents, 10 May 1932.

could appoint such a person? In May 1935 the Crusader Council invited the shrewd and energetic President of the Auckland University College Evangelical Union, Archie Morton, to join them, so that discussions could commence.[34] On 23 July a conference of the Crusader Council and the Executive of the Auckland E.U. recommended the formation of an Inter-Varsity Fellowship. Archie Morton wrote to the other Evangelical Unions to advise them of the recommendation, and took the opportunity to forward a design for an I.V.F. badge, demanding an immediate verdict on both.[35]

Agreement seemed likely, for earlier in the year the Australian who was on his way to take up the position of General Secretary of the Canadian I.V.F. had visited the various E.U. executives and assured them that they 'were strong enough to do it'.[36] Meanwhile readers of the Crusader Movement prayer letter were assured that: 'There is a rising tide of blessing among the E.U.s ... This vital department of evangelical witness is on the eve of great things.'[37] Despite this encouragement the other Evangelical Unions were cautious. The Otago University students were fearful of condemnation by the churches, and were then angered when Archie Morton brushed aside their cautions.[38] Morton answered their complaints by introducing to the Crusader Council the daughters of Dr. Pettit who were students at Otago but were in favour of the proposal. The next meeting of the Crusader Council endorsed the proposal to hold an Inter-Varsity Fellowship conference at Roseneath school, Wellington at Easter 1936 concurrent with the Inter-Varsity sports tournament for which students could get travel concessions.[39]

It was at this conference that the Inter-Varsity Fellowship of

[34] Wellington, SU Archives, Crusader Movement Minutes, vol 1 pp. 262–6 (meetings of 21 May and 18 June 1935).

[35] *Ibid.* pp. 266–70 (meeting of 23 July 1935); Wellington, TSCF Archives, A2c/006, A.U.C.E.U. Executive to E.U. Executive members, 30 July 1935.

[36] Christchurch, H. Thomson, 'Substance of a Conference between Mr. C. Stacey-Woods, Dr. J.M. Laird, Mr. M. Wilson and the Executive of the Otago Evangelical Union in the home of Mrs. Cree Brown, 2nd term, 1935', question 11.

[37] Wellington, SU Archives, Crusader Prayer Letter, 5 September 1935.

[38] Wellington, TSCF Archives, A2c/007, Scheme for I.V.F. (N.Z.). Summary of replies to A.U.C.E.U.; A2c/010, Graham Miller to B. Williams, 30 September 1935.

[39] Wellington, SU Archives, Crusader Movement Minutes, vol 1 pp. 274–7 (meeting of 31 August 1935).

Evangelical Unions in New Zealand was formed. Agreement was not achieved without some tensions. In particular Morton continued to ride roughshod over delegates from the other Unions. Sensitivities were not assuaged by a sermon by the visiting Irish-American evangelist J. Edwin Orr, for this sermon urged the students to confess their sins openly. The paramount sin proved to be bitterness against the unrepentant Morton.[40] The formation of the I.V.F. did not in fact relieve the pressure on the Crusader Movement. Despite some financial support from the Crusader Council it was not until 1938 that the first I.V.F. staff member was appointed, and subsequently the world war made it difficult to find staff.

The character of the Inter-Varsity Fellowship was affected by its context. Dr. Pettit's address at the first I.V.F. conference publicly rehearsed the failings of the Student Christian Movement, although in an exchange of letters in the S.C.M. magazine the authority of the Bible rather than liberal theology assumed prominence as the key point at issue.[41] By the thirties the heady modernism of the S.C.M. ten years before had evaporated, and some genuine attempts were made to appease evangelicals, especially at Otago University.[42] In the southern towns some students chose to be members of both organisations. But the I.V.F. was necessarily separatist in policy, and this was an official part of its constitution. After this policy was questioned by a speaker at the 1939 I.V.F. conference, the Rev. W.A. Orange warned the General Committee of the likelihood of either 'open persecution' or 'social corruption or defiling influence', and urged members to 'beware of (a) kindness towards as of [sic] people who are not of sound doctrine (b) endeavouring to obtain in the movement representation of all denominations'.[43] These remarks may seem strange ones to come from an Anglican clergyman. They can only be understood if the characteristic distinction made by evangelicals between Movement and Church is recalled. The Inter-Varsity Fellowship and the Crusader

---

[40] Lineham, 'Evangelical Witness at Canterbury University' p. 10.
[41] *I.V.F. Papers No. 2* pp. 22–36; and letters to *The Student* cited in *ibid.* pp. 12–17.
[42] Wellington, Alexander Turnbull Library, SCM Archives, file 33, Jean Archibald to College Executives, 24 March 1932.
[43] Wellington, TSCF Archives, IVF General Committee Minutes, vol 1, pp. 37–8 (meeting of 12 May 1939).

Movement rigorously avoided anything which seemed to them to encroach upon the task of the Church. Unlike the Student Christian Movement they had no recognised position in the eyes of churchmen. Since clergy were particularly sensitive about anything which drew people away from church services, the I.V.F. became very cautious about Sunday events, including involvement in mission services.[44] The Churches were in effect seen as bodies whose essential function was the conduct of Sunday services.

The I.V.F. thus came to perceive of the Church as an institution confined to church buildings, and the services and sacraments held there. This essentially congregational and institutional view of the Church enabled them to justify the Crusader groups and Evangelical Unions as christian clubs in specific secular contexts, which were responsible for a localised witness in that context. Worship took place in the church; witness took place in the E.U. (In fact biblical instruction and sermons were equally important aspects of the life of the E.U., but this teaching focussed on essential truths which the Churches could not be assumed to emphasize.) This view of the respective roles of Church and Movement reflects the denominational spread of evangelical students. Anglicans and Presbyterians had to work with Baptists and Brethren. A clear separation of the roles of Church and Movement was thought to be the preference of church leaders. The distinction between Movement and Church has always been a somewhat unclear one for members of protestant denominations, for denominations themselves have some of the characteristics of Movements. But this subtle point was not one which pioneer evangelicals could dare to consider.

All these attitudes and tensions played their part in creating a space for evangelical student movements. In their turn these pioneering movements led after the Second World War to other denominational and inter-denominational evangelical bodies. To some extent these later movements emerged in a secure evangelical world, and felt less need to defer to church sensitivities. Some were far more stridently lay and un-ecclesiastical. Some were less preoccupied with theological questions. Yet in effect the issue of the

---

[44] Wellington, TSCF Archives, A2d/002, Ivan Moses, Memorandum to Executive on the Nature and Scope of I.V.F., July 1946.

scope for inter-denominational movements continued to face all the para-church organisations of the protestant world. To some extent their interest in ecclesiological questions is inversely proportionate to the opportunities they find for their activities. In the new world of New Zealand evangelicalism in the thirties, it was a problem of peculiar relevance.

Massey University
Palmerston North, New Zealand

THE OXFORD GROUP MOVEMENT
BETWEEN THE WARS

by D.W. BEBBINGTON

IN July 1935 Lady Margaret Hall, Oxford, was the setting for an international gathering that attracted thousands of the eminent and the curious, many of them churchmen.[1] Similar 'house-parties' had been held every year since 1930.[2] At free periods during the day, recalled Beverley Nichols, an enthusiast on his first visit, 'the High Street seemed afire with shining faces';[3] last thing at night attenders could enjoy a 'lemonade and biscuit' party in the Toynbee Room.[4] The main business, however, consisted of sessions where those present listened to testimonies of changed lives, of how people had 'surrendered' and were now 'all out for God'. These were the main annual meetings of the Oxford Group.

The animating spirit was Dr Frank Buchman, 'tall, upright, stoutish, clean-shaven, spectacled, with that mien of scrupulous, shampooed, and almost medical cleanness, or freshness, which is so characteristic of the hygienic American'.[5] Buchman was in fact a Pennsylvania Lutheran minister who after a decisive spiritual experience during the Keswick Convention of 1908 had turned into a highly professional evangelist.[6] Personal conversation including a direct challenge to confess past sins, what he called 'soul surgery', became in his hands a powerful tool for winning converts.[7] He arrived in Britain in 1920 fresh from a successful evangelistic tour in the Far East and spent the academic year trying to put his technique into practice among Cambridge undergraduates. A Rugby blue was converted and, as he put it, set about 'tackling

---

[1] *The Times* 9 July 1935 p. 11.
[2] G.F. Allen, 'The Groups in Oxford' *Oxford and the Groups* ed R.H.S. Crossman (Oxford 1934) p. 25.
[3] Beverley Nichols, *All I could never be* (London 1949) p. 248.
[4] *The British Weekly* 13 July 1933 p. 295.
[5] Harold Begbie, *Life Changers* (London 1923) p. 34.
[6] W.H. Clark, *The Oxford Group* (New York 1951) caps 3–4.
[7] H.A. Walter, *Soul Surgery* 6 edn (London nd).

other men'. It was he who by bearing testimony at Oxford in the spring of 1921 made the initial impression on what was to become the headquarters of the movement.[8] House-parties were at first held in Cambridge, but Oxford proved a more fertile mission field. Despite aloofness by most Evangelical clergy, a policy recommended by Bishop Chavasse, by 1927 the movement could assemble 120 undergraduates for a pre-term meeting.[9] Younger clergymen were soon won over. A college chaplain, Geoffrey Allen, was drawn in when he capitulated to guidance to buy a new dressing gown as an aid to early rising.[10] In these years the Group deliberately sought no publicity. Buchman remained based in America and the other leaders' time was fully occupied.[11] Up to about 1930 the movement in Britain was largely confined to the universities.

From 1930 to 1934, however, the Oxford Group spread over much of the country. Sheer dedication was partly responsible. Teams of 'life-changers' spoke of their own surrender with compelling sincerity. Many were prepared to travel abroad for the purpose at their own expense. It was on such a trip to South Africa in 1928 that a team first attracted the label 'Oxford Group', but most campaigns were in Britain. The first was at Worthing in 1927, with a larger operation at Edinburgh in 1930 and others elsewhere in subsequent years.[12] The consequences often snowballed. During the Edinburgh campaign, for instance, an Oxford undergraduate spoke at a Methodist Bible class from 3 to 10 p.m. Numbers of young people gave themselves to Christ, continued to meet afterwards in weekly groups and carried the message to other Methodist churches in Scotland.[13] The culmination was an onslaught on London in the autumn of 1933 involving some 500 workers.[14] Circumstances as well as zeal were responsible for the impact. These were depression years in which Britain's abandonment of the gold standard and high unemployment sapped national morale. The Oxford Group claimed to offer the solution, and, as though to

[8] Begbie, *Life Changers*, cap 4.
[9] *The Record* 18 Nov. 1932 p. 689. Allen, 'Groups', p. 18.
[10] Geoffrey Allen, *He that Cometh* (London 1932) p. 34.
[11] A.J. Russell, *For Sinners Only* (London 1932) p. 109.
[12] Allen, 'Groups' pp. 20, 17, 24.
[13] *The Methodist Recorder* 4 Feb. 1932 p. 17.
[14] *Times* 9 Oct. 1933 p. 19.

vindicate the claim, frequently paraded George Light, chairman of the Unemployed Workers' Association of Warwickshire, to testify to the change in his life.[15] The Nazi seizure of power and the increasing likelihood of European war also generated a sense of crisis that the movement was quick to exploit.[16] In this atmosphere the message of the teams was heard the more readily.

The greatest advantage of the Group was its image. In an era of successful youth movements, it was young – a corollary, initially, of its university base. There was youthful exuberance in the discussion of religion 'with such freedom, sincerity, gaiety and wholehearted joy'.[17] Traditional theological language was discarded and contemporary slang took its place. The new Grouper rector in the best fictional account of the movement, John Moore's *Brensham Village*, uses expressions like 'scrumptious', 'ripping' and 'awfully jolly'. First names were *de rigueur*. 'The Groupers', comments Moore, ' ... would have addressed the Holy Apostles themselves by their Christian names, or rather they would have abbreviated them and called Saint Peter Pete.'[18] Meetings were punctuated by laughter. 'It's such fun', was a pet phrase.[19] In this hearty ethos athletes were naturally heroised. From testimonies at an early London rally a correspondent concluded that the young people were 'as keen on sport as on religion'.[20] The excitements and amusements of life were to be relished. There was, for instance, no taboo on the theatre.[21] Adherents had been, in the words of an apologist, 'reborn to the world as well as reborn to God'. It was all very unstuffy and up-to-date: 'We are Moderns'.[22] And this image was sedulously cultivated by attention to publicity. One coup was the placing of a Group slogan on four million milk-bottle tops.[23] Another was the conscious adoption of the title 'Oxford Group' in 1931 shortly before the celebration of the

[15] *Record* 15 Dec. 1933 p. 740. Marjorie Harrison, *Saints run Mad* (London 1934) pp. 132, 141.
[16] E.g. B.H. Streeter in *Times* 10 May 1935 p. 10.
[17] *Record* 29 Apr. 1932 p. 261.
[18] John Moore, *Brensham Village* (London 1966 edn) pp. 162, 171.
[19] *Record* 14 Oct. 1932 p. 617.
[20] *Methodist Recorder* 28 Jan. 1932 p. 4.
[21] E.g. *Groups* July 1935 p. 47.
[22] 'The Layman with a Notebook', *What is the Oxford Group?* (London 1933) pp. 4, 130.
[23] Tom Driberg, *The Mystery of Moral Re-Armament* (London 1964) p. 144.

centenary of the Oxford Movement, so that the inevitable confusion of the two would attract greater public notice. The implication that the university had somehow given the Group its *imprimatur* was strongly resented long before, in 1939, A.P. Herbert, as MP for the university, unsuccessfully tried to prevent the registration of the title with the Board of Trade.[24] Although Buchman was barred from access to the B.B.C.,[25] he recruited journalists to support the cause. Hugh Redwood of *The News Chronicle*, Paul Hodder-Williams of *The British Weekly* and Herbert Upward of *The Church of England Newspaper* all enthused over the movement in the 1930s.[26] And most of all A.J. Russell of *The Sunday Express* brought Buchmanism into the headlines with *For Sinners Only*, a *pot-pourri* of conversion narratives published in 1932. In a year it had sold 117,000 copies in Britain alone and, if it struck some as 'a bath of treacle', it drew many others towards the Group.[27] Buchman and his acolytes were masters in projecting an attractive image.

Although it is difficult to define who belonged to the Oxford Group on account of its rejection of the notion of membership, several eminent names were attracted. Episcopal backing came preeminently from Foss Westcott, Metropolitan of India, for of the home bishops only Cyril Bardsley of Leicester, who at one time in Groupist fashion kept a book for noting down guidance, came close to adhesion.[28] Archbishop Lang went out of his way to commend the movement, even troubling to send a congratulatory message to Buchman's sixtieth birthday dinner.[29] Winnington-Ingram, bishop of London, tempered official support with criticism, provoking the comment that he played the part of Innocent III in relation to Saint Francis – not approving but blessing.[30] After consultations at Lambeth in October 1933, a battery of bishops issued statements similarly qualifying general praise with particular

[24] *Ibid.* cap 6.
[25] *Times* 16 July 1937 p. 12.
[26] *Record* 20 Nov. 1931 p. 729, 6 Aug. 1937 p. 510, 20 Nov. 1931 p. 729.
[27] *British Weekly* 6 July 1933 p. 273. Harrison, *Saints* p. 2. F.C. Raynor, *The Finger of God* (London 1934) pp. 35, 48, 157, 206, 246.
[28] *Times* 21 Sept. 1933 p. 6. Russell, *Sinners* p. 286.
[29] Driberg, *Mystery* p. 190. *Times* 1 June 1938 p. 11.
[30] *Times* 9 Oct. 1933 p. 19.

censures.[31] A scattering of senior clergy like Provost Margetson of Edinburgh fully associated themselves with the Group, but the best Anglican catches were two Oxford theologians, L.W. Grensted, Oriel Professor of the Philosophy of the Christian Religion, and B.H. Streeter, a distinguished New Testament scholar and Provost of Queen's College.[32] Wider Anglican opinion was also more appreciative than might be expected for a brash American import. H.D.A. Major for the Modern Churchmen's Union bestowed his approval chiefly because of the neglect of hellfire and 'blood theology'.[33] Evangelicals, as represented by *The Record*, initially gave a welcome, if a cautious one, on precisely the opposite ground that, although the Group did not emphasise the atonement, it might be guided into more truth.[34] Amongst liberal Evangelicals the movement made some of its early headway in 1931.[35] Although *The Church Times* criticised its lack of social conscience, several Anglo-Catholic voices were raised on behalf of the movement: Fr W.S.A. Robertson of St. Ives (Hunts) reported that the Group had brought 'a new sincerity, and a courageous missionary-heartedness' to his 'young altar-servers'.[36] Clerical involvement was disproportionately Anglican, but uncommitted interest was, if anything, more widespread outside the Church of England. Presbyterians from north and south of the border attended house parties, and Dr John Carlile, editor of *The Baptist Times*, gave the movement his patronage.[37] Much stronger backing came from within Congregationalism and Methodism. Some of the earliest provincial inroads of the Group were among Congregationalists, and in March 1932 the denomination's moderators, though not without reservation, affirmed its value.[38] Many travelling teams were organised by Methodists, the young W.E. Sangster defended

[31] H.H. Henson, *Retrospect of an Unimportant Life* 2 vols (London 1943) 2 p. 290. *Times* 3 Nov. 1933 p. 7, 22 Nov. 1933, p. 19.

[32] *Record* 20 May 1932 p. 325. Russell, *Sinners* cap 19. Henson, *Retrospect* 2 p. 328.

[33] H.D.A. Major, 'The Group Movement', *The Meaning of the Groups* ed F.A.M. Spencer (London 1934) p. 124.

[34] *Record* 17 June 1932 p. 388.

[35] *Ibid* 20 Nov. 1931 p. 729.

[36] Sidney Dark, *Not Such a Bad Life* (London 1941) pp. 229–30. *British Weekly* 6 July 1933 p. 272.

[37] *Times* 9 July 1935 p. 11. Russell, *Sinners* p. 142. *British Weekly* 13 July 1933 p. 295.

[38] *Record* 20 Nov. 1931 p. 729. *Times* 19 Mar. 1932 p. 15.

the Group doctrine of guidance and the rising Leslie Weatherhead, without joining, was red-hot in its favour. As 'the greatest religious force in the world', he declared, it would lead to 'a revival even more far-reaching and significant than that of the Wesleys'.[39] Committed laymen included Sir Lynden Macassey, Leader of the Parliamentary Bar, Austin Reed, the men's outfitter, and a goodly number of military and naval officers.[40] The one cabinet minister to draw close, at least for a while, was Ernest Brown, Minister of Labour and a leading Baptist.[41] Although the 225 MPs who signed a petition favouring registration as the Oxford Group in 1939 undoubtedly included many with virtually no interest, two years earlier ten MPs were prepared to write a letter to *The Times* implying considerable allegiance to its position.[42] Of the peers, although several attended Group gatherings, only Lord Addington, a bachelor who gave much of his time to local government, threw himself into the cause.[43] Lord Salisbury, a senior Conservative statesman, was sufficiently impressed to address a rally, but stopped short of identification with the Group.[44] Even if few of the well-known plunged into the movement, far more respected and applauded its work.

There was nevertheless stern opposition. Dr Whittingham, bishop of St. Edmundsbury and Ipswich, failed to see 'the notes of sanity and judgment, of the calm strength of high and sustained purpose'.[45] Bilbrough of Newcastle thought the Group's literature feeble, Williams of Carlisle dismissed the movement as more American than Oxford and Rawlinson, who became bishop of Derby in 1936, had long believed it 'extremely peculiar – one might almost say, grim'.[46] The most strenuous opponent, however, was Hensley Henson, bishop of Durham, who in March 1933 published a charge branding the movement as anti-intellectual, adolescent in style and

---

[39] Raynor, *Finger* pp. 116–17. Paul Sangster, *Doctor Sangster* (London 1962) pp. 92, 103. *British Weekly* 27 July 1933 p. 340.

[40] *British Weekly* 6 July 1933 pp. 273, 278. *Times* 9 July 1937 p. 11, 29 July 1935 p. 14.

[41] *Times* 28 July 1937 p. 11, 7 Aug. 1937 p. 6.

[42] *Ibid.* 8 June 1939 p. 8, 16 July 1937 p. 12.

[43] Driberg, *Mystery* pp. 56, 190. *Times* 10 Aug. 1937 p. 7.

[44] Henson, *Retrospect* 2 p. 376. *Times* 30 Mar. 1937 p. 17.

[45] *Times* 10 Nov. 1933 p. 17.

[46] *Record* 26 May 1933 p. 311. *Times* 12 Oct. 1933 p. 7. Driberg, *Mystery* p.17.

limited in its conception of Christianity.[47] Six months later he returned to the assault with a powerful letter to *The Times* that merely hinted at 'the darkest shadow on the movement – I mean the trail of moral and intellectual wrecks which its progress leaves behind'.[48] It is clear Henson found the Oxford Group distasteful, an 'Essay in Corybantic Christianity'.[49] Hardly less harsh, though much less eloquent, were condemnations by conservative Evangelicals. Their Fellowship of Evangelical Churchmen was warned of the Group's dangers and deficiencies in September 1932, and in the following year Thomas Houghton, an extreme Protestant clergyman from Norfolk, denounced Buchmanism as apostasy.[50] For long caught between approving and disapproving brethren, the Oxford Evangelical leadership under Christopher Chavasse eventually came down publicly against the Group in June 1932.[51] Something like an official Anglo-Catholic rejection of Groupism was published by the Faith Press in 1933. Ivor Thomas, MP, argued with some panache that 'what is valuable in it may be easily obtained in historical Christianity, so that where it is useful it is superfluous, and where it is not superfluous it is pernicious'.[52] The formal Roman Catholic response, issued by the Catholic Truth Society, contended that the Groupist idea of listening-in to the Holy Ghost had implications 'contrary to natural morality', while M.J. D'Arcy for the Jesuits preferred the Spiritual Exercises of Saint Ignatius.[53] Ronald Knox, as Roman Catholic chaplain to Oxford, derived his unfavourable impressions from local gossip. It was reported, he remarked, 'that one college chaplain was induced to resign by undergraduates commonly coming to him and asking him to forgive them for having described him as the worst chaplain in Oxford'.[54] To the anathemas of churchmen, journalists like Tom Driberg added racier critiques.[55] And opposition was capped by

---

[47] H.H. Henson, *The Oxford Groups* (London 1933).
[48] *Times* 19 Sept. 1933 p. 8.
[49] Henson, *Retrospect* 2 p. 290.
[50] *Record* 30 Sept. 1932 p. 581. Thomas Houghton, *Buchmanism* (London 1933).
[51] *Record* 24 June 1932 p. 402.
[52] Ivor Thomas, *The Buchman Groups* (London nd [1933]) p. 2.
[53] Driberg, *Mystery* p. 193. M.J. D'Arcy, 'The Groups and the Spirit of Worship' *Oxford* ed Crossman pp. 180–1.
[54] R.A. Knox, 'The Group Movement' *Meaning* ed Spencer p. 88.
[55] Driberg, *Mystery* pp. 16–17.

disdainful observations from senior members of Oxford, like Miss
Barbara Gwyer, Principal of St. Hugh's, who felt a horror for
religious commotion among undergraduates. 'Are not "my station
and its duties", by faithful worship hallowed', she asked, 'a young
Christian's first and sufficient concern?'[56] It was natural for those
of conservative taste, like Gwyer or Henson, to combine with
those of conservative outlook in religion, like conservative Evangelicals and Roman Catholics, in withstanding the Oxford Group.

The controversy surrounding Buchman's movement focused on
four issues. First, there were its most distinctive practices: sharing,
that is private confession of sins with a group or individual, or else
public witness to a changed life; and guidance, that is the silent
seeking of divine direction, especially through an early-morning
'quiet time'. Sharing was open to ridicule, as when *The Daily
Herald* gleefully reported a young woman confessing to having
thought, 'Fancy Mavis coming to Communion in an orange
blouse!'[57] Although some High Churchmen saw a welcome analogy
between sharing and the confessional,[58] critics condemned the
technique as over-introspective or (in its public form) as giving
scope for egoistic display.[59] Most serious, it was often alleged,
were the risks of discussing sex. In one much publicised incident
the Group was denounced at a Foyles' Literary Luncheon in
honour of Buchman, by an actress of all people, as 'shocking,
indecent and indelicate'.[60] While apologists for the movement
explained that sex matters were never discussed before mixed audi-
ences,[61] suspicion of confession lingered on this point – and,
according to Ronald Knox, did much to whet undergraduate curiosity.[62] If sharing might seem immoral, guidance could seem
irrational. The method of sitting with a blank mind and a pencil
awaiting 'luminous thoughts' to jot down, widely practised among
Buchmanites, was held by the bishop of London to be dangerous.
'You cannot divest yourself', he declared in a sermon, 'of common

[56] Miss B.E. Gwyer, 'Comments of an Educationalist' *Oxford* ed Crossman p. 68.
[57] Harrison, *Saints* p. 81.
[58] E.g. M.L. Smith and Francis Underhill, *The Group Movement* (London 1934) p. 33.
[59] E.g. *Record* 4 Dec. 1931 p. 769, 18 Nov. 1932 p. 689.
[60] Driberg, *Mystery* p. 55.
[61] E.g. *Record* 7 Oct. 1932 p. 601.
[62] Knox, 'Group' p. 84.

sense, instinct, reason, and conscience'.[63] There was a likelihood of neglecting other means of guidance and of giving expression 'to the mysterious depths of the subconscious'.[64] And again such behaviour could appear ridiculous. A journalist attending a house-party was amused to be told to ask God's guidance over the amount to leave as a tip.[65] Yet Groupers stoutly defended seeking guidance: what was it other than two-way prayer?[66] Non-rational it might be, but, like discussion of sex, it implied a degree of psychological awareness unusual in the religious circles of the 1930s.

Secondly, there were the alleged deficiencies of the movement. It was held to be unthinking, so undogmatic as to be entirely untheological. To some supporters like Commander Sir William Windham, this was its great attraction: it was 'a practical religion which they could all accept'.[67] As J.W.C. Wand pointed out, only by avoiding doctrinal disputes could the Group appeal to people of differing religious backgrounds.[68] Yet the movement met the charge of theological sterility by drawing Streeter and the con-tinental theologian Emil Brunner into its ranks,[69] and also by producing in Grensted's *The Person of Christ* (1934) a distinctively Groupist Christology. And in reply to the frequently repeated charge, especially from Evangelical quarters, that the Groupers failed to stress the doctrine of the cross, it was claimed that the atonement was central to their work.[70] A parallel criticism was neglect of worship and the sacraments. It was true that at house-parties hymns were rare and intercessory prayer unknown.[71] But Groupers avoided holding meetings in church hours, encouraged participation in the sacraments of members' own churches and contended that they were not attempting to supplant the existing denominations. 'Our only organisation', Buchman declared, 'is the

---

[63] *Times* 6 Nov. 1933 p. 11.
[64] Christopher Chavasse in *Record* 18 Nov. 1932 p. 689.
[65] Harrison, *Saints* pp. 55–6.
[66] E.g. 'Layman', *Group* p. 69.
[67] *Times* 27 Sept. 1933 p. 12.
[68] J.W.C. Wand, 'The Groups and the Churches' *Oxford* ed Crossman pp. 163–4.
[69] Emil Brunner, *The Church and the Oxford Group* trans David Cairns (London 1937) p. 18.
[70] E.g. A.J. Russell, *One Thing I Know* (London 1933) pp. ix–xi.
[71] Harrison, *Saints* p. 108.

Church'.[72] Hensley Henson insisted on the contrary that, since the Group provided for all the spiritual needs of its members, other systems were superfluous and would naturally be abandoned. A sectarian logic was at work.[73] Although there was contemporary evidence of young people preferring Group activities to those of their church,[74] in the long term Henson was proved wrong. The Group remained a movement pursuing Fabian tactics within the churches, aiming gradually to leaven the lump. Buchman was scrupulous to observe certain ecclesiastical niceties, arranging, for instance, that the London campaign should be inaugurated by a commissioning service in St. Paul's Cathedral complete with episcopal benediction.[75] Insofar as the Group lacked a churchly sense, it was because it deliberately functioned as a complement to the churches. It was a bridge between the religious organisations and a secularising society.

Thirdly, the movement was charged with elitism, with being 'The Salvation Army of the upper classes'.[76] It seemed to concentrate exclusively on 'the well-to-do, the cultured, the leisured, and the intelligent'.[77] House-parties (themselves an institution taken over from Society) were expensive, costing from eleven to fifteen shillings a day.[78] London rallies began at 8.45 p.m. to allow time for dinner beforehand.[79] Buchman and the inner circle resided in London at Brown's Hotel, Mayfair, much used by the aristocracy.[80] There was little sign of an active social conscience. Life-changing, as Grensted admitted, was so central as to make social concern a 'very secondary interest'.[81] Sensitivity to this point drove Buchman to order a mission in the deprived East End parish of St. Mark's, Victoria Park, but, along with a subsequent lunch in Buchman's honour at a trade union club, it was very much a token gesture.[82] Occasionally reports were heard of teams including shop and office

[72] Brunner, *Church* p. 93.
[73] Henson, *Groups* p. 48.
[74] E.g. *Methodist Recorder* 28 Jan. 1932 p. 17.
[75] *Times* 9 Oct. 1933 p. 19.
[76] *Record* 27 Jan. 1933 p. 55.
[77] Smith and Underhill, *Movement* p. 36.
[78] Harrison, *Saints* p. 30.
[79] *Methodist Recorder* 19 Oct. 1933 p. 3.
[80] Russell, *Sinners* p. 22.
[81] L.W. Grensted, 'Conclusion' *Oxford* ed Crossman p. 200.
[82] Harrison, *Saints* pp. 30–2. Driberg, *Mystery* pp. 125–6.

workers or domestic servants and gardeners,[83] but the main impact was on the middle and upper-middle classes. It was a matter of conscious strategy. 'The surest way to help the masses', according to a defender of the Group, 'was through the conversion of their leaders in industry and politics and Church'.[84] The names of 'key people' were unashamedly exploited. In the dawning media age, Buchman knew the power of well-known personalities.

The fourth major ground of criticism was political. The Group, alleged L.P. Jacks, Principal of Manchester College, Oxford, was as authoritarian as Fascism: did it not proclaim 'the Dictatorship of the Holy Spirit'?[85] On the other hand the Buchmanite Group, according to Hensley Henson, 'reminds us irresistibly of the Russian Soviet, and 'Frank's' sovereignty in the one system is not wholly unlike that of Lenin or Stalin in the other'.[86] The charge had substance. Methodist Groupers found themselves outlawed by the leadership round Buchman for undertaking campaigns without checking their guidance and broke away in disgust.[87] But there was more to the criticism than an analogy with totalitarianism. In 1934 W.H. Auden drew attention to Fascist sympathies within Buchman's movement, and in the previous year two Nazi Groupers had appeared at the Oxford house-party.[88] Buchman travelled to the 1936 Olympic Games in Berlin, probably met Heinrich Himmler, head of the Gestapo, and on his return to New York gave an interview in which he declared, 'I thank heaven for a man like Adolf Hitler'.[89] With his German-speaking background, Buchman cherished the illusion that the Führer might surrender to God; and he also perceived Hitler as a bulwark against Communism. Buchman already entertained the fervent anti-Communism that was to become his main plank in the Cold War era. In Berlin he observed that England was 'seething with Communism'; and he

---

[83] *Methodist Recorder* 4 Feb. 1932 p. 17. J.C. Winslow, *The Church in Action* (London 1936) p. 62.
[84] Allen, 'Groups' p. 22.
[85] L.P. Jacks, 'Group Unity and the Sense of Sin' *Oxford* ed Crossman pp. 117–18.
[86] Henson, *Groups* p. 48.
[87] Raynor, *Finger* pp. 108–11, 170–1.
[88] W.H. Auden, 'The Group Movement and the Middle Classes' *Oxford* ed Crossman p. 101. *British Weekly* 13 July 1933 p. 295.
[89] Driberg, *Mystery* cap 4.

frequently paraded the former Fife Communist organiser James Watt on his platforms to commend 'a revolution by consent'.[90] With increasing continental success from the autumn of 1934, Buchman does seem to have been more attracted by the public display and militaristic atmosphere of the European dictatorships. Oxford house-parties were replaced after 1935 by camps, flags, broadcasts and national assemblies. 'After a silent period of communion', during the 1936 national assembly at Castle Bromwich, 'bugles were sounded and drums beaten as 1,000 young men marched to the front followed by a contingent of girls.'[91] There had been a change of ethos even before, in May 1938, Buchman announced the slogan that was to supersede 'Oxford Group' as the movement's title: 'Moral Re-armament'.[92] But it would be wrong to read back this later, more politicised, mood into the early 1930s. During the earlier phase the Group, though internally authoritarian, was minimally political.

In the early 1930s the Oxford Group, as the nature and range of comments on it have shown, made a significant impression on religion in Britain. If by 1935 the 'slogans that were once so fresh are becoming jejune with over-use',[93] for a while there was a widespread revival atmosphere. Apart from bodies under Buchman's ultimate control, there sprang up groups that felt free to go beyond his techniques by incorporating Bible study and missionary support in their programmes.[94] Methodists even created a complementary network of Cambridge Groups.[95] The idea of team missions was taken up by Bryan Green of the Oxford Pastorate, and Bishop Bardsley recommended his Leicestershire parishes to form 'a cell or group' of laymen round the vicar for evangelism.[96] A Methodist layman, no doubt one of many, reported adopting the early-morning quiet time, and W.E. Sangster was directed by the Group's insistence on moral absolutes towards the traditional

[90] *Ibid.* p. 65. *Times* 27 Sept. 1933 p. 12. Russell, *Sinners* p. 143.
[91] *Times* 27 July 1936 p. 9.
[92] F.N.D. Buchman, *Remaking the World* (London 1958 edn) pp. 45-8.
[93] *Groups* Jan. 1935 p. 376.
[94] Frank Child, 'The Group in the Parish' *Meaning* ed Spencer p. 6.
[95] W.H. Beales, *The Hope of His Calling* (London 1933).
[96] G.I.F. Thomson, *The Oxford Pastorate* (London 1946) p. 111. Joan Bayldon, *Cyril Bardsley, Evangelist* (London 1942) p. 170.

The Oxford Group

Wesleyan ideal of holiness.[97] Perhaps the most significant legacy consisted of those converted or mobilised through the movement who did not remain as it evolved into MRA but carried their activism into church life. Looking back from the 1960s, Geoffrey Allen, by then bishop of Derby, commented that 'I learned many things through my time with the Oxford Group in the early 1930s; but I became dissatisfied with some of the later developments'.[98] The relatively small scale of MRA operations in Britain must not blind us to the earlier impact of the movement. It was successful because for a few years the Group provided what was wanted by an educated generation that recognised the deficiencies of human rationality, saw no point in the paraphernalia of theology and worship, idolised great names and longed to re-make the world. Since it was an association and not a church bearing a weight of tradition, the Group could adapt its image to fit the bill. It was the genius of Buchman to fine-tune the movement so accurately that it projected a mass appeal. What Hensley Henson intended as a jibe was in fact a measure of Buchman's achievement: 'The organization of the Groupist movement reflects the distinctive character of the age'.[99]

Stirling University

[97] *Methodist Recorder* 10 Nov. 1932 p. 20, 8 Apr. 1937 p. 15.
[98] Driberg, *Mystery* p. 269.
[99] Henson, *Groups* p. 48.
I am glad to acknowledge the support from the British Academy, the Carnegie Trust for the Universities of Scotland and the Whitley Trust that made possible the research on which this paper is based.

ABBREVIATIONS

AASRP	*Associated Archaeological Societies Reports and Papers*
AAWG	*Abhandlungen der Akademie [Gesellschaft to 1942] der Wissenschaften zu Göttingen* (Göttingen 1843–)
AAWL	*Abhandlungen der Akademie der Wissenschaften und der Literatur* (Mainz 1950–)
ABAW	*Abhandlungen der Bayerischen Akademie der Wissenschaften* (Munich 1835–)
Abh	Abhandlung
Abt	Abteilung
ACO	*Acta Conciliorum Oecumenicorum*, ed E. Schwartz (Berlin /Leipzig 1914–40)
ACW	*Ancient Christian Writers*, ed J. Quasten and J.C. Plumpe (Westminster, Maryland/London 1946–)
ADAW	*Abhandlungen der Deutschen* [till 1944 *Preussischen*] *Akademie der Wissenschaften zu Berlin* (Berlin 1815–)
AF	*Analecta Franciscana*, 10 vols (Quaracchi 1885–1941)
AFH	*Archivum Franciscanum Historicum* (Quaracchi/Rome 1908–)
AFP	*Archivum Fratrum Praedicatorum* (Rome 1931–)
AHP	*Archivum historiae pontificae* (Rome 1963–)
AHR	*American Historical Review* (New York 1895–)
AKG	*Archiv für Kulturgeschichte* (Leipzig/Münster/Cologne 1903–)
AKZ	*Arbeiten zur Kirchlichen Zeitgeschichte*
ALKG	H. Denifle and F. Ehrle, *Archiv für Literatur- und Kirchengeschichte des Mittelalters*, 7 vols (Berlin/Freiburg 1885–1900)
Altaner	B. Altaner, *Patrologie: Leben, Schriften und Lehre der Kirchenväter* (5 ed Freiburg 1958)
AM	L. Wadding, *Annales Minorum* 8 vols (Rome 1625–54); 2 ed, 25 vols (Rome 1731–1886); 3 ed, vol 1–, (Quaracchi 1931–)
An Bol	*Analecta Bollandiana* (Brussels 1882–)
Annales	*Annales: Economies, Sociétés, Civilisations* (Paris 1946–)
Ant	*Antonianum* (Rome 1926–)
APC	*Proceedings and Ordinances of the Privy Council 1386– 1542*, ed Sir Harris Nicholas, 7 vols (London 1834–7)
—	*Acts of the Privy Council of England 1542–1629*, 44 vols (London 1890–1958)
—	*Acts of the Privy Council of England, Colonial Series (1613– 1785)* 5 vols (London 1908–12)
AR	*Archivum Romanicum* (Geneva/Florence 1941–71)
ARG	*Archiv für Reformationsgeschichte* (Berlin/Leipzig/ Gütersloh 1903–)

ABBREVIATIONS

ASAW	*Abhandlungen der Sächsischen Akademie [Gesellschaft* to 1920] *der Wissenschaften zu Leipzig* (Leipzig 1850–)
ASB	*Acta Sanctorum Bollandiana* (Brussels etc 1643–)
ASC	*Anglo Saxon Chronicle*
ASI	*Archivio storico Italiano* (Florence 1842–)
ASL	*Archivio storico Lombardo*, 1–62 (Milan 1874–1935); ns 1– 10 (Milan 1936–47)
ASOC	*Analecta Sacri Ordinis Cisterciensis [Analecta Cisterciensia* since 1965] (Rome 1945–)
ASOSB	*Acta Sanctorum Ordinis Sancti Benedicti*, ed L. D'Achery and J. Mabillon (Paris 1668–1701)
ASP	*Archivio della Società [Deputazione* from 1935] *Romana di Storia Patria* (Rome 1878–1934, 1935–)
AV	Authorised Version
AV	*Archivio Veneto* (Venice 1871——); [1891–1921, *Nuovo Archivio Veneto*; 1922–6, *Archivio Veneto–Tridentino*]
B	*Byzantion* (Paris/Boston/Brussels 1924–)
Bale *Catalogus*	John Bale, *Scriptorum Illustrium Maioris Brytanniae Catalogus*, 2 parts (Basel 1557, 1559)
Bale, *Index*	John Bale, *Index Britanniae Scriptorum*, ed R.L. Poole and M. Bateson (Oxford 1902) *Anecdota Oxoniensia*, medieval and modern series 9.
Bale, *Summarium*	John Bale, *Illustrium Maioris Britanniae Scriptorum Summarium*, (Ipswich 1548, reissued Wesel 1549)
BEC	*Bibliothèque de l'Ecole des Chartres* (Paris 1839–)
Beck	H-G Beck, *Kirche und theologische Literatur im byzantinischen Reich* (Munich 1959)
BEFAR	*Bibliothèque des écoles françaises d'Athènes et Rome* (Paris 1876–)
BEHE	*Bibliothèque de l'Ecole des Hautes Etudes: Sciences Philologiques et Historiques* (Paris 1869–)
Bernard	E. Bernard, *Catalogi Librorum Manuscriptorum Angliae et Hiberniae* (Oxford 1697)
BF	*Byzantinische Forschungen* (Amsterdam 1966–)
BHG	*Bibliotheca Hagiographica Graeca*, ed F. Halkin, 3 vols + 1 (3 ed Brussels 1957, 1969)
BHI	*Bibliotheca historica Italia*, ed A. Ceruti, 4 vols (Milan 1876–85) 2 series, 3 vols (Milan 1901–33)
BHL	*Bibliotheca Hagiographica Latina*, 2 vols + 1 (Brussels 1898–1901, 1911)
BHR	*Bibliothèque d'Humanisme et Renaissance* (Paris/Geneva 1941–)
Bibl Ref	*Bibliography of the Reform 1450–1648, relating to the United Kingdom and Ireland*, ed Derek Baker for 1955–70 (Oxford 1975)
BIHR	*Bulletin of the Institute of Historical Research* (London 1923–)

ABBREVIATIONS

CF	*Classical Folia, [Folis 1946–59]* (New York 1960–)
CGOH	*Cartulaire Générale de l'Ordre des Hospitaliers de St.-Jean de Jerusalem (1100–1310)*, ed J. Delaville Le Roulx, 4 vols (Paris 1894–1906)
CH	*Church History* (New York/Chicago 1932–)
CHB	*Cambridge History of the Bible*
CHistS	*Church History Society* (London 1886–92)
CHJ	*Cambridge Historical Journal* (Cambridge 1925–57)
CIG	*Corpus Inscriptionum Graecarum*, ed A. Boeckh, J. Franz, E. Curtius, A. Kirchhoff, 4 vols (Berlin 1825–77)
CIL	*Corpus Inscriptionum Latinarum* (Berlin 1863–)
Cîteaux	*Cîteaux: Commentarii Cisterciensis* (Westmalle 1950–)
CMH	*Cambridge Medieval History*
CModH	*Cambridge Modern History*
COCR	*Collectanea Ordinis Cisterciensium Reformatorum* (Rome/Westmalle 1934–)
COD	*Conciliorum oecumenicorum decreta* (3 ed Bologna 1973)
Coll Franc	*Collectanea Franciscana* (Assisi/Rome 1931–)
CR	*Corpus Reformatorum*, ed C.G. Bretschneider and others (Halle, etc. 1834–)
CS	*Cartularium Saxonicum*, ed W. de G. Birch, 3 vols (London 1885–93)
CSCO	*Corpus Scriptorum Christianorum Orientalium* (Paris 1903–)
CSEL	*Corpus Scriptorum Ecclesiasticorum Latinorum* (Vienna 1866–)
CSer	*Camden Series* (London 1838–)
CSHByz	*Corpus Scriptorum Historiae Byzantinae* (Bonn 1828–97)
CYS	*Canterbury and York Society* (London 1907–)
DA	*Deutsches Archiv für [Geschichte,-Weimar 1937–43] die Erforschung des Mittelalters* (Cologne/Graz 1950–)
DACL	*Dictionnaire d'Archéologie chrétienne et de Liturgie*, ed F. Cabrol and H. Leclercq (Paris 1924–)
DDC	*Dictionnaire de Droit Canonique*, ed R. Naz (Paris 1935–)
DHGE	*Dictionnaire d'Histoire et de Géographie ecclésiastiques*, ed A. Baudrillart and others (Paris 1912–)
DNB	*Dictionary of National Biography* (London 1885–)
DOP	*Dumbarton Oaks Papers* (Cambridge, Mass., 1941–)
DR	F. Dölger, *Regesten der Kaiserurkunden des oströmischen Reiches (Corpus der griechischen Urkunden des Mittelalters und der neuern Zeit*, Reihe A, Abt I), 5 vols: 1 (565–1025); 2 (1025–1204); 3 (1204–1282); 4 (1282–1341); 5 (1341–1543) (Munich/Berlin 1924–65)
DRev	*Downside Review* (London 1880–)

ABBREVIATIONS

DSAM	*Dictionnaire de Spiritualité, Ascétique et Mystique*, ed M. Viller (Paris 1932–)
DTC	*Dictionnaire de Théologie Catholique*, ed A. Vacant, E. Mangenot, E. Amann, 15 vols (Paris 1903–50)
EcHR	*Economic History Review* (London 1927–)
EEBS	Ἐπετηρισ Ἑταιρειας Βνξαντινων Σπονδων (Athens 1924–)
EETS	*Early English Text Society*
EF	*Etudes Franciscaines* (Paris 1899–1938, ns 1950–)
EHD	*English Historical Documents* (London 1953–)
EHR	*English Historical Review* (London 1886–)
Ehrhard	A. Ehrhard, *Uberlieferung und Bestand der hagiographischen und homiletischen Liberatur der griechischen Kirche von den Anfangen bis zum Ende des 16. Jh*, 3 vols in 4, *TU*50–2 (=4 series 5–7) 11 parts (Leipzig 1936–52)
Emden (O)	A.B. Emden, *A Biographical Register of the University of Oxford to 1500*, 3 vols (London 1957–9); *1500–40* (1974)
Emden (C)	A.B. Emden, *A Biographical Register of the University of Cambridge to 1500* (London 1963)
EO	*Echos d'Orient* (Constantinople/Paris 1897–1942)
ET	English translation
EYC	*Early Yorkshire Charters*, ed W. Farrer and C.T. Clay, 12 vols (Edinburgh/Wakefield 1914–65)
FGH	*Die Fragmente der griechischen Historiker*, ed F. Jacoby (Berlin 1926–30)
FM	*Histoire de l'église depuis les origines jusqu'à nos jours*, ed A. Fliche and V. Martin (Paris 1935–)
Foedera	*Foedera, conventiones, litterae et cuiuscunmque generis acta publica inter regis Angliae et alios quosvis imperatores, reges, pontifices, principes vel communitates*, ed T. Rymer and R. Sanderson, 20 vols (London 1704–35), 3 ed G. Holmes, 10 vols (The Hague 1739–45), re-ed 7 vols (London 1816–69)
Franc Stud	*Franciscan Studies* (St Bonaventure, New York 1924–, ns 1941–)
Fredericq	P. Fredericq, *Corpus documentorum inquisitionis haereticae pravitatis Neerlandicae*, 3 vols (Ghent 1889–93)
FStn	*Franzikanische Studien* (Münster/Werl 1914–)
GalC	*Gallia Christiana*, 16 vols (Paris 1715–1865)
Gangraena	T. Edwards, *Gangraena*, 3 parts (London 1646)
GCS	*Die griechischen christlichen Schriftsteller der erste drei Jahrhunderte* (Leipzig 1897–)
Gee and Hardy	*Documents illustrative of English Church History* ed H. Gee and W.J. Hardy (London 1896)

GEEB	R. Janin, *La géographie ecclésiastique de l'empire byzantin;*
CEM	*1, Le siège de Constantinople et le patriarcat oecumenique,* pt 3 *Les églises et les monastères* (Paris 1953);
EMGCB	2, *Les églises et les monastères des grands centres byzantins* (Paris 1975) (series discontinued)
Golubovich	Girolamo Golubovich, *Biblioteca bio-bibliografica della Terra Sante e dell'oriente francescano:* series *1, Annali,* 5 vols (Quaracchie 1906–23) series 2, *Documenti* 14 vols (Quaracchi 1921–33) series 3, *Documenti,* (Quaracchi 1928–) series 4, *Studi,* ed M. Roncaglia (Cairo 1954–)
Grumel	V. Grumel, *Les Regestes des Actes du Patriarcat de Con-*
Regestes	*stantinople,* 1: *Les Actes des Patriarches,* 1: 381–715; II: 715–1043; III: 1043–1206 (Socii Assumptionistae Chalcedonenses, 1931, 1936, 1947)
Grundmann	H. Grundmann, *Religiöse Bewegungen im Mittelalter* (Berlin 1935, 2 ed Darmstadt 1970)
Guignard	P. Guignard, *Les monuments primitifs de la règle cistercienne* (Dijon 1878)
HBS	*Henry Bradshaw Society* (London/Canterbury 1891–)
HE	*Historia Ecclesiastica*
HistSt	*Historical Studies* (Melbourne 1940–)
HJ	*Historical Journal* (Cambridge 1958–)
Hjch	*Historisches Jahrbuch des Görres Gesellschaft* (Cologne 1880–, Munich 1950–)
HKS	Hanserd Knollys Society (London 1847–)
HL	C.J. Hefele and H. Leclercq, *Histore des Conciles,* 10 vols (Paris 1907–35)
HMC	*Historical Manuscripts Commission*
Holzapfel	H. Holzapfel, Handbuch der Geschichte des Fran-
Handbuch	ziskanerordens (Freiburg 1908)
Hooker,	*The works of ... Mr. Richard Hooker,* ed J. Keble, 7 ed
Works	rev R.W. Church and F. Paget, 3 vols (Oxford 1888)
Houedene	*Chronica Magistri Rogeri de Houedene,* ed W. Stubbs, 4 vols *RS* 51 (London 1868–71)
HRH	*The Heads of Religious Houses, England and Wales, 940– 1216,* ed D. Knowles, C.N.L. Brooke, V.C.M. London (Cambridge 1972)
HS	*Hispania sacra* (Madrid 1948–)
HTR	*Harvard Theological Review* (New York/Cambridge, Mass., 1908–)
HZ	*Historische Zeitschrift* (Munich 1859–)
IER	*Irish Ecclesiastical Record* (Dublin 1864–)
IGLS	*Inscriptions grèques et latines de la Syrie,* ed L. Jalabert, R. Mouterde and others, 7 vols (Paris 1929–70) in progress

ABBREVIATIONS

IR	*Innes Review* (Glasgow 1950–)
JAC	*Jahrbuch für Antike und Christentum* (Münster-im-Westfalen 1958–)
Jaffé	*Regesta Pontificum Romanorum ab condita ecclesia ad a. 1198*, 2 ed S. Lowenfeld, F. Kaltenbrunner, P. Ewald, 2 vols (Berlin 1885–8, repr Graz 1958)
JBS	*Journal of British Studies* (Hartford, Conn., 1961–)
JEH	*Journal of Ecclesiastical History* (London 1950–)
JFHS	*Journal of the Friends Historical Society* (London/Philadelphia 1903–)
JHI	*Journal of the History of Ideas* (London 1940–)
JHSChW	*Journal of the Historical Society of the Church in Wales* (Cardiff 1947–)
JIntH	*Journal of Interdisciplinary History* (Cambridge, Mass., 1970–)
JLW	*Jahrbuch für Liturgiewissenschaft* (Münster-im-Westfalen 1921–44)
JMH	*Journal of Modern History* (Chicago 1929–)
JMedH	*Journal of Medieval History* (Amsterdam 1975–)
JRA	*Journal of Religion in Africa* (Leiden 1967–)
JRH	*Journal of Religious History* (Sydney 1960–)
JRS	*Journal of Roman Studies* (London 1910–)
JSRAI	*Journal of the Royal Society of Antiquaries of Ireland* (Dublin 1871–)
JSArch	*Journal of the Society of Archivists* (London 1955–)
JTS	*Journal of Theological Studies* (London 1899–)
Kemble	*Codex Diplomaticus Aevi Saxonici*, ed J.M. Kemble (London 1839–48)
Knowles, *MO*	David Knowles, *The Monastic Order in England, 943–1216* (2 ed Cambridge 1963)
Knowles, *RO*	, *The Religious Orders in England*, 3 vols (Cambridge 1948–59)
Knox, *Works*	*The Works of John Knox*, ed D. Laing, Bannatyne Club/Wodrow Society, 6 vols (Edinburgh 1846–64)
Laurent, *Regestes*	V. Laurent, *Les Regestes des Actes du Patriarcat de Constantinople*, 1: *Les Actes des Patriarches*, IV: *Les Regestes de 1208 à 1309* (Paris 1971)
Le Neve	John LeNeve, *Fasti Ecclesiae Anglicanae 1066–1300*, rev and exp Diana E. Greenway, 1, St Pauls (London 1968); 2, Monastic Cathedrals (1971) *Fasti Ecclesiae Anglicanae 1300–1541* rev and exp H.P.F. King, J.M. Horn, B. Jones, 12 vols (London 1962–7) *Fasti Ecclesiae Anglicanae 1541–1857* rev and exp J.M. Horn, D.M. Smith, 1, St Pauls (1969); 2, Chichester (1971); 3, Canterbury, Rochester, Winchester (1974); 4, York (1975)

Lloyd, Formularies of Faith	*Formularies of Faith by Authority during the Reign of Henry VIII*, ed C. Lloyd (Oxford 1825)
LRS	Lincoln Record Society
LQR	Law Quarterly Review (London 1885–)
LThK	*Lexicon für Theologie und Kirche*, ed J. Höfer and K. Rahnes (2 ed Freiburg-im-Breisgau 1957–)
LW	*Luther's Works*, ed J. Pelikan and H.T. Lehman, American edition (St Louis/Philadelphia, 1955–)
MA	*Monasticon Anglicanum*, ed R. Dodsworth and W. Dugdale, 3 vols (London 1655–73; new ed J. Caley, H. Ellis, B. Bandinel, 6 vols in 8 (London 1817–30)
Mansi	J.D. Mansi, *Sacrorum conciliorum nova et amplissima collectio*, 31 vols (Florence/Venice 1757–98); new impression and continuation, ed L. Petit and J.B. Martin, 60 vols (Paris 1899–1927)
Martène and Durand	E. Martène and U. Durand, *Veterum Scriptorum et Monumentorum Historicorum, dogmaticorum, Moralium*
Collectio	*Amplissima Collectio*, 9 vols (Paris 1729)
Thesaurus	*Thesaurus Novus Anedotorum*, 5 vols (Paris 1717)
Voyage	*Voyage Litteraire de Deux Religieux Benedictins de la Congregation de Saint Maur*, 2 vols (Paris 1717, 1724)
MedA	*Medium Aevum* (Oxford 1932–)
Mendola	*Atti della Settimana di Studio*, 1959– (Milan 1962–)
MF	*Miscellanea Francescana* (Foligno/Rome 1886–)
MGH	*Monumenta Germaniae Historica inde ab a.c. 500 usque ad a. 1500*, ed G.H. Pertz and others (Berlin, Hanover 1826–)
AA	*Auctores Antiquissimi*
Ant	*Antiquitates*
Briefe	*Epistolae 2: Die Briefe der Deutschen Kaiserzeit*
Cap	*Leges 2: Leges in Quart 2: Capitularia regum Francorum*
CM	*Chronica Minora 1–3 (= AA 9, 11, 13) ed Th. Mommsen (1892, 1894, 1898 repr 1961)*
Conc	*Leges 2: Leges in Quart 3: Concilia 4: Constituones et acta publica imperatorum et regum*
DC	*Deutsche Chroniken*
Dip	*Diplomata in folio*
EPP	*Epistolae 1 in Quart*
Epp Sel	*4: Epistolae Selectae*
FIG	*Leges 3: Fontes Iuris Germanici Antique, new series*
FIGUS	*4: Fontes Iuris Germanici , in usum scholarum*
Form	*2: Leges in Quart 5: Formulae Merovingici et Karolini Aevi*
GPR	*Gesta Pontificum Romanorum*
Leges	*Leges in folio*

Lib	*Libelli de lite*
LM	*Ant 3: Libri Memoriales*
LNG	*Leges 2: Leges in Quart 1: Legs nationum Germanicarum*
Necr	*Ant 2: Necrologia Germaniae*
Poet	*1: Poetae Latini Medii Aevi*
Quellen	*Quellen zur Geistesgeschichte des Mittelalters*
Schriften	*Schriften der Monumenta Germaniae Historica*
SRG	*Scriptores rerum germanicarum in usum scholarum*
SRG ns	*Scriptores rerum germanicarum in usum scholarum, new series*
SRL	*Scriptores rerum langobardicarum et italicarum*
SRM	*Scriptores rerum merovingicarum*
SS	*scriptores*
SSM	*Staatschriften des späteren Mittelalters*
MIOG	*Mitteilungen des Instituts für österreichische Geschichtsforschung* (Graz/Cologne 1880–)
MM	F. Miklosich and J. Müller, *Acta et Diplomata Graeca medii aevi sacra et profana*, 6 vols (Vienna 1860–90)
Moorman, *History*	J.R.H. Moorman, *A History of the Franciscan Order from its origins to the year 1517* (Oxford 1968)
More, *Works*	*The Complete Works of St Thomas More*, ed R.S. Sylvester and others Yale edition (New Haven/London 1963–)
Moyen Age	*Le moyen âge. Revue d'Histoire et de philologie* (Paris 1888–)
MRHEW	David Knowles and R.N. Hadcock, *Medieval Religious Houses, England and Wales* (2 ed London 1971)
MHRI	A Gwynn and R.N. Hadcock, *Medieval Religious Houses, Ireland* (London 1970)
MHRS	Ian B. Cowan and David E. Easson, *Medieval Religious Houses, Scotland* (2 ed London 1976)
MS	Manuscript
MStn	*Mittelalterliche Studien* (Stuttgart 1966–)
Muratori	L.A. Muratori, *Rerum italicarum scriptores*, 25 vols (Milan 1723–51); new ed G. Carducci and V. Fiorine, 35 vols in 109 fasc (Città di Castello/Bologna 1900–)
NCE	*New Catholic Encyclopedia*, 15 vols (New York 1967)
NCModH	*New Cambridge Modern History* 14 vols (Cambridge 1957–70)
nd	no date
NEB	*New English Bible*
NF	*Neue Folge*
NH	*Northern History* (Leeds 1966–)
ns	new series
NS	New Style
Numen	*Numen: International Review for the History of Religions* (Leiden 1954–)

ABBREVIATIONS

OCP	*Orientalia Christiana Periodica* (Rome 1935–)
ODCC	*Oxford Dictionary of the Christian Church*, ed F.L. Cross (Oxford 1957), 2 ed with E.A. Livingstone (1974)
OED	*Oxford English Dictionary*
OMT	*Oxford Medieval Texts*
OS	Old Style
OHS	*Oxford Historical Society*
PBA	*Proceedings of the British Academy*
PG	*Patrologia Graeca*, ed J.P. Migne, 161 vols (Paris 1857–66)
PhK	Philosophisch-historische Klasse
PL	*Patrologia Latina*, ed J.P. Migne, 217 + 4 index vols (Paris 1841–64)
Plummer, Bede	*Venerabilis Baedae Opera Historica*, ed C. Plummer (Oxford 1896)
PO	Patrologia Orientalis, ed J. Graffin and F. Nau (Paris 1903–)
Potthast	*Regesta Pontificum Romanorum inde ab a. post Christum natum 1198 ad a. 1304*, ed A. Potthast, 2 vols (1874–5 repr Graz 1957)
PP	*Past and Present* (London 1952–)
PPTS	*Palestine Pilgrims' Text Society*, 13 vols and index (London 1896–1907)
PRIA	*Proceedings of the Royal Irish Academy* (Dublin 1936–)
PRO	Public Record Office
PS	Parker Society (Cambridge 1841–55)
PW	*Paulys Realencyklopädie der klassischen Altertumwissenschaft*, new ed G. Wissowa and W. Kroll (Stuttgart 1893–)
QFIAB	*Quellen und Forschungen aus italienischen Archiven und Bibliotheken* (Rome 1897–)
RAC	*Reallexion für Antike und Christentum*, ed T. Klauser (Stuttgart 1941)
RB	*Revue Bénédictine* (Maredsous 1884–)
RE	*Realencyclopädie für protestantische Theologie*, ed A. Hauck, 24 vols (3 ed Leipzig, 1896–1913)
REB	*Revue des Etudes Byzantines* (Bucharest/Paris 1946–)
RecS	Record Series
RGG	*Die Religion in Geschichte und Gegenwart*, 6 vols (Tübingen 1927–32)
RH	*Revue historique* (Paris 1876–)
RHC	*Recueil des Historiens de Croisades*, ed Académie des Inscriptions et Belles-Lettres (Paris 1841–1906)
Arm	*Historiens Arméniens*, 2 vols (1869–1906)
Grecs	*Historiens Grecs*, 2 vols (1875–81)
Lois	*Lois. Les Assises de Jérusalem*, 2 vols (1841–3)
Occ	*Historiens Occidentaux*, 5 vols (1844–95)

ABBREVIATIONS

Or	*Historiens Orientaux*, 5 vols (1872–1906)
RHD	*Revue d'histoire du droit* (Haarlem, Groningen 1923–)
RHDFE	*Revue historique de droit français et étranger* (Paris 1922–)
RHE	*Revue d'Histoire Ecclésiastique* (Louvain 1900–)
RHEF	*Revue d'Histoire de l'Eglise de France* (Paris 1910–)
RHR	*Revue de l'Histoire des Religions* (Paris 1880–)
RR	*Regesta Regum Anglo-Normannorum*, ed H.W.C. Davis, H.A. Cronne, Charles Johnson, R.H.C. Davis, 4 vols (Oxford 1913–69)
RS	*Rerum Brittanicarum Medii Aevi Scriptores*, 99 vols (London 1858–1911), *Rolls Series*
RSCI	*Rivista di storia della chiesa in Italia* (Rome 1947–)
RSR	*Revue des sciences religieuses* (Strasbourg 1921–)
RStI	*Rivista storica italiana* (Naples 1884–)
RTAM	*Recherches de théologie ancienne et médiévale* (Louvain 1929–)
RV	Revised Version
Sitz	*Sitzungsberichte*
SA	*Studia Anselmiana* (Roma 1933–)
sa	sub anno
SBAW	*Sitzungsberichte der bayerischen Akademie der Wissenschaften*, PhK (Munich 1971–)
SCH	*Studies in Church History* (London 1964–)
ScHR	*Scottish Historical Review* (Edinburgh/Glasgow 1904–)
SCR	*Sources chrétiennes*, ed H. de Lubac and J. Daniélou (Paris 1941)
SF	*Studi Francescani* (Florence 1914–)
SGra	*Studia Gratiana*, ed J. Forchielli and A.M. Stickler (Bologna 1953–)
SGre	*Studi Gregoriani*, ed G. Borino, 7 vols (Rome 1947–61)
SMon	*Studia Monastica* (Montserrat, Barcelona 1959–)
Speculum	*Speculum, A Journal of Medieval Studies* (Cambridge, Mass., 1926–)
SpicFr	*Spicilegium Friburgense* (Freiburg 1957–)
SS	*Surtees Society* (Durham 1835–)
SS Spoleto	*Setimane di Studio sull'alto medioevo*, 1952– , Centro Italiano di studi sull'alto medioevo, Spoleto 1954–)
STC	*A Short-Title Catalogue of Books Printed in England, Scotland and Ireland and of English Books Printed Abroad 1475–1640*, ed A.W. Pollard and G.R. Redgrave (London 1926, repr 1945, 1950)
Strype, *Annals*	John Strype, *Annals of the Reformation and Establishment of Religion … during Queen Elizabeth's Happy Reign*, 4 vols in 7 (Oxford 1840)
Strype, *Cranmer*	John Strype, *Memorials of … Thomas Cranmer*, 2 vols (Oxford 1824)

Strype, Grindal	John Strype, *The History of the Life and Acts of ... Edumund Grindal* (Oxford 1821)
Strype, Memorials	John Strype, *Ecclesiastical Memorials, Relating Chiefly to Religion, and the Reformation of it ... under King Henry VIII, King Edward VI and Queen Mary I*, 3 vols in 6 (Oxford 1822)
Strype, Parker	John Strype, *The Life and Acts of Matthew Parker*, 3 vols (Oxford 1821)
Strype, Whitgift	John Strype, *The Life and Acts of John Whitgift*, 3 vols (Oxford 1822)
sub hag	*subsidia hagiographica*
sv	*sub voce*
SVRG	*Schriften des Vereins für Reformationsgeschichte* (Halle/ Leipzig/Gütersloh 1883–)
TCBiblS	*Transactions of the Cambridge Bibliographical Society* (Cambridge 1949–)
Tchalenko	G. Tchalenko, *Villages antiques de la Syrie du Nord*, 3 vols (Paris 1953–8)
THSCym	*Transactions of the Historical Society of Cymmrodorion* (London 1822–)
TRHS	*Transactions of the Royal Historical Society* (London 1871–)
TU	*Texte und Untersuchungen zur Geschichte der altchristlichen Literatur* (Leipzig/Berlin 1882–)
VCH	*Victoria County History* (London 1900–)
VHM	G. Tiraboschi, *Vetera Humiliatorum Monumenta* 3 vols (Milan 1766–8)
Vivarium	*Vivarium: An International Journal for the Philosophy and Intellectual Life of the Middle Ages and Renaissance* (Assen 1963–)
VV	*Vizantijskij Vremennick* 1–25 (St Petersburg 1894–1927), ns 1 (26) (Leningrad 1947–)
WA	D. *Martin Luthers Werke*, ed J.C.F. Knaake (Weimar 1883–) [*Weimarer Ausgabe*]
WA Br	*Briefwechsel*
WA DB	*Deutsche Bibel*
WA TR	*Tischreden*
WelHR	*Welsh History Review* (Cardiff 1960–)
Wharton	H. Wharton, *Anglia Sacra*, 2 parts (London 1691)
Whitelock, Wills	*Anglo-Saxon Wills*, ed D. Whitelock (Cambridge, 1930)
Wilkins	*Concilia Magnae Britanniae et Hiberniae A.D. 446–1717*, 4 vols, ed D. Wilkins (London 1737)
YAJ	*Yorkshire Archaeological Journal* (London/Leeds 1870–)
Zanoni	L. Zanoni, *Gli Umiliati nei loro rapporti con l'eresia, l'industria della lana ed i communi nei secoli xii e xiii, Biblioteca Historica Italica*, 2 series, 2 (Milan 1911)

ZKG	*Zeitschrift für Kirchengeschichte* (Gotha/Stuttgart 1878–)
ZOG	*Zeitschrift für osteuropäische Geschichte* (Berlin 1911–35) = *Kyrios* (Berlin 1936–)
ZRG	*Zeitschrift der Savigny-Stiftung für Rechtsgeschichte* (Weimar)
GAbt	*Germanistische Abteilung* (1863–)
KAbt	*Kanonistische Abteilung* (1911–)
RAbt	*Romanistische Abteilung* (1880–)
ZRGG	*Zeitschrift Religions- und Geistegeschichte* (Marburg 1948–)
Zwingli, Werke	*Huldreich Zwinglis Sämmtliche Werke*, ed E. Egli and others, CR (Berlin/Leipzig/Zurich 1905–)